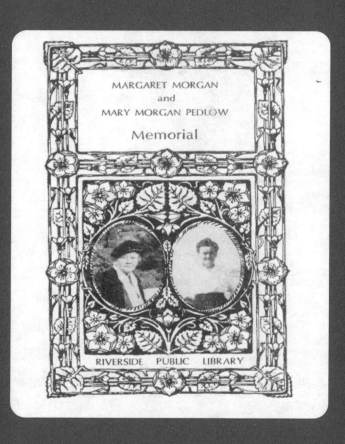

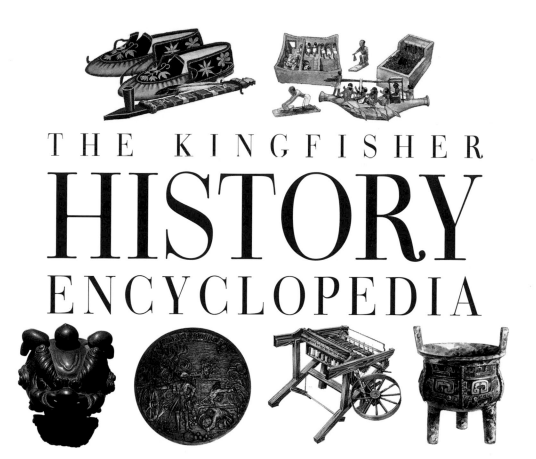

THE KINGFISHER
HISTORY
ENCYCLOPEDIA

KINGFISHER

NEW YORK

Copyright © 2004 by Kingfisher
Published in the United States by Kingfisher,
175 Fifth Ave., New York, NY 10010
Kingfisher is an imprint of Macmillan Children's Books, London.
All rights reserved.

Distributed in the U.S. by Macmillan, 175 Fifth Ave., New York, NY 10010
Distributed in Canada by H.B. Fenn and Company Ltd., 34 Nixon Road,
Bolton, Ontario L7E 1W2

LIBRARY OF CONGRESS CATALOGING-IN-PUBLICATION DATA
The Kingfisher history encyclopedia.—1st ed.
p. cm.
Includes index.
Summary: A reference guide to world history, featuring a time line,
key date boxes, and biographies of historical figures.
1. World history—Juvenile literature. [1. World history.]
I. Kingfisher Books.
D20.K558 1999
909—dc21   98-50409   CIP AC

CONTRIBUTORS
Jane Birch, Teresa Chris, Neil Grant, Ken Hills, Julian Holland,
Palden Jenkins, Elizabeth Longley, Fiona Macdonald, Hazel Martell,
Mike McGuire, Theodore Rowland-Entwhistle, Giles Sparrow
2012 edition: with thanks to Professor Ben Fortna, School of Oriental and African Studies,
University of London, U.K.

ISBN: 978-0-7534-6875-3

Kingfisher books are available for special promotions and premiums. For details contact:
Special Markets Department, Macmillan, 175 Fifth Ave., New York, NY 10010.

For more information, please visit www.kingfisherbooks.com

First American Edition published in 1999
This updated edition published in 2012
Printed in Singapore
9 8 7 6 5 4 3 2 1
1TR/0612/UTD/TWP/128GEMA

THE KINGFISHER
HISTORY
ENCYCLOPEDIA

KINGFISHER
NEW YORK

CONTENTS

INTRODUCTION

Often, fact is stranger than fiction. Your *Kingfisher History Encyclopedia* is packed full of fascinating facts and real-life stories about the people, places, and events of the past that have shaped the colorful, but still turbulent world that we know today. The causes and effects of the actions and events are explained in full, giving a vivid picture of how leaders, tyrants, artists, and scientists who lived hundreds of years ago have left a legacy that still impinges on people's lives in the twenty-first century.

Use your *Kingfisher History Encyclopedia* to discover past events and find out how people have lived their lives over the last 40,000 years—from Stone Age cave dwellers to the Anglo-Saxons, from the Aztecs and Incas of Mesoamerica to the Manchus in China, and from the American Revolution to United Nations peacekeeping.

This user-friendly encyclopedia contains many features to help you look things up easily, or just have fun browsing. The in-depth coverage of each historical period also makes the encyclopedia perfect for all your school projects and homework assignments.

The clear, informative text is accompanied by key date boxes, colorful photographs, and superb illustrations and maps. At-a-glance world maps at the beginning of each chapter highlight the major events that happened during a particular time period. These are arranged according to continent or area of the world. At the end of each of the ten chapters, there are three special feature spreads that give an overview of the arts, architecture, and science and technology of the featured time period. Finally, there is a Ready Reference section at the back of the book containing lists of names and dates for quick and easy access.

Whether you use your *Kingfisher History Encyclopedia* for homework, or just dip into it at random, it will add considerably to your understanding of the past, and will stimulate you to explore the lives of our ancestors further.

◄ Man-made structures tell us a great deal about the past. One of the largest and most famous is the Great Wall of China. Its construction was ordered by the first Qin emperor, Shi Huangdi, around 221 B.C., to keep out invaders from the north. Stretching for 4,000 mi. (6,400km), the wall was built by joining together shorter walls that had been built earlier. The wall has been rebuilt many times. Most of the wall that can be seen today was constructed during the Ming dynasty (1368–1644).

WHAT IS HISTORY?

The word "history" comes from the ancient Greek word *histo* meaning "know this." In Greek, "I know" also meant "I have seen," and *historeo* came to mean "learn by inquiry." The Greeks thought that the only way to know something was to either see it for themselves, or ask questions about it. The Greek historian Thucydides wrote that too many people often believed the first story they heard.

Ancient Greeks understood the essence of history. First, historical knowledge must be based on evidence. Second, history is not one story, but several. Third, everything must be checked for mistakes. Historians try to find out not only what happened, but why it happened.

The ancient Egyptians left administrative and religious records, using a writing system called hieroglyphics, on paper made from papyrus.

"History" has come to mean many things. It is an account of past events, in sequence of time; it is the study of events, their causes and results; and it is all that is preserved or remembered about the past. For evidence, historians use written accounts, artifacts such as weapons and tools, and spoken (oral) accounts. To remember something, people write it down, or mark it in some way. This is because events, even important ones, disappear from memory or become confused. Our lives may seem different from people's lives in the past, but some things have not changed—Roman roads are still used every day and games like chess were played centuries ago.

Documentary evidence is very important to historians. English families that have had a connection with one place stretching back over 1,000 years may find a reference to their family in the *Domesday Book*, compiled in 1086. It records who owned land, who lived there, how much it was worth, and what taxes were paid.

LOCAL HISTORY

Oral history is a good source of local history. Listening to the recollections of older people, looking at their photographs, and sharing their memories reveals a lot about the past. Family history is a branch of local history. Photographs of family members may reach as far back as great-great-grandparents. Important family events were often recorded in the front of a family bible. Local record offices store diaries, letters, census returns, old photographs, records of large estates, school textbooks, and business accounts from firms that have long stopped trading. Church records give details of baptisms, marriages, and funerals.

Buildings often tell us a lot about the past. In the early 1600s, the great Mogul emperor Akbar was buried in this highly decorated tomb, which still stands in the city of Fatehpur Sikri in India.

THE WORK OF HISTORIANS

The first real historian was Herodotus. He used the Greek word *historia* to mean "investigation." Although Herodotus was writing at a time when everyone believed their lives were controlled by the gods, he also looked for rational explanations and was the first person to look at the cause and effect of events. Sometimes history is written by those who play a major part in it. Julius Caesar wrote about the wars in Gaul (France), and Winston Churchill wrote about World War I and II. Not all historians witness the events they write about. Most depend on accounts and documents produced at the time. Those who write history should always be aware of any bias or prejudice in themselves and in other writers. Bias means being influenced by a particular point of view, and prejudice literally means "judging before"— before all the facts have been looked at. Historians also have to avoid the mistake of writing about the past as if all events were leading with a fixed purpose to the present.

THE WORK OF ARCHAEOLOGISTS

Archaeology is the study of the peoples of the past by the scientific analysis of the things they leave behind. Archaeologists study objects (artifacts), features (buildings), and seeds or animal bones (ecofacts). Archaeology can tell us about societies that existed before written records were made, and add to our knowledge of civilized societies.

Archaeologists treat the things they find as clues to the lives of the people who used them. They can sometimes discover the reasons for great changes in the societies they are studying. Kathleen Kenyon, digging at the site of Jericho in 1952, found out that its walls were destroyed in biblical times, but by fire—not by the sound of trumpets! Archaeology can often present historians with evidence that makes them reexamine their views of early societies. In 1939, at Sutton Hoo in England, the remains of an Anglo-Saxon treasure ship were discovered. The artifacts found there are evidence of a society from the so-called "Dark Ages" that are far from primitive.

Since the 1950s, archaeologists have been concerned with finding general theories that explain the changes that occur in human societies. They now try to find out why farming developed in Mexico around 7000 B.C. or why the first cities grew in the Near East. Computers can be used to process the statistics and they have made this sort of study much faster and more efficient.

Artifacts such as coins, pottery, tools, and weapons are sometimes found in great abundance. Studying them can add to our

Delicate *netsuke* give an insight into Japanese life in the 1700s.

This selection of items found by archaeologists in the wreck of the ship *Mary Rose* shows us what a sailor was likely to take to sea in 1536. They include a pouch, a whistle, a comb, and a rosary.

knowledge of social and military history. Ecofacts, such as animal bones, skins, and plant seeds, help identify the jobs people did and what they ate. Pictures and paintings can also provide valuable information. We can tell a lot about what people looked like, and what they did, from cave paintings, frescoes, portraits, and pictures in stained glass.

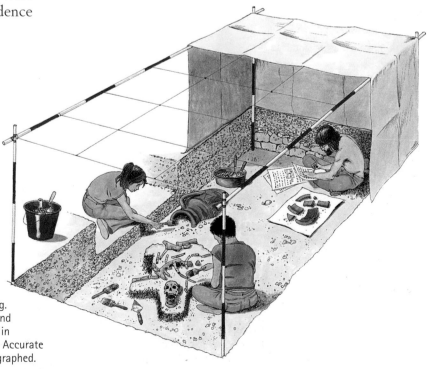

When digging, archaeologists try to avoid damaging anything. A grid is used to locate and record the exact position, size, and condition of finds. All earth removed from a site is collected in pails and later sifted in case any small find has been missed. Accurate written records are made and each level of the site is photographed.

THE ANCIENT WORLD

40,000–500 B.C.

This is the earliest history of humanity, as it evolved from cave dwellers to village-dwelling farmers to populations in towns, up to and including the first advanced civilizations. It was around 40,000 B.C. that humans first built their own homes, made music, and painted pictures on the walls of caves. It was not until around 8000 B.C. that the first farming and trading villages were built, and another 5,000 years—250 generations— passed before important civilizations appeared in Egypt and Mesopotamia.

▲ The first peoples lived in caves and made fire by using a bow to spin a stick against another piece of wood to create sparks.

◀ The ancient Egyptians believed in life after death. They worshiped many gods, including Osiris, the god of the dead, whose image is seen here in a painting on the tomb of Horemheb.

THE WORLD AT A GLANCE 40,000–500 B.C.

Though there is fossil evidence that the earliest humans evolved at least 130,000 years ago on the continent of Africa, their lives were extremely simple compared to ours. By 40,000 B.C., humans had learned how to use fire to keep themselves warm, cook food, and scare away wild animals. From being hunters and gatherers of wild fruit, berries, and seeds, they slowly found out how to grow crops and keep domestic animals. Around 8000 B.C., life became more complex as farming villages developed in the Middle East. It was much later that other parts of the world developed in this way. During the next 3,000 years, important basic activities such as building, tilling the land, pottery, copperworking, sewing, and animal breeding were introduced.

It was not until 3000 B.C. that the first towns were built, beside rivers in Egypt, Mesopotamia, and China. By 2600 B.C., large constructions such as the pyramids in Egypt, the stone circles in eastern Europe, and the first temples in Peru were built. Around the same time, the people in the kingdom of Kush in East Africa were learning to work metal, and Chinese astronomers first observed an eclipse of the sun. Civilization had come into being.

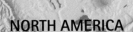

NORTH AMERICA

NORTH AMERICA

In ancient times, North Americans hunted animals and foraged for food on a vast continent with no civilizations. Although these peoples lived off the land, they still had their beliefs, medicines, tools, and simple homes. The first steps toward civilization were made about 700 B.C. by the Adena people in the woodlands of what is now Ohio. They built temple mounds, lived in villages, and worked with copper.

MESOAMERICA AND SOUTH AMERICA

MESOAMERICA AND SOUTH AMERICA

Farming was established in Mexico (Mesoamerica) by 3000 B.C., and by 2000 B.C., the Peruvians of the Andes had also developed farming communities. The growing population lived in permanent villages and over hundreds of years these gradually grew larger and became towns. By 2600 B.C., large temples had been built on the coast of Peru— around the same time as the earliest stone circles in eastern Europe and the pyramids in Egypt began to appear. At the same time, the Olmec civilization emerged in Mexico. By 500 B.C., the Maya in Mexico were also building pyramids.

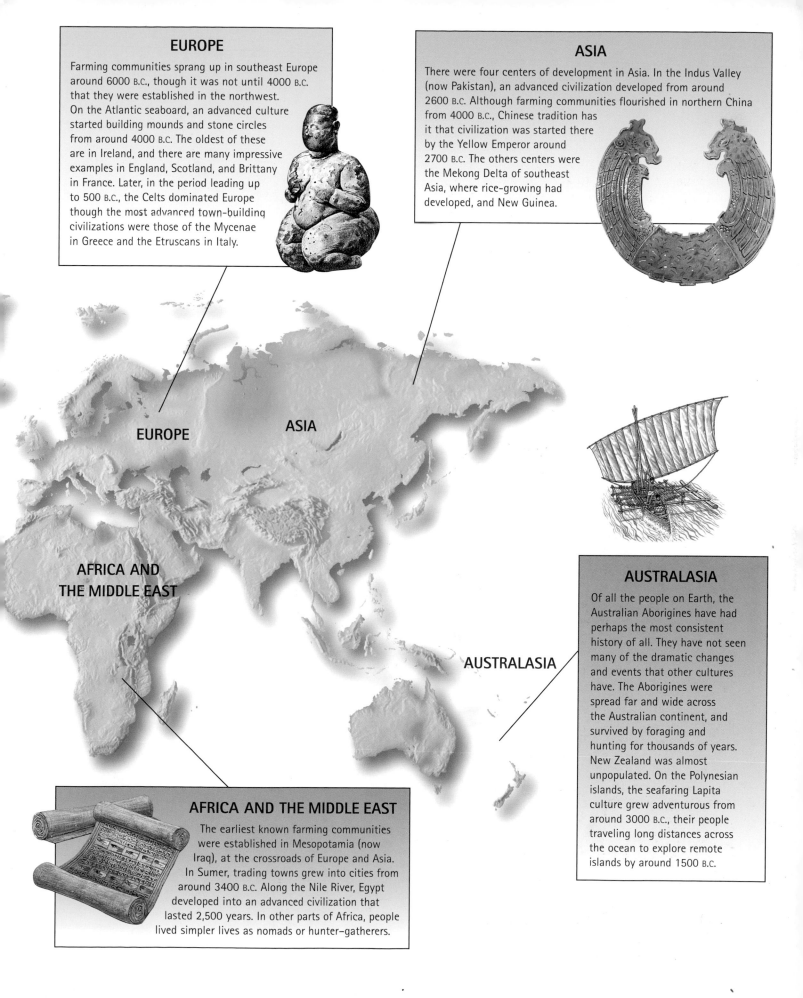

EUROPE

Farming communities sprang up in southeast Europe around 6000 B.C., though it was not until 4000 B.C. that they were established in the northwest. On the Atlantic seaboard, an advanced culture started building mounds and stone circles from around 4000 B.C. The oldest of these are in Ireland, and there are many impressive examples in England, Scotland, and Brittany in France. Later, in the period leading up to 500 B.C., the Celts dominated Europe though the most advanced town-building civilizations were those of the Mycenae in Greece and the Etruscans in Italy.

ASIA

There were four centers of development in Asia. In the Indus Valley (now Pakistan), an advanced civilization developed from around 2600 B.C. Although farming communities flourished in northern China from 4000 B.C., Chinese tradition has it that civilization was started there by the Yellow Emperor around 2700 B.C. The others centers were the Mekong Delta of southeast Asia, where rice-growing had developed, and New Guinea.

EUROPE

ASIA

AFRICA AND
THE MIDDLE EAST

AUSTRALASIA

AUSTRALASIA

Of all the people on Earth, the Australian Aborigines have had perhaps the most consistent history of all. They have not seen many of the dramatic changes and events that other cultures have. The Aborigines were spread far and wide across the Australian continent, and survived by foraging and hunting for thousands of years. New Zealand was almost unpopulated. On the Polynesian islands, the seafaring Lapita culture grew adventurous from around 3000 B.C., their people traveling long distances across the ocean to explore remote islands by around 1500 B.C.

AFRICA AND THE MIDDLE EAST

The earliest known farming communities were established in Mesopotamia (now Iraq), at the crossroads of Europe and Asia. In Sumer, trading towns grew into cities from around 3400 B.C. Along the Nile River, Egypt developed into an advanced civilization that lasted 2,500 years. In other parts of Africa, people lived simpler lives as nomads or hunter-gatherers.

THE FIRST HUMANS 40,000–10,000 B.C.

The earliest humanlike creatures evolved over a period of several million years. Our closest true human ancestors have developed only within the last 50,000 years.

The earliest hominids (humanlike creatures) were the *Australopithecines.* Many of their bones have been found in East Africa. They walked upright and made simple tools from pebbles. They were probably not true humans because their brains were very small in comparison.

Early peoples used flints of different shapes for making scrapers, knives, arrowheads, and borers.

PROTOHUMANS

Homo habilis (handy human) appeared about two million years ago. This hominid had more skills, and lived alongside the last of the Australopithecines. The most advanced early human was *Homo erectus* (upright human), and remains have been found in Africa and Asia. By learning to use fire to cook and keep warm, *Homo erectus* was able to move from place to place.

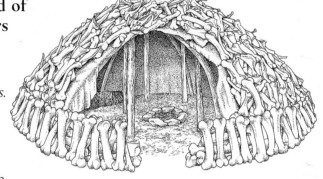

This shelter, discovered in the Ukraine, was made of wood covered with animal skins weighed down with mammoth bones. It was built to survive harsh winters and fierce winds.

NEANDERTHALS

About 200,000 years ago *Homo sapiens* (wise human) developed from *Homo erectus.* At the same time another human type, the *Neanderthal*, adapted to the colder climates of the last Ice Age, spreading through the continent of Europe and the Middle East. The Neanderthals developed many different simple stone tools, though their language was limited. They did not survive into modern times— the last known Neanderthals died out in Spain around 28,000 years ago.

THE ICE AGE

The last Ice Age, at its height around 16,000 B.C., had a major influence on how early people developed. It was the most recent of several ice ages that have occurred over the last 2.3 million years. With much water trapped in ice, the sea level was about 300 ft. (90m) lower than today. As a result there was dry land between Siberia and Alaska, between Australia and New Guinea, and between Britain and Europe, that allowed people to migrate.

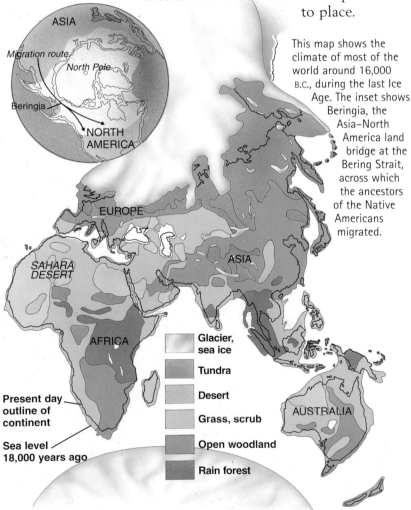

ASIA

Migration route

North Pole

Beringia

NORTH AMERICA

EUROPE

ASIA

SAHARA DESERT

AFRICA

AUSTRALIA

This map shows the climate of most of the world around 16,000 B.C., during the last Ice Age. The inset shows Beringia, the Asia–North America land bridge at the Bering Strait, across which the ancestors of the Native Americans migrated.

Glacier, sea ice

Tundra

Desert

Grass, scrub

Open woodland

Rain forest

Present day outline of continent

Sea level 18,000 years ago

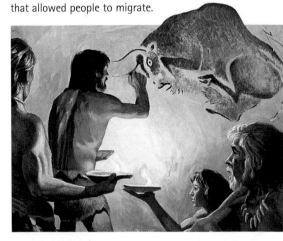

In places such as Lascaux in southwest France, Ice Age people made cave paintings, possibly to honor the spirits of the animals they hunted for food and clothing.

CRO-MAGNONS

The humans of today are probably descended from the Cro-Magnons, a group of hunter-gatherers who seem to have entered Europe from the Middle East and eventually replaced the Neanderthals. These people gathered fruits, berries, and roots and hunted wild animals. They lived in simple caves and shelters. Around 40,000 years ago, they had developed mentally to become more like modern humans, with more ideas and a larger vocabulary. They began creating artworks, including cave paintings in France, Spain, and the Sahara. They made jewelry, figurines, clothes, shelters, tools, and hunting weapons.

▲ This is a tented encampment in eastern Europe about 25,000 years ago. Using this camp as their base, the hunters gathered their food, using skins for clothes and shelter, and bones for tools and ornaments. This way of life demanded teamwork and cooperation among the community.

◀ Using a bow to spin a stick against a piece of wood, heat was built up by friction to create fire. This could take 10–20 minutes.

The Cro-Magnons made jewelry from stones, bones, ivory, shells, and teeth. It was often buried in graves.

Cave-dwelling hunters tackled very large animals, such as mammoths, but they also brought back a variety of smaller animals, including hares and deer.

THE FIRST FARMERS 10,000–4000 B.C.

People's lives changed greatly with the development of agriculture. Slowly they discovered how to domesticate animals and began to cultivate plants for crops.

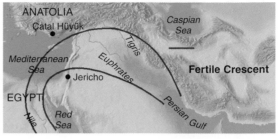

Early civilizations of the Middle East grew up in the Fertile Crescent, an ideal area for farming and settled village life, for trade, and later for building towns.

People first worshiped mother-goddesses about 25,000 years ago. They believed that, like the Earth, these goddesses gave life to all living things.

Wheat and barley were crossed with grasses to breed new strains. They were used to make bread, the staple of human diet in every early civilization.

The earliest farmers settled nearly 10,000 years ago in the Fertile Crescent in the Middle East. Here people grew wheat and barley. They kept goats, sheep, pigs, and cattle that they used for meat, milk, hides, wool, and to carry things. The improvement in the design of simple tools allowed people to clear land more effectively, build villages, and stay in one place. Later, agriculture developed in fertile areas in China, northwest India, Iran, Egypt, southern Europe, and Mexico.

DOMESTICATION

The first animal to be domesticated was the dog, as early as 10,000 B.C. Dogs were used for herding and as night guards. The horse, goat, and sheep were also domesticated. Farmers learned how to breed animals in order to change their characteristics. A number of species spread as well—chickens and pheasants, for example, originated in the Far East. Meanwhile, some animals, such as aurochs, were hunted to extinction.

IRRIGATION

One of the most important inventions was irrigation, a system of supplying cultivated land with water. Farmers in the Fertile Crescent and Mesoamerica dug channels to carry water to their crops. Using reservoirs and sluiceways, land lying far from rivers could be made fertile. In Egypt and China, annual floods were controlled to provide irrigation. In wetter climates, drainage was also important. After many generations, some farmers started bartering goods with neighbors and travelers, leading to the growth of trade and the founding of the first towns and civilizations.

▶ Nomadic peoples followed wild herds or moved from season to season. They went where the pickings or the weather were best. They used temporary homes and simple tools. When tribes met they would trade items, hold festivals, and arrange marriages.

◀ In early villages, people thatched their houses, kept their animals in pens and pastures, and tended vegetable patches. They developed new techniques for storing food, fertilizing fields, and making tools.

SUMER AND AKKAD 5000–1600 B.C.

The first people to settle in Mesopotamia were the Sumerians more than 7,000 years ago. They built a number of independent city-states—the first civilization.

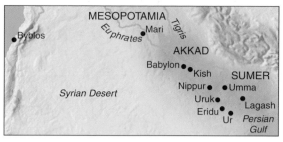

The fertile Tigris and Euphrates river valleys acted as the birthplace of trading cities, extending their influence far and wide—an attractive target for marauding warriors.

The Sumerian civilization consisted of a number of city-states—cities that were also independent nations. Some of these cities lasted for 3,000 years. They were located on important trade routes along the Tigris and Euphrates rivers. Their traders traveled to Egypt and India.

In 2360 B.C., Sargon of Akkad invaded Mesopotamia, carving out the world's first empire.

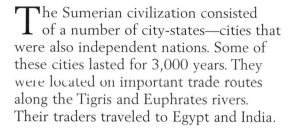

Scribes and accountants were important, and involved in all aspects of Sumerian daily life, including trade, law, and religion.

SUMERIAN CITIES

Each city-state had fine public buildings, markets, workshops, and water systems. There was a royal palace and a *ziggurat*, on top of which was a shrine dedicated to the god of that city. Around the public buildings were houses. Beyond these lay the farmers' fields and the marshlands of the Mesopotamian rivers.

READING AND WRITING

The Sumerians devised one of the earliest writing systems, *cuneiform*. From about 3200 B.C. they wrote on clay tablets, and scribes held a key role in their society. Thousands of tablets have survived, containing accounts, records, sacred scripts, and letters. The contents of their graves have shown that the Sumerians were wealthy and their craftspeople skilled.

INTERNAL STRIFE

Around 2900 B.C., with city populations growing, power shifted away from the priesthoods which had been all-powerful—commerce gradually becoming more important than religion. Rivalry between different cities grew, and they fought each other for supremacy. They were also invaded by tribes from Persia, Arabia, and Turkey who wanted to share the cities' wealth and power.

AKKAD AND UR

Eventually, the city of Akkad grew dominant. The city was led by Sargon, who created the world's first empire around 2334 B.C. His rule brought more order—but it also brought cruelty and violence. Around 2100 B.C., as Akkad declined, the city of Ur took its place, rising to prominence for a century. After its fall, Assyria and Babylon grew to dominate the area.

This reed house was occupied by early Sumerians before bricks were used. Reed houses were still built by Marsh Arabs until recently.

ZIGGURATS

Built of sunbaked clay bricks, ziggurats towered impressively over the river plains. Building them demanded careful architecture and engineering. The shrine at the top was dedicated to the god of the city. Here, priest-kings performed rituals to benefit the cities and their lands and to appease the gods.

The great ziggurat at Ur

ANCIENT EGYPT 4000–1800 B.C.

Ancient Egypt was surrounded by deserts, but it was green and fertile because of the Nile River. It flooded every year, depositing rich, silty soil along its banks.

The Egyptians loved to wear lucky charms. Their favorites were carved stone scarabs. The scarab beetle was sacred to the sun god, Ra.

Papyrus is a stiff paper made from papyrus reeds. The Egyptians glued sheets of it together to make scrolls. Administrative and religious texts were written in hieroglyphs.

The Egyptians used the Nile for transportation and cultivated the land alongside it. They grew wheat and barley for bread and beer, and flax for linen; they raised cattle as beasts of burden. Egyptians had a highly developed religion and advanced medical, astronomical, and engineering knowledge.

THE PHARAOHS

For most of their history, Egyptians were united in one kingdom. Administrators and priests ran everyday affairs, but the head of society was the pharaoh—a living god. People believed that ceremonies he performed kept the good will of the gods, kept the Nile flowing, and kept society in order. When the pharaoh died, his body was mummified and placed inside a stone sarcophagus in an imposing tomb, along with jewelry, clothing, furniture, and food—everything he would need for eternity. Sacred writings on the tomb walls were meant to protect him in the afterlife.

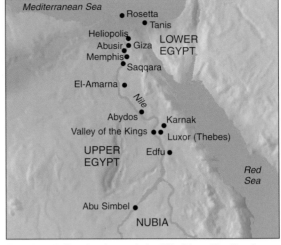

Egyptian civilization hugged the Nile River. The flood plains of the delta were rich and highly populated, though cities stretched a long way up the Nile. Riverboat transportation was important to traders.

EGYPTIAN SOCIETY

Most people in Egypt were farmers. They gave part of their produce to the local temple as taxes. Very few people could read and write, and schooling was only for boys. Those who could write were called scribes. It was they who went on to become the priests and administrators who ran the country for the pharaoh. But at the heart of Egyptian life was communication with the gods.

PYRAMIDS

From around 2630 B.C., Egyptians built many pyramids, the most famous being the Great Pyramid at Giza. No one knows exactly why the shape was chosen, but the scale and dimensions suggest astronomical, mathematical, and spiritual purposes. By building such great monuments, the pharaohs sought to please the gods and to leave a significant, permanent mark on history. Some of the long stone blocks above the king's Chamber weighed 60 tons, and around 2.3 million of them were used.

The Great Pyramid, the first of three pyramids at Giza and the tomb of the pharaoh Khufu, had many passageways and chambers.

King's chamber
Grand gallery
Queen's chamber
Entrance
New passage
Underground chamber

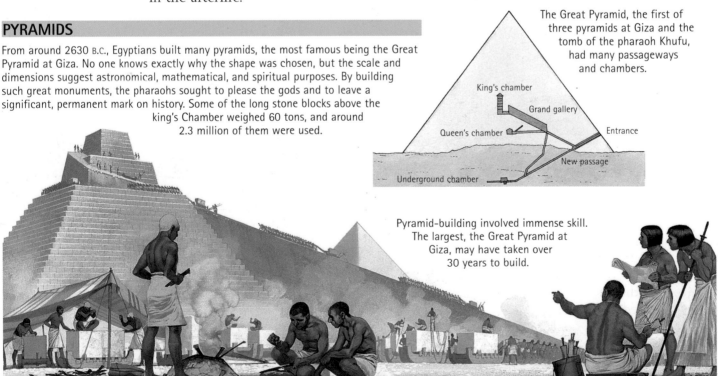

Pyramid-building involved immense skill. The largest, the Great Pyramid at Giza, may have taken over 30 years to build.

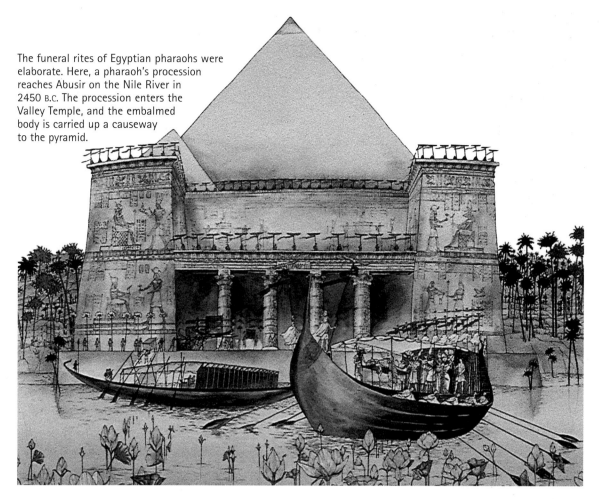

The funeral rites of Egyptian pharaohs were elaborate. Here, a pharaoh's procession reaches Abusir on the Nile River in 2450 B.C. The procession enters the Valley Temple, and the embalmed body is carried up a causeway to the pyramid.

EGYPTIAN GODS

Horus was the sky-god, and his spirit entered the living pharaoh. His eyes were the sun and the moon.

Ptah, the creator-god, invented the arts. He was the local god of the capital, Memphis.

Hathor, the goddess of love and beauty, once raised the sun up to heaven on her horns.

Isis, sister and wife of Osiris, was the mother of Horus. She had great magical powers.

Re-Horakhty, the sun-god and Horus joined together, is shown with the sun on a hawk's head.

Osiris was the god of the dead. In his realm, souls were judged for their worthiness.

Toward this end the Egyptians created remarkable works of stone carving. They built enormous pyramids and temples. Tall obelisks were cut from one block of stone. No effort or expense was spared to honor the gods—or the pharaoh, who was their living link with humanity. The Egyptians developed a way to preserve the body of their god-king, and many building projects were undertaken to provide him with a tomb for his eternal protection. In time, everyone who could afford it would have their preserved bodies placed in tombs, with treasures for the afterlife and sacred scrolls to guide them to it.

RETURN TO GREATNESS

After the time of the first pharaohs and the pyramid builders, there was a decline that lasted for over 100 years. With no strong ruler, the people felt the gods had abandoned them. Then, around 2040, Mentuhotep became pharaoh, brought order, and restored Egypt's greatness. This period was called the Middle Kingdom.

The pharaohs reorganized the country and again built pyramids, although not as large as those at Giza. Some of Egypt's finest art and literature was produced during the Middle Kingdom.

Egypt had been isolated from the rest of the world at this time. Ancient Egyptians were not great travelers, sailors, or conquerors, but great Middle Kingdom rulers such as Amenemhat I and Senwosret III expanded Egypt's boundaries. They built forts to protect the country, and created a strong army. They invaded countries such as Nubia to take control of gold reserves.

KEY DATES

3300 Growth of towns in lower Nile valley and development of hieroglyphics
3000 Upper and Lower Egypt united
2920 The first pharaohs
2575 Old Kingdom, capital Memphis—high point of Egyptian civilization
2550 The Great Pyramid is completed
2040 Middle Kingdom—expansion and development
1550 New Kingdom—Egypt at its largest and wealthiest

MEGALITHIC EUROPE 4500–1200 B.C.

In Spain, France, Ireland, Britain, and Sweden there are ancient megalithic monuments, remains of an ancient civilization that built large stone temples.

A megalith in Portugal. No one really knows the purpose of these chambers—they were possibly built as tombs, or places for meditation or healing. They range in age from 4,000 to 6,000 years old.

One of the most impressive monuments from this period is Stonehenge, in southern England. It was built in three stages from 3000 B.C. onward, forming a circle of huge, dressed (shaped), upright stones linked by lintels (beams). Scientists think that it was used as a temple, a place to study the stars, and to calculate the calendar. Even older and larger than Stonehenge is the Avebury stone circle, a few miles to the north. It is a much larger ring of stones that have not been dressed.

Many other stone circles in a variety of shapes and sizes are found elsewhere in Britain, with names like the Merry Maidens, Long Meg, and Callanish.

The Ring of Brodgar in the Orkney Islands, off northeast Scotland, is about the same age as Stonehenge. The stones there are all tall, thin, and pointed.

Stoney Littleton long barrow, near Bath in southwest England, has several small chambers that would have been used for ancestral burial purposes over a number of years.

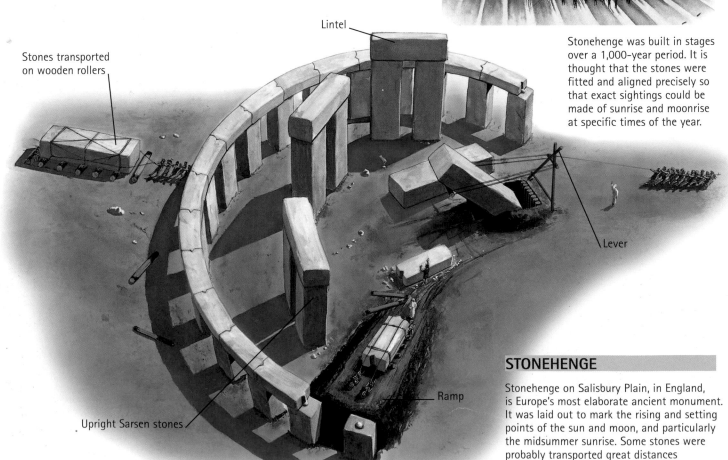

Lintel

Stones transported on wooden rollers

Stonehenge was built in stages over a 1,000-year period. It is thought that the stones were fitted and aligned precisely so that exact sightings could be made of sunrise and moonrise at specific times of the year.

Lever

Ramp

Upright Sarsen stones

STONEHENGE

Stonehenge on Salisbury Plain, in England, is Europe's most elaborate ancient monument. It was laid out to mark the rising and setting points of the sun and moon, and particularly the midsummer sunrise. Some stones were probably transported great distances before being erected.

Copper ore was laboriously dug by hand in this deep mine near Salzburg in eastern Austria, around 1200 B.C. The ore was transported to the surface in sacks and crushed with heavy stone hammers.

KEY DATES

4500	Farming develops in western Europe
4300	First megaliths built in Brittany and Ireland
3000	Building of Stonehenge begins
3200	Stone circle building period starts
2400	Copper first comes into use in western Europe
2000	Peak of megalith building period. Stonehenge construction almost complete

MAINLAND EUROPE

Stone circles have been found in the west of Ireland that are even older than those in Britain. At Carnac in Brittany, in northwestern France, there is an impressive series of avenues made up of 3,000 large stones, stretching for several miles. Brittany also has many single standing stones, called menhirs. Standing stones are found all over Europe from Spain to Ireland and Scotland to Sweden.

Many stone chambers (barrows) were covered with soil to make a mound—they are found in France, Ireland, and England. There are also "quoits," made up of three vertical stones with a single large slab balanced on top.

Another remarkable collection of megalithic monuments is in Malta. Some of the oldest have walls made of massive stones. Several of the temples contain dressed stones carved with simple designs. The most remarkable Maltese monument is the Hypogeum, an underground temple carved on three levels deep into the rock.

The remains of megalithic homes have been found at Skara Brae in the Orkney Isles north of Scotland. These stone houses were engulfed in sand and preserved for thousands of years. They have helped us to reconstruct a picture of life in ancient times.

THE INDUS VALLEY 4000–1800 B.C.

The early peoples of the Indian subcontinent lived on the banks of the Ganges and Indus rivers. The first civilization sprang up in the Indus Valley, now in Pakistan.

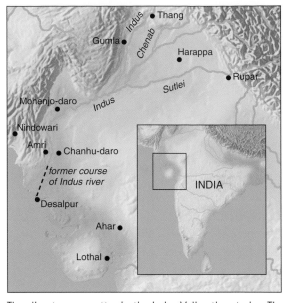

The climate was wetter in the Indus Valley than today. The rivers were used not only for trade and transportation, but also for irrigation of the flat lands of the valley.

The two largest cities in the Indus Valley around 2000 B.C. were Mohenjo-Daro and Harappa, each with around 40,000 people. They were among the world's largest cities at the time. At the center of each lay an artificial mound which served as a citadel (stronghold). On this mound stood a large granary which, to the population, served as a kind of central bank. These forgotten cities were only discovered in the 1920s.

Indus seals like this were attached to bales of merchandise. They have been found not only in Mohenjo-Daro, but also as far away as Sumer. This is evidence of a wide trade network.

CITY LAYOUT

Around the citadel the city buildings were arranged in a grid pattern—administration buildings, markets, storage areas, workshops, houses, and temples. Each house was built around a courtyard, and had rooms, a toilet, and a well. Buildings were made from mud bricks baked in wood-fired ovens. The citadel at Mohenjo-Daro had a bathhouse, as well as private and public baths and meeting places.

Brick-lined shafts like this are found in the courtyards of Mohenjo-Daro. They may have been wells or used for cool storage of grains and oil.

These ruins are all that remain of the 4,000-year-old city of Mohenjo-Daro.

FARMERS AND CRAFTWORKERS

Among other crops, the farmers of the Indus Valley grew barley, wheat, cotton, melons, and dates. Elephants and water buffalo were tamed to work in the fields. The area had many skilled potters who used wheels for throwing pots—a new technology at the time. Harappans used stone tools and made knives, weapons, bowls, and figures in bronze. They had an advanced system of waste-disposal that included the building of covered drains and the installation of garbage chutes.

THE END OF A CIVILIZATION

No one knows who the people of the Indus Valley were or where they came from. We do not understand their writing, either. The area had similarities to Sumer, but also major differences. The city dwellers traded with the cities of Sumer; they also traded with the tribespeople of India and central Asia. The Indus Valley civilization lasted 800 years, but came to an end about 3,700 years ago. No one knows why it ended, but there are various possible causes: floods; disease; a breakdown in trade, the economy, or civil order; or immigration and takeover by the Aryans who moved into India from central Asia. All trace of the cities lay buried under sand until they were rediscovered in the 1920s.

These are the excavated remains of the Great Bath at Mohenjo-Daro. The people appear to have placed great importance on hygiene and access to water. They may also have used the baths for sports and ceremonies.

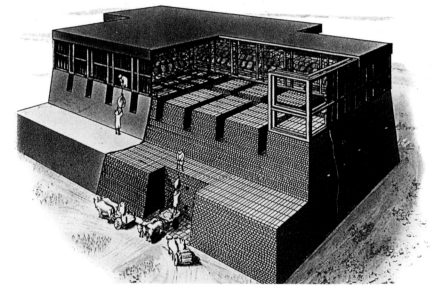

▲ The storehouses at the center of the cities were very valuable to the inhabitants—they could have had religious as well as practical significance, since grain may have been regarded as sacred.

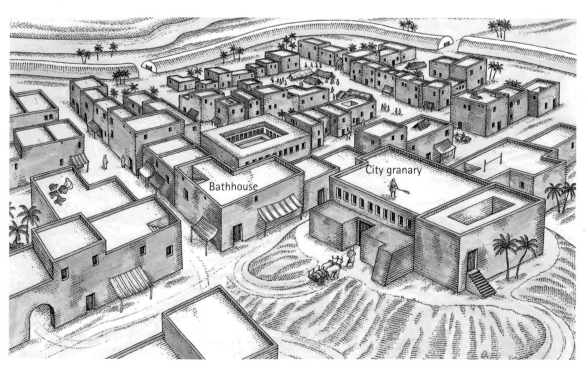

Bathhouse

City granary

◀ An artist's impression shows Mohenjo-Daro at the height of its prosperity. Unlike Sumerian cities, it was built in a grid pattern, suggesting orderly government and planning. The bathhouse had its own indoor well, and what seems to have been a granary had a sophisticated storage and ventilation system.

15

ANCIENT CRETE 3000–1450 B.C.

The earliest European civilization began on the island of Crete about 4,500 years ago. It is called the Minoan civilization after the legendary King Minos.

Stories say that Minos built a labyrinth (maze) in which he kept a Minotaur, a creature with the head of a bull and the body of a man. The Minoan civilization was at its height from 2200 to 1450 B.C. The Minoans owed their prosperity to their abilities as seafarers and traders.

Crete was well placed for trading with and influencing other areas. In the end, this was the Minoans' undoing, since the Mycenaeans envied their civilization and eventually invaded.

MINOAN CITIES

The Minoans built several large cities connected by paved roads, each of them a small city-state. At the heart of each city was a palace with a water supply, decorations, windows, and stone seats. Minoan craftsmen were renowned as potters and builders. They also made beautiful silver and gold jewelry. The capital, Knossos, had the grandest palace. It had splendid royal apartments, rooms for religious ceremonies, workshops, and a school.

Minoans were expert shipbuilders. They traveled around the Aegean Sea and to Egypt in boats like this, carrying their pottery and other craftworks far and wide.

The internal walls of the palace were plastered and decorated with large, magnificently painted pictures.

DOWNFALL OF A CIVILIZATION

Advanced Minoan civilization came to a sudden and mysterious end in about 1450 B.C. A volcanic eruption on the nearby island of Thera had already been a major disaster, overwhelming much of Crete. The end came when Knossos was invaded by the Mycenaeans who greatly admired the Minoans and took their ideas to the European mainland. In Crete lay the roots of the later Greek classical civilization.

This figure was found at Knossos. It combines the snake cult of Crete and worship of the mother-goddess. The figure itself wears the typical clothing of a Minoan woman.

The massive royal palace at Knossos, 500 ft. sq. (150m sq.), was several stories high and built from wood, stone, and clay. A large courtyard, was in the center. Royal apartments were on the east of the court, on the first floor.

The walls of the state rooms at Knossos were elaborately decorated. The wall painting shows the sport of bull leaping. The bull was a sacred symbol of power, and the ability to vault over its horns symbolized the mastering of its strength.

THE MYCENEANS 2000–1200 B.C.

Mycenae was a city on the southern peninsula of Greece. It was the center of the first Greek civilization, which developed after that of the Minoans in Crete.

The ruins of the Lion Gate at Mycenae, the main entrance to the city, built around 1300BC. It was one of the few ways through the walls, which were built with huge stones and were easy to defend.

This gold mask was found in a grave in Mycenae by archaeologist Heinrich Schliemann. He thought it was Agamemnon's mask—modern scholars think it belonged to a man who lived 300 years earlier.

This beautiful gold goblet from Mycenae clearly demonstrates the skill of the local craftsworkers. It shows men hunting bulls, a common theme at that time.

The Mycenaeans (known as Achaeans) migrated to Greece from the Balkans around 2000 B.C. Mycenaean civilization began as a series of hillside villages occupied by people speaking an ancient form of the Greek language. By about 1650 B.C., many villages had grown into fortified towns, with rich palaces and luxurious goods that rivaled those made by the highly skilled Minoans. Mycenae consisted of about 20 city-states.

MYCENAEAN TOMBS

Before they built fortresses and cities the Mycenaeans buried their leaders in elaborate "beehive tombs." These were built of large stone blocks, shaped to form a great dome. One tomb at Mycenae, the Treasury of Atreus, has a doorway nearly 20 ft. (6m) high, that opens into a chamber 43 ft. (13m) high and 46 ft. (14m) wide. It was once lined with bronze plates. The richness of these tombs shows that a great deal of money and effort was spent on royalty and the aristocracy. One king had as many as

400 bronzesmiths and hundreds of slaves. Wealthy Mycenaeans treasured the gold that they imported from Egypt. Skilled craftworkers made gold cups, masks, flowers, and jewelry; even their swords and armor were inlaid with gold.

EXPANSION AND DOWNFALL

Around 1450 B.C., the Mycenaeans conquered Crete and established colonies around the Aegean Sea and on the islands of Rhodes and Cyprus. They traded throughout the Mediterranean, particularly with Phoenicia, Egypt, and Italy. However, around 1200 B.C., Mycenae fell to invading wandering raiders called the Sea Peoples. Many Mycenaeans were forced to flee to other countries.

This reconstruction shows the city of Mycenae as it probably looked at the height of its power. The royal palace on the hilltop was built on several levels.

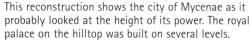

SHANG DYNASTY 1766–1122 B.C.

The earliest civilizations in China from around 3200 B.C. grew up on the banks of the three largest rivers: the Huang He, Chang Jiang, and Xi Jiang.

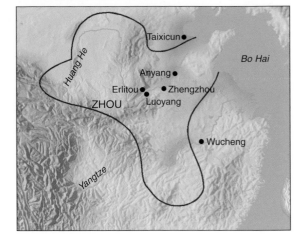

Shang civilization was based around the Huang He River in the north, though it also influenced central China. Later, the Zhou dynasty extended control over a larger area.

Like the people of Sumer, Egypt, and the Indus Valley, Chinese farmers relied on the country's rivers for transportation and water to grow their crops—paddy fields needed floods in springtime to help the rice grow. But the Chinese also faced two dangers: major floods and devastating raids by tribes from the north and west.

A piece of bronze Shang money, cast in the shape of a spade. This may have been made to slot into a case or sheath where several coins would be kept.

EARLY CULTURES

The first small towns appeared around 3000 B.C., during the Longshan period, around the Huang He (Yellow River) in the north. According to tradition, Huangdi, the Yellow Emperor, was the first emperor from around 2700 B.C. The first dynasty was that of the Xia (Hsia), who ruled for four centuries from 2200 B.C. Yu, its founder, is credited with taming the rivers by building dikes to stop floods, and also irrigation channels.

TANG AND THE SHANG

The earliest dynasty we have evidence for was the Shang, founded by Emperor Tang. The Shang ruled north China for more than 600 years. They lived in a string of cities along the Huang He, with the capital at Anyang. The city had many large palaces and temples, built mainly of carved wood. The Zhou dynasty replaced the Shang in 1122 B.C.

The Shang people grew millet, wheat, and rice, and also mulberries for feeding silkworms, from which they produced silk. They kept cattle, pigs, sheep, dogs, and chickens, and hunted deer and wild boar. The Shang used horses to draw plows, carriages, and chariots. Early in their history, they used cowrie shells as money, later switching to bronze. They were skilled in working bronze and jade, and made highly decorated practical and religious objects.

▼ Tradition says that silk was discovered by Empress Xiling Ji around 2690 B.C. She was the wife of the legendary Yellow Emperor, Huangdi, who was reputed to have brought civilization, medicine, and writing to China. The empress found that silkworms fed on mulberry leaves, so she had mulberry groves planted. Silk was spun into a fine textile that was so valued it was even used as a form of money. Silk manufacture remained a closely kept secret by the Chinese for about 3,000 years.

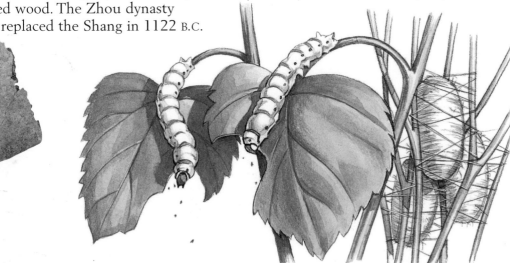

This is an oracle bone from the 1300s B.C. Large numbers of these have been found, engraved with early Chinese pictograms (picture writing). Diviners used these to interpret the future.

KEY DATES

3000 The first Chinese towns appear, during the Longshan culture
2700 Huangdi, the "Yellow Emperor," becomes emperor
2200 Period of Xia dynasty—Yu is the emperor
1766 Foundation of the Shang dynasty by Emperor Tang
1400 Peak of the Shang period
1122 Zhou dynasty displaces the Shang

BRONZE

Bronze is a mixture of copper and tin, which, when polished, looks like gold. The Shang became strong through their bronze-working, since it was a hard metal with many uses in tools, household items, and weapons. Bronze was also used for adornments, artistic, and religious items. It was cast in clay molds carved with patterns. Across the world, bronze represented a technological breakthrough.

CHINESE WRITING

Around 1600 B.C., the Shang developed the earliest forms of Chinese calligraphy— a pictorial writing in which each letter represents a whole word. The Chinese script we know today evolved from Shang writing. The Shang worshiped their ancestors, who were seen as wise guides for their way of life, and they used oracles to help them make decisions.

▼ When found in 1970, this bronze vessel held well over 300 pieces of jade. It was designed during the Shang period as a vessel for storing large amounts of wine and was known as a *pou*. The high quality and intricate design show that by this time bronze casting was a highly developed art. Other bronze vessels, called *jue*, with three legs and a long spout, were used for pouring wine during ceremonies.

▲ The ancient Chinese cooked sacrificial food in large bronze decorated vessels like this one. It had long legs so that it could stand over a coal fire.

Shang warriors fought in cumbersome armor made of bamboo and wood, padded with cloth. Early Chinese were warlike, and tribes used to fight long feuds. Centralized states such as the Shang developed to stop the feuding between warlords.

THE HITTITES 1600–1200 B.C.

Around 1650 B.C., a number of small city-states were united, through warfare. The result was the rich and powerful Hittite kingdom.

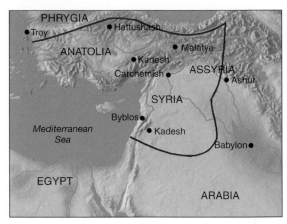

The Hittite territories at their peak, around 1300 B.C. They fought with the Egyptians, Assyrians, and Phrygians, and their empire disappeared in less than a century.

This Hittite rock-carved relief at Yazilikaya shows the protector-god Sharruma with the goddess Ishtar in the background. The relief was carved around 1250 B.C.

The Hittites consisted of several tribes and they spoke as many as six languages among them. One was the language of the Hatti, the original occupants of Anatolia. The Hittites were the first use iron—a metal that replaced the softer bronze.

This Hittite stela (carved standing stone) from Anatolia (Turkey) shows a woman doing her spinning, while she speaks to a scribe who holds a clay tablet and pen.

THE HITTITE EMPIRE

The Hittites were a warlike people. They controlled the supply of iron, and they used chariots, which gave them a great military advantage. They worshiped around 1,000 gods, chief of which was a storm-god. Early on, in 1595 B.C., they sacked Babylonia, plummeting it into a dark age. Gradually they conquered Anatolia, Syria, and the Levant (Lebanon), challenging the hold that the Assyrians and Egyptians had on the area.

The Hittites carved many works of art on boulders, shaping only part of the rock and leaving the rest in its natural form. This sphinxlike gateway once guarded a Hittite settlement located at Alaca, in what is now modern Turkey.

The Hittites adopted civilized ways, such as writing, from other peoples. They also introduced the horse into the Middle East from China. Men were dominant in society, and they were rich and well traveled. The Hittites reached their peak around 1300 B.C. The Hittites survived many threats until they fell to the Sea Peoples. Finally, they were destroyed and occupied by the Phrygians, who came from the Balkans, to the north. The Hittites were never heard of again, but they had had a strong influence on their neighbors.

BABYLON 1900–700 B.C.

Ur's domination of Mesopotamia was followed by many invasions. Around 1894 B.C. the Babylonians replaced their rulers with a dynasty that lasted 300 years.

A local boundary stone from Babylon is carved with prayers that ask the gods to protect the owner's land.

The Babylonians began to dominate southern Mesopotamia under their sixth ruler, Hammurabi the Great (1780–50 B.C.). He was a highly efficient ruler, famous for the code of laws that he laid down, and he gave the region stability after turbulent times.

Babylon became the central power of Mesopotamia. The armies of Babylonia were well-disciplined, and they conquered the city-states of Isin, Elam, and Uruk, and the strong kingdom of Mari. But Mesopotamia had no clear boundaries, making it vulnerable to attack. Trade and culture thrived for 150 years, but then the Hittites sacked Babylon in 1595 B.C.

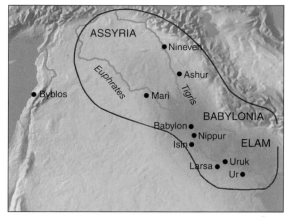

Under Hammurabi and his successors, Babylon controlled the whole of Mesopotamia. However, it became vulnerable to invasion from the north and west.

Its cities continued for 100 years under different foreign rulers. Then, for 500 years, Babylon was overshadowed by Assyria before its next rise to greatness.

EARLY SCIENCE

The mathematicians of Babylonia devised a system of counting based on the number 60, from which we get the number of minutes in an hour and the degrees (60 x 6) in a circle. Babylonian scholars developed early sciences and astrology from the knowledge they gained from the Sumerians.

Hammurabi was famous for his detailed code of laws. Well known to us today is "An eye for an eye, and a tooth for a tooth," prescribing punishments for personal crimes. The laws brought all of Babylon under a uniform legal system. They protected the weak from the strong, and regulated business and land ownership.

This stela shows Shamash, the god of justice, giving Hammurabi the instruction to formulate a code of laws. Underneath are inscribed the laws that Hammurabi codified, for all to see. In this way, people were shown that the laws were given to Hammurabi by the gods.

Skilled archers helped Babylon to defend itself against the Assyrians and many other invaders—Kassites, Aramaeans, Elamites, and Hittites. Its wealth, and its location at the meeting place of roads from Asia to the Mediterranean, was envied by jealous neighbors.

THE ASSYRIANS 1900–612 B.C.

While Babylonia ruled southern Mesopotamia, the warlike Assyrians dominated the north. Their kingdom lay in the valley of the upper Tigris River.

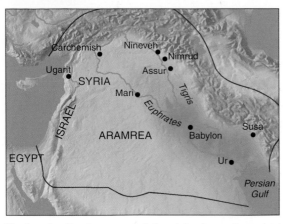

The Assyrian Empire grew and shrank in phases. It reached its greatest extent at the end, around 650, covering the whole of the Fertile Crescent. When Ashurbanipal died, Egypt and Babylon broke away and the empire collapsed.

Ashurbanipal was the last great ruler of Assyria. A ruthless soldier, he was also a patron of the arts, building the great library at Nineveh and vast gardens stocked with plants from all over the known world.

King Adadnirari I, the country's first powerful ruler (1770–50 B.C.), enlarged the Assyrian lands and took the boastful title "King of Everything." He and his successors were fierce dictators, who did not allow individual states to be independent. Assyria grew rich through the activities of its trading families, who sold textiles and metals far and wide.

COLLAPSE AND REBIRTH

As Assyria grew in size, rebellions by its conquered subjects increased. Eventually, Assyria fell to the Hurrians (relatives of the Hittites). The Hurrians dominated Assyria for over 250 years. As their overlordship dwindled, Assyria grew in strength again. Its next period of greatness lasted for 300 years. It reached its height under Tiglathpileser I (1115–1093 B.C.), who led many campaigns against neighboring lands. Assyria eventually dominated the whole region, including Babylon.

ASHURBANIPAL'S PALACE

The Assyrian king was an absolute ruler with very active involvement in all matters of state. In his magnificent palace, Ashurbanipal, surrounded by his advisors, heard the cases presented by the people. The palace was large, with extensive gardens. As a patron of learning, the king ordered many historic records from Babylon and Sumer to be written down, and texts on mathematics, chemistry, and astronomy were produced. Literary texts such as the *Epic of Gilgamesh* and the story of the Flood, from Akkadian times, were also recorded. All of these were destroyed by invaders after Ashurbanipal's death, though many records survived.

The Assyrian king meets his courtiers and administrators.

The Assyrians believed that the winged lion from Ashurbanipal's palace could ward off evil.

Here, Assyrian workers bring in materials for the building of a new palace, supervised by their king. Oarsmen in hide-covered boats tow a raft along the Tigris.

ASSYRIA FLOURISHES

From about 1076 B.C., Assyria and Babylonia were overrun by Aramaean tribes from Syria. But 150 years later, Ashurdan II and his successors reconquered the Assyrian Empire. The capital was moved to Nineveh, and buildings were erected and irrigation schemes undertaken. Assyrian kings expanded their lands to control all trade routes and suppress troublesome neighbors. The Assyrian Empire was at its greatest extent under Tiglathpileser III (745–727 B.C.), when it included the lands of Babylon, Syria, Palestine, Cyprus, northern Arabia, and Egypt.

ASSYRIAN LIFE

The Assyrians were great builders and erected magnificent cities, temples, and palaces. The men wore long coatlike garments and were bearded. Women wore a sleeved tunic and a shawl over their shoulders. It was not unknown for men to sell their wives and children into slavery to pay off debts.

The Assyrians were experts at siege warfare. Their battering-rams knocked holes in city walls; then scaling ladders and mobile towers helped the men climb over. The soldiers protected themselves with large shields.

KEY DATES

2500	Assyrians settle the upper Tigris valley
1900	Growth of Old Assyria
1680	Assyria falls to the Hurrians (until 1400)
1300–1200	Assyrian expansion
1076	Assyria falls to the Aramaeans (until 934)
730–630	Assyrian expansion at its greatest
612	Fall of Assyria to the Babylonians and Medes

THE FINAL CHAPTER

The last and greatest ruler of Assyria was King Ashurbanipal. He was a scholarly king and during his reign he created a huge library in Nineveh, his capital. The ancient records of Sumer and Akkad were preserved on clay tablets, together with literature and histories, mathematics, and astronomy from ancient times. When Ashurbanipal died in 627 B.C. the Assyrian empire fell to the Babylonians and Medes.

Ishtar was the goddess of war to the Assyrians. To the Babylonians she was the mother-goddess.

THE HEBREWS 1800–587 B.C.

The Hebrews first settled in Palestine about 4,000 years ago. They came to Palestine from Ur, although no one knows exactly where they came from before then.

Their name meant "the people from the other side" of the Euphrates River. Their story is told in the Bible. According to the Old Testament, the leader of the first Hebrews was Abraham, a shepherd who lived in Ur. Abraham traveled with his family first to Syria and then to Canaan (now Palestine), where they finally settled.

Solomon (965–928 B.C.) was one of the wiser kings of history and he carried out his royal duties fairly. His rule brought order and peace, and Jerusalem became one of the richest cities of the period.

After Solomon's death, Israel split into two different states, Israel and Judah—this weakened them against outside attack and led to their downfall.

EARLY YEARS

Abraham's grandson, Jacob (also called Israel), had twelve sons. He is said to have started the twelve tribes of Israel, which were named after his sons. When famine struck Canaan, Jacob led his people to safety in Egypt. Later, they became slaves of the Egyptians until Moses led them out of Egypt and took them back to Canaan, probably around 1200 B.C. There, led by Joshua, they fought the Philistines (Palestinians) for the right to settle and establish the land of Israel. Tradition has it that they used the sound of trumpets to bring down the walls of the city of Jericho.

THE FIRST STATE OF ISRAEL

Around 1020 B.C., the Philistines began to threaten the Hebrews. To defend themselves, the Hebrews banded together and appointed Saul their first king. His successor, David, united all the tribes, made Jerusalem the new nation's capital, and added a number of other territories. As defensive measures, his son Solomon built several new cities and a wall around the capital. The great temple at Jerusalem was his most famous work. He was a peace-loving and wise king.

SOLOMON'S TEMPLE

Solomon built an impressive temple in Jerusalem, at great expense, to house the Israelites' holy treasure, the Ark of the Covenant, which contained Moses' Ten Commandments. The Temple became the focus of Jewish culture. It is said that Solomon's temple had walls inlaid with precious jewels, and that it was designed in accordance with mathematical principles learned from the Egyptians.

The Judaean desert, often mentioned in the Bible, is a landscape of astounding beauty. It was probably greener in ancient times because of a milder climate.

According to the Bible, Solomon was a wise king. It is said that two women came before him with a child, each claiming to be its mother. Solomon suggested that he cut the child in two, so each mother could have half. One woman broke down and gave up her claim. Solomon recognized her as the true mother, and gave her the child. His reign marked the peak of Israel's history. After he died, his people argued and divided into two nations: Israel and Judah.

TROUBLES AND DISPERSION

After a rebellion by the Israelites, the Assyrians captured Israel in 721 B.C., and then Judah in 683. The Jews scattered in various directions, and many were carried away to Assyria as slaves. Nebuchadnezzar of Babylon crushed a Jewish rebellion in 597 and most of the Jews were taken to Babylon. During that exile, much of the Old Testament of the Bible was written down. This was the beginning of the *diaspora*, the dispersion of the Jews, which lasted into the 1900s.

This copy of a wall-painting from Beni Hasan in Middle Egypt shows a group of Semitic, or Asiatic, people, very possibly Hebrew, entering Egypt to trade.

A Jewish man blows on a *shofar*, a ram's horn fitted with a reed to amplify the sound it makes. It is possible these were used to bring down the walls of Jericho—or at least to frighten the inhabitants into opening the gates. The shofar is one of the world's oldest musical instruments, and it is blown on Jewish holy days. The woven prayer-shawl is called a *tallith*.

KEY DATES

c.1800	Abraham and the Hebrews move to Canaan
c.1200	Moses and Joshua take the Jews to Canaan
c.1020	Saul becomes king of the Hebrews
c.1000	David becomes king of the Hebrews
965–928	Solomon, king of Israel, reigns
721	Assyrians invade Israel, dispersing many Jews
587	Babylonians destroy Jerusalem and deport most of the Jews to Babylon

25

EGYPT, THE NEW KINGDOM 1550–1070 B.C.

The New Kingdom is the third major division of Egyptian history. It was a time of artistic achievement, military might, prosperity at home, and prestige abroad.

In Ancient Egypt, the dead were embalmed and tightly wrapped in cloth, a process called mummification, so that they would "live" forever. The mummy was put inside a coffin that was often highly decorated.

After the Middle Kingdom, a weak and divided Egypt was dominated by the Hyksos from Canaan, for 100 years. They ruled in Lower Egypt, the north. Around 1550, an Upper Egyptian royal family rose and battled to oust the Hyksos and reunite the whole country. In 1532 they succeeded. Ahmose established the 18th dynasty and became the first pharaoh of the New Kingdom—Egypt's Golden Age.

THE NEW KINGDOM

One of its early pharaohs, Thutmose I, conquered Palestine and the lands west of the Euphrates around 1500 B.C. During the rule of Amenhotep III, the New Kingdom, with its capital at Thebes, was rich and prosperous. Farmers and workers lived simply, but the nobility had a luxurious lifestyle. By law, men and women were equal, and women owned property. Women were able to follow one of four main professions: priestess, midwife, dancer, or mourner. Apart from the nobles, scribes and priests held the most important positions in Egyptian society.

AKHENATEN

The strangest ruler was Amenhotep IV (1353–35 B.C.). He attempted to change Egyptian religion by replacing its many gods and complex traditions with worship of only one god: Aten. He changed his name to Akhenaten and built a new capital at El-Amarna, dedicated to Aten. His queen, Nefertiti, was not of royal birth and may not have been Egyptian. When Akhenaten died, the priests of the old gods regained control, and worship of Aten was discouraged. The dead king's name was removed from every monument and record. His new city was abandoned and it was as if he had never existed.

Prosperous Egyptians were buried with jewelry, pottery, and models showing activities such as baking, brewing, and fishing. These models provide vivid details about the everyday life of the Egyptians.

This solid gold mask lay over the face of Tutankhamen's mummy. His tomb was found in the Valley of the Kings, in 1922, and the mummy with its sumptuous mask was revealed to stunned onlookers in late 1925.

A New Kingdom royal palace contained living quarters, but a large part would have been used for official duties. In a hall such as this, the pharaoh would award honors, receive ambassadors and dignitaries, and accept tribute.

THE END OF GREATNESS

Most New Kingdom rulers were buried in the Valley of the Kings, in tombs cut deeply into the rock. But robbers still broke in. Only one tomb survived, almost intact, to modern times, that of the boy-king Tutankhamen, who succeeded Akhenaten and died not yet twenty years of age. Egypt stayed powerful for a time, especially under Seti I and his son Ramses II—the Great—of the 19th dynasty (1307–1196 B.C.). Over time, rulers became weaker. Priests took control, and finally Egypt fell to a succession of foreign invaders. The Greeks conquered Egypt and ruled for around 300 years. Finally, Egypt became a Roman territory. Her monuments fell to ruins, her history and writings were forgotten.

Egyptian doctors treated their patients with a combination of medical practice and religious magic.

◀ Early Egyptian ships were flat-bottomed, suitable only for river transportation. Later they began to make larger, heavier ships with deeper, rounded bottoms that could be used for sea travel. These ships greatly increased Egypt's ability to trade goods with the lands bordering the Mediterranean Sea.

▲ Hatshepsut was the daughter of the great Thutmose I and widow of the weak Thutmose II. After her husband's death she took the throne and ruled as pharaoh in her own right. She wore male clothing and even the traditional false beard worn by the pharaohs.

◀ Kahun was an Egyptian town built of mud bricks. The houses had two levels, plus a flat roof on which people spent much of their time. Trades and crafts occupied different areas in the town, as they do in modern Eastern cities. A pyramid was connected to Kahun by a causeway. On the edge of the town was a temple.

27

THE PHOENICIANS 1500–500 B.C.

The Phoenicians were the greatest seafarers of the ancient world. They lived along a coastal strip in the Levant at the eastern end of the Mediterranean Sea.

The Phoenicians were the first to make transparent glass like this perfume bottle, on a large scale.

Phoenicians were famous for ivory carvings, like this finely detailed head.

The Phoenicians, who were merchant adventurers, lived in a string of independent city-states with good harbors in what is now Lebanon. Originally from Canaan, they were not interested in farming the land, but in seafaring, manufacturing, and trading.

TRADE AND CRAFTS

The Phoenicians traded overland with merchants carrying valuable goods from as far away as India and China to the west. The goods were sent by sea to Egypt, Greece, Italy, and north Africa. This trade made Phoenicians prosperous and powerful. They saw the rise and fall of the Minoans and Mycenaeans, and actively helped the rise of Greece and then Rome. The Phoenicians were skilled craftworkers, making glassware, metal items, jewelry, and cloth. They also invented glass-blowing. The port of Tyre was famous for Tyrian purple dye, a rich color worn by Greeks and Romans as a sign of status.

This is how a Phoenician warship probably looked. It was a galley with a ram for attacking other ships.

PHOENICIAN PORTS

The Phoenician ports in the Levant were Ugarit, Sidon, Byblos, and Berytus (Beirut). The main port was Tyre which, according to tradition, was founded 4,750 years ago. The city had close links with Israel. Hiram, king of Tyre, supplied King Solomon with mighty beams of Lebanon cedarwood and with craftworkers to build his great temple in Jerusalem.

The Phoenician Temple of Obelisks at Byblos in the Levant, the Phoenicians' homeland. The use of this site goes back at least 4,000 years, to the same time as the Minoans.

Starting in Cyprus, the Phoenicians gradually spread westward and set up many colonies around the Mediterranean. The most important was Carthage in North Africa, which became a large city. Other colonies were in Spain, Malta, Sicily, Morocco, and Sardinia. Later the Phoenicians colonized Cadiz and Tangier, founding trading posts down the coast of West Africa. Eventually, their homeland was invaded by the Babylonians around 570 B.C., so the colonies became independent, with Carthage as their chief port.

The main Carthaginian deity was the warrior god, Baal Haamon, connected with fertility. This is the temple of Salambo Tophet, from around 700 B.C. where worshipers sacrificed and buried children.

EXPLORATION

Around 600 B.C., the Egyptians commissioned the Phoenicians to sail around the coast of Africa. This voyage took three years. Regular trade with distant countries rich in tin and silver, like Britain, started around 450 B.C. The Phoenicians' downfall came in 200–100 B.C., when Rome, which was seeking to control the Mediterranean, fought them and destroyed Carthage.

The Phoenicians sailed from port to port throughout the Mediterranean, trading valuable goods and transporting them for others. Here a Phoenician trading ship docks in an Egyptian city. Phoenicians did not control great areas of land as other nations sought to do, but they were nevertheless very influential. They connected the different parts of the ancient world.

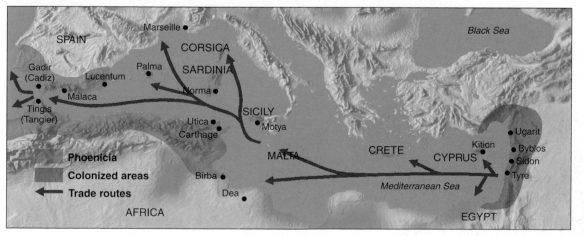

The bold sailors from the city-states of Phoenicia founded many colonies along the coasts of the Mediterranean, trading throughout that sea and venturing into the Atlantic, sailing to West Africa and Britain.

AFRICA 6000–200 B.C.

Although the earliest human remains have been found in Africa, not much was known until recently of the continent's history before 1500 B.C., except for Egypt.

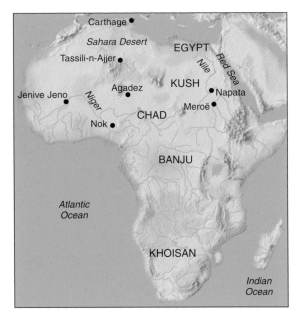

Today the Sahara forms a great desert barrier between northern and central Africa, but in about 6000 B.C. that barrier did not exist. Rock drawings and paintings show that the climate was much wetter, and that more people were able to live in the Sahara. The land began to dry up after around 3500 B.C., but desert trade towns and routes remained open, providing a link between northern and central Africa.

These are Masai women of recent times, from what is now Kenya. They are dressed in traditional ceremonial clothes.

These ancient rock paintings of warriors from Oum Echna in the Sahara, date from before 3500 B.C. when the Sahara was habitable grassland.

NUBIA AND KUSH

Egyptian culture spread up the Nile to Nubia (now Sudan). The kingdom of Kush grew out of Nubia from 2000 B.C. onward. Kush was valuable to Egypt as a trading partner and a source of gold. Egypt conquered Kush in 1500 B.C., to secure gold deposits there but in 750 B.C. was itself conquered by the Kushites, who founded the 25th dynasty of pharaohs. Kush never had a Bronze Age, but went straight from using stone to using iron. The capital was moved from Napata, its religious center, to Meroë, because Meroë was surrounded by rich iron ore deposits.

Africa, a vast continent, has many different environments in which many diverse cultures have grown up. North Africa was dominated by Egyptian and Mediterranean cultures. South of the Sahara Desert people lived without being affected directly by them.

This meant that Kush became an important center of ironworking, supplying Egypt, Babylon, Arabia, and Ethiopia. Meroë imitated Egypt, and it preserved many Egyptian traditions for the future at a time when Egypt itself was going through cultural changes. Ethiopia was also an important, though self-contained, area of culture with religious traditions of its own.

These ruined pyramids are at Meroë, east of today's Khartoum. The kingdom of Meroë developed from Nubia, a kingdom once influenced by Egypt.

CENTRAL AND SOUTHERN AFRICA

Around the Niger River lived farming tribes, with a few trading towns. Downstream, the Nok nation of Nigeria became ironworking and village-dwelling craftspeople. To the east there were the nomadic shepherds and village-dwelling people of Chad. Across central Africa, Bantu peoples were moving south from Nigeria, taking ironworking and farming with them. Southern Africa was occupied by shepherds as well as hunter-gatherers known as the Khoisan.

KEY DATES	
3000	Desertification of the Sahara begins
2750	Farming begins in West Africa
700	Nubian kingdom of Kush flourishes
600	Growth of Nok culture, Nigeria, and Meroë
200	Jenne-jeno, the first African city, is established

▲ A wall painting in the tomb of Sobekhotep shows foreigners bringing tribute to the pharaoh. Here, a group of African peoples bring gifts prized by the Egyptians: from Nubia, gold in large rings; from farther south, logs of ebony and fly whisks made from giraffe's tails, and fruit and a small monkey, and, finally, a baboon.

▶ Rock paintings and relief carvings are found across much of the Sahara. This cattle-herding scene was painted on rock in the Tasili area in the central Sahara. The artist has even recorded the color patterns of the individual cows.

AMERICA 1500–350 B.C.

The first Americans arrived in North America overland from Asia in the Ice Age when the sea level was lower. Over thousands of years they populated South America.

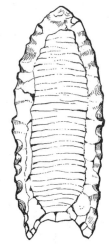

A Folsom point, a type of arrowhead found at Folsom in North America, dating from 9000 B.C.

Many early Americans remained hunters, fishers, and food gatherers, but in two separate areas, new civilizations developed—Mesoamerica (Mexico), and Equador and Peru.

THE OLMECS OF MEXICO

In Mesoamerica, some 9,000 years ago, the Native Americans settled and grew crops of Indian corn, beans, and pumpkins. Small villages sprang up in which the people made pottery and wove cloth. Out of this culture, around 1500 B.C., the first American civilization was born. The city-dwelling Olmecs built their capital at La Venta, near the Gulf of Mexico. The Olmecs built large earth and stone pyramids as centers for religious worship, and they produced huge sculptures and fine jade carvings. Many of their sculptures mix human and jaguar-like features. The Olmecs also had their own kind of writing and a sophisticated calendar system. Their neighbors, the Zapotecs and Maya, also developed advanced city civilizations.

This fine stone bowl is a magnificent example of the Chavín people's skill in stone carving. It was the work of a sculptor living in Peru 2,500 years ago.

CIVILIZATION IN THE ANDES

The first fishing and farming villages in South America were in northern Peru. About 2,800 years ago a more advanced culture appeared, called the Chavín. The Chavín people made pottery, wove cloth on looms, built in stone, and made elaborate carvings. The largest building in their capital was three stories high. Inside was a maze of rooms, corridors, and stairs.

KEY DATES

2600	Ceremonial centers built in Peru
2200	Farming villages founded in Mexico
1200	Olmec towns and ceremonial centers built
850	Chavín culture grows
600	Earliest Maya temple-pyramids built
350	Decline of the Olmecs

▲ This is one of eight enormous heads carved from basalt by the Olmecs; some are almost 10 ft. (3m) tall. They may represent early rulers, and each wears a distinctly different head covering.

▶ Dating from around 1200 B.C., this Olmec "altar" was probably a throne. The figure of an Olmec ruler sits in the niche underneath.

ARYAN INDIA 1500–500 B.C.

About 3,500 years ago the Aryans, a band of tough warriors and shepherds, fled south across the Hindu Kush mountains to settle in the subcontinent of India.

A natural disaster, maybe drought or disease, or a civil war, made the Aryans flee from their homelands in southern Russia. They spread out to Anatolia and Persia as well as India. They lived in tribal villages, probably in wooden houses, unlike the brick cities of the Indus Valley people.

Gautama Siddhartha (c.563–483 B.C.) was a prince. He saw the suffering of the people and left his family to search for truth. He later attained enlightenment, becoming known as Buddha. He taught a kinder faith that respected all living beings.

THE ARYANS IN INDIA

Aryans counted their wealth in cattle and sheep. They were not as advanced as the Indian peoples, but they were tougher. They were warriors and gamblers, beef-eaters and wine drinkers, and loved music, dancing, and chariot racing. Gradually, they settled down and adopted many of the ways of the native Indians, becoming crop growers and ironworkers. Among the crops was rice, unknown to the Aryans but already grown in the Indus Valley.

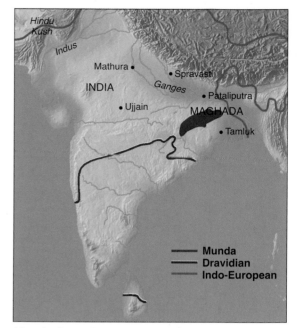

After the Aryans invaded northern India, many of the native people, the Dravidians and the Munda, moved to the southern and eastern parts of India.

HINDU CULTURE

The use of the plow and irrigation systems enabled the Aryans to grow enough crops to support large towns. By 500 B.C. there were 16 major kingdoms in northern India, the most prominent being Maghada. Maghada was the birthplace of the Mauryan Empire and of two new religions—Jainism and Buddhism.

The Aryans had no form of writing. Like many ancient peoples, they passed on their history and religious beliefs by word of mouth. These traditions, called the *Vedas*—the Books of Knowledge—were written down much later. The oldest of these is the *Rig-Veda*, a collection of more than 1,000 hymns, composed in their language, Sanskrit. Most of what we know about the Aryans' daily lives in ancient times comes from the *Vedas*, the ancient "old testament" of the Hindus. Unlike other faiths, Hinduism was not started by one teacher—its beliefs accumulated gradually over time.

▲ The Aryans introduced the caste system, headed by the educated Brahmin priests who ruled the country. The Kshatriyas were warriors, and the Vaisyas were traders and farmers. The darker skinned native Dravidians were servants and workers. It was impossible to change caste or marry outside it.

◄ One of the chief Hindu deities is Shiva, the transformer, who is both a creator and destroyer, the lord of change. He is depicted dancing in a halo of flames.

THE FOUNDING OF ROME 753–510 B.C.

According to tradition, the city of Rome was founded in 753 B.C. by local tribespeople who had established their camps on Rome's seven hills.

Legends say that early Rome was ruled by local kings, of whom Romulus was the first. The citizens were Sabines and Latins, who united to form one town, thinking of themselves as Romans. They were influenced by their neighbors to the north, the Etruscans, and traders from Greece and Carthage, who brought in new ideas about culture and society.

According to legend, Rome was founded by twin brothers, Romulus and Remus, grandsons of King Numitor. The king's wicked brother Amulius put the babies in a basket to float down the Tiber River to their deaths. However, they were rescued and suckled by a she-wolf. They founded Rome, but quarreled, and Remus was killed. Romulus became the first king of Rome.

ETRUSCANS

The Etruscans, whose kingdom was called Etruria, lived in a group of city-states which emerged around 800 B.C. They were farmers, metalworkers, seafarers, and traders and liked music, games, and gambling. They were greatly influenced by the Greeks, adopting the Greek alphabet, wearing himaton (robes), and believing in Greek gods. Many of their ways were passed to the Romans, who eventually took Greek-style culture to its ultimate expression.

In its early days, Rome was surrounded by Etruscans, Samnites, and others. Greeks and Phoenicians also had colonies in and around Italy. As Rome expanded, it had to overcome these older societies.

Legend has it that seven successive kings ruled Rome for 240 years. Kings did not have complete power—they had to contend with an assembly of nobles, who grew more influential as time passed.

KINGS OF ROME

The kings of Rome wore togas with purple borders. In processions, the kings were preceded by standard-bearers who carried a *fasces* (a bundle of rods and an ax blade), a symbol of power representing the king's right to rule over everyone else.

This terracotta sarcophagus of an Etruscan husband and wife was made around 510 B.C. Women had more status in Etruscan society than they did among Greeks or Latins, where they were kept in the background.

An assembly had a say in electing the king and what he could do, especially in war. The kings formed armies to defend Rome. There were arguments between the kings and the patricians (the leading families). The kings represented the old ways, and urban Rome was changing. The new elite of patricians eventually overthrew the monarchy in 509 B.C., and declared Rome a republic. It was the first republic in the history of the world. The Romans did not plan to become a great imperial power—at first they wanted only to protect themselves and fight off their interfering neighbors. However, within 500 years, Rome was to become the center of the Western world, taking over from the Greeks.

KEY DATES	
800	The Etruscan civilization emerges
753	Traditional date for the founding of Rome
509	Foundation of the Roman Republic
400	Decline of Etruria

▲ The Etruscans left little writing, but their paintings were vivid. This one from a tomb shows lyre and flute players.

▲ A *fasces* was a symbol of power in Rome. The wooden rods symbolized punishment, and the ax represented life and death.

◄ Greek art and dress greatly influenced the Etruscans. The figures in the tomb of the Augurs—diviners or soothsayers—at Tarquinia, painted around 500 B.C., clearly show Greek touches.

BABYLON REVIVED 626–539 B.C.

Tribespeople from the west, called Chaldeans, migrated into Assyria and Babylonia from about 1100 B.C. Several Chaldeans served as kings under their Assyrian overlords.

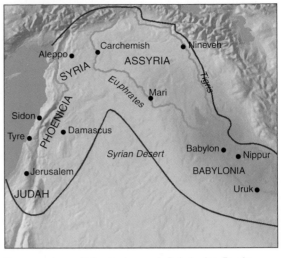

The map shows Nebuchadnezzar's Babylonian Empire at its fullest extent, controlling all of the lands known as the Fertile Crescent.

Nebuchadnezzar reigned for 43 years and his reign was marked by many military campaigns. Twice he subdued revolts in Judah, and when Phoenicia rebelled he besieged its chief port, Tyre, for thirteen years.

In 626 B.C., a Chaldean king called Nabopolassar took power, declared Babylonia independent, and threw off the Assyrian yoke. Nabopolassar then crushed the Assyrians in 612 B.C. His son Nebuchadnezzar drove the Egyptians back into Egypt and took Syria.

NEBUCHADNEZZAR

Nebuchadnezzar was one of the most famous kings of Babylonia. He came to power in about 605 B.C. His story is told in the Bible, in the Book of Daniel. He invaded many of the former Assyrian lands and the deserts west of Babylon. Among other conquests, Nebuchadnezzar captured Jerusalem and forced thousands of Jews to live in Babylon as prisoners because they had been rebellious. He made Babylon the master of all the lands within the Fertile Crescent.

BABYLON

Nebuchadnezzar devoted most of his time to making Babylon still more beautiful, a capital of the world. He had huge walls built around the city, and he named the main gate after the goddess Ishtar. He also built the Hanging Gardens—stepped gardens overlooking the city. He built a large bridge over the Euphrates River, and an enormous ziggurat, the Temple of Marduk or Bel (the "tower of Babel"). Nebuchadnezzar built himself a fine palace and he also improved the other cities. He encouraged the worship of the old god Marduk, seeking to revive Babylon's and Sumer's former greatness. Nebuchadnezzar ruled for more than 40 years, but in his later years he suffered from spells of madness.

▲ Flanked by lions and owls, the goddess Ishtar wears a crown of lunar horns. Ishtar was the chief goddess of the Babylonians.

▶ Babylon was a seafaring nation, situated on the Euphrates River. Great reed boats were built that traveled as far as India and East Africa. It was also the focus of land routes from Asia to the West.

THE CITY OF BABYLON

The Greek historian, Herodotus, described Babylon as the most splendid city in the world. It was already ancient when Nebuchadnezzar rebuilt it with new temples, palaces, roads, walls, gates, and a bridge across the Euphrates. The Temple of Marduk, or Bel, a Sumerian-style ziggurat, was very tall and became known as the Tower of Babel. The Greeks regarded the Hanging Gardens as one of the wonders of the world. Babylon was a metropolis with markets and workshops selling and making everything imaginable. It supplied Greeks, Indians, Persians, and Egyptians with all kinds of goods.

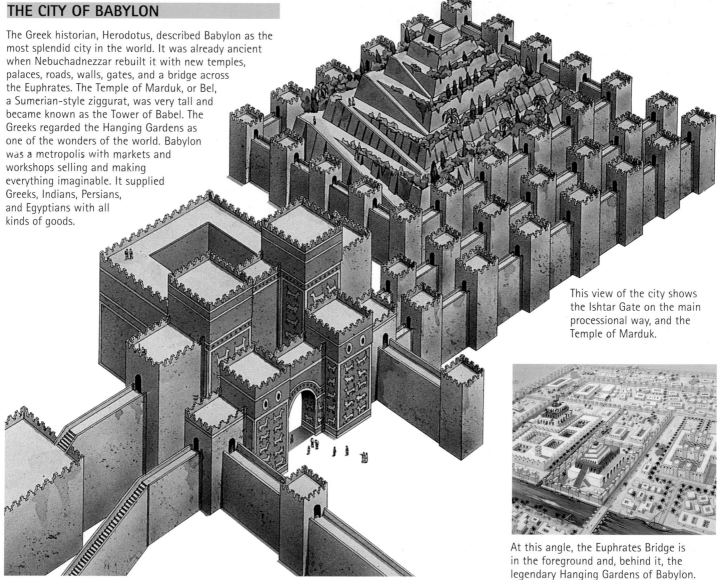

This view of the city shows the Ishtar Gate on the main processional way, and the Temple of Marduk.

At this angle, the Euphrates Bridge is in the foreground and, behind it, the legendary Hanging Gardens of Babylon.

DECLINE AND FALL

The Babylonian Empire survived for only six years after Nebuchadnezzar died. His son, Awil-Marduk (given the name of "Evil Merodach" in the Bible), reigned for three years before being assassinated. Two other kings, one of them a child, reigned for just three more years.

A Syrian prince, Nabu-Na'id, then seized power in Babylon, and tried to persuade the people to worship his own god, Sin, rather than Marduk. He made Belsharusur (Belshazzar) co-ruler.

Meanwhile, in Persia, a new young king, Cyrus II, had risen to power after taking the throne in 557 B.C. He had ambitions to take over Mesopotamia and found a Persian empire. In pursuit of this goal, he invaded Babylonia and captured the city of Babylon in 539 B.C. Nabu-Na'id was deposed and his son killed by the invading forces. Cyrus the Great, as he became known, freed the rebellious Jews who had been made captive in 586 B.C. by the young Nebuchadnezzar.

Babylonia was then ruled by the Persians for more than two relatively peaceful and stable centuries, until the time of another youthful king, Alexander the Great, who defeated the Persians and captured Babylon in 331 B.C., making it his capital.

KEY DATES

853 Assyria takes control of Babylon
626 Babylonians rebel against the Assyrians
612 Nineveh (Assyria) sacked by the Babylonians and the Medes
604 Nebuchadnezzar becomes king—Babylon's peak
539 Babylon conquered by Cyrus the Great of Persia

GREEK DARK AGE 1100 – 600 B.C.

When many of the Mycenaeans fled around 1200 B.C., Greece entered its "Dark Age." This left a gap which was filled by a new people, the Dorians.

There is no written history of this period, which lasted over 500 years. The Dorians did not have the culture or the skills of the Mycenaeans. They spoke a different kind of Greek, and they did not yet write things down.

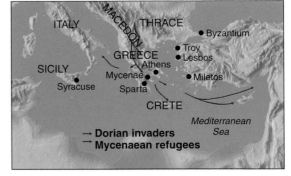

Many of the city-dwelling Mycenaeans were scattered by wandering raiders or "Sea Peoples," and those who remained were country dwellers. The Dorians, from the Balkans, marched in and dominated Greece from 1100 B.C.

HISTORIC SAGAS

The Dorians preserved memories of the Mycenaean age by telling long poetic sagas. When they adopted writing from the Phoenicians, they wrote down these poems. Two poems, Homer's *Iliad* and *Odyssey*, tell of the siege of Troy and one of its heroes, Odysseus. Objects found in Mycenaean graves match Homer's descriptions.

CITY LIFE

During the Dark Age, people abandoned town life to live in tribes ruled by warlords. By 600 B.C. city life had revived and overseas colonization began. Power was held by tyrants (mayors) or oligarchies (groups of leaders). Trade, population, and prosperity grew. After times of unrest around 500 B.C., some cities, such as Athens, appointed reformers to reorganize government, law, and trade. This was the beginning of Classical Greece.

Homer was a blind bard who, around 800 B.C., composed the epic poems the *Iliad* and *Odyssey*, which described people and events. He probably gathered together all the legends of Mycenae and retold them. Homer would have sung or recited his sagas to an audience.

Greek warfare developed during the Dark Age. Heavily armed foot soldiers, called *hoplites*, fought in a close formation known as a *phalanx*. They fought as a unit, covering each other.

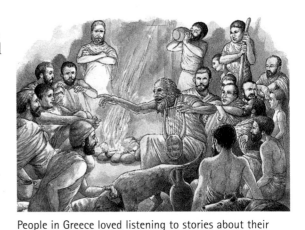

People in Greece loved listening to stories about their gods and heroes. Here, a Dorian bard is telling poetic histories to the people. The bards were not only entertainers and teachers, they also carried news of events to people.

THE ZHOU DYNASTY 1122–221 B.C.

The Zhou dynasty ruled China for over 800 years. They brought China a golden age—the growth of towns, trade, and early Chinese imperial culture.

The Zhou (pronounced Chou) began as a group of wandering herders who had settled in the fertile Wei Valley in western China. They ousted the last king of the Shang dynasty, who was cruel and a drunkard. The Zhou domain was not a single kingdom, but a collection of large estates, whose rulers owed loyalty to the king. Society was divided into rich nobles, common people, and slaves. A merchant class also developed. The Zhou introduced ironworking to China, using the metal for weapons, domestic items, and farm tools such as plows. Iron made farming easier and gave Zhou soldiers an advantage in war.

These Zhou iron battle-axes from around 500 B.C. were made at the beginning of the "Period of Warring States."

ROYAL DECLINE

After a few centuries, royal authority declined, and China entered an unstable "Springs and Autumns" period. The king held official power, though he was dictated to by the strongest lord of the time. Later, the "Period of Warring States" followed, which was dominated by warlords. During this troubled period, early classical Chinese thought took shape—this was the time of Confucius and Lao–Tzu, philosophers and sages. At this time the idea of a centralized Chinese imperial state came into being.

Confucius, Lao–Tzu, and the Buddha as a child, painted during the 1700s. They were all alive at around the same time, but it is thought that only Confucius and Lao–Tzu are likely to have met.

The people living in this ancient Chinese village of the earlier Zhou period would have been isolated and self-sufficient.

This picture of an archer on horseback was stamped on a clay tile, made during the Zhou dynasty. The bow is similar to those used later in the West.

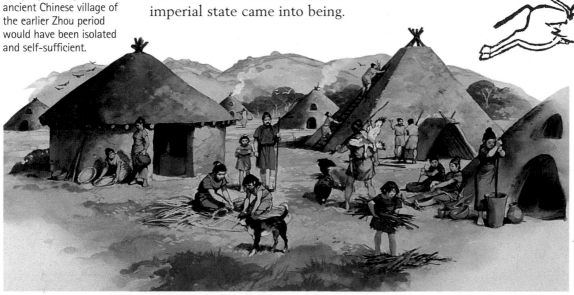

39

THE PERSIAN EMPIRE 559–331 B.C.

Iran used to be known as Persia. Its people comprised two groups, the Medes and the Persians, who migrated to Persia from central Asia about 2,800 years ago.

Darius I (548–486 B.C.) was a great general who extended the empire east and west, reorganizing it into 20 provinces. He built good roads as well as a new royal capital at Persepolis. From Lydia in Anatolia, he introduced gold and silver money to Persia. Darius called himself *Shahanshah*, king of kings.

At first the Medes were very powerful. Then, nearly 2,550 years ago, Cyrus, the ruler of the Persians, rebelled against the Medes and seized control. Cyrus the Great made Persia the center of a mighty new empire. His capital was at Ecbatana on the Silk Road, now buried under the modern city of Hamadan.

CONQUERING KINGS

Cyrus commanded a mighty army of cavalry and skilled archers. Taking advantage of the weaknesses of his neighbors, he conquered an empire extending from the Mediterranean to Afghanistan. His son Cambyses invaded Egypt. The Persians gained the support of their subjects by ruling fairly. Darius I eventually extended the empire into India and Greece. He also reorganized it, appointing *satraps* (governors) to each province. They paid him taxes in cereals, silver, and agricultural produce.

This frieze was carved in low relief on a thin stone at the Palace of Apadana, Persepolis. These works of art covered the walls and stairways of the palace.

UNITING THE ANCIENT WORLD

Darius built roads and market towns to reach all parts of his huge empire, and encouraged trade by introducing a standard coinage. The Persians controlled the western end of the Silk Road from China, and all trade from India to the Mediterranean. This wealthy, cosmopolitan empire linked most of the ancient civilizations of the time. However, it relied on the strength of its rulers. Eventually, the Greeks brought the empire down and took it over.

▶ The tomb of Cyrus the Great was built at Pasargadae in Iran. Cyrus is regarded as the author of the world's first charter on human rights.

This is a Persian infantryman. The Persian army was successful because of its clever use of strategy. It covered tremendous distances during its campaigns.

RELIGIOUS TEACHING

In religion, the Persians followed the teachings of a Persian prophet named Zarathustra (in Greek, Zoroaster). Zoroaster had adapted the ancient Persian tribal religion, which the Persians had brought with them from central Asia. They worshiped one god, Ahura Mazda, who they believed was locked in divine battle with Ahriman (representing sleep) and Satan (representing evil).

   Although Zoroastrianism did not become a world religion, it later influenced many other faiths including Christianity. This influence can be clearly seen in the biblical Book of Revelations.

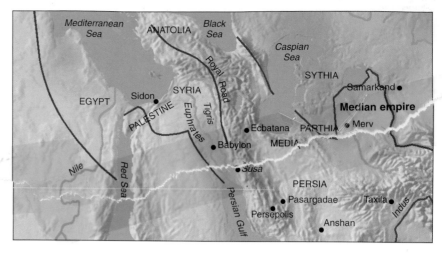

An impression from a cylinder seal, with cuneiform writing on the left, shows Darius I hunting a lion from a chariot with a bow and arrow. The winged figure overhead is an image of Ahura Mazda, main god of the Persians.

KEY DATES

c.850–750 The Medes and Persians migrate into Iran
c.600 Zoroaster reforms the ancient Persian religion
559–525 Cyrus the Great creates the Persian Empire
521–486 Darius expands empire to its high point
480 Greeks halt Persian expansion at Salamis
331 Fall of Persia to Alexander the Great

This map shows the Persian Empire at its greatest extent under Darius. Susa became its administrative center and Persepolis was its center of state. The Royal Road was built to speed communications.

Darius built himself a grand palace in his new capital city of Persepolis. The staircase of the palace was carved with this procession of dignitaries in ceremonial attire.

THE ARTS 25,000–500 B.C.

Since the earliest days, humans have decorated objects, made adornments, and represented ideas in artistic ways. This is a crucial part of the development of culture.

The early people who lived in Europe some 25,000 years ago made little clay models of goddesses and animals. These are thought to be totems or religious objects to help encourage the fertility of the land or to communicate with the spirits of the animals. Some ancient peoples painted vivid pictures deep inside caves showing animals, tribal shamans, and hunting scenes.

ARTISTIC SKILLS

Once people started leading more settled lives, they began to make pottery and other decorated items. In China, the people of Yang Shao painted pots with geometrical patterns on them. As copper and bronze replaced stone for weapons and tools, metalworkers became important, and the tools and objects they made were richly decorated. They did this not just to make them beautiful. By carving gods or sacred symbols on their tools or weapons, they believed that they would make them more effective.

This Olmec figure is carved in green jade. It represents a jaguar spirit associated with Tláloc, the god of rain and fertility.

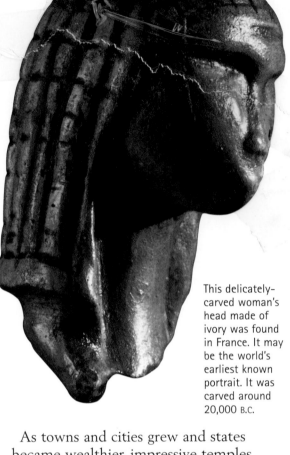

This delicately-carved woman's head made of ivory was found in France. It may be the world's earliest known portrait. It was carved around 20,000 B.C.

As towns and cities grew and states became wealthier, impressive temples, palaces, and other monumental buildings were decorated with carvings and paintings showing what life was like. From the frescoes of Mycenae to the Egyptian tomb paintings and from Olmec carvings to Chinese painted pottery, the art of these ancient people has given us an insight into their way of life.

▲ This fish from the Egyptian New Kingdom is a bottle for cosmetics. It was made around 1200 B.C. from strips of colored glass wrapped around a core. The ripples were made by drawing a point across the glass before it hardened.

▶ This elaborate game board was found in a cemetery in the Sumerian city of Ur. It is around 4,500 years old. Sadly, the rules of this game have not survived.

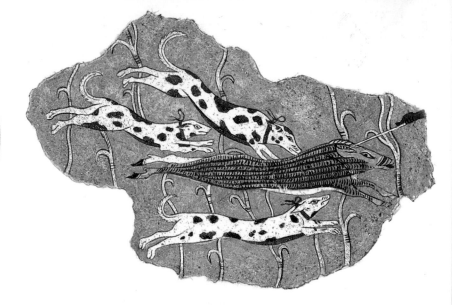

The Chinese valued jade, which they saw as a pure material with which to work. They carved many objects from it, like this intricate open ring which was probably worn by a wealthy Chinese woman around 1000 B.C.

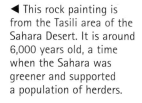

WRITING

Writing was originally a work of art, made up of pictures representing ideas or objects. Around 1000 B.C., the Phoenicians invented the world's first alphabet. It had 22 characters; all were consonants, none were vowel sounds. The "pictograms" of ancient China represented whole words—one pictogram might mean "mountain" or "town." Modern Chinese characters still represent concepts like this, instead of sounds.

▲ A fresco is a picture painted on damp plaster, so that the color sinks in deeply to last a long time. This fresco of dogs on a boar hunt was painted on a wall in Mycenae, about 1500 B.C.

◀ This rock painting is from the Tasili area of the Sahara Desert. It is around 6,000 years old, a time when the Sahara was greener and supported a population of herders.

The Greeks heavily influenced Etruscan art, as can be seen in this picture painted around 500 B.C. in the Tomb of the Leopards at Tarquinia. The reclining banqueters at a funeral are asking for another jar of wine.

ARCHITECTURE 40,000–1500 B.C.

The earliest humans lived in caves or any other natural shelter they could find. Eventually, people started making more comfortable homes and other buildings for themselves, using wood, mud, and stone.

The first bricks were shaped from mud and left to harden in the hot sun.

The houses of the New Stone Age city of Çatal Hüyük in Anatolia, Turkey, were built in 6000 B.C. They were so tightly packed that there were no streets. People walked along the rooftops.

The first buildings people made were tents of animal skins supported on wooden poles. In some places, they used mammoth bones to weight the structure down.

MUD-BRICK HOUSES

Around 6000 B.C., people started to build homes using dried mud and wood. They covered the walls with fine plaster, on which they painted decorations with pigments taken from plants. The floors were bare, or covered with straw or animal hides. Furniture, such as as tables and beds, was also made from mud bricks.

ROOFING MATERIAL

To keep out the weather, early people made roofs of wooden poles covered with twigs and leaves, straw or thick mats of soil known as sods. In hot climates, roofs were made flat to reflect the sun's rays, keeping the buildings cool. Houses in Jerusalem had flat roofs, each one with a parapet, or low wall, to stop visitors falling over the edge. In temperate climates, roofs were made sloping so that rainwater would run off quickly. Around 4000 B.C. the Sumerians of Mesopotamia built their homes entirely from marsh reeds. They used several layers of reeds to create large, curved roofs, but these roofs did not survive very long; they needed to be replaced every few years.

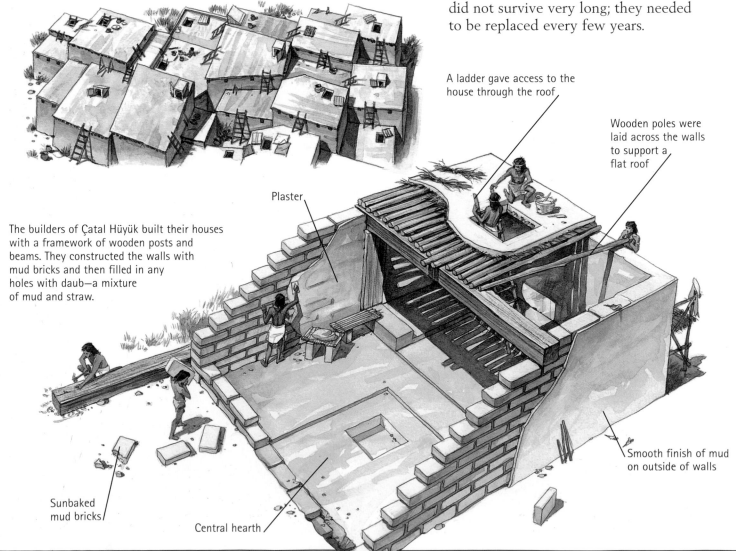

The builders of Çatal Hüyük built their houses with a framework of wooden posts and beams. They constructed the walls with mud bricks and then filled in any holes with daub—a mixture of mud and straw.

Plaster

A ladder gave access to the house through the roof

Wooden poles were laid across the walls to support a flat roof

Smooth finish of mud on outside of walls

Sunbaked mud bricks

Central hearth

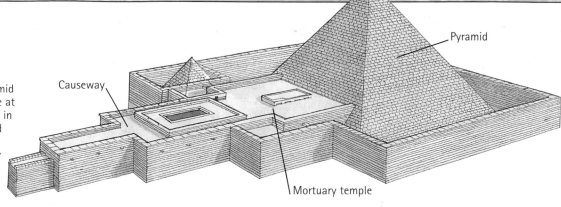

Pyramids housed the bodies of Egyptian kings. The stone pyramid complex of the pharaoh Sahure at Abusir near Memphis was built in about 2450 B.C. A causeway led directly from a lake formed by the Nile floods to the mortuary temple. The body was then buried in the pyramid.

Pyramid

Causeway

Mortuary temple

BUILDING WITH STONE

Around 3000 B.C., people in Europe, Egypt, South America, the Middle East, and China started to use stone as building material. At first they used uncut stone. Then, as metal tools were developed, they cut and shaped the stone into large, rectangular slabs. The blocks of stone were laid one on top of the other. Flat or sloping roofs spanned the walls.

Not all these early buildings were built for people to live in. Some were made for religious purposes, and others as tombs for the dead or shelters for farm animals. They include the pyramids and temples of Egypt and South America, the ziggurats of the Middle East, and monuments such as Stonehenge in Britain. Unlike those made from mud and wood, many stone buildings have survived to the present day.

The first builders used stone tools. Later builders had metal tools which were more efficient.

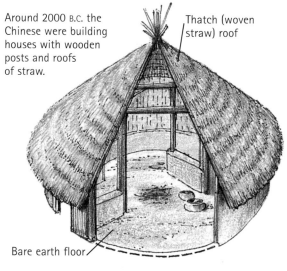

Around 2000 B.C. the Chinese were building houses with wooden posts and roofs of straw.

Thatch (woven straw) roof

Bare earth floor

Skara Brae, in the Orkney Islands off the coast of Scotland, was a small farming settlement with stone houses. Inside, there were stone cupboards and beds. The settlement was buried by sand at the height of a fierce storm 4,500 years ago.

VILLAGE LIFE IN EUROPE

The first European farmers made their house walls of hurdles of woven twigs, plastered with clay to keep out the wind and rain. They often decorated the walls with colorful pigments taken from plants.

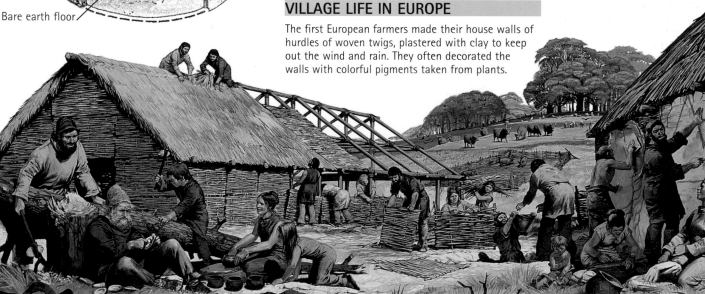

SCIENCE AND TECHNOLOGY 25,000–500 B.C.

The early history of the world is often divided into periods named after the materials used for the technology of the time—stone, bronze, or iron.

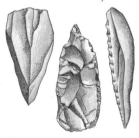

The first tools were made of any available hard stone. Flint made a greater variety possible, allowing the making of sharper edges. A knife-like blade, a borer, and a sharp point are shown here.

The three main divisions are Stone Age, Bronze Age, and Iron Age. These divisions cover different periods of time in different parts of the world, and they represent periods of development rather than specific historic dates. For example, in Çatal Hüyük in Turkey the use of copper started around 6200 B.C., but for Aboriginal Australians, the Stone Age continued almost until the present day.

THE SPREAD OF TECHNOLOGIES
In ancient China, the Bronze Age started around 2700 B.C., and it lasted for over 2,000 years. In other places, technologies were introduced through foreign contact. In Africa, ironworking started around 800 B.C., when it was imported from Egypt, leading them out of the Stone Age. One of the most significant inventions was the wheel, first used by the Sumerians more than 5,000 years ago; it needed flat surfaces such as roads to run on. Boats were important, powered by paddles or poles, then oars and sails—these were the best means of travel, and many early civilizations depended on rivers and boats for transportation.

The Cro-Magnons of around 40,000 years ago used implements of wood, bone, and stone. They knew how to prepare animal skins for clothes and shelters and how to shape objects into useful tools.

MAKING LIFE EASIER
Many farming, domestic, and military implements were needed. They ranged from needles and eating utensils, pots and furniture, spades and saws, to swords and battering rams—all invented to meet different needs over the centuries. Each of them made life easier and better. These objects allowed urban civilizations to come into being and flourish.

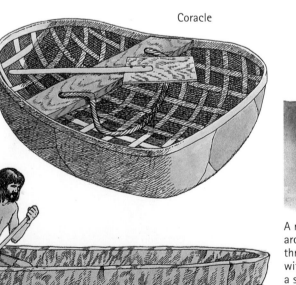

The first boats were dugouts, made from a single tree trunk. Later, more complex boats were made, such as the coracle, made of animal skins fixed over a wooden frame. These were first built around 6,000 years ago in Britain.

Coracle

Dugout

A reconstruction of a loom from Iron Age Europe of around 500 B.C. It was used for weaving colored woolen threads into cloth. The vertical threads, weighed down with clay loomweights, were moved back and forth while a shuttle was passed between them to bind the threads together as a woven material. Such cloth was a great step forward from the use of skins.

No one knows when the wheel was invented. It was probably first made from a sliced log, or it might have developed from potters' wheels. Carts were certainly in use in Sumer more than 5,000 years ago. These carried large loads over longer distances. From the cart came an important weapon of war, the chariot, which speeded up battle charges. The wheel was also used as a pulley to lift heavy loads. New forms of woodworking allowed the building of lighter wheels, and metals made stronger axles.

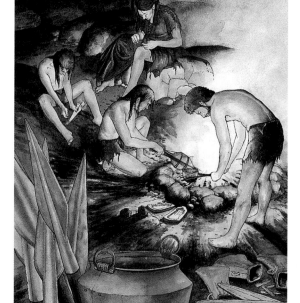

Early smelters used bellows to heat a fire to a temperature where a metal such as copper would melt into liquid. This was then poured into molds. When cooled, the metal product would be finished with polishing and sharpening. Later, copper and tin were mixed to make the much harder bronze.

This bronze bucket and highly decorated ax head were made in Europe around 600 B.C.

FROM ABACUS TO COMPUTER

All of the technologies in use today have their roots in this prehistoric period. In modern times we use computers, but counting systems, such as the abacus, were invented thousands of years ago.

WHEN IT HAPPENED

c.9000 B.C.	Arrowheads first made in North America
c.8000 B.C.	First farming in Mesopotamia
c.3000 B.C.	The wheel is used on chariots in Mesopotamia
c.2700 B.C.	Chinese start making bronze and weaving silk
c.2500 B.C.	Bricks are first used for building in the Indus Valley
c.1500 B.C.	Iron is smelted by the Hittites in the Middle East

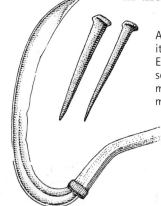

An iron dagger with its sheath from ancient Europe, and a Roman scythe and nails. Nails made woodworking much easier and quicker.

THE CLASSICAL WORLD
499 B.C.–A.D. 500

This was the great age of ancient Greece and Rome. These two extraordinary civilizations were responsible for shaping much of the world we live in today. By about 100 B.C., the ancient world was dominated by four empires. The Roman Empire was the most powerful, stretching from Europe to North Africa. In the Far East, the Han dynasty controlled almost all of what is now China, and the Middle East was ruled by the Sassanids. In India, the Gupta family held power. But, by about A.D. 450, these four empires had collapsed.

▲ Sages and philosophers traditionally influenced Chinese society, but they came under attack during the modernizing Qin period.

◀ The Temple of Olympian Zeus in Athens, Greece, was begun in the 500s B.C., but not completed until the 100s B.C.

THE WORLD AT A GLANCE 499 B.C.—A.D. 500

The classical civilizations that thrived during this period set many trends and patterns for later times. Discoveries by the Greeks form the foundation of the modern knowledge of biology, mathematics, physics, literature, philosophy, and politics. Alexander the Great spread Greek ideas into much of Asia. Later, by A.D. 100, the Romans took Greek culture farther afield into Europe and North Africa. Farther east, the Han dynasty controlled large areas of China, and the Guptas spread classical Hindu culture throughout much of India.

In these empires, life was mainly secure and peaceful, with strong governments and armies. But they soon came under attack from tribes of nomads called barbarians, and the cost of fighting these was high. By about A.D. 450 the great empires had collapsed.

At about the same time, the city of Teotihuacán in Mesoamerica was at its height. Its neighbors, the Maya, built great cities and roads, and dominated Mesoamerica until the 1400s.

NORTH AMERICA

North American tribes were spread thinly across the continent. They led simple lives—hunting, gathering, and farming in a variety of environments. In the Ohio area, the Hopewell culture built towns and ceremonial mounds, marking the first civilization north of Mexico. About A.D. 500, the Anasazi culture began to develop in Utah, Arizona, and New Mexico.

NORTH AMERICA

MESOAMERICA AND SOUTH AMERICA

MESOAMERICA AND SOUTH AMERICA

In Mexico and in Peru, a number of civilizations grew. They had their greatest periods between A.D. 1 and A.D. 600. In Mexico, the great trading city of Teotihuacán, with its pyramids and palaces led the way. The Maya were beginning a civilization that would develop writing and astronomy. Quite separately, in Peru, the city of Tiahuanaco grew, high in the Andes. On the Peruvian coast, the Chavin, Nazca, and Moche cultures also began to establish themselves.

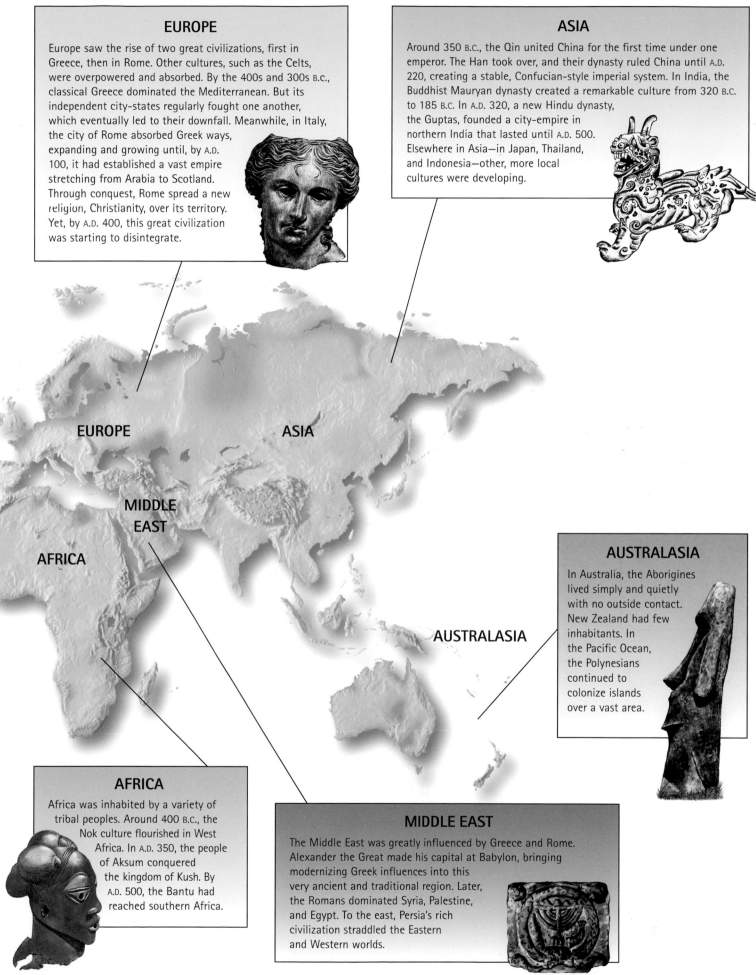

EUROPE

Europe saw the rise of two great civilizations, first in Greece, then in Rome. Other cultures, such as the Celts, were overpowered and absorbed. By the 400s and 300s B.C., classical Greece dominated the Mediterranean. But its independent city-states regularly fought one another, which eventually led to their downfall. Meanwhile, in Italy, the city of Rome absorbed Greek ways, expanding and growing until, by A.D. 100, it had established a vast empire stretching from Arabia to Scotland. Through conquest, Rome spread a new religion, Christianity, over its territory. Yet, by A.D. 400, this great civilization was starting to disintegrate.

ASIA

Around 350 B.C., the Qin united China for the first time under one emperor. The Han took over, and their dynasty ruled China until A.D. 220, creating a stable, Confucian-style imperial system. In India, the Buddhist Mauryan dynasty created a remarkable culture from 320 B.C. to 185 B.C. In A.D. 320, a new Hindu dynasty, the Guptas, founded a city-empire in northern India that lasted until A.D. 500. Elsewhere in Asia—in Japan, Thailand, and Indonesia—other, more local cultures were developing.

EUROPE

ASIA

MIDDLE EAST

AFRICA

AUSTRALASIA

AUSTRALASIA

In Australia, the Aborigines lived simply and quietly with no outside contact. New Zealand had few inhabitants. In the Pacific Ocean, the Polynesians continued to colonize islands over a vast area.

AFRICA

Africa was inhabited by a variety of tribal peoples. Around 400 B.C., the Nok culture flourished in West Africa. In A.D. 350, the people of Aksum conquered the kingdom of Kush. By A.D. 500, the Bantu had reached southern Africa.

MIDDLE EAST

The Middle East was greatly influenced by Greece and Rome. Alexander the Great made his capital at Babylon, bringing modernizing Greek influences into this very ancient and traditional region. Later, the Romans dominated Syria, Palestine, and Egypt. To the east, Persia's rich civilization straddled the Eastern and Western worlds.

CLASSICAL GREECE 600–337 B.C.

Ancient Greece was made up of independent city-states, each with its own laws and customs. Here, the Greeks created a new society with new ideas.

Athens led the way in the development of richly painted pottery.

E ach city-state or *polis* grew up on the plains, and the mountains around them provided natural limits and defenses. Citizens built high, strong walls around their cities, and an *acropolis* (fort) was erected on a high place inside the walls. At the heart of each city was the *agora*, a large open space used for meetings and markets.

The Aegean Sea was well placed for the founding of a maritime civilization, with cities dotted along both coastlines, and easy access to the Mediterranean Sea.

CITIES AND COLONIES

The two most important city-states were Athens and Sparta. There were many other cities, such as Corinth, Chalcis, Miletos, Smyrna, and Eretria, each with its own way of life, customs, and forms of government. The city-states expanded to build colonies northward on the Black Sea, in Cyrenaica on the coast of north Africa (Libya), Sicily, southern Italy, and even as far away as the southern coasts of France and Spain. Greek city-states were very competitive with each other.

GREEK CULTURE

The Greeks created a new society with new ideas. They fought hard for their freedom, especially against the Persians who threatened Greece. Being traders, sailors, and adventurers, the Greeks influenced many faraway cultures. Philosophers, doctors, and scientists taught a new way of thinking, based on observation and discussion. Old rural traditions died off as the cities grew to dominate the countryside. New art, architecture, and sciences were created.

Here, the traders of a Greek colonizing expedition, around 500 B.C., draw their ships up onto the beach to start business. The newly built walled city would contain a marketplace, temples, law courts, and government offices as well as houses, workshops, and defenses.

◀ At the battle of Salamis, c. 480 B.C., 380 Greek ships, called *triremes*, faced a Persian force of 1,200 ships. The more mobile triremes drove the Persians into a confused huddle. Persian defeats on land and at sea led them to withdraw from Greece.

EDUCATION

The sons of freemen were sent to school, and girls were taught weaving and household skills by their mothers. Starting at the age of six or seven, the boys learned reading, writing, dancing, music, and athletics. They wrote on wax tablets, using a stick called a *stylus*.

◀ Here, Greek children study a number of subjects with their tutors. ▼ This painting shows a schoolboy being tested by one of his tutors.

DISUNITY BETWEEN CITY-STATES

Athens, Sparta, and other city-states united to fight off Persian invasions for 60 years, and triumphed at the battles of Marathon and Salamis around 480 B.C. However, from 431 B.C. they spent more than 25 years fighting each other in the Peloponnesian War because Sparta feared the growth of Athenian power. The independent Greek cities, therefore, never united as one country. This disunity eventually resulted in an invasion around 330 B.C. by Philip II of Macedon, father of Alexander the Great.

KEY DATES	
800s	The first city-states founded in Greece
594	Reform of the Athenian constitution
540s	Persians conquer Ionia (eastern Aegean)
480	Persian invasion ends
431–404	Peloponnesian Wars: Athens against Sparta
404	Athens falls to Sparta
371	Sparta declines—Thebes now main city-state
337	Philip of Macedon invades Greece

A silver four-drachma "owl" piece was the most common coin in the ancient Greek world. Issued in Athens, one side carried a picture of Athena, goddess of wisdom and patron and protector of Athens. The other side carried a picture of an owl, Athena's symbol, carrying an olive branch.

Greek philosophers have had a great impact on history, and their works are still studied today. The freethinking atmosphere in Athens stimulated questioning and discussion on many different subjects. Herodotus and Thucydides were famous Greek historians, and Plato, Socrates, and Aristotle were philosophers and scientists.

GREEK CITY-STATES 600–337 B.C.

There were many Greek city-states. Athens and Sparta were the leading cities, constantly fighting each other to dominate Greece.

Greek theaters were built so that everyone could see the stage and hear the actors. Greek plays often had a strong moral message, and many Greek dramas survive to this day.

Athens and Sparta had very different beliefs and ways of life. Athens was a busy, cosmopolitan trading city run by public debate and decision making—a center for new ideas and trade from all over the known world. Athens became great through prosperity and invention. Sparta was steered by its king, and had a very strictly ruled and militaristic society. Sparta threatened Athens' leadership with a well-trained and superior army. Athens was the birthplace of democracy under the reformers Kleisthenes (around 500 B.C.) and Pericles (around 460 B.C.). Voting was enjoyed by freemen, but not by women, foreigners, or slaves. By 400 B.C. it was the leading city-state, controlling the seas and a number of colonies abroad. Many cities paid tribute to Athens for protection and trade advantages. Its statesmen, soldiers, writers, architects, philosophers, artists, and mathematicians had a wide influence.

The sculpted head of a Greek goddess. The Greeks made their gods look very human, introducing realism into their art. In later centuries, this artistic realism reached as far as India and Japan, where statues of the Buddha were also made in a realistic style.

Cities such as Corinth, Thebes, Samos, and Byzantium also made up the culture now known as classical Greece. Being smaller than Athens and Sparta, they often had to ally themselves with each other to survive—sometimes switching sides. Each made its own special contribution to Greek culture.

▲ When a politician became unpopular, citizens voted to ostracize or exile him by scratching his name on a piece of broken pottery called an *ostraka*.

◄ In Athenian politics there were long, heated debates in which orators had a great influence. This was a new kind of government: democracy.

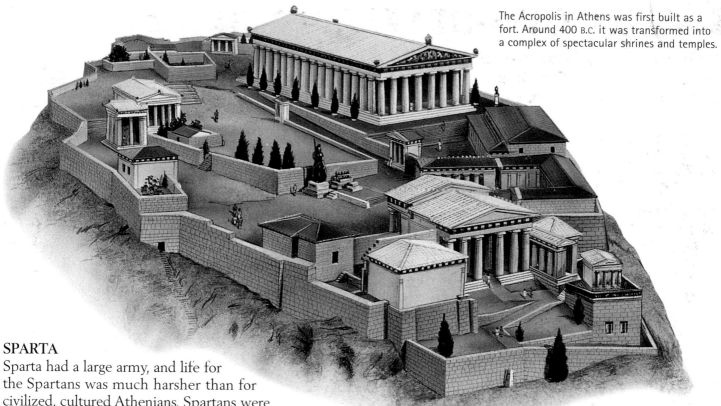

The Acropolis in Athens was first built as a fort. Around 400 B.C. it was transformed into a complex of spectacular shrines and temples.

SPARTA

Sparta had a large army, and life for the Spartans was much harsher than for civilized, cultured Athenians. Spartans were renowned for their strength, dedication, and courage. Sparta relied on a vast population of land slaves called *helots* to provide food. A helot rebellion in 464 B.C. lasted for 20 long years, until the Spartans created an army to control the slaves—the first dictatorial "police state." Spartan life was tough from birth onward: babies who were weak or sick were left to die on the mountainside. Boys were given strenuous training in military skills and sports from the age of seven until they were 20, when they became citizens. Then they joined the army. Even when married, Spartans ate and slept in communal barracks until they were 30 years old.

▲ Greek city houses were built around a courtyard with a large kitchen. Flat roofs provided extra living space in the summer.

▼ In this Greek agricultural scene, a shepherd is guarding his sheep, pigs are being herded, olives are being pressed, and the oil is being sold to a merchant.

ALEXANDER THE GREAT 336–323 B.C.

After the end of the disastrous Peloponnesian War, the age of Spartan domination did not last long. By 359 B.C. Philip of Macedon controlled all of Greece.

Alexander was one of the greatest generals of all time. In 13 years, he united Greece, Egypt, and Babylon, spreading Greek ("hellenistic") ideas and customs far and wide.

Philip of Macedon was assassinated in 336 B.C., shortly after he had invaded Greece. His son Alexander was only 20 years old when he became king. He set out to destroy the Persian threat to Greece—and to gain Persia's wealth.

His first campaign in 334 B.C. gave him control of Asia Minor, and he quickly took Syria and Egypt. By 331 B.C., Persia had fallen and Alexander had taken Babylon. He then embarked on a program of exporting Greek culture and city building to the lands the Greeks invaded. He was a modernizer, and many people welcomed, or at least accepted, the Greeks. Alexander then marched to central Asia and India. In India, his soldiers refused to go farther. They withdrew to Babylon, Alexander's

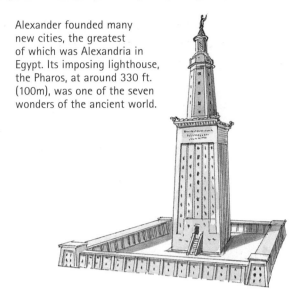

Alexander founded many new cities, the greatest of which was Alexandria in Egypt. Its imposing lighthouse, the Pharos, at around 330 ft. (100m), was one of the seven wonders of the ancient world.

new capital. In 323 B.C., at the age of 32, Alexander suddenly died of fever. His generals were left to battle for shares of the Greek Empire, which now stretched from Egypt to India.

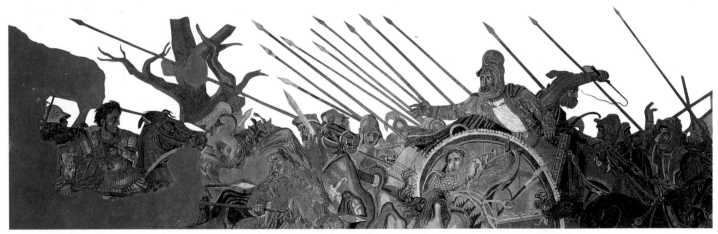

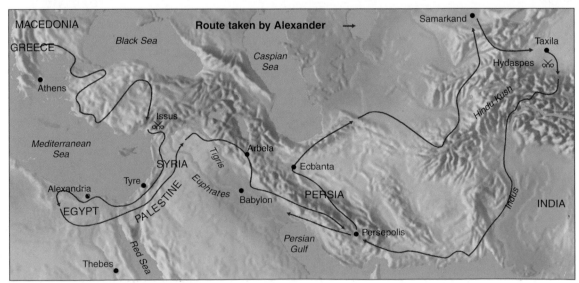

Route taken by Alexander →

MACEDONIA
GREECE
Black Sea
Caspian Sea
Athens
Issus
Mediterranean Sea
SYRIA
Tigris
Arbela
Tyre
Alexandria
Euphrates
Ecbanta
PALESTINE
EGYPT
Babylon
PERSIA
Persian Gulf
Persepolis
Red Sea
Thebes
Samarkand
Taxila
Hydaspes
Hindu Kush
Indus
INDIA

This Greek painting shows Alexander beating the Persian king, Darius, at the battle of Issus, in Syria, in 333 B.C. Alexander eventually took over the whole Persian Empire.

◄ In just a few years, Alexander's troops marched many thousands of miles, building new cities, peopling them with Greeks, and modernizing whole countries with Greek ideas and trade. Babylon became the new capital of the Greek Empire.

INDIA: THE MAURYAN EMPIRE 321–233 B.C.

The Mauryan Empire was founded by Chandragupta. It extended from Bengal to the Hindu Kush and united all the lands of northern India.

Asoka said, "All people are my children." He set out to create a kind of heaven on Earth in Mauryan India.

Chandragupta took power in Maghada in 321 B.C., and within ten years he had invaded most of northern India. He was a good organizer, and India became prosperous under his influence. His son Bindusara (293–268 B.C.) extended the empire far into southern India.

ASOKA THE EMPIRE BUILDER

Chandragupta's grandson, Asoka (268–233 B.C.), was the greatest Mauryan ruler. He enlarged the empire, which was inhabited by peoples of more than 60 different beliefs and languages. Asoka was a Hindu, but he adopted Buddhism after seeing a particularly horrific battle. He adopted the Buddhist moral rules of good conduct and nonviolence and brought peace, culture, dignity, and prosperity to his subjects. He built up the religion from a small sect, and sent out missionaries as far as Indonesia, central Asia, and Egypt. He had many stone pillars erected around India, covered with moral and religious guidelines for his people. Asoka was one of history's fairest monarchs.

The lion capital at Sarnath, erected by Asoka, has been adopted by modern India as one of its national emblems. The column on which it stood marked the place where Buddha preached.

The Mauryans made sure that there was plenty of food available by developing large irrigation and farming schemes across India, such as these rice paddies in the Ganges Valley of northern India.

MAURYAN LIFE

On a practical level, Asoka tried to improve the conditions of his people. He had reservoirs and irrigation systems built and wells dug, and he set up rest houses at regular intervals along the roads of the empire, to encourage travel and trade and to bring together all its different regions into one system. Asoka also employed a large secret police to help him run his diverse empire. Although Asoka tried to unite the empire, under his rule religious differences between Hindus, Buddhists, and others actually became more distinct. After his death the Mauryan Empire soon became weak and India fragmented into small kingdoms.

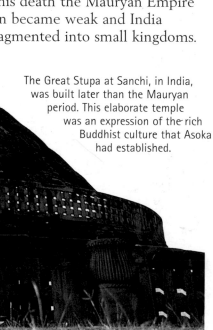

The Great Stupa at Sanchi, in India, was built later than the Mauryan period. This elaborate temple was an expression of the rich Buddhist culture that Asoka had established.

CHINA: THE QIN DYNASTY 221–206 B.C.

The warlike Qin tribes of western China conquered their neighbors from 350 B.C. onward. By 221 B.C. they had built the empire from which China takes its name.

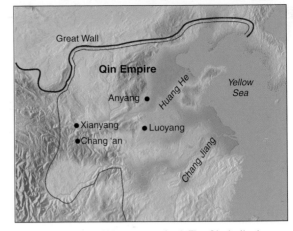

For the first time, China was united. The Qin built the Great Wall to protect it from tribes from the north. The Qin capital was Xianyang on the upper Yellow River, the area where the Qin originated.

King Zheng of Qin (pronounced "*Chin*") united most of China in just ten years, ending the Warring States period. He changed his name to Shi Huangdi (meaning "First Emperor") and founded the first imperial dynasty of China.

The ancient Chinese were great inventors. They invented the wheelbarrow, which they used to carry both goods and people in the 2nd century B.C.— Europe only adopted it 1,000 years later.

IMPERIAL CHINA

Shi Huangdi reorganized the government, bringing everything under central control. He standardized all weights and measures, Chinese writing, and even the width of wagon wheels; he made laws and institutions in the Qin tradition, and introduced a single currency. He was a ruthless modernizer, abolishing the powers of the feudal aristocracy and sending out administrators to run the regions. He built roads and canals, and improved farming with irrigation and drainage schemes. To protect China from barbarians, construction began on the Great Wall, much of which still exists today. He established imperial traditions that remained consistent through different dynastic periods over 2,000 years. In 221 B.C., Shi Huangdi destroyed many traditional literary works, including those of Confucius, and even executed 400 scholars, to ensure modernization.

THE MANDATE OF HEAVEN

Shi Huangdi was a warrior who used cavalry rather than chariots. He was used to being obeyed, and some of his actions made him very unpopular. Yet he commanded respect and achieved results, and he used his power to make changes quickly and to unite China. He also had principles. He believed that the emperor had been given the "mandate of heaven" by the gods, and that he must earn the support of the gods by governing well. This principle meant that the emperor could also be deposed if he misgoverned the country.

Sages and philosophers traditionally influenced Chinese society and government and also played a religious role. As preservers of knowledge, they came under attack during the modernizing Qin period.

Life was bustling in a typical Qin town of a few thousand people, with its market, buildings, and defenses.

58

KEY DATES

350s	Qin becomes a militaristic state
315	Qin becomes the leading state in China
256	Qin annexes the state of Zhou (Luoyang)
230	King Qin Zheng begins to unify China by force
221	Qin dynasty unites the country for the first time in one empire
214	To protect China from Hun raids, construction of the Great Wall begins
212	Shi Hunagdi burns all historical documents, books are banned, and Chinese script standardized
209-202	Civil war between competing warlords
202	Founding of the Han dynasty by Liu Bang

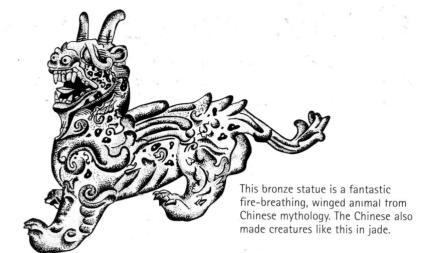

This bronze statue is a fantastic fire-breathing, winged animal from Chinese mythology. The Chinese also made creatures like this in jade.

THE QIN LEGACY

Shi Huangdi died in 210 B.C., and four years later the Qin dynasty was overthrown because the changes and laws they made were too harsh. A civil war broke out. The idea of a united empire, however, had become fixed in the minds of the people. An ordinary man, named Liu Bang, who had become a Qin official, founded a new dynasty and, as a result, gained popular support. The Han dynasty was to rule for 400 years, on the basis that Shi Huangdi had established.

Shi Huangdi's tomb housed his body and possessions for use in the afterlife. It also contained 7,000 larger-than-life terracotta soldiers. Each face was realistic and may have represented the actual faces of a specific soldier.

THE GREAT WALL OF CHINA

The Qin used large numbers of forced laborers to build much of the Great Wall. It was 1,400 mi. (2,250km) long and built from packed earth and rubble. Stone, bricks, and mortar were added later. The scale of this operation shows how important it was to the Chinese to keep the raiding tribes of the north out. These tribes preyed on Chinese security and prosperity, and China suffered greatly before the wall was built and the raiders beaten off.

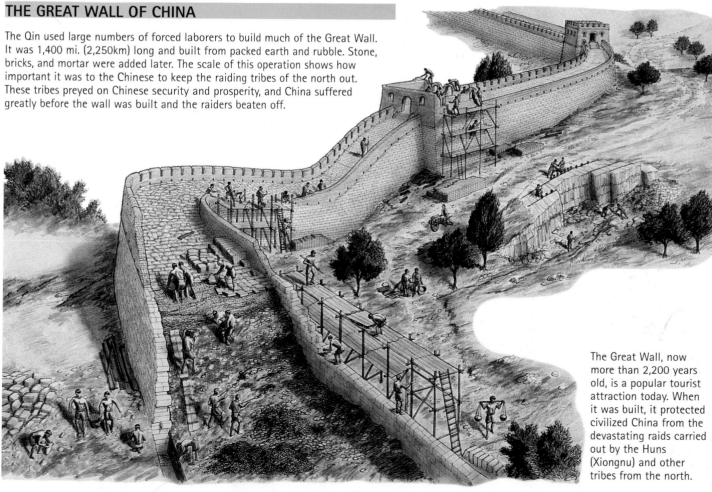

The Great Wall, now more than 2,200 years old, is a popular tourist attraction today. When it was built, it protected civilized China from the devastating raids carried out by the Huns (Xiongnu) and other tribes from the north.

AFRICA 500 B.C.–A.D. 500

Most of Africa was unaffected by outside influences. In West Africa, new nations were being formed, and migration was changing southern Africa.

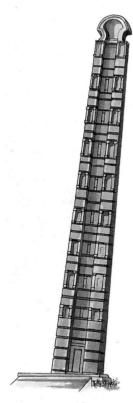

The introduction of the camel to the Sahara brought major changes around 100 B.C. Caravans were able to cross the desert carrying gold, ivory, gums, spices, and slaves. Trading towns became established in West Africa: Jenne-jeno, Niani, Yelwa, and Nok were on rivers or at the edges of deserts and rain forests. These towns were the capitals of the first budding African states. North–south trade passed through Meroë and Aksum, bypassing the Sahara into the regions now known as Chad, Rwanda, and Kenya.

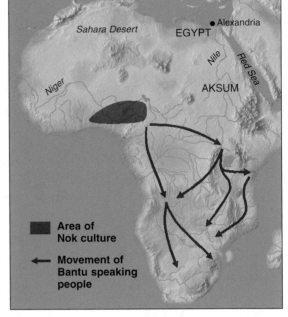

Africa had four main centers of cultural growth: Aksum (Ethiopia), the Berber north African coast, negro West Africa, and the developing Bantu areas farther south.

This terracotta head from Nok is a fine example of sculpture that flourished from 400 B.C. to A.D. 200.

AKSUM

Meroë collapsed in 350 B.C., and Aksum, on the Red Sea coast of Ethiopia, grew rich exporting ivory, precious stones, and perfumes to Arabia, Greece, and Rome, reaching its peak in A.D. 350. Around that time its king, Ezana, adopted Christianity. Cities and great monoliths were built. Aksum thrived until A.D. 1000.

BANTU EXPANSION

Farming, Bantu-speaking people from Nigeria gradually migrated south and east, and by A.D. 500 they had occupied central and southern Africa, leaving the rain forests to the pygmies and the Kalahari Desert to the Khoisan bushmen. On Africa's east coast the Bantu had started to trade with Greeks and Romans.

Greek trading missions on the east African coast bought medicinal herbs, aromatic gums, jewels, and gold from the Bantu-speaking tribespeople of the hinterlands.

To smelt iron, iron ore was put into an earthen furnace. Bellows were then used to raise its temperature to extract metal from the ore.

The leaders of Aksum were very religious. They built tall monoliths like this at places of importance, such as over royal tombs.

JUDEA 600 B.C.–A.D. 135

Since their 60-year exile in Babylon, from 597 B.C., the Jews, with their different religious beliefs, had grown further apart from their Near-Eastern neighbors.

The *menorah*, a Jewish ceremonial candlestick, was shaped by Moses to signify the seven days of Creation. One stood in the Temple at Jerusalem.

The Western Wall in Jerusalem is at the site of the Temple that was destroyed by the Romans in A.D. 70.

The ancient fortress of Masada is where besieged Jewish rebels committed suicide in A.D. 73 rather than surrender to the Romans.

The Jews worshiped one god, Yahweh, built synagogues, and observed strict religious laws. On returning from exile in Babylon in 538 B.C., they emphasized Jewish law and beliefs, and set themselves apart from non-Jews, or Gentiles. Palestine was under Greek rule and many Jews fought to stop their influence destroying Jewish traditions.

ROMAN PALESTINE

After Greek rule, Judea was independent for nearly 80 years before being conquered by Rome. The Romans appointed Herod as king of Judea in 37 B.C. Jewish people were free to travel and trade, and many left to settle elsewhere. When Pontius Pilate became Judea's Roman governor in A.D. 26, life became hard for the Jews. They loathed the Romans and their taxes. After much rebelliousness, the Romans forced the Jews to leave Judea in A.D. 135.

THE ROMAN REPUBLIC 509–27 B.C.

Rome was by now run by patricians (the ruling class). They sought to expand Rome's interests, first in Italy and later throughout the Mediterranean.

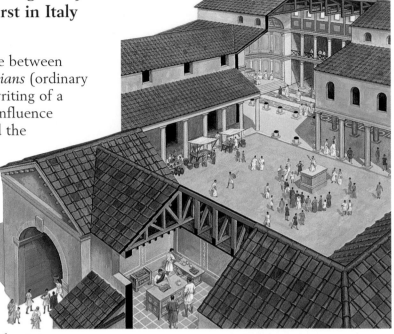

There followed a struggle between the patricians and *plebeians* (ordinary people), which led to the writing of a legal code and to plebeian influence in government. This formed the backbone of the Republic. Seeking protection from attack, the Romans entered a series of wars that, by 270 B.C., gave them control of most of Italy. Rome soon clashed with Carthage over trade in the Mediterranean. The Punic Wars that followed lasted 60 years. During this period, the Carthaginian emperor, Hannibal, led his army across the Alps to invade Italy. After a series of victories by Hannibal, the brilliant Roman general, Scipio, set off to Africa to attack Carthage. This forced Hannibal back to Carthage, where he was finally defeated by Scipio. The Romans soon established new cities, building order and prosperity and giving conquered peoples a form of Roman

The central square or *forum* of a Roman town was where people met each other, announcements were made, markets were held, and where the town hall, treasury, and law courts were located.

citizenship if they cooperated. By 44 B.C. the Romans ruled Spain, France, Europe south of the Danube, Anatolia, and northern Africa, dominating the Mediterranean. In less than 200 years, the Romans had become the controlling force in the West.

Jars like this *amphora* were used to store and transport olive oil and wine throughout the Roman Empire.

The Colosseum in Rome, an enormous stadium, was used for gladiatorial contests, sports, and the gory killing of animals, captured enemies, and slaves.

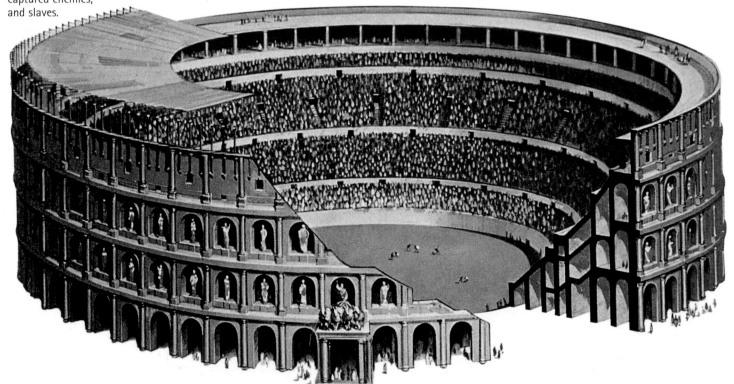

THE END OF THE REPUBLIC

In 100 B.C., friction grew between the patricians and plebeians. The army was opened up to landless citizens, who were rewarded for their services with land and status in the colonies. Power struggles between generals ended in civil war, and, in 44 B.C., Julius Caesar became dictator for life. Alarmed Republicans assassinated him, and the Republic soon ended.

Vital to the growing empire was the system of roads built to speed up trade, mail delivery, and troop movements. On the right, a water-carrying aqueduct is being built over a road.

THE PUNIC WARS

Expanding their influence, the Romans came up against the Phoenicians in Carthage. The Punic Wars (264–241 and 218–202 B.C.) began over a fight for Sicily, but grew to threaten the great cities of Rome and Carthage. The Carthaginian general, Hannibal, nearly won, after invading Italy from the Alps. The Roman general, Scipio Africanus, avoided a head-on battle, instead attacking Spain in 206 and then Carthage itself in 202 B.C. The Phoenicians lost everything, and the Romans then dominated the Mediterranean Sea and its trade.

Hannibal's army marched from Spain, over the Alps, and into Italy. It was so formidable that the Romans avoided confronting it. They attacked Carthage instead, and forced Hannibal to rush back to defend it.

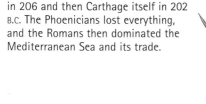

The Carthaginians used African elephants to frighten the Roman troops. When they crossed the Alps, most of the elephants died.

Hannibal was a brilliant strategist and a modest man who carried out maneuvers no one believed could work. The Romans beat him only by outwitting his strategy.

63

THE ROMAN EMPIRE 27 B.C.–A.D. 475

After Julius Caesar's death in 44 B.C., Romans preferred dictatorship to chaos. Octavian, his successor, gradually took control. He became the first emperor.

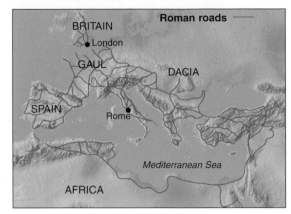

The Roman Empire dominated most of the Western world, uniting it into one economic system, under one goverment.

Octavian was Caesar's nephew. He was an able politician, getting himself elected as Consul (president) year after year. He called himself *princeps* ("first citizen"), not king. Renamed Augustus ("imposing one"), he reorganized the government and empire and imposed peace. Under him, trade extended as far as East Africa, India, and China, and the empire's towns, roads, and territories grew ever larger.

Julius Caesar was a ruthless and ambitious general and politician who conquered the Celts of Gaul and later became Rome's first dictator for life—an appointment that angered Republicans and led to Caesar's murder.

Heavily armed Roman legionnaires: a *centurion* (officer) with a *ballista* (catapult), a legionary (soldier), and a standard-bearer.

ROMAN EMPERORS

Emperors relied more on the army than on the Roman people for support. Patricians no longer had great power. Many had moved to rich country estates and the far provinces. Most of the Roman emperors chose their successors; some unpopular or controversial ones were deposed by soldiers. In A.D. 68–69, four emperors were deposed in one year. From A.D. 100, Rome was ruled by strong emperors—Trajan, Hadrian, Antoninus, and Marcus Aurelius—most of whom were not actually Roman. By A.D. 117 the empire had grown too large and Rome's soldiers could no longer be paid with booty, slaves, and land taken in conquest. The burden on Rome grew.

When attacking a fortress, legionnaires would form a protective shield like this—a *testudo* (tortoise), that advanced slowly under fire from stones and arrows.

THE ROMAN ARMY

Soldiers joined the army to gain rewards of promotion, land, or power—especially if they were not Roman. This meant that soldiers dominated the empire and its colonies, becoming landowners and the ruling class. The army was very international, often hiring barbarians as mercenaries. Legions fought in such faraway places as Scotland, Morocco, and Arabia. Roads, forts, and border walls were built to maintain security.

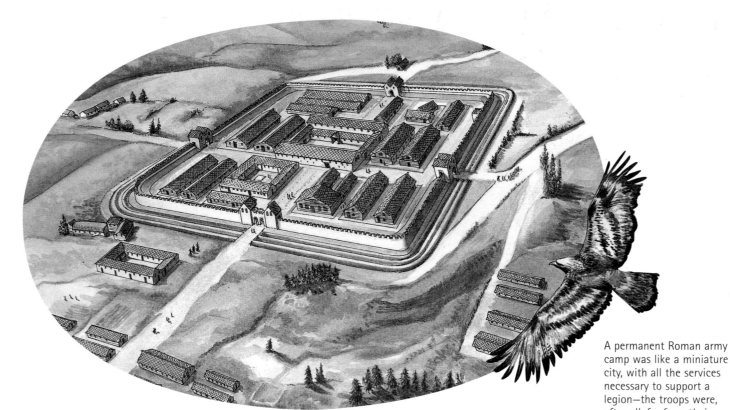

A permanent Roman army camp was like a miniature city, with all the services necessary to support a legion—the troops were, after all, far from their homes in other parts of the empire. These military bases were located in the areas that were most in need of permanent protection.

THE ROMAN EMPIRE

The final conquests, in the century following Augustus, had been in Britain, Syria, Palestine, and Egypt. The Jews and British had been difficult to beat, and the Parthians impossible. However, most of the conquered peoples adapted. People in Gaul, North Africa, Syria, Britain, and Hungary adopted Roman ways and thought of themselves as Roman citizens. Running a huge empire was difficult, and it was united by business, not religious or ethnic ties. Provincial peoples were allowed to get on with their lives, as long as they obeyed the rules set by the Romans.

The Appian Way, a major road from Rome to the southeast coast, was built in 312 B.C. Soldiers, traders, and travelers could now travel along it very quickly.

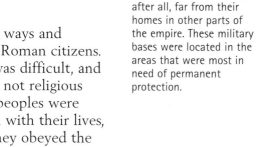

KEY DATES

509 B.C.	Roman republic founded
496	Romans defeat Latins at Battle of Lake Regillus
493	Roman-Latin alliance forms the Latin League, which fights the Etruscans
390	Rome sacked by Celts
306	Romans defeat Etruscans
300s	Romans expand to dominate Italy
264–202	Punic Wars and the fall of Carthage
146	Rome takes Greece
50s	Caesar conquers France
49–31	Civil War between competing generals
27 B.C.	Octavian: end of republic, growth of empire
A.D. 160	Plague and crisis cut population and trade
212	Roman citizenship granted to all inhabitants of the empire
286	Diocletian divides and reorganizes the empire
324	Founding of Constantinople
370	Barbarian attacks on the empire
410	The Visigoths sack Rome—rapid decline of the city results
476	Fall of the last emperor, Romulus Augustus

ROMAN LIFE 509 B.C.–A.D. 475

The Romans did not really invent many things to advance their civilization—they took what had already been invented and developed it further.

Everyday objects like this key were handmade in specialized workshops.

The Romans used olive oil to fill lamps to light their homes.

The Roman way of life became known as *Romanitas*—everything that had to do with being a citizen of the empire. It was not just an empire—it was a system, a single market, and a union of different lands, sharing a developed way of life.

THE POWER OF THE PEOPLE

The Greeks created democracy and the Romans took it further. Democracy meant government by patricians, the ruling class, although plebeians (ordinary people) had some influence in elections. Slaves—mostly non-Roman—had no power at all. Roman democracy worked well for a time, but in the end it was misused. It was replaced by the rule of an emperor.

THE SENATE

The Republic was ruled by an elected Senate, a group of patricians who selected two consuls each year to act as presidents. These presidents were advised by the Senate. Later, Roman soldiers gained greater power than the ordinary people, and the consuls became military dictators. After the death of Augustus, Rome was ruled by a succession of emperors who held absolute power.

URBAN LIFE

The largest cities of the empire were Rome, Alexandria, and Antioch, with over 100,000 inhabitants in each. Other Roman cities had 10,000–50,000 inhabitants. Each city was carefully laid out with its official buildings and public squares, baths, a stadium, markets, workshops, and storehouses, as well as living quarters for each social class.

A ROMAN TOWN

The Romans were superb builders. They built roads across the countryside and walls around their towns for protection. People went to the public baths to wash, relax, and meet friends. There were temples dedicated to gods and goddesses. Business was done in the forum, originally the city's marketplace.

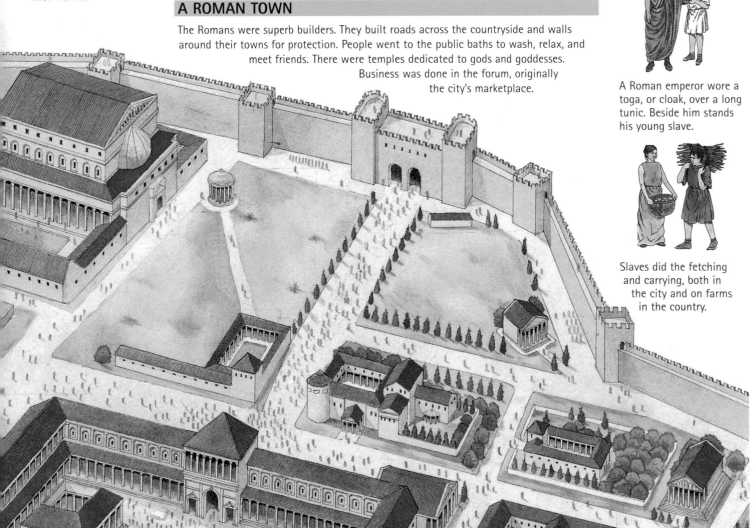

A Roman emperor wore a toga, or cloak, over a long tunic. Beside him stands his young slave.

Slaves did the fetching and carrying, both in the city and on farms in the country.

KEY DATES

200 B.C.	Growth of classical Roman art, architecture, and literature
103	Revolt by slaves in Rome
91	War between Rome and Italian cities
88	Civil war in Rome
c.30 B.C.	The poet Virgil and the historian Livy at work
A.D. 64	Start of persecution of Christians in Rome, under Nero
100	The empire reaches its greatest extent
160	Thousands of Roman citizens die from the plague
200	The empire's road system is completed
260	Beginning of barbarian incursions
313	Constantine decrees religious tolerance
410	Fall of the empire

The Romans used chariots drawn by horses for races and fast travel. Races were held in sports arenas. Goods were carried in carts drawn by strong, heavy oxen.

THE COUNTRYSIDE

As Roman life developed, farms were bought and reorganized by rich city-dwellers or awarded to soldiers as estates. Tenants, peasants, and slaves did the work, growing produce for sale in the cities. Large quantities of food and materials were transported from the farms to Rome and other cities. In addition, the legions required feeding, so the country estates were prepared for large-scale and profitable food production.

EVERYDAY LIFE

Life in Rome was in many ways similar to city life today. High-rise houses, traffic problems, shopping, waste disposal, hustle, and bustle were all common features. Rome was also a meeting place for people from all over the empire, and the people communicated in the common tongues, Latin and Greek. It was a money economy and a very complex society with different classes, belief systems, and several different religions.

A COUNTRY VILLA

Wealthy Romans lived in large town houses. They also had grand villas in the country. Some villas were run as large farms. The owner and his family could enjoy a comfortable house and garden, with a heating system to keep them warm in the winter. Many large farms used slave labor to grow highly profitable crops of grain or olives, or to raise sheep and goats for milk, meat, and hides.

THE CELTS 500 B.C.–A.D. 43

The Celts were a loose grouping of tribes living in southern Germany from around 1500 B.C. By Roman times, the Celts dominated much of Europe.

Around 500 B.C., the Celts were the dominant European power. They had expanded from a heartland in what is now southern Germany. They were not a nation, but more a confederation of individual tribes with a shared culture. Their influence eventually stretched from Spain to Britain, Germany, and northern Italy, and as far as central Anatolia.

CELTIC LIFE

The Celts were tribal farmers who gathered around their chiefs' *oppidae* or strongholds. These were often hill forts, and some of them later became villages or towns. Most Celts were homesteaders and small farmers, living in a variety of tribes. Sometimes these tribes divided, with one group moving to another place, so that certain tribes might be spread through different areas. The Celts were bound together by the Druids, who were learned priests, lawmakers, bards, and wise men. They also had gifted musicians, artists, and metalworkers. Their jewelry, pottery, weapons, and drinking vessels were often decorated with intricate designs and geometric shapes. The Celts traded with Rome, Greece, and other countries, but they were not much influenced by these civilizations.

This Celtic bronze shield was made around A.D. 100. Set with precious stones, it was more likely to have been made for ceremonial use than for use in battle.

Vertcingetorix was a Gaulish chief who organized a successful rebellion against Julius Caesar's invasion of Gaul in 52 B.C., but he was later forced to surrender.

A Celtic chief and members of his tribe feast in their timbered hall while listening to the poetic songs of a bard. Laws, history, stories, news, and religious teachings were communicated by the druidic bard.

This bull's head appeared on a huge bronze ceremonial cauldron found at Gundestrup in Denmark. Animal figures, like this, and geometric designs were a popular feature on pieces of elegant Celtic metalwork.

POWER AND LAW

Each Celt was a free person with individual rights. Druidic justice was famous, and bonds of loyalty within each tribe were strong. The chiefs were elected by tribespeople, and the high kings by the chiefs. Both could be deposed if they did not do a good job.

Celtic roundhouses were made of timber and thatch, with wattle-and-daub (or sometimes stone) walls. Smoke floated out through the thatched roof, but rain was unable to seep in. Sleeping space was around the inside of the wall, and cooking and washing were done around the central fire.

▼ The Celtic stag-god Cernunnos or Hurn was hammered and chiseled into the side of this large bronze cauldron around 1,900 years ago.

CELTIC WARRIORS

Known as fierce warriors (the women also fought), the Celts used iron to make their weapons and tools. In 390 B.C., they sacked Rome, and in 280 B.C. they raided Greece and Anatolia, seeking booty. Sometimes they even fought among themselves. The Romans exploited this when conquering Gaul (France) and Britain. The British Celtic leader, Caradoc (Caractacus), was betrayed by other Celts. Disunited, the British warriors lost their independence in A.D. 43–80. The Celts came to accept Roman rule and later fought with the Romans against Germanic barbarians. The Celts were also the first European Christians. After the fall of Rome, Celtic ways in Europe survived only in Ireland, Cornwall, Brittany, and parts of Scotland and Wales.

Boudicca was the queen of the Iceni of the East of England. She headed a rebellion against the occupying Romans in Britain in A.D. 60 in which seventy thousand Romans were killed. However, the rebellion was eventually crushed, and Boudicca committed suicide.

CHINA: THE HAN DYNASTY 202 B.C.– A.D 220

The Han was the first long-lasting dynasty of united imperial China. Han China enjoyed stability and greatness and was a fine example of civilization.

For 400 years from 202 B.C. to A.D. 220, China was ruled by emperors of the Han dynasty. They were more lenient and stable than the Qin, and practiced fair Confucian principles of law and administration.

This bronze model of a prosperous man in his carriage was found in the tomb of the Han general, Wuwei. It was probably made around A.D. 100.

THE EARLY HAN

The dynasty was founded by Liu Bang, a commoner who was popular because he relaxed the harsh laws, cut taxes, and favored the people. The capital was Chang'an, which, after 100 years, became the world's largest city.

It was at the end of the Silk Road along which China traded with Persia and Rome. Han China saw itself as the "Middle Kingdom," the center of the world. There was a great flowering of culture, wealth, and learning. At this time, Han China was as large and developed as the extensive Roman Empire. The Han developed a system of administration by highly educated officials called mandarins. People who wanted to work as public officials had to take an examination on the writings of Confucius.

▲ A ceramic horse and rider made in Han China around 80 B.C. Stirrups were not introduced into China until around A.D. 300.

▼ Here, Chinese soldiers of the Han period engage in battle. Lacking stirrups, the horsemen on both sides were easily knocked to the ground during fighting at close quarters.

THE MARTIAL EMPEROR

Wu Di, the "Martial Emperor," reigned for 55 years from 141 B.C. He added part of central Asia, Korea, and much of southern China to his empire. At great expense, he beat back the Xiongnu (Huns) of Mongolia, who often raided China. He improved the mandarin administration, built schools, canals, cities, and buildings, and encouraged foreign contact. Buddhism was introduced to China during this high point in the country's long history.

The emperor's many representatives were always treated with great respect. The speedy transportation of officials from one place to another was helped by stations where fresh horses were provided.

◀ Emperor Kuang-Wu declared himself ruler and ruled from A.D. 25-57.

WANG MANG

During the following century, the Han grew weak, while the nobles grew ever stronger. A courtier, Wang Mang, rebelled, took power, and ruled from A.D. 9–23. He introduced many changes and reforms, favoring the people against landowners and nobles, and reforming land rights and the judicial system. Eventually the nobles overthrew Wang Mang, and the Han dynasty was restored.

THE LATER HAN

The Han produced exquisite objects of wood, lacquer, and silk. They also replaced many of the writings that had been destroyed by the Qin. Chinese inventors were far ahead of the rest of the world. Their invention of paper took centuries to reach the West. Many of the cities they built were large and elegant. However, the population had grown, and rebellions among landless and poor peasants became frequent. Barbarians again attacked the borders, and warlords took over the army. The last Han emperor gave up his throne in A.D. 220 and the empire fell apart.

City streets in Han China were crowded. The muddy roads were full of carts, chariots, and traders. Craftsmen, letter writers, storytellers, and astrologers also plied their trade noisily in the open air.

CHRISTIANITY A.D. 30–400

Around the time that Jesus of Nazareth was born there were many faiths and sects in the Roman Empire. Within 400 years, Christianity became dominant.

The Chi-Rho symbol, or labarum, was adopted by early Christians. Its P and X are the first two letters in the Greek spelling of Christ. The symbol Chi-Rho itself is a short form of the word *chreston*, or "good omen."

The Jewish people believed that a Messiah (savior) would be born to lead them. At the time that Jesus of Nazareth was born, Judea was suffering under Roman rule. At about the age of 30, Jesus began publicly teaching, and it is said that he performed many miracles, such as healing. The Jewish authorities accused him of blasphemy and he was tried before the Roman governor, Pontius Pilate. He was crucified, but his followers reported seeing him alive after his death.

A CHURCH IS BORN

This "resurrection" formed the basis of a new faith, breaking with old Jewish traditions and founded by Jesus' closest disciples, the apostles. It gradually spread among both exiled Jews and non-Jews throughout the Roman world. Early followers—especially Paul—taught that Christianity was open to anyone who chose to be baptized. By A.D. 300, it had spread to Egypt, Aksum, Syria, Armenia, Anatolia, Greece, Rome, France, Britain, and India.

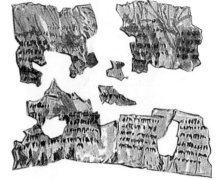

The Essenes were a Jewish sect. Their abandoned scrolls, found in a cave at Qumran near the Dead Sea, in 1947, included one which deals with the Messiah and what was to happen after he appeared.

Christians kept their faith quietly, because the Roman authorities often persecuted them, and caused many of them to go into hiding. Many died a painful death in the arena. In Egypt, a group of Christians withdrew to the desert to live as hermits. They were the first Christian monks.

JESUS OF NAZARETH

Jesus was born in Bethlehem, in Judea. Around the age of 12, in discussions with learned rabbis at the temple, Jesus showed himself to be special. Nothing more is known about his life until he was around 30 years of age. He then began a public life of teaching. Jesus attracted large crowds. He used parables—stories that taught lessons by example. Love and respect for others was at the heart of his teaching. Three years after he began his mission, the Romans put him to death.

A painting of Jesus as he was portrayed in the first centuries after his death.

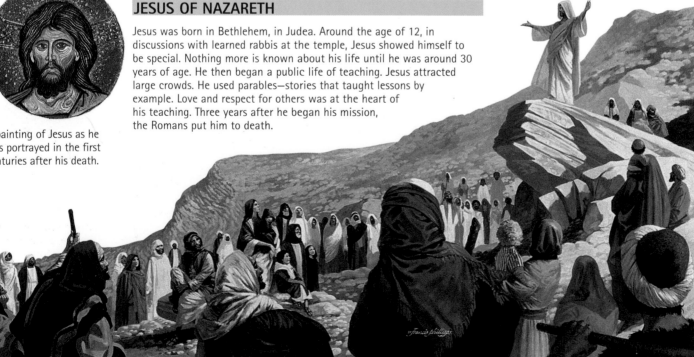

KEY DATES

3 B.C.	Probable year of the birth of Jesus of Nazareth, in Bethlehem
30	Approximate date of the crucifixion of Jesus Christ
45–64	The missions of Paul to Greece, Anatolia, and Rome
65–100	The Christian Gospels are written
180	Foundation of early Church institutions
249–311	Periodic persecutions of Christians in the Roman Empire
269	St. Anthony establishes Christian monasticism in Egypt
313	Emperor Constantine recognizes the Christian church
325	Church doctrine formalized
337	Constantine is baptized on his deathbed

STATE RELIGION

Religious persecution in the Roman Empire was halted when Emperor Constantine recognized Christianity in A.D. 313. Later it became the official state religion. Constantine called the first council of all bishops, at Nicaea, urging them to resolve their differences and write down one doctrine—the Nicene Creed. Politically, he saw the Church as a way of bringing new life to his empire. His actions defined Christianity, greatly affecting Europe and, eventually, most of the rest of the world. It also meant that the ideas of some teachers were outlawed as "heresies," and this led to the disappearance of many aspects of the faith. It also led to death or exile for those who disagreed with the doctrine. The Gnostic (Egyptian), Celtic, and Nestorian churches were examples of branches that eventually died out—although the Nestorians journeyed to Persia and as far as China to prevent this.

In the A.D. 300s , an Egyptian Christian, Anthony, traveled to the Sinai desert and began the monastic tradition. St. Catherine's monastery, at the base of Mt. Sinai, is one of the oldest monasteries in the area.

Constantine changed the church from a sect into a powerful institution. Legend has it that he adopted the Christian symbol after being told in a dream to paint it on his soldiers' shields before a crucial battle outside Rome in A.D. 312—a battle he won.

PARTHIANS AND SASSANIDS 238 B.C.–A.D. 637

The Parthians were Asiatic nomads who had moved south into Persia around 1000 B.C. About 300 B.C., the Parni tribe, later to become their rulers, joined them.

The Parthians were famous for horseback fighting. They would gallop away from the enemy as if fleeing, and then turn and shoot backward at their pursuers. This led to the term "Parthian shot."

Shapur I became the Persian shah (emperor) in A.D. 242. Two years later he shocked the Romans by defeating them. Shapur was the greatest of the Sassanid shahs and ruled for 30 years.

The Parthians and the Parni lived in northern Iran under Persian and then Greek Seleucid rule. The head of the Parni became the Seleucid governor of Parthia. Then, in 238 B.C., he declared independence and made himself high king over a number of local chiefs in the land. The Parthians adopted existing local ways of doing things (Greek, Persian, Babylonian), rather than inventing their own, although in time they adopted more and more Persian customs. Parthia grew prosperous through Silk Road trade from China.

RISE AND FALL OF THE PARTHIANS

The greatest Parthian leaders were two brothers, both called Mithradates. Little is known of Parthia, except that the Parthians conquered Babylonia and Bactria (Afghanistan) and were friendly with Han China. They fought the Romans regularly, stopping the Roman expansion eastward. Their army was strong and well-organized. Famous for horseback fighting, they swept into battle at great speed, behind a hail of arrows, and were able to quickly overwhelm all armed opposition.

THE RISE OF THE SASSANIDS

The Parthian wars with Rome were costly and unpopular. After 450 years of superiority in Persia, they became a spent force. In A.D. 225, this made it possible for a local king named Ardashir to overthrow the Parthians. Ardashir ruled over a Persian dynasty, the Sassanids. He made the Parsee faith (Zoroastrianism) into the state religion of Persia. This was a new idea, later copied by Constantine of Rome. Ardashir led the Persians into a new period of greatness.

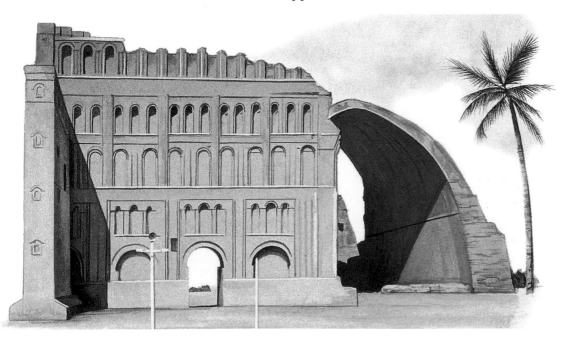

Around A.D. 275, Shapur I built a wonderful palace at Ctesiphon in Babylonia, of which only these ruins remain. Ctesiphon became a wealthy city and a major center for the area, communicating with the West and with China.

SHAPUR I OF PERSIA

The Sassanid shahs (emperors) wanted to carry on in the ancient traditions of old Persia, and they also wanted to reclaim the lands Darius had once ruled before they were conquered by Alexander the Great. Their court at Ctesiphon (near Babylon) became the focus for a brilliant culture, and the wealthy empire became Rome's greatest rival. Shapur I was an outstanding Sassanid ruler. He fought the Romans and even captured the Roman emperor Valerian, and had him killed. Shapur conquered Armenia, Syria, Bactria, and Sogdiana (Afghanistan), and the Indus Valley (Pakistan). At home, Shapur sponsored a cultural flowering of Persia that centered on Zoroastrian religious ideas. In 480, Persia suffered a religious revolt and the invasion of hordes of Huns from Mongolia. After these problems were dealt with, Shah Khosru II conquered Egypt and Byzantium. However, he was killed, a civil war broke out, weakening Persia. Sassanid Persia collapsed when the newly inspired Muslim Arabs conquered the area in 637, eventually converting the Persians to Islam.

KEY DATES

238 B.C.	Parthian Arsaces I declares independence from Seleucia
141	Mithradates invades Mesopotamia
53	Parthians destroy the Roman army in Syria
A.D. 225	Sassanids overthrow the Parthians
240–272	Shapur I—Sassanid Persia at its high point
480s	Hun invasions of eastern Persia
616	Khosru II conquers Egypt
637	Persia falls to the Muslim Arabs

Parthian and Sassanid wealth came through trade on the Silk Road which passed through Parthia from China to the West. This carved life-size figure of Hercules was placed by the Silk Road to guard the route.

In 260, Shapur I captured the Roman emperor Valerian in battle and forced him to submit. He then had him killed, stuffed, and put on display. Shapur hoped to become the world's greatest emperor, and his capital, Ctesiphon, near Babylon, was one of the grandest of the time.

THE AMERICAS 500 B.C.–A.D. 500

During this period there were many different cultures in the Americas. By A.D. 100, the city-state of Teotihuacán had grown to dominate Mexico.

An eagle's claw cut from a sheet of mica (a flat, glassy mineral that forms rock) by the Hopewell Indians of Ohio in around A.D. 200.

Except for visits by Pacific Polynesians to Peru during the A.D. 300s, the Americas were isolated from the rest of the world. Even so, Teotihuacán, dominated by its enormous Pyramid of the Sun, was the world's fifth largest city, with 200,000 people.

NORTH AMERICA

Several culture groups existed here. The nomadic, buffalo-hunting Plains Indians occupied the Midwest, and the woodland tribal nations lived in the Northeast. In the Mississippi Valley, the copper-working, trading Hopewell culture was in decline by A.D. 500. In the Southwest, the village-dwelling, corn-growing Hohokam and Mogollon peoples were thriving. On the West Coast and in the North, simpler hunting, fishing, and food-gathering societies such as the Makah and Inuit flourished.

There were many different cultures in the Americas. Apart from the urban civilizations, such as Teotihuacán, there were many simpler cultures scattered throughout the region.

MESOAMERICA

The Olmecs (1200–300 B.C.) and the Zapotecs (1400–400 B.C.) were the earliest civilizations in Mexico. The Zapotecs were noted for their learning and were the first Americans to develop writing (800 B.C.). They also had a mathematical calendar system, which they later taught to the Maya and the people of Teotihuacán.

THE GREAT SERPENT MOUND

No one knows exactly who built the Great Serpent Mound. It is possible that it was the Adena Indians, predecessors to the Hopewell culture. It was built in what is now Ohio, somewhere between 1000 B.C. and A.D. 700. This mound, some 1,300 ft. (400m) long, may have been a ceremonial center depicting the cosmic serpent (a symbol of the life force in nature) eating the cosmic egg. This would probably have symbolized the eternal cycle of death and rebirth, or represented the incarnation of the life force.

A carved stone sculpture from Teotihuacán. Surprisingly unwarlike, this city nevertheless had a great influence on all other neighboring cultures—especially through its crafts and other goods.

TEOTIHUACÁN

As the Olmecs and Zapotecs declined, the city-state of Teotihuacán, founded around 200 B.C., grew to dominate Mexico by A.D. 100. At its height 600 years later, Teotihuacán was larger than ancient Rome. It was built in a planned grid system, with impressive temple complexes and pyramids, many craft workshops, trading markets, and foreign residents' quarters. It was the largest trading city in the Americas, linking and supplying North and South America. Teotihuacán influenced other Mexican cultures such as the Maya, and it imported materials from as far away as the Great Lakes and Colombia. It was surrounded by other cities, but it was unusually peaceful. It mysteriously declined around A.D. 600, although the Aztecs carried its heritage on into later times.

This is one of the stone stepped Mayan pyramids at Tikal, Guatemala. At the top of the steps stands a temple. Around 300 B.C. (possibly even earlier), the Maya began building huge temple complexes. The one at El Mirador covers over 6 sq. mi. (16 sq km.)

SOUTH AMERICA

In Ecuador, the state of Moche, at its peak around A.D. 300, made fine pottery, textiles, and metalwork. Farther south, the city of Tiahuanaco, 12,200 ft. (3,660m) above sea level beside Lake Titicaca in the Andes, was inhabited by 40,000 people and featured enormous stone temples and palaces. Founded around 300 B.C., the city reached its golden age around A.D. 500.

KEY DATES
350 B.C. Earliest Maya city-states appear
300 B.C. Tiahuanaco, Peru, founded (peak A.D. 500, abandoned 1000)
200 B.C. Teotihuacán founded (peak A.D. 500)
200 B.C. Moche culture, coastal Ecuador (peak A.D.300, conquered 700)
100 B.C. Hopewell culture (peak A.D. 300, ended 800)
A.D. 300 Beginning of Classical period of Maya civilization (until 800)
300 Mogollon culture, North America
400 Hohokam culture, North America (until 1450)

A shell carving of a priest or official who served at Palenque, one of the main ceremonial centers of the Mayan civilization.

THE GUPTA DYNASTY A.D. 320–510

The Guptas became emperors of northern India in A.D. 320 and remained in power for 200 years. The stage was set for them by a people called the Kushans.

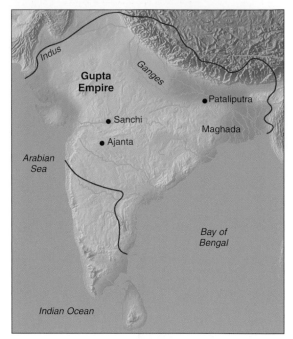

The Guptas ruled most of India and were responsible for its golden age. Their capital, Pataliputra, was one of the largest cities in the world at that time.

The Kushans were Greek-influenced Asian nomads in Bactria (now northern Afghanistan). They founded a kingdom there in A.D. 25, then moved north into Turkestan and farther south into Afghanistan and India, dominating the area by 100. Their greatest king was Kanishka (100-130), a Buddhist who supported social tolerance and the arts. Controlling most land trade across Asia, the wealthy Kushans gave stability to Asian trade. Around 240, however, Shapur of Persia took much of their land, and they never recovered.

The Guptas were minor princes in Maghada. Chandragupta I married a Maghada princess and became king in 320. He started the Gupta tradition of aiding the arts and religions and helped develop Indian society.

Krishna ("the first wise man") is one of the ten incarnations of the god Vishnu. He is associated with love and wisdom, and is featured in the *Mahabharata* and *Bhagavad Gita*, two great Hindu holy books.

THE GUPTA MAHARAJAHS

Chandragupta's son Samudragupta continued in his father's footsteps. Ruling from 335 for 45 years, he expanded Gupta rule by force and diplomacy across northern India and into southeastern India. His own son Chandragupta II (380-414) took Gupta India to its high point, one of the greatest times of Indian history. Skandagupta (455-467) beat off an invasion of India by Huns from central Asia. However, the Gupta Empire had been ruled through a loose arrangement of local *rajahs* (kings) under the Gupta *maharajah* (emperor), and after Skandagupta died, many local kingdoms broke away. By 510, the Guptas had been beaten by another wave of Hun invaders, and India broke up into *rajputs* (small kingdoms). An alliance of these rajputs beat off the Huns again in 528. India remained divided for 650 years, except for a period when Sri Harsha, a religious rajah of Kanauj (606-647), succeeded in uniting northern India for 40 years.

These large seated stone Buddhas are in Cave 17 of the vast complex at Ajanta. Each of the images is shown with different *mudras*, the symbolic hand gestures still used in Indian dancing.

AJANTA CAVES

The Ajanta caves were rediscovered by a group of British officers on a tiger hunt in 1819. The 29 caves near Bombay were created by Buddhist monks between 200 B.C. and A.D. 650, using hammers and chisels. They were built as a monastic retreat, and the walls were covered with fine paintings that depict stories from the life of the Buddha. There were also many sculptures. The caves mark the peak of the religious culture of India, in which yoga and meditation were fully developed. Not far away, at Ellora, other caves contain art from the Hindu, Buddhist, and Jain religious traditions which, during the tolerant Gupta period, thrived happily alongside one another.

▲ The elaborately carved Chaitya Hall in the Ajanta caves complex was used as a temple and a hall for meditation and philosophical debates.

◄ A wall painting from Ajanta shows musicians and dancers entertaining the royal household. Actors, magicians, acrobats, and wrestlers would also have taken part in this entertainment.

GUPTA CULTURE

The Gupta maharajahs succeeded one another as good and strong rulers. Copying Asoka, they set up monuments inscribed with religious texts all over India. They built new villages and towns, putting Hindu brahmins (priests) in charge. Agriculture and trade flourished. Indians migrated as far as Indonesia, and Buddhism spread to China. Both Hindu and Buddhist cultures developed. The Hindu sacred epics, the *Mahabarata* and the *Ramayana*, were written at this time. Kalidasa, India's great poet and dramatist, wrote about love, adventure, and the beauty of nature. The Buddhist university at Nalanda had an impressive 30,000 students. This was India's golden age, its classical era of music, dance, sculpture, art, and literature.

The Buddhist Wheel of Life. The eight main spokes represent the eight different states of being that Buddhists identify in the cycle of reincarnation of souls—only one of which is waking daily life.

KEY DATES

A.D. 75–100 The Kushan invasion of India

100–130 Kanishka— the peak of the Kushan period

320–335 Rule by Chandragupta I (founder of the Gupta Empire)

335–380 Rule by Samudragupta (conquers northern and eastern India)

380–414 Rule by Chandragupta II (Gupta Empire at its peak)

470s Decline of the Gupta Empire

505 Gupta Empire ends

THE DECLINE OF ROME A.D. 200–476

In 165, a plague swept through the Roman Empire and dramatically reduced the population. Rome's subsequent decline lasted three hundred years.

The plague lasted for two years and was followed from 180 by the rule of the mad emperor Commodus, uprisings in Africa and Britain, and a succession of quickly toppled and inadequate emperors. The government at home was falling apart, and Rome was in chaos.

The emperor Diocletian created a *tetrarchy* (rule of four) to administer the two halves of the empire. The tetrarchy consisted of two emperors helped by two lieutenants.

PROVINCIAL CHANGES
Power shifted to the provinces where the people wanted to keep their Roman status. The Parthians in the east and the British in the north created trouble, and a new force was appearing: the barbarians. Marcomanni, Goths, Franks, Alemanni, and Vandals were pressing in, and in 260–272 the Romans had to abandon Hungary and Bavaria to them. Parts of the empire such as Gaul, Britain, and Syria, were becoming separate and the Roman economy was also declining.

From 250–550 the Romans were constantly battling with Germanic and Asiatic barbarians, who sought to join the empire, to raid it for booty, or to bring it down.

THE EMPIRE DIVIDES
In 284, the emperor Diocletian decided that the empire was too large for one man to rule and divided it into two, the Greek-speaking East and the Latin-speaking West. He appointed a co-emperor called Maximilian to rule the western half. The army was reorganized and enlarged to 500,000 men, and taxes were changed to pay for it. Provinces were reorganized to make them more governable. Romanitas was promoted by emphasizing the emperor's divine authority.

The vast empire grew too large and complex to rule, so Diocletian divided it. This meant that the rich East was not inclined to help the embattled West, so the West ground to a halt. High taxation levels meant that many Romans cared little—it was cheaper to live without the empire.

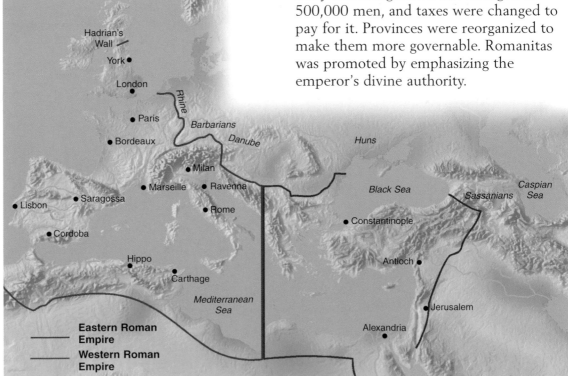

Eastern Roman Empire / Western Roman Empire

CONSTANTINE

Constantine ruled as emperor from 312 to 337.

Constantine saw himself as the savior of the Roman Empire. He decided to use the growing strength of Christianity to build a new culture in the empire. Calling bishops to a number of councils, he made them settle church doctrine and become organized. He favored the Christians, whom he considered to be less corrupt and self-seeking than the Romans. However, he was not a Christian himself until he converted on his deathbed. He was the last strong emperor of the Roman Empire. By moving the capital to Constantinople and founding the Byzantine Empire, however, he also weakened the West and hastened Rome's eventual downfall. The Roman Catholic church continued to be a cultural and religious force in the West long after Rome fell.

▲ Constantine's arch in Rome was built to bring back a spirit of victory and supremacy to Rome, after a century of many disappointments. However, Rome's real achievements at the time were not as great as the arch was meant to suggest.

◄ A detail from the arch of Constantine shows Roman soldiers besieging the town of Verona in 312. This battle was part of Constantine's war against his coemperor Maxentius. The arch was dedicated in 315.

THE END OF THE EMPIRE

Emperor Constantine tried to revive the empire. He favored and promoted Christians, built churches, and held church councils, making Christianity a state religion. In 330 he moved the capital to Byzantium, calling it Constantinople. This city became as grand as Rome, and the west grew weaker and poorer. The western half of the empire, under attack by the barbarians, collapsed after Rome was sacked in 410 and 455. The last emperor was deposed by the Goths in 476. Following this, the western empire was replaced by a number of Germanic kingdoms. The empire in the East, known as the Byzantine Empire, lasted until 1453. Though many Roman ways were adopted by the barbarians, the Roman Empire was at an end.

KEY DATES

165–167	Plague sweeps through the Roman Empire
167–180	The Marcomanni Wars against the first barbarians
250	Emperor worship made compulsory under Decius
250–270	Barbarians attack the empire from the north
276	Emperor Tacitus killed by his troops
286	Diocletian divides the empire in two and rules eastern empire; Maximilian rules western
324	Constantinople founded as the new imperial capital
370	Arrival of Huns in Europe: Germans seek refuge in empire
378–415	The Visigoths rebel and ravage the empire
406	Roman withdrawal from Britain, Gaul, and Iberia
410	The Visigoths sack Rome
441	The Huns defeat the Romans
476	Death of the last Roman emperor

Emperor Justinian continued the fight against the barbarians. This gold coin was minted in 535 to celebrate his general Belisarius' defeat of the Vandals.

THE BARBARIANS A.D. 1–450

The term barbarian means "outsider"—and Romans thought them to be uncivilized. They lived in small farming communities and were ferocious warriors.

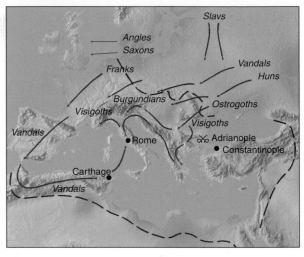

A map showing the complex movements of the main barbarian tribes around 370–450, as they occupied different parts of the western Roman Empire.

An ornate bronze brooch, commonly used by barbarians to fasten their cloaks, is an example of the fine craftsmanship of these people. This piece of jewelry was made around 400 in a style that was fashionable in Denmark and later in Saxon England.

The Germans living in southern Sweden and northern Germany moved south and pushed the Celts west. The Romans tried to control the Germans and were seriously beaten by them in A.D. 9. The Romans traded with some friendly German tribes, and recruited some into the Roman army. Some tribes, such as the Franks, Alemanni, and Goths raided the empire in 260–270, and the Romans had to make peace and settle them.

THE HUNS

The Huns (Xiongnu) had been evicted from Mongolia by the Chinese. They swept into Europe, settling in Hungary around 370. The German tribes panicked, pushing into the empire for safety. The Romans settled many of them, though the Vandals in Greece rebelled, and by 410 they sacked Rome itself. From 440–450, the Huns ravaged Greece, Germany, and Gaul, destroying everything. An alliance of Romans and Germans defeated them, but the empire was then in decline. After Attila the Hun attacked northern Italy, the western empire finally broke down.

THE NEW EUROPEANS

As Rome collapsed, barbarians settled in Germany, Italy, Spain, Britain, and France, gradually adopting many Roman customs. By 800, the Frankish king Charlemagne ruled an empire spanning Germany and France. The Visigoths settled in Spain, and the Vandals took Carthage. The Huns retreated to Romania and the Ukraine. The Lombards settled in Italy and founded a strong kingdom under King Odoacer. The Burgundians settled in eastern France, and the Saxons and Jutes took England.

A scene based on a Roman tomb carving from around 200 shows Roman soldiers in a fierce battle with German barbarians.

This relief from the obelisk of Theodosius was erected in Constantinople in 390. The stone carvings show the emperor receiving the submission of the barbarian peoples. Theodosius was the last emperor of a united Roman Empire (379–395), and an enthusiastic Christian. He was of barbarian blood, born of Germans who had joined the Roman Empire.

▼ This painting shows Attila the Hun marching on Paris during his army's invasion of Gaul in 452.

ATTILA THE HUN

Attila became king of the Huns (Xiongnu) in 433. He set up a new Hun homeland in Hungary after they had massacred, looted, and taken slaves throughout eastern Europe (433–441). The Huns then devastated the Balkans and Greece (447–450), forcing the Romans to pay gold to save Constantinople. The Huns later invaded Gaul and northern Italy, but they were beaten by a combined Roman and Visigoth army. In 453, Attila took a German wife and died suddenly in bed, possibly from poisoning. Attila was a military genius and a great Hun leader. When he died, the Huns migrated eastward to the Ukraine and caused no more trouble in the West.

◀ Attila the Hun was highly respected, mainly because no one could beat him and his soldiers. When he died, the Huns fell.

KEY DATES

70 B.C.	Germans migrate to Gaul, beating the Celts
56	Julius Caesar sends the Germans out of Gaul
A.D. 9	German rebellion against the Romans
200	Germans form a confederation
260	Barbarians move into the Roman Empire
367	Scots, Picts, and Saxons attack Roman Britain
451–454	Huns devastate Gaul and northern Italy

JAPAN 300 B.C.—A.D. 800

Japan is one of the oldest nations in the world. People have been living there from around 30,000 B.C. Classical Japan took shape from around 300 B.C.

In ancient times, Japan was occupied by the Ainu people. The Ainu were unique, and not related to any other tribe. Today's Japanese people moved onto the islands in prehistoric times, from Korea and Manchuria on the mainland. They forced the Ainu onto the northernmost island, Hokkaido.

THE YAYOI

Around 300 B.C., the Yayoi were beginning the rise that would make them Japan's predominant tribe. They introduced bronze and iron and also rice and barley from Korea and China. They shaped Japanese culture and the Shinto religion, in which nature spirits (*kami*) and tribal ancestors were worshiped. Tradition says that Jimmu, the legendary first emperor (*tenno*), great-grandson of Ameratsu, "Goddess of the Sun," appeared in 660 B.C. In fact, if he existed at all, it was probably several hundred years after this.

The Ainu, or Ezo, did not look like modern-day Japanese—they had lighter complexions and much more hair, like these two tribal elders. The Ainu had no written language, and, because they were looked down on by the Japanese, there are few records of their history.

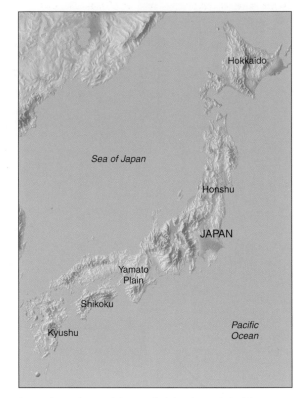

Japan is made up of four main islands, and the biggest, Honshu, has always been the dominant one. In early times, the indigenous Ainu people were squeezed out of Honshu and north onto the island of Hokkaido.

THE YAMATO

Around A.D. 167, an elderly priestess called Himiko of the Yamato tribe became ruler. She used her religious influence to unite about 30 of the Japanese tribes. Himiko sent ambassadors to China, and from that time Chinese culture and, later, Buddhism, influenced the Japanese. The Yamato increased in power during the A.D. 200s. Today's Japanese emperors can trace their ancestry to the Yamato, who claimed descent from the sun goddess. During this period, until 646, much of Japan was united as one state, and it invaded southern Korea. With the establishment of Buddhism during the 500s, Shinto was threatened. Around 600, Prince Shotoku reformed the Yamato state, centralizing it in the Chinese style and reducing the power of the tribal lords. Temples and towns were built, and there was great cultural development. The 700s saw Japan's golden age. Rivalry between Shinto and Buddhism was also resolved by merging both into a common Japanese religious culture.

A painted scroll from the A.D. 300s shows a Yamato court lady being dressed by her servant. The boxes are for cosmetics.

84

THE SHINTO RELIGION

Shinto is the ancient nature religion of Japan. Its mythology was written down in the 700s, in the *Kojiki* and the *Nihongi*. Shinto worshipers believed in the power of natural energies and spirits, or kami. Shinto priests sought to please the spirits, attracting their support and protection. In Shinto, it is believed that all life began in a cosmic egg that formed in the primordial chaos. The egg separated and became the gods (kamis), and the union of two kamis brought the Earth into being, with Japan as their special home. The sun goddess also came from this marriage, and the emperor was thought to descend from her. Many influences entered Shinto from Buddhism, and both religions coexisted throughout Japanese history, although there were periods of rivalry.

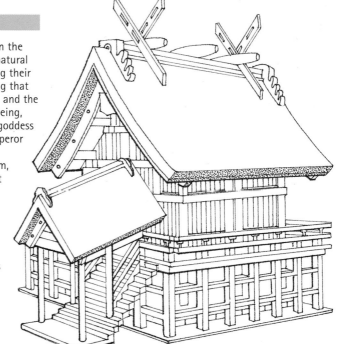

▶ This is a reconstruction of a Shinto shrine at Izumo, an area known for its places of Shinto worship. The priests held ceremonies of renewal and purification there at special times of the year to appeal to the kami to send them bumper crops and give the people good health and fertility.

▲ Shinto priests were originally tribal shamans. In later times, their traditions, dress, and temples became more formal, in response to the challenge from Buddhism.

▶ This is the main gate of the Shinto Kasuga shrine at Heian. These gates not only served the usual purpose, they also marked the energy lines along which the spirits traveled to reach the temple, which was carefully placed in a special location.

THE NARA PERIOD

A permanent capital was established at Nara around 710. Gradually, the emperor became a ceremonial figure, serving as the representative of the gods. Government was controlled by officials and monks and there were greater political struggles. In 794, the emperor moved the capital to Heian (Kyoto), where a new phase of Japanese history began. Japan had developed from a tribal land to become a strong state. Little has been recorded about the life of ordinary people, because records were only kept about the imperial court and temples.

KEY DATES

300 B.C.	Beginning of the Yayoi culture
A.D. 239	Queen Himiko sends an embassy to China
300	The Yamato period—farming, towns, ironworking
366	The Japanese invade southern Korea (until 562)
552	Full introduction of Buddhism
593–622	Prince Shotoku creates a Chinese-style centralized state
646	Yamato period ends
710	Nara becomes permanent capital (the Nara period)
794	Emperor Kammu moves his court to Heian (Kyoto)

In Shinto, small clay figures were used as totems to bring good fortune to places or to the souls of the dead in the afterlife.

THE MAYA 300 B.C.–A.D. 800

The Maya lived in what is now southern Mexico and Guatemala. They created a civilization that was at its peak while the Roman Empire was crumbling.

The Mayan heartland moved from the south in early times to the center around Tikal. After A.D. 800 the Maya lived in the north of Yucatán.

The engraved figures found in Mayan ruins often show richly dressed people, such as this priest with his ornate headdress. He appears to be holding a knife in his left hand.

The Maya existed as far back as 2000 B.C. Over the centuries, by draining marshy land and building irrigation systems, they became successful farmers, able to support a large population. In the early phase, from 300 B.C. to A.D. 300, they built many cities in Guatemala, Belize, and southern Yucatán, each with its own character and artistic style. Their cities had temple pyramids, a fortified palace, marketplaces, workshops, and living quarters.

MAYAN CLASS SYSTEM

The Maya had a class system: the nobles, priests, rulers, officials, and their servants lived in the cities while ordinary people lived on the land, going into the cities for markets and religious festivals. There was an alphabet of 800 hieroglyphs, and the Maya studied advanced mathematics, astronomy, and calendar systems. As in ancient Greece, each city was an independent city-state, and there was feuding between them, usually to demand tribute and take prisoners. Around A.D. 230, a violent volcanic eruption blew apart Mount Ilopango in the south, and covered a large area with ash. The southern cities had to be abandoned, and this marked the end of the "pre-classic" period of Mayan civilization.

THE CLASSIC PERIOD

Between 300 and 800, Mayan civilization reached its peak. Many new cities were built in Yucatán. The dominant city was Tikal, although Palenque, Yaxchilán, Copán, and Calakmul were also important.

The Maya wrote in hieroglyphs (picture writing), which are found carved on huge stone monuments and written in books made of bark paper.

The Maya played a ball game which may have had religious importance to them as a kind of oracle. In vast courts they bounced a solid rubber ball back and forth using their hips, thighs, and elbows, aiming for a hoop in the side wall. The ball probably represented the sun.

The Maya were skilled craftspeople, making stone sculptures, jade carvings, decorated pottery, paintings, advanced tools, and gold and copper objects. They built roads and shipping lanes to encourage trade. Their mathematical system counted in 20s, and used three symbols: a bar for "five," a dot for "one," and a shell for "zero."

HUMAN SACRIFICE

The Maya practiced blood sacrifice. They viewed this life and the afterlife as equal worlds, and killing people for religious purposes, to please the gods and ancestors and to bring fertility and prosperity, was an acceptable thing to do. In later times, ambitious building projects meant that peasants had to supply ever more food and labor, and hostage-taking wars to capture sacrificial victims drastically cut the population. The agricultural system collapsed, and with it the cities. By 950, most central Mayan cities lay in ruins—though a later phase followed. Mayan peoples still live in Central America.

These were the four kinds of people at the top of the Mayan social pyramid: an official, a warrior, a noble, and a priest.

MAYAN CITIES

In the early days of Mayan city building, the largest city was El Mirador, founded in 150 B.C., and had a population of 80,000 people by A.D. 100. It was abandoned around A.D. 150. Tikal, ruled by its king Stormy Sky, later became the largest city, with some 100,000 people around 450. Most cities were impressive and planned in grids. They were built around the ceremonial centers, and often oriented to astronomical events such as the rising and setting points of the sun. The religious basis of Mayan cities and their use of pyramids resembled that of the ancient Egyptians 2,000 years earlier.

Mayan cities were carefully laid out, with numerous sacred shrines and temples covering many acres of land, and large open spaces, platforms, and meeting places.

87

THE POLYNESIANS 2000 B.C.–A.D. 1000

The Polynesians were a unique people of the Pacific islands. They were remarkable sailors, venturing far into the Pacific Ocean in search of new homelands.

A carved effigy of the god Tangaroa Upao Vahu, the first of the Polynesian gods. Polynesians believed that Tangaroa created the world and brought them to it from the heavens.

In their mythology, the Polynesians say they came from the heavens, through a mystical land often thought to be Hawaii. Historians and language experts believe they may originate in Taiwan, migrating in open canoes to the Philippines around 3000 B.C., then to the Bismarck archipelago off New Guinea around 2000 B.C. They carried with them pigs, dogs, and chickens, as well as fruit and vegetables (coconuts, taros, yams, breadfruit, and bananas). From these people, the Lapita culture developed. Its people used shells to make tools and they also made pottery which had intricate and beautiful patterns.

POLYNESIAN TRAVELS

The Polynesians developed large oceangoing canoes that could be sailed or paddled at great speed. They made use of the winds and ocean currents to help them on their way. These were stabilized boats, built with outriggers or doubled up like catamarans, so that they could withstand the wind and waves of the open sea. With these boats they were able to move between the many island groups of the Pacific.

KEY DATES

2000 B.C.	Growth of the Lapita culture in Melanesia
1300 B.C.	Migration to the "Polynesian triangle" around Fiji
200 B.C.	Migration to Tahiti and the Marquesas
A.D. 300	Migration to Rapa Nui—visits to America
400	Migration to the Hawaiian islands
850	Occupation of Aotearoa—birth of the Maori culture

MIGRATION

The Polynesians embarked on planned journeys of discovery. They were great navigators, and had advanced knowledge of the stars, ocean currents, winds, and wildlife. Around 1300–1000 B.C. the Polynesians moved to New Caledonia, Vanuatu, Fiji, Samoa, and Tonga, and then to Tahiti and the Marquesas Islands by 200 B.C. They reached Easter Island by A.D. 300, and Hawaii by 400. Some of them migrated to Aotearoa (New Zealand) by 850, where they settled and became known as the Maori. On the islands they bred animals and used the vegetables and fruit they carried to plant new crops that are now found throughout the islands.

These are two of the main types of oceangoing Polynesian canoes. On the left, the outrigger canoe, with carrying racks, would have been useful for island hopping; the double canoe, with shelters and a larger capacity, would have been valuable for longer journeys.

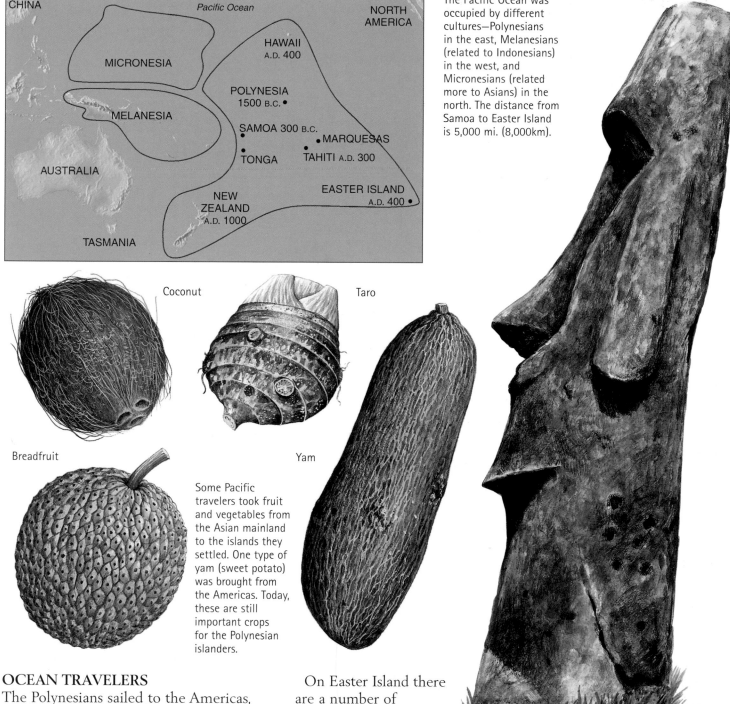

The Pacific Ocean was occupied by different cultures—Polynesians in the east, Melanesians (related to Indonesians) in the west, and Micronesians (related more to Asians) in the north. The distance from Samoa to Easter Island is 5,000 mi. (8,000km).

Coconut

Taro

Breadfruit

Yam

Some Pacific travelers took fruit and vegetables from the Asian mainland to the islands they settled. One type of yam (sweet potato) was brought from the Americas. Today, these are still important crops for the Polynesian islanders.

OCEAN TRAVELERS

The Polynesians sailed to the Americas, bringing back the sweet potato, and they traded with some of the Aborigines in Australia. They crossed thousands of miles of open sea in their explorations and migrations. On the Pacific islands, they lived in tribal societies ruled by chiefs, and they became experts in wood carving. They were isolated from Asia and Indonesia, where towns and nations were developing. It was only when European explorers such as Captain Cook arrived in the region in the 1700s that they began to be influenced by outsiders.

On Easter Island there are a number of remarkable and unique stone sculptures of heads measuring up to 40 ft. (12m) high. They are thought to have been built by the Polynesians. However, Polynesians did no stone carving elsewhere, and it is probable that the carvings are much more ancient, possibly built by an earlier people for unknown reasons. Meanwhile, in Aotearoa, the Maori developed their own separate tribal culture, growing in number to 250,000 and splitting into village farmers and warrior societies.

On Easter Island (Rapa Nui) there are over 500 of these enormous stone sculptures. They are carved from soft volcanic rock; each head weighs more than 50 tons. The statues were placed at *ahu* sites—areas in the open air that were intended for religious worship. About 200 years ago, every Easter Island statue was pushed face down—no one knows why.

THE ARTS 500 B.C.–A.D. 500

During this period, the arts were developed increasingly for their own sake, and less for the religious, royal, or traditional purposes of previous millennia.

The arts were gradually being developed to express creativity and decorate houses, streets, and everyday objects. The wealth accumulated by empires and urban traders was used to sponsor and support artists, leading to major advances in artistic creation. There was more realism—the Greeks and Romans made statues and paintings which directly and accurately represented people and life around them in a new way. In Greece, the finest art was produced in the classical period, and this reached its height about 400–300 B.C. Through the campaigns of Alexander the Great, Greek ideas about artistic realism reached as far as India; and the spread of Buddhism took them farther east to China, Japan, and southeast Asia. Roman artists copied the work of the Greeks, and developed their own, sometimes harshly realistic style.

This pot was made in Roman Britain around A.D. 200, the time of Britain's first "industrial revolution." It shows a gladiator yielding in battle and asking for mercy.

Throughout the empires of this period, the houses of the rich were decorated with bright paintings on the walls, statues, reliefs, and mosaics. Buildings were adorned with elaborate carvings and paintings. In Africa and the Americas, artistic styles developed separately from elsewhere, and China too had its own styles, which were unique.

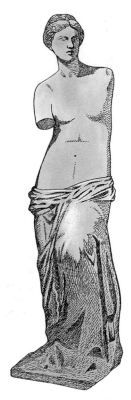

This figure of the goddess Aphrodite, now known as the Venus de Milo, was sculpted in 130 B.C. by Alexandros of Antioch in the Greek style. Though a goddess, she is portrayed as a person in realistic form, showing human feelings or "pathos."

◀ This vase was owned by a man named Leandros, whose name is written across the top. The vase itself, in the shape of the head of an African woman, may be from one of the Greek colonies in northern Africa.

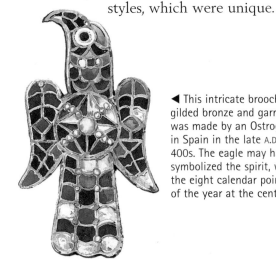

◀ This intricate brooch of gilded bronze and garnets was made by an Ostrogoth in Spain in the late A.D. 400s. The eagle may have symbolized the spirit, with the eight calendar points of the year at the center.

A sculpture from the tomb of a Roman blacksmith, shows his assistant using a bellows to heat up metals in a furnace, the smith at his anvil, and the tools of his trade.

This head from a shrine at Taxila in northern India was fashioned in the Greek style, although it is Buddhist in origin.

THE EMERGENCE OF NEW IDEAS

In China and Mexico, writing was composed of pictures rather than letters, mixing ideas with artistic expression. The Chinese made objects from wood coated with lacquer, and they also painted on silk. During the same period, the Greeks pioneered the theater, portraying real-life situations. They were the first to represent moods and emotions in their art. Since creativity is natural to humans, every culture, whether simple or sophisticated, had its own art forms, carved in wood or stone, written or painted on papyrus or bark, sewn into clothing and tapestries, or cast in metals. New ideas emerged through the arts, and during this important period many different styles were established, some continuing up to the present day.

These Chinese cranes from the late Zhou dynasty (around 300 B.C.), were coated with lacquer, a natural varnish, which was painted on in layers, and set until it became hard. Cranes were seen as the bringers of good news and grace.

A pottery model of a watchtower made in later Han China around A.D. 100. Such towers were built to guard noblemen's estates from unwanted visitors—they may also have had religious significance.

A copper raven made by the Hopewell people of eastern North America around 100 B.C. The Hopewell controlled rich reserves of very pure copper, which they exported as far as Mexico.

This Mayan stone carving shows a shaman in ceremonial dress entering a mystical world.

ARCHITECTURE 500 B.C.–A.D. 500

The growth of empires and cities led to the construction of many public buildings. The most magnificent were the ones for state and religious use.

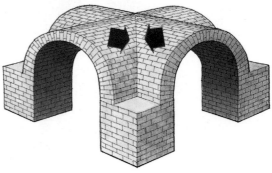

The Romans developed a technique to build vaulted passageways. They found that one vault could cross another and still support a heavy building on top.

In the cities of the developed world of the time, buildings were constructed from stone for strength and durability, and often faced with a decorative stone such as marble to make them look impressive. They were built by hand, although tools and devices such as scaffolding had been developed that made construction of large buildings and sophisticated arches possible. Many buildings today are not much more advanced than they were 2,000 years ago. The Greeks were skilled architects. The study of mathematics helped them design well-proportioned buildings that suited their surroundings. By 300 B.C., the Greeks had also developed town planning, designing whole cities in detail and arranging the streets in a grid pattern. The city builders of Mesoamerica also used urban planning. In other places, cities evolved from their former origins as villages, forts, harbors, or road junctions with a more random pattern of design.

Greek, Roman, Indian, and Chinese builders had virtually the same hand tools used today. These included saws, chisels, pincers, planes, and hammers.

The Parthenon in Athens, completed in 432 B.C., was one of the finest of all Greek temples. The columns were developed from the idea of tree-trunk supports. Stone-dressing became an advanced art, and complex scaffolding was used to allow the building of enormous structures.

ROMAN DEVELOPMENTS

The Romans adopted many Greek ideas, but also discovered new techniques. One was how to make concrete in around 200 B.C. At first they used it in foundations, but soon it was also used in the construction of walls and huge domed roofs. They also developed arches for buildings, bridges, and aqueducts. By A.D. 200, Roman cities had apartment buildings, called *insulae*, that were four or five stories high. Roman cities were a foretaste of the densely packed cities of today—Rome had an enormous traffic problem.

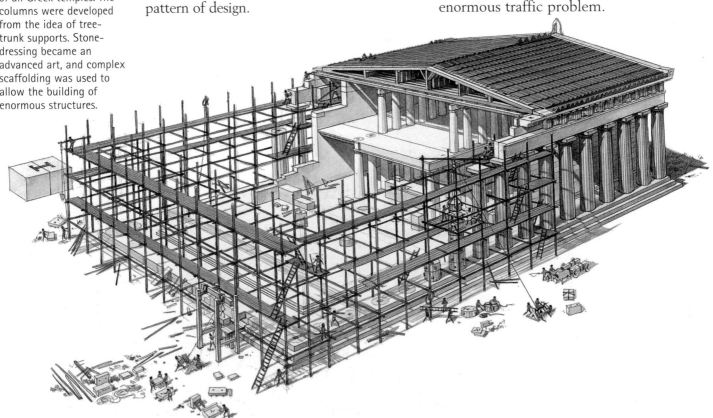

This multiarched aqueduct, built around A.D. 378, was designed by Roman engineers to carry water to the new city of Constantinople.

LARGE-SCALE BUILDING

Engineering works became much more ambitious and sophisticated. Paved, drained, and raised roads were built in the Roman Empire, Persia, India, China, and Mexico. They allowed much faster transportation and the use of carts to carry bigger loads. Water was channeled into canals or along raised aqueducts to supply the cities. In Mesoamerica, enormous pyramids and other structures were built in impressively large religious centers. All this engineering work involved the assembling and organization of large numbers of people, as well as food supplies and building materials. Architects, surveyors, and engineers were in demand, to select materials and supervise construction. This represented a tremendous growth in practical skills, as well as knowledge of mathematics and engineering principles.

The specialized construction trades that we know today developed from this time. All over the world, building techniques improved gradually, even in simpler societies and villages—although their use of wood, which rots and falls apart, means that few traces of their buildings remain. In cold climates, new methods of dealing with cold and damp were developed. In hot climates, cool and shady buildings were built, with arches, good light, and ventilation. The Maya built high pyramids to be able to reach above the tree level of the jungles around them. Construction principles remain the same today.

These are the ruins of Gaochang, a city built by the Han Chinese on the Silk Road to the West. The Silk Road cities were rich and cosmopolitan, and accommodated travelers from many different lands.

Mayan pyramids were built without cranes and bulldozers. Millions of blocks of stone were prepared and erected, and when building the upper parts, everything was carried up by hand. This must have been a work of tremendous coordination.

SCIENCE AND TECHNOLOGY 500 B.C.–A.D. 500

Rapid progress was made in China and Europe because of greater investment, more sophisticated ideas, and larger-scale projects.

The wealth and security found in the growing empires meant that great advances could be made. Some advances were made as solutions to practical problems or as the result of newly available materials. Others were made by urban people who had the leisure to study. The Greek philosopher Aristotle (384–322 B.C.) is considered to be one of the founders of Western science. He, and several other scientists, philosophers, geographers, and doctors of his time, pioneered a rational approach to the world, based on observation. They questioned how and why things worked the way they did. China, too, was the source of many inventions, from gunpowder to magnetic compasses and calculators (abacuses).

The abacus was widely used in China at the beginning of this period. It was an early calculator that allowed the computation of difficult sums. Modern computers became faster only in the early 1980s.

The Archimedes screw is a device for lifting water from one level to another. It takes its name from the Greek inventor Archimedes (287–212 B.C.) who lived in Syracuse on the island of Sicily.

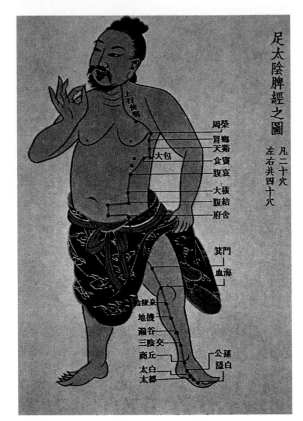

In acupuncture, the Chinese used the tips of needles to stimulate nerves to treat illnesses. This chart shows the parts of the body where the needles are placed. Acupuncture is still practiced today and has become widely used in the West in modern times.

Papermaking was first developed in Han China around A.D. 105, and paper documents soon became common. It took over 1,000 years for papermaking to reach Europe.

A TIME OF PROGRESS

All cultures had their scientists, doctors and researchers—they were distancing themselves from the past and adopting new ideas. Businessmen were interested in investing in these ideas to make money. Knowledge and sophisticated technologies were gradually improving: new strains of plants, new medicines, mathematical systems, ways of piping water, recording information, and forging metals were developed. This was a time of progress that slowed down as the world became more insecure from the A.D. 300s onward.

WHEN IT HAPPENED

450 B.C. In Nigeria, people of the Nok culture smelt iron in furnaces
250 B.C. Greek mathematician and inventor Archimedes active
200 B.C. The Romans first use concrete
10 B.C. The Romans start using cranes in construction
A.D. 78 Chang Heng, inventor of the seismograph, is born in China
100 Paper-making invented in Han China
127 Ptolemy (Egypt) writes about music, astronomy, mathematics, and geography
270 Magnetic compass used in China

A Greek doctor examines a young patient. The Greeks adopted a scientific approach to medicine and made extensive studies of human anatomy. They laid the foundations of Western medicine.

This coin-operated machine was used to sell sacred water at a Greek temple. A falling coin triggered the mechanism to release a measure of the sacred water into a container.

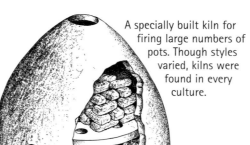

A specially built kiln for firing large numbers of pots. Though styles varied, kilns were found in every culture.

This cubit rule and curved calipers were used by Han scientists in China to accurately measure the width and thickness of objects.

This Roman water mill was built around A.D. 100. The waterwheel's rotation was transferred through wooden shafts and gearwheels to the millstones which ground the grain. Large mills had six or more waterwheels arranged in a line along a riverbank. Waterwheels were also used in China to raise water from rivers into irrigation channels to water the fields.

EARLY MIDDLE AGES
501–1100

This period used to be called the Dark Ages because historians thought that civilization ended when the Roman Empire fell. Many people now call these years the Early Middle Ages because they mark the start of the period that separates ancient and modern history. The former Roman Empire split into two: the western part peopled by farmers, skilled metalworkers, and shipbuilders; the eastern part became the Byzantine Empire. The Chinese and Arabs still led the way in science and technology. Buddhist and Christian religions were spread through trade, while Islam was spread through military conquest.

▲ The Carolingian Renaissance inspired this ivory carving, from the 800s, of St. Gregory and other scholars at work.

◄ This Mayan stone carving from the 900s was found in the ruins of the city of Chichén-Itzá on the Yucatán Peninsula of Mexico.

THE WORLD AT A GLANCE 501–1100

After the fall of the Roman Empire, new countries and peoples emerged in Europe. The lives of these people were governed by the Christian Church and a rigid social system, later called feudalism.

Between Europe and the Far East, there was a huge area containing many different people who all shared the same religion, Islam. Farther north, Slavic countries such as Russia and Bulgaria were also forming.

China was still culturally and scientifically far ahead of the rest of the world. Its influence spread all over Asia, and to Japan, where the arts flourished.

In North America, the first towns were being built, and the Toltec civilization developed in Mexico. In South America, huge independent empires, such as the Huari Empire, were forming.

Contact between the civilizations of the world was very limited. Only a few countries traded with each other. But Islam was gradually spreading over the whole of northern Africa through conquest and trade.

NORTH AMERICA

NORTH AMERICA

In about 700, two separate town cultures began to develop in North America. One was the Temple Mound culture around the Mississippi area—a culture that traded far across the continent in copper and goods. Another was the Anasazi *pueblo* (village) culture in the Southwest, where people lived in stone pueblos connected by roads. The Anasazi had an advanced religion. Elsewhere, many Native American tribes grew bigger and stronger, though they were still mainly farming and hunting peoples, living either in permanent villages or as nomads. Far to the northeast, in Newfoundland, the first white men arrived—the Vikings settled there for a short time around the year 1000.

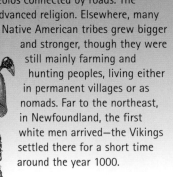

MESOAMERICA AND SOUTH AMERICA

MESOAMERICA AND SOUTH AMERICA

Around 600–700, the great Mexican city of Teotihuacán was at its greatest. Decline began around 750, both there and among the Maya farther south. But the Mayan Empire of city-states survived this whole period. From 900 to 1100, the warlike Toltecs flourished in Mexico. In Peru, in South America, the city-states of Tiahuanaco in the Andes and the Huari near the coast grew larger and more developed. Tiahuanaco preceded the Inca Empire. By 1000, the Huari Empire was replaced by the Chimú Empire, which was developing around Chan Chan in northern Peru.

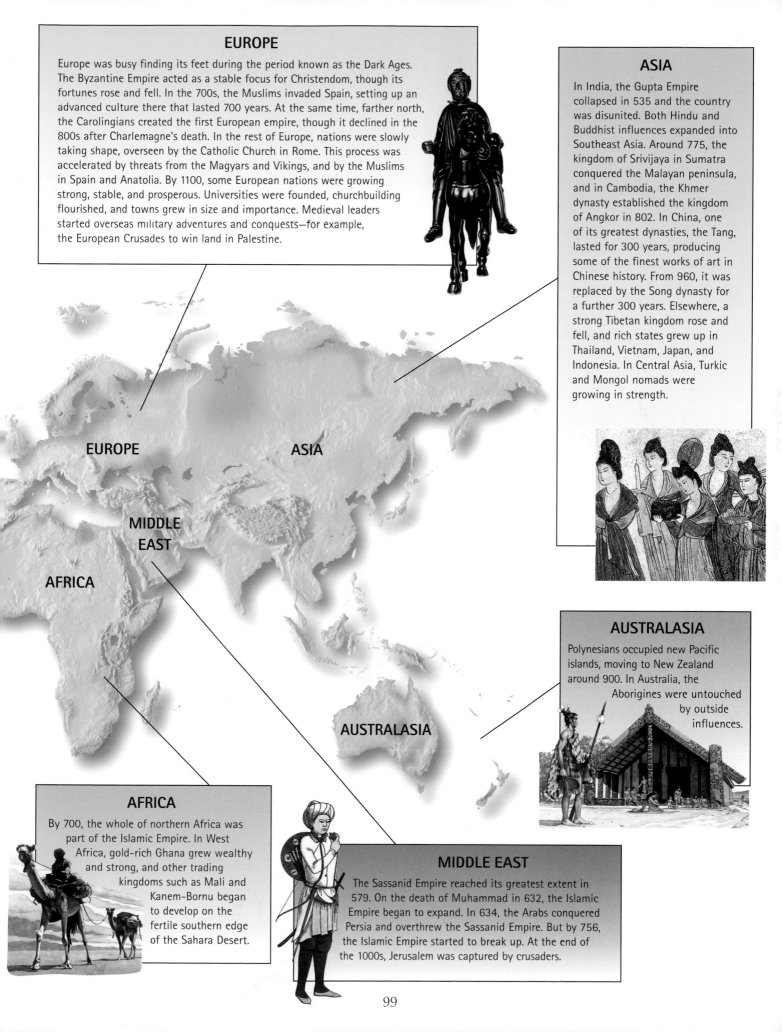

EUROPE

Europe was busy finding its feet during the period known as the Dark Ages. The Byzantine Empire acted as a stable focus for Christendom, though its fortunes rose and fell. In the 700s, the Muslims invaded Spain, setting up an advanced culture there that lasted 700 years. At the same time, farther north, the Carolingians created the first European empire, though it declined in the 800s after Charlemagne's death. In the rest of Europe, nations were slowly taking shape, overseen by the Catholic Church in Rome. This process was accelerated by threats from the Magyars and Vikings, and by the Muslims in Spain and Anatolia. By 1100, some European nations were growing strong, stable, and prosperous. Universities were founded, churchbuilding flourished, and towns grew in size and importance. Medieval leaders started overseas military adventures and conquests—for example, the European Crusades to win land in Palestine.

ASIA

In India, the Gupta Empire collapsed in 535 and the country was disunited. Both Hindu and Buddhist influences expanded into Southeast Asia. Around 775, the kingdom of Srivijaya in Sumatra conquered the Malayan peninsula, and in Cambodia, the Khmer dynasty established the kingdom of Angkor in 802. In China, one of its greatest dynasties, the Tang, lasted for 300 years, producing some of the finest works of art in Chinese history. From 960, it was replaced by the Song dynasty for a further 300 years. Elsewhere, a strong Tibetan kingdom rose and fell, and rich states grew up in Thailand, Vietnam, Japan, and Indonesia. In Central Asia, Turkic and Mongol nomads were growing in strength.

EUROPE

ASIA

MIDDLE EAST

AFRICA

AUSTRALASIA

Polynesians occupied new Pacific islands, moving to New Zealand around 900. In Australia, the Aborigines were untouched by outside influences.

AUSTRALASIA

AFRICA

By 700, the whole of northern Africa was part of the Islamic Empire. In West Africa, gold-rich Ghana grew wealthy and strong, and other trading kingdoms such as Mali and Kanem-Bornu began to develop on the fertile southern edge of the Sahara Desert.

MIDDLE EAST

The Sassanid Empire reached its greatest extent in 579. On the death of Muhammad in 632, the Islamic Empire began to expand. In 634, the Arabs conquered Persia and overthrew the Sassanid Empire. But by 756, the Islamic Empire started to break up. At the end of the 1000s, Jerusalem was captured by crusaders.

THE BYZANTINE EMPIRE 476–1453

Byzantium inherited the eastern half of the Roman Empire, surviving nearly a thousand years until, finally, it was taken over by the Ottoman Turks.

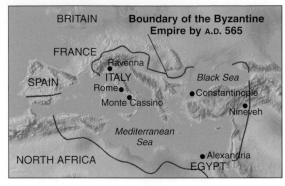

Centered on the strategic city of Constantinople, Byzantium controlled east–west trade and for long periods dominated the Mediterranean Sea and the Black Sea.

Justinian ruled Byzantium for 38 years with his wife Theodora. They were lawmakers and reformers, and they restored the empire's power and lands. They gave shape to the sophisticated culture of Byzantium, building great churches and acting as patrons of art and literature.

▼ Byzantium was often under attack. Its navy had a secret weapon invented by Kallinikos in 677 called "Greek Fire," a mixture that burst into flames when it touched water. It was made from lime, sulfur, and petroleum.

Constantinople, the eastern Roman capital, had been built by Emperor Constantine on the site of the ancient Greek port of Byzantium. When the Roman Empire collapsed in 476, the city became the capital of the new Byzantine Empire. The edges of the Roman Empire's territories had been captured by barbarians, so the early emperors of Byzantium, Anastasius (491–518) and Justinian (527–565), fought to reclaim Rome's former territories. During Justinian's long reign, he sent able generals—Belisarius, Narses, and Liberius—to add North Africa, much of Italy, and southern Spain to its list of reclaimed territories. However, many of these gains were soon lost under his successors.

A revival followed when Emperor Heraclius (610–641) reorganized the empire and brought state and church closer together. He beat back the Sassanid Persians, who had occupied Syria, Palestine, and Egypt. Under his rule, Constantinople became a rich center of learning, high culture, and religion. The city was well placed for controlling trade between Asia and Europe. The empire produced gold, grain, olives, silk, and wine, which were traded for spices, precious stones, furs, and ivory from Asia and Africa.

▲ This pictorial map shows Constantinople in 1422, not long before it fell to the Ottomans. It became a Muslim city, and was renamed Istanbul in 1453. The city stood on a promontory called the Golden Horn.

This classic Byzantine Orthodox mosaic is on the inside of a church dome in Ravenna, Italy. It shows Jesus being baptized by John the Baptist. The presence of the god of the Jordan River identifies the place of the baptism.

The Byzantines made elaborate crosses, icons, caskets, and other sacred relics. These became an important part of life in the Orthodox Church.

▼ Saint Sophia, the Church of the Holy Wisdom, was built in Constantinople for Justinian around 530. It took 10,000 people to build it. Later it became a mosque, and it is now a museum.

KEY DATES

476	Fall of the last Roman emperor
491–518	Emperor Anastasius in Constantinople
527–565	Emperor Justinian's generals reconquer former territories
610–641	Emperor Heraclius expands Byzantium
633–640	Arabs take Syria, Egypt, and North Africa
679	Bulgars overrun Balkan territories
976–1026	Basil II rebuilds the empire
107	Seljuk Turks take Anatolia
1204–61	Norman Crusaders capture Constantinople
1453	Fall of Byzantium to the Ottoman Turks

The Byzantine basilica of St. Apollinare was built near Ravenna in Italy during the 500s. In this period, Byzantine architecture was gradually steering away from the old Roman styles.

The Byzantine Empire declined during the 700s—the Arabs twice tried to take Constantinople itself. However, under Basil II (976–1025), the empire flourished again. Then, soon after Basil died, Anatolia was lost to the Turks, and the empire again declined. It was taken over by the Crusaders for 50 years during the 1200s, but it was reclaimed again by Michael VIII in 1261. Finally, the city of Constantinople was taken by the Ottoman Turks in 1453. The sophisticated Byzantine culture had been the most lively and creative in Europe, and the Orthodox faith had spread as far as Russia and eastern Europe.

MONASTICISM 269–1216

**To escape the busy city of Alexandria, a group of
Christians formed a community in the Egyptian desert.
This marked the beginning of the monastic tradition.**

Monks and nuns led
simple lives, studying,
praying, and caring
for the sick.

In the first 200 years of Christianity,
some Christians had lived as hermits on
remote islands or in deserts, spending their
time in prayer. In 269, an Egyptian hermit,
Anthony of Thebes, brought several
hermits together to form a community—
the first monastery. This idea spread to
other countries, where other monasteries
and convents were established. Some of
these communities were linked by a
shared set of guidelines. The most famous
was the rule of St. Benedict, founder of
the Monte Cassino monastery in Italy,
around 529. In the Benedictine order,
monks worked and worshiped together.

A page from the *Book of Durrow*, written and illustrated
around 675 by Irish monks. Beautifully decorated
manuscripts were meticulously produced by hand.

By 900, other orders had appeared. The
Cluniacs in France followed strict rules
of poverty and chastity, reacting against
growing corruption in the Church. The
Cistercians, founded around 1115, were
even stricter, with some monks spending
all their time in prayer and administration
while "lay" brothers did the heavy work.
St. Francis of Assisi founded the
Franciscans to preach and care for the
poor, and St. Dominic founded an order
devoted to preaching and teaching.

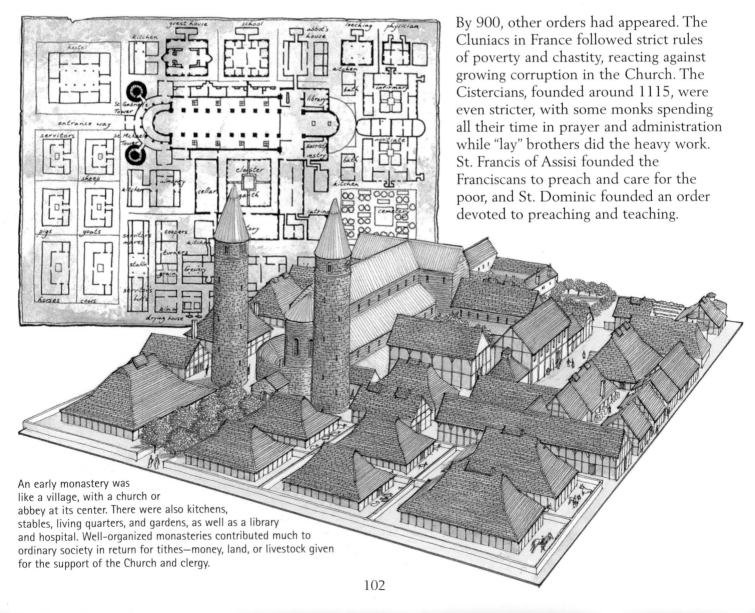

An early monastery was
like a village, with a church or
abbey at its center. There were also kitchens,
stables, living quarters, and gardens, as well as a library
and hospital. Well-organized monasteries contributed much to
ordinary society in return for tithes—money, land, or livestock given
for the support of the Church and clergy.

Many monasteries had schools and libraries where specially trained monks copied out books by hand. Some learned monks wrote new books on history, medicine, and philosophy, as well as religious doctrine.

MONASTERIES AND SOCIETY

Life in a monastery was spent praying, sleeping, and working. Each monk or nun received food, a room or cell, and a habit, or clothing, and they were provided for all their lives. This was more than most ordinary people had, so there was no shortage of new members. Although monks and nuns lived apart from the world, monasteries still played an important role in everyday life.

SEATS OF LEARNING

The best way to get an education was by joining a monastery. Monasteries had libraries of classical and biblical texts—the basis for much of the learning of the time. Great works were written by monks such as the Venerable Bede, famous for his history of England, completed in 731. Some monks stayed in monasteries, and some became parish priests, while others became clerks to kings and bishops. Most monasteries provided shelter for travelers and pilgrims. They also cared for the poor and treated the sick, with medicines made with herbs from the monastery gardens.

KEY DATES	
269	St. Anthony founds the first monastic community in Egypt
c.540	St. Benedict writes his Benedictine monastic rule
c.930	Cluniac monastic reform movement
c.960	Byzantine Orthodox monastic orders set up
1054	Orthodox and Catholic churches split apart
1115	Founding of Cistercian monastery of Clairvaux
1209	Franciscan order receives papal approval
1216	Dominican order founded

The *Book of Kells* is a book of Gospels begun on the island of Iona off the coast of Scotland and completed in Ireland. The pages were illuminated (decorated) in the Celtic style between 650 and 690. This page from the book features St. Matthew.

The Venerable Bede was a monk who lived in Jarrow in northeast England. He is known as the "father of English history" because he wrote *The Ecclesiastical History of the English People*. Bede was the first historian to date events from the time of the birth of Jesus—most other writers of the time related dates to reigns or notable events.

SUI AND TANG CHINA 589–907

The Sui dynasty reunited China after 370 years of division, but it lasted only 30 years. It was followed by the Tang dynasty, which lasted nearly 300 years.

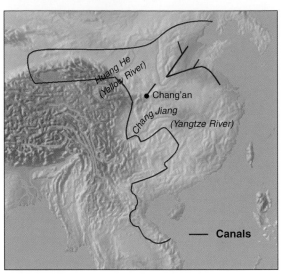

China grew in size during the Tang period. It expanded into central Asia, and many large projects were started, such as the canal system and irrigation schemes.

From the fall of the Han to the rise of the Sui, China was divided into three kingdoms—Wei in the north, Shu in the west, and Wu in the south. There was constant warfare, as well as nomad invasions from Mongolia and Tibet. Many towns were ruined, and the population fell. Devastation in the north led to migrations southward, making the south more politically important. During this time, Buddhism became more widespread in China, bringing in many foreign ideas. Finally, in 581, Yang Jian, a general from Wei, overthrew his rulers and founded the Sui dynasty. By 589 he had unified China.

The Tang people believed that dragons symbolized the energies of the Earth and that all things should be in harmony with one another. These beliefs even influenced their thinking about building practices.

SUI DYNASTY

Yang Jian renamed himself Emperor Wen. Before he came to power, taxes were high and people were drafted into the army for long periods of time. As emperor, he cut taxes and abolished compulsory military service, governing firmly from his capital, Chang'an. He also encouraged the development of agriculture by setting up irrigation schemes and redistributing land. All these things helped make the country wealthy.

The second Sui emperor was Yang Di. Under Yang Di's rule, China's Grand Canal was rebuilt so that it linked the main rivers of China. He also had palaces and pleasure parks built. The money for them was raised by ordering people to pay ten years' tax in advance. The peasants rebelled and, in 618, Yang Di was killed.

TANG DYNASTY

The second Tang emperor, Taizong (626–649), reorganized government, cut taxes, and redistributed land. The reorganization of this united empire was far in advance of anything found

Rice paddies need controlled watering and large-scale drainage works. The Tang dynasty created conditions in which such large-scale projects became possible.

This wall painting from a tomb shows the Tang princess Yung Tai, who was forced to commit suicide at the age of 17 for criticizing her grandmother, Empress Yu. In China, obeying and submitting to one's parents and elders was considered to be very important.

THE GRAND CANAL

Started by the Sui and completed by the Tang, the Grand Canal was an enormous undertaking. It stretched over 500 mi. (800km) from the Huangho River to the Yangtze, and linked the major cities and capitals of the north with the rice-growing and craft-producing areas of the south. Road travel from north to south was difficult, and sea travel was hampered by typhoons and pirates. The canal allowed safe, long-distance, freight-carrying transportation, to bind China's northern and central regions closer together.

in other parts of the world. This stable period marked the beginning of nearly 300 years which promoted Chinese excellence in the arts, science, and technology. Between 640 and 660, Tang China expanded into central Asia, seeking to keep troublesome nomads from controlling the Silk Road. The Chinese went as far as modern-day Korea, Afghanistan, and Thailand. After Taizong's time, a rebellion by An Lushan in Beijing in 755 challenged Tang rule, and the Tang never fully recovered. Imperial rule became a formality, and power shifted to regional governors and courtiers. The Tibetans also defeated the Chinese in central Asia and there were more rebellions during the 800s. By 907 the Tang dynasty had collapsed and there followed a period of civil wars that lasted until 960.

KEY DATES	
589	Yang Jian unites China, founding Sui dynasty
602–610	Military actions in Taiwan, Vietnam, Korea, and central Asia
618	Tang dynasty founded by Li Yuan
626–649	Emperor Taizong—expansion of Tang China
640–660	Chinese expansion in central Asia and Korea
755–763	An Lushan's rebellion—Tang power declines
870s	Major peasant rebellions throughout China
907	Tang dynasty collapses

These ceramic ornaments are examples of the foreign animals that would have been seen in the Tang capital, Chang'an. The camel carried silk, and the horse, larger than the Chinese variety, originated in central Asia. Chang'an lay at the Chinese end of the Silk Road and was the world's largest city, with two million people.

ISLAM 622–750

Islam established itself very quickly and influenced many other civilizations. Within 150 years it had grown into a huge empire guided by religious principles.

This is a Muslim portrayal of the Archangel Gabriel (Jizreel). Gabriel is recognized by Muslims as the messenger of Allah to the prophet Muhammad.

The prophet Muhammad, who founded the religion called Islam, was born in Mecca in 570. At the time, the Arab peoples worshiped many different gods. Muhammad became a successful, widely-traveled trader, and was influenced by the Judeo-Christian belief in just one God. When he was 40 years old, his life changed: he saw the Archangel Gabriel in a series of visions. Muhammad then wrote down the *Koran*, the Muslim holy book, under dictation from Gabriel. He was instructed to teach about prayer, purification, and *Allah*, the one God. The word *Islam* means "surrender to Allah."

When Muhammad started teaching, the rulers of Mecca felt threatened by his ideas. Muhammad and his followers had to flee to Medina in 622 and the Muslim calendar counts its dates from this flight—the *Hegira*. In Medina, Muhammad organized a Muslim society, building a mosque. His following grew quickly—many Arabs were poor and Islam preached a fairer society. In 630, Muhammad recaptured Mecca and became its ruler. He kept nonbelievers out and banned idol-worship. Muhammad died in 632.

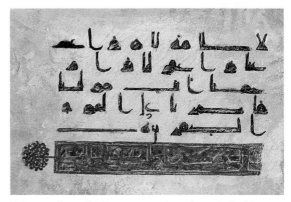

This page from the *Koran* was written in early Arabic lettering style during the 800s. One aspect of the new Islamic culture was its artistic and cultural creativity.

ISLAMIC EXPANSION

The new Muslim *caliph* (leader), called for a *jihad*, or holy war. Within ten years, under Caliph Umar, the Arabs conquered Syria and Palestine (defeating the Byzantines), Mesopotamia and Persia (bringing down the Sassanids), as well as Egypt and Libya. After the death of Caliph Uthman, there were disputes between his successor, Muawiya, and Ali, Muhammad's son-in-law. Ali's murder in 661 led Muslims to split permanently into two factions—the Sunnis, and the Shiites, who were followers of Ali.

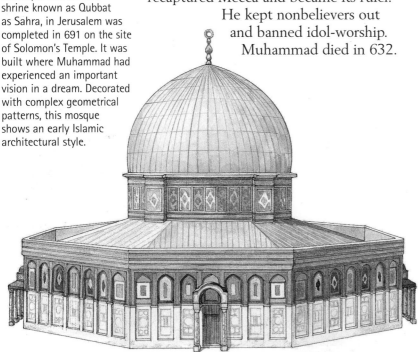

The Dome of the Rock, the important Muslim shrine known as Qubbat as Sahra, in Jerusalem was completed in 691 on the site of Solomon's Temple. It was built where Muhammad had experienced an important vision in a dream. Decorated with complex geometrical patterns, this mosque shows an early Islamic architectural style.

Muslims traveled widely, as explorers and traders, and carried ideas about Islam with them. Their faith decreed that they should make at least one pilgrimage to Mecca.

◀ At the battle of Yarmuk, in Syria, in 636, Muslim forces defeated a Byzantine army twice their size. This was a major loss for Byzantium, and the Muslims captured Syria and Palestine, the most prosperous part of the Byzantine Empire. They took Jerusalem and established the beginnings of a large empire.

▼ Arabic knowledge of medicine, healing, and surgical technique was well advanced for this time. This picture shows doctors setting a broken limb.

THE UMAYYAD DYNASTY

In 661, the Arabs established a capital at Damascus, and Muawiya became the first Umayyad caliph. Territorial expansion followed—Muslim armies invaded central Asia, Afghanistan, Armenia, northern Africa, and even Spain. They twice attacked Constantinople, without success. When they invaded Europe, they were defeated by the Franks in France in 732 and had to retreat. The Umayyads organized their empire in the Byzantine style. They were tolerant and did not force conversion to Islam. Many people converted because Muslims were seen as genuine liberators, bringing an end to the old order, establishing clear laws, and increasing trade. Arabic became a universal language across Islam, except in Persia which was mainly Shiite and retained its distinct culture. This common language helped ideas and knowledge to spread quickly from one place to another.

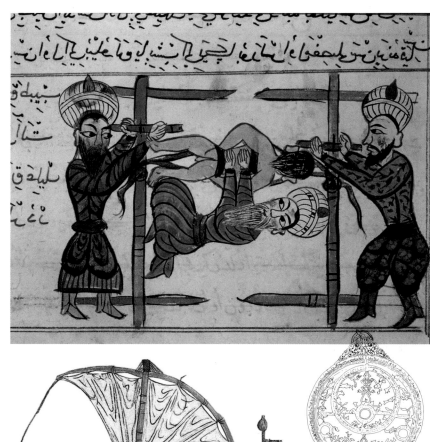

Arabs were good astronomers. The astrolabe allowed them to navigate at sea—and in the desert.

The Arabs sailed in *dhows*. These wooden boats had large triangular sails and carried cargo and passengers.

KEY DATES	
610	Muhammad experiences his first vision
622	The *Hegira*—the flight from Mecca to Medina—takes place
630	Muhammed takes Mecca and forms an Islamic state
636–642	Muslims take Palestine, Syria, Persia, and Egypt
656–661	Caliphate of Ali—dispute between factions
661–680	Founding of Umayyad dynasty
711	Arabs invade Spain
732	Franks defeat the Arabs at Poitiers, France
750	Umayyad dynasty overthrown by the Abbasids

PERSECUTION OF THE JEWS 70–1300

After rebelling against Roman rule, the Jewish people went into exile. Toleration in their new lands was often followed by severe persecution.

▲ The *Magen David* (Star of David), is an ancient symbol. It first appeared as a symbol of Judaism around 960 B.C.

▼ A rabbi teaches his pupil "Hillel's Golden Rule" during the late 1300s in Germany. There was a strong emphasis on education to preserve Jewish culture and to ensure survival.

During A.D. 66–73, the Jews of Judea fought against their Roman rulers. The Romans massacred many, and in A.D. 70, destroyed the Great Temple of Jerusalem. Jews were barred from entering Jerusalem under penalty of death. In A.D. 116, Jewish rebellions in Roman-controlled Egypt, Cyrene, and Cyprus were also crushed. There was continual unrest in Judea. During the Second Jewish Revolt, A.D. 132–135, hundreds of thousands of Jews were massacred or sold as slaves. Jerusalem was razed to the ground and the Romans built a new city on the site, naming it Aelia Capitolina. On the mount where the Great Temple had stood was a new temple, dedicated to Jupiter. Survivors were driven from Judea to join established communities in Babylon, Anatolia, Greece, and northern

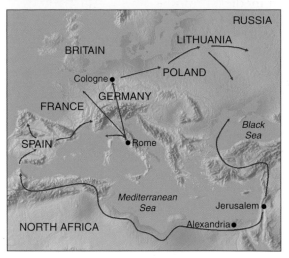

The arrows show the approximate movement of Jewish people during the *Diaspora* (dispersal) and the early stages of persecution during the 1100s.

Africa. The *Diaspora*, or dispersal of the Jewish people, that began with the Babylonian exile in 586 B.C., grew in momentum.

After Constantine, Christian Romans became increasingly intolerant. They expected Jews to become Christians, and in the 400s downgraded their citizenship. Some Jews moved even farther away, to Germany and Spain. They established small, close communities in cities, keeping to their own traditions and maintaining contact through international networks. As a result, the two great Jewish traditions arose—the Ashkenazic Jews in Germany, whose popular language is Yiddish, and the Sephardic Jews, whose language is Ladino.

In the Near East, Spain, and northern Africa, Jewish communities prospered. Under Islamic rule, they enjoyed security and protection from their enemies.

EUROPEAN ANTI-SEMITISM

In medieval Europe, Jews could not own property or join armies. Instead, they became skilled craftworkers, doctors, and traders. Eventually they were allowed to be moneylenders, which was forbidden to Christians, who considered lending money for interest a sin. Kings and traders protected the Jews who provided this service. Ordinary people, however, resented what they saw as affluence during generally hard times.

By 1100, the Crusades had begun, and feelings towards non-Christians had hardened. Across Europe, people turned against some Jews, and forced them to live in particular areas of cities called "ghettos." Many others were persecuted or expelled from their homes. Thousands of Jews were killed during the Crusades (1092–1215). Jews were also expelled from England in 1290 and from France in 1306. Many fled from Spain and Germany to eastern European countries.

▲ In medieval times, Jewish moneylenders were heavily involved in financing the economic growth of Europe, particularly in Venice and Genoa in Italy.

▼ After about 1000, German Christians began to blame the Jews for the death of Jesus. Many were persecuted, tortured, and killed.

KEY DATES	
66–132	Jewish revolts and the Roman expulsion of the Jews
700s	Jews find refuge in the new Arabic Empire
1100s	Persecutions in France and Germany
1189	Jewish massacre in York, England
1215	Lateran Council allows Jews to lend money
1290	Expulsion of Jews from England
1280	Early Jewish ghetto in Morocco

Accused of being the killers of Christ and other crimes, many Jews were tortured and killed by Christian medieval knights during the 1200s.

NORTH AMERICA 500–1492

The first North American towns appeared in the Mississippi valley during the 700s. In Colorado, the Anasazi were building villages called *pueblos*.

Across North America there were very different cultures, ranging from town dwellers along the Mississippi and Ohio Rivers to self-sufficient, village-dwelling people on the Pacific coast and the nomadic tribes of the Plains.

The Iroquois were a confederation of hunting tribes who lived in the woodlands of what is now New York State. They lived in village communities, gathering food, hunting, and trading with other tribes.

The first true North American towns appeared along the Mississippi and Ohio Rivers. Now known as the Temple Mound culture, each town had a central plaza with up to 20 rectangular earth mounds around it. On top of these were temples for the dead. A palisade (wooden wall) surrounded the plaza. Outside, up to 10,000 people lived in longhouses with adobe (dried mud) walls and thatched roofs. The people traded along the rivers, possibly taking copper from Wisconsin to Mexico. They hunted for meat and were also farmers. They grew corn, sunflowers, beans, and pumpkins.

They made war with tribes such as the Algonquin and first used bows and arrows around 800. The Temple Mound culture reached its peak during the 1100s, but mysteriously disappeared by 1450. Elsewhere, permanent village cultures were developing. The Woodland Americans of the east were farmers, hunters, and traders.

The Plains Tribes, who were usually nomadic buffalo hunters, began building riverside farming villages around 900. On the Pacific coast, there were many food-collecting, hunting, and fishing peoples. Some of them already lived in permanent villages and had well-developed societies. In the far north, the hunting Inuit were even trading with Vikings around 1000. The Cree, Chippewa, and Algonquin tribes of Canada lived their lives close to nature and had little contact with foreigners and traders.

The Sioux or Dakota peoples followed the buffalo herds as they migrated across the midwestern plains. The Sioux *tepees* were built of buffalo skins draped around a framework of sloping poles. They could be dismantled easily and carried by the Sioux as they traveled.

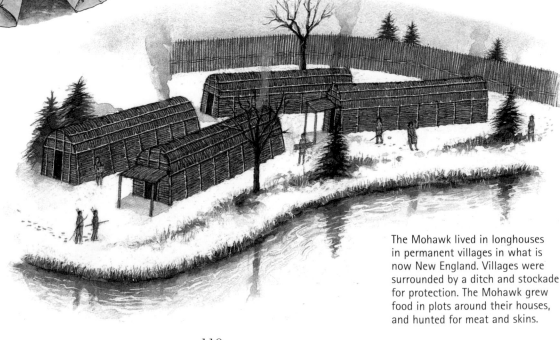

The Mohawk lived in longhouses in permanent villages in what is now New England. Villages were surrounded by a ditch and stockade for protection. The Mohawk grew food in plots around their houses, and hunted for meat and skins.

PUEBLO CULTURES

In the Southwest, several cultures thrived between 700 and 1300. These were the Anasazi, Hohokam, and Mogollon, the predecessors to today's Hopi. They were trader-farmers living in small towns. After 700, these people moved from pit houses—large roofed-over holes—into large, multistory communal buildings, some housing up to 250 people. They used irrigation systems and relied on "skywatchers"—knowledgeable shamans who predicted the rains. By 1300, these unique cultures had disappeared.

KEY DATES	
300	Growth of Anasazi, Mogollon, Hohokam cultures
800	Agricultural growth in many cultures
800	Founding of the first Mississippi towns
1000–1200	Southwestern and Mississippi cultures at their peak
1300	Decline of Anasazi, Mogollon, and Hohokam cultures
1450	Mississippi towns depopulated
1500	Europeans arrive on East coast

THE ANASAZI PEOPLE

Anasazi, a Navajo word, means "ancient ones who are not us." The Anasazi grew corn, beans, squash, and cotton, and lived in *pueblos* (tribal towns) with unique buildings nestling high up in canyons. They were known for their pottery, textiles, and artwork. Around Chaco Canyon, a network of 125 villages was linked by 250 mi. (400km) of roads. The Anasazi had advanced shamanic religious rituals, with large tribal trance dances. They had unique knowledge and legends, and constructed underground ceremonial chambers called *kivas*.

◀ Religious ceremonies played an important role in pueblo life. These masked men are performing a ceremony to make rain fall on the desert so that their crops will grow.

▼ The Cliff Palace, sheltering under a cliff at Mesa Verde, Colorado, was built by the Anasazi. It housed around 250 people, who lived as a closely knit community. In front of the ruined palace are ceremonial *kivas* (without their roofs), which were originally used for religious purposes.

BULGARS AND SLAVS 600–1453

Bulgaria and Kiev had a significant influence on eastern Europe. Their adoption of Orthodox Christianity affected both their peoples and the Orthodox church.

During the mid-800s, Cyril and his brother Methodius devised the Cyrillic alphabet, based on Greek letters, for use in writing the Slavonic languages.

The Bulgars were the descendants of the Huns, who settled beside the Volga River in Russia, and reached the height of their power around 650. Then the Khazars from lower down the Volga destroyed their kingdom. As a result, many Bulgars migrated to the Danube area, dominating the local Slavs and founding a Bulgar state. Byzantium took action against them, especially when the Bulgars killed their emperor in battle in 811. In the 860s, two missionaries, Cyril and Methodius, were sent to convert the Bulgars and draw them into Byzantium's influence. This helped, but the quarrels did not end until the Bulgars were beaten in 1014. To punish them, Basil II had 14,000 Bulgars blinded, and the Bulgar khan died of shock.

Vladimir, Grand Prince of Kiev (c.956–1015), interviewed Catholic and Orthodox Christians, Muslims, and Jews, and opted for the Orthodox faith, probably for political as much as religious advantages. Vladimir was the youngest son of Grand Prince Svyatoslav, who brought down the Khazars. Vladimir conducted campaigns to secure Kiev's territories.

ORTHODOX DIPLOMACY

In Byzantium, the state and the church were closely linked. Religious and diplomatic missions were sent out and, in this way, Byzantium converted the Bulgars to Christianity. Catholic Rome and Orthodox Constantinople competed for influence in eastern Europe. Kiev adopted the Orthodox beliefs, and a Russian Orthodox culture was born there. Cyrillic lettering, still used today by Russians and Bulgarians, was invented by Cyril the missionary and his brother Methodius. By the time Byzantium fell in 1453, Russia had become the home of Orthodoxy.

When the Bulgars killed the Byzantine emperor Nicephorus in 811, they made his skull into a goblet to take to their khan, Krum. The Byzantine emperors called the Bulgar khans *czars*—a name that was adopted later by Russian rulers.

The Church of Intercession, an example of early Orthodox church construction in Russia, was built at Bogolyubovo in 1165.

THE RISE AND FALL OF KIEV

The Slavs came from what is now Belarus. The first states in Russia were Slavic, and led by Swedish Viking traders (*Ros*, or "oarsmen"). The greatest Ros leader was Rurik, who founded Novgorod, Smolensk, and Kiev. The Vikings traded with Baghdad and Constantinople, and Kiev grew rich as a trading city. The Vikings considered themselves a superior class, mixing only gradually with the Slavs. In 988, the Kievan prince Vladimir converted to Christianity, marrying a Byzantine princess. He then made the nobility and people adopt Christianity. This brought Kiev new trade, culture, and respectability abroad. Under Jaroslav the Wise (1019–54) Kiev was a center of splendor and influence that rivaled Constantinople, with diplomatic connections across Europe.

Churches were built, and the first Russian laws were written, as well as the first works of Russian art and literature. Kiev was on the steppes (plains) of the Ukraine, and vulnerable to nomadic warriors such as the Pechenegi who threatened, and the Polovtsy who sacked, the city. After Jaroslav died, the state of Kiev broke up, and the Russians retreated into safer northern areas. Here a new Russia was being established, centered around the growing city of Moscow.

A central theme of Orthodox culture was the icon, or holy image, which was believed to have spiritual and healing powers. Icon painting spread from Byzantium, through Kiev, into later Russian culture.

This helmet from the 1200s belonged to the prince of a small principality called Suzdal, once part of Kievan Russia.

113

THE CAROLINGIANS 751–843

The Carolingian dynasty established Europe's first rich and powerful empire. These people were the former Germanic "barbarians" known as the Franks.

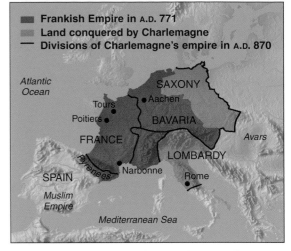

Charlemagne's empire unified most of western Europe. Its capital, Aachen, lay not far from the capital of today's European Union in Brussels.

Map legend:
- Frankish Empire in A.D. 771
- Land conquered by Charlemagne
- Divisions of Charlemagne's empire in A.D. 870

The Franks had settled in what is now Belgium and northern France. Their leader, Clovis (481–511), of the Merovingian dynasty, established a capital at Paris. Clovis became a Christian and earned Rome's support. He united the Frankish tribes, defeated the Gauls, the Alemanni (a confederation of Germans), and the Visigoths, and created a kingdom resembling today's France. His sons consolidated this, but quarrels broke out. Power fell to Charles Martel, who led the Franks against the invading Muslims at Poitiers in 732. Charles founded the Carolingian dynasty, and in 751, under his son Pepin, the Carolingians replaced the Merovingians as Frankish rulers. In 768, Pepin's sons, Carloman and Charlemagne, inherited his kingdom. Carloman died in 771, and Charlemagne took full control. He first conquered the rest of France, and then what is now Germany, Italy, and the Netherlands, creating an enormous European empire. In central Europe he quelled the Saxons and the Avars, forcing them both to accept Christianity.

This gold image of Charlemagne, inset with precious stones and known as a reliquary, was made in Germany around 1350, to hold parts of Charlemagne's skull.

CHARLEMAGNE'S CORONATION

Obtaining the blessing of the Church gave a nation greater respectability. For the pope, Charlemagne's grand coronation in 800 was a political move against Constantinople—there was now a Christian empire in the West as well as in the East. Charlemagne offered to marry the Byzantine empress Irene, but this was unacceptable to many people. Missions were sent to Charlemagne from Persia and the Baghdad Caliphate, as well as from the rulers of Europe. Had Charlemagne's empire remained intact, European history might have been very different.

Pope Leo III crowned Charlemagne Holy Roman emperor in 800.

Holy Roman emperors were crowned in the Palatine Chapel, Aachen.

THE CAROLINGIAN RENAISSANCE

Charlemagne supported the Roman church, favoring its influence in his kingdom. In return, in 800, the pope crowned Charlemagne as the first Holy Roman emperor. Charlemagne was a lawmaker and founded schools, cathedrals, and monasteries run by Irish, British, and Italian monks. He also invited scholars, scribes, architects, and philosophers to his court. His capital at Aachen became the chief center of learning in western Christendom. Charlemagne died in 814. His successor Louis the Pious ruled successfully but, on his death in 843, the empire was divided between his three sons. The empire later became two countries: Germany and France. The Carolingians ruled Germany until 911 and France until 987.

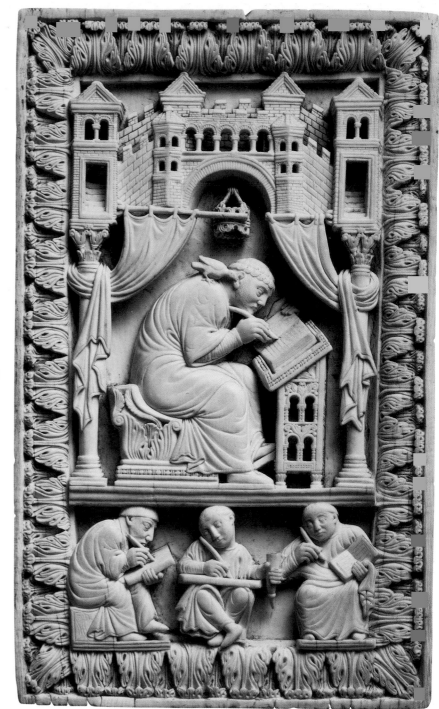

BEATISSIMO papaedamaso bieronimus

Charlemagne was a great military leader who, once he had invaded lands, tried to improve conditions and encourage the poor to improve their standard of living.

▲ The Carolingian Renaissance inspired this ivory carving of St. Gregory and other scholars at work, in 850–875. The Aachen scholars created a new script called *minuscule*, with clear, rounded letters, but Charlemagne never learned to write.

KEY DATES	
486–510	France united by Merovingian king, Clovis
732	Charles Martel beats the Arabs at Poitiers
751	Pepin, the first Carolingian king
768	Charlemagne becomes Carolingian king
782	Charlemagne defeats the Saxons
790s	Charlemagne defeats the Avars in Austria
800	Pope crowns Charlemagne
814	Charlemagne dies
843	Carolingian Empire divided into three

THE ABBASID DYNASTY 750–1258

During the 500 years of rule by the Abbasid dynasty, the Islamic Empire was unified, its culture flourished, and Baghdad became one of the world's greatest cities.

The stories for *The Thousand and One Nights* came from many different countries, including India, Syria, and Egypt. The stories feature Ali Baba, Sinbad the Sailor, and Aladdin.

In 750, there were disagreements between the Arabs as well as dissent among the invaded peoples. The Umayyads were overthrown by the Abbasid family who then ruled the Islamic world for 500 years. The Abbasids were descended from Muhammad's uncle, al-Abbas. Under al-Mansur, their first caliph, they moved their capital to the new city of Baghdad in 762, and adopted many Persian and Greek traditions. Their most famous ruler was Harun al-Rashid (786–809), the fifth caliph. From 791 until 806, he fought a long war with the Byzantine Empire, which he eventually won. Parts of the empire sought independence, but Harun al-Rashid managed to suppress them. In spite of these wars he found time to encourage learning and the arts, bringing together Persian, Greek, Arab, and Indian influences. Baghdad became a world center for astronomy, mathematics, geography, medicine, law, and philosophy. The court in Baghdad was the setting for much of *The Thousand and One Nights*, a book still

enjoyed today. Under later caliphs, various provinces became independent, but they still followed Islam, its law, and culture. The Abbasid caliphs increasingly lost power and became spiritual figureheads. The Muslim empire separated into emirates, whose fortunes rose and fell at different times. Yet the Muslim world acted as one civilization with many different centers.

When Harun al-Rashid became caliph in 786, he ended a decade of uncertainty and rivalry in the Islamic Empire.

This elaborately decorated tile, made in Persia during the 1100s, shows that Islamic art in the Abbasid period was very rich and sophisticated.

This decorated Persian bowl was made during the Abbasid dynasty. It shows how Muslim artists created new styles with intricate designs.

People came to the Abbasid court in Baghdad from all over the empire, even from as far away as central Asia and Spain.

116

GHANA 700–1240

Ghana was the first truly African state. Most Africans still lived in tribal village societies, but Ghana, a center of the gold trade, opened up new possibilities.

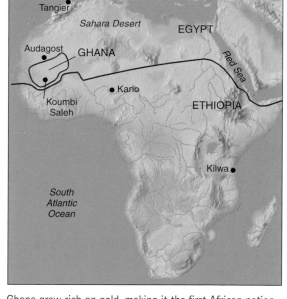

Ghana grew rich on gold, making it the first African nation. Its capital, Koumbi Saleh, was very cosmopolitan. Gold was transported north to Morocco, Tunisia, the Nile, and Arabia.

Prester John was a legendary king who was said to rule over a Christian empire in the heart of Africa.

The medieval kingdom of Ghana lay farther north, inland from today's nation of Ghana. Its roots lay in the 300s, when the African Soninke tribes were ruled by the Maga, a Berber clan from Morocco. The Berbers had mastered transsaharan camel travel, and traded salt for gold from the Soninke. When the Arabic Muslims invaded northern Africa there was an upsurge in the gold trade, and by 700, Ghana was rich and important as a trading center. In 770, the Soninke ousted the Maga, and built a nation under Kaya Maghan Sisse, who became Soninke king around 790. Ghana's capital was the city of Koumbi Saleh, where Africans and Berbers met and traded. During the 800s, Arab traders described Ghana as "the land of gold." The gold came from Ashanti and Senegal to the south and west, and trade routes led north and east to Morocco, Libya, and Aksum, and so on to Europe and Asia.

Ghana reached its peak during the 900s, controlling both the gold and salt trades. Other goods that passed through Ghana included woolen cloth and luxury items from Europe, and leather goods and slaves from the south. In 990, Ghana took over the neighboring Berber kingdom of Audagost—making Ghana 500 mi. (800km) across. In 1076, however, it fell to the Almoravids, a puritanical Berber Muslim sect. The Almoravids ruled Morocco and Spain, but they fell in 1147, and power returned to Ghana until, in 1240, the country became part of a new African nation, Mali.

Berber and Arab traders transported goods hundreds of miles across the Sahara Desert with camel caravans. Without traders, Ghana and its successors, Mali and Songhai, would not have become rich nations.

FUJIWARA JAPAN 800–1200

During the late 800s, the Fujiwara clan became the rulers of Japan on behalf of the emperor. During the Fujiwara period, art and literature flourished in Japan.

Japanese horses were dressed with many ornaments on their harnesses. This horse bell would probably have been worn on the horse's hindquarters.

From the early 300s, Japan had been ruled by an emperor. If an emperor died while his eldest son was still young, a regent, usually someone in the emperor's family, was chosen to rule until the new emperor grew up. In the 800s the Fujiwara clan gained importance at the Japanese court when Fujiwara Yoshifusa's daughter married the emperor. By tradition, children were brought up by their mother's family, and so the Fujiwaras brought up the next emperor.

An illustration from the *The Tale of Genji*, a novel about the complexities of Fujiwara court life. It was written by Lady Murasaki Shikibu, a lady-in-waiting to the empress.

Court life was very formal, with rules for everything. This man is reading a letter. Even the color of the letter paper and the way it was folded were considered important.

This meant that Fujiwara Yoshifusa was the first regent from outside the imperial family, marking the start of the Fujiwara period. More Fujiwara daughters were married to future emperors and the Fujiwara family grew powerful. Soon, every emperor had a permanent Fujiwara regent, who controlled the running of the country while the emperor spent his time on religious and court matters. For 300 years, the Fujiwara family dominated Japan.

The Great Torii Gate, at Itsukushima or Miyajima-Shrine Island was built during the 800s. It is part of a classic Shinto shrine. The torii stood as a kind of divider, to separate the sacred areas of the temple from the nonreligious parts.

118

FUJIWARA CULTURE

During the Fujiwara period Japanese art and literature flourished. This happened at the imperial court in Kyoto, among nobles on their estates, and in the temples, so ordinary people saw little of it. The rich and powerful were very insulated from the rest of society. Great works of art were painted, and literature was written in a new style—notably, Lady Murasaki Shikibu's classic *The Tale of Genji*. Until that time, the Japanese had tended to imitate Chinese styles. Clans favored by the Fujiwaras prospered. Then other clans, largely of military families, began to grow more powerful, and the provinces and clan estates started to act increasingly on their own behalf. They fought among themselves until the Fujiwaras could no longer control the country. During the 1100s, there were many rebellions until, finally, the Gempei civil war broke out in 1180, and the Fujiwara were replaced by the powerful Minamoto shoguns.

KEY DATES

794	Japanese court moves to a new capital at Heian (Kyoto)
858	Fujiwara Yorifusa becomes regent
930	Fujiwara gain full dominance: economic reforms
c.1000	Peak of artistic and literary expression in Japan
1180–85	Gempei civil war: rise of the Minamoto shoguns

This clay figure of a protector-god stood outside Shinto temples to protect them from demons. The clothing worn by this figure is typical of a Japanese warrior of the 700s.

The hondo or main hall of Kiyumizudera Temple at Kyoto (Heian) was built during the 700s. Japanese buildings were usually made of wood so that they could survive earthquakes. Sadly, many of these fine wooden buildings were destroyed by fire instead.

MAGYARS AND BOHEMIANS 896–1273

During this period, central Europe had no real nations. Bohemia and Poland were Slavic heartlands, and Hungary was occupied by Asiatic Magyars.

Duke Wenceslas, prince of Bohemia in the 920s, tried to modernize his country and convert it to Christianity. He was famous for his charity and fairness. His pagan brother, Boleslav, opposed him and had him killed in 929. Later, Wenceslas was made a saint, and he is the patron saint of the Czech Republic.

The Magyars were Asian horse-riding nomads from the steppes (plains) of today's Kazakstan. Seeking a new homeland, they raided central Europe and, under prince Arpad in the late 800s, they occupied Hungary. Just 25,000 Magyars defeated all the Slavs by using speed and shock tactics. Then they started raiding Germany, Italy, and France for slaves and riches. For decades, they sacked monasteries and ruined farms, torturing and killing people in the process. They were so fast, they could be attacked only when weighed down with their booty. Eventually, the German emperor Otto I defeated them in 955. Under Prince Geiza (972–997) the Magyars made peace, adopted Christianity, and settled down as nobles ruling the Slavs. In 1000, Pope Sylvester II crowned Stephen I Magyar king of Hungary. Stephen's reign brought peace and prosperity—he was later canonized. By 1200, Hungary was a strong nation. But in 1241 the Mongols swept in, devasting the country just as the Magyars had once done.

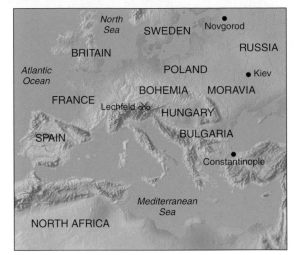

In the forests of central Europe, various new states developed among the Slavonic tribes from about 800 to the late 1200s: Hungary, Bohemia and Moravia (now the Czech Republic), and Poland.

Prince Arpad, a Magyar, led his people from Asia into Europe, founding the Magyar Arpad dynasty and the nation of Hungary. This is his statue in Budapest, the Magyar capital, which straddles the Danube River.

The Magyars rode strong Asiatic horses, and they could cover long distances very quickly. This helped them become the scourge of Europe for 55 years, raiding Germany, France, and Italy, weakening many states and killing many people.

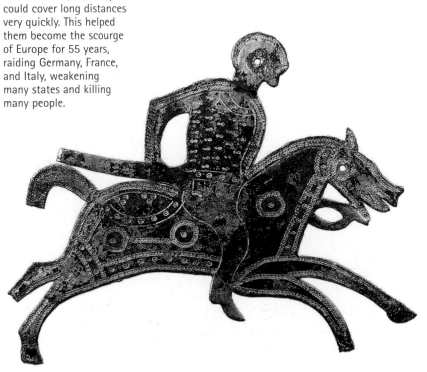

POLAND

The Polish tribes were united by Miesko I around 960, and became Christian. His son Boleslav Chrobry tried to unite all Slavic lands, including Bohemia, Moravia, and Kiev, but later the Poles had to retreat. Though the church and German influences brought the Poles together, the provinces were disunited, and this weakness was to prove significant when other countries tried to take parts of Poland. Nevertheless, Poland as a Slavic nation became established at this time.

MORAVIA AND BOHEMIA

Northwest of Hungary and southwest of Poland were the Slavonic states of Moravia and Bohemia (now the Czech Republic). Moravia was established by Duke Moymir in 830, who freed it from Carolingian domination. During the 800s, Bohemia was part of the Moravian Empire. The Germans tried to reclaim Bohemia from the Moravians, but there was a Slav revolt in 874. Moravia was reunited under Sviatopluk, who made peace and expanded the country. In 906, the Magyars destroyed Moravia.

Meanwhile, around Prague, a new Bohemian state was developing. One national character of this time was Duke ("good king") Wenceslas, noted for his charity. Bohemia took over Moravia in 1029, gaining recognition from the Holy Roman Empire by 1086. Many German traders moved in, and expanded the local economy. The peak of Bohemian power came under Ottokar II, who took over Austria in 1251. He lost it to Rudolf the Hapsburg in 1273. Bohemia was overrun by the Germans in 1300, but it remained a distinct country linked with Moravia.

King Stephen, later canonized, receives the crown of Hungary from Pope Sylvester II, making him Apostolic King. This alliance helped Hungary become respectable, and it helped the pope gain influence in central Europe.

This crown was given to King Stephen by Pope Sylvester in 1000. The symbolic effect of such crownings was to give a nation recognition and to bind it into the European order of the time.

Each country has its national hero. For Hungary, it is St. Stephen. This statue of Stephen on his horse was erected in 1902.

KEY DATES

830	Moymir establishes the Moravian state
896–907	Prince Arpad, leader of the Magyars
906	Moravia falls to the Magyars
920	Wenceslas tries to modernize Bohemia
955	Defeat of the Magyars, ending Magyar raids on Europe
960	Unification of Poland under Miesko I
997–1038	St. Stephen, king of Hungary
1241	Collapse of Hungary after Mongol raids
1260	Peak of Bohemian power and prosperity
1308	Bohemia and Moravia come under German control

ANGLO-SAXON BRITAIN C.600–1066

The arrival of the Angles, Saxons, and Jutes in Britain during the 400s and 500s created a new people, the English, who were to dominate Britain.

The Romans left Britain around 410. There was a brief revival of power for the now romanized British. In 446, the British high king, Vortigern, invited German Saxons from the Rhineland to enter Britain as mercenaries to support in his struggle with the Picts. The Saxons gained a foothold in the southeast, but were held off between 500 and 539, by the now legendary British leader Arthur. After a battle in 552, the Saxons started taking over southern and central England. Many Britons were killed or lost their lands; many emigrated to Wales, Cornwall, Ireland, Scotland, Brittany, and northwest Spain.

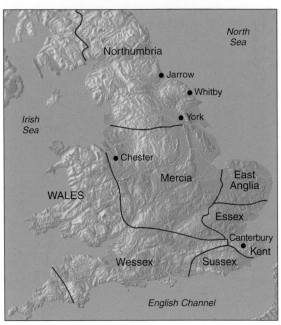

England was divided into seven kingdoms. From 878 Northumbria, East Anglia, and much of Mercia came under Viking control and formed the Danelaw.

The Angles buried their kings, with their possessions, in ships, to take them to the afterlife. This gold clasp comes from a famous burial ship of the early 600s, discovered at Sutton Hoo, in eastern England.

Vortigern, the British high king, hired German mercenaries, but failed to pay them. In revenge, they set out to conquer Britain. Settlers soon followed, beaching their boats and wading ashore with cattle and sheep.

THE BIRTH OF ENGLAND

In the wake of the German invaders, many of their countrymen emigrated to England. During the 500s and 600s, they slowly populated the country. British towns, villages, and farms were abandoned, and the Celtic Christian church retreated with them. The Germans brought new farming and ownership patterns, and their pagan tribal groupings gradually took the shape of kingdoms. Seven kingdoms were eventually formed: East Anglia, Mercia, and Northumbria (ruled by the Angles); Essex, Sussex, and Wessex (ruled by the Saxons); and Kent (ruled by the Jutes).

In 597, the pope sent Augustine to convert the English. These converts coexisted with the pagans, but there were disputes with Celtic Christians. These were settled at the Synod of Whitby in 664, where the Celts agreed to submit to papal authority. The seven kingdoms often fought to claim the title "Bretwalda" (lord of Britain). In the 600s, the Northumbrian kings Edwin, Oswald, and Oswy, and in the 700s, the Mercian kings Ethelbald and Offa, gained supremacy. Egbert of Wessex was the first king of a united England, in 829.

▼ This statue of King Alfred the Great stands at Wantage, his birthplace. Alfred was one of England's great leaders. He created laws based on justice and encouraged education.

STRUGGLES FOR POWER

In 789, the first Vikings appeared in England, and by the middle of the 800s they had started to settle. When Alfred the Great was king of Wessex in 871, the Vikings were threatening to overrun his kingdom. Alfred fought nine battles against them in one year alone. He finally defeated them in 878 and made them sign the Treaty of Wedmore. which divided England in two—the Saxon west and Danelaw in the east. Alfred was a lawmaker, a scholar, and a just king. In his time, texts were translated into early English, and *The Anglo-Saxon Chronicle*, an important history book, was begun. By 940, Danelaw had been won back from the Danes. England was reunified under Edgar (959–75), but in 1013 the Danes returned, and England was ruled until 1035 by the Danish king, Canute the Great. There was better cooperation between the Danes and Saxons under Edward the Confessor. In 1066, Harold II, having just fought invading Norwegians in Yorkshire, was beaten by invading Normans, under Duke William.

▲ The Ruthwell Cross, carved in a Celtic style by Saxon monks during the 700s, was richly decorated with scenes from the Gospels.

KEY DATES

446	Arrival of Jutish mercenaries led by Hengist and Horsa
560 onward	Large-scale immigration of English Saxons
597	Augustine arrives to convert English Saxons
793	The first Viking raid, on Lindisfarne monastery
870 onward	Immigration of the Danes into Danelaw
871–99	Alfred the Great crowned king of Wessex
1013	The Danes conquer all of England
1066	The Normans, led by Duke William, conquer England

▼ English Saxon society had three classes— thanes or nobles, churls or freemen, and serfs or slaves. In this picture, serfs are harvesting barley.

THE HOLY ROMAN EMPIRE 962–1440

Otto I became king of Germany in 936. He wanted to revive the old Roman Empire and was crowned as the first Holy Roman emperor by the pope in 962.

The Holy Roman Empire was neither particularly holy, nor Roman. Founded by Charlemagne in 800, it was concerned with the power of kings and it was German. After Charlemagne's death the Carolingian Empire gradually broke up, and France and Germany were separated. In Germany, a high king was elected as an overlord so that he could bind together the many independently ruling dukes, counts, and bishops. The first of these overlords was Conrad I of Franconia, elected in 911. Later, the ambitious Otto I (936–973) wanted to revive the Roman Empire. Otto brought stability by uniting all of the rulers who owed him allegiance and by defeating the Magyars.

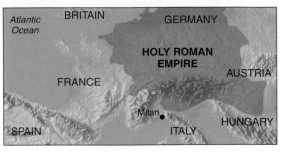

The Holy Roman Empire united all of the German-speaking peoples and extended its power into Italy, both to protect and to try to control the popes.

Otto conquered Bohemia, Austria, and northern Italy. After 25 years, he had the pope crown him Emperor Augustus, founding an imperial tradition that lasted 850 years until 1806. His empire became a revived Holy Roman Empire.

Otto I was on the throne of Germany for 37 years. He made the Holy Roman Empire a great and lasting institution by uniting his country's regional rulers and making them cooperate with him.

The Holy Roman emperor had the right to be crowned by the pope in Rome. Many popes and emperors disagreed over questions of power and authority, and this led to problems because each side wanted to interfere in the other's affairs.

Henry IV went to see the pope at Canossa, in January 1077, to settle a dispute over power. Pope Gregory VII kept him waiting outside in a snowstorm for three days before forgiving him and removing the ban of excommunication.

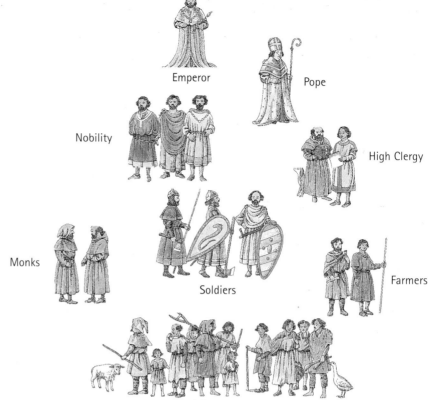

Emperor

Pope

Nobility

High Clergy

Monks

Soldiers

Farmers

Laborers

POPES AND EMPERORS

Several popes wanted help in ruling Christian Europe but often came into conflict with the emperors. Catholics had to obey the pope, so he was powerful. Popes wanted to choose emperors, and emperors wanted to choose popes and control Church affairs. Finally, Emperor Henry IV and Pope Gregory VII clashed—in 1075, Gregory said Henry had no right to choose bishops. In revenge, Henry said that Gregory was no longer pope. Gregory excommunicated him, which meant that Henry was no longer recognized by the Christian Church and his subjects did not have to obey him. In 1077, Henry asked to be forgiven. The quarrel over choosing bishops was finally settled in 1122, but there were more disputes, which led to a gradual separation of church and state.

KEY DATES	
911	Conrad I of Franconia is elected German king
936–973	Otto I strengthens the Holy Roman Empire
955	Otto I defeats the Magyars
1056–1106	Henry IV in conflict with the pope
1122	Concordat of Worms: an agreement between emperor and pope
1200	Peak of the political power of the Roman Catholic Church
1300	Popes lose political power
1440	Holy Roman Empire passes to the Austrian Hapsburg dynasty

▲ Noblemen usually supported the emperor against the pope, but sometimes they rebelled. Soldiers usually supported the nobles, who gave them land; and peasant laborers were employed by soldiers and nobles. Similarly, monks supported clerics, who supported the pope. These were "feudal" relationships, where a person gave allegiance and taxes in return for protection, land, or rights. Everyone was bound into feudal relationships throughout society.

In 1100, the pope and the Holy Roman emperor signed an agreement at St. Peter's Cathedral, in Worms, in southwestern Germany. The agreement ended a long-running dispute over who was responsible for the appointment of bishops.

CAPETIAN FRANCE 987–1328

In France, the Carolingian dynasty was followed by the Capetians in 987. Founded by Hugh Capet, the dynasty's aim was to unite France as a proud nation.

The dynasty founded by Hugh Capet died out in 1328. Monarchs of the later French royal houses of Valois and Bourbon claimed indirect descent from him.

Capet was the nickname given to Hugh Capet, the dynasty's founder, because of the short cape he wore when he was a lay abbot. As Duke of Francia, he had been the chief vassal of the last Carolingian king, and was himself elected French king. His position was not very strong: from Paris, he ruled northern France, but the dukes of Normandy, Burgundy, and Aquitaine were nearly as powerful as he was.

THE MAKING OF FRANCE

The aim of the Capetians was to unite France and build it up as a proud and prosperous nation. Capetian influence and French nationalistic feeling grew under Louis the Fat (1108–37), who made alliances with Church leaders against the Germans and the English.

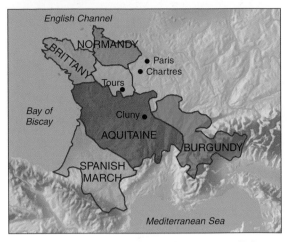

When Hugh Capet came to power, France was split into large dukedoms. Marriages and shifting political alliances meant that France was kept divided for some time. The Capetians' aim was to unite France under one rule.

Unlike the kings, the dukes were more interested in the fortunes of their own dynasties than those of France as a whole. Marriage alliances allowed land to pass out of central control, and this was to become a problem.

The Oratory at St. Martin d' Aiguilhe is an imposing structure in Burgundy. This part of France was ruled by the mighty dukes of Burgundy, against whose power the Capetian kings could not complete.

Hugh Capet is shown here receiving the keys of the town of Laon from Bishop Asselin, its local ruler.

FRENCH AND NORMANS

In 1152, King Louis VII's wife, Eleanor of Aquitaine, divorced him—he was away on Crusades too often. She then married Henry II, the French-Norman king of England, putting Aquitaine under Norman rule. France was then split into two halves, and this led to conflict. By 1214, the French had regained some of the Norman land, and by 1226, Louis VIII had strengthened France greatly. This process was continued by Louis IX (St. Louis), who conquered the south and overcame several rebellious nobles. However, the dukes still held much power, and the Normans exploited this. They wanted to control France. The question of Norman power in France was not resolved and, after the Capetians fell in 1328, a century of war began between the English and French. The Capetians had given France nationhood and stability, but this had taken some time to achieve.

This painting depicts the excommunication of Robert II, king of France (996–1031) and son of Hugh Capet. This happened because Robert made a questionable marriage.

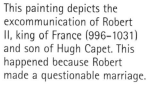

ABBEYS AND CATHEDRALS

In medieval times there were two major employers: the kings and the Church. Many churches, monasteries, and cathedrals were built during the 1100s and 1200s, but not only for religious reasons. The building stimulated the economy, provided employment, and symbolized greatness, stability, and wealth. Also, the Church acted as a European religious overlord to kings, and it was in the interest of kings to attract the favor of the pope. The new churches of the time were symbols of progress and prosperity as well as places of worship.

Jumièges Abbey was built around 1040 as part of a drive by the Capetians to make France into an influential kingdom supported by the pope.

The Capetians made France stable and wealthy. One result of this was the building of great cathedrals such as Chartres. Construction began in 1195, and it took 35 years to complete.

THE AMERICAS 500–1200

In Mesoamerica, the Toltecs came into prominence following the destruction of Teotihuacán. Meanwhile, in South America two new civilizations were developing.

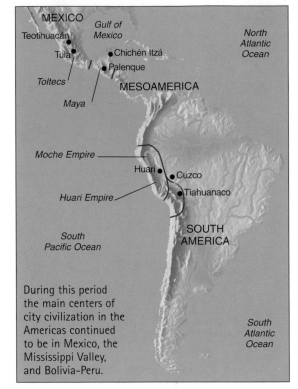

During this period the main centers of city civilization in the Americas continued to be in Mexico, the Mississippi Valley, and Bolivia-Peru.

The Toltecs were very militaristic. Their temples were guarded by stone statues of warriors such as this one from Tula.

By 600, Teotihuacán was in decline, and around 750 it was burned to the ground, possibly by tribes from the north. Various peoples tried to assume control, and around 900, the Toltecs established a capital at Tula. It became the center of a military state and trading network that reached from Colorado to Colombia. In 1000, far away in Yucatán, a faction of the Toltecs invaded the Mayan Empire, expanding the northern Mayan city of Chichén Itzá. The Toltec Empire came to an end in 1168, when it was overrun, and Tula was destroyed. Soon afterward, the Aztecs moved into the area.

THE LATER MAYA

Many Mayan cities were abandoned around 800, although some still flourished in northern Yucatán from 900 onward. Around 1000, Yucatán was invaded by Toltecs, who stayed there until 1221, building a copy of Tula at Chichén Itzá. Warrior chiefs took power from the priests, and caused crafts such as pottery, art, and literature to decline in quality.

The Toltecs were beaten by the Maya from Mayapán, whose Cocom dynasty dominated Yucatán for 200 years until civil war broke out in 1480. The Spanish arrived during the 1500s, but the last Maya city-state, Tayasal, did not fall until 1697.

THE PYRAMIDS OF ETOWAH

Etowah was one of the towns of the Mississippian culture in North America. This city culture spread far beyond the Mississippi valley—Etowah was near today's Atlanta, and famous as a source of mica, a transparent form of rock which could be split into fine sheets, like glass. The Etowans used tools of copper and stone, and built earthen pyramids with temples or the palaces of their chiefs on top. Their cities often had 10,000–20,000 inhabitants. They traded with Mexico and the Great Lakes area, and they made items to trade with the village-dwelling tribes of North America.

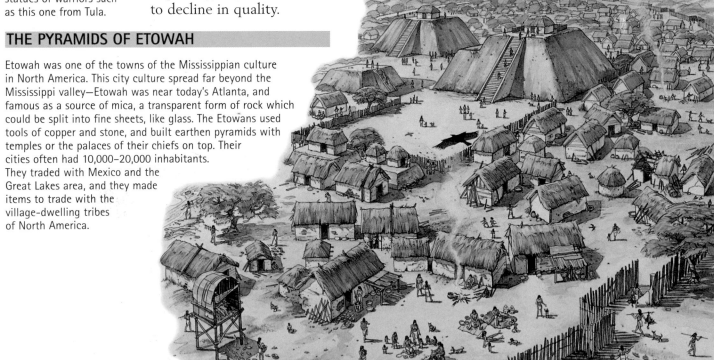

TIAHUANACO AND HUARI

Civilization in South America was based in two places. One was at Tiahuanaco, a large temple-city 12,000 ft. (3660m) above sea level near Lake Titicaca in Bolivia. Between 600 and 1000, it had a population of 100,000. The people of Tiahuanaco made distinctive pottery and jewelry, massive stone dry-stack walls, and enormous temple-stones. They created a string of towns stretching to the coast and into the Brazilian rain forests. The other civilization was Huari, which included remnants of several earlier local cultures such as Nazca and Moche. This was a powerful military empire, covering over half of modern Peru. Huari and Tiahuanaco may have followed the same religion, but Huari was militaristic and Tiahuanaco was peaceful. The two empires prospered until about 1000, when they were both abandoned, possibly because of drought.

KEY DATES	
600	Teotihuacán is sacked and burned
800	Toltec migration into central Mexico
900	Toltecs establish a city-state at Tula
1000	Tiahuanaco and Huari abandoned
1168	Tula destroyed
1200	Building of the Mississippian temple-cities
1200	Rise of the Aztecs and the Incas

This pottery image of a god from Huari, decorated with corn, was probably honored by farmers to help grow their crops.

This bowl from the Mimbres people of the southwest had a hole made in it to "kill" the bowl. It was then buried with its owner.

▲ This is one of the many massive carved stone figures of Tiahuanaco, erected around 700. Tiahuanaco, near the southern edge of Lake Titicaca, was ruled by a priesthood according to religious principles. The city had several large temples.

▲ This earring from Huari is made of stone inlaid with bone and shell. The Huari people also made beautiful jewelry and small objects out of gold.

◄ The sun god Viracocha was carved on the Gateway of the Sun at Tiahuanaco around 600. This giant gateway opened into the Kalasasaya, the largest of the city's building areas and the main temple.

THE VIKINGS c.600–1000

The Vikings have a reputation as raiders and violent warriors. But they were also traders and settlers, whose impact on European history has been great and lasting.

During the 700s, the Vikings began to venture from their homelands in Norway, Denmark, and Sweden in search of adventure, treasure, and better farmland. They made excellent wooden ships that could sail on rough seas and up rivers, and landed easily on beaches. At first they raided rich monasteries and coastal towns, and later they sailed up the Rhine, Seine, and Loire rivers to attack inland cities. Local rulers bought them off with silver and gold. Not all Vikings were raiders. Many were farmers looking for new land or traders seeking business. They were first-class sailors and traders, and ventured as far as Constantinople and Baghdad in search of conquest or trade.

Viking coins minted in the 800s were made of real silver or gold, so the coins themselves were actually worth the value they represented.

Viking men and women wore everyday clothes that were both practical and fashionable. Their gold and silver jewelry was sometimes broken up and used as money.

VIKING LONGSHIPS

The Vikings built superb boats, with sturdy keels acting as frames, which made the ships faster and more seaworthy. The boats were capable of being sailed or rowed. They could also be hauled by teams of men across land when necessary—even being dragged long distances overland in Russia, to get from one river to another. They could be beached easily without the need for a harbor. A dragon's head on the bow was intended to scare off evil spirits, sea monsters, and enemies.

For the cremation of a Viking headman, the dead body was placed on a ship with his belongings, for use in the next life, and a slave girl was often sacrificed. The ship was set alight by a close relative, naked to symbolize how we enter and leave life naked.

VIKING TRADERS AND SETTLERS

In Britain, the Vikings settled mainly in northern and eastern England, northern Scotland, the Isle of Man, and Ireland. In Ireland they destroyed many monasteries and founded the first towns. In France, the Vikings settled in Normandy, which had been given to them by the French king in 911 to discourage their raiding. In 1066, as Normans, they invaded England, and in the early 1070s, southern Italy, and Sicily. Vikings also settled in Iceland, and some sailed on to Greenland and North America. Others entered the Mediterranean, raiding southern France, Spain, and Byzantium. Beaten back by the Byzantines, Vikings sold them their services as traders and warriors instead. Swedish Vikings took over the Baltic Sea, and built trading towns such as Visby, Novgorod, and Kiev. Sailing down Russia's rivers, they met Bulgar, Khazar, Byzantine, and Arab traders. By 1000 the Vikings had settled down, and their Nordic homelands became Christian nations. They had an enormous effect on the future of northern Europe: they established trading routes and towns; founded Russia, greatly influenced Holland, Poland, Britain, France, and Ireland; and weakened the Carolingian Empire. Their descendants, the Normans, were influential in Europe and led the Crusades. Because of the Viking raiders, people had to rely on local feudal lords, and exchanged work, produce, and fighting men for protection. Gradually, Europe became more disunited, fighting grew frequent, and gaps grew between the rich and poor.

▲ The Vikings were skilled metalworkers. This is a die, used for stamping a pattern onto hot metal. It shows two shamans with weapons, poised for ritual animal sacrifice.

▼ The Viking town in Denmark called Hedeby, was well known for its craftworkers and traders. Hedeby was one of the ports from which the Vikings sailed far and wide.

THE NORMANS C.800–C.1200

The Normans invaded England in 1066 and soon ruled the Saxon and Viking English, the Welsh, and the Irish. They also wielded influence farther afield.

William the Conqueror, Duke of Normandy, was king of England from 1066 to 1087.

The Normans were Danish overlords who lived in Normandy from 900 onward. They had absorbed Carolingian and Christian ideas. There were not many of them, but they were tough warrior lords. William the Conqueror was crowned on Christmas Day 1066—in France he had been only a duke, but now he was also the English king.

NORMAN RULE

After the Norman invasion of 1066 many of the English protested. William put down rebellions brutally, taking English land and giving it to his Norman nobles, for them to rule the local areas. He gave land to the Church in order to gain its support, replacing English with French bishops, and he encouraged French traders and craftworkers to settle in England. The Normans built large castles, churches, monasteries, and great cathedrals, and many towns grew up around them. The nobility spoke French, and the ordinary people spoke early English. A central administration and tax system was established, and a tax assessment of England's land and wealth, the *Domesday Book*, was made. Norman rule was harsh. They were mainly interested in wealth and power, and used England as a base for foreign adventures that the English had to finance. However, England developed economically, and within 100 years the Normans began the invasion of Wales, Ireland, and Scotland. England was changing—its landscape, towns, and culture were all influenced by the Normans. By 1140 there was a disagreement over who should rule the country. This weakened the king and strengthened the nobles' power. A new Norman dynasty, the Plantagenet was founded in 1154, and its first king, Henry II, ruled England and half of France. During this time, the English class system, dominated by nobles, began to develop.

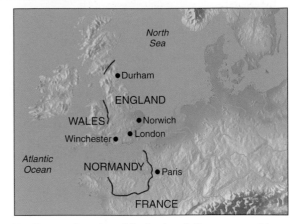

The Norman invasion of England took five years, and it raised the Normans from provincial French vassals to being the wealthy rulers of a whole country.

▲ William the Conqueror was succeeded by two of his sons. William II ruled from 1087–1100, Henry from 1100–1135. They established firm Norman rule, but it collapsed under the next king, Stephen, who died in 1154.

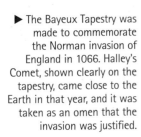

▶ The Bayeux Tapestry was made to commemorate the Norman invasion of England in 1066. Halley's Comet, shown clearly on the tapestry, came close to the Earth in that year, and it was taken as an omen that the invasion was justified.

THE NORMANS IN EUROPE

The Normans were also busy elsewhere in Europe. Around 1060, Norman soldiers under Robert Guiscard invaded Sicily and southern Italy, to support the pope against the Byzantines and Arabs. As a result, they were favored by the pope and often protected him. In the 1200s, they became leaders of the Crusades. Through political marriages, and by serving as knights, papal agents, bishops, and royal courtiers, Norman lords formed a feudal network which became very influential across Europe in the 1200s. In these feudal relationships, a noble who pledged allegiance and gave military support to a king was rewarded with lands and titles. These nobles then ruled estates and provinces, demanding loyalty of their followers and in exchange rewarding them with lands and positions of power. And so feudalism that started in France became established throughout Europe.

To honor ancient traditions, local law courts were often held outdoors. The lord of the manor was the judge. This court, or assize, held in 1072, met to decide whether some lands belonged to the Bishop of Bayeux, in Normandy, or to Canterbury Cathedral.

THE FEUDAL SYSTEM

Under the feudal system, people held land in exchange for services. It developed during the 700s under the Franks and was introduced to England by the Normans. In exchange for receiving estates and titles, Norman nobles paid taxes to the king, provided knights, and raised armies. Nobles gave their knights land in exchange for military service and taxes. A knight had to have *villeins* (peasant workers) to manage his land. The villeins lived in villages near the manor house. In exchange for a farm or house, they worked for the lord of the manor, paying him in crops or money.

Stories about heroic knights and courtly love between lords and ladies were very popular in Norman England.

THE SELJUK TURKS 1037–1243

The Seljuks invaded the Middle East from 1037 onward, ending Arabian domination of the Islamic world and opening the way for the Ottomans.

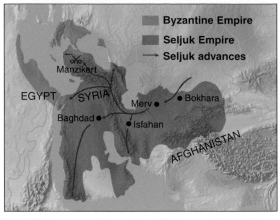

The Seljuks streamed down from Bokhara to Baghdad, and later, westward into Anatolia, almost as far as Constantinople. Anatolia (Turkey) then became Muslim.

This minaret at the Jami mosque in Simnan, Iran, shows typical Seljuk patterns in its elaborate brickwork. The Seljuks became Muslims around 970, and considered themselves defenders of the Islamic faith.

The Turks were originally a family of tribes living in Turkestan, central Asia. They split up during the 500s, and spread to Russia, China, India, and Persia. Some Turks abandoned the nomad life to become administrators and mercenary warriors. They served the Abbasids, Fatimids, and others, and sometimes rose to high office. Turks such as the Seljuks, Ottomans, Mamluks, Bulgars, and Khazars soon began to have great influence. They also joined forces with the Mongols. The Turkish cities of Samarkand and Bokhara grew wealthy and cultured in Islamic times.

SELJUK EXPANSION

To the east of the Caspian Sea lived a Turkic group called the Ghuzz, or Turkomans. The Seljuk broke away from the Ghuzz in 950, moving south and west. The Abbasid caliph in Baghdad was having difficulties, and he asked the Seljuks for their help. Led by Tughril Beg, the Seljuks invaded Persia and occupied Baghdad by 1055. The Abbasid caliph appointed Tughril as sultan under him—in effect, he gave the Abbasid Empire to the Seljuks. In this way, the Seljuks rose from being a simple nomadic tribe to rulers of the Islamic world.

Alp Arslan, Tughril's nephew, became sultan in 1063. He took Syria and Armenia and raided Anatolia. In 1071, the Byzantine emperor fought back. Alp Arslan hired Norman and Turkish mercenaries and marched into Armenia. The armies met at Manzikert. The Seljuks won because they pretended to be defeated and ran away. When the Byzantines pursued them, they turned around and badly defeated the Byzantine army. The Seljuks captured the Byzantine emperor and held him for ransom. This victory laid the foundation of what later became the Ottoman Empire. Alp Arslan was a compassionate leader and ruled the empire well. With his blessing, many Turkomans and Seljuks moved into Anatolia.

Like most nomads from the Asian steppes, the Seljuks were great horsemen. Using the new invention of stirrups, they could stay on horseback and fire arrows accurately in battle. This picture shows them defeating the Byzantines at the battle of Manzikert.

MALIK SHAH

The Seljuk Empire reached its greatest power under the rule of Alp Arslan's son, Malik Shah (1072–92). He was a patron of the sciences and the arts and built fine mosques in his capital, Isfahan. His minister, Nizam al-Mulk, was respected as a statesman. During this time, Seljuks took over Anatolia (Turkey) completely, and founded the Sultanate of Rum right next to Constantinople. On Malik Shah's death, the Seljuk Empire broke up into small states, and a variety of Seljuk, Mamluk, and Kurdish sultanates continued through the 1300s, all under the eye of the Abbasid caliph in Baghdad. Then, in 1220, the Mongols overran the area, finally occupying Baghdad in 1258.

▲The Tomeh or Friday mosque was built in Isfahan, Persia, in the Seljuk style. The Seljuks were great patrons of learning, architecture, and culture.

KEY DATES	
950	The Seljuks break away from the Ghuzz Turks
1038	Seljuks conquer Khorasan (Afghanistan)
1055	Seljuks conquer Baghdad
1071	Seljuks defeat the Byzantines at Manzikert
1072	Peak of the Seljuk Empire
1081	Founding of the Seljuk sultanate of Rum
1092	Death of Malik Shah—Seljuk Empire breaks up
1243	Mongol invasions: Seljuks become Mongol vassals
1258	Mongols destroy the Abbasid caliphate

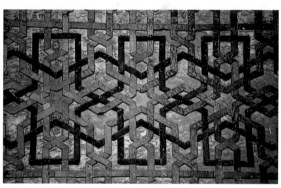

▲This is a tiled detail from the tomb of the Seljuk sultan Kaykavus I at Sivas in Turkey. The Seljuks produced beautiful and intricate patterns that were used to adorn their religious buildings.

◄Though the Seljuks brought new life to the Abbasid Empire, life in the Muslim world went on very much as before. This scene shows what a souk, or indoor trading hall, in Baghdad, would have looked like during the 1100s.

CHINA: THE SONG DYNASTY 960–1279

The Song (or Sung) dynasty created the third united Chinese Empire. This was a time of great innovation and took China into a long period of cultural eminence.

This Song temple painting from the 1100s shows disciples of the Buddha feeding the poor.

After the Tang dynasty fell in 907, China became fragmented. In the Huang He Valley, five emperors tried to start new dynasties over 53 years. None succeeded until Song Taizu took power in 960, founding the Song dynasty. He brought the many warlords and armies under control, and by both military and diplomatic means began to reunify China. This took 16 years and was completed by his brother, Song Taizong, the second Song emperor, in 979.

THE NORTHERN SONG PERIOD

Now surrounded by other states, China under the Song was smaller than in Tang times. In the northwest was Xixia, which was Tibetan; in the northeast was Liao, ruled by Mongol Khitans; in the southeast was Nan Chao, a Thai state; and in the south was Annam, a Vietnamese kingdom. The Song emperors worked hard to make peace with all of them.

Until the Jin invaded the north in 1127, the Song ruled all of China. They were then forced to move south where they prospered for another 150 years until the Mongols invaded.

Agriculture expanded and the population grew—especially in the south, which was now wealthy and important. By the end of the Song period there were probably around 100 million people living in China.

▼ Song artists often painted landscapes with small central features in them. This example of landscape painting from the Song period is called "Fisherman."

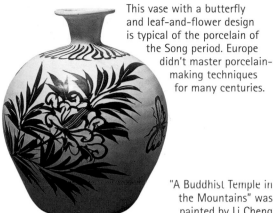

This vase with a butterfly and leaf-and-flower design is typical of the porcelain of the Song period. Europe didn't master porcelain-making techniques for many centuries.

"A Buddhist Temple in the Mountains" was painted by Li Cheng during the 900s.

THE SOUTHERN SONG PERIOD

In 1068, the prime minister, Wang Anshi, reformed the government. He simplified the tax system and reduced the size of the huge army. Although these cuts saved money, they also made invasion easier. In 1127, northern China was attacked by the Jin, and the Song capital, Kaifeng, was lost. The Song withdrew to Hangzhou, south of the Yangtze, and the north was then ruled by the Jin until Kublai Khan's Mongols took over in 1234. Hangzhou became a large, beautiful city, with canals, parks, and fine buildings. The Southern Song lasted until 1279, when southern China was overrun by the Mongols.

The Song period saw great prosperity and advancement in new technologies, arts, and literature. They invented gunpowder rockets, clocks, movable-type printing, paddle-wheel boats, magnetic compasses, and waterpowered machinery. Landscape painting, fine porcelain, poetry, and theater flourished. Banking and trade became important, towns grew large, and new crops were introduced. Song China could have become even greater, had it not been brought down by the Mongol invaders.

KEY DATES

907	Fall of the Tang dynasty
960	Song Taizu founds the Song dynasty
979	Song Taizong completes unification of China
1000	Culture and the economy thrive in China
1068-86	Wang Anshi's reforms
1127	The Jin take northern China: the Song retreat to Hangzhou
1234	The Mongols conquer northern China, ousting the Jin
1279	The Mongols conquer southern China: Song period ends

CHINESE PORCELAIN

Throughout the world, pottery had been made of clay that produced a chunky and rough finish. Around 900, the Song dynasty Chinese invented porcelain, which was made from kaolin, a fine white clay. Their craftworkers made smooth and delicate porcelain which, when used with special glazes and painting styles, could be beautifully decorated— making each piece a work of art. During this period, Chinese emperors even had factories built to make porcelain specially for their palaces. Porcelain production soon became an enormous industry in China.

Song emperors had ceramic factories built to supply fine porcelain.

This porcelain wine vessel stands in another vessel used for warming.

137

THE ARTS 501-1100

During this period, most artistic expression was for religious purposes. But religious authorities did encourage the development of arts, music, and crafts.

Churches, mosques, and temples attracted the finest craftworkers and musicians. Religious feeling encouraged them to stretch their talents to create delicate, elaborate works. Gifted people were usually educated by religious authorities. Ordinary people bore many hardships, but religion allowed them to think of higher matters and pray for better times, at least in the afterlife. Even tough, warlike rulers often had a gentle, religious side to them, and they brought artists, musicians, poets, and thinkers to their courts, turning a court into a cultural center. This earned a ruler not only God's approval, but also that of society and learned scholars.

Monastic scribes illuminated their lettering with religious pictures, using red lead, gold, silver, and special inks. Some scribes would spend years on each book using styles that showed Greek, Roman, Egyptian, Celtic, and German influences.

Temples, churches, and mosques were wealthy and used the arts to communicate religious stories and ideas. At this time most people could not read or write, and in many areas religious ceremonies were performed in foreign languages. So pictures, music, carvings, mosaics, and architecture were all used for teaching and raising people's spirits. Each culture developed its own artistic, musical, and literary style.

▲ Alfred the Great of Wessex was very religious. This was the top of a bookmark that he may have had made for a priest to keep his place when reading the Bible. The words around the edge say "Alfred had me made."

▼ For the ship-burials of their chieftains, the Vikings created elaborate decorations carved in wood or inlaid with metals. Vikings were not just warriors, but also skilled craftworkers and lovers of fine objects.

A picture of St. Mark from the Irish *Book of Kells* shows Celtic knotwork and spirals mixed with early Christian styles from Rome, Egypt, and Byzantium.

Byzantine churches were decorated with mosaics and holy pictures called icons. In Europe's monasteries, monks spent long hours copying books by hand. They illuminated, or decorated, the capital letters of texts and borders of pages with detailed designs. Muslims specialized in calligraphy, or beautiful handwriting, and in making elaborate geometrical patterns on their buildings. Buddhists in Asia painted stories of the life of the Buddha. In Tang and Song China, they painted and carved new kinds of landscape art and natural images. In Mexico, manuscripts, stone carvings, and murals, or wall paintings, were common.

▲ A Byzantine mosaic inside the dome of the Arian Baptistry in Ravenna, Italy, shows Jesus being baptized by John the Baptist. The twelve Apostles, each carrying a crown, are depicted around him. Each individual figure in the painting is a work of art in itself.

◄ Under Islamic law, artists were not allowed to paint pictures of people or animals—this was thought to be idolatry, the worship of idols. As a result, artists used calligraphy and decorated texts with geometric designs and flowing patterns of leaves and flowers.

During the Song dynasty, fine porcelain was also made for export. This special pale green bowl, called a celadon, was said to crack or change color if poison was put into it, and was much valued by vulnerable leaders.

ARCHITECTURE 501–1100

Building styles varied throughout the world, ranging from simple structures in remote villages to grand architectural works in cities and empires.

Building styles varied across the world. In hot, humid climates, buildings were made to keep people cool and shaded, while in cold climates they needed to offer protection from wind, rain, snow, and chill. Where trees were plentiful, buildings were made entirely of wood. This was especially true in northern Europe and Japan. Even the first castles were built of wood, although many were later replaced using more durable stone. In warmer climates sunbaked bricks, or adobe, were used. Bricks and stone were more difficult to work with, but the builders of churches, mosques, and palaces often used them, hoping to leave a lasting mark on history. With advances in building techniques, architectural styles became more complex, frequently featuring arches, lofty roofs, and domes. Minarets, pagodas, and church spires became taller, and their shapes more graceful.

Motte and bailey castles were common all over western Europe. If attacked, villagers could shelter within the castle. But the village itself was still vulnerable to burning and looting.

In later castles of the Middle Ages, outer walls were built to enclose settlements, sometimes around whole towns. The Normans were masters of castle-building—but the Japanese, Arabs, and Maya were also skilled in the art.

Muslims built minarets beside mosques so that the *muezzin*, or caller, could climb them to call the people to prayer. The design of these minarets, and of the cupolas, or onion-shaped domes, on top of the mosques themselves, is typical of Muslim architecture.

Villages like this Saxon one in England, with its central hall and a stockade, were common across the world. Different materials and styles were used, but the structure and layout were usually the same.

The Hagia Sophia (Saint Sophia) in Constantinople was built during the early 500s. An immense work of Byzantine architecture, it was later converted into a mosque by the Ottomans. It is now a museum.

Fortifications were made taller and bulkier. By 1000, fine buildings for traders, markets, and trade guilds were also appearing. Cities, such as Hangzhou, Teotihuacán, Cordoba, and Kanauj were built on a grand scale. A more secular, or nonreligious, style was slowly emerging, establishing designs to be followed by architects in later times. However, the majority of people still lived in simple structures. American tepees, European log cabins, Arabic tents, and Indonesian longhouses, built quickly with simple materials, more than satisfied their inhabitants' needs. They were probably often more comfortable to live in than drafty stone castles or grand palaces.

In Aotearoa (New Zealand), the Maoris constructed wooden buildings. They were carved with stone tools, and they often added carved bone, colorful shells, and stones for special features, such as the eyes of their gods.

▲ Norman builders had only simple equipment to help them build great cathedrals and castles. Their methods were often ingenious, and they were very skilled. Building methods like those used by the Normans did not change fundamentally for nearly 1,000 years, until the introduction of steel and concrete.

▶ Supporting the great weight of the roof, the pillars and arches of Durham cathedral in England have a typical Norman, or "Gothic," style, which developed around 1100. Not only beautiful in shape, these lofty, light-filled buildings were also well built and have stood for many hundreds of years.

SCIENCE AND TECHNOLOGY 501–1100

During this period, the world's greatest inventors and scientists were Chinese and Arabic. Europeans were far behind, and Americans mainly copied their ancestors.

Many advances in science and technology were made independently by the Chinese and the Arabs. However, there was contact between them, so they also learned from each other. The Arabs were influenced by many new ideas from India and Persia; for example, the use of the number zero and the decimal counting system came from India. While all cultures across the world knew about herbal medicines and their uses, the Chinese and the Arabs were the most advanced. Arabic doctors wrote medical books which were studied by both Chinese and Europeans. The Chinese understood how vaccination worked—this arose from their knowledge of acupuncture. They made magnetic compasses that could be used for navigation at sea and in the desert, and they invented gunpowder for fireworks and as a signaling device. It was the Europeans, several centuries later, who first used it in guns. Chinese ships, called junks, were the world's largest, and only the Vikings could match their seamanship.

The inventor Su Song built this clock tower in 1090, at Kaifeng, the Song capital. It was powered by water dripping onto a wheel. A gong sounded to mark the hours.

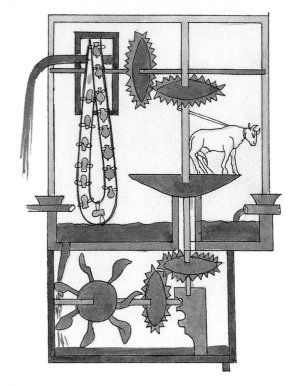

The Arabs further developed the technical knowledge of ancient Greece, Persia, and India. They built machines like this, which raised water using the power produced by the falling water, the animal's movement, and the gears.

The Chinese invented paddle-wheel riverboats, and they designed large wooden machines for making cloth, irrigating fields, and lifting heavy weights. They also invented wood-block printing, dyes, paints and paintbrushes, and developed new types of vegetables.

▲ Grain crops were cut with a scythe (right). Using a flail (left), the grain was separated from the husks by tossing it up into the air where the lighter chaff blew away.

► Charcoal was used as a fuel in metal smelting. Wood was roasted in a smoldering, smothered fire. It slowly dried out, leaving charcoal behind.

◄ During this period the Arabs made significant advances in the use of medicine. In this illustration from an Arabic manuscript of the 1100s, a doctor and an apothecary—a pharmacist or druggist—are making an herbal medicine which they could use to counteract the effects of poisons.

BOOKS AND IDEAS

One of the greatest advances during this period was printing. From the 500s, the Chinese had used wooden blocks, or woodcuts, that were carved to print a whole page. They soon progressed to using movable type for individual letters, so that pages could be made up and printed quickly in large quantities. In the mid-700s, the Chinese technique of papermaking was passed on to the Arabs, who later passed it to Europe. The Arabs were skilled in astronomy and mathematics, and they drew the most accurate maps available at the time. The Muslim cities of Cairo, Baghdad, Cordoba, and Samarkand were home to the world's first universities. However, these developments did not result in a technological revolution, because the pace of development had slowed down in China and the Muslim world by 1100.

▶ The Arabs were great astronomers, drawing star constellations as human figures. This is one called Cepheus. They also invented the astrolabe, which measured the angles of stars to the horizon, for use in navigation and star charts.

WHEN IT HAPPENED

593 Woodblocks used for printing in China
595 Decimal counting used in India
700 Waterwheels to drive mills in Europe
700 Major advances in chemistry in Baghdad
751 Technique of papermaking spreads from China to the Muslim world
810 Algebra invented in Persia; Arabs adopt decimals
868 Earliest known printed book is produced in China
900 Arabic advances in astronomy
900 Chinese develop porcelain

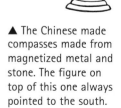

▲ The Chinese made compasses made from magnetized metal and stone. The figure on top of this one always pointed to the south.

◄ The Chinese used fireworks in religious ceremonies. They made fireworks that could operate from big dragonlike kites high up in the sky.

THE MIDDLE AGES

1101–1460

During the Middle Ages, empires rose and fell around the world. Many wars were undertaken in the name of religion. In Europe, alliances were made and quickly broken and a sense of nationalism began to grow. European traders ventured as far afield as China, camel caravans trudged across the Sahara and Venetian ships sailed the Mediterranean Sea with their goods. These were times of faith and fortune, of war and torture, famine and wealth.

By the end of the Middle Ages, learning had become a possibility for everyone who could read.

▲ The Krak des Chevaliers, in what is now Syria, was the largest and strongest castle built by the crusaders. It was garrisoned by 2,000 men, but finally fell to the Saracens in 1271.

◀ The French king, Saint Louis IX, embarks in Aigues Mortes in 1248 for the seventh Crusade to the Holy Land.

THE WORLD AT A GLANCE 1101–1460

During this period, trade increased people's knowledge of many parts of the world, but it also helped spread the Black Death, a disease carried by the fleas that lived on rats found on ships. In Europe, the Black Death killed a fourth of the population.

Information about Africa was spread by Arab traders who sailed down the east coast of the continent. They brought with them stories of vast inland empires, rich with gold, and centered on large stone cities. In West Africa, the kingdom of Mali flourished.

In the Far East, the Khmer Empire of Cambodia was at its height. In Japan, military rulers called shoguns were supported by samurai warriors, and were virtual dictators of their country.

The Mongols conquered much of Asia and Europe to form the largest empire of all time—although it was to be short-lived. Their success was based on brilliant military tactics and superb horsemanship.

In the Americas, the Aztecs built their capital city of Tenochtitlan in the center of Lake Texcoco in Mexico, while in South America, the Inca Empire was expanding by conquering neighboring tribes.

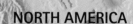

NORTH AMERICA

NORTH AMERICA

During medieval times, the Mississippian Temple Mound culture had reached its peak, even though it faded almost completely during the 1400s. In the Southwest, the Anasazi, Mogollon, and Hohokam pueblo cultures declined during the 1200s.

MESOAMERICA AND SOUTH AMERICA

MESOAMERICA AND SOUTH AMERICA

The Toltecs fell around 1200, and this allowed a second phase of growth for the Maya in southern Mexico. But then the warlike Aztecs started building an empire in the 1400s in central Mexico. Their island capital, Tenochtitlan, became one of the world's greatest cities. Yet the most influential people in the Americas were the Incas who, from small beginnings in Cuzco, Peru, conquered and united many city-states and cultures in the Andes region during the 1400s. They became the largest American empire.

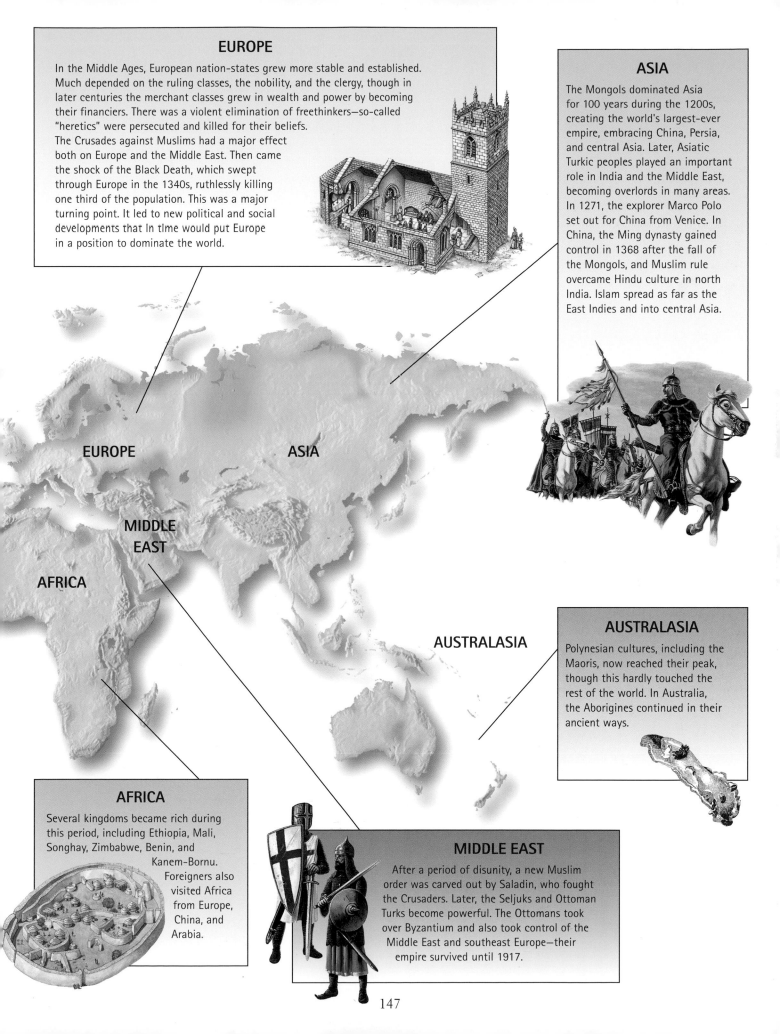

EUROPE

In the Middle Ages, European nation-states grew more stable and established. Much depended on the ruling classes, the nobility, and the clergy, though in later centuries the merchant classes grew in wealth and power by becoming their financiers. There was a violent elimination of freethinkers—so-called "heretics" were persecuted and killed for their beliefs. The Crusades against Muslims had a major effect both on Europe and the Middle East. Then came the shock of the Black Death, which swept through Europe in the 1340s, ruthlessly killing one third of the population. This was a major turning point. It led to new political and social developments that In tlme would put Europe in a position to dominate the world.

ASIA

The Mongols dominated Asia for 100 years during the 1200s, creating the world's largest-ever empire, embracing China, Persia, and central Asia. Later, Asiatic Turkic peoples played an important role in India and the Middle East, becoming overlords in many areas. In 1271, the explorer Marco Polo set out for China from Venice. In China, the Ming dynasty gained control in 1368 after the fall of the Mongols, and Muslim rule overcame Hindu culture in north India. Islam spread as far as the East Indies and into central Asia.

EUROPE

ASIA

MIDDLE EAST

AFRICA

AUSTRALASIA

AUSTRALASIA

Polynesian cultures, including the Maoris, now reached their peak, though this hardly touched the rest of the world. In Australia, the Aborigines continued in their ancient ways.

AFRICA

Several kingdoms became rich during this period, including Ethiopia, Mali, Songhay, Zimbabwe, Benin, and Kanem-Bornu. Foreigners also visited Africa from Europe, China, and Arabia.

MIDDLE EAST

After a period of disunity, a new Muslim order was carved out by Saladin, who fought the Crusaders. Later, the Seljuks and Ottoman Turks become powerful. The Ottomans took over Byzantium and also took control of the Middle East and southeast Europe—their empire survived until 1917.

THE CRUSADES 1095–1291

Palestine became the center of a struggle for political and religious power when the pope called for a crusade to free the Holy Land from Muslim control.

To Christians and Muslims, Palestine was the Holy Land, a place of pilgrimage for hundreds of years. After the Arabs conquered Palestine in 637, Christian pilgrims were still able to visit Jerusalem safely, but this changed with the arrival of the Seljuk Turks. In 1095, Pope Urban II called on Christians to free Palestine from Muslim rule. Knights and ordinary people set out, led by Peter the Hermit and Walter the Penniless. Most of them never reached Palestine, and the rest became a wild, hungry mob. In 1099, a well-disciplined Crusader army recaptured Jerusalem, massacring its inhabitants.

They established four so-called Latin States, or kingdoms in Palestine and Syria. At first the Saracens, as the Crusaders called the Seljuk Turks, left the Crusader kingdoms alone.

The Crusaders wore heavy armor and rode large stallions, and the Muslims, called Saracens, wore light armor and rode mares. Both armies were formidable looking, but the Saracens were more mobile.

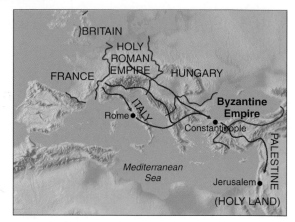

At first the Crusaders traveled overland from France and Italy to Palestine, but, to avoid having to fight the Seljuk Turks in Anatolia, they started to go by sea from Venice.

Some of the heads of the Christian kingdoms behaved badly toward the Muslims. In 1187, Saladin defeated the Christians at Hattin and recovered Jerusalem. In 1191, England's Richard I ("the Lionheart") led an army to the Holy Land. He took Cyprus and the city of Acre, which had been under siege by Christian forces, but he was unable to recapture Jerusalem. He and Saladin signed a treaty sharing the Holy Land, including Jerusalem—the Christians founded a "Second Kingdom" of the holy city with its heart at Acre.

The Crusaders built Norman-style castles in Palestine and Syria. The Krak des Chevaliers in Syria, built by the Knights Hospitallers, was besieged by the Muslims in 1271. They eventually starved the Crusaders into surrender.

Saladin (c.1137–1193), a pious leader, led his people in a *jihad* or holy war against the Crusaders.

Richard I of England (1157–1199), known as the Lionheart (on the right), led an army of knights to the Holy Land in 1191, on the third Crusade. They failed to recapture Jerusalem, but Richard was able to secure a five-year peace treaty with Saladin. This allowed European pilgrims to visit the holy places again. On his return to England, in 1192, he was captured by Leopold of Austria and then Henry VI, the Holy Roman emperor, who held Richard for ransom for about a year. He finally reached England in 1194.

The fourth Crusade began in 1202, but the Crusaders were unable to pay Venice for transportation. So, in exchange for transportation, they agreed to loot Constantinople on Venice's behalf. In 1212, up to 50,000 children from France and Germany set off for Palestine, but most of them died of hunger or became slaves—this is known as the Children's Crusade. The fifth Crusade to Egypt failed; the last three crusades (1218–1272) were also unsuccessful. In 1291, Palestine was finally conquered by the sultan of Egypt.

Louis IX, of France (1226–1270), was deeply religious. He led the seventh Crusade (1248) and was captured. He also led the eighth, but died of plague.

KEY DATES

1096–99	First Crusade takes Palestine and Syria
1187	Saladin wins back Jerusalem
1189–92	Third Crusade
1202–04	Fourth Crusade loots Constantinople
1212	Children's Crusade—a tragic failure
1218–21	Fifth Crusade—a failure
1228–29	Sixth Crusade—partly successful
1291	Acre is lost—the last Crusades

▼ At the decisive battle of Hattin in 1187, Saladin tricked the Crusaders onto a hill on a hot day. While the Crusaders roasted in their metal armor, he surrounded and defeated them. Saladin then went on to win back Jerusalem.

KNIGHTHOOD 1100–1400

Knights were trained horseback warriors drawn from the nobility. They played an important part in the Crusades and other wars during the Middle Ages.

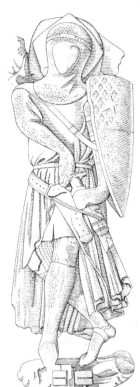

The crossed legs of this carved effigy on the tomb of a Norman knight show that he had been on a crusade to the Holy Land.

In return for lands, lordships, and power, nobles did military service for their kings. They were wealthy enough to have large horses, armor, and attendants (squires). Often the younger sons of nobles became knights to gain riches or honors, because the eldest son usually inherited his father's estates. Knights were particularly important in the Crusades. Some went on crusades to gain power and lands; others went for sincere religious reasons and to protect pilgrims. But knighthood was not just about fighting. A knight was expected to be cultured, fair, and honorable, to help the weak, and protect the poor. This was known as chivalry; unfortunately, many knights did not live up to these high ideals.

A squire kneels to help his master arm himself for battle. Plate armor made from steel was not introduced until the 1300s. Before that, knights wore chain mail.

THE LIFE OF A KNIGHT

A boy began his training around the age of seven, becoming a page in the household of a knight or nobleman. By 14, he became a squire, who served at table, helped his master put on his armor, and accompanied him into battle. Later, if he performed his duties well, he was also made a knight. Knights practiced their skills in mock battles called tournaments. In these, most knights carried a scarf or glove from a lady, to show they were fighting on her behalf. Richard I of England and Louis IX of France were famous for their support of the romantic ideals of chivalry. In the Crusades, some knights took monastic vows of chastity and poverty, and joined the Templars, Hospitallers, or Teutonic Knights. The Knights Templars were so trusted that they carried people's money for them. As a result, the Templars became bankers and were very powerful in Europe. However, by 1312, the Templars were abolished for malpractices, such as dishonesty in business and heresy.

KEY DATES

1095	Pope Urban II calls for the Crusades
1113	Knights Hospitallers founded
1118	Knights Templars founded
1208	Albigensian Crusade against the Cathars
1227	Teutonic Crusades against pagan Lithuania
1291	End of the Crusades in Palestine
1312	Knights Templars dissolved by the French king

Two important Crusader orders of knights were the Knights Templars (left) and the Knights of St. John, or Hospitallers (right). The Hospitallers set up a hospital for pilgrims in Jerusalem, and the Templars guarded the original site of the Temple in Jerusalem.

The tradition of the troubadours started in southern France just before 1100. These minstrel-poets sang songs of romantic love, chivalry, and religion.

Axes, pikes, and swords were the main weapons that knights used during the Crusades.

In tournaments, knights jousted against each other to show their knightly skills and bravery. Although they used blunt swords and lances, knights were often killed or maimed. Mock sieges and assaults on castles were also staged.

In 1227, the German Teutonic Knights were sent to colonize Prussia (now Lithuania). Other knights were sent on missions within Europe—such as the Albigensian Crusade sent by the pope to subdue the Cathars. The Cathars were Christians living in southwestern France who disagreed with the pope.

From the 1300s, knighthood became more of a royal honor than a military role. Some knights performed worthy tasks, helping people in difficulty and bringing justice; other knights sought power or wealth for themselves. Knights often argued, which was one reason why the Crusades eventually failed.

HENRY OF ANJOU 1154–1189

Henry of Anjou became Henry II, the first Plantagenet king of England, in 1154. With his lands in France he became one of the most powerful rulers in Europe.

Henry II (1133–89) was a man of great humor but he also had a violent temper. Through his strong rule, he brought a period of peace and prosperity to both England and France.

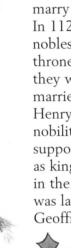

Eleanor of Aquitaine (c. 1122–1204), wife of Louis VII of France, had no children, so the marriage was annulled. She then married England's Henry II.

▲▶ Thomas à Becket (c.1118–70), Henry's chancellor, became Archbishop of Canterbury in 1162. He frequently opposed the king, and in 1170, was murdered in Canterbury Cathedral (right). This was a mistake that Henry much regretted.

Henry of Anjou was William the Conqueror's great-grandson. His mother, Matilda, was the widow of the Holy Roman emperor Henry V, who had died in 1125. She was the daughter of Henry I of England, who named her his heir after his sons had died. Henry I also wanted to strengthen his hold on Normandy, so, in 1128, he had Matilda marry Count Geoffrey of Anjou in France. In 1127, Henry had forced the English nobles to accept a woman as heir to the thrones of England and Normandy, but they were now furious that Matilda had married into a French royal house. When Henry died in 1135, the Church and the nobility split, and most threw their support behind Matilda's cousin Stephen as king. Civil war broke out in 1139, but in the end, Stephen remained king. He was later forced to make Matilda and Geoffrey's son, Henry of Anjou, his heir.

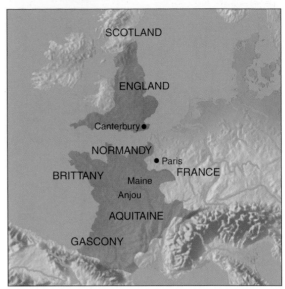

Henry ruled over a greater area of France than the French king, Louis VII. He also ruled England, and eventually spread his influence to Wales, Scotland, and Ireland.

When Henry of Anjou became Henry II of England at the age of 21, he inherited the French provinces of Anjou, Maine, and Touraine from his father, and Normandy and Brittany from his mother. In 1152, he married Eleanor, the abandoned wife of the French king Louis VII, thus gaining Aquitaine. As a result of this, he ruled England and two thirds of France.

HENRY AND BECKET

Henry was an energetic ruler and traveled widely throughout his kingdom. He was well educated and cultured, and his court at Chinon in France was attended by many erudite scholars and troubadours (minstrels). Henry brought his nobles firmly under control, improved the laws of England, and forced the Scots and Welsh to obey him. When Norman nobles took control in Ireland, he subdued them and made himself king of Ireland in 1172. Henry chose capable ministers, among them Thomas à Becket, who became his chancellor. When Henry made him Archbishop of Canterbury, Becket began to assert the rights of the Church. After years of quarrels, Henry is said to have exclaimed, "Who will rid me of this turbulent priest?" Four knights took him at his word and killed Becket. Henry later did penance for this crime.

Henry's empire was a family possession, not a country, and he planned to divide it among his four sons. They squabbled over this and then revolted against him. Two of them died, leaving Richard (the Lionheart) and John. Richard became king of England in 1189, and was followed after his death in 1199 by John. Henry had been a great and creative king, who had set up English common law, but he died in 1189, feeling that his life had been a failure. After his death, his sons lost most of his French lands, and the new order that Henry had built in England soon disintegrated.

KEY DATES

1122	Eleanor of Aquitaine is born
1133	Henry of Anjou born
1139	Eleanor of Aquitaine marries Louis VII of France; marriage later annulled
1152	Henry marries Eleanor of Aquitaine
1154	Henry becomes king of England
1157	Submission of the king of Scotland
1162	Thomas à Becket becomes Archbishop of Canterbury
1166–76	Legal reforms in England
1170	Murder of Thomas à Becket
1171	Henry becomes king of Ireland
1173	Thomas à Becket made a saint
1174	Rebellions by Henry's sons
1189	Henry dies in France

Eleanor of Aquitaine died in 1204. Her tomb in the abbey church at Frontrevault, in western France, lies next to that of one of her sons, Richard I. Her husband, Henry II, who died in 1189, lies nearby.

After the murder of Becket, the pope demanded that Henry do penance and be flogged. This was done, and Henry expressed his regrets. He was later pardoned.

LIFE IN A CASTLE

Castles were large buildings that were cold and drafty to live in. They were military fortresses that also housed the lord's soldiers and servants. Towns soon grew outside the castle walls. In the lord's dwellings, the lady's servants lived in the top room, where linen and clothes were stored. Under this was the master bedroom, where the lord and lady slept. Below this was the *solar*, the lord's private living room, and on the ground floor were the great hall and a secure storeroom for the master's weapons and valuables.

IRELAND 700–1350

This period of Irish history saw increasingly permanent domination by foreigners, following invasions first by the Vikings and then by the English.

▲ Strongbow, or Richard de Clare (c. 1130–1176) invaded Ireland from Pembroke, in Wales. He became king of Leinster.

▼ MacMurrough Kavanagh, king of Leinster, rides to make peace with the Earl of Gloucester during the Norman invasions.

Ireland was inhabited mainly by Gaelic Celts who lived in about 150 *tuath* or tribes. They frequently feuded and warred, which became a hindrance to Ireland's prosperity. Then, in 432, a man arrived who changed the course of Irish history— St. Patrick. He traveled around Ireland converting Irish chiefs to Christianity and preaching peace. By 600, Ireland had become Europe's main Christian center, and Irish monks preached all across Europe. In 795, the Vikings invaded the island, and for the next 40 years raided and destroyed monasteries. By 840, they began to settle, founding towns such as Dublin, Waterford, Cork, and Limerick. From these, they traded and mixed with the Irish people, adopting many of their customs.

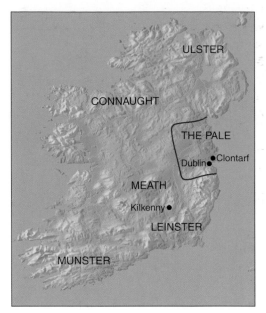

In medieval times, there were five kingdoms in Ireland. All that was left of direct Norman rule was a small area around Dublin called the Pale.

The rest of Ireland was still traditionally Irish. By now, the five largest kingdoms were Ulster, Leinster, Munster, Connaught, and Meath. In 976, Brian Boru, king of Munster, set about invading his neighbors. By 1011, he dominated Ireland, but on his death other local kings fought to be high king. The last strong high king was Turlough O'Connor of Connaught. After he died in 1156, two kings became rivals. One of these, Dermot MacMurrough of Leinster, asked for help from the Normans in England.

THE COMING OF THE ENGLISH

The Earl of Pembroke, or "Strongbow," supported Dermot MacMurrough in return for marrying his daughter and inheriting Leinster. In 1170, Strongbow and other Norman nobles invaded, seizing Irish lands for themselves. This alarmed the king of England, Henry II, who proclaimed himself overlord of Ireland. Many Irish, fearing chaos, supported him and the Norman nobles submitted. Like the Vikings before them, many Normans soon adopted the customs of the Irish. However, in 1366, Lionel, Edward III's son and governor of Ireland, ordered the Irish-Norman families to stop speaking Gaelic and marrying Irish women. This demand was not accepted, and the Irish-Normans now looked upon the English as interfering foreigners. By the late 1400s English rule existed only in the Dublin area, called "the English Pale."

KEY DATES

432	St. Patrick introduces Christianity to Ireland
795	The start of Viking raids—destruction of Irish monasteries
840	Vikings settle, establishing coastal trading towns
1014	Brian Boru, king of Munster, defeats Vikings at the Battle of Clontarf
1148	Richard de Clare becomes Earl of Pembroke
1166	Rory O'Connor becomes first king of Ireland since 1014
1170	Norman invasion of Ireland led by Richard de Clare
1171	Richard de Clare becomes king of Leinster; Henry II annexes Ireland
1366	Irish-Normans revolt against English orders banning Gaelic and mixed marriages
1530s	Henry VIII reimposes English control

During the unsuccessful English campaigns in Ireland, between 1367 and 1400, ships had to carry provisions across the Irish Sea to the English troops.

▼ On the Rock of Cashel, in County Tipperary, site of royal fortifications since the 300s, stand the ruins of St. Patrick's Cathedral. Given to the Church in 1101, the cross (far left) is where the kings of Munster were traditionally crowned.

SHOGUNS AND SAMURAI 1200–1500

The shoguns were generals who acted as governmental dictators, and the samurai were Japanese knights. They both dominated Japan for almost 700 years.

A samurai's main weapons were a bow made of boxwood or bamboo and one or two single-edged swords. Samurai were strictly trained from childhood, following a code called *bushido*—the warrior's way.

The Fujiwara family had held power in Japan for 300 years since the 800s. However, their influence broke down when local dissent spread and when they ran out of daughters, the traditional brides of the emperor. For a time, some of the former emperors ruled. Then the Taira clan took over briefly until a rival clan, the Minamoto, rallied under Minamoto Yoritomo and seized power. Yoritomo assumed the title *sei-i tai shogun*, which means "barbarian-conquering great general." In 1192, he set up the Kamakura shogunate, through which he ruled Japan from his estate, Kamakura, near Edo (Tokyo). His powers were unlimited. From that time on, shoguns ruled Japan as military dictators until 1868. When Yoritomo died in 1199, the Hojo family, a branch of the Taira clan, became regents to the shoguns, and held power in an unofficial capacity until the Kamakura shogunate ended in 1333.

Minamoto Yoritomo (1147–1199) was an ambitious nobleman who saw his chance in the chaos that followed the breakdown of the power of the Fujiwara. Yoritomo ruthlessly crushed his enemies, including many of his own family. He set up the shogunate, a rigid feudal system that affected the whole country with him—the first shogun—as its head.

Japanese government was complicated. The emperor was a ceremonial figure to whom everyone bowed down, but the shogun had the real power. The regents to the emperors and shoguns also had influence, as did the *daimyos* or lords, who jostled for position at court and frequently battled over land. As a result, a class of warriors, or *samurai*, developed, who fought for the daimyos.

Samurai had elaborate decorated armor and many rituals. They were not only warriors who followed the code of *bushido*—the observance of very rigid rules that affected everything they did—but also had to be trained in the arts and religion.

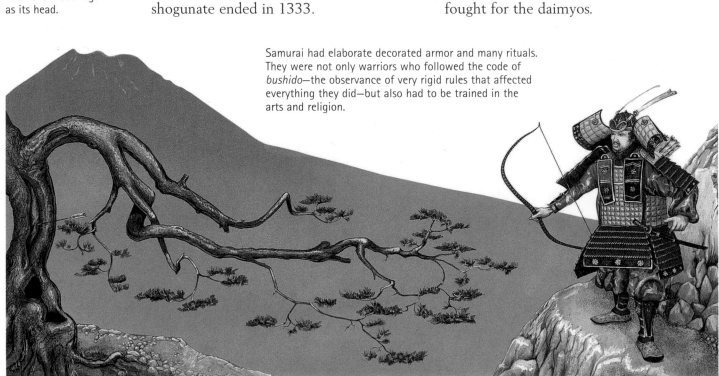

▶ During the 1100s, Zen, a branch of Buddhism, spread from China to Japan. It had simple but strict rules, which the samurai followed. Buddhist shrines, like this gateway, were also built in the Chinese style.

As with European knights and Muslim warriors, religion and war were very closely connected for a samurai. He took a long time dressing and arming himself for battle, with strict rules of cleanliness and ritual.

KNIGHTS OF JAPAN

The samurai were knights who were prepared to fight to the death for their daimyos, to whom they swore undying loyalty. Like the European knight, a samurai believed in truth and honor, and had a strict code of conduct called *bushido*. Before combat, a samurai would shout his name and those of his ancestors, and boast of his heroic deeds. In battle he fought hand to hand, often using two swords at once. If defeated or captured by his enemy, he had to commit ritual suicide (*hara-kiri*) in order to save face. At times, rivalry between samurai was destructive.

In 1333, the Ashikaga clan overthrew the Kamakura shogunate and the emperor, putting a new emperor in power. He appointed them as shoguns, this time in Kyoto. However, there was frequent samurai fighting between daimyos. This increased until the Onin civil war broke out, lasting from 1467–77, and Japan split into nearly 400 clan-states. The Kyoto emperors became powerless and impoverished. Despite this, trade and culture grew in Japan, centered on the daimyo estates. For ordinary people, the daimyo wars brought high taxcs, insecurity, and disruption to their lives.

THE SAMURAI IN BATTLE

Samurai battles were very ritualistic. They involved prayer and posturing (making oneself look strong) beforehand, with shouting and noisemaking using rattles and gongs to frighten the enemy. Individual samurai would undertake duels and contests. Often, battles were like a dance or a ceremonial game of chess. However, samurai warfare was deadly once they joined in full battle. During the Ashikaga period (1338–1573), much of the fighting deteriorated into meaningless squabbles for honor and plots of land.

157

EUROPEAN TRADE 1100–1450

Trade and industry rapidly grew to provide services for rising populations. Merchants and bankers thrived and found new influence from meeting society's needs.

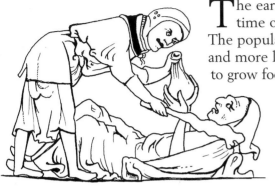

The perils of travel in medieval times are shown in this drawing of a highwayman stealing a traveler's money. Highwaymen often lay in wait for their victims at roadsides.

In a medieval town, markets were usually held once a week. Livestock, food, metals, cloth, leather, and woodwork were all sold there, and people met to discuss local affairs.

The early Middle Ages was a time of growth for Europe. The population was increasing, and more land was cultivated to grow food. This led to surplus produce for trading. Towns grew larger, with regular trade fairs at places like Troyes, Lyons, Kiev, Antwerp, Frankfurt, Leipzig, London, and Krakow. River links and shipping routes were busier. Instead of exchanging goods (bartering), money was used, and increasingly, people went into business for profit. Jewish traders, Knights Templars, and certain business families specialized in moneylending and the safekeeping of valuables. Italy was the richest part of Europe. Venice and Genoa were large independent seaports and banking centers, buying spices, silks, and other luxuries from the East. Goods from Asia came through Byzantium, Egypt, and Syria, and from Africa through Tunisia and Morocco. They were traded for cloth, furs, hides, iron, linen, timber, silver, and slaves.

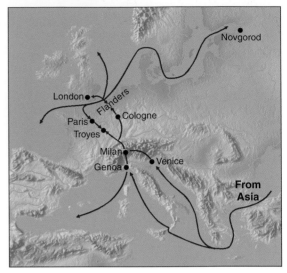

In the 1100s, cities and ports grew along trade routes in Europe. Italian merchants attended fairs such as that at Troyes to buy Flemish cloth and sell Asian goods.

Most of Europe's money was silver, but the Asian countries traded in gold. This caused problems, so the Templars, Jewish traders, and Italian merchants invented banking, with bills of exchange and "promissory notes" that could be used instead of cash. Industries grew in the Rhineland (Germany), northern France, Flanders, and England, importing materials like copper, alum, wool, and charcoal, and exporting goods and clothes.

THE GROWTH OF COMMERCE

A new class of merchants and skilled craftworkers appeared. Merchants grew rich through buying and selling, but they also risked loss because of highway robbery or piracy on the high seas where cargoes and fortunes could be lost. Trading companies, cities, and organizations like the Hanseatic League in the Baltic Sea worked together to protect trade, and opened offices in ports and marketplaces. To protect their trade, the Venetians and Genoese became Mediterranean naval powers. Around 1350, in Genoa, insurance services were offered, to protect traders against loss and bankruptcy. Banking families such as the Fuggers in Augsburg, Germany, and the Medicis in Florence, Italy, grew in wealth and influence. A new commercial order was developing, and kings, nobles, and clerics slowly lost power as they grew dependent on merchants and indebted to bankers. Soon, this new class began to influence the decisions of kings.

In Europe, posthouses and taverns were built along main roads. They provided refreshments, a place to stay, and a change of horse for merchants, pilgrims, and other travelers.

THE HANSEATIC LEAGUE

In 1241, two German towns, Hamburg and Lübeck, set up a *Hansa* or trading association, which developed into the Hanseatic League in 1260, and involved many former Viking towns. They carried food and raw materials from eastern Europe in exchange for manufactured goods from the west. The Hanseatic League dominated trade between England, Scandinavia, Germany, and Russia during the 1300s.

The seal of Danzig, one of the leading Hansa towns.

Hanseatic merchants used these sturdy ships to carry goods between Baltic and Atlantic ports. They established warehouses, customs, banking systems, and defensive structures.

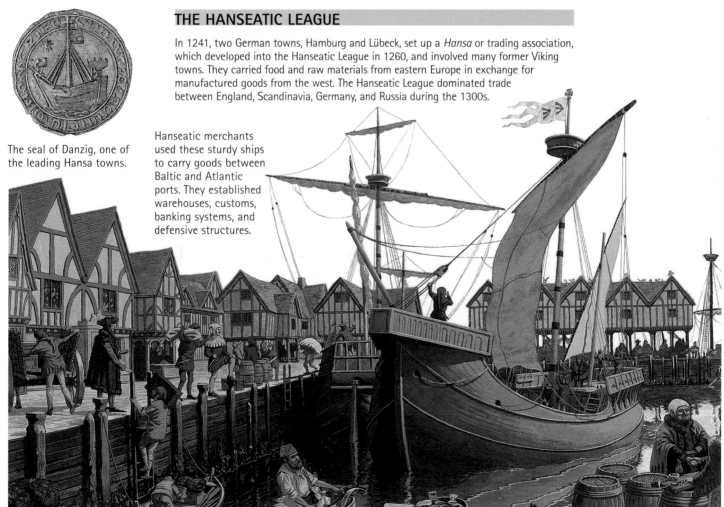

159

VENICE 1100–1500

During medieval times, the city-state of Venice dominated most of the trade between Europe, Asia, and Africa—becoming rich and powerful in the process.

▲ Four bronze horses, dating from around 300 B.C., were seized by the Venetians at the sack of Constantinople in 1204, during the fourth Crusade. The Crusades allowed Venice to grow even richer and more influential.

Venice was originally built on stilts and piles driven into the mud of a marsh. Between the built-up islands were canals which can be seen in this bird's-eye view and map of the city from the 1500s.

Venice had been founded in Roman times by the Veneti, a Romanized tribe that withdrew to the marshes to avoid raids by the Celts, Hannibal, and others. Their town was built on stilts and piles driven into the mud, with canals between the built-up islands they had constructed. There was no land to farm, so the early Venetians fished in the sea. Gradually, their small boats began to venture farther afield to trade. By 1100, Venice had become a very wealthy place, and its rich traders were living in sumptuous palaces. Protected by the sea, the city did not have to spend time and money on the building of elaborate fortifications. Its ships sailed around the Mediterranean, trading with the Byzantines and Arabs, who themselves traded with Russia, Asia, and Africa. Imported goods were sent overland into Europe. The cosmopolitan population of Venice—Jews, Germans, French, Italians, and Arabs—introduced many new ideas.

St. Mark's Cathedral was built to house the relics of St. Mark as well as other treasures which the Venetians had looted from Alexandria and Constantinople.

GROWTH OF VENETIAN POWER

During the 1100s, the Venetians expanded their influence by taking an active part in the Crusades. As the power of Byzantium declined, Venice took over its trade, and used several well-placed islands like Corfu and Crete as ports. After fighting off its great Italian rival, Genoa, during the 1300s, Venetian ships dominated all trading and cargo transportation between Europe and the East, and reached the height of its power during the 1400s. Venice did not own much land, but it controlled so much business that its silver dinars and gold ducats were used everywhere as money.

VENETIE M.D

Like other places in medieval Italy, Venice was a city-state and largely independent. Its rulers were called doges, from the Latin word *dux*, which means "leader." Doges were elected for life and came from the most powerful families in Venice. They had almost absolute power over the government, the army, and the Church. But, after 1140, they lost most of their powers, which were transferred to a Great Council.

▲ The Lion of St. Mark was made by the Italian sculptor Vittore Carpacchio around 1500 and has been Venice's emblem for centuries.

◀ Convoys of ships sailed to the Levant to buy cotton, silk, and porcelain from China, spices from Zanzibar and Indonesia, and gems and ivory from Burma. Venice was famous for its lace and glassware.

KEY DATES

726	First doge is elected
800s	The rise of Venice as a trading port
1081	Venetians gain trade privileges in Byzantium
1090s	Arab dominance of Mediterranean trade ends
1192	Venice transports Crusaders to Constantinople by ship
1381	Venice defeats Genoa, to dominate all trade
1400s	The economic center of Europe shifts north

Venetian banks lent money and underwrote contracts, guaranteeing payment if things went wrong. Banks encouraged trade, but their interest rates were high.

CHARTER AND PARLIAMENT 1215–1485

In England, in the 1200s, there was a growing struggle between the kings and the lords. The absolute power of kings was being questioned by those they ruled.

This is the great seal of King John, affixed to the bottom of the Magna Carta. John's seal showed his consent, and so turned the charter into the law of the land.

King John of England, the youngest son of Henry II, was given to violent outbursts of temper. Not surprisingly, he soon angered his barons in English-ruled Anjou and Poitiers, and he lost those lands to France. In England, he taxed his barons heavily and ruled so harshly that they rebelled. The barons threatened John, and demanded that he recognize their traditional rights and obey the law.

King John (1199–1216), quarrelled with his nobles, who turned against him, and forced him to sign the Magna Carta.

THE MAGNA CARTA

In 1215, the barons met King John in a meadow called Runnymede, beside the Thames River. There, they forced him to put his seal on the Magna Carta, or "great charter." This document covered many important areas, including weights and measures, the powers of sheriffs, and the legal rights of freemen and boroughs (towns). The king agreed to obey the law himself, and he was not allowed to raise taxes without the agreement of his Great Council of nobles. No sooner had John agreed to the charter than he went back on his word. A civil war broke out, but John soon died, leaving the throne to his young son who became Henry III. The charter was reissued, and in 1225, it became the law of England. Henry III was incompetent and he spent large sums of money, so the barons banded together again, this time led by Simon de Montfort. They forced Henry to agree to consult the Great Council in all major matters. Like his father, Henry III went back on the deal, but de Montfort defeated him in battle at Lewes in 1264. Simon de Montfort and the Council then ruled England in Henry's name.

In 1215, John was forced to put his seal on the Magna Carta at Runnymede. John did not actually sign the charter, and possibly could not even write.

THE POWER OF PARLIAMENT

In 1265, Simon de Montfort called a new Parliament of two chambers, the House of Lords (previously the Great Council of nobles and bishops,) and the House of Commons. The House of Commons was made up of two knights from every shire and two people (burgesses) who represented each borough. Later, Edward I (1272–1307), a successful ruler, reformed England's law and administration; he created a Model Parliament which included even more representatives from the country. However, the king still held power. In 1388, there was a major clash and the "Merciless" Parliament removed some of King Richard II's rights.

As time went on, Parliament's powers gradually grew. The House of Commons slowly gained greater power, although it was mostly the richer classes that were represented in Parliament. Full-scale democracy only arrived in the 1900s.

KEY DATES

1215	King John reluctantly affixes his seal to the Magna Carta
1216	King John dies. His nine-year-old son, Henry III, becomes king
1225	The Magna Carta becomes the law of England
1227	Henry III, now aged 20, begins to rule
1258	Council of nobles set up
1265	Simon de Montfort's Parliament is called
1272	Edward I becomes king of England
1295	Edward I's Model Parliament
1307	Edward II becomes king of England
1388	The "Merciless" Parliament (against Richard II)

▶ Simon de Montfort (c.1208–1265) was a Norman baron who became Earl of Leicester. In 1264–65 he virtually ruled the country on behalf of the king.

▲ Henry III, is pictured here at his coronation in 1216. He ruled for 55 years. He lost much of his power as king because he was not a good ruler. He was more interested in the arts and in building churches.

Bishop   Lord   Lady   Knight   Merchant   Nun

Peasant

Queen

King

These were the different social classes of the time, in order of power from the king downward. The largest number of people were peasants, who had no power at all. Some lords and priests treated them fairly, allowing them to voice their concerns, but this was rare.

MALI AND ETHIOPIA 1240–1500

In West Africa, the Mali Empire grew powerful by controlling the gold trade. In the east, the Christian empire of Ethiopia was isolated by the spread of Islam.

In 1240, Sundiata Keita, the ruler of the small Malinke kingdom in West Africa, brought about the collapse of the nation of Ghana, and established a new nation called Mali. He set up a well organized state that possessed fertile farmlands beside the Niger River. Under Sundiata's rule, Mali controlled the gold trade and became rich and powerful. Many of the camel caravan routes across the Sahara Desert led to Mali's fine cities, such as Koumbi Saleh, Djenne, and Timbuktu.

Mali's trading cities exported ivory, gold, and slaves to the Muslim world, and to Venice and Genoa in Europe. In exchange, they imported salt, cloth, ceramics, glass, horses, and luxuries. Timbuktu and Djenne became centers of learning, where Muslims mingled with Africans. Timbuktu had a university and 100 schools. Mali reached the height of its power, and also became Muslim, under Sundiata's grandson Mansa Musa (1307–37). He made a pilgrimage to Mecca in 1324, taking 500 slaves and 90 camels loaded with gold. In 1325, Mali overpowered Songhay, lower down the Niger River, but in 1464 Songhay's ruler declared independence. Mali's decline had begun in 1350, and by 1500, it had been conquered by Songhay.

Mali had important links with the Muslim world. The Great Mosque at Timbuktu was designed by As-Saheli, an Egyptian.

Timbuktu was a prosperous city on the Niger River. It was a key destination of many caravan routes across the Sahara and had schools, a university, mosques, and markets.

This is part of a Catalan map of northwest Africa from the 1300s. It shows major towns and trading routes, and features Mansa Musa, the great ruler of Mali.

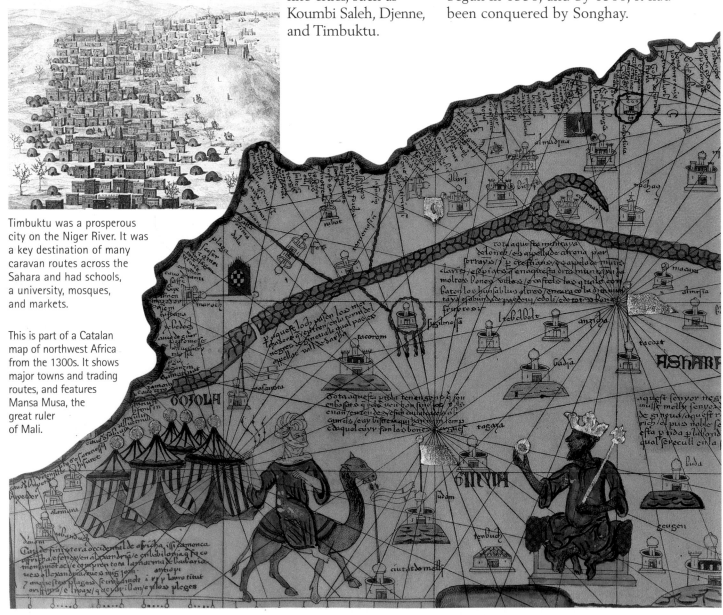

THE GREAT MOSQUE AT DJENNE

During the 1100s, when Mali was founded and Islam was adopted, Mansa Musa ordered a mosque built in the ancient city of Djenne, a center for the gold trade. The present Great Mosque, finished in 1907, was built of mud brick in the traditional style.

THE FOUNDING OF ETHIOPIA

In East Africa, the old nation of Aksum had collapsed around 1000. Ethiopia (Abyssinia) was founded by the Jewish Zagwe dynasty around 1137. Most Ethiopians practiced Coptic Christianity. Their church was cut off by the spread of Islam, but there was contact with Christianity through an Ethiopian monastery in Jerusalem. Lalibela became emperor in 1190, moved the capital from Aksum and built a new one at the holy city of Roha, later renamed Lalibela in his honor.

In 1270, Yekuno Amlak founded the Solomonic dynasty—they claimed descent from Solomon and the Queen of Sheba. Ethiopia expanded its borders into the mountains of East Africa, taking in many tribes. It was a unique country, untouched by others for a long time, isolated from the rest of the world by its mountain location. However, having been at its strongest during the 1300s and 1400s, it was plagued by internal discord in the 1500s. In medieval Europe, Ethiopia was regarded as a mysterious Christian kingdom, with a mythical king called Prester John. The very last emperor of Ethiopia, Haile Selassie, who ruled from 1930 to 1974 was a descendant of Yekuno.

The Ethiopians built cross-shaped churches, carved and hollowed out of solid rock. Both of these pictures are of the Church of St. George at the holy city of Lalibela, one of 11 such churches built in the 1200s.

KEY DATES	
1137	Founding of Ethiopia by the Zagwe dynasty
1190s	Lalibela built as the capital of Ethiopia
1240	Sundiata Keita founds the state of Mali
1270	Yekuno Amlak founds the Solomonic dynasty; Ethiopia expands
1307–37	Mansa Musa, Mali's greatest ruler
1350	Mali goes into slow decline
1300s–1400s	High point of Ethiopian culture
c.1500	Songhay overwhelms Mali

BENIN AND ZIMBABWE 1100–1480

Benin was an advanced kingdom in the tropical forests of West Africa. Zimbabwe was a gold-mining centre in the high grasslands of southeast Africa.

This lifelike ivory mask shows an *oba* or king of Benin. The oba would have hung it around his waist on ceremonial occasions.

Benin was situated in what is now southeastern Nigeria. It was the longest lasting of the forest kingdoms of rain-forested West Africa. Its capital, Benin City, was founded in about A.D. 900 and was at its most prosperous during the 1400s. The city had wide streets lined with large wooden houses and was enclosed by walls 25 mi. (40km) long. The palace of the *oba* (king) was richly decorated with bronze plaques and carvings. The city's busy traders dealt in cloth, ivory, metals (especially bronze), palm oil, and pepper. Benin was famous for its art, especially sculptures using pottery, ivory, or brass.

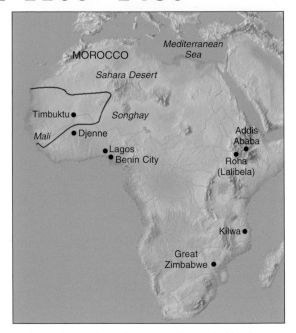

During medieval times, there were four main kingdoms that flourished in Africa: Mali (later overwhelmed by Songhay), Ethiopia, Benin, and Zimbabwe.

This Benin bronze shows an oba seated on his throne, with two subjects. kneeling before him. The Benin cast bronzes by the "lost wax" process. A wax model was carved, then covered with clay to make a mold. The wax would be melted away, and molten bronze would be poured into the mold. Many copies could then be made using this process.

Benin flourished under the leadership of Oba Eware the Great, who ruled from 1440 to 1473. He modernized and expanded Benin. Usually, warring African states made slaves of their prisoners, but Benin avoided this—so when the Portuguese began buying slaves from West Africa in the 1500s, Benin did not join in the slave trade. This protected it from European colonization until 1897.

Many of the peoples of West Africa lived in tribal villages, herding animals and growing crops. The grasslands of central Africa (shown here) were very different environments from the tropical forests of the west.

ZIMBABWE

Zimbabwe grew prosperous from its large reserves of copper and gold. Dug from over one thousand mines, much of it was bought by Arab traders on the east coast from the 900s onward. They built the only towns in southern Africa, and Zimbabwe is best known for its walled palace city, Great Zimbabwe, built between 1100 and 1400. However, little is known of the Zimbabweans. They were not great warriors, so Zimbabwe did not expand its borders by military means.

Around 1450, Zimbabwe was absorbed into the Shona kingdom of Rozvi (Mwenemutapa), named after a line of strong kings. This warrior kingdom took control of most of what is now Zimbabwe and Mozambique. It continued to trade gold and copper with the Arabs and grew rich from this. This changed when the Portuguese settlers tried to gain control of the mines. Rozvi fought against this for some time, but by 1629, the mines had fallen under Portuguese control. Nevertheless, Rozvi survived until the 1830s.

This is a bronze head of an *oni*, or king, of Ife, from the 1300s. He is wearing the headdress of a sea god. Ife was a kingdom that once bordered Benin.

GREAT ZIMBABWE

One intriguing African mystery is the walled city of Great Zimbabwe, after which modern Zimbabwe is named. The massive stone structures were built with granite blocks between 1000 and 1400, but nobody knows why or by whom. A *zimbabwe* is a stone-built enclosure, of which there were many in southeast Africa, but this was the largest and grandest.

The ruins of the Great Enclosure can be seen today on the 60-acre (24ha) site of Great Zimbabwe.

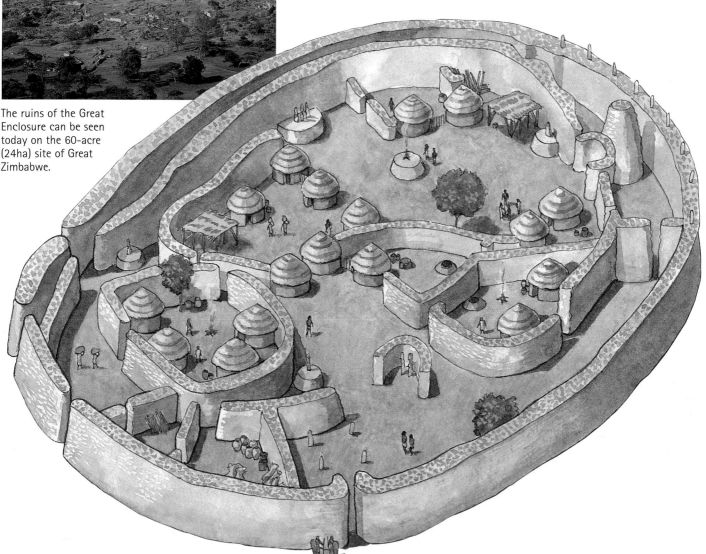

RELIGION IN THE MIDDLE AGES 1100–1500

In the Middle Ages, religious institutions worldwide had grown powerful and influential. This brought enormous benefits, but also led to corruption.

St. Francis of Assisi (1182–1226) founded the Order of Franciscan Friars in 1210. Two years later, he founded the Poor Clares, an order for women.

By 1200, even the newest religion, Islam, was 500 years old. Religions had become major institutions, and were established in the traditions of every country. In many places, everyday life had become difficult—there was poverty and hardship, and those not suffering from these often experienced corruption and crime. Many religious people began to feel that it might be beneficial to withdraw from the world and worship God by becoming hermits, monks, and nuns. This made monastic communities attractive. In Europe, China, and Tibet, monastic traditions, with their strict rules and simple lifestyles, grew strong. Monasteries provided the local community with health care, education, employment, and refuge. They encouraged pilgrimages and provided a positive influence during troubled times.

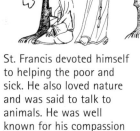

St. Francis devoted himself to helping the poor and sick. He also loved nature and was said to talk to animals. He was well known for his compassion and for caring for small creatures. He was made a saint two years after his death.

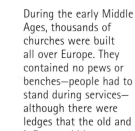

During the early Middle Ages, thousands of churches were built all over Europe. They contained no pews or benches—people had to stand during services—although there were ledges that the old and infirm could lean on.

This is the Church of St. Peter in Rome as it looked in the Middle Ages. Built in Roman times in 325, it became the pope's headquarters, until it was demolished in 1506 and replaced by a much grander Renaissance church.

RELIGIOUS POWER

The priesthood was influential in politics as well as religion. In Europe, there was rivalry between popes and kings, priests, and lords—and even between competing popes. The Church became corrupt—priestly posts and the forgiveness of sins could be bought. In Islam, there was no strong priesthood, but there were many different Muslim groups

In Mayan and Toltec Mexico, priests were all-powerful, and demanded blood sacrifice of their people. Worldwide, many people had a simple faith, but no real religious education. In Europe, religion was taught in Latin, and in India it was taught in Sanskrit—languages that most people did not understand. Pilgrimage was important—Muslims went to Mecca, Christians to Rome and Jerusalem, and Buddhists and Hindus to holy mountains and temples. Many people could not improve their lives, so they prayed for a better life in heaven (Christians, Muslims, and the Maya), or in their next life (Hindus and Buddhists). Around the world great temples, cathedrals, churches, and mosques were built—some of the finest architecture of the time.

168

The Great Mosque at Cordoba in Muslim Spain was one of the most elegant buildings ever erected. Over a thousand pillars held up the roof—this made the interior light and airy, an important feature of buildings in hot climates.

RELIGION AND CULTURE

During the Middle Ages, great religious thinkers were at work. Scholars such as Meister Eckhart in Germany, Thomas Aquinas in Italy, Maimonides and Ibn Arabi in Egypt, Marpa the Translator in Tibet, Ramanuja in India, and Dogen in Japan shaped the ideas of the age. Religion became a part of everyday life, affecting the arts and sciences, medicine, government, and society. It formed the heart of the world's many cultures. But there was a growing gap between what people believed and what they practiced. Some thought it was all right to pray on holy days and break the rules the rest of the time. Some temples and churches became so rich and corrupt that many people began to question their faith.

▲ Mosques were built in many countries, from Africa to India—even in parts of China. These are the ruins of the mosque at Kilwa, a Muslim city-state off the coast of East Africa that traded with Zimbabwe.

▼ This is a Buddhist monastery in Tibet. Buddhism, with its belief in reincarnation, was introduced to Tibet in A.D. 749. Tibetan monks are called *lamas*.

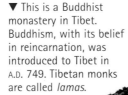

◄ Quetzalcóatl was a god honored by the Toltecs, the Maya, and the Aztecs. He was the god associated with civilization and learning, and with the spiritual protection of the priesthood.

THE MONGOL EMPIRE 1206–1405

The Mongols created the largest empire in history. Their presence was felt strongly in China, Russia, and Islam, though their empire was not very long lasting.

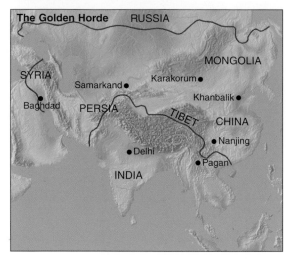

At its greatest extent, in the 1200s, during the reign of Kublai Khan, the Mongol Empire extended from the Pacific Ocean to the Black Sea.

Genghis Khan (c.1162–1227) was a great leader, general, and organizer. During one campaign, his army traveled at breakneck speed—275 mi. (440km) in just three days. He died after falling from a horse.

In 1180, a 13-year-old boy was made leader of his tribe when his father was poisoned. The boy was named Temujin, and his tribe, the Yakka Mongols, were a warlike nomadic people in Mongolia. Two thirds of the tribe promptly deserted him, but Temujin soon reunited them and went on to take over other Mongol tribes. In 1206, at a meeting of the *khans* (chiefs), Temujin was hailed as Genghis Khan, "Emperor of All Men." He promised that future generations of Mongols would lead lives of luxury. Genghis Khan began a career of conquest, by training a ruthless, fast-moving, and well disciplined army. His hordes terrified their opponents, killing anyone who did not surrender or change sides. In a series of outstanding campaigns, Genghis Khan conquered Turkestan, northern China, and Korea, then swung westward to overrun Afghanistan, Persia, and parts of Russia. Part of his success came from the fact that his opponents were not united.

MONGOL EXPANSION

After Genghis died, Ogodai and Monke Khan conquered Armenia, Tibet, more of China, and then ravaged eastern Europe. Ghengis's grandson, Kublai Khan, completed the conquest of China. He made himself first emperor of the Yuan dynasty (1271–1368). Some aspects of Mongol rule were good—they gave women status, encouraged scholars, respected different religions, and helped trade. They opened the Asian Silk Roads to East-West travelers. Other aspects were not so good—their ruthless armies destroyed cities and massacred many. However, the Song in southern China were able to resist them for 20 years before they fell, and the Delhi Sultanate stopped them from invading India. By 1260, Mongol expansion had ended.

In battle, the Mongols were unstoppable. Their bows fired farther than any had before, their horses were fast, and their tactics tricked many of their opponents.

The Mongols were a nomadic people from the plains of Mongolia who lived in portable *yurts*—large, round tents made of hides or cloth. They herded cattle, sheep, goats, and horses. Even when they invaded cities, their army stayed outside in yurt encampments.

THE BARBAROUS TAMERLANE

From 1275, a Venetian merchant named Marco Polo spent 17 years at the court of Kublai Khan. His stories gave Europeans their first picture of China and its wealth. After Kublai Khan's death in 1294, the mighty Mongol Empire began to break up. Some khans, such as the Chagatais in Turkestan, the Ilkhans in Persia, and the Golden Horde in southern Russia, kept smaller empires for themselves. Cruel though the Mongols were, none was as barbarous as the great Mongol-Turkish ruler of Samarkand, Tamerlane, or Timur (1336–1405). His army went on the rampage between 1361 and 1405, and brutally overran Persia, Armenia, Georgia, Mesopotamia, Azerbaijan, and the Golden Horde.

Despite his cruel reputation, Tamerlane was a great patron of the arts, astronomy, and architecture in Samarkand. Generally, however, the Mongols left no lasting mark on the world, except for the destruction they brought. China and Russia became poor, the Muslim world was in turmoil, and even European countries like Poland and Serbia suffered greatly. After Tamerlane's death in 1405, the great, bloodstained Mongol adventure was over, except in Russia and Turkestan.

In battle, the Mongols wore light armor made of leather and iron. They were so fast and ruthless that most of their opponents gave up in fear. Large silk flags streamed behind them. Anyone who opposed them was destined to die.

MONGOL SPORTS

The Mongols loved horseriding, wrestling, and archery. The great khans encouraged sport as a way of developing battle skills and discovering talented soldiers. There were many sports contests, and military promotion could be gained from success in these. Participating in sports also fostered teamwork, which was one of the Mongols' greatest strengths.

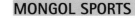

From an early age, Mongol boys practiced archery and wrestling.

The Mongols adopted the ancient Persian game of polo.

AZTECS AND INCAS 1100–1500

Two great civilizations were founded in the Americas within about a hundred years of each other: the Inca Empire in Peru and the Aztec Empire in Mexico.

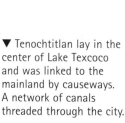

The Aztec god Huitzilopochtli was sometimes depicted as a snake. This image is made of wood, and covered with jade stones.

Legends say that the Aztec people originally came from northern Mexico. Then, in 1168, on the instructions of their god Huitzilopochtli (often depicted as a snake), they began to migrate southward. They eventually settled in the valley of Mexico, where they set up farming communities. Around 1325, during a time of warfare, they moved to a safe site on an island in Lake Texcoco. This is the site of present-day Mexico City.

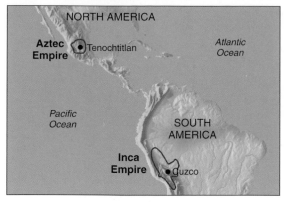

The Aztec and Inca empires developed independently of each other in North and South America. By the beginning of the 1500s, they had both expanded and had great influence over their regions.

The Great Temple lay at the heart of the island city of Tenochtitlan. On top of the pyramid were shrines to the gods Tláloc and Huitzilopochtli. The monument in front of it was dedicated to Quetzalcóatl.

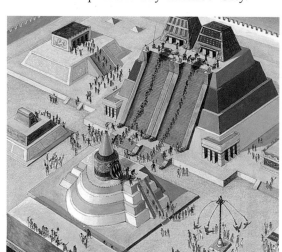

▼ Tenochtitlan lay in the center of Lake Texcoco and was linked to the mainland by causeways. A network of canals threaded through the city.

THE CITY OF TENOCHTITLAN

The Aztecs created garden-islands in Lake Texcoco on which to grow food. They also started to build a great city, called Tenochtitlan. It was easily defended, since it could be reached only by the causeways (raised roads) that the Aztecs had built across the lake. The Aztecs traded throughout Mexico, and their men served in the armies of other cities in return for payment. Under their great leader, Itzcóatl who ruled from 1427–40, they began to conquer these neighboring cities, eventually building up the Aztec Empire which, by 1500, stretched coast to coast.

THE INCA EMPIRE

According to tradition, Manco Capac and his sister, Mama Ocllo, were the first rulers of the Incas around 1200. They called themselves "the Children of the Sun." The Incas lived in a valley high in the Andes mountains, in what is now Peru. There they built a city called Cuzco, and others such as Machu Picchu. *Cuzco* means "navel" or "center of the world." For 200 years, the Incas lived there, isolated from the rest of the world. However, under Pachacutec, a brilliant general and their emperor from 1438 to 1471, the Incas began a time of conquest. By 1500, they had created an extensive empire.

The Inca ruler Pachacutec leads his army into battle. Inca soldiers used *bolas* (slingshots that consisted of a stone attached to a length of string), wooden spears, swords, and star-shaped clubs for weapons. Under Pachacutec's leadership, the Incas successfully conquered the neighboring tribes.

Gold, silver, and precious stones were used to craft beautiful objects for noble families. The objects also played a role in religious rituals.

MACHU PICCHU

Machu Picchu was a remarkable Inca mountaintop city that was so well concealed that it was only rediscovered in 1911. High in the Andes, the city was one of the last strongholds of the Incas against the invading Spaniards. It was built using stones that fit together precisely, without mortar. Machu Picchu was a spiritual center, with an astronomical observatory and temples.

MEDIEVAL EXPLORERS 1270–1490

In the Middle Ages, many bold men made long, and often dangerous, journeys to distant lands. These new contacts improved trade and spread political influence.

Prince Henry the Navigator (1394–1460) was responsible for the port city of Ceuta in Morocco. This led to his fascination with ships. He sponsored expeditions and the work that led to a new ship, the caravel. He encouraged more precise mapmaking and seafaring instruments. The sailors he trained were the first Europeans to undertake long sea voyages. Soon the Portuguese opened up new routes around Africa to India and the Far East.

The first medieval explorers were the Vikings, who went as far as America, Morocco, and Baghdad. The first account of central Asia was written by a Franciscan friar, John of Pian del Carpine, who visited the Mongol khan on behalf of Pope Innocent IV in 1245. The best known European traveler was Marco Polo, a young Venetian who journeyed to meet Kublai Khan in China and remained there for many years. Returning in 1295, he composed a vivid account of his travels.

Between 1325 and 1350, Ibn Battuta, a Moroccan lawyer, traveled to Russia, central Asia, India, southern China, and Africa, writing detailed descriptions of his travels. Admiral Zheng He was sent by the Chinese Ming emperor Yongle on seven naval expeditions between 1405 and 1433. His fleet sailed to Indonesia, India, Persia, Mecca, and East Africa, establishing diplomatic relations and extending China's political influence over maritime Asia. Zheng He took back gifts to the emperor, including spices and exotic animals.

Camel caravans took Muslim travelers and traders across the deserts of Africa and Asia, making them some of the most traveled people of the medieval period.

PRINCE HENRY THE NAVIGATOR

Henry was a son of the king of Portugal. At the age of 21, he discovered treasures in Morocco that had been carried overland from Songhai and Senegal in West Africa. He was curious to know if these places could be reached by sea. So, after about 1420, Henry paid Portuguese sailors to explore the coast of Africa. Encouraged by their discoveries, he built a school of navigation at Sagres in Portugal, to train sailors for further voyages of discovery.

Kublai Khan sent Marco Polo on various journeys, including to the Chinese borders of Tibet. Polo told of how they burned bamboo on their campfire, which caused loud crackling noises that terrified the horses. However, the noise also scared off wild animals.

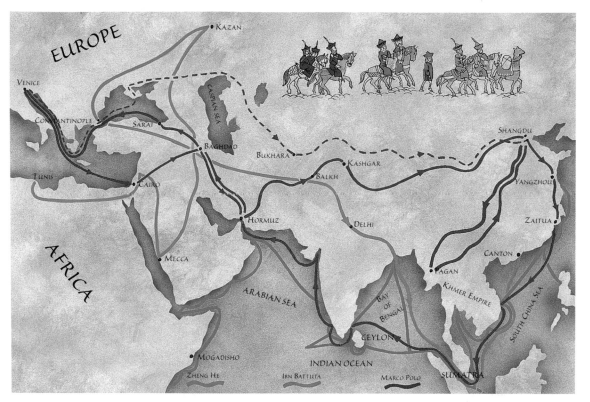

The incredible journeys of medieval travelers covered thousands of miles. The greatest of these travelers were Marco Polo, Ibn Battuta, and Zheng He.

Marco Polo first visited China with his father, a Venetian trader. He stayed there longer, playing an active role in the court of Kublai Khan. He was even sent on missions for the khan around China and to Pagan in Burma.

Marco Polo was away from Venice for 25 years. His overland journey to China took four years, and the return journey by sea from China to Persia, then overland, took three. He acted as a regional governor and ambassador for the khan while in China. The khan welcomed many foreigners, and he found Europeans to be very unusual, exotic visitors.

By the time Prince Henry died in 1460, Portuguese explorers had reached what is now Sierra Leone. Henry's work inspired later Portuguese explorers to sail farther down the coast of West Africa, seeking a sea route to India and the Far East. The world was now on the verge of a great expansion of international contact. The Chinese could have been the first international travelers, but its emperors preferred isolation, and traders were discouraged from travel. Muslims had also traveled far and wide, though by 1500 they had lost their urge to expand further. Meanwhile, the Europeans were about to change their inward-looking policies and seek new horizons.

Ibn Battuta (1304–68) was a lifelong traveler from North Africa who wrote lengthy accounts of his journeys. He traveled to Africa and Russia, to Morocco and India, and by sea to southern China. His stories were the most accurate and useful of all the accounts written by medieval travelers.

Admiral Zheng He's fleet of huge oceangoing junks were specially built for his expeditions. On his first voyage, his fleet consisted of 62 of these ships.

175

THE HUNDRED YEARS' WAR 1337–1453

The Hundred Years' War was a series of short, costly wars in which the English kings tried to dominate France, but met great resistance.

John of Gaunt (1340–1399) was one of the sons of Edward III. As regent (1377–1386) for his nephew Richard II, he was the most powerful man in England.

In 1328, Charles IV of France died. The French barons gave the throne to his cousin, Philip VI, but Charles's nephew, Edward III of England, challenged him. Philip confiscated Edward's French lands, and in 1337 war broke out. At the start of the conflict, which actually lasted 116 years, the English defeated a French fleet in the English Channel at Sluys, then invaded France, winning a major battle at Crécy, and capturing Calais. Both sides ran out of money and had to agree to a truce, which lasted from 1347 until 1355. In 1355, a fresh English invasion took place, led by Edward's heir, Edward, whose nickname was the Black Prince. He won a resounding victory at Poitiers. The Treaty of Brétigny in 1360 gave England large parts of France. But a new campaign followed, and England lost most of her French possessions.

The English longbow (left) shot farther and faster than ever before. The French crossbow (right) was easier to load and fire than a longbow, but much slower.

In the late 1360s, both thrones were inherited by children—Charles VI of France and Richard II of England. Richard's uncle, John of Gaunt (for Ghent in Belgium, his birthplace), ruled for him. In 1396, Richard II married Charles VI's daughter, Isabelle, and a 20-year truce was agreed.

▲ Edward, (1330–1376), father of Richard II, wore black armor and so was called "the Black Prince."

▶ Edward III, (1312–1377) invaded France in 1346. His army of 10,000 defeated a French army twice its size at Crécy. The English easily outshot the French crossbows.

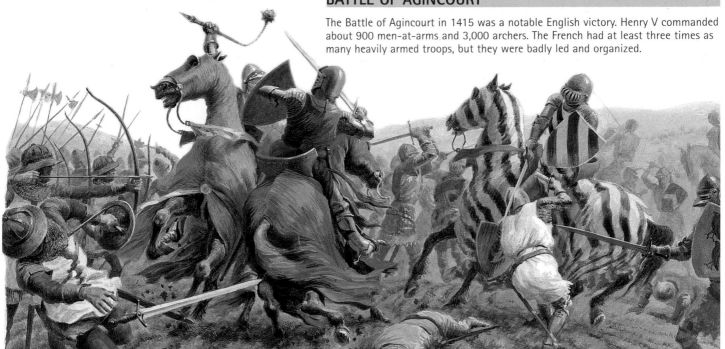

BATTLE OF AGINCOURT

The Battle of Agincourt in 1415 was a notable English victory. Henry V commanded about 900 men-at-arms and 3,000 archers. The French had at least three times as many heavily armed troops, but they were badly led and organized.

THE END OF A COSTLY WAR

After a long truce the war began again in 1415. Henry V (1387–1422), England's adventurous king, revived his country's claim to the French throne. England still held Calais and parts of Bordeaux. Henry captured Harfleur in Normandy and heavily defeated the French at Agincourt. Henry then occupied much of northern France. Charles VI made him heir to the French throne in 1420. He also married Charles's daughter, Catherine of Valois. Henry died just 15 months later, leaving the throne to his infant son, Henry VI. Charles VI died soon after.

In support of the claim, Henry's uncle, John, Duke of Bedford, besieged Orléans. The French forces, led by a 17-year-old peasant girl, Joan of Arc, successfully defended the town. Joan claimed she saw visions and heard voices telling her to free France. She escorted the new but uncrowned king, Charles VII, to Reims to be crowned. However, Joan was soon defeated at Paris and captured by the Burgundians. They sold her to the English, who burned her as a witch. Sporadic fighting went on for some years afterward. The French recaptured their lands by 1453, ending the war. Only Calais remained English. This had been a kings' war—but it was the people who had paid the price.

KEY DATES

E = English victory, F = French victory

1340	Battle of Sluys (E), at sea
1346	Battle of Crécy (E)
1347	Battle of Calais (E)
1356	Battle of Poitiers (E)
1372	Battle of La Rochelle (F), at sea
1415	Battle of Agincourt (E)
1428	Battle of Orléans (F)
1450	Battle of Formigny (F)
1451	Battle of Bordeaux (F)

At the age of 17, Joan of Arc (1412–1431) led the French against the English, during France's darkest hour. The English accused her of being a witch, because she claimed she had visions and heard voices telling her to drive the English out of France.

Joan of Arc was burned at the stake in 1431. Five hundred years later, in 1920, she was made a saint.

177

THE BLACK DEATH 1347–1351

The Black Death was one of the worst disasters in history. It resulted in the death of around a third of the population of the Middle East and Europe.

European towns were filthy, with rubbish, rats, and human excrement in the streets. Human waste was thrown out of windows and trodden underfoot. The lack of basic hygiene was the reason that the plague spread so fast.

The Black Death killed about 25 million people in Europe alone, and probably millions more in Asia. It began as bubonic plague. Its name comes from spots of blood under the skin that turned black and from swellings (buboes) in the groin and armpits. Most victims died horribly, shortly after symptoms appeared. Bubonic plague was transmitted to humans by fleas on rats—it could not be passed from person to person. But if pneumonia developed in a plague victim, the infection became pneumonic plague, which could be passed on to another person. It was highly contagious, spread rapidly, and most victims died.

The disease was carried from southern China or Burma, through central Asia, along the Silk Road to Baghdad and the Crimea. In 1347, it arrived by ship at Genoa, in Italy, and spread to Paris and London in 1348, and Scandinavia and Russia in 1349. No one was safe from it.

The Black Death was carried by fleas on rats. It may have spread from an area in southern China or Southeast Asia.

Rats were common in houses, ships, and food storerooms, so the disease spread rapidly through the population.

In the art of the time, the Black Death was depicted as a skeleton riding furiously on horseback.

THE IMMEDIATE EFFECTS

The Black Death devastated whole regions: houses stood empty, villages and towns were abandoned, and people in some trades and even some entire areas were completely wiped out. Baghdad and Mecca were emptied. Doctors, priests, and the people who buried the plague victims also died. In the end, fields were littered with unburied corpses. Society and the economy in Europe began to disintegrate.

▶ The Black Death spread through Europe from Genoa. Some areas, including Ireland and parts of France lost 10 percent of their population. Other areas, including northern Italy, eastern England, and Norway, lost as much as 50 percent.

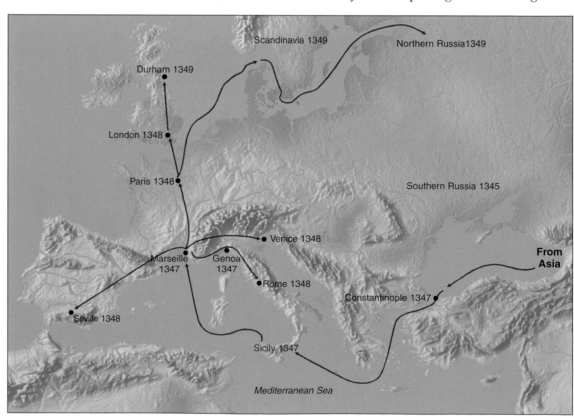

Scandinavia 1349

Northern Russia 1349

Durham 1349

London 1348

Paris 1348

Southern Russia 1345

Venice 1348

Marseille 1347

Genoa 1347

Rome 1348

Seville 1348

Constantinople 1347

From Asia

Sicily 1347

Mediterranean Sea

THE LONG-TERM EFFECTS

The Black Death destroyed many people's faith in God. To them it appeared to have no logic, killing good as well as bad people. Farms were abandoned and churches were empty. Until the onset of the Black Death, Europe usually had a surplus of labor and low wages, but the shortage of workers now made wages soar. Many country people began moving into the empty towns, working for actual money for the first time. The already weak feudal system collapsed. There were revolts. Europe and the Muslim world were in shock. Over the next 100 years, many things changed. The medieval period was making way for a new, more questioning, world.

People burned the clothes of the dead to try to stop the plague from spreading. This didn't work because the disease was caused by fleas living on rats that were found everywhere at the time.

▲ It was important to remove infected bodies quickly, even when people were still bewailing the loss of their loved ones. Criers went around the streets calling "Bring out your dead!"

◀ At night, plague carts were loaded with corpses to be taken away and buried. The Black Death spread quickly in towns because of the crowded housing conditions and lack of hygiene. Even isolated monasteries did not escape since the disease was carried there by infected people pleading for help.

179

CHINA: THE MING DYNASTY 1368–1644

After a long campaign, the Mongols were driven out of China. There then followed 150 years of peace and prosperity under the Ming dynasty.

Emperor Hong Wu (1328–1398) reorganized the administration of China and set up colleges for training mandarins (civil servants). Candidates for these posts had to pass examinations in literature and philosophy.

Kublai Khan was a great Chinese emperor, but he was a foreigner. When he died in 1294, he was followed by a series of feeble Yuan emperors, famines, and much hardship. The last Yuan emperor, Sun Ti, was a bad ruler. The Chinese people were tired of being ruled harshly by foreigners. They found a Chinese ruler in Zhu Yuan Zhang, who had been a monk and, during bad times, a beggar. As a rebel bandit chief, he had a ready-made army. He also proved to be an excellent general.

After a 13-year campaign, he captured Beijing, drove the Mongols back to Mongolia, and became emperor in 1368. He founded the Ming ("bright") dynasty, and took the name Hong Wu ("very warlike"). He moved the capital south to the fortified city of Nanjing. Hong Wu ruled China for 30 years as a dictator, guarding against Mongol incursions and restoring order and

▼ In Beijing, the Ming emperor Yongle built the Forbidden City, which only the emperor and his household were allowed to use. This is a typical building inside the imperial complex.

Art, literature, and ceramics had developed during the Song and the Yuan dynasties. This vase demonstrates another period of excellence in the arts under the Ming.

prosperity to his country.

Hong Wu left his throne to a grandson, Jianwen (born Zhu Yunwen), but he was overthrown four years later by his uncle Zhu Di, who became Emperor Yongle (pronounced *Yong-lay)* in 1403.

PEACE UNDER THE MING

China grew great again under Yongle, who was emperor from 1403 to 1424. Roads, towns, and canals were rebuilt, and when he moved to Beijing, he built the great halls, palaces, and temples of the Forbidden City. Learning and the arts flourished. Trade and industry were encouraged, and, unusually, China looked outward, exporting goods and spreading Chinese influence abroad. The Muslim admiral Zheng He was sent on long voyages to India, the Middle East, and Africa. After Yongle's reign, however, China lost interest in other countries. Many Chinese settled in Southeast Asia, and became involved with the growing "China trade." Government administration was improved and, apart from problems with piracy and Mongol attacks, flourished for a century.

From 1517 onward, the Portuguese and other Europeans arrived on the coast, trading mainly in Guangzhou (Canton). In the late 1500s, there was a series of emperors who were disliked and wasteful, and there were attacks on the borders. Trade declined, corruption and banditry grew, and there was famine and rebellion. In 1592, the Japanese invaded neighboring Korea, thereby threatening the security of China. Rebels eventually took over much of China, and in 1644, the Ming dynasty finally fell.

Gardening and landscaping developed into a very special art form in China and Japan. Water was an important ingredient in this exquisite Chinese ornamental garden.

KEY DATES	
1353–54	The Black Death breaks out across China
1368	The Ming dynasty is founded by Zhu Yuanzhang
1403–24	The reign of Ming Emperor Yongle
1517	Arrival of the first European traders in southern China
1552–55	Major attacks on shipping by pirates off the coast of China
1582	Growing corruption and decline
1592	The Japanese invade Korea, threatening China's security
1644	Fall of the Ming dynasty

This brush holder, from the Ming period, is made of carved lacquer. Lacquer is a thick varnish painted in many layers onto wood. It sets hard, making a very strong material that is often used by the Chinese.

Landscape painting also became a highly developed art form under the Ming. This classic Ming landscape painting by Tang Yin is entitled "Dreaming of Immortality in a Thatched Cottage."

CONSTANTINOPLE 1204–1453

The Byzantine Empire lasted 1,000 years. The Ottoman Turks eventually reached the doorstep of Constantinople, and had taken over the city by 1453.

The Byzantine basilica of St. Sophia in Constantinople was turned into a mosque after the Ottoman takeover in 1453. The minarets were added at this time.

Byzantium was the empire of one city— Constantinople. In the later centuries of its dominance, foreign powers moved ever closer to the city, and Byzantine territory was much reduced. The Byzantines were slowly losing heart. In 1204, Frankish and Norman Crusaders had taken Byzantium, renaming it "the Latin Empire." The Greek Byzantines regained it in 1261, but Byzantium did not recover. A series of civil wars also weakened the empire.

THE OTTOMAN TURKS

Around 1070, before the Crusaders arrived, the Seljuk Turks had entered Anatolia, where they founded the sultanate of Rum. The Mongols destroyed it around 1240, and by 1280 the Ottoman Turks had started settling southeast of Constantinople. The Ottomans built up their empire quickly. They encircled the city and crossed into Europe, where, in 1361, they took Adrianople, making it their capital. Tamberlane defeated them in 1402, but from 1430 onward the Ottomans continued their expansion into Europe.

The Ottomans were in control of most of Greece, Bosnia, Albania, and Bulgaria by 1450, and tried to conquer Hungary. All that was left of the Byzantine Empire was Constantinople itself. In 1453, the Turks, led by Mehmet II, made a final assault on the city. The last Byzantine emperor, Constantine XI, had 10,000 men whereas Mehmet had between 100,000 and 150,000. The Turks even dragged 70 of their ships overland, bypassing Constantinople's outer sea defenses, to attack by surprise. Protected by strong walls, the Byzantines held out for 54 days until finally Mehmet's best troops overran the city, ending the Byzantine Empire.

A *janissary*, here in ceremonial dress, was an elite soldier of the Ottoman army. The first janissaries were young Christian prisoners of war whose life was spared if they converted to Islam and fought for the Turks.

Teams of oxen and thousands of soldiers dragged 70 small galleys of Mehmet II's fleet over a neck of land into an unprotected stretch of sea near Constantinople. They were able to bypass the Byzantine sea defenses and besiege the city.

Mehmet II was one of the most successful Ottoman sultans. He was well educated, built many public buildings, and repopulated Istanbul with people from all parts of his empire.

A NEW BREED OF MUSLIMS

The Byzantine Empire had given birth to an outstanding medieval culture. Its decline was slow. It changed from a great power into a small country possessing a long history, but with little future. The Ottoman Turks, replacing the Byzantines, wanted to be involved in Europe. Many of their administrators were captured Europeans. The Ottomans were a new breed of Muslims who came from the East yet looked West. They occupied the traditional territory of the Byzantine Empire—the Balkans, the Black Sea, Anatolia, and Syria, and also invaded other lands. After Mehmet and his army overran Constantinople in 1453, the name of the city was changed to Istanbul, but life continued as before. However, the Muslims were now much closer to Europe, which caused the Europeans concern.

▲ This fresco from the Moldovita monastery in Romania, depicts the Ottoman siege of Constantinople in 1453, the final hour of Byzantine Empire's 1,000-year history.

◄ Castles were strategically built to guard the Bosphorus, the narrow sea route that connected the Black Sea with the Mediterranean.

KEY DATES

1071	The Seljuks defeat the Byzantines, occupying Anatolia
1204	Crusaders capture Constantinople
1243	The Mongols destroy the Seljuk sultanate of Rum
1261	Byzantines retake Constantinople
1280	The Ottomans in Anatolia move close to Constantinople
1389	Ottomans defeat the Serbs in Kosovo
1391	Ottomans defeat European Crusaders in Romania
1453	The final fall of Constantinople

THE KHMER EMPIRE 802–1440

The Khmer Empire was created in 802, when the Khmer people were united by Jayavarman II. It reached its peak under Suryavarman I and Suryavarman II.

Around 400, the Khmer had created a state called Chen-la which was at its strongest around 700 under Jayavarman I. Previously Hindu, the Khmer adopted Buddhism during this time. Chen-la declined, and, after a brief occupation by the Javanese, a new Khmer state was created in 802 by Rajah Jayavarman II. He was a "god-king" or *devarajah* (like the Tibetan Dalai Lama today). He ruled from a city called Angkor Thom, near a lake called Tonle Sap. The Khmers wrote books on paper, palm leaves, and vellum. Fire, rot, and termites have long since destroyed them, but it is possible to learn about the Khmers from Chinese histories, and from the many carvings in the ruins of Angkor Thom ("great city") and Angkor Wat ("great temple") nearby.

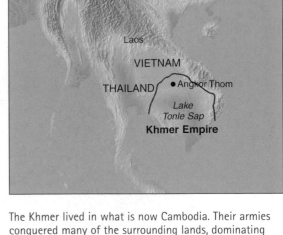

The Khmer lived in what is now Cambodia. Their armies conquered many of the surrounding lands, dominating mainland Southeast Asia during the 1100s.

The building of Angkor Thom, originally called Yasodharapura, was started just before 900. The richly decorated temple complex of Angkor Wat was built between 1113 and 1150.

The temple complex of Angkor Wat was richly decorated with many carved sandstone figures. After the temple was abandoned in the 1400s, they were swallowed up by the jungle and not rediscovered until the 1800s.

▼ Angkor Wat, a huge temple complex built of red sandstone, was surrounded by walls and a moat 590 ft. (180m) wide and 2.5 mi. (4km) long. The temple had three main enclosures (representing the outer world) surrounding an inner holy shrine.

The Khmer armies, which may have included hundreds of war elephants, fought many battles and conquered most of the surrounding lands, including Thailand and Champa (southern Vietnam). The empire reached its peak between 1010 and 1150, under Suryavarman I and Suryavarman II. During the 1200s, the people grew tired of serving the devarajahs through forced labor, and Khmer life began to break down. In 1444, invading Thai armies forced the Khmer to abandon Angkor. From then on, Cambodia was dominated by the Thai kingdom of Siam.

KHMER DAILY LIFE
The Khmer were builders, craftworkers, fishermen, farmers, and warriors. Many lived in houses perched on stilts around Tonle Sap. Their main food was rice, and their special irrigation systems produced three crops a year. The kings were still Hindus, but most of the population was Buddhist. They held elaborate religious ceremonies in connection with the seasons of the year. They traded with India and Java, and also with China, bartering spices and rhinoceros horn for porcelain and lacquerware. The royal women of the court wore skirts, leaving the upper part of the body bare. They were encouraged to study law, astrology, and languages. Men wore only a loose loin covering.

▲ Many of the temple carvings at Angkor Wat show the daily lives of the Khmer people as well as telling the stories of their sacred myths and battles.

This masterpiece of carved architecture is one tower of the Bavon temple, built in the 1100s in the capital city Angkor Thom.

KEY DATES
c.400	Founding of Chen-la, after the fall of Funan
c.700	Chen-la reaches its peak of development
802	Jayavarman II founds the Khmer nation by uniting the people
880s	The Khmer conquer the Mon and Thai peoples
900	Angkor Thom founded
1050–1150	The Khmer Empire at its high point under Suryavarman I and Suryavarman II
1113–50	Angkor Wat is built
c.1215	Death of last Angkor king, Jayavarman VII; empire starts to fall into decline
1444	Angkor abandoned after Thai invasions led by Ayutthaya

These heavenly dancers were carved on one of the walls at Angkor Wat in about 1200.

THE ARTS 1101–1460

This was a period of consolidation and improvement in the arts. The sense of invention and creativity of the early Middle Ages was developed further and refined.

Each noble family in Europe had its own coat of arms. Heraldry used many different symbols to tell a story about the family's history and aims.

During the late Middle Ages, artistic creativity around the world was blossoming. Medieval arts and music had developed, refining the styles and techniques created in the previous 500 years. There were now grander institutions, such as the Church, requiring artistic works, and there was a growing number of patrons—rich people who bought works of art and sponsored artists.

The arts of the Tang and the Song in China reached new heights of refinement in the Yuan and Ming periods. Ceramics, literature, music, theater, landscape painting and gardening, lacquerware, and sculpture all flourished.

This enamel reliquary, decorated with scenes depicting the murder of St. Thomas à Becket in Canterbury Cathedral in 1170, was made in England in 1220.

In Japan, local styles replaced the imported Chinese styles which had been adopted earlier. In comparison, the Toltecs and Aztecs took on and adapted earlier styles from Teotihuacán and the Maya. Islamic art, now a long-standing tradition, was modernized by different schools of thought in Spain, Morocco, Egypt, and Samarkand. In Europe, most art and music was created for the Church, including stained glass, tapestry, and choral music. During the 1300s and 1400s, some artists, working privately, began to paint pictures in a realistic style.

▼ During the Ming dynasty, the Chinese made ornamental blue-and-white pottery in the imperial factories. Later, many pieces were exported to Europe.

◄ Stained-glass windows were made from pieces of colored glass, joined together with strips of lead. This window, in Canterbury Cathedral in southern England, depicts medical subjects and was made in 1280.

These two Aztec women are making cloth. One is spinning raw cotton into yarn for the other to weave on a belt loom. It is given this name because one end was tied to the woman's belt.

In Europe there was a tradition of street theater at markets and festivals. Popular plays were performed on the back of a wagon, or on a makeshift stage.

In Europe, there were mystery plays based on the Bible or on traditional myths, and poems about heroes such as Charlemagne and King Arthur. Geoffrey Chaucer wrote about courtly love and ordinary people. Books were available to a wider public as they began to be written in local languages, rather than in Latin.

Wooden furniture and wall panels were often carved with scenes from stories. This scene is from *The Pardoner's Tale* by Geoffrey Chaucer from his great *Canterbury Tales*. It shows Death teaching a lesson to three men.

The temple complex at Angkor Wat, in present-day Cambodia, was built during the peak of the Khmer Empire in the 1100s. Its sandstone walls were carved with pictures of the Khmer people, their daily lives, myths, and battles.

ARCHITECTURE 1101–1460

Throughout the world, remarkable craftsmanship and technical advances led to the construction of imposing and elegant buildings during the Middle Ages.

Most castle walls had slots called loopholes. They were narrow on the outside and wide on the inside, letting the archers shoot out, but attackers could not shoot in.

Freemasons, or masons, were skilled and valued workers. They cut and shaped stones accurately for use in building.

Most people in Europe built houses with wood because it was cheap and plentiful. Unfortunately, it caught fire easily and tended to rot. Therefore, important buildings were constructed in stone. Castles and city walls were built with thick, well-laid stones. Cathedrals were designed in a new Gothic style. Instead of the rounded arches and sturdy pillars of the older Romanesque style, they had pointed arches, slender pillars, and high stained-glass windows. Worldwide, buildings were becoming finer in shape and less bulky. The carved decorations of Khmer temples, the roofs of Ming palaces, and temples in China, and the expert woodwork found in Japan made this an architecturally rich period.

MUSLIM ARCHITECTURE

The arrival of the Ottoman Turks in the Muslim world brought a new lease on life to Islamic architecture. Earlier Islamic styles gave way to Seljuk and Persian influences, different from earlier styles in detail and shape. The newest Muslim architecture came from Turkey, Morocco, Afghanistan, and Samarkand, where arches, domes, pillars, and mosaics were developed.

Roughmasons placed the stones in the wall, according to the numbers put on them by the masons.

Under the direction of an experienced master mason, a large team of people would be needed to build a castle. Ropes, pulleys, wooden scaffolding, and horses were all used to carry the materials to where they were needed.

Gothic-style cathedrals were taller and lighter than earlier ones. They were built according to carefully worked out engineering principles, and they took years to build.

Tamerlane, the last great Mongol leader, was buried in a beautiful jade-covered vault in Samarkand. This is one of the finest examples of Islamic art from this period.

In South America, high in the Andes, the Inca city of Machu Picchu was a remarkable feat of engineering. Here, the Incas built high walls of massive stones which fit together so exactly that not even an earthquake could move them. The city still stands today.

The Tibetans built monasteries clinging to precipitous Himalayan mountainsides—such as the Potala in Lhasa. During the 1200s, the Ethiopians carved Christian churches out of solid rock, making them safe from any form of attack. These rock-cut churches still survive, as do many other grand buildings around the world from this period.

Stonecutters left their own special marks to identify their work. Some of them also carved the faces of people they knew on the gargoyles and other decorations around the churches they built.

In India and Southeast Asia, stonecutting was at a peak of development during this period. This ornately carved stone gate guarded the entrance to a temple in Orissa, India.

SCIENCE AND TECHNOLOGY 1101–1460

The spread of knowledge from China and Muslim countries led to a new fascination with learning that swept through Europe in the Middle Ages.

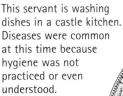

The Chinese, the Indians, and the Arabs were still ahead of the rest of the world in science and technology. Crusaders returning to Europe from Palestine brought with them Arabic knowledge of medicine, technology, astronomy, and mathematics. The city-states of Venice and Genoa, exposed to Asian influences through trade, often received these ideas first. The great Italian mathematician, Fibonacci, based his work on knowledge gleaned from Arabic texts. In England, Roger Bacon, one of the earliest Western scientists, based his ideas of reflection and refraction on works brought in from Muslim Spain and Egypt.

Eyeglasses for farsighted people were first worn in about 1285. Those for nearsighted people were not invented until around 1430.

PRINTING

Knowledge of papermaking spread to Europe from Arabia at the end of this period. The Koreans and Chinese had also invented movable-type printing, and this was later developed in Europe, setting off a revolution in knowledge. But for most of this period, all books were still written by hand, and most people in Europe could not read.

This servant is washing dishes in a castle kitchen. Diseases were common at this time because hygiene was not practiced or even understood.

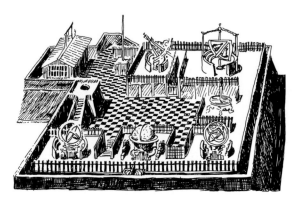

The great Mongol emperor of China, Kublai Khan, founded the Institute of Muslim Astronomy in Beijing in the 1200s, to observe important planetary events. China had a special government astronomy department.

ADVANCES IN CHINA

Chinese writing and education was very advanced, and Chinese medicine, mathematics, and other sciences were already well developed. The government administrators, called mandarins, were actually required to be scholarly. This helped the progress of Chinese sciences and technologies. The Mongols also brought foreign ideas with them, which would later benefit Ming China.

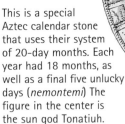

This is a special Aztec calendar stone that uses their system of 20-day months. Each year had 18 months, as well as a final five unlucky days (*nemontemi*) The figure in the center is the sun god Tonatiuh.

Monks distilled alcohol (aqua vitae—the water of life) from wine to make alcoholic beverages. Fermented cereals were used to make whiskey.

Waterpowered wheels were used to drive simple machinery such as the hammer used in ironworking (shown here). This process made metalworking much easier.

THE SPREAD OF KNOWLEDGE

There was a new spirit of inquiry in the air. The Arabs learned from the East, and the Europeans learned from the Arabs. When the first Westerners, such as the Venetian Marco Polo, went East, they took European ideas with them. More knowledge from ancient Greece came to Europe after the fall of the Byzantine Empire, when many scholars fled from Constantinople to Italy. When Admiral Zheng He sailed from China to India, Arabia, and Africa, his fleets carried scholars and collectors to gather items and information from the places they visited.

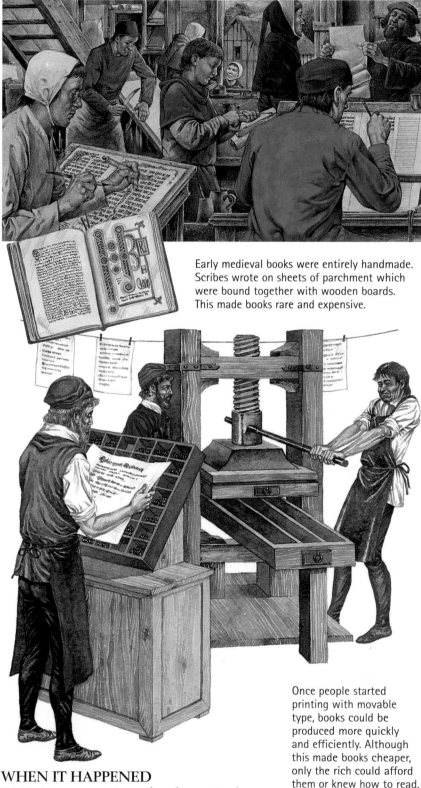

Early medieval books were entirely handmade. Scribes wrote on sheets of parchment which were bound together with wooden boards. This made books rare and expensive.

Once people started printing with movable type, books could be produced more quickly and efficiently. Although this made books cheaper, only the rich could afford them or knew how to read.

The Chinese were skilled ironworkers. A group of workers can be seen here forging a large ship's anchor in the 1300s.

WHEN IT HAPPENED

1100 Returning Crusaders bring Arabic knowledge back to Europe
1202 Fibonacci, an Italian mathematician, writes about Hindu-Arabic numbering
1260 Englishman Roger Bacon describes the laws of reflection and refraction
1275 First human dissection carried out
1397 Movable type produced in Korea

THE RENAISSANCE

1461–1600

This period marks the start of modern history. Muslims still dominated much of Europe and Asia. The Ottomans in the Middle East and the Moguls in India took Islamic culture to new heights. The Aztecs and Incas dominated the Americas. In Europe, a new world was coming into being. Europeans questioned their traditions and beliefs. They sailed the oceans, explored new ideas, and European society changed greatly—becoming more complex, freethinking, and materialistic.

▲ The Inca celebrated two festivals of the sun. One was in June, the other in December. The emperor led the ceremonies, attended by officials from all over the empire, in the great square at Cuzco.

◄ This is a detail from "Madonna of the Magnificat," painted by Italian Renaissance artist Sandro Botticelli in 1465.

THE WORLD AT A GLANCE 1461–1600

Europeans started to emerge from the narrow confines of the Middle Ages to travel beyond their continent. In 1461, European seafarers, traders, and colonists were on the brink of setting out to find new routes to the Far East, and to explore and exploit the rest of the world. For the first time, continents were brought into direct contact with each other.

In Mexico and South America, the Aztec and Inca empires were at their height, but with the arrival of the Spanish, the Aztec capital of Tenochtitlan was destroyed and the Incas were forced to retreat to the mountains of Peru. By 1533, the Spanish had turned the native population into slaves and the original inhabitants were nearly wiped out by disease and mistreatment. The invaders turned their attention north, but it was some years before North America would feel the real effects of their arrival.

African civilizations also came under European influence, but it was confined to the coast. The heart of Africa remained undisturbed. China was still ruled by the Ming dynasty. Although the arts flourished, society had begun to stagnate under its rule.

In Europe, the movement now called the Renaissance was fueled by Greek scholars fleeing from the fall of Constantinople, who brought with them the knowledge of ancient Greece and Rome.

NORTH AMERICA

Europeans first arrived here about 1500, though colonies were not really started until the 1600s. The Mississippian culture was in decline from the 1450s, and the Pueblo peoples of the Southwest were now past their peak. Other native peoples were having their own political and religious problems, as well as matters of trade with other tribes—all the time unaware of the white man's impending threat to their way of life.

NORTH AMERICA

MESOAMERICA AND SOUTH AMERICA

MESOAMERICA AND SOUTH AMERICA

Disaster struck the whole region. The richly advanced civilizations of Mexico and the Andean regions were generally on an upswing when the Spanish arrived. But both the Aztecs, in the 1520s, and the Incas in the 1530s, were quickly subjugated by these strange foreigners, whom they had welcomed at first. Trickery, followed by European diseases, killed millions. The Spanish and Portuguese quickly took over, establishing plantations, mines, and cities in the search for gold, wealth, and glory. The majority of early immigrants were actually Africans, brought over as slaves to work the plantations. But it was the European bosses and priests who, by 1600, ran what was to be become Latin America. Those indigenous Americans who survived were suddenly the subjects of new masters.

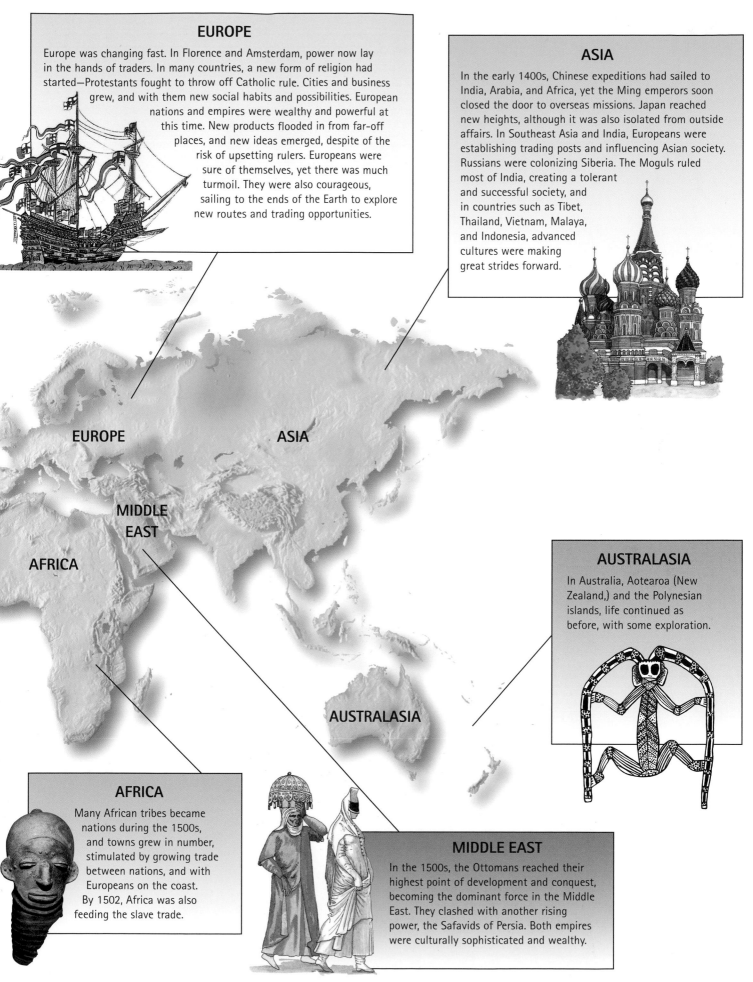

EUROPE

Europe was changing fast. In Florence and Amsterdam, power now lay in the hands of traders. In many countries, a new form of religion had started—Protestants fought to throw off Catholic rule. Cities and business grew, and with them new social habits and possibilities. European nations and empires were wealthy and powerful at this time. New products flooded in from far-off places, and new ideas emerged, despite of the risk of upsetting rulers. Europeans were sure of themselves, yet there was much turmoil. They were also courageous, sailing to the ends of the Earth to explore new routes and trading opportunities.

ASIA

In the early 1400s, Chinese expeditions had sailed to India, Arabia, and Africa, yet the Ming emperors soon closed the door to overseas missions. Japan reached new heights, although it was also isolated from outside affairs. In Southeast Asia and India, Europeans were establishing trading posts and influencing Asian society. Russians were colonizing Siberia. The Moguls ruled most of India, creating a tolerant and successful society, and in countries such as Tibet, Thailand, Vietnam, Malaya, and Indonesia, advanced cultures were making great strides forward.

EUROPE

ASIA

MIDDLE EAST

AFRICA

AUSTRALASIA

In Australia, Aotearoa (New Zealand,) and the Polynesian islands, life continued as before, with some exploration.

AUSTRALASIA

AFRICA

Many African tribes became nations during the 1500s, and towns grew in number, stimulated by growing trade between nations, and with Europeans on the coast. By 1502, Africa was also feeding the slave trade.

MIDDLE EAST

In the 1500s, the Ottomans reached their highest point of development and conquest, becoming the dominant force in the Middle East. They clashed with another rising power, the Safavids of Persia. Both empires were culturally sophisticated and wealthy.

195

THE AZTECS 1430–1520

During the 1400s, the Aztecs dominated Mexico from the wondrous city of Tenochtitlan, dominated by pyramids, on an island in the middle of a lake.

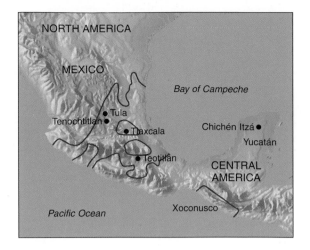

The Aztecs dominated the center of Mexico from coast to coast, including several cities. They also influenced much wider areas to the north and south.

▲ Priests were powerful in Aztec society. They did not marry, and they were responsible for conducting all of the many ceremonies in the Aztec 260-day calendar. They also carried out human sacrifices, using knives with blades made from very sharp stone, such as chalcedony, flint, or obsidian.

The Aztecs had started to expand in 1430, under the emperor Itzcóatl, and by 1500, they controlled a large empire in Mexico. Tenochtitlan had a population of about 300,000, and was at its most powerful, under Montezuma II (also known as Moctezuma II). In order to feed everyone, food was grown on artificial islands, or *chinampas*, built up in Lake Texcoco, in the middle of which the city stood. Conquered lands provided corn, beans, and cocoa, cotton cloth, and gold, silver, and jade for Aztec craftworkers. Traders bought turquoise from the Pueblo Indians in the north, and from the south came brightly colored feathers, which were used to make elaborately decorated capes, fans, headdresses, and shields. Aztec society was organized along military lines. All young men served in the army from the age of 17 to 22. Some stayed longer than this, because even a peasant could rise to be an army commander if he was good enough.

HUMAN SACRIFICES

One of the main tasks of the army was to take many prisoners of war. The prisoners were sacrificed in Tenochtitlan, at the huge pyramid-temples in the middle of the city. Religious blood sacrifice was important to the Aztecs who sacrificed to many different gods. All of these gods were believed to need a great deal of human blood—especially the god of war, Huitzilopochtli. This armed aggression and human sacrifice gradually turned the Aztecs' neighbors against them.

▶ Ordinary Aztecs lived in huts with thatched roofs. They ate pancakes made from cornmeal, with spicy bean and vegetable fillings, very like Mexican tortillas today.

This ceremonial headdress from the 1500s is made mainly of quetzal feathers. Parrot feathers in brown, crimson, white, and blue were also used.

RISE AND FALL OF THE AZTECS

The Aztecs traded far and wide around Mexico, into what is now the United States, and south to Colombia. They sold high-value items made by craftworkers—clothing, jewelry, and household and ceremonial items. They also exacted tribute—payments made by cities to keep the Aztecs from invading them. The capital, Tenochtitlan, was one of the world's best-planned cities. The streets and canals were laid out in a grid pattern on its lake island, and arranged around a huge ceremonial area of pyramids, temples, palaces, and gardens. Three wide causeways linked the city to the mainland. But the Aztecs' greed for sacrificial victims meant that, when the Spanish arrived in 1519, their neighboring societies helped them conquer the Aztecs by the following year.

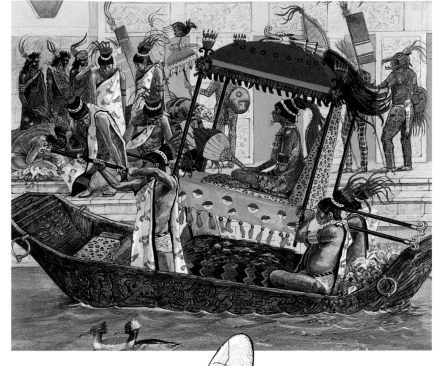

The emperor was treated like a god, and he could be spoken to only by priests and nobles. Ordinary people had to keep their eyes down when the ruler traveled through the capital.

◀ This terracotta statue bears the hideously grinning skull face of the Aztec god of death. The Aztecs used human skulls to make masks. They encrusted them with turquoise and seashells and lined them inside with red leather.

▼ Three long causeways linked Tenochtitlan to the mainland. Traders traveled far and wide from the city, and some of them acted as spies for the emperor. The causeways were also a good defense for the city. When the Spanish arrived, it was trickery and disease, not direct attack, that helped them overcome the Aztecs.

THE INCA EMPIRE 1438–1533

For a century, the Incas ruled a vast, well-organized, mountaintop empire, high in the Andes in South America. Their empire was obliterated by the Spanish.

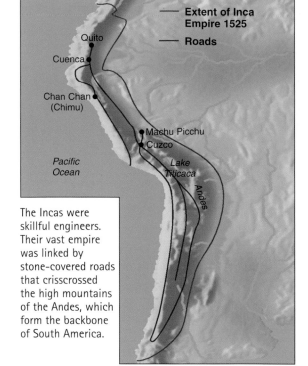

The Incas were skillful engineers. Their vast empire was linked by stone-covered roads that crisscrossed the high mountains of the Andes, which form the backbone of South America.

This golden pendant made by the Incas has markings showing mathematical patterns. These had a religious and calendrical significance for the Incas.

The Inca ruler was known as the *Sapa Inca*. He was believed to be descended from Inti, the sun god, who gave him the right to rule. He was also worshiped as a god himself. The Sapa Inca ran the country from Cuzco, thought to be Inti's home. Royal officials oversaw and directed everything in all parts of the empire. They looked after the affairs of the cities, and made sure the factories and workshops that produced pottery, textiles, and decorative metal objects, as well as the farms, were all working efficiently. Writing was unknown to the Incas, so they kept all their records on *quipus*. These were cords with knots tied in them to convey information, such as records of population and taxes. At its greatest period in 1525, the empire stretched for 2,200 mi. (3,500km). The cities, towns, and villages were all linked by a network of roads. Communication was provided by relay runners.

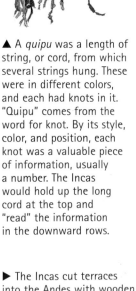

▲ A *quipu* was a length of string, or cord, from which several strings hung. These were in different colors, and each had knots in it. "Quipu" comes from the word for knot. By its style, color, and position, each knot was a valuable piece of information, usually a number. The Incas would hold up the long cord at the top and "read" the information in the downward rows.

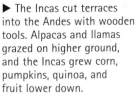

▶ The Incas cut terraces into the Andes with wooden tools. Alpacas and llamas grazed on higher ground, and the Incas grew corn, pumpkins, quinoa, and fruit lower down.

INCA EXPANSION

When Pachacuti became the Sapa Inca in 1438, he began to expand his lands around Cuzco. In 1450, he conquered the Titicaca basin; and in 1463, he went to war against the Lupaca and Colla tribes. Under his son Topa's command, the Inca army defeated the neighboring Chimu Empire in 1466, and Topa continued to expand the empire after he became the tenth Sapa Inca in 1471. During the next 15 years, he conquered lands far to the south, and later took control of lands to the north and west.

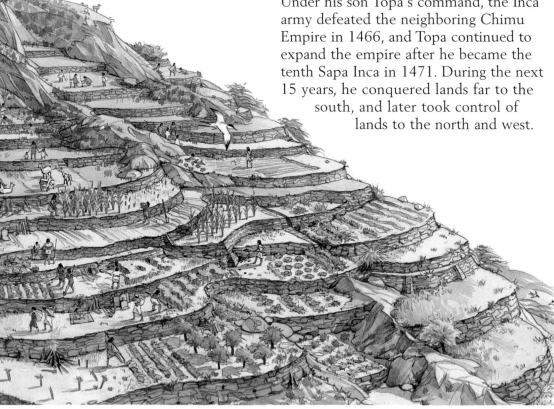

RISE AND FALL OF THE INCAS

The Incas reached a very high level of technology and organization, and came up with ingenious ways of farming on steep slopes, and building bridges, roads, and towns high in the mountains.

Topa built many of these roads and towns. Topa's son, Huayna Capac, the Sapa Inca from 1493, further expanded the empire, building a second capital at Quito. When he died in 1525, the empire was divided between his sons: Huascar ruled the south, and Atahualpa the north. This division led to civil war just before the Spanish landed in 1532. The invaders took advantage of the road system while the Incas argued among themselves, and the Spanish were able to destroy the empire by 1533.

KEY DATES	
1200	Manco Capac establishes the Inca dynasty and capital of Cuzco
1350	Local expansion of the Incas under Mayta Capa
1438	Pachacuti becomes the Sapa Inca
1450	Pachacuti greatly enlarges the Inca Empire
1466	Topa Inca overruns the Chimu Empire
1485	Topa Inca conquers Chile and Peru
1493	Quito becomes the second capital
1525	Huayna Capa dies, and civil war breaks out between Cuzco and Quito
1532	The Spanish invade the Inca Empire
1533	The Spanish destroy the Inca Empire

▲ Two main roads ran the length of the empire. They were connected with every town and village by smaller roads. Goods were carried by trains of llamas. Quipus were delivered by relay runners.

▲ Relay runners carried official messages and packages throughout the empire. Each runner ran about 1 mi. (1.5km) before the next one took over. To make sure of a quick changeover, a runner announced his approach by blowing on a conch shell.

◄ Each year, the Incas would celebrate the Great Festival of the sun, to give thanks for the growth of crops and the continuation of life, and to pray for blessings in the future—not unlike the Christian festival of Easter.

THE RECONQUEST OF SPAIN 1469–1516

The reconquest of Muslim-ruled Spain by the Spanish began during the 1100s. The country was fully reunited 300 years later, under Ferdinand and Isabella.

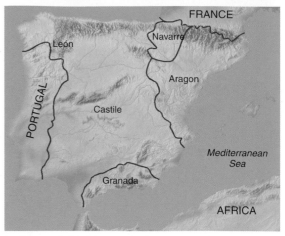

Spain was divided for much of the 1400s, though the uniting of Aragon and Castile in 1479 made the eventual union of Spain almost inevitable.

Ferdinand (1452–1516) succeeded to the throne of Aragon. He was a tough politician and ruled Spain together with his wife, Isabella.

Isabella (1451–1504) inherited the kingdom of Castile. She and her husband, Ferdinand, eventually became rulers of all Spain.

After the fall of the Roman Empire, Spain had been ruled by the Visigoths for 300 years. Then came the invading Berbers (Moors) from northern Africa in 711, establishing a Muslim caliphate which lasted from 756 until 1031. At this time, Christians in the north of Spain started pushing southward. They started a *reconquista* (reconquest) which, by 1235, had limited the Muslims to Granada in the south of the country.

However, Catholic Spain was divided into several countries—León, Castile, Navarre, and Aragon. In the 1400s, León had joined with Castile, making Castile and Aragon the two largest. The first step toward finally uniting Spain was made in 1469 when Ferdinand, heir to Aragon, married Isabella of Castile. When the king of Castile died in 1474, Isabella and Ferdinand succeeded him as joint rulers of his kingdom. Five years later, Ferdinand inherited Aragon and made Isabella joint ruler of Aragon as well.

▼ The Christian armies of Aragon and Castile defeated the Moors in 1492, and the Moors were driven back to North Africa where they were shown no mercy.

THE SPANISH INQUISITION

Many Muslims and Jews had converted to Christianity and stayed in Spain, making a great contribution to its culture. But their success was resented. The king and queen decided that all non-Christians should leave Spain. They wanted to find those who had "converted" but still followed the old religion secretly. Spain used religion as a political weapon. The pope gave permission for an Inquisition, a court that investigated heresy, but the Spanish misused the power and imprisoned, tortured, and killed thousands of people.

THE REUNIFICATION OF SPAIN

In 1492, fourteen years after the Spanish Inquisition began, Moorish Granada was recaptured by Aragon and Castile. Many Muslims and Jews were expelled or forcibly converted—as many as 200,000 Jews left the country. This persecution resulted in many skilled and able people moving away to France, Germany, and the Ottoman Empire.

In the same year, Ferdinand and Isabella sponsored the voyage of Christopher Columbus—they were seeking a sea route to India and China, but instead found the Americas. This began a period of Spanish conquest that brought about the downfall of the Aztecs, Maya, and Incas.

Ferdinand and Isabella had five daughters, one of whom, Catherine of Aragon, married Henry VIII of England. But Ferdinand and Isabella had no son, and descent passed through their daughter Joanna the Mad. When Isabella died in 1504, Ferdinand acted as regent for the young Joanna. In 1515, Navarre joined Castile, and Ferdinand finally became king of a united Spain. Joanna's son, Charles V, eventually became the Hapsburg emperor, the most powerful ruler in Europe. Under his rule, Spain experienced its golden age.

Boadbil, the last Moorish emir of Granada, leaves the city after the conquest by Aragon and Castile in 1492, ending a long era of Muslim rule in Spain.

KEY DATES

1248	The Christians reconquer most of Spain
1469	The marriage of Ferdinand and Isabella
1474	Isabella inherits Castile
1478	The Spanish Inquisition is established
1479	Aragon and Castile are united
1492	The conquest of Granada—end of Muslim rule in southern Spain. Christopher Columbus' expedition to India is financed by Isabella
1504	Isabella dies
1515	Navarre joins Castile—Spain is finally united
1516	Ferdinand dies

During the Spanish Inquisition, books that were written by people suspected of heresy were burned. This painting by Pedro Berruguete not only celebrates the Catholic victory in Spain, but also vividly illustrates the power of the Inquisition.

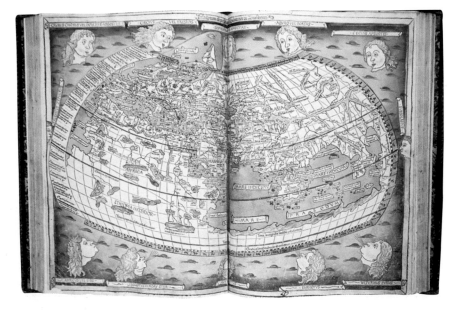

A map of the world taken from Ptolemy's *Geographia*, shows how the world was thought to look in 1486, before world exploration by Europeans really began.

THE RENAISSANCE 1450–1600

The Renaissance was a bridge from medieval to modern culture. It was a revolutionary period in the arts and sciences that eventually changed the whole world.

Developed in the 1440s, Gutenberg's printing press with movable type made books available to people throughout Europe for the first time.

Renaissance architects copied the elegant styles of Ancient Greece and Rome for buildings such as the Tempietto in Rome.

During the 1300s, life in Europe had been affected by wars, peasant revolts, and the Black Death. The old order was dying, and people were seeking something new. In medieval times, the Church had dominated the arts, education, and learning. People had accepted what they were told without asking questions. Then, in the 1300s, Italian scholars began to take an interest in the writings of the ancient Greeks and Romans—ideas that arrived in Europe from Byzantium and the Arab world. This interest grew when, in 1397, Manuel Chrysoloras, a scholar from Constantinople, became the first professor of Greek at the University of Florence in northern Italy. Scholars became fascinated by the questions that ancient philosophers dealt with. From these studies grew a belief system called *humanism*. Suddenly people, not God, were considered responsible for choosing the course of their lives. After the fall of the Byzantine Empire and Muslim Spain in the 1400s, many scholars moved to Italy and northwestern Europe, taking many old manuscripts and ideas with them.

▼ Sandro Botticelli (1445–1510) was an Italian artist famous for his religious and mythological paintings, such as "The Adoration of the Kings." He was sponsored by the influential Medici family of Florence.

During the Renaissance, the ideal person was the "universal" man or woman. This was someone who was educated to be skillful in a variety of subjects including literature, painting, science, music, and philosophy.

THE PEAK OF THE RENAISSANCE

The Renaissance affected art and science, architecture and sculpture. Ideas became more realistic, more human, and less dominated by religion. Paintings and statues were more lifelike, music explored new feelings, and books asked real-life questions. Rich families such as the Medicis and the Borgias in Italy and the burghers of Holland became patrons of the arts and sciences. Printed books helped to spread new ideas. The Renaissance reached its peak in the 1500s, mainly in cities such as Venice, Florence, Antwerp, and Haarlem. People looked closely at the world, made detailed scientific observations, collected exotic objects, and considered new ideas.

THE NEW SPIRIT OF INQUIRY

Some people studied plants and animals. Others investigated astronomy and geology. Sometimes their findings brought them into conflict with the Church. When Nicolaus Copernicus (1473–1543) realized that the Earth moved around the sun, he dared not publish his views until he was actually on his deathbed. He feared the reaction of the Church, which continued to insist that the Earth stood at the center of the universe.

This new spirit of inquiry and interest in humanity eventually led some people to question the authority of the Church. Thinkers such as Jan Hus in Bohemia and John Wycliffe in England began to question the Church openly. People's own opinions became more important—rulers and the Church could no longer do just as they pleased.

THE BIRTH OF A MODERN WORLD

Demand for change led to advances in science and art, and even caused some people to set sail for unexplored lands. New universities encouraged new ideas. Money and trade also became significant. Foods and products such as coffee, sugar, tobacco, potatoes, pineapples, porcelain, and cotton were imported to Europe from Africa, America, India, and China.

No longer bound to the land by feudalism, people began to move around. Many of them went to cities to seek their fortune. Northwestern Europe grew in importance, and power shifted slowly from the nobles and clerics to the bankers and politicians. These changes marked the beginning of a modern world that was to develop rapidly over the next 400 years.

The Dutch scholar and humanist Desiderius Erasmus (1467–1536), was critical of the Catholic Church and, later, of the Reformers, especially Luther.

EVERYDAY LIFE IN FLORENCE

Florence, in Italy, was one of the great centers of Renaissance learning and art. Lorenzo de' Medici became joint ruler of the city with his brother Giuliano, in 1469, and was a powerful patron to many writers, artists, and scientists. The city grew rich from trade and commerce, its people wore fine clothes, and its streets thronged with skilled craftspeople.

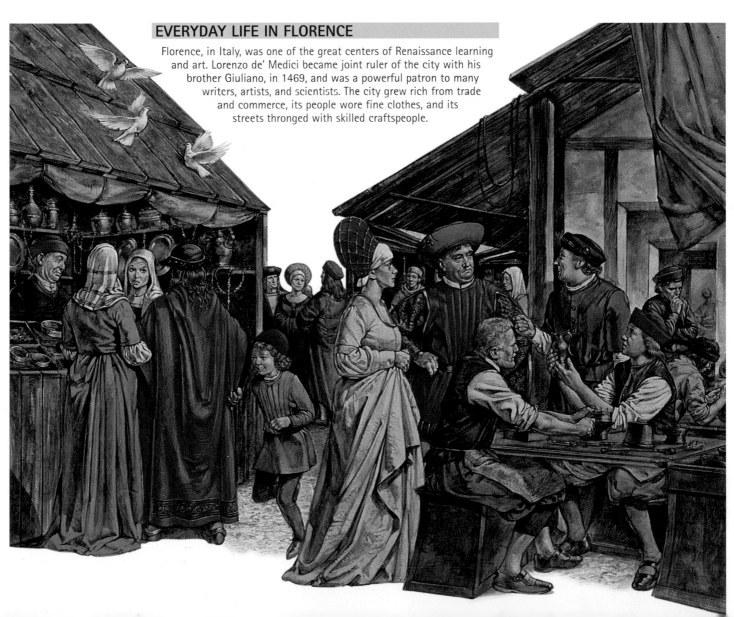

ITALY 1460–1530

During this period, Italy was divided into small states. This made for great variation—some states were progressive while others were more conservative.

To further the ambitions of her father, Rodrigo, (Pope Alexander VI), Lucrezia Borgia (1480–1519) was married three times. With her third husband, the Duke of Ferrara, she became a great patron of the arts. Their court became a magnet for artists and writers. She is also known for her devotion to causes involving children and education.

Many Italian states, such as Florence, Venice, and Rome, were really large cities. Others were ruled by dukes, as in Mantua, Milan, Urbino, and Ferrara. Most of these states were ruled by families who had grown rich from trade and commerce in the late Middle Ages.

The most powerful family of the time was the Medici family of Florence. They had made a great fortune during the 1300s through banking and moneylending. The best known of the Medicis is Lorenzo, who became joint ruler of Florence with his brother in 1469. He was a cunning statesman and banker as well as a patron of writers, artists, philosophers, and scientists. He was eager to promote his family and saw his second son become pope. Under Lorenzo's influence, Florence became one of the most beautiful and prosperous cities in Italy, and a center of the Renaissance. Lorenzo helped make the form of Italian spoken in Florence into the language of the whole country.

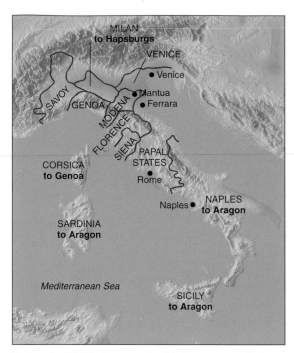

During the Middle Ages, much of Italy was controlled by the Holy Roman Empire. Following a power struggle between emperors and popes, many cities formed their own independent states.

Another family, the Borgias, sought power through the Church and the military. Two Borgias became pope. One of them, Rodrigo, schemed to help his children. When he died, the family's power collapsed.

The Medici villa at Florence was built in 1480 for Lorenzo the Magnificent by Renaissance architect Giuliano da Sangallo.

LORENZO DE' MEDICI

In 1469, when he was 20 years old, Lorenzo became joint ruler of Florence with his brother Giuliano. He was the grandson of Cosimo de' Medici, who was the second Medici to hold power in Florence. Lorenzo's brother was killed in a plot by a rival family in 1478. Lorenzo did everything he could to further his family's interests—his second son Giovanni became Pope Leo X—and to build a large gathering of scholars and creative people. He was the first patron of the artist Michelangelo. He maintained and expanded the family traditions of banking and government.

Lorenzo de´ Medici (1449–1492)—"The Magnificent"—ruled Florence from 1478 to 1492.

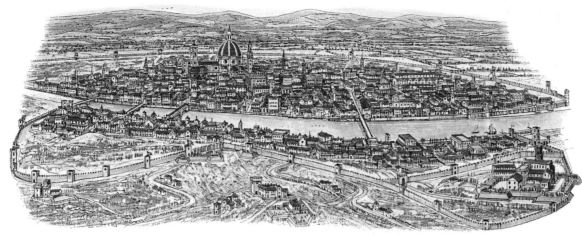

The magnificent city of Florence was at the height of its powers during the late 1400s. Ruled by the Medicis, it became home to many great artists, architects, writers, and scientists of the Renaissance. Florence also became one of Europe's main business and banking centers.

The Sforzas were a great family of Milan. Ludovico Sforza (1452–1508), was a man of taste, but also one with ruthless ambition. He ruled as regent for his nephew, the duke of Milan, but made himself the real center of power. He made alliances with Rodrigo Borgia and married a daughter of the powerful d'Este family, from Ferrara. Ludovico's court attracted great artists from all fields, among them Leonardo da Vinci.

Families like the Medicis represented "new money," with new values and ideas. They paid for exploration, centers of learning, public works, and new, imported products. People traveled to Italy to learn new ideas, which were taken back to other parts of Europe, and Europeans flocked to Florence, Venice, and Milan to gain support for their own ideas. Although future centers of modern development were to be in northwestern Europe, much of the energy of the early Renaissance came from the city-states of Italy.

Raphael was influenced by the work of Da Vinci and Michelangelo in Florence. This is his "Deposition of Christ," which he painted in 1507 at the age of 24. The following year Pope Julius II asked him to do a major work in the Vatican in Rome.

Wealthy Renaissance people enjoyed a very comfortable life. In addition to palaces or large city residences, many had country villas where they welcomed groups of visitors. They would spend time hunting, holding parties, discussing literature, and writing poetry.

EUROPEAN EXPLORERS 1460–1600

During the second half of the 1400s, European sailors and navigators planned voyages which would take them far beyond the limits of the world they knew.

In 1488, Bartholomeu Dias (1450–1500) sailed around Africa's Cape of Good Hope in a terrible storm—thereafter it was feared as the "Cape of Storms."

Vasco da Gama (1469–1525) rounded the Cape of Good Hope in 1497, and sailed up the east coast of Africa. With the help of an Indian sailor, he then crossed the Indian Ocean to Calicut in India, returning home with a cargo of spices. He went back to India to defend Portuguese interests and was made viceroy of India in 1524.

The urge to explore was partly a result of a new interest in the world, encouraged by the Renaissance; but the main intention was to bypass the Islamic world in order to set up new trading links with India and the Far East, the source of spices and other luxuries. Until the fall of the Byzantine Empire in 1453, spices were brought overland to Constantinople and then carried across the Mediterranean to Europe. In spite of their expense, spices were essential. The only way to preserve meat was by salting it. Adding spices helped hide the salty taste, and they also concealed the taste of meat which had spoiled despite being salted.

The Portuguese had set up harbors and forts along the west coast of Africa, trading with the Africans in gold, ivory, and silver. Gradually, they sailed farther south, and in 1488, Bartholomeu Dias sailed around the tip of southern Africa—pushed by a fierce gale. His frightened, exhausted crew refused to go any farther. Nine years later, Dias helped Vasco da Gama plan a voyage around the Cape of Good Hope to Calicut in India.

A sailor's personal property from the year 1536, salvaged from the wreck of Henry VIII's flagship, the *Mary Rose*. It includes a pouch, a whistle, a rosary, and a comb.

Vasco da Gama was followed by Pedro Cabral who returned from India with a cargo of pepper. This encouraged other navigators to try to sail farther east. In 1517, the Portuguese had reached China, and nearly 30 years later they had arrived in Japan. The Portuguese were driven not only by trading possibilities, but also by a determination to spread Christianity to the peoples of the East.

▶ Vasco da Gama's small ships were a development of the traditional caravel, with its triangular lateen sail. His ships had both square and lateen sails, making them more maneuverable and adaptable on the seas.

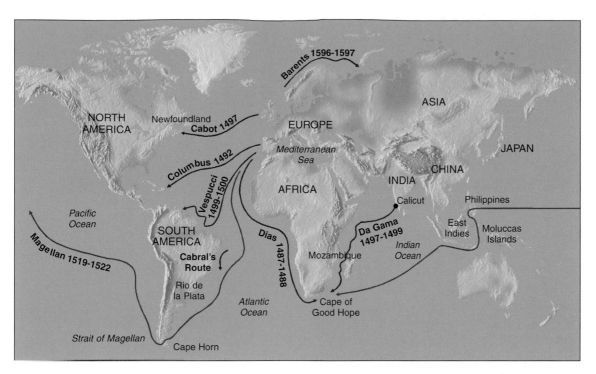

Barents 1596-1597

Cabot 1497 Newfoundland

Columbus 1492

Vespucci 1499-1500

Magellan 1519-1522

Pacific Ocean

NORTH AMERICA

SOUTH AMERICA

Cabral's Route

Rio de la Plata

Strait of Magellan

Cape Horn

Atlantic Ocean

EUROPE

Mediterranean Sea

AFRICA

Dias 1487-1488

Mozambique

Cape of Good Hope

ASIA

CHINA

JAPAN

INDIA

Calicut

Da Gama 1497-1499

Indian Ocean

East Indies

Philippines

Moluccas Islands

◀ Navigators from Europe tried many routes to reach the Spice Islands, the Moluccas. They discovered more than they expected, opening up new routes and laying the foundations of future empires.

▲ Although Portuguese by birth, Ferdinand Magellan (1480–1521) sailed for Spain. He led the first expedition to sail around the world, and gave the Pacific Ocean its name.

WESTWARD EXPLORATION

While the Portuguese sailed east, the Spanish sailed west. In 1492, Columbus found the West Indies. Amerigo Vespucci reached South America in 1499, but didn't realize until his voyage of 1501 that he had found a new continent. In 1497, John Cabot, a Venetian sponsored by England's Henry VII, discovered Newfoundland. In 1535, Jacques Cartier sailed up the St. Lawrence River, claiming the area for France. Ferdinand Magellan rounded South America in 1519. He died in the Philippines, but part of his crew returned to Spain in 1522—the first explorers to sail around the world.

CHRISTOPHER COLUMBUS

In 1492, Queen Isabella sponsored Christopher Columbus, a navigator from Genoa in Italy, to find a western route to India. It is possible that he knew of America from Viking tales he had heard in Iceland. Most people believed the world was much smaller than it really was. When Columbus reached a group of islands across the Atlantic, he called them the West Indies. They were in fact the islands of the Caribbean. Columbus made three more voyages there, but it is not known whether he really knew if they were America or Asia.

Christopher Columbus (1451–1506) first went to sea at the age of fourteen. He was shipwrecked and washed up on the coast of Portugal.

◀ When Christopher Columbus and his crew landed on Guanahani in the Bahamas, he claimed it for Spain.

THE SONGHAY EMPIRE 1460–1603

Songhay replaced and enlarged the state of Mali. During the 1200s, Mali itself had replaced Ghana as the dominant gold-trading nation of West Africa.

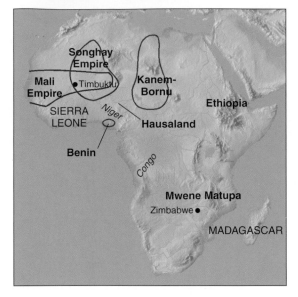

Early European explorers who settled on the coasts of Africa knew nothing about its rich interior. Songhay traded its gold and slaves for luxury goods and salt.

When Europeans arrived in Africa in the 1460s, the continent had many states and kingdoms. Tradition has Songhay founded in the 600s by a Berber Christian called al-Yaman, beside the Niger River. By 1200, the rulers moved to Gao, farther up the Niger, where they converted to Islam. Songhay became part of Mali in 1325, after Gao was captured by Mansa Muse, the Muslim emperor of Mali. In 1464, Sonni Ali made Songhay independent again and expanded its territory, taking over Mali, including Timbuktu and Jenne. Songhay became rich and powerful, dominating West Africa. Sonni Ali was cruel and immoral, and persecuted religious people. He drowned in 1492, and in 1493, Askia Mohammed I founded a new dynasty. Under his leadership, Songhay grew, trading gold, first with the Arabs, then with the Portuguese. Askia was a good ruler—he respected religious beliefs and rebuilt Songhay's society. Timbuktu again became an international center of learning.

This terracotta head from Songhay was made in the 1400s. It was probably part of a larger statue of a prominent person who lived in Songhay.

THE DECLINE OF SONGHAY

In 1528, Askia Mohammed I was deposed by his son, and a succession of weak and corrupt rulers followed. Songhay grew weaker, and finally fell to the Moroccans in 1591. Songhay was not the only state in West Africa. To the east was Kanem–Bornu, an African empire which grew around Lake Chad. By 1100, it had become a center of Muslim civilization, reaching its peak under Idris Aloma, who came to power in 1571 and ruled until 1603.

Gao, once the capital of Songhay, housed the tomb of the greatest king of Songhay, Askia Mohammed I, who ruled from 1493 to 1528.

SAFAVID PERSIA 1500–1722

At the beginning of the 1500s, Persia regained independence under the Safavid dynasty. Persia soon became one of the leading cultures of the world.

▲ This military standard from Safavid Persia was used in ceremonies to honor those who had been killed in battle. It was made of precious metals and richly inlaid with precious stones.

Persians had been prominent in the Abbasid Empire since 642, and then again under the Seljuks and Mongol Ilkhans. After a period of disorder, the Safavid dynasty came to power after the they captured the city of Tabriz in 1501, making Persia independent. Their leader was Ismail I who had himself crowned *shah*, or ruler. The name "Safavid" came from Ismail's ancestor Safi od-Din, a Sufi holy man who lived around 1300. By 1508, Ismail controlled all of Persia and most of Mesopotamia. He established Shiite Islam as the state religion. Doctrinal differences, together with disputes over land, led to a long series of Muslim religious wars between the Shiite Safavids and the Sunni Ottomans. They started in 1514 when the Ottoman sultan, Selim I, invaded western Persia. Under the Safavids, Persia developed its own identity after centuries of foreign domination, and the powerful dynasty lasted for 200 years.

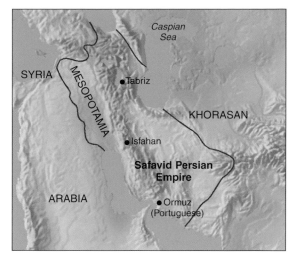

Under the Safavids, Persia again became independent and a major power in the region. They made friends and traded with the Portuguese, though they were troubled by the Ottomans to the west and the Turks to the east.

Safavid Persia was continually under pressure from Ottomans in the west and Turks in the east, until the reign of Abbas I who made peace and created a cultural renaissance in Persia. After his death in 1629, a series of weak shahs followed, and the Safavids were brought down by invading Afghans in 1722.

ABBAS THE GREAT

The Safavid dynasty reached its peak under Shah Abbas the Great (1571–1629), who ruled from 1587. A good military leader, he made peace with the Ottomans and drove the Uzbek Turks out of eastern Iran. He moved his capital to Isfahan and made it into one of the world's finest cities, with a magnificent palace and mosque. Covered bazaars (markets) surrounded the main square, trees and streams flanked the market square, and a central avenue had gardens on both sides. Abbas the Great set in motion a revival of Persian culture, creating lasting friendly relations with Europe, and entertaining foreign visitors.

◀ This 17th-century painting shows Abbas I defeating the Uzbeks.

▲ Complex geometric and natural patterns decorate the mosque at Isfahan.

TUDOR ENGLAND 1485–1603

During the Tudor period, England grew great and powerful. It forged a strong new identity, broke its ties with Rome, and sowed the seeds of an imperial future.

Henry Tudor (1457–1509) came to power in 1485.

Henry VIII (1491–1547) brought about great changes in England.

The Tudors, a Welsh family, rose to power after the confusion of a long civil war, the Wars of the Roses (1455–1485). The first Tudor king, Henry VII, banned private armies and put down any nobles who opposed him. He enriched his own finances and those of the nation. In 1509, when the young Henry VIII became king, England was an important power in Europe. Henry married Catherine of Aragon, daughter of Spain's Ferdinand and Isabella, and spent 15 years as a pleasure-seeking Renaissance-style ruler, while Thomas Wolsey ran the government. After wars against France and Scotland Henry became more politically aware. In 1521, he wrote a treatise attacking Luther, and the pope gave him the title Defender of the Faith. He had only one living child, Mary, and Henry wanted a male heir, so

Henry VIII loved banquets. He was well-educated, played several musical instruments, and wrote songs. He also enjoyed lively discussions on religion, art, and politics.

he asked the pope's permission to divorce Catherine. He was refused. At this time, new religious ideas and demands for Church reform were common, so Henry broke with Rome and made himself head of the Church in England.

DISSOLUTION OF THE MONASTERIES

Between 1536 and 1540, Henry closed 800 monasteries. He turned 10,000 monks and nuns out and sold or gave away their lands. He did this to break the power of Rome in England, and to raise money. He founded the Protestant Church of England, though he was not enthusiastically Protestant—Protestantism really developed under Elizabeth I.

Henry VIII rebuilt the English navy, and his pride and joy was the *Mary Rose*. In 1536, he went to Portsmouth to watch it sail. However, the ship's balance was affected by the 700 sailors on deck, and it capsized and sank.

Henry married six times, and during his reign, strengthened English control of Wales and Ireland, established a large navy, and planned various colonial and commercial ventures. He was succeeded in 1547 by his only son, Edward VI (1537–1553) who died at the age of sixteen. During his reign, the Church of England grew stronger. Edward was followed by his half-sister, Mary I (1516–1558). Devoutly religious, she tried to restore England to Catholicism.

THE FIRST ELIZABETHANS

When Mary died, her sister Elizabeth I came to the throne. Elizabeth was hard-working, popular, and intelligent. She refused to marry, and she made her own decisions. The Catholic Mary, Queen of Scots, Elizabeth's cousin, was found guilty of plotting against her, but Elizabeth resisted pressure to have her executed for many years. Elizabeth aided European Protestants and sent out English pirates against Spanish ships. She made a settlement between English Catholics and Protestants, and fought a war with Spain, defeating the Spanish Armada. England began to develop overseas ventures, and at home its industries and economy grew. This was Shakespeare's time, when English culture and society flowered, laying the foundations for a period of imperial English greatness.

Elizabeth I (1533–1603) became queen of England and Ireland in 1558. She ruled for 45 years and, due to her active involvement in government, England went through a period of stability, as well as cultural and economic expansion.

MARY, QUEEN OF SCOTS 1542–1587

Mary Stuart became queen of Scotland in 1542 when she was only a week old. Her father, James V, was the nephew of Henry VIII, and this encouraged the Catholic Mary to claim the English throne. She was educated in France and married the heir to the French throne in 1558. After his death in 1560, Mary returned to Scotland where she proved unpopular. She abdicated and fled to England in 1568. As a focus for Catholic dissent against Elizabeth, Mary became involved in plots and was imprisoned in Fotheringay Castle, where she was executed in 1587 on a charge of treason.

THE PORTUGUESE EMPIRE 1520–1600

Portuguese seafarers and traders paved the way for European colonialism around the world. At its height, their trading empire spanned the whole globe.

This ornamental African mask from Benin shows the oba (king) wearing a headdress carved with representations of Portuguese merchants.

The Portuguese were the leading seafaring explorers of Europe. They had long been fishermen, accustomed to the high seas. Henry the Navigator began the training of sailors in the mid-1400s, and sent ships down the west coast of Africa. There were large profits at stake in the trade of exotic goods. Portuguese explorers reached the East Indies (Indonesia) in the early 1500s, following the Muslim trade routes to the Moluccas (Spice Islands), which were rich in the spices such as cinnamon, cloves, and nutmeg, that Europe wanted. To control this valuable trade, the Portuguese conquered the Moluccas and seized many of the best-placed ports on the Indian Ocean. They also visited China. Because Portuguese traders needed to sail around Africa in order to return to Lisbon, forts were set up at various places along the African coast to supply and protect the ships.

▲ The Portuguese were the first Europeans to trade with West African countries. This brass plaque from Benin shows Portuguese men symbolically holding up the pillars supporting the palace of the oba of Benin.

▼ The Portuguese Empire at its greatest extent in about 1600 was far-flung, but very profitable. Trading posts and ports to service ships were positioned in strategic locations along the major trade routes.

▲ In the 1500s, Benin craftspeople carved items such as this ivory saltcellar, for export to Europe. Around the base are figures of Portuguese noblemen.

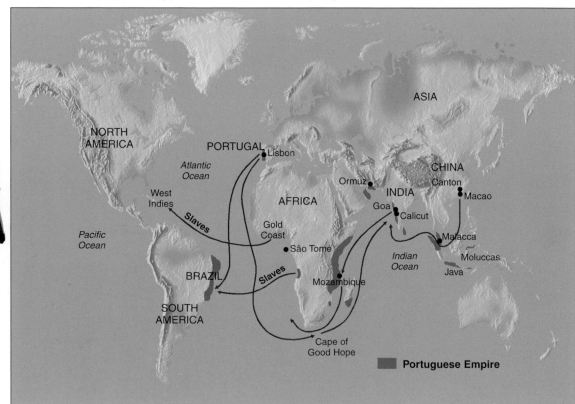

NORTH AMERICA

PORTUGAL • Lisbon

Atlantic Ocean

West Indies

Slaves

Pacific Ocean

Gold Coast

• São Tomé

BRAZIL

Slaves

SOUTH AMERICA

AFRICA

ASIA

Ormuz •

Goa

CHINA
Canton
• Macao

INDIA

• Calicut

Malacca

Moluccas

Java

Indian Ocean

Mozambique

Cape of Good Hope

■ **Portuguese Empire**

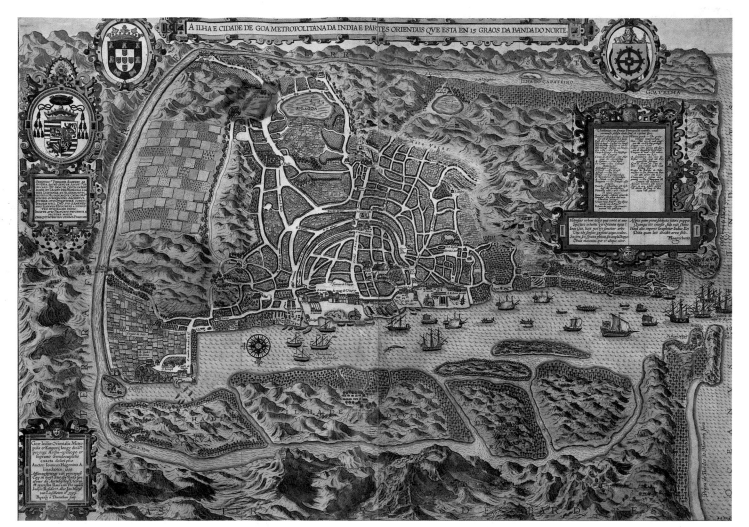

A ILHA E CIDADE DE GOA METROPOLITANA DA INDIA E PARTES ORIENTAIS QVE ESTA EN 15 GRAOS DA BANDA DO NORTE.

THE START OF THE SLAVE TRADE

From Africa, the Portuguese bought gold and slaves to work on their sugar plantations. The first ones were on the African island of Sâo Tomé, but the sugar was inferior and the market collapsed. Problems grew. In the 1570s, a slave named Amador led a major revolt. Raids by pirates were a continuing threat. Sâo Tomé became only a place where slaves were loaded onto ships bound for Brazil—and so the transatlantic slave trade began.

At its height in the 1500s, the Portuguese Empire did not possess large areas of colonial land like the Spanish, but they did hold well-placed, valuable trading posts and plantations. These included Angola and Mozambique, the islands of Cape Verde, Madeira, and the Azores; the bases of Ormuz (Persia), Goa and Calicut (India), and Colombo (Sri Lanka); and trading posts in the Far East, such as Macao (China), the Celebes, Java, and Malacca.

KEY DATES

1419	The Portuguese reach Madeira
1471	The Portuguese reach Asante and Benin
1488	Dias rounds the Cape of Good Hope
1498	Vasco da Gama reaches India
1500	Cabral explores the coast of Brazil
1505–20	Asian trading posts founded in Goa and Malacca
1520	Magellan discovers the Moluccas (Spice Islands)
1530	First Portuguese colony established in Brazil
1534	First African slaves are brought to Brazil

The port of Goa in India was an important trading link in the Portuguese Empire. It is shown here in a map made in 1595 by a Portuguese–Dutch engraver, Johannes Baptista van Doetechum the Younger.

Before the Portuguese arrived in the Moluccas, its rulers enjoyed high profits from the lucrative spice trade. Under Portuguese rule the local rulers were bypassed. Spices from the Moluccas included cloves, nutmeg, pepper, cinnamon, and ginger.

THE REFORMATION 1520–1618

During the Reformation, a new kind of Christianity, with many new groups and sects, developed. This led to social divisions and eventually war across Europe.

John Calvin (1509–1564) was born in France and was originally named Jean Chauvin. He was a strict Protestant and believed that God had already ordained the future and that only those chosen by God (the Elect) would be saved.

Europe suffered a series of violent religious civil wars. There were many massacres, and people accused of being heretics were burned at the stake.

By the early 1500s, the new ideas of the Renaissance led some people to challenge the teachings of the Roman Catholic Church. The way its leaders ran the Church was strongly criticized. Priests, monks, and nuns no longer led lives of poverty, celibacy, and simplicity, and popes and bishops were too interested in money and power. People sought Church reform. This became known as "the Reformation." It had started quietly over 100 years before, but gained momentum in 1517 when Martin Luther, a German priest, nailed a list of 95 statements (theses) to the church door at Wittenberg, criticizing the role of the Church. Luther hated the sale of "indulgences"—the forgiveness of sins in exchange for money. He hoped that his list would lead to healthy debate, but he was accused of heresy (going against Church beliefs), and excommunicated from the Catholic Church in 1521.

The Reformation in the 1500s meant that Europe was divided roughly north–south over religious beliefs— Protestant to the north and Roman Catholic to the south. This division also happened within individual countries such as France, and later led to civil war.

THE EARLY PROTESTANTS

Luther had gained support in Germany and Switzerland, setting up his own Lutheran church. Other groups, such as Quakers, Anabaptists, Mennonites, and Moravian Hussites did the same. After a conference in 1529, they were all called Protestants. Ulrich Zwingli led the Reformation in Switzerland. His views were more extreme, and this led to a civil war in which Zwingli was killed. He was followed by John Calvin, who gained followers in France, Germany, and Holland. He established the Reformation in Switzerland and influenced John Knox, who took the Reformation to Scotland. Some groups pooled all their property to form communities, taking over whole towns.

▲ Martin Luther (1483–1546) believed that people are saved by faith alone, not by buying indulgences. He wanted faith to be based on the Bible, not on corrupt religious traditions. He believed that church services should be in the local language, not Latin. The cartoon on the right shows the devil dictating Luther's sermons to him.

The Council of Trent met three times between 1545 and 1563. It began a major reform within the the Catholic Church and sought to stop the spread of Protestantism.

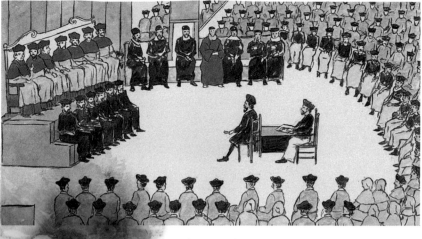

▲ The Catholic Church used pictures for teaching, and this 1470 woodcut from Germany shows a good Catholic on his deathbed, being given the last rites.

THE COUNTER-REFORMATION

In 1522, Pope Adrian VI admitted there were many problems in the Roman Catholic Church, but following his death, nothing more was done until 1534, when Paul III became pope. This was the year Henry VIII of England broke away from Rome. Paul began to reform the Church in a movement known as the Counter-Reformation. He began by encouraging the preaching and missionary work of an Italian order of friars called the Capuchins. Six years later, he approved the founding of the Society of Jesus, or Jesuits, which had been started by Ignatius Loyola, to spread Catholicism. He also called together a group known as the Council of Trent, in 1545, to decide on further Church reforms. The council enforced vows of poverty and set up Church colleges (seminaries) to educate monks, nuns, and priests. All this led to a revival of Catholic faith and active opposition to the Protestants.

However, the religious dispute in Europe grew into a political one when Philip II of Spain tried to restore Catholicism in England, France, and Holland by force. Other rulers took sides. Civil war erupted in France, and Protestant Holland revolted against Spanish domination. Eventually, the Thirty Years' War broke out in 1618.

▼ Julius II, pope from 1503 to 1513, was concerned with politics, and was a great patron of the arts. Popes after him were forced to reform the Church from within.

KEY DATES

1517	Luther's 95 Theses, announced at Wittenberg, Germany
1522	Luther's Bible is published in German
1523	Zwingli's Program of Reform established in Switzerland
1530s	Protestant social movements and revolts in Germany
1534	England separates from the Roman Church
1540s	Calvin establishes Protestant church in Geneva
1545	The first Council of Trent—the Counter-Reformation begins
1562–98	The Huguenot Wars in France
1566	Calvinist church founded in the Netherlands
1580s	Increase of tension between European rulers
1618	Outbreak of the Thirty Years' War (until 1648)

THE OTTOMAN EMPIRE 1453–1600

Following the taking of Constantinople in 1453, the Ottoman Empire soon became a force to be reckoned with in the Middle East and around the Mediterranean.

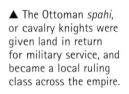

When Constantinople fell to Mehmet II in 1453, the Ottoman Empire began its golden age. The former Byzantine capital was renamed Istanbul, and became the center of an enormous empire, which at its peak, stretched from Algeria to Persia and Hungary to Arabia. The empire was founded by Osman I in 1301, and by 1389, it had extended into Europe. The Mongols halted its expansion for a while, but, after taking Constantinople, Mehmet II quickly conquered 12 kingdoms and 200 cities in Anatolia and the Balkans. Then Selim I gained Syria, Arabia, and Egypt between 1512 and 1520.

▲ The Ottoman *spahi*, or cavalry knights were given land in return for military service, and became a local ruling class across the empire.

▼ By 1566, the Ottoman Empire stretched into three continents. Süleyman had built up a strong navy and won control of the Mediterranean. He also dominated the Red Sea and Persian Gulf.

SÜLEYMAN THE MAGNIFICENT

Süleyman the Magnificent ruled for 46 years from 1520. He conquered Belgrade and Hungary, but failed in his siege of Vienna, the capital of the Holy Roman Empire. He later took Mesopotamia, Armenia, and the Caucasus region. The Ottomans gained control of the eastern Mediterranean and Black Sea (thereby dominating Venetian and Genoan trade), and also North Africa and the Ukraine.

Women in the Ottoman Empire led a secluded life. Outside their home they had to wear a veil and could only meet men from their own families.

To his own people, Süleyman was known as *Qanuni*, the Lawgiver, because he reformed the Ottoman administration and the legal system. He gave shape to the Ottoman Empire, enriching everything from architecture to courtly life. He was a poet, scholar, and patron of the arts, and he rebuilt much of Istanbul.

Europeans called him Süleyman the Magnificent because of the splendor of his court and his military victories in Europe. These included a series of campaigns in which he captured Belgrade in Yugoslavia in 1521, and threw the Crusader Knights of St. John out of Rhodes in 1522. His greatest victory was at Mohacs in Hungary in 1526; his siege of Vienna in 1529 threatened the heart of Europe; and he took the Muslim holy city of Mecca in 1538. Meanwhile, the Turkish fleet, under the pirate Barbarossa (Khayr ad-Din Pasha), attacked and ravaged the coasts of Spain, Italy, and Greece.

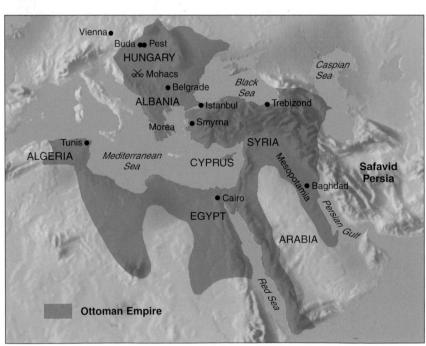

Vienna
Buda •• Pest
HUNGARY
⚔ Mohacs
• Belgrade
Black Sea
Caspian Sea
ALBANIA
• Istanbul
• Trebizond
Morea
• Smyrna
Tunis •
SYRIA
ALGERIA
Mediterranean Sea
CYPRUS
Mesopotamia
Safavid Persia
• Baghdad
• Cairo
EGYPT
Persian Gulf
ARABIA
Red Sea

Ottoman Empire

Süleyman the Magnificent (1494–1566), became sultan in 1520 and turned the Ottoman Empire into a vast and rich Sunni Muslim empire straddling three continents.

MUSLIM WARS

Süleyman waged three campaigns in the east against the Safavid Empire of Persia. This was a war between Muslims— between the Sunni Ottomans and the Shiite Persians. Süleyman took Baghdad, but the eastern border of the empire was never secure. The wars between the two empires lasted throughout the 1500s and diverted Ottoman attention so that they did not advance further into Europe.

THE START OF A SLOW DECLINE

When Süleyman died, his son Selim II became sultan. Selim led a life of leisure, while his ministers and generals ran the empire. The Ottomans themselves were not many in number. They relied on taking Russian and North African slaves, and drafting one in five boys from their European territories, to train them as administrators and soldiers. Ordinary people were left alone as long as they were obedient and paid taxes, and no one was forcibly converted to Islam. The Ottomans relied on Greeks, Armenians, Venetians, and other foreigners as traders, making the Ottoman Empire international in character. However, by 1600, the empire had begun a long, slow decline.

▲ Süleyman's greatest victory was at the battle of Mohacs in 1526 where he crushed the Hungarian army. His army overwhelmed an alliance of central European nations and killed the king of Bohemia.

▼ Süleyman's failure to capture Vienna, the capital of the Holy Roman Empire in 1529 prevented him from moving farther into Germany and central Europe. Ottoman advances halted there. The use of cannons was a fairly recent development in warfare.

KEY DATES	
1453	The Ottomans take Constantinople
c.1460	Greece, Serbia, and Bosnia taken
1512–20	Selim I takes Syria, Arabia, and Egypt
1522	Süleyman takes Rhodes from the Knights of St. John
1526	Battle of Mohacs: Hungary taken
1529	Siege of Vienna (failed)
1534	Süleyman takes Baghdad and Armenia
1538	Süleyman takes the holy city of Mecca
1540s onward	The flowering of Ottoman culture
1566	Death of Süleyman, the Ottoman Empire passes its peak

INDIA: THE MOGULS 1504–1605

The Islamic world was changing. India, a divided subcontinent, was invaded by the Moguls. They established a strong Empire in the north of India.

Babur (1483–1530), born in Turkestan, was the first Mogul emperor in India. He died in Agra.

Babur, a descendant of Genghis Khan and Tamerlane, led a tribe in Turkestan called the Moguls—the name Mogul is a variation of the word "Mongol." Driven out by the Uzbeks, they invaded Kabul in Afghanistan in 1504. Then they set their sights on India, a patchwork of often-warring Hindu and Muslim states. After an experimental attack in 1519, 12,000 Moguls swept through the Khyber Pass into India in 1526, invading the Delhi sultanate, the greatest power in India.

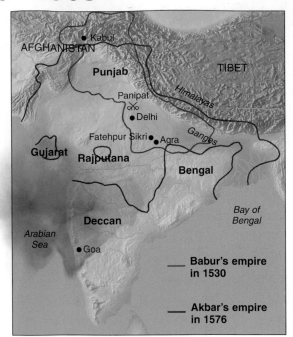

Expanding outward from Delhi, the Mogul Empire grew to cover all of northern India and much of central India. Although it was Muslim-ruled, it accommodated the many faiths and cultures of India.

Babur and his followers were Muslims. When they invaded India, the Ottoman Empire supplied them with guns and soldiers. Babur's troops also rode swift horses which easily outmaneuvered the Indians' slower elephants. This helped them defeat a much larger Indian army at a battle in which the sultan of Delhi was killed. After this victory, Babur made Delhi his capital. When Babur died in 1530, his son Humayun became ruler.

◀ Painted by a Persian, this picture shows Babur (left), his ancestor Tamerlane, and Babur's son Humayun (right).

▲ Babur had a full-scale account of India written. It details the nature, people, and customs of his empire.

Humayun invaded western India, but in 1540, the Surs chased out the Moguls, forcing them back into Persia. Humayun returned in 1555, overcame the Surs, and moved back to Delhi. A year later, before he was able to win back the whole empire, Humayun was killed in an accident.

AKBAR EXPANDS THE EMPIRE

Humayun's succesor was Babur's grandson, Akbar. He became emperor at the age of 13 and ruled until his death in 1605. Akbar was a great military leader and wise ruler. His army pushed west into Gujarat and east into Bengal—the richest province in northern India. It produced rice and silk, which provided Akbar with his main source of income. By 1576, Akbar controlled all of northern India.

Although Akbar was a Muslim, many of his subjects were Hindus, and to keep the peace, he married a Hindu princess. He believed in religious tolerance, bringing the Hindus into the government and encouraging their overseas trade. He set up a well-organized empire with professional administrators.

MOGUL GREATNESS

During this period, India traded profitably with Africa, the Ottomans, Europe, and the Far East. By this time, the Portuguese had trading posts and ports in India. The country also had the world's largest textile industry. Akbar welcomed Christian Jesuits and Persian artists to his court, and he tried unsuccessfully to create a new religion for India. He built schools for children as well as a new capital city at Fatehpur Sikri. The city combined Muslim and Hindu styles of architecture.

KEY DATES	
1504	The Moguls seize Kabul
1526	Delhi becomes the Mogul capital in India
1556	Akbar the Great, the greatest Mogul emperor, begins reign
1571	Fatehpur Sikri becomes the new capital
1605	Jahangir becomes Mogul emperor (Nur Jahan rules 1611-22)
1628	Shah Jahan, Mogul emperor
1658	Aurangzeb, the last great Mogul emperor
1707	Beginning of the decline of the Moguls
1803	The fall of the last Mogul stronghold to the English

AKBAR, THE THIRD MOGUL EMPEROR

Akbar inherited the Mogul Empire at the age of 13, and he ruled for nearly 50 years. He invaded Rajasthan, Gujarat, Bengal, Kashmir, and the Deccan to rule most of India. He taxed farming peasants less, encouraged traders, and introduced a very efficient government and military service. This served later Mogul emperors and their people well. Though Akbar could not read, he welcomed scholars of all religions, artists, and foreign travelers to his court. His greatest success was in making peace with the Hindu majority of the Indian population, ending many Hindu–Muslim conflicts.

Akbar (1542–1605) believed in religious toleration. His own beliefs included ideas from different religions. In 1575, he set up a center for the study of religion through the exchange of ideas. Akbar found, however, that the scholars were not as broad-minded as he had hoped—each one argued without really listening to anyone else's point of view.

◀ Although some local rulers rebelled against Akbar's rule, they were soon defeated. Here, the rebel Bahadur Khan is shown yielding to Akbar.

▼ At Fatehpur Sikri, Akbar built a capital city with a mixture of Muslim, Hindu, and other architectural styles as the center for his new religion. He was buried in this tomb.

THE CONQUISTADORES 1519–1550

The Spanish conquistadores were soldiers and adventurers who invaded the Americas. In doing so, they destroyed the great Aztec and Inca civilizations.

Hernán Cortés (1485–1547) returned to Spain where he died in poverty.

Francisco Pizarro (c.1475–1541) marched on the Incas in 1532. He was murdered in Lima.

Soon after the navigators had found the Americas, Spanish adventurers, known as *conquistadores* (conquerors), followed them. After conquering many Caribbean islands, they explored the American mainland, hoping to find treasure. In 1519, about 500 Spanish soldiers, led by Hernán Cortés, reached the Aztec city of Tenochtitlan, where, at first, they were welcomed. It is thought that the Aztec emperor, Montezuma II, believed that Cortés was the god Quetzalcóatl, whose return he had been awaiting. The Spanish tricked and captured Montezuma, and Cortés ruled in his place. When Cortés left, the Aztecs rebelled and defeated the remaining Spanish. With the help of an interpreter, Cortés then won the support of the neighboring tribes who had been conquered by the Aztecs. In 1521, he returned to Tenochtitlan with a native army and destroyed the city.

At first Montezuma welcomed Cortés to Tenochtitlan, showering him with gifts. This goodwill died when the Spanish seized power. Most of the Aztecs soon died of diseases brought by the foreigners.

THE END OF THE INCA EMPIRE

Another conquistador, Francisco Pizarro, landed in Peru in 1532, seeking to conquer the Incas. An Inca civil war was already in progress between Huascar and Atahualpa, the sons of Huayna Capac. Atahualpa killed Huascar with the help of the Spanish, but Pizarro then had Atahualpa executed. The Incas soon surrendered, and by 1533 their vast empire was in Spanish hands.

THE CAPTURE OF ATAHUALPA

In 1532, Pizarro, with only 159 men against a large Inca army, kidnapped the Inca leader, Atahualpa. He was a god to the Incas, which, to them, made Pizarro more powerful than the gods. The Incas soon yielded, and Atahualpa was executed. Like the Aztecs, the Incas were tricked into submission, and a whole civilization died.

THE SPANISH EMPIRE 1533–1600

Spain's occupation of large areas of the Americas brought harsh conditions and disease to the Native Americans. By 1600, Spain had the largest empire.

After the fall of the Aztecs and Incas, the king of Spain added their territories to his empire. The Aztec Empire became the Viceroyalty of New Spain in 1533. Later in the 1500s, it also included parts of California, Arizona, and New Mexico. The land of the Incas became the Viceroyalty of Peru. Many people from Spain emigrated to live in this new Spanish Empire. The colonies were ruled by the Council of the Indies, based in Spain. Many of the laws made for the colonies show that the Spanish government tried to make sure that the Native Americans were not badly treated. But it was impossible to prevent the colonial Spaniards from treating them cruelly. Native Americans were forced to mine silver and work as slaves. Millions died because they had no resistance to European diseases such as measles and smallpox. The colonists were followed by Spanish missionaries, who destroyed temples and idols and set up churches in their place, trying to convert the Native Americans.

The conquistadores were followed by missionaries, who tried to convert the Native Americans— by force, if necessary. They destroyed their temples and made the people build churches in their place.

The Spanish forced the Native Americans to mine gold and silver, which was then sent back to Spain. The harsh conditions and new diseases brought by the Spanish decimated the population of Mexico, which fell from 25 million in 1500 to just one million in 1600.

The Spanish Empire continued to expand under the reign of Philip II (1556–1598). Most of the Philippine Islands were conquered in 1571. Then, in 1578, King Sebastian of Portugal was killed in Morocco. Philip was his closest relative, so he inherited the Portuguese Empire. By 1600, the Spanish had the world's largest empire, but they were losing power. Philip's opposition to the Protestants in Europe led to expensive wars that used up the gold and silver from the Americas.

▲ The Spanish took new foods, such as pineapples, tomatoes, potatoes, cocoa, peppers, and sunflowers back to Europe.

► The Spanish Empire was large and yielded vast wealth, especially from gold and silver mined in Mexico and Peru.

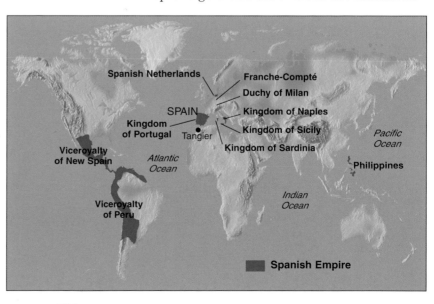

Spanish Netherlands
Franche-Compté
Duchy of Milan
SPAIN
Kingdom of Portugal
Tangier
Kingdom of Naples
Kingdom of Sicily
Kingdom of Sardinia
Viceroyalty of New Spain
Atlantic Ocean
Pacific Ocean
Philippines
Indian Ocean
Viceroyalty of Peru
Spanish Empire

221

THE HAPSBURGS 1273–1556

The Hapsburg family came from Habichtsburg in Switzerland. They dominated European politics for more than 600 years, from the 1200s until 1914.

Charles V (1500–1558) became king of Spain in 1516 and Holy Roman emperor in 1519. In 1553, he gave the imperial crown to his brother, and two years later gave his kingdoms (Spain, the Netherlands, the Americas) to his son Philip.

▼ After Charles V's death, the Austrian Hapsburgs ruled the Holy Roman Empire. The Spanish Hapsburgs ruled Spain, the Netherlands, parts of Italy, and Latin America.

The Hapsburg family took its name from their castle in Switzerland—Habichtsburg, or "Hawk's Castle." By 1200, the Hapsburg lands were in Austria. After 1438, the Holy Roman emperor was almost always a Hapsburg. In the late 1400s, Maximilian I (1459–1519) expanded Hapsburg influence by advantageous marriages. His son, Philip of Burgundy (1478–1506), married Joanna the Mad, a daughter of Ferdinand and Isabella of Spain. Their son, Charles V, was to be the most powerful Hapsburg of all.

When Philip died in 1506, Charles inherited Burgundy and the Netherlands. In 1516, Ferdinand of Spain left him Spain and Naples, and in 1519 he inherited the Holy Roman Empire from Maximilian. This led to rivalry with Francis I of France, and their countries were at war for most of Charles's reign. A devout Catholic, Charles did not like the spread of Protestantism. He called two diets, or assemblies, to reconcile the differences with the Lutherans, but both failed. In 1546, he took up arms against some of them—the League of Schmalkalden.

Rudolf I (1218–1291) was elected king of Germany in 1273, and became the first Hapsburg Holy Roman emperor, although never officially crowned. The title, Holy Roman emperor, remained in the Hapsburg family until 1806.

Charles defeated the League in 1547, but later had to agree to their demands. By 1556, he had spent much of Spain's wealth fruitlessly, and was exhausted by war. He retired to a monastery, after dividing his lands between his son Philip (who gained Spain, the Netherlands, and the American colonies) and his brother, Ferdinand (who gained Austria and the Holy Roman crown).

The double-headed eagle was the emblem of the Holy Roman Empire. The power of the emperors decreased in the 1500s, as some of the German states became more powerful.

DENMARK

NETHERLANDS

FRANCE

Burgundy

GERMANY

SWITZERLAND

AUSTRIA

HUNGARY

Navarre

PORTUGAL

Aragon

FLORENCE

PAPAL STATES

SPAIN

Castile

Kingdom of Sardinia

NAPLES

Ottoman Empire

SICILY

TUNIS

———— Extent of Holy Roman Empire

▓ Hapsburg lands

KEY DATES

1020	Habichtsburg, the family home, is built
1459–1519	Maximilian I expands Hapsburg influence
1506	Charles V inherits Burgundy and the Netherlands
1516	Charles V inherits Spain and Naples
1519–56	Charles V, Holy Roman emperor
1546	War between the Hapsburgs and the Protestants
1618–48	Thirty Years' War between the Catholics and the Protestants

THE SPANISH ARMADA 1588

The Armada was sent by Europe's most powerful country to invade an increasingly ambitious England. Its failure led to 300 years of English rule on the seas.

Francis Drake (1543–1596) was a pirate and adventurer. After raiding gold from Spanish galleons in the Caribbean, he was made first a captain and later an admiral, and helped defeat the Spanish Armada. In 1580, he was the first Englishman to sail around the world—on his ship, the *Golden Hind*.

Philip II ruled Spain and its empire from 1556 to 1598. His strong Catholic beliefs provoked revolts in Holland and Spain, led to war with the Ottomans and England, and sucked Spain into the French Wars of Religion. His absolute rule and military activities left Spain economically ruined, despite the gold and silver Spain received from the Americas. Spain did not like England. Elizabeth I had turned down Philip II's marriage proposal. British pirates often raided Spanish colonies and fleets. Worst of all, England was Protestant.

In 1588, Philip sent the Armada from Lisbon to attack England. Its 130 galleons carried 8,000 sailors and 19,000 soldiers. Delayed by storms, the Armada was sighted and harassed by the English as far as Calais, where it was due to meet

It was important for Elizabeth I to defeat the Armada. She did not like her brother-in-law Philip II, and she had ambitions for England, helped by England's victory.

another Spanish fleet that did not arrive.

During the night, the English caused havoc by sending in fireships, and then pounding the escaping ships with gunfire. A strong wind blew the remaining ships into the North Sea. The Armada sailed around Scotland, and only half of the ships finally returned to Spain. This was an enormous setback for the Spanish.

▲ Philip II (1527–1598) ruled Spain from 1556 until his death. He believed that he had a mission to win worldwide power for Spain and the Roman Catholic Church. He married Mary Tudor (Mary I) of England.

▶ Philip II sent his Armada against England in August 1588. The Spanish had larger ships, but the English ships were faster and more maneuverable. The defeat of the Armada meant the end of Spain as a great naval power.

FRENCH WARS OF RELIGION 1562–1600

The spread of the Protestant faith led to problems in some parts of Europe—nowhere more so than in France, which suffered from 36 years of bloody civil wars.

In 1598, Henry IV of France signed the Edict of Nantes, granting the Huguenots freedom of worship and a place in French society. This ended the French Wars of Religion.

Catherine de Médicis (1519–1589) was the daughter of Lorenzo de' Medici and wife of Henry II of France. She ruled France as regent for her young son Charles IX.

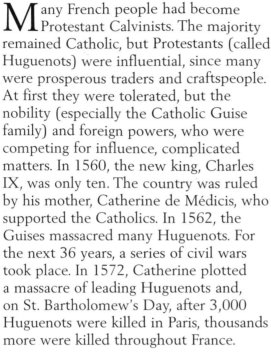

Many French people had become Protestant Calvinists. The majority remained Catholic, but Protestants (called Huguenots) were influential, since many were prosperous traders and craftspeople. At first they were tolerated, but the nobility (especially the Catholic Guise family) and foreign powers, who were competing for influence, complicated matters. In 1560, the new king, Charles IX, was only ten. The country was ruled by his mother, Catherine de Médicis, who supported the Catholics. In 1562, the Guises massacred many Huguenots. For the next 36 years, a series of civil wars took place. In 1572, Catherine plotted a massacre of leading Huguenots and, on St. Bartholomew's Day, after 3,000 Huguenots were killed in Paris, thousands more were killed throughout France.

◀ Henry of Navarre, a Protestant, married into the royal Valois family, but he was imprisoned by the Catholics. He eventually became Henry IV and ruled from 1589 to 1610.

Moderate people were horrified at this bloody massacre, and conflict now grew between extremists and moderates as well as between Catholics and Huguenots. In 1574, Henry III (1551–1589), another of Catherine de Médicis' sons, became king. He was also influenced by his mother, and civil war continued. In 1576, Henry made a settlement between all sides. This was known as the Edict of Beaulieu, but it failed to stop the turmoil.

In 1572, Henry of Guise persuaded Catherine de Médicis to allow the murder of a Huguenot admiral. In the events that followed, many thousands more were killed.

THE WAR OF THE THREE HENRYS

In the same year as the Edict of Beaulieu, an extremist Catholic group, led by Henry of Guise, was formed to oppose the settlement, and the religious difficulties increased. The Catholics, allied with Spain and other Catholic countries, tried to block the Huguenot Henry of Navarre from inheriting the throne. This led to the War of the Three Henrys, involving King Henry III, the Huguenot Henry of Navarre, and the Catholic Henry of Guise. Henry III lost control, and war broke out. Henry of Guise tried to take the throne and, in 1585, he banned the Protestant religion. In 1589, Henry III had Henry of Guise murdered. However, Henry III was then assassinated by a fanatical monk.

Henry of Navarre became King Henry IV of France, and to calm things, he decided to convert to Catholicism in 1593. The Huguenot Wars finally ended in 1598 with the Edict of Nantes, which allowed religious freedom and equality to all. There was to be more trouble in the 1600s, however, and by the 1680s, many Huguenots had left France for their own safety.

▲ In France and the rest of Europe, it was common for Protestants to be accused of heresy. The punishment for this crime was usually to be burned alive at the stake. The soul of the heretic was supposed to burn and be sent down to hell.

◀ Many Huguenots were skilled traders, craftspeople, and educated townspeople. It was important for France to keep them, since they ran many industries and professions. After 1685, many of them left France for other countries or the colonies, taking their skills and wealth with them.

KEY DATES

1533	Catherine de Médicis marries Henry II of France
1559	Henry II dies and is succeeded by his son Francis II who dies after a year; Catherine de Médicis is regent
1560	Charles IX becomes king, at the age of 10; Catherine again acts as regent
1562	The Massacre of Vassy marks the beginning of the Huguenot Wars
1570	Peace and limited rights are agreed for the Huguenots
1572	The Massacre of St. Bartholomew's Day
1574	The moderate Henry III becomes king
1576	Edict of Beaulieu—a pact that imposes tolerance of the Huguenots
1585–89	War of the Three Henrys
1589	Henry of Navarre becomes king of France
1593	Henry of Navarre (Henry IV) converts to Catholicism
1598	The Edict of Nantes grants religious freedom and equality to all

RUSSIA 1462–1613

During this period, Russia grew from a collection of small principalities into a great country. Its isolation ended, allowing it to play a major role in history.

Ivan III (1440-1505) was the first ruler of all Russia. He made Moscow his capital. By the time he died from alcoholism, he had set Russia on a new course.

▲ Ivan III adopted the Byzantine symbol of the double-headed eagle as his own emblem—both Byzantium and Russia looked east and west.

After the decline of Kiev around 1060, Russia survived as an assortment of separate small principalities such as Novgorod, Smolensk, Kiev, and Vladimir. This suddenly changed when the Mongols, under Batu Khan, invaded in 1238. They burned Moscow and damaged Kiev. The Khanate of the Golden Horde (or Tartars) dominated Russia by demanding tribute in money and soldiers, and the Russians cooperated to avoid trouble. (In the 1300s, Kiev was absorbed into Lithuania for a time.)

In 1263, Moscow had a new ruler, Prince Daniel, who gradually expanded its territories. Slowly, Moscow began to dominate the other Russian states. In 1380, the Muscovites defeated the Golden Horde, although the Tartars carried on raiding Moscow and demanding tribute until 1480, when Ivan III finally defeated them. Ivan III, or Ivan the Great, came to the throne of Moscow in 1462. He expanded Moscow and gave it a sense of pride, introduced a legal code, and declared himself "ruler of all Russia." In 1472, he married Sophia, the niece of the last Byzantine emperor, and appointed himself as the protector of the Eastern Orthodox Church, calling Moscow "the third Rome."

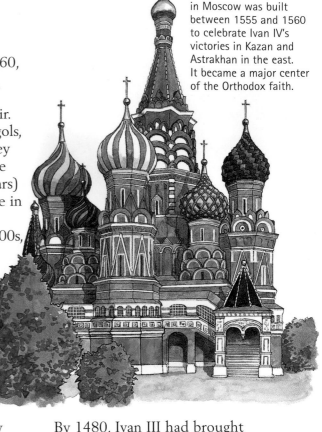

St. Basil's Cathedral in Moscow was built between 1555 and 1560 to celebrate Ivan IV's victories in Kazan and Astrakhan in the east. It became a major center of the Orthodox faith.

By 1480, Ivan III had brought Novgorod and other cities under his control. He rebuilt Moscow's famous *Kremlin* (citadel). When he died in 1505, he was succeeded by his son Vasili III, who ruled until 1533. Vasili III was succeeded in turn by Ivan IV, his three-year-old son.

▼ The boyars of Russia had been independent until Ivan the Terrible brought them under his control. They then joined the growing trade with the West in fur, timber, and other raw materials.

IVAN THE TERRIBLE

Ivan IV, or "Ivan the Terrible," was the Grand Prince of Moscow from 1533 to 1584. He was crowned as the first *czar* (emperor) in 1547. His harsh upbringing left him with a violent and unpredictable character, but his nickname meant "awe-inspiring" rather than "terrible." He improved the legal system as well as reforming trading links with England and other European countries—Russia had until then been isolated. He captured Kazan and Astrakhan from the Tartars, pushing on toward Siberia. Ivan reduced the power of the boyars (the nobility) by instituting a kind of secret police, to bring the country under stronger control. He set many patterns for the future, and established strong central control by the czars. In 1581, in a fit of anger, he killed his son and heir Ivan, and so was succeeded by his second son, Fyodor, who was mentally unstable.

THE ROMANOV CZARS

After Ivan IV died in 1584, Boris Godunov ruled as regent until Fyodor died in 1598. Boris made himself czar, despite opposition from the boyars. He promoted foreign trade and defeated the Swedes, who sought to invade Russia. When he died in 1605, Russia entered eight years of civil war, as rival forces fought for the throne. Eventually, Ivan IV's great-nephew Mikhail Romanov (1596–1645) gained the throne in 1613. He was czar for thirty years, founding the Romanov dynasty, which ruled until 1917.

▲ The Kremlin was the center of Moscow. It was actually a fort and many palaces, churches, and cathedrals were rebuilt within the protection of its walls by Ivan III. It became the symbol of the centralized power of the czars.

◄ Ivan the Terrible visited the seat of the patriarch of the Russian Orthodox Church at Zagorsk, in order to have himself anointed and confirmed as the head of the Orthodox Church.

Ivan IV (1530-1584) was a strong ruler who truly set the course of Russia's expansion. Known as the Ivan the Terrible, he had a formidable personality.

KEY DATES

1238	Invasion of Russia by the Mongols
1263	Moscow begins to grow larger
1462–1505	Ivan III, the Great, strengthens Moscow
1472	Ivan III appoints himself protector of the Eastern Orthodox Church
1480	End of Tartar dominance of Russia
1505–33	Vasili III is ruler
1533–84	Ivan IV, the Terrible, expands Russia
1584–98	Fyodor is czar and Boris Godunov regent
1598–1605	Boris Godunov rules as czar
1605–13	Civil war between rival boyars
1613	Mikhail Romanov, first of the Romanovs, becomes czar

DUTCH INDEPENDENCE 1477–1648

The Netherlands was a fast-developing Protestant area with a promising future, but ruled by Catholic Spain. The Dutch wanted to control their own affairs.

William of Orange (1533–1584)—"the Silent"—became Spanish governor of part of the Netherlands in 1559. He disagreed with Philip II's treatment of the Protestants and turned against Spain. He led the Dutch Revolt from 1567 to 1572, and in 1573 became a Calvinist. Philip offered a reward for his death. In 1584, having escaped one assassination attempt, he was killed by a fanatical Catholic, Balthasar Gérards.

After the collapse of Charlemagne's empire in the 800s, the Netherlands, made up of 17 provinces in what is now Belgium, Luxembourg, and the Netherlands, were very fragmented since they belonged to various ruling families. In the 1300s and 1400s, the dukes of Burgundy, Philip the Bold and John the Fearless, acquired Flanders (Belgium) and the Netherlands. These lands stayed under Burgundy's control until Charles V, inheritor of Burgundian lands and a member of the Hapsburg dynasty, made them a Spanish possession in 1516. This did not suit the people of the Netherlands, since most of them were Protestant. The fight for independence started when Charles's son Philip II became king of Spain in 1556. He resisted the Protestant tide and tried to take complete control. He sent the Duke of Alba as governor to the Netherlands with orders to use terror, if necessary, to crush any opposition.

The Duke of Alba executed two leaders of the independence

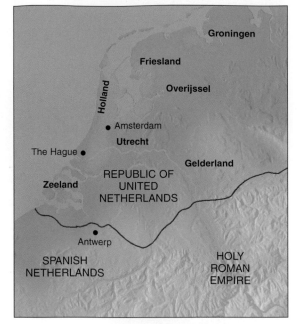

The United Provinces grew richer as the marshy land was drained and developed. As a Protestant country with growing trade and industry, independence from Spain, an old-fashioned imperial power, became necessary.

movement, and this resulted in the Dutch Revolts—led by William of Orange. The more ruthless the Duke of Alba became, the more the opposition grew. There were public executions, towns were pillaged, and whole populations were massacred. The Dutch used many guerrilla tactics, such as the flooding of the lowlands, to halt the Spanish advance. In 1576, Spanish troops sacked Antwerp, one of Europe's richest ports, and ended its prosperity.

▲ A cartoon of the time shows the aristocratic Duke of Alba trying to stamp out heresy in the Netherlands by trampling on the bodies of executed Protestants.

▶ During the siege of Louvain in 1571, the heroic Dutch successfully used every possible means to overcome the superior armed might of the Spanish.

STRUGGLE AND INDEPENDENCE

Many merchants and bankers moved to
Amsterdam, rebuilding it into a fine city
defended by canals and a growing navy.
They developed modern trade, banking,
and industry, becoming one of Europe's
main Protestant centers. Spain brought
the Catholic southern provinces (Belgium)
back under its control, but in 1581, seven
Protestant northern provinces declared
themselves independent. Fortunately for
them, Spain was busy fighting France,
England, and the Ottomans, and so
was unable to stop the Dutch.

This struggle for independence was a
religious war and a fight between modern
Dutch town-dwelling burghers and the
traditional Spanish royal hierarchy. Led by
William of Orange, the Dutch declared
the Republic of the United Netherlands.
A truce followed in 1609, but it was not
until 1648 that Spain officially recognized
Dutch independence.

▶ The plundering of the rich city of Antwerp by the
Spanish in 1576 was the last straw for the Dutch. From
then on, they were determined to get rid of the Spanish.

KEY DATES	
1477	The Netherlands become a Hapsburg possession
1516	The Spanish take control of the Netherlands
1568	The Dutch Revolt begins
1576	The sack of Antwerp—a turning point
1581	The Northern Provinces declare independence
1609	Truce—the Dutch effectively win the war
1648	Dutch independence fully recognized

▲ Battle is joined on
the Zuider Zee, east of
Amsterdam, between the
naval might of Spain and
the small boats of the
Dutch in 1573. As with
the Armada, the smaller
boats outmaneuvered
the Spanish vessels and
sank many of them.

NORTH AMERICA 1460–1600

North America was a land of many different peoples, each with their own traditions, way of life, and culture. The arrival of the Europeans was disastrous for them.

The tribes of the Iroquois wore masks during important tribal ceremonies. The masks represented the spirits of mythological creatures.

▲ The French explorer Jacques Cartier (1491–1557) sailed up the St. Lawrence River in what is now Canada, and claimed the area for France. One of his men drew this map of the Huron town of Hochelaga— now the city of Montreal.

▶ The Miami tribe of Ohio made clothing from hides and furs. Skins were cleaned and stretched, then cut and sewn into garments and moccasins. Women did most of the domestic work and crop-growing, but they also held power in tribal decision-making.

When the Europeans first arrived in America in the 1500s, there were millions of Native Americans, in hundreds of tribes and many nations. They did not believe that they owned the land but thought that it was held in common for the entire tribe. Each tribe had its own customs, language, and way of life, according to where it lived. For example, on the Plains where wild animals such as buffalo were plentiful, the Cheyenne and Pawnee lived a nomadic lifestyle, hunting and trapping. Hunters on the Plains sometimes camouflaged themselves in animal skins when they went in search of prey. The animals they caught provided them with meat, and also with skins for clothing and shelters. Tribes who lived on the coast or by lakes made wooden canoes and fished for their food. Other tribes were village-dwelling farmers, who grew crops, herded animals, and hunted and fished.

Some Native Americans built totems to the spirits of nature, often with an eagle at the top to represent the farseeing powers of Great Spirit.

In the Southwest, people living in villages, called *pueblos*, grew crops of corn, squash, and beans by building dams to irrigate the dry land. They had roads, complex societies with strong religious traditions, and they traded with the Aztecs and other native peoples.

Along the Mississippi River, an advanced city civilization had thrived, although it was in decline from 1450 onward. The Mississippians supplied Native American tribes with tools, cloth, valuables, and goods brought from far away.

People on the east coast lived by farming corn, beans, and tobacco in plots around their villages, and they engaged in local trade and barter. In the Northeast, Native American fields and clearings reminded European settlers of home—with the result that the region gained the name "New England." Many tribes were part of confederations or nations related by blood, tradition, or political agreements. Sometimes disagreements between tribes led to war.

The people of the northeastern woodlands made decorated moccasins and ceremonial pipes which were used to celebrate special occasions.

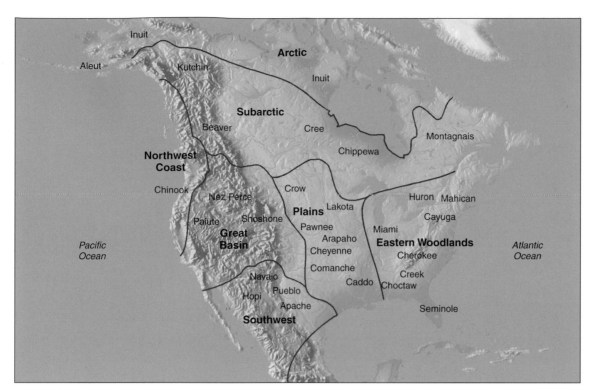

Inuit
Aleut
Kutchin
Arctic
Subarctic
Inuit
Beaver
Cree
Montagnais
Chippewa
Northwest Coast
Crow
Chinook
Nez Perce
Huron Mahican
Lakota
Cayuga
Plains
Paiute
Shoshone
Pawnee
Miami
Great Basin
Arapaho
Cheyenne
Eastern Woodlands
Cherokee
Pacific Ocean
Atlantic Ocean
Comanche
Navajo
Caddo
Creek
Hopi
Pueblo
Choctaw
Apache
Southwest
Seminole

The American tribes were very diverse. The map shows where the main tribes of Native Americans lived in 1500, before Europeans arrived and started driving them off their lands. At this time there were about six million Native North Americans. These numbers fell drastically as the colonists spread west across the continent.

▼ The Chippewa lived in wigwams made of bent branches and covered with an outer layer of skins or birchbark to fend off the winter cold.

THE ARRIVAL OF THE EUROPEANS

Like the Aztecs and the Incas, none of the Native American tribes had horses or wheeled transportation before the Europeans arrived. Their knowledge of metal was limited, and most of their tools were made from wood or stone. Their weapons were bows and arrows, slingshots, and spears. At first, some tribes were friendly to the Europeans, and even helped them survive. But things changed disastrously for the native peoples when more aggressive European settlers arrived. Whole villages of Native Americans died from European diseases such as smallpox and the measles. Others were killed in disputes, and the rest were driven off their lands.

▶ The nomadic Plains Indians lived in *tepees*. In the evenings, stories were told, both to entertain and to pass on the history, customs, laws, and ways of the tribe. They also held tribal councils to settle disputes and decide the tribe's future.

JAPAN AND CHINA 1467–1644

After first welcoming the Europeans, the Japanese began to see dangers in foreign influence. Meanwhile, in China, the Ming dynasty was losing control.

In 1467, civil war broke out among the great feudal lords of Japan. The emperor had lost most of his power, and even the shogun had very little influence over the running of the country. For more than 100 years, private armies of samurai fought each other in the struggle to dominate Japan. During these civil wars, Europeans began to visit the country. The first to arrive were Portuguese sailors, in 1542. Seven years later, a Spanish Jesuit missionary, Francis Xavier, began trying to convert the Japanese to Christianity. Other traders and missionaries followed and were welcomed at first.

As well as introducing a new religion to Japan, the Europeans also brought firearms with them. Some samurai looked down on these, believing they were the weapons of cowards, but others quickly saw their advantages in battle. One samurai, Oda Nobunaga (1534–1582), equipped his men with muskets (guns) and with their help, captured Kyoto, the capital, in 1568.

Jesuit missionaries entered China in the 1500s with the emperor's permission. They converted tens of thousands to Christianity.

Hideyoshi (1536–1598) broke the traditional power of the feudal lords and the Buddhist temples, but his plans to build a Japanese Empire failed.

STRUGGLE AND CIVIL WAR

Nobunaga was wounded and later committed suicide, but his work was continued by Hideyoshi, who became Kampaku, or chief imperial minister, in 1585. He planned a great Japanese Empire that would include China. Hideyoshi invaded Korea in 1592 and 1597, but failed to conquer it. He died in Korea. Hideyoshi had appointed Tokugawa Ieyasu (1543–1616) as his son's guardian, but a power struggle broke out. Ieyasu defeated his rivals at the battle of Sekigahara in 1600. He became the first shogun of the Tokugawa dynasty in 1603. Hideyoshi and Ieyasu took strong central control of Japan and its trading, banning foreigners, Christianity, and overseas travel.

BATTLE OF NAGASHINO

At the battle of Nagashino in 1575, Oda Nobunaga armed his 3,000 men with muskets bought from the Portuguese. They defeated a much larger force of mounted samurai, who were armed with the traditional weapons of swords and bows and arrows. This was a turning point in Japan—the beginning of modern times in which European influences played a part. The Japanese tried to control these influences, banning Christians and foreign traders. But the Europeans sided with certain lords in southern Japan, and European goods and ideas crept in.

MING CHINA

By 1500, the Ming dynasty was weakening. The emperor stopped Chinese ships from sailing beyond coastal waters, but allowed foreign ships to visit China. Japanese pirates were also attacking the coast, making these waters dangerous for sailors. In 1517, European traders arrived, and in 1557, the Portuguese were permitted to settle in Macao. Some Jesuit priests were allowed into Beijing.

Defeating Mongol invasions and the Japanese invasion of Korea destabilized China. Famines, rising taxes, and official corruption led to unrest. In 1641, rebels took over parts of China, and in 1644, the Manchus from the north were called in to help drive out the rebels in Beijing. The Manchus, taking advantage of this chaos, took over and set up their own Qing dynasty of emperors.

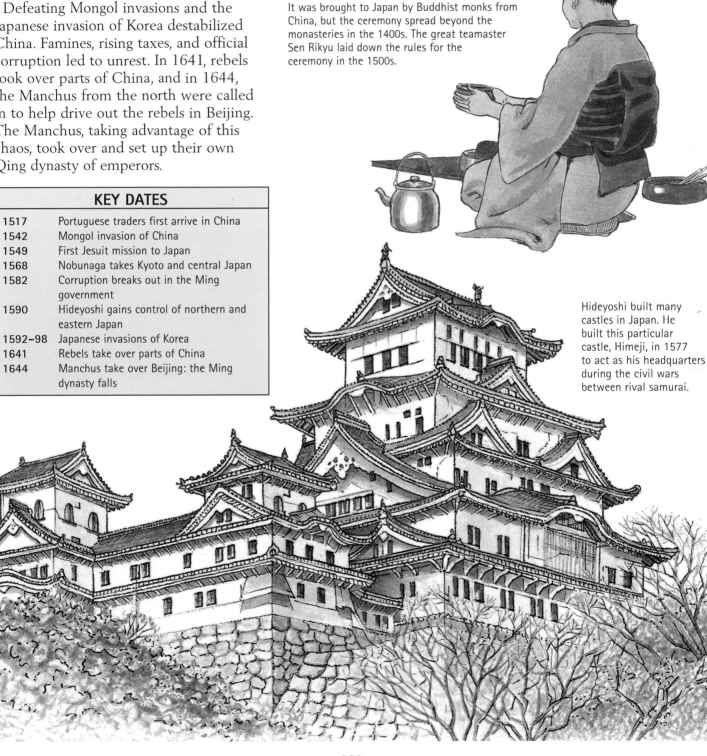

◄ To protect themselves from Japanese pirates, the Chinese developed floating mines (water bombs). This idea eventually reached the West.

► The Japanese Tea Ceremony is called *cha-no-yu*. It was brought to Japan by Buddhist monks from China, but the ceremony spread beyond the monasteries in the 1400s. The great teamaster Sen Rikyu laid down the rules for the ceremony in the 1500s.

KEY DATES

1517	Portuguese traders first arrive in China
1542	Mongol invasion of China
1549	First Jesuit mission to Japan
1568	Nobunaga takes Kyoto and central Japan
1582	Corruption breaks out in the Ming government
1590	Hideyoshi gains control of northern and eastern Japan
1592–98	Japanese invasions of Korea
1641	Rebels take over parts of China
1644	Manchus take over Beijing: the Ming dynasty falls

Hideyoshi built many castles in Japan. He built this particular castle, Himeji, in 1577 to act as his headquarters during the civil wars between rival samurai.

233

THE ARTS 1461–1600

In Europe, the Renaissance heavily influenced painting, sculpture, and architecture. Art also flourished in the Ottoman, Safavid, and Mogul empires.

Though they had their roots firmly in tradition, the arts were now evolving with an exciting new imagination and increasing vigor. In Europe especially, Renaissance thinking strongly influenced all the arts—painting, sculpture, theater, music, and architecture, as well as education and religion, all flourished. Artists such as Titian, Holbein, Raphael, Dürer, Leonardo da Vinci, Brueghel, Botticelli, and Michelangelo were all at work, developing new, more realistic representations. In Britain, there was a flowering in literature and drama—especially as a result of the works of the playwright William Shakespeare.

The arts were becoming more public and popular, and not simply the domain of king and Church. The new middle classes—traders and professionals—paid for most of it, and it became fashionable to be a patron of the arts.

In Europe, organs and harpsichords were popular instruments. An organ was played by one person, while another operated the bellows supplying the air needed to play it.

Though the Incas did not have potter's wheels, they made detailed and beautiful pottery from coils of clay fashioned into elegantly decorated shapes.

◄ In Persia, new styles developed showing natural motifs, such as these flowers on a tile on a wall in the Masjid-i Jomeh Mosque in Yazd, Persia.

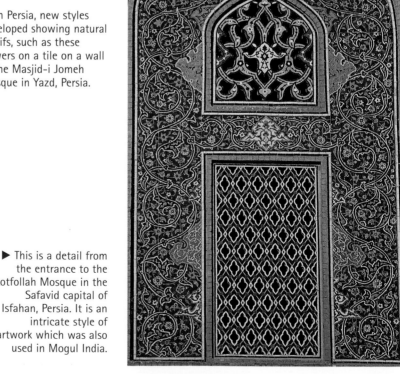

► This is a detail from the entrance to the Lotfollah Mosque in the Safavid capital of Isfahan, Persia. It is an intricate style of artwork which was also used in Mogul India.

In the Americas, the Aztecs and the Incas created new styles of ornaments in gold and silver, although they did not know how to make metal tools. They also developed new forms of architecture in the building of their cities. In Eurasia, the Ottoman Turks brought Islamic and European styles closer together, drawing on creative people from Spain, Italy, and Egypt to develop a new architecture and literature. Russia, a new country, combined Byzantine, European, and Tartar styles in its churches and buildings.

The arts were also flourishing in Safavid Persia and Mogul India, combining and developing Persian, Muslim, and Hindu styles. However, in China and Japan there was less innovation because of the growing isolationism of their leaders. In Africa, earlier civilizations were starting to lose their momentum as they came face to face with European colonists.

▲ Realism was important to Renaissance Europeans. Michelangelo's statue of Moses, carved around 1513, clearly showed the muscles and veins in arms and legs.

The work of the 16th-century Italian artist Tintoretto demonstrates the new realistic style of the Renaissance. However, the theme of the painting, St. George slaying the Dragon, is traditionally religious.

The Globe Theater, where Shakespeare's political and social plays were performed, was built in London in 1599.

Iznik pottery from the Ottoman Empire was made according to Persian styles, but also depicted European themes.

ARCHITECTURE 1461–1600

Building design was developing worldwide, and the most exciting advances were in Renaissance Europe, where new architectural styles were emerging.

During the Renaissance period the Europeans started overtaking the previously more advanced cultures of China, India, and the Muslim world. This was true not only in architecture, but also in the arts, and science and technology. In Europe, the nobility and the rich started building themselves comfortable palaces and stately homes, instead of the fortified castles of the Middle Ages. Townhouse design was also developing. The improved technology of glass-making meant windows could be larger. In England, some large buildings such as Hampton Court were built with handmade bricks, while others were still made largely of wood. This was a fire hazard in towns, where narrow streets allowed flames to spread quickly from building to building. Waste and sewage disposal was not yet developed.

Inside the houses, furniture was made from wood and was often ornately carved. Walls were paneled with wood, and ceilings were decorated with plaster. Formal gardens were first laid out at this time. Especially popular were herb gardens, which provided flavorings for food and cures for ailments.

English and Dutch townhouses in the 1500s were being built up to five stories high. Windows had many small panes of glass, and woodwork was often elaborately carved. In Amsterdam, many of these houses still survive.

Hampton Court Palace is a classic English Tudor building. It was built by Cardinal Wolsey and given to Henry VIII. The fortified appearance represented past medieval styles rather than a need for defense.

Across the world, many new buildings were larger and grander. Italian cathedrals, Japanese castles, Mogul buildings in India, Ottoman architecture in Istanbul, and Persian buildings in Isfahan reached new heights of elegance. New capital cities were planned, and thousands of builders and craftspeople were employed to build them. However, at the same time, the vast majority of people still lived in the simplest of dwellings.

Mortise   Dovetail
and tenon

▲ The strength of a timber-framed building was in the joints between the timbers. If these were made correctly, the building would hold together even if it was pushed over. The most used joints were mortise and tenon, and dovetail.

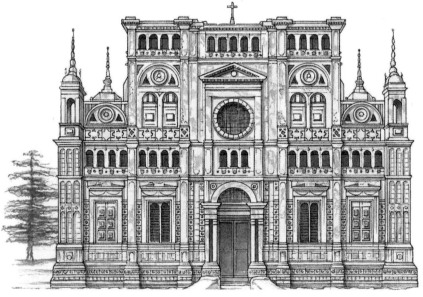

Catholic churches of the Renaissance period, such as this one in Pavia, Italy, were very ornate and complex. This elaborate style was also used in the building of Catholic churches in Latin America. Protestant churches were much plainer and simpler in style.

▶ The dome of the cathedral in Florence was designed by Brunelleschi in the 1430s. The tower was so large that no one knew how to build a dome to cover it. Brunelleschi solved the problem by studying ancient Roman architecture, and erected a crane on the top to complete its construction.

▶ The Golden Temple was built in Amritsar, India, to serve as the spiritual center for the new Sikh religion. Sikhism had developed in the Punjab during the Mogul period of religious tolerance.

THE PRECISION OF THE INCAS

One of the most interesting architectural developments took place in South America before the Spanish invasion. Many of the Inca people lived in mountainous areas, where building was very difficult. The temples, palaces, and houses of the Inca city of Machu Picchu, high in the Andes, were built with stone blocks, which fit together ingeniously without the use of mortar. This took tremendous patience and skill, especially since the Incas only used tools made of stone. The ruined city is still one of the architectural marvels of the world.

▼ The Incas built on simple lines, usually based on squares and rectangles. They had no rounded arches or carvings to decorate their buildings, and the stones were joined together without mortar. Inca cities were carefully planned.

▲ Inca stonework was shaped very precisely with stone hammers. This was followed by polishing and sanding down to make the fit between the stones exact. This helped make buildings both earthquake-proof and very durable.

SCIENCE AND TECHNOLOGY 1461–1600

In contrast to the rest of the world, a new spirit of inquiry was awakening in Europe. This gave birth to a growing revolution in science and technology.

By 1500, windmills had become more advanced, and were used for grinding grain and pumping water. The Dutch used them to drain and reclaim the wetlands of the Netherlands.

An astrolabe

A backstaff

A magnetic compass

In much of the world, research and development of new ideas and technologies was slowing down. Ming China was in decline and becoming isolated, and India, Persia, and the Ottoman Empire were not as inventive as they had been previously. However, when European travelers arrived on their shores, Asians were interested in the new ideas and inventions—guns, astronomical knowledge, clocks, new tools, and shipbuilding methods—that they brought with them. The Koreans invented ironclad ships, based on the ideas brought in by a Dutch visitor. Meanwhile, Native American cultures, before the European settlers arrived and destroyed them, tended to adapt and improve the technologies of their forefathers. Both the Aztecs and the Incas fully exploited these improvements when building their great cities.

▲ Long sea journeys required improved navigational aids for calculating position and direction. The astrolabe was Arabic and, with the backstaff, was used to figure out a ship's latitude. The compass, first used by the Chinese in the 1100s, was used to keep a ship on course.

▶ The Italian Leonardo da Vinci was both an artist and an inventive genius. Among his many designs are these sketches for making flying machines. Although in practice they did not work, and it was not until 1902 that humans could fly, his work pointed the way to the future.

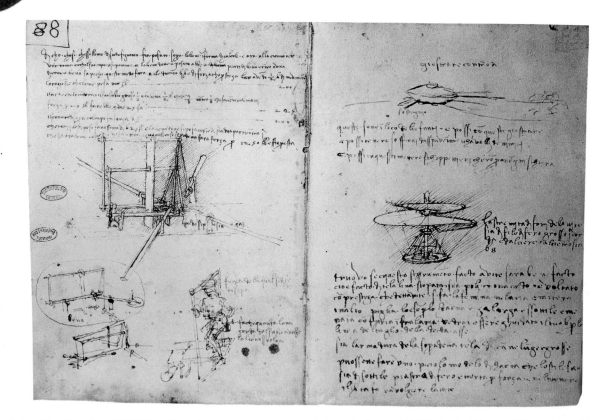

A REVOLUTION IN EUROPE

The revival of learning in Europe during the 1400s and 1500s led people to start observing the world around them. They explored and experimented to find out how things really were, rather than just accepting what they were told by the Church. Sometimes this led to clashes with the Church, as was the case with Galileo in 1615, after he had invented thermometers, telescopes, and developed ideas about gravity, mathematics, and astronomy. Many outstanding ideas and inventions were produced at this time. The first successful watch was invented in 1504, and the microscope in 1590. People studied the structure of the human body, and in 1543, Andreas Vesalius published some of the first accurate descriptions of human anatomy.

Tycho Brahe (1546–1601) carefully mapped and studied the heavenly bodies. The king of Denmark had an observatory built for him on the island of Hveen, complete with instruments, library, laboratory, and living quarters. The telescope had not yet been invented, but Brahe established the positions of 777 stars by naked-eye observation.

Although the pace of development had slowed considerably, the Chinese still produced beautiful porcelain. This Ming porcelain bowl, depicting boys playing, was made in the late 1400s.

Traditional medieval ideas about alchemy, astrology, geometry, and herbal medicine also thrived, led by such thinkers as Paracelsus, Kepler, and Nostradamus. Scientific and exploring societies were founded. Some inventors such as Leonardo da Vinci were even thinking about airplanes, helicopters, and submarines. This flourishing of genius in Europe marked the beginning of a scientific and technological revolution, which was to continue into the future. It laid the foundations for today's modern world.

▼ During the Renaissance, scholars began to study mathematical theory. This was essential for their scientific experiments.

WHEN IT HAPPENED

1492 Martin Behaim makes the first globe
1504 Peter Heinlein invents the watch
1512 Nicolaus Copernicus suggests that the Earth moves around the sun.
1518 Royal College of Physicians founded in London
1528 First manual on surgery is published
1540 Michael Servetus discovers the circulation of the blood
1546 Mapmaker Gerardus Mercator identifies the Earth's magnetic poles
1600 William Gilbert writes about magnetism and electricity

TRADE AND EMPIRE

1601–1707

The Europeans were now beginning to take
over the world. The biggest impact was in the
Americas. British and French settlers occupied
the east coast of North America, and Spanish
conquistadores had already taken over Mexico
and South America. European trading posts
were now dotted around the world—only Japan
kept them out. In Europe, this century brought
a tragic mixture of wars, revolution, and
devastation, as well as enormous growth
and progress in the sciences and arts.

▲ In 1620, a ship called the *Mayflower* sailed from Plymouth in England,
carrying pilgrims to a new life in North America.

◄ The Taj Mahal, near Agra in India, was built in the 1600s by Shah
Jehan as a mausoleum for his wife, Mumtaz Mahal.

THE WORLD AT A GLANCE 1601–1707

The 1600s were the age of the absolute ruler. In Europe, India, China, and Japan, power was concentrated in the hands of the kings, emperors, and shoguns who ruled the land. The great exception was England where an elected, rebellious Parliament overthrew and executed the king, Charles I. Although his son, Charles II, was later invited to take the throne, he was only granted limited powers.

At this time, although embroiled in wars, Europe spread its influence worldwide, while countries such as India and China enriched Europe with their products, art, and ideas.

Many thousands of Europeans sailed across the ocean to North America to seek a better life, or to try to set up communities where they could worship as they wished, free from the interference of hostile governments.

The 1600s also saw another kind of movement of people. The terrible trade in slaves tore millions of Africans from their homes and transported them across the Atlantic to work on American plantations.

NORTH AMERICA

The first European colonies in North America were founded in Virginia and Quebec, and others soon followed. By 1700, the early colonies in North America were well established and attracting more and more people. At first, the settlers were cautiously accepted by the Native Americans, but soon the settlers were shooting at them, or selling them guns with which to fight each other. Initially, the settlers had a limited impact, but the Native Americans soon found themselves losing land. Sometimes they rebelled, but this was increasingly unsuccessful. In the West, life went on as before for Native Americans. The white man had not reached that far yet.

NORTH AMERICA

LATIN AMERICA

LATIN AMERICA

This region was now dominted by the Spanish and Portuguese, and the plantations, mines, and cities grew in size and number. The colonial governments were ruthless, and missionaries undermined and deliberately destroyed native cultures. Many indigenous peoples felt their gods had left them and accepted their fate in despair. They were often forced to work for their invaders, or to retreat to remote places. For the Spanish, there was unlimited wealth.

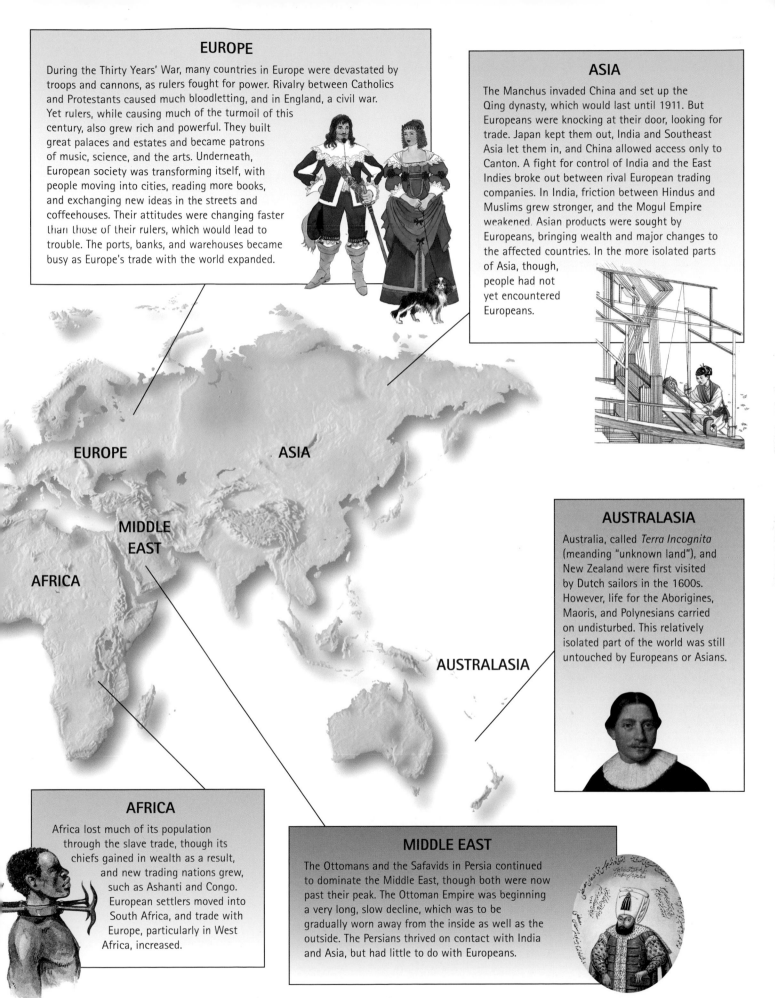

EUROPE

During the Thirty Years' War, many countries in Europe were devastated by troops and cannons, as rulers fought for power. Rivalry between Catholics and Protestants caused much bloodletting, and in England, a civil war. Yet rulers, while causing much of the turmoil of this century, also grew rich and powerful. They built great palaces and estates and became patrons of music, science, and the arts. Underneath, European society was transforming itself, with people moving into cities, reading more books, and exchanging new ideas in the streets and coffeehouses. Their attitudes were changing faster than those of their rulers, which would lead to trouble. The ports, banks, and warehouses became busy as Europe's trade with the world expanded.

ASIA

The Manchus invaded China and set up the Qing dynasty, which would last until 1911. But Europeans were knocking at their door, looking for trade. Japan kept them out, India and Southeast Asia let them in, and China allowed access only to Canton. A fight for control of India and the East Indies broke out between rival European trading companies. In India, friction between Hindus and Muslims grew stronger, and the Mogul Empire weakened. Asian products were sought by Europeans, bringing wealth and major changes to the affected countries. In the more isolated parts of Asia, though, people had not yet encountered Europeans.

EUROPE

ASIA

MIDDLE EAST

AFRICA

AUSTRALASIA

Australia, called *Terra Incognita* (meaning "unknown land"), and New Zealand were first visited by Dutch sailors in the 1600s. However, life for the Aborigines, Maoris, and Polynesians carried on undisturbed. This relatively isolated part of the world was still untouched by Europeans or Asians.

AUSTRALASIA

AFRICA

Africa lost much of its population through the slave trade, though its chiefs gained in wealth as a result, and new trading nations grew, such as Ashanti and Congo. European settlers moved into South Africa, and trade with Europe, particularly in West Africa, increased.

MIDDLE EAST

The Ottomans and the Safavids in Persia continued to dominate the Middle East, though both were now past their peak. The Ottoman Empire was beginning a very long, slow decline, which was to be gradually worn away from the inside as well as the outside. The Persians thrived on contact with India and Asia, but had little to do with Europeans.

243

JAPAN IN ISOLATION 1603–1716

The Tokugawa shoguns brought stability to Japan after years of chaos. Fearing disruptive influences from foreigners, they sealed Japan from the outside world.

Shinto religious traditions remained strong under the Tokugawas, but the role of the temples in politics and the economy was reduced.

In 1603, Tokugawa Ieyasu (1543–1616), head of a powerful family, became shogun—largely by political maneuvering and military force. Edo (later renamed Tokyo), the small fishing village that had been his headquarters, became his capital. Here, Ieyasu began to build what became the world's largest castle. He retired in 1605, and made his son Hidetada shogun. But Ieyasu continued to control the government until his death.

Ieyasu thought that there were two threats to Japan: the violent rivalry between *daimyos* (lords) that had caused great instability, and the growing foreign influence. He placed the daimyos under constant watch in Edo and kept them so busy organizing—and paying for—the building of the palace there, that they had no time to make trouble and no money for soldiers.

Japan is a fertile and well-populated country, with many valleys and plains separated by mountains. These geographical extremes made it difficult to unify during this period.

JAPAN

Hokkaido

Honshu

Edo ●

● Kyoto

● Nagasaki

● Deshima

▲ There were important technical and cultural advances in Japan during this time. However, because of Japan's "closed door" policy to foreigners, these advances were not seen by the outside world. These exquisite Japanese porcelain figures date from this period.

When the foreign missionaries and traders began to involve themselves in Japanese politics, Ieyasu realized that their ideas could lead to more violence. For the sake of harmony, the shogun placed restrictions on them. The strongest Christian influence was in Nagasaki. In 1638, after a revolt there, the shogun had 37,000 converts killed, and banned Christianity.

▶ Nijo Castle in Kyoto was built in the 1600s for the Tokugawa Bakufu, the ambassador to the emperor. Even though the emperor was by now largely powerless, it was still important for the shogun to remain on friendly terms with him.

JAPAN BECOMES PROSPEROUS

Following the rebellion by Japanese Christians in Nagasaki, only a few Dutch and Chinese traders were allowed into Japan. Japanese people were not allowed to go abroad, and those who lived away from the country were not allowed to return. Christian priests were ordered to leave or be killed, and their churches were torn down. Japanese Christians were executed. Life became strictly regulated, and the country was sealed off from outside influences. Tokugawa rule gave Japan almost 250 years of peace.

Japan grew more prosperous because it now operated as one country. Merchants and farmers were encouraged to expand their businesses, and traditional *daimyos* and samurai warriors lost their positions and grew poor. Like Europe, Japan was changing from a feudal society into a trading economy. Cities and towns grew larger, and the population expanded greatly during the 1600s and 1700s. Though Japanese society still kept its strict rules of behavior, people were becoming better educated.

There were temporary setbacks to Japan's growth during this period. In 1684, the fifth Tokugawa shogun, Tsunayoshi, introduced some reforms inspired by Buddhist scholars of the 1100s. They were not popular. In 1703, the capital, Edo (Tokyo), was destroyed by an earthquake and fire. However, in 1716, a reforming shogun, Yoshimune, came to power and Japan's isolation from the rest of the world began to break down.

▲ The Tosho-gu Temple at Nikko, built during the 1600s, was dedicated to Ieyasu, who, after his death, was looked on as a saint.

◄ Sumo wrestling began in 1624. It was encouraged as an alternative to samurai warriors killing each other. Wrestlers were selected when young. They trained for many years.

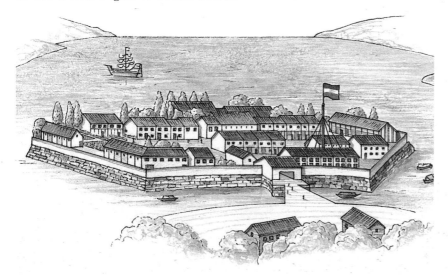

◄ The Dutch were permitted to occupy the island of Deshima in Nagasaki Bay as a trading base. A few ships were allowed to visit each year, exchanging foreign goods for Japanese silks and other products. The Dutch were not allowed to cross onto the Japanese mainland.

KEY DATES

1603	Ieyasu founds the Tokugawa Shogunate
1609	Small Dutch trading base established on the island of Deshima in Nagasaki Bay
1612	Persecution of Nagasaki Christians begins
1637	Portuguese traders banned and expelled
1637–3	The Shimabara Rebellion in Nagasaki
1684	Hardship after Tokugawa Tsunayoshi's reforms
1703	Edo (Tokyo) destroyed by earthquake and fire
1716	Yoshimune, a reformer, comes to power

THE STUARTS 1603–1649

The Stuart dynasty came from Scotland. In England, they faced a complicated political situation that led to six years of civil war and the downfall of a king.

Apparently, James I (1566–1625) stammered and dribbled. But he was an intelligent king who did his best in a difficult situation, and during his time, England and Scotland moved closer to being united. He was not popular. He believed in divine right, which claimed that a ruler could do as he wished and was responsible only to God.

Queen Elizabeth I, the last Tudor monarch of England, died in 1603 without an heir. James VI of Scotland, son of Mary, Queen of Scots, succeeded her as James I of England. James was descended from Henry VIII's sister and Elizabeth's aunt, Margaret Tudor, who had married the Scottish king, James IV, in 1503. His family, the Stuarts, had ruled Scotland since 1371.

England and Scotland now had the same king, but they still remained separate countries. James dreamed of uniting them, but many English and Scottish people were opposed to this. He tried to make peace between Catholics, Anglicans, and Puritans. The Puritans were extreme Protestants who wished to abolish church ceremony and music, bishops, church hierarchies, and other "popish" traditions. James angered them by refusing to go as far as they wanted. But he ordered a new translation of the Bible, the King James Bible, to try to bring Christians together.

As England's prosperity grew under Tudor and Stuart rule, many towns were renewed. They were not planned, but rebuilt along existing winding streets.

THE GUNPOWDER PLOT

Catholics in England were frustrated by Protestant intolerance toward them, and, although James I tried to please everyone, opinions pulled in conflicting directions. Some Catholics saw violence as the only way to gain toleration for Catholicism, though many disliked this idea. A small group plotted to kill both the king and parliamentarians by blowing up Parliament during its ceremonial opening on November 5, 1605. One of the conspirators was Guy Fawkes, who was discovered guarding barrels of gunpowder in the cellars of Parliament. He and the other plotters were arrested, tortured, and put to death. After this, attitudes toward Catholics hardened.

JAMES THE SPENDER

James made peace with Catholic Spain to try and ease tensions between European Catholics and Protestants, and Britain was at peace for 20 years. But in 1624 James was drawn into the Thirty Years' War in Germany on the Protestant side, supporting his son-in-law, Frederick. James fell deeply into debt. The cost of running the country was growing and James himself was a lavish spender. He believed Parliament should obey him without question and grant whatever he asked for. But Parliament and the king's ministers had grown stronger in Tudor times, and he clashed with them when his demands for money were refused.

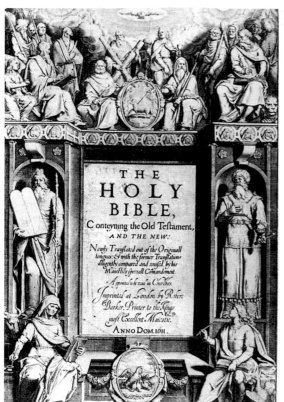

The King James Bible, or Authorized Version, published in 1611, was carefully translated under James I's guidance, in order to serve as the one Bible for Anglicans, Puritans, and Catholics. It was admired because of the beauty of its language, and has survived to this day. It is still used in some churches.

KEY DATES

1603 James I becomes king of England
1605 The Gunpowder Plot to blow up Parliament
1608 James disagrees with Parliament over money
1621 James again disagrees with Parliament
1625 Charles I becomes king
1629 Charles closes Parliament
1637 Charles's court splits after a crisis
1640 Charles recalls Parliament—clashes follow
1642 The English Civil War begins
1649 Charles I is executed by parliamentarians

Charles left London and raised an army. He was defeated in 1646, and handed power to Parliament, but he then escaped to continue the Civil War. Finally, Charles was recaptured, brought to trial, and executed in 1649. For 12 years following the English Civil War, England had no king.

▼ During Tudor and Stuart times, the wealthy gained more power and influence. However, disagreements increased between the different groups, especially over money, business, and religious matters.

CHARLES I

James I tried to please everyone. He was unpopular in England because he made mistakes, and because he was Scottish and his Danish wife, Anne, was Catholic. His belief in the rights of the king was also disliked. When he died in 1625, his son Charles became king and inherited his lack of popularity.

Charles I (1600–1649) also disliked parliamentary interference, and handled situations badly. People took sides and supported either the king or Parliament. This became a battle between traditional and modern ideas. When, in 1629, Parliament refused to give Charles more money and allow him to rule in his own way, he sent the parliamentarians home and tried to govern without them.

Charles ruled without Parliament for eleven years, but his court and ministers were divided over many important questions. Charles also angered the Scots, who thought he had become too English, and lost their support. Parliament, called back in 1640, united against him. It tried to limit his powers and suppress his supporters. In 1642, Charles tried to arrest five parliamentary leaders, but Parliament, including the nobility, opposed him fiercely.

EARLY AMERICAN SETTLERS 1607–1650

When the first Europeans arrived, Native Americans were unsure about them. Little did they know that these settlers would eventually come in their millions.

The Plymouth Colony settlers were hardy, but not farmers. They would have starved if a Native American named Squanto had not made friends with them and showed them how to survive by growing corn and catching fish.

For a century after John Cabot discovered Newfoundland in 1497, most Europeans regarded North America as unimportant. They did not appreciate its potential, and saw little economic value there. Their main interests were in finding a sea route to Asia and acquiring easy riches by raiding Spanish galleons laden with gold in the Caribbean. Early explorers returned home without finding the gold, exotic cities, and sea passages to Asia that they had sought. Both Cartier's French colony at Quebec (1534–1541) and Raleigh's English colony at Roanoke (1584–1590) failed. However, a Spanish settlement founded in 1565 at St. Augustine in Florida survived. Only in 1607–1608, when new colonies were founded at Quebec and Jamestown, did the Europeans realize that the new lands might be valuable. From 1600 onward, many Europeans, wishing to escape religious strife and war at home, sailed to North America to start a new life.

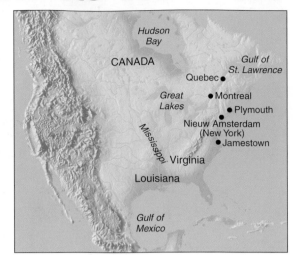

The place names of modern northeast America show that most of the successful early European settlers came from either England or France.

The first successful English colony, founded in 1607 at Jamestown, Virginia, was almost wiped out by disease, hunger, and troubles with the Native Americans, but it survived. The colony's leader, John Smith, wrote a book that attracted even more settlers.

▲ A group of Puritans, known as the Pilgrim Fathers, landed at Plymouth, Massachusetts, in 1620 and founded the first permanent colony in North America. The colony flourished and gave rise to a new nation founded on the principles of liberty and justice.

▶ The *Mayflower* carried 102 Puritan colonists and 47 crew members in cramped conditions. Escaping from religious persecution, they set out from Plymouth, England, in 1620 and landed near Cape Cod. There they founded a small settlement which they also named Plymouth.

THE NEW AMERICANS

English colonist John Rolfe introduced tobacco growing to the settlers in 1612. The crop earned them money and Jamestown prospered. As the demand for tobacco increased, the tobacco growers needed more land, which they took from the native people. This struggle for land led to bitter wars between colonists and Native Americans. The arrival in Massachusetts of the Pilgrims in 1620 marked a turning point—they had come to stay, and to live according to Puritan principles. In 1625, the Dutch established a colony on Manhattan Island, today's New York City. French colonists also arrived, settling north of the St. Lawrence River in what is now Canada.

Fur trading, particularly in beaver skins, became profitable because of the high demand in Europe. From the 1630s onward, more Puritan refugees and migrants from England arrived. They had no hope of return, and, though life was hard, the New England colonies thrived.

▲ When the Puritans landed in America in 1620 they knew nothing about living in this new wilderness. Food ran short, and many of the settlers died from disease and exposure. Nearly half of them died during the first winter, and only 54 were still alive the following spring.

KEY DATES	
1492	Columbus arrives in the Americas
1497	Cabot lands in Newfoundland
1513	Spanish Ponce de León explores Florida
1540	Coronado (Spanish) enters New Mexico
1534–41	Cartier (French) explores the St. Lawrence
1584–90	Raleigh's English Roanoke colony (fails)
1607	Jamestown, Virginia (English), founded
1608	Champlain establishes Quebec and New France
1620	Arrival of the Pilgrims in New England
1625	Dutch settle in New Amsterdam (New York)

By 1700, there were about 400,000 Europeans in North America, and the New England colonies were well established. Whole communities had moved there from Europe, and before long they were self-supporting. Harvard College was founded near Boston in 1636.

THE SWEDISH EMPIRE 1560–1721

Sweden's greatest king, Gustavus Adolphus, and his reforming chancellor, Axel Oxenstierna, made Sweden into a great, modern Protestant power.

Gustavus Adolphus (1594–1632) was a brave and inspiring leader, and he governed Sweden well. He made a modernized state with impressive cities, industries, and a strong army. He ruled for 21 years from 1611.

▲ Count Axel Oxenstierna (1583–1654) was Sweden's chancellor for 42 years from 1612. He was a great reformer. After Gustavus Adolphus' death, Oxenstierna ran the country for a further 22 years under Queen Christina. He masterminded Sweden's growth into a modern Protestant power.

In 1520, Sweden, led by King Gustavus Vasa, rebelled against Denmark and gained independence. The Swedes then started to break the dominance of the Hansa League over the Baltic Sea region. Although Sweden was sparsely populated, it had a strong government and a growing trade with England and Holland. The Swedes fought in Estonia, eventually conquering the country by 1582. In later campaigns they gained Karelia, east of Finland, and Lapland in the north.

Gustavus Adolphus was born in 1594. He became king of Sweden in 1611, at the age of 17. He was to become Sweden's greatest king. A devout and educated Protestant, he spoke many languages. He had Sweden's towns rebuilt, and its industries flourished. Its frontline army was only 40,000 strong, but Gustavus made it the best in Europe. By 1629, he had defeated the armies of Denmark, Russia, and Poland, making Sweden the leading military power in northern Europe.

Gustavus Adolphus built a great fleet and made Sweden the dominant Baltic state. His flagship, the *Vasa*, however, capsized and sank on its maiden voyage in 1628.

Gustavus' fellow Protestant princes in Germany faced defeat in the Thirty Years' War. If Germany became Catholic, then Sweden would be isolated, so Gustavus Adolphus declared war on Emperor Ferdinand II of Austria. In July 1630, Gustavus landed an army in Germany. In 1631, at Breitenfeld near Leipzig, the Swedes defeated the emperor's army.

▶ The island city of Stockholm was one of Europe's finest capitals. It is shown here in an engraving by Franz Hogenberg, made around 1579, during Stockholm's years of greatness.

SWEDEN'S ERA

In the spring of 1632, the Swedish army occupied Munich and advanced against Vienna, Ferdinand's capital. At the battle of Lützen, the emperor's forces retreated in disorder, but Gustavus died in battle. There was a temporary setback in 1634 when the Swedes were defeated at the battle of Nördlingen. Their fortunes soon turned when they defeated the Catholics at Jankau in 1645. In 1655, they entered Poland, and in 1658 took southern Sweden from the Danes. Under Charles XII, they overcame the Danes, Russians, Poles, and Saxons. But in 1709 they ventured too far—into the Ukraine. Tired and far from home, they were defeated by the Russians and, by 1721, all Swedish gains south of the Baltic and in Russia had been lost.

▲ Tidö Castle in Sweden was built around 1620. During this period, Sweden developed from a simple agricultural nation into a great European power.

KEY DATES

1520	Sweden gains independence from Denmark
1523–60	Gustavus Vasa modernizes Sweden
1580	Sweden conquers Estonia
1611–32	Gustavus Adolphus reigns as king of Sweden
1620s	Sweden becomes the leading northern power
1630–34	Sweden successful in the Thirty Years' War
1643–45	Swedish victories against Denmark and Austria
1697–1708	Many Swedish victories throughout Europe
1709	Swedes defeated by the Russians
1721	Sweden in retreat—the end of its period of dominance

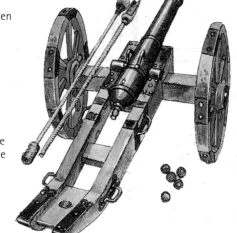

▶ Gustavus Adolphus equipped his army with new guns which could be easily transported and manhandled by the soldiers. Through their extensive knowledge of mining, the Swedes had become masters in metallurgy and the use of explosives. They applied this knowledge to war.

THE BATTLE OF LÜTZEN

The Swedes fought alongside the Protestant Germans against the Catholic forces of imperial Austria at Lützen. The Catholic army was much larger, and the Protestant attack was delayed by foggy conditions. But good tactics and bravery helped the Protestants break through and rout the Catholics. Gustavus Adolphus, who always led his troops from the front, was killed. However, his fellow general, Bernard, Duke of Saxe Weimar, kept fighting, and after a full day's battle, the Catholics fled in chaos.

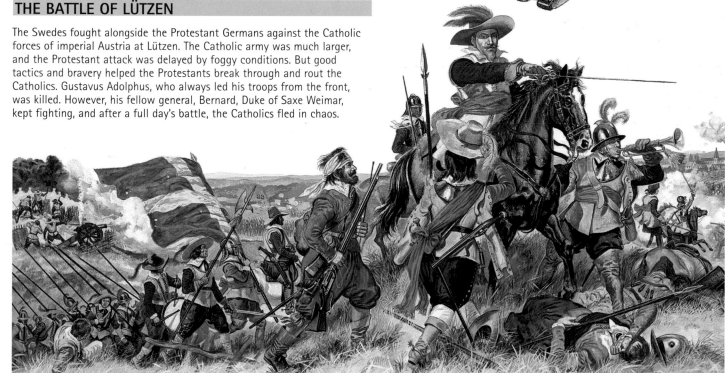

THE THIRTY YEARS' WAR 1618–1648

The Thirty Years' War was the world's first modern war. Starting as a religious conflict between Catholics and Protestants, it ended as a fight for power in Europe.

Ferdinand II of Austria (1578–1637) was a Catholic. He tried to impose his religion on all his subjects.

Frederick (1596–1632), the "Winter King" of Bohemia, was the son-in-law of England's James I.

In 1618, tensions exploded in Bohemia between Catholics and Protestants, and between the Hapsburgs and other royal houses. Ferdinand II, the Holy Roman emperor, had inherited the Bohemian throne in 1617 and two years later, in 1619, the Austrian throne. Until that time, the Hapsburgs had been neutral in matters of religion. Bohemia had long been Protestant, but Ferdinand was Catholic, and he unwisely forced Bohemia to become Catholic. This resulted in the Bohemians revolting against him.

In 1619, the German rulers who elected the Holy Roman emperor met at Prague. They deposed Ferdinand II as king of Bohemia and made Frederick, a Protestant, king in his place. This resulted in a series of wars, fought mainly in Germany, which eventually involved most of Europe for the next thirty years.

At first, the Catholics won most of the battles, with Spanish Hapsburg help and money. In 1625, the Danes joined the Protestants, but to no avail. The Catholics had two outstanding generals, Count Wallenstein and Count Tilly, whose troops fought well, and by 1629, the Protestant allies were in trouble.

The use of guns and cannons increased the destruction and cost of the war. The matchlock musket was improved by the Swedes to make it lighter and faster to reload.

SWEDEN ENTERS THE WAR

Frederick fled and a Catholic prince, Maximilian of Bavaria, was appointed king of Bohemia. The struggle then moved northward. Led by Wallenstein, the emperor's army defeated the Danes and overran northern Germany. It seemed that nothing could stop Ferdinand from forcing Germany to become Catholic until, in 1630, Protestant Gustavus Adolphus of Sweden entered the war. He took back northern Germany, soundly defeating the Catholics in battles at Breitenfeld and Lützen. But the battles took their toll. Tilly was killed at Breitenfeld, and Gustavus Adolphus died at Lützen.

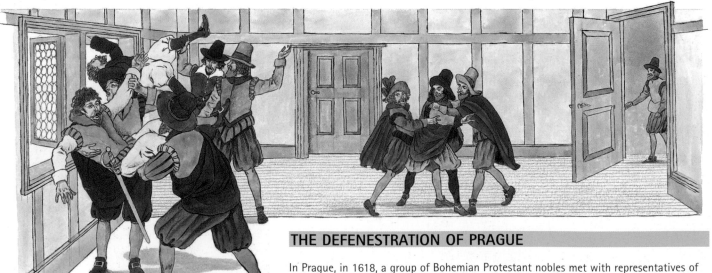

THE DEFENESTRATION OF PRAGUE

In Prague, in 1618, a group of Bohemian Protestant nobles met with representatives of the Catholic Hapsburg emperor. Their arguments became so heated that the Bohemians threw the emperor's men out of a window—in other words, defenestrated them—of Hradcany Castle, the Hapsburg stronghold. This violent action is known as the "Defenestration of Prague" and sparked the Thirty Years' War.

The French entered the war in 1635, a year after the Swedes were beaten at Nördlingen. The French minister Cardinal Richelieu already supported the Protestants because he opposed the ambitious Hapsburgs. The same year, the German Protestant princes withdrew from the war, bankrupt and defeated. Many alliances switched, and the conflict grew even more complicated. The French advanced into Catholic Bavaria to overcome the Spanish Hapsburgs and Sweden defeated the Austrian Hapsburgs. When the French and Swedes were poised to take over Bavaria and threaten Austria, the Hapsburg emperor asked for peace.

THE RESULTS OF THE WAR

During this long war, large guns and mercenary troops had been used. This had been expensive and caused great devastation. Troops looted whole areas of Germany and at times even switched sides. Germany was ruined, and the Netherlands and Switzerland gained independence; however, France, Sweden, and Holland grew stronger. Some states gained land and others lost it. One German state, Brandenburg–Prussia, grew stronger and was to become even more important. The Hapsburgs lost their power, and the Holy Roman Empire grew weaker. Germany broke down into 300 small states. Many European governments became secular, which meant that they no longer forced religious beliefs on their subjects. The Peace of Westphalia, which ended the war, was the first major European treaty of modern times.

▲ One of the worst events of the Thirty Years' War was the destruction of the German city of Magdeburg by the Catholics under Count Tilly in 1631. Until then, Tilly had been highly respected across Europe.

▶ The Catholic Count Albrecht Wallenstein (1583–1634) was an outstanding general. He became rich from the war, and tried to build his own empire in northern Germany. This made him very unpopular with the emperor, and eventually led to his downfall.

▼ Wallenstein and his men were murdered at Eger in Germany in 1634, when it was discovered that he was using the war as a way of creating power for himself.

KEY DATES	
1618–20	Bohemian revolt against Austria
1625–27	Denmark joins the Protestants
1629	Protestant Germans losing the war
1630	Gustavus Adolphus of Sweden joins the war, overrunning northern Germany
1631	Tilly storms and destroys Magdeburg
1631–32	Protestant victories at Breitenfeld and Lützen
1634	Protestants are defeated at Nördlingen. Count Wallenstein is murdered
1635	Protestant Germans make peace—France joins the war
1645	French and Swedish victories in Germany
1648	The Peace of Westphalia treaty ends the war

FRANCE AND RICHELIEU 1624–1661

Louis XIII became king at the age of nine. He later appointed as his chief minister the man who was to make France the leading nation in Europe.

Marie de Médicis (1573–1642) was queen of France, then regent to her son Louis XIII. She clung to power, but was banished in 1617. Richelieu helped her make peace with her son in 1620. But when she tried to replace Louis in 1630, she was permanently exiled to Brussels.

In 1624, Louis XIII of France appointed Cardinal Richelieu as his chief minister. They worked together for eighteen years. Richelieu's ambition was to unify France into one centrally ruled country and make it great. Regional dukes held a lot of power, so he set out to reduce their influence. In 1628, he also dealt harshly with the troublesome French Protestant Huguenots. Richelieu was disliked by Catholic leaders, nobles, and judges because he stopped many of their privileges, and the high taxes he levied caused mass revolts. He believed in strong control, and used force to get his way.

The clothing of the French nobility was elaborate. Wigs, hats, and clothes were a sign of status. This was a French army officer's clothing when on campaign.

Abroad, Austria and Spain were the main threats to France. The Hapsburgs ruled both countries and, if they joined forces, France would be vulnerable. By 1631, during the Thirty Years' War, Hapsburg Austria controlled most of Germany and threatened to dominate Europe.

Louis XIII (1601-1643) was the son of Henry IV and the second king of the Bourbon line. He became king as a boy in 1610 and assumed power in 1617. He was very influenced by Cardinal Richelieu, but he outlasted Richelieu by one year, and left the throne to his young son, Louis XIV.

CARDINAL RICHELIEU

Armand du Plessis, the Duke of Richelieu (1585–1642), became a bishop in 1607 and a cardinal in 1622. He entered the council of the regent, Marie de Médicis, in 1616, and became chief minister in 1624. Richelieu believed in absolutism—the right of the king to do what he wanted. He believed the king was responsible to God, not to the Church, the nobility, or the people. Richelieu used spies effectively and suppressed all opposition. He trained his successor, Cardinal Mazarin, who continued Richelieu's policies and ruled as regent for the young Louis XIV until 1661. In many European countries, this was a time when chief ministers were very powerful.

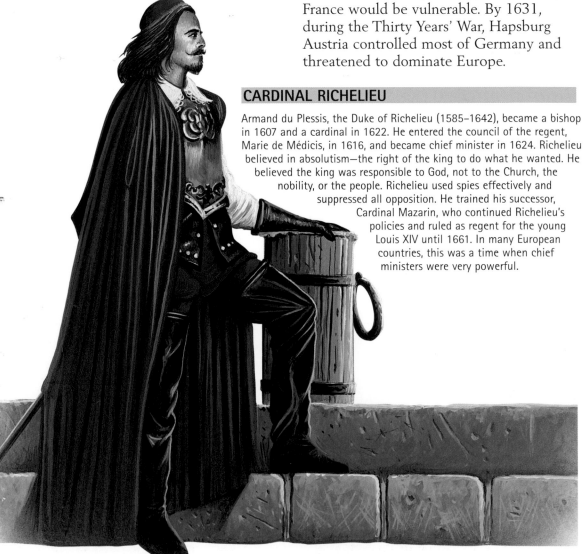

La Rochelle was the stronghold of the Protestant Huguenots, who had developed their own army and navy. Richelieu besieged the port in 1628 and broke their power. In this painting, Louis XIII is depicted visiting the scene of the siege in October of that year.

FRANCE BECOMES STRONGER

To weaken Austria, Richelieu paid Sweden, the Netherlands, and Denmark to fight a common enemy, the Hapsburgs. In 1635, France declared war on Spain (which ruled Belgium and Burgundy). The fighting went on until 1648 and outlasted Richelieu, but his plans succeeded. He tried to extend France to what he thought were its natural frontiers—the Pyrenees in the southwest and the Rhine in the east.

When Richelieu died in 1642, his follower Cardinal Mazarin continued his policies. France replaced Spain as Europe's greatest power. A revolt by the French nobility, called the Fronde, was put down in 1653. When Louis XIV came to the throne he was only five, and Mazarin ruled as regent. By the end of Mazarin's life, in 1661, France had changed greatly. It had grown larger, stronger, and richer; its armies had become the finest in Europe, and Louis XIV was to be its greatest king.

▶ The royal flag of the ruling Bourbon kings of France acted as the French flag until 1790, the time of the French Revolution.

▼ Richelieu allowed the Protestant Huguenots religious freedom, but he fought to break their political and military power. This grisly massacre of Huguenots was initiated by Richelieu.

DECLINE OF SPAIN 1598–1700

After a century of greatness, Spain went through a long, slow decline that arose from its refusal to recognize the changing times, and its failure to adapt to them.

Philip III (1578–1621) became king of Spain, but his real interests were religious, not political. During his reign, Spain began to lose its place in the world as a great European and colonial power.

▼ Wealth from the New World was not just spent on wars. Philip II had built the magnificent palace at El Escorial, near Madrid, at the end of the 1500s. Its library housed a priceless collection of Greek, Latin, and Arabic manuscripts.

When Philip III became king of Spain in 1598, his country was bankrupt. The Spanish army was outdated, and the government was corrupt and incompetent. Spain had amassed great riches from the Americas, but their value had decreased because Europe was by now flooded with Spanish gold and silver.

The opportunity to make easy fortunes had rotted Spanish society, and sensible ways of making money, such as promoting and developing trade, education, and crafts, had been ignored. Yet Spain's empire was still the largest in the world, consisting of most of South and Central America and a large part of North America, as well as the Philippines and settlements in Asia and Africa. Philip had no interest in politics, and Spain was run by his ministers. The first of these, the Duke of Lerma, used his position to make himself very rich. His greatest mistake was expelling the Moriscos in 1606.

The most famous Spanish author at this time was Miguel de Cervantes (1547–1616), who wrote *Don Quixote*. The book tells the story of a foolish landowner who sees himself as a brave knight and has a series of amusing adventures with his squire, the peasant Sancho Panza.

The Moriscos were Muslim Moors who had stayed in Spain and converted to Christianity. Lerma suspected that they were plotting against the government. However, the Moriscos were extremely hardworking and skilled, and Spain could not afford to lose them.

At this time, the Roman Catholic Church was more powerful even than the king or his ministers. Through the Inquisition it supervised and controlled every aspect of Spanish life. Religious issues were considered to be more important than any economic interests, and the nation grew steadily poorer.

THE END OF THE HAPSBURGS

In 1621, Philip III was succeeded by his son Philip IV. His reign was disastrous. The Spanish support of the Catholic cause in the Thirty Years' War and the wars against Richelieu's France had all proved very costly, and Spain had gained little. By now the flow of treasure from America had dwindled. At home, a revolt in Catalonia plunged Spain further into debt. In December 1640, a mass rising in Portugal ended its union with Spain, leading to further losses. However, fighting continued and Spain did not recognize Portugal's independence until 1668.

Philip IV was followed in 1665 by his four-year-old son, Charles II, the last Hapsburg king of Spain. When Charles grew up he failed to produce an heir and was succeeded by Philip of Anjou, grandson of France's Louis XIV.

Philip V introduced a new order into Spain, but the country was now no longer a great power. A European war was fought over who should rule Spain— the Hapsburgs or the French Bourbons. The result, in 1713, was that Spain lost its possessions in Italy, as well as Gibraltar and Belgium. The Hapsburg dynasty lost Spain to the Bourbons.

This painting shows Charles II receiving Holy Communion at El Escorial, with a pomp and splendor that was at odds with the reality of a country in decline.

SPANISH DECLINE

Spain had experienced one century of brilliance and wealth, and one century of decline. It had failed to recognize the new order in northern Europe, with the great economic development led by Protestants. The Catholic order in Spain had failed to modernize itself, and tried to keep power in the hands of nobles, bishops, and kings. As a result, Spain failed to develop after its spectacular growth around 1492, and by 1700 other European countries had surpassed it.

Charles II, who was king for 35 years until his death in 1700, was depicted in paintings as a grand monarch, but his reign was not successful. He failed to produce an heir and was the last Hapsburg king of Spain.

KEY DATES	
1598	Spain loses war with France after interfering in French affairs
1598–1621	Philip III is king of Spain
1606	Expulsion of the Moriscos from Spain
1621–48	Spain loses the Netherlands
1621–65	Philip IV is king of Spain
1640	Portugal and its empire separate from Spain
1648	Spain finally accepts Dutch independence
1665–1700	Charles II reigns as the last Spanish Hapsburg king
1701–13	The War of the Spanish Succession— Spain loses possessions in Italy, Belgium, and Gibraltar
1700–46	Philip V is the first Bourbon king of Spain

EAST INDIA COMPANIES 1600–1700

The East India Companies were powerful trading organizations set up by the English, Dutch, and French to protect their business interests in southeastern Asia.

The ships of the East India Companies, first used for trading, were also converted into warships for use against pirates, Asians, and ships from other companies.

In 1600, the English East India Company was formed in London. Its purpose was to unite the English traders doing business in southeastern Asia. There was cut-throat competition for trade in this area which had first been controlled by the Spaniards and the Portuguese. During the 1600s, the contest for this lucrative trade with the East was between the Dutch, English, and French.

The Netherlands followed England and set up a Dutch East India Company in 1602, with its headquarters in Amsterdam and also at Batavia (Jakarta) on the island of Java. The French formed their own East India company later, in 1664.

These organizations became immensely powerful. Trading was only one of their activities—they also had a political influence. They armed their ships to fight at sea and maintained private armies. The East India companies set up military as well as trading bases and made treaties with local rulers around them. They waged war on neighboring nations and on each other. In many ways they behaved like independent states.

In the 1600s, many European travelers visited India. Through them, knowledge of the impressive history and culture of India began to reach Europe.

The English lost the contest to control the spice trade in the East Indies to the Dutch. India then became the center of English activities, and by 1700, they had sole trading rights in India, with a number of key ports, notably Calcutta, Madras, and Bombay. The Dutch had ports on the Cape in South Africa, in Persia, Ceylon, Malaya, and Japan, and also dominated the Spice Islands (now Indonesia). The French were less successful in their attempt to dominate India. Many private fortunes were made. Sailors and traders often died of disease or fighting. Some made homes in Asia, founding European centers in India, Southeast Asia, and China.

▲ In 1652, the Dutch founded a base at the Cape of Good Hope (Cape Town) as a staging post for ships on the long voyage from Europe to the Far East. This later became a Dutch colony.

▶ The English colony of Madras was a major port for exporting cotton goods. It was also the center of a region noted for making cloth with brightly colored designs and scenes from Indian life.

258

THE DUTCH EMPIRE 1660–1664

The Dutch Empire was founded on worldwide trade. During the 1600s, their huge merchant fleet helped the Dutch to become a powerful trading nation.

Amsterdam was the center of European banking in the 1600s. A bank was founded there in 1609 that deposited and loaned money to finance trade.

▲ Peter Stuyvesant (c.1610–1672) was the harsh governor of the New Netherland colony in North America from 1647 to 1664. He was against religious freedom. He was hated both by the Native Americans and the colonists. In 1664, they surrendered without a fight to a small English fleet.

▼ The Dutch Adrian Reland made this folding map of Java around 1715. Java had been ruled by many different local rulers until the Dutch East India Company took control in 1619. Java remained a Dutch colony until 1949.

By 1600, Amsterdam was Europe's busiest port, with warehouses, banks, and trading houses, as well as a large fleet of ships. Frustrated by their exclusion from South America by the Spanish and Portuguese, the Dutch headed for the Far East. They founded an East India Company for their traders. They took control of trade from the Spice Islands or "East Indies," seizing Java and the Moluccas from the Portuguese.

The Dutch East India Company established its headquarters at Batavia (Jakarta) on the island of Java (now part of Indonesia) in 1619. The company maintained an army and a powerful fleet of ships that drove the English and the Portuguese out of the East Indies and seized Ceylon, the port of Malacca, and several ports in India. The company even set up a trading post in Japan—the only Europeans allowed to do so.

In 1652, the Dutch occupied the Cape of Good Hope on the southern tip of Africa, as a midway point on the long journey from the Far East to Europe. From there, Dutch ships were able to take the shortest route to the East Indies, straight across the Indian Ocean.

EXPANSION AND CONTRACTION

The huge merchant fleet of the Netherlands was also busy elsewhere. In 1621, the Dutch West India Company was founded across the Atlantic. By 1623, 800 Dutch ships were engaged in the Caribbean, trading in sugar, tobacco, animal hides, and slaves. The company established a colony in Guiana, and they captured Curaçao. For a while, they controlled northeastern Brazil.

In North America, the company founded the colony of New Netherland along the Hudson River in 1624. From there they exported furs, timber, and other goods bought from Native Americans.

Eventually, the Dutch lost their naval supremacy to the English and their empire suffered. They lost Ceylon, Malacca, and the Cape to the English, and were left with just their Southeast Asian empire.

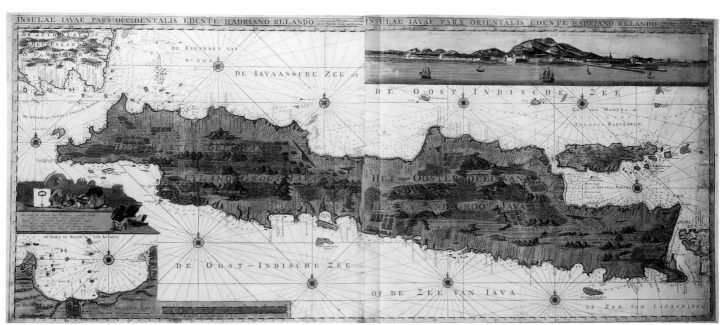

ENGLISH CIVIL WAR 1642–1660

The English Civil War was fought between supporters of the king and supporters of Parliament. For five years the country was run by a dictator, Oliver Cromwell.

Charles I (1600–1649) came to the throne of England in 1625, the same year that he married Henrietta Maria of France. His belief in the divine right of the king first led to clashes with Parliament and eventually to the English Civil War.

▲ Oliver Cromwell (1599–1658) went to college in Cambridge and studied law in London. He was first elected to Parliament in 1628, representing Cambridge. He recruited and trained Parliament's New Model Army. He was a strict Puritan and believed that God had chosen him to perform His will.

The English Civil War was fought between supporters of King Charles I and supporters of Parliament. Like his father, James I, Charles believed in divine right, claiming that his right to rule came directly from God. This belief put Charles at odds with Parliament.

Charles became king in 1625 and immediately began to quarrel with Parliament over his right to imprison people who opposed him over religion, and taxes. In 1629, he dissolved Parliament, and, for 11 years, tried to rule alone.

In 1637, Charles attempted to impose the Anglican form of public worship on the Scots. The Presbyterian Scots rebelled, raising an army that, in 1640, occupied part of northern England. Charles recalled Parliament to ask for money to put down the rebellion by the Scots, but Parliament demanded reforms. Civil war broke out after Charles tried to arrest his five leading parliamentary opponents. In 1642, fighting broke out all over the country between Royalists (supporters of the king), known as Cavaliers, and supporters of Parliament, known as Roundheads.

■ Parliament's Headquarters

▲ Royalist Headquarters

During the Civil War, the west and north generally supported the king, and the south and east supported Parliament, though there were local divisions across the country. The first major battle took place at Edgehill in 1642; the last at Worcester in 1651.

The king made Oxford his capital, and his forces at first held the advantage. However, Parliament secured the support of the Scottish army, and in the long run, proved superior, for it had the money to maintain a professional army. This New Model Army led by Sir Thomas Fairfax decisively defeated Charles's forces at Naseby in 1645. The king surrendered in 1646, after Oxford fell to the Roundheads.

Cavalier

Roundheads

▶ The king's Cavalier forces were crushingly defeated by the New Model Army of the Roundheads at the battle of Naseby in 1645. This was the decisive victory for Parliamentary forces during the English Civil War.

Charles was imprisoned on the Isle of Wight, where he plotted to start the war again with Scottish help. A second phase of fighting broke out, with Royalist risings and a failed invasion attempt by the Scots. In 1648, parliamentarians who still respected the king were removed from Parliament by Oliver Cromwell. The remaining Rump Parliament, as it was called, found Charles guilty of treason and executed him in 1649.

OLIVER CROMWELL

After Charles' execution, Parliament abolished the monarchy, and England became a Commonwealth. Parliament governed the country, but had an ongoing struggle with the army. In 1653, Oliver Cromwell emerged as a strong leader and ruled the country as Lord Protector. Cromwell clashed with some parliamentarians and was forced to govern with the help of army generals. He fought a war with the Dutch over trade and control of the seas, took control of Ireland, and planned colonial expansion.

His dictatorship was not universally popular because of his use of force and high taxes he imposed. But he introduced education reforms and gave more equality to the people. In 1658, Cromwell died and was succeeded by his son Richard. He was not an effective ruler and the army removed him. The English people wanted a king again, and in 1660, the son of Charles I took the throne as Charles II.

THE TRIAL OF CHARLES I

Charles was unpopular because he married a Catholic. He also imposed high taxes to pay for wars that people did not want, as well as trying to limit the powers of Parliament—he dissolved it for 11 years. At his trial and execution, he behaved with great dignity, and this won him some sympathy. At his execution, Charles put on an extra shirt so that people would not think that, when he shivered from the cold, he was shivering with fear. His body was secretly buried by his supporters at Windsor Castle.

◄ The seal of the House of Commons depicts the Commonwealth Parliament in session in 1651.

▼ Shortly after the end of the Civil War, there were two disasters in London. The first was the Great Plague, which arrived from Europe, and killed about 20 percent of London's population in 1665. Then, in 1666, the Great Fire destroyed most of the city.

CHINA: THE QING DYNASTY 1644–1770

The Qing dynasty was founded by the Manchus, a Siberian people who lived in Manchuria. The Qing dynasty would rule China from 1644 to 1911.

The Manchus came to conquer China from lands lying north of the Great Wall. During the Manchu period, the size and population of China grew, and the troublesome Mongols were finally defeated.

This intricate gold flower-shaped brooch was made during the Manchu period and was exported to Europe.

▼ The grand houses and ornamental gardens of the upper-class Qing Chinese are depicted on this ebony paneled Coromandel screen, made in 1672. Such screens could have up to 12 panels and were shipped to Europe from the Coromandel coast in India.

The Ming dynasty of emperors had ruled China since 1368. But heavy taxation had made their rule unpopular and rebellions broke out all over the country. The last Ming emperor, Chongzhen, hanged himself as peasant rebels overran his capital, Beijing. In the confusion that followed, the Manchu chieftain Dorgon led an army south from Manchuria. He occupied Beijing and set up the Qing ("pure") dynasty. His nephew Shunzhi was the first Qing emperor.

Resistance to the Manchus continued in China's southern provinces, and 40 years went by before all of China submitted to their rule. The Manchus lived separately from the Chinese in closed-off areas. Marriage between Chinese and Manchus was forbidden. Chinese men were even compelled to wear their long hair in *queues* (pigtails) to show that they were inferior to the Manchus.

However, both Chinese and Manchus were employed as civil servants to run the empire. As time passed, the Manchus adopted Chinese customs and were eventually accepted. They were few in number, so they had to be careful not to be too excessive in their treatment of the Chinese. They brought new life and efficiency to the country without disturbing the nation's customs.

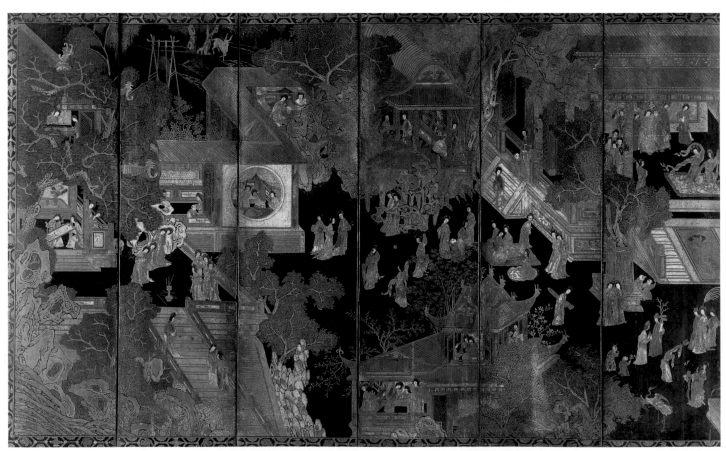

A RICH AND POWERFUL EMPIRE

At first China prospered under Qing rule. The empire grew and trade increased, particularly with Europe. Chinese silk and porcelain were considered the finest in the world, and their cotton goods were inexpensive and of high quality. Huge quantities of Chinese tea were sold abroad when tea drinking became fashionable in Europe in the 1700s.

The empire became so rich and powerful that its rulers were able to treat the rest of the world with contempt. Under Emperor Kangxi's rule (1661–1722), foreign traders were forced to kneel whenever his commands were read out. The Manchus also forced several nations into vassal status, including Tibet, Annam (now Vietnam), Burma, Mongolia, and Turkestan, making the Chinese Empire the world's largest at the time. They made a deal with the Russians over land and trade.

Early on, there were some rebellions in southeast China and among ethnic minorities, who protested against Chinese people moving into their areas. But, on the whole, the Qing period brought peace, prosperity, and security to China. The population grew dramatically from 100 million in 1650 to 300 million in 1800, and Chinese (Han) people spread out to the west and southwest of China. In the late 1700s, however, corruption and decline began to set in.

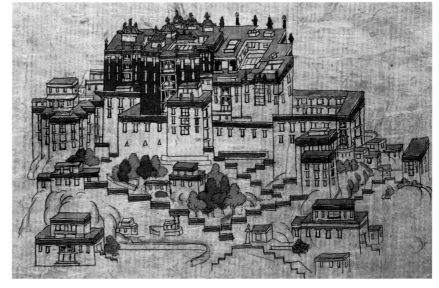

▲ Tibet (Xizang) was ruled by a Buddhist leader called the Dalai Lama. The third Dalai Lama rebuilt the Potala monastery in Lhasa, the capital, as his residence in 1645. The Dalai Lamas came under the influence of the Mongols, but the Qing army invaded and by the mid-1700s, Tibet was part of the Chinese Empire.

◄ This enameled porcelain vessel from the late 1600s imitated the shape and design of the bronze ritual vessels of ancient Shang China.

◄ The Chinese silk industry employed thousands of workers, especially women, to weave silk into cloth on looms. Silk cloth was made for use in China and for export to Europe. Cotton was also imported and then made into cloth for export. The weavers of the port of Su-Chou were particularly famous for their silks.

KEY DATES

1644	The Manchus found the Qing dynasty in Beijing
1644–60	Manchu forces conquer most of China
1661	The island of Formosa is captured from the Dutch by supporters of the defeated Ming; Kangxi becomes second Qing emperor
1674–81	Rebellions in the south, soon suppressed
1683	Manchu forces capture the island of Formosa from supporters of defeated Ming
1689	Russians swap Siberian land for trade in China
1696	The Manchus defeat the Mongols in Mongolia
1717–20	War against the Mongols to control Tibet
1750s	Chinese invade Tibet and Turkestan
1760s	Chinese invade Burma, making it a vassal state

THE SUN KING 1643–1715

Louis XIV was determined to make France a great nation. The whole life of France revolved around him and he became the most powerful ruler in Europe.

Louis XIV (1638–1715) became king in 1643 at the age of five. His mother, Anne of Austria, ruled as regent on his behalf for eight years until 1651. In 1648, the people of Paris, burdened for many years by heavy taxes, rose in revolt. Louis was forced to flee the city. The revolt, called the Fronde, collapsed in 1653. Louis decided this would never happen again and, in 1661, at the age of 22, took control. He turned France into an absolute state, ruled solely by the king. In 1665, Louis appointed Jean Colbert as his Controller-General of Finance. Colbert made France the best-run country in Europe. He reorganized taxes and reformed laws. New industries were set up. He had roads, canals, and bridges built, and he greatly expanded the French navy and merchant fleet. Louis and the royal family moved into a magnificent new palace at Versailles in 1682. Heads of the noble families of France were also made to live there so that Louis could keep an eye on them.

Louis XIV sent his general, the Duc de Vendôme, to help the Bourbon king of Spain, Philip V. Here, Vendôme inspects Austrian banners after the battle of Villaviciosa.

As Louis grew older, he came under the influence of others and became more rigid, especially in his religious beliefs. Conflict developed. In 1685, he revoked the Edict of Nantes, and no longer showed tolerance toward the Huguenots.

To Louis, France's natural boundaries were the Alps, the Pyrenees, and the Rhine. He plunged France into war to expand it to these borders. The French army became the largest, most formidable fighting force in Europe. But Louis lost most of the land he had gained. He left his grandson and heir, Louis XV, a country under rigid control and nearly bankrupt from war.

▲ Louis XIV wanted France to be a great cultural center. He helped develop the arts, including ballet. In 1661, he set up the Royal Academy of Dance. Here the king himself dances as the sun god Apollo in *The Ballet of the Night* in 1653—an event that lasted an incredible twelve hours. It is because of this performance that Louis came to be called the Sun King.

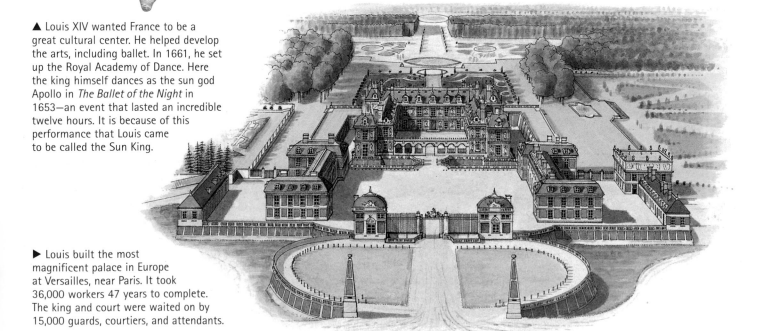

▶ Louis built the most magnificent palace in Europe at Versailles, near Paris. It took 36,000 workers 47 years to complete. The king and court were waited on by 15,000 guards, courtiers, and attendants.

DECLINE OF MOGUL INDIA 1605–1707

After the death of Akbar the Great, the Mogul Empire began to decline. The warlike Marathas and the British eventually caused its disintegration.

Mumtaz Mahal was Shah Jahan's favorite wife. She died in childbirth in 1629, after 19 years of marriage. The magnificent Taj Mahal, a masterpiece of Mogul architecture, was built in memory of her.

Akbar, the founder of the Mogul Empire in India, died in 1605. His son Jahangir (1569–1627) succeeded him, but was not interested in ruling. He preferred the company of painters and poets, so he lavished his energies and money on constructing splendid buildings and elaborate gardens. Meanwhile, his beautiful, ambitious wife, Nur Jahan, ruled the country. Shah Jahan (1592–1666) succeeded his father Jahangir as emperor in 1628. He extended the empire, and by 1636, he had conquered the Deccan in central India. His end was tragic. In 1657, he fell ill, and his four sons quarreled over his succession. Aurangzeb (1618–1707), the third son, imprisoned his father, killed his brothers, and seized the throne.

Shah Jahan conquered the Deccan in central India and rebuilt Delhi as the capital of the Mogul Empire. Imprisoned by his son in 1657, he died in captivity.

Aurangzeb conquered much of the rest of India, but he could not overcome the warlike Marathas on the west coast. He was a fanatical Muslim. Most of his subjects were Hindus, and he persecuted them without mercy. Opposition to him grew. The Marathas overran the Deccan, and revolts broke out across India. After Aurangzeb died in 1707, the empire began to break up. The 1700s saw many wars, and the provincial governors (*nawabs*) became more independent. The Marathas and the British began to take over the Mogul lands.

TAJ MAHAL

Shah Jahan built the Taj Mahal near Agra as a tomb for Mumtaz Mahal ("Chosen One of the Palace"). The beautiful building was made of white marble inlaid with patterns of semiprecious stones, and took 11 years to build. The whole complex took a total of 22 years to complete.

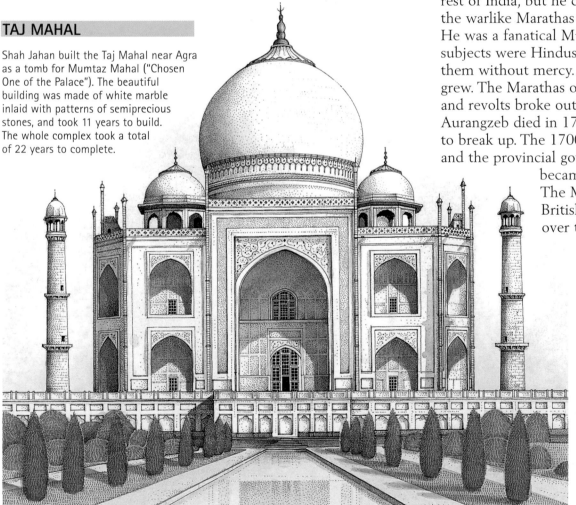

KEY DATES	
1605	Jahangir, emperor for 23 years
1608	The English arrive in India
1611–22	Nur Jahan, Jahangir's wife, rules
1628	Shah Jahan, emperor for 30 years
1658	Aurangzeb, last great Mogul, 49 years
1660s	Rise of the Marathas, the Moguls' opponents
1707	Beginning of decline of the Moguls

THE OTTOMAN EMPIRE 1602–1783

After the reign of Süleyman the Magnificent, the Ottoman Empire entered a long and slow decline. Nevertheless, the empire survived until 1923.

Sultan Osman II (1603–1622) ruled from 1618. He was young, strict, and fond of archery. He restricted the power of the Janissaries (senior army officers), but they took over, had him killed, and replaced him with Mustafa I.

In 1565, Süleyman the Magnificent decided to invade Malta, occupied at the time by the Crusader Knights of St. John. Although the Turks greatly outnumbered the Knights, their invasion was not successful, and they had to withdraw after several months. Süleyman died in 1566. In 1571, when the Ottomans tried to invade Venetian-ruled Cyprus, their invasion force was destroyed by a combined fleet from the navies of Venice, Spain, and the Papal States, at Lepanto off the coast of Greece. In 1602, a long and costly war broke out with Safavid Persia, with no gain. Plagues and economic crises also hit Istanbul. Once-profitable trade routes linking Asia, Africa, and Europe were bypassed as new sea routes around Africa and land routes through Siberia opened.

THE EMPIRE FADES

The Thirty Years' War in Europe gave the Ottomans some peace. But when, in 1656, they tried to invade Crete, the Venetians blocked the Dardanelles (the narrow sea passage from the Mediterranean to the Black Sea), threatening Istanbul itself. This caused panic, and the sultan, Ibrahim, was deposed by army officers. A new grand vizier (chief minister), Mehmet Kuprili, took charge. He reformed the economy and army, and Ottoman fortunes revived.

The next vizier, Kara Mustafa, tried to invade Hapsburg Vienna for a second time in 1683. The defenders of Vienna held out for two months until an army of Germans and Poles arrived to defeat the Turks. The Austrians invaded Hungary, the Venetians took part of Greece, and the Russians threatened Azov in the Ukraine. Another vizier, Mustafa Kuprili, took office in 1690. He managed to drive back the Austrians, but he was killed in 1691. During the 1690s, the Ottomans finally lost Hungary and Azov. Their European empire was saved only because Austria went to war with France.

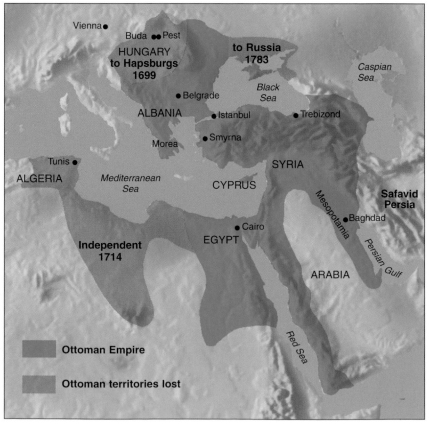

▲ Sultan Mustafa I (1591–1639) was mentally unstable. He ruled twice—between 1617–1618 and again between 1622–1623.

▶ The Ottoman Empire was still large, but it was slowly falling apart at the seams as its prosperity dwindled.

THE EMPIRE SHRINKS

Between 1710 and 1720, the Ottomans regained Azov and Greece, but they lost Serbia and parts of Armenia. They also lost control of most of northern Africa—Algeria, Tunisia, and Libya. Officially, these countries were still Ottoman, but were actually independent. In 1736, the Russians attacked again, and by 1783, they had taken the Crimea and most of the Ukraine—the Ottomans no longer controlled the Black Sea. In Anatolia, local chiefs were rebelling, and in Istanbul, people were worried about the future.

The Ottoman Empire was still strong, but it had lost much of its trade and wealth. The progress made in the early days of the Ottoman Empire in religion, the arts, and social advances, slowed. The Ottomans' only friends, the Moguls, were also in decline, while the Europeans were advancing rapidly. But the Ottoman Empire was not yet finished.

▶ A Turkish miniature, made in 1610, shows a festival of musicians called to entertain the sultan in Istanbul. To keep the sultans separate from politics and the people, they were looked after lavishly. The authority of the sultans was finally weakened by a series of bloody contests for power among the ruling families.

▼ The siege of Vienna in 1683 marked the farthest point of the Ottoman Turks' advance into Europe. The defenders of Vienna held out for two months, just long enough for a slow-moving army of Germans and Poles to arrive. The Turks were utterly defeated in a 15-hour battle on September 12, 1683.

THE AGE OF REASON 1600–1750

By the mid-1600s, the ideas of the Renaissance had spread through most of Europe. New discoveries were being made about the world and human beings.

New ideas in science and philosophy were debated in salons such as that of Ninon de Lenclos (1620–1705). Such salons were the breeding-ground for the Age of Reason in Europe.

John Locke (1632–1704) was an English philosopher who examined the nature and scope of human understanding.

Within a few hundred years, the people of Europe had witnessed great changes. Ships were now traveling to far-off lands, bringing back goods and knowledge from other cultures. Europe had become a money-based economy, with new and larger cities and towns. Literature, theater, and opera had made great strides. Kings and nobles lived on elegant estates, isolated from the rest of the population. Ministers and civil servants controlled governments. New thinkers had introduced radical ideas.

Life was now very different for everyone, rich and poor. People began to question and doubt the truth of many commonly held ideas. The words of the Bible and the philosophers of ancient Greece no longer satisfied everyone. Many people began to believe in their ability to think things out for themselves. At the same time, new discoveries were being made about the world and the heavens, and about other countries and human beings. There was an urge to examine, research, experiment, and discuss anything and everything, to cross a new frontier of scientific inquiry. This revolution in scientific methods and ways of thinking became known as the Age of Reason.

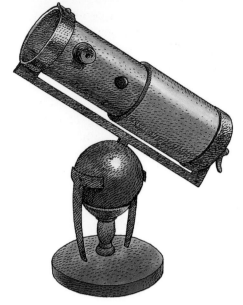

Sir Isaac Newton (1642–1727) produced a reflector telescope that sharpened and magnified the vision of distant stars. Astronomy became a more accurate science.

Travelers went to Japan, Armenia, Mexico, Arabia, and Africa, to explore and report back on what they found. New medicines (as well as diseases) arrived from far-off lands. Doctors began opening corpses to study the body's organs and their functions. Botanists collected and started to classify plants; chemists experimented with compounds. During the 1600s, telescopes, barometers, pendulum clocks, calculating machines, and air pumps were all invented.

THE ROYAL OBSERVATORY

The Royal Greenwich Observatory was founded by Charles II, himself an astronomer, and was built by Christopher Wren in 1675. The first Astronomer Royal was John Flamsteed, a noted astronomer of the time. The observatory was built to produce accurate star charts and tables of planetary motion for sailors. Greenwich became a center for the study of time. Greenwich Mean Time, the world's time standard, was established in 1880. For centuries, Greenwich was a leading observatory—until London's pollution and electric streetlighting in the 1900s made it necessary to move its astronomical work to other, less polluted places in England.

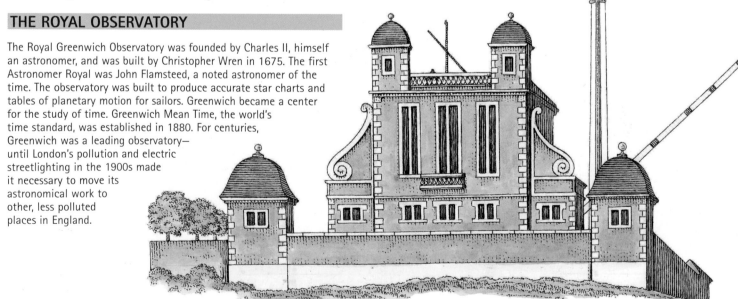

LOGIC AND NEW IDEAS

Mathematicians such as Leibnitz and Descartes worked with geometry and calculus. Galileo and Newton studied gravity, and Kepler worked on planetary motion. Tycho Brahe cataloged the stars; Snellius, Huygens, and Grimaldi researched the behavior of light; and Boyle studied gases. Mechanical objects followed a logic that made sense, and this logic was also applied to human society and politics. Francis Bacon developed the idea of the perfect state. Others wrote about government, the rights of people, and the "contract" between rulers and ruled.

New institutions grew up where these ideas could be discussed. Cardinal Richelieu's Académie Française was founded in 1635. Early members of the Royal Society in England were the chemist Robert Boyle, the physicist Isaac Newton, the diarist Samuel Pepys, and the architect Christopher Wren. In the new smoke-filled coffeehouses and teahouses around Europe, people were talking to each other as never before. A new, nonreligious, "rational" way of seeing things took shape. The work of René Descartes, Isaac Newton, Francis Bacon, Galileo, and many others formed the foundation for today's knowledge of the world.

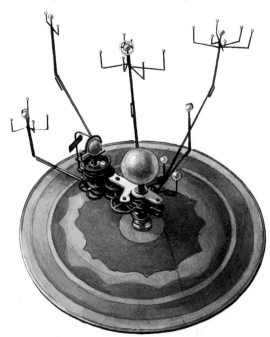

▼ The first orrery was built in 1700 to demonstrate the movements of the planets around the sun, and moons around the planets. A handle turns the planets.

In 1652, the first coffeehouse was opened in London. People discussed business and politics and exchanged information. The most famous was Lloyd's coffeehouse, which served people who insured shipping.

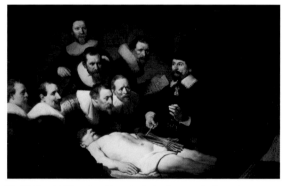

Until the 1600s, the Church forbade people to cut open human corpses for study. This painting by Rembrandt shows Dutch doctors examining the dissection of a body.

Galileo Galilei (1564–1642) was an astronomer, mathematician, and physicist. He offended the Catholic Church by teaching that the Earth revolves around the sun.

Galileo's early telescopes were primitive, but they helped him discover four of Jupiter's moons.

KEY DATES

1608	Hans Lippershey, a Dutch optician, invents the first telescope
1609	Galileo studies the heavens; Kepler formulates Laws of Planetary Motion
1628	Harvey discovers blood circulation
1635	Académie Française founded
1637	Descartes' Analytical Geometry explained
1644	Evangelista Torricelli, an Italian scientist, publishes his theory on the barometer
1647	Pascal invents an adding machine
1657	Huygens builds a pendulum clock
1660	A barometer is used to forecast the weather
1666	Newton formulates Laws of Gravitation
1673	Leibnitz invents a calculating machine
1705	Edmund Halley predicts return of comet in 1758
1735	Carl Linnaeus classifies plants and animals
1742	Anders Celsius devises Celsius scale of temperature

SLAVERY AND PIRATES 1517–1810

The early development of many colonies in the Americas was carried out by pirates, the owners of sugar plantations, and millions of African slaves.

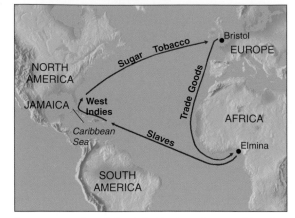

From ports such as Bristol, finished goods were shipped for sale in West Africa. Once the goods had been sold in Africa, the ship would be loaded with slaves to take to the West Indies. The final leg of the voyage would bringa cargo of sugar back to Europe.

West Africa was rich in gold. Arabs called the area "Guinea" and Europeans borrowed the word. In 1663, a guinea coin of Guinea gold was issued by order of Charles I.

Within a hundred years of Columbus' landing in 1492, most of the native peoples of the Caribbean islands, the Arawaks and Caribs, were dead as a result of European mistreatment and diseases. By the early 1600s, the Caribbean was a battleground. The Spanish, French, English, and Dutch all fought for the islands they called the West Indies. Some islands changed hands several times in a fierce contest for trade and for land to establish European colonies.

English, French, and Dutch privateers became pirates to make their fortune. They were often sponsored by their governments, since they caused trouble for the Spanish, captured islands, established settlements, and made good profits. Some were later sent out as admirals or colonial governors. Francis Drake sailed around the world between 1577 and 1580, raided Spanish ships, and returned home rich. Captain Kidd was enlisted to help control pirates, but joined them instead. Edward Teach (Blackbeard) and Captain Morgan raided Spanish settlements and galleons in the Caribbean. They paved the way for the establishment of colonies. The Spanish lost gold to the pirates, but this did not stop them from colonizing the Americas.

THE SLAVE TRADE

In Europe, tea and coffee were becoming fashionable, and this led to a huge demand for sugar to sweeten them. Sugar grew well in the climate of the West Indies, but its cultivation needed many workers. Local labor could not be found, because many of the original islanders had died, and so the colonists imported slaves from West Africa.

Europeans saw nothing wrong with using Africans as slaves. They were bought cheaply, crammed into ships, and then sold to plantation owners. Two thirds of them died, either on the voyage or from disease, harsh treatment, and overwork. Even so, by 1800, there were nine million African slaves in the Americas.

Newly captured slaves were chained together by the neck or feet. Iron collars stopped the slaves from running away.

▲ Iron manacles (handcuffs) that could not be opened without special tools were used to hold slaves' arms together.

▶ Whole families and villages of Africans were shipped to the Americas as slaves. Many did not survive the journey. West Africa, the Congo, and Angola lost much of their populations.

270

Slaves harvested the sugarcane on plantations in the Caribbean. Landowners grew wealthy. They often returned to Europe where they lived well, and left their plantations in the hands of managers.

THE TRIANGLE OF TRADE

The European-owned sugar plantations in the Caribbean were often very large. They had warehouses, boatyards, churches, slave quarters, and the landowner's grand house. A triangle of trade developed, taking finished goods from Europe to West Africa, slaves from West Africa to the Americas (the Middle Passage), and plantation products back to Europe. The profitable markets in Europe for sugar, tobacco, oils, and other products were exploited. Piracy, plantations, and slavery were driven by the urge for profit. Slavery continued into the 1800s. Most of today's African–Americans are the descendants of slave ancestors.

▶ Long before Europeans arrived, there was an established tradition of slaves captured in tribal conflicts, and often traded or sold. For centuries, the Arabs had traded slaves on the eastern African coast. When the Portuguese arrived they used the slaves in their colonial ventures.

HENRY MORGAN

Welsh Captain Morgan (1635–1688), pirate, was the scourge of the Caribbean between the 1660s and 1680s. He organized fleets of buccaneers, attacked Spanish galleons in midocean, and seized their treasures. Much of the booty went to England, to reward investors who sponsored his voyages. He captured Porto Bello in 1668, sacked Maracaibo in 1669, and took Panama in 1671. Later, he was knighted for his services against the Spanish, and was made lieutenant governor of Jamaica in 1674. He died in 1688, aged 53. Buccaneers like Morgan helped England's economy to prosper.

AFRICAN STATES 1550–1700

In the 1600s, Africa was a patchwork of different peoples and kingdoms. Each had its own customs, form of government, language, and gods.

During this period, the nations of Africa were developing rapidly. If the Europeans had not arrived, the African nations would probably have advanced their cultures much farther. Although Europeans did not have a great influence until the 1800s, they bought gold, exotic items, and slaves, and sold guns, cloth, tools, and finished goods. By doing so, traditional African trade and society were changed. Some areas, such as West Africa, lost many people to slavery. Social divisions increased as chieftains and traders made profitable deals with the Europeans. Some chiefs even sold their own people into slavery.

The largest African state was Songhay. European traders on the coast took the gold and slave trade away from Songhay, and its wealth collapsed. In 1591, a Moroccan army crossed the Sahara and invaded the country. South of the Sahara, new states had emerged, including Mossi, the city-states of Hausaland, and Kanem-Bornu, and Darfur. These Muslim states traded with the Ottomans and Arabs.

The West African kingdom of Benin is famous for its bronzes. This ram's head was made in the 1600s for a chief, who would have worn it on his belt.

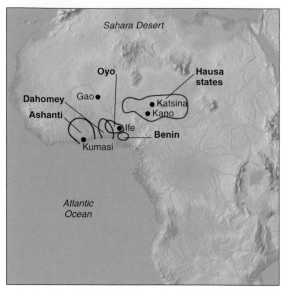

Gao, Katsina, and Kano adopted the Muslim faith, brought to West Africa across the Sahara by the Arabs. The coastal kingdoms kept their own religions. Much of northeast Africa was under Ottoman control.

In the east, Christian Ethiopia was surrounded by Muslim countries. Muslims in some parts of the country rebelled, ravaging Ethiopia. The Portuguese arrived and drove out the Muslims in 1543, and Ethiopia was left in peace. Along the east and west coasts, the Portuguese built forts and slave depots. These attracted Africans to the coasts and encouraged chiefs to grow rich by joining in the slave trade.

▲ This Ashanti helmet was decorated with gold animal horns and charms. Europeans were unable to buy slaves with gold from the Ashanti because they had all they needed. Instead they paid for them with guns that increased Ashanti military power.

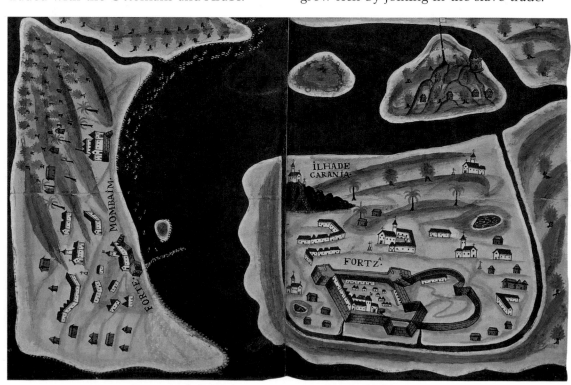

► The Portuguese built forts around the coast of Africa. This pictorial map, made in 1646, shows the fort at Mombasa on the east coast (now in Kenya).

DAHOMEY AND ASHANTI

A number of states occupied the forest zone along the west African coast. In 1625, a new kingdom called Allada was founded by King Akaba. Between 1645 and 1685, it merged with two other kingdoms to become Dahomey. This new state grew wealthy from the gold and slave trades. Dahomey was overrun in 1747 by Yorubas from Oyo (now in Nigeria). Dahomey became notorious to Europeans because, when its chief died, thousands of slaves were sacrificed so they could accompany him to the afterlife.

West of Dahomey lay Ashanti. In 1689, Osei Tutu founded the powerful Ashanti confederacy and built its capital at Kumasi. It grew wealthy from trade in cola nuts, gold, and slaves. The important Portuguese-controlled fort and trading post at Elmira in Ashanti was taken over by the Dutch in 1637.

Africa provided the slaves needed to work the rapidly growing plantations in the Americas. Millions were shipped across the Atlantic. Many died either during slave wars between African states to capture slaves or on the terrible voyage across the Atlantic ocean—the Middle Passage. To lose such an enormous number of its people was a catastrophe for Africa.

▲ A tribal celebration in the kingdom of Lovango in the Congo region in 1686. After the arrival of the Europeans, tribal security and unity gradually gave way to increased social distrust and control by greedy chiefs.

▶ A European trader offers brandy to the chief of the Alcaty tribe, in Senegal, West Africa, in exchange for water, around 1690.

KEY DATES

1570	Rise of Kanem-Bornu as a major nation
1575	Portuguese first settle in Angola
1588	The English Guinea Company is founded
1600	Mwenemutapa at its zenith
1625	New kingdom of Allada set up by King Akaba
1637	Dutch drive Portuguese from the Gold Coast
1652	Dutch East India Company founds Cape Town
1660s	Rise of Bambara kingdoms in West Africa
1685	Founding of Dahomey from three kingdoms
1689	Osei Tutu founds the Ashanti Empire
1701	Military expansion of Ashanti by Osei Tutu

◀ Here an *oba* (ruler) of Benin rides in a procession of his people. Once the richest state in West Africa, by 1700, the kingdom of Benin was on the wane. It was overwhelmed by the growing strength of the Yoruba people and the kingdom of Oyo.

IRELAND 1540–1800

English Protestant rule in Ireland was finally and forcibly imposed during the 1600s. There was resistance, but this was brutally crushed by the English.

The Irish never liked English rule. Henry II of England had conquered most of Ireland in 1171, and for the next 400 years English monarchs had struggled to maintain their authority there. Relations became more strained as time passed. The problem was mainly religious. The Irish were Catholic and the English had become Protestant. Irish priests encouraged rebellion by teaching that the English were heretics with no rightful authority over Ireland. But the English took strong measures to keep the Irish under their control. They dissolved many old monasteries and sold the land to families who supported their rule. The Irish reacted with frequent revolts. In 1556, Mary I sent troops into central Ireland to forcibly remove some of the native Irish and give their land to English settlers.

▲ James Butler, the Duke of Ormonde (1610–1688), governed Ireland for Charles I of England.

▼ The town of Drogheda was beseiged in 1641 by Catholic Irish forces led by Sir Phelim O'Neill.

PLANTATIONS AND REVOLT

The established hold of the English was further extended in 1580. English colonists were promised wealth and opportunity, and they quickly developed the land and new towns. But their colony was destroyed in 1598 by an Irish attack. A revolt broke out in Ulster, a purely Irish area, but was suppressed by 1603. The English started a plantation there, mostly with Puritan Scots settlers, strengthened by fortified towns such as Londonderry. Some Irish fought back, but many left. By the mid-1600s, the Catholics of Ulster were outnumbered by Protestants.

In 1642, an Irish uprising began, and thousands of Protestant settlers were killed. Engaged in the English Civil War, Cromwell did not tackle the uprising until 1649. He arrived with a large army and crushed the Irish with a brutality that has never been forgiven. Local people were moved to poor land in the west of the country, and English soldiers were given the land to settle. Catholics now owned less than half the land in Ireland.

HARSH PROTESTANT RULE

Irish hopes were briefly raised when Catholic James II became king of England. His daughter married William of Orange from Holland, commander of a grand alliance of countries fighting France. William became king of England in 1688. James, the "Old Pretender" escaped to Ireland. Eventually James's army (the Jacobites) met William's at the battle of the Boyne in 1690, and William triumphed.

This series of events marked a turning point in Irish history. Harsh laws were introduced that banned Catholics from owning guns. They were also forbidden to be involved in politics, to hold land, to receive education, and even to own large horses. Catholics converting to the Protestant faith were given land taken from those that remained Catholic. Communities broke apart, with some Irish accepting their lot, others resisting, and yet more leaving the country. But, while the 1700s were relatively peaceful, new trouble was brewing. When Wolfe Tone led a rebellion in the 1790s, many Irish people were killed, a French invasion was fought off, and the rebellion cruelly crushed. However, the English were forced to realize that the Irish Catholics were there to stay.

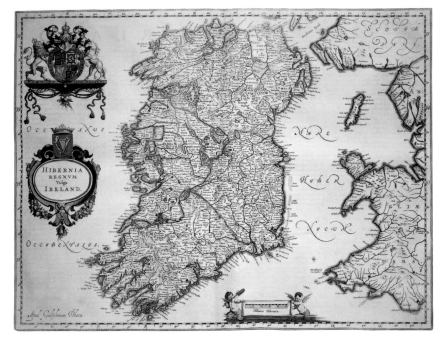

This map of Ireland was made by a Frenchman in 1635. Fourteen years later, Cromwell arrived with a large army and brutally suppressed an uprising against English rule. Many Irish people were moved to poor land in the west.

Being Catholic, James II was the great hope of the Irish Catholics. However, European power politics became caught up in the Irish question, and the English, under William III, had to defeat James.

KEY DATES

1556	Mary I starts Protestant plantations in Ireland
1580	Further plantation settlements established
1598	Revolts across Ireland, especially in Ulster
1642	Irish uprising against English control
1649	Cromwell's suppression of the Irish revolt
1690	Battle of the Boyne—a Protestant victory
1798	Wolfe Tone's nationalist rebellion

THE BATTLE OF THE BOYNE

This decisive battle took place near Drogheda in 1690. The army of the recently deposed James II, last of the Stuart kings, was outnumbered by the Protestant army of William III. When William's troops crossed the Boyne River, James's troops fled. James went into exile in France, and William's rule in England was strengthened by the victory.

RUSSIAN EXPANSION 1613–1725

At the beginning of Peter the Great's reign, Russia was a backward state. Peter began the process that turned Russia into one of the world's superpowers.

Peter the Great (1672–1725) is here portrayed as a cat.

I n 1682, at the age of ten, Peter I, known as Peter the Great, became joint czar of Russia with his half-brother Ivan V. Their half-sister Sophia Alekseyevna ruled as regent while they were young. Ivan was feebleminded, which Peter found very frustrating. In 1689, Peter seized complete control. At the beginning of his reign, Russia was a relatively backward state compared with the countries of western Europe. Peter's ambition was to make Russia a great European power.

◀ Peter encouraged fine craftsmanship. He gave this jeweled cup to his son Alexis in 1694. He could also be cruel. In 1718, he imprisoned and tortured Alexis to death.

▶ Czar Peter had enormous energy and was constantly at work making laws, drilling troops, planning towns, building ships, and even extracting teeth. He was careful with money, and gave most of his income to the state. He died after diving into the Neva River in the winter to rescue some drowning sailors.

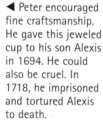

The boyars had been Russia's ruling class since the 900s. When Peter returned from Europe, he abolished their powers. He made them cut off their beards as part of his plan to modernize Russia.

RUSSIA LOOKS WESTWARD

Russia was a vast and potentially wealthy country. Its explorers were pushing east into Siberia. The Ural Mountains, rich in minerals, had been opened up, bringing new resources. Peter wanted to shift Russia's focus away from the East, and to make it look westward. This involved reducing the power of the boyars (nobles). The boyars had been the hereditary ruling class in Russia for 700 years, and they wanted to preserve tradition and further their own interests.

Peter realized that Russia would remain in isolation until it secured an outlet to the West, either through the Baltic, which was dominated by Sweden, or the Black Sea, which was dominated by the Ottomans. Russia had no ports except Archangel in the far north, which was frozen solid during the winter months.

To gain a warm-water port, Peter set out to conquer coastal territory. He captured Azov on the Black Sea from the Ottomans (though he later lost it again). In 1700, he went to war against Sweden, defeating Charles XII at Poltava in the Ukraine. In the peace treaty that followed he gained Estonia and Livonia. This gave him the foothold he needed on the Baltic coast.

PETER AND THE WEST

Peter centralized the government, and brought the Orthodox Church under state control. He changed the role of the nobility, and required them to serve him.

In 1697, Peter began an 18-month tour of western Europe, especially Holland and England, seeking to learn the ways and skills of the West. He traveled widely, disguised as an ordinary citizen, and visited factories, hospitals, almshouses (houses for the poor), and museums. To learn the art of shipbuilding, Peter worked as a carpenter in various European shipyards. Subsequently, he hired hundreds of the craftsmen and technicians to teach their skills to the Russian people.

On his return to Russia, Peter created a new civil service organized along European lines, and made his courtiers adopt Western dress and manners. He built factories, canals, and roads, and founded new industries. He improved the army and built a navy, and founded St. Petersburg as his new capital.

Although Peter was very enthusiastic, he could also be forceful and cruel, which lost him support. Peter's plan was only half-complete when he died in 1725, but he had started a process that was later to turn Russia into one of the superpowers of the modern world.

▲ When Peter the Great visited England, few knew that he was the czar of Russia. He was an inquisitive man and questioned everyone he met. He enjoyed the practical aspects of woodworking and shipbuilding.

◀ In spite of Peter's many reforms, Russian peasants continued to live in poverty. They often starved during the long, harsh Russian winters.

▼ Peter the Great brought many European architects and craftspeople to build his grand new capital at St. Petersburg. It was designed in the new Baroque style which was spreading across Europe. He is shown here discussing the plans with an architect in 1703.

THE GREAT NORTHERN WAR 1700–1721

Following a war between Sweden and other northern European countries, Sweden lost most of its empire, and Russia became the leading power in the Baltic.

This painting shows King Charles XI of Sweden (1655–1697) and his family. The future Charles XII (1682-1718) is held by his mother, Queen Eleonora.

This map shows the Swedish Empire at its greatest extent in 1660. Sweden was the largest military power in northern Europe and was in an ideal position to invade Russia in 1708.

The Great Northern War was fought between Sweden and other northern European powers, led by Peter the Great of Russia. At stake was control of the Baltic Sea and the lands around it. In 1700, Sweden was attacked by Denmark, Saxony, Poland, and Russia. Sweden's Charles XII was only 18, and his enemies hoped to take advantage of his inexperience. But Charles proved to be a born leader. He defeated the Russians at Narva in Estonia, forcing Saxony, Poland, and Denmark out of the war and putting a new king on the Polish throne. Eight years later, Charles invaded Russia. But the bitter winter of 1708–1709 set in, and the Russians retreated, destroying everything as they went. The Swedes ran short of food, and struggled against repeated Russian attacks. By the spring, Charles's army was just half its original size.

At the battle of Poltava in June 1709, the Russians beat the Swedes, and Charles fled to Turkey. He returned to Sweden in 1714, and beat off a Danish invasion in 1716. He invaded Norway and was killed there in 1718. Without Charles, and exhausted by 20 years of fighting, the Swedes agreed peace terms in 1721.

▲ This bronze plaque shows the taking of Narva in Estonia by the Swedes. During the battle, 40,000 Russian soldiers were crushingly defeated by an army of 8,000 Swedes. This was a tremendous victory for the young Charles XII of Sweden.

▶ The Battle of Poltava, near Kiev, in the Ukraine, in 1709, brought Sweden's power and dominance in the region to an end. Peter the Great's army was larger and better equipped, and the Swedes were tired, hungry, and far from home.

THE SPANISH SUCCESSION 1701–1713

When Charles II of Spain died in 1700 he left no heir. The question of who should succeed him led to the War of the Spanish Succession.

John Churchill, Duke of Marlborough (1650–1722), commander of the allied forces, won great battles at Blenheim, Ramillies, Oudenarde, and Malplaquet.

Prince Eugene of Savoy (1663–1736) fought the Turks at the siege of Vienna in 1683. By 1701, he had become commander-in-chief of the Austrian forces and fought at the battles of Blenheim and Oudenarde.

The French Bourbons and the Austrian Hapsburgs both claimed the Spanish throne. Before Charles II died in 1700, they had signed an agreement dividing his empire. But Charles's will left his lands to Philip of Anjou, the grandson of Louis XIV of France. Louis ignored his earlier agreement with the Hapsburgs, and chose to back Philip instead. But an alliance between France and Spain was not acceptable to every country in Europe.

By 1701, western Europe was at war. Organized by William III of England, England, the Netherlands, most German states, and Austria formed a grand alliance against France. In 1704, a French army was overwhelmed at Blenheim by a combined force under the Duke of Marlborough. He won three more victories over the French in the Spanish Netherlands. In 1706, an Austrian army under Prince Eugene of Savoy drove the French from Italy.

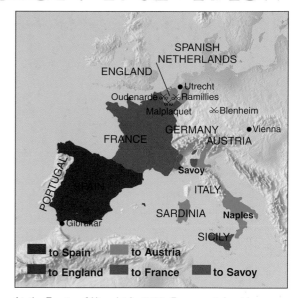

At the Treaty of Utrecht in 1713, France retained her frontiers. Austria took the Spanish Netherlands and Naples, England gained Gibraltar and Newfoundland. Philip V remained king of Spain.

The allies then invaded Spain, but the French forces pushed them out again, leaving Louis' grandson Philip V on the Spanish throne. The long war had exhausted both sides and, in 1713, a peace treaty was signed at Utrecht.

THE BATTLE OF BLENHEIM

In 1704, the Battle of Blenheim was fought in Bavaria among four armies and several nations. The French and Bavarians were marching on Vienna. The armies of Marlborough and Eugene intercepted them at Blenheim, and in the ensuing battle, 12,000 allies and 30,000 French and Bavarians were killed. However, it was a victory for Marlborough and Eugene, and Vienna was saved.

COLONIAL AMERICA 1600–1700

Settlers were arriving on the North American continent in large numbers. These European peoples shaped the character of future life in the "New World."

▲ William Penn (1644–1718) was a wealthy Quaker who founded Pennsylvania in 1681. He set out to welcome people who had suffered religious persecution and hardship.

▼ The Quaker Society of Friends was founded in England in the mid-1600s. They were Puritans and disliked priestly control of the Church. Quakers, including women, were encouraged to preach and speak out.

The French and Spanish made up the majority of the early European settlers, but they were later overtaken by the English and Germans. The majority were Protestants who had suffered persecution. Within 20 years of the first Puritans arriving, there were 20,000 English people living in Massachusetts. The colony developed rapidly, with Boston as its capital. Some of these colonists preferred the land in Connecticut. Others founded Rhode Island because they disliked Puritan religious restrictions.

In 1625, at the mouth of the Hudson River, New York had started out as a Dutch colony. When the English took over in 1664, English, German, and a variety of other nationalities settled there. It soon grew into a large cosmopolitan city of traders and craftspeople. Farther down the coast in 1681, in repayment of a debt, the English king gave Pennsylvania to a group of Quakers led by William Penn. Penn was a religious idealist and dreamed of a "holy experiment"—a new society. He helped poor people from Europe settle in the colony. Many English, Scottish, Irish, and German settlers moved there to start a new life.

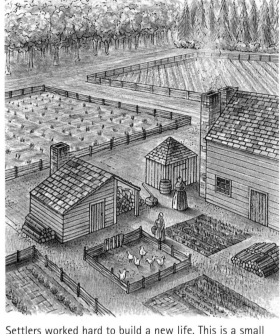

Settlers worked hard to build a new life. This is a small family farm in Maryland (previously New Sweden). The family kept cattle, pigs, and chickens and grew wheat, vegetables, tobacco, and cotton.

Farther south, the Carolinas and Virginia grew in size after the English Civil War, when King Charles II granted land there to his royalist supporters. They established profitable plantations growing tobacco, cotton, rice, and indigo. The settlers imported slaves from Africa to work the land from 1619 onward. Soon the majority of the people were slaves.

The Puritans of New England had a high regard for education. In 1636, the Massachusetts government founded Harvard College in Cambridge.

PIONEERING SETTLERS

In the southwest, Spanish–Mexican pioneers pushed up into New Mexico, and built a capital at Santa Fe in 1609. This was a colony of forts, mines, and trading posts. With Florida also in their hands, the Spanish might have taken all of North America, but Spain lost its control over the seas and they missed their chance. The French had settled around the St. Lawrence, the Great Lakes, and the Mississippi. As colonists, traders, fur-trappers, and pioneers, they were few in number. By 1700, there were 12 English colonies along the Atlantic coast, with some 250,000 English compared to only 20,000 French. Germans, Dutch, Swedes, Bohemians, Lithuanians, and other nationalities all found homes in different areas. The new America was being built by hardworking, ordinary people rather than distant European governments.

NATIVE PEOPLES

At first, the Native Americans and European settlers both gained from mixing together and in some cases, coexisting peacefully. But as more settlers arrived, native lands were seized. There were several atrocities, and native distrust of and resistance to the settlers grew. Local conflicts arose, leading to war in the 1670s. The settlers won, and native resistance declined. Some native peoples were actively driven from their homelands. As European takeover became certain, a gradual tide of Indian migrations began.

▼ The first elected representatives of the colony of Virginia, together with its governor and council, met in 1619 at Jamestown to make the laws.

▼ Fur was an important commodity that the settlers exported to Europe. Here, two French fur traders meet Native Americans near Lake Superior.

SALEM WITCH TRIAL

In 1692, several young girls in the town of Salem, Massachusetts, claimed that they had been bewitched by a West Indian slave, named Tituba. Most people of the time believed in witchcraft and the Puritans of Salem took fright. This led to the trial and execution of 14 women and 6 men accused of witchcraft. Several people died in prison, and 150 more awaited trial. Eventually, the madness was stopped by the governor, William Phips, and by a respected Congregational preacher, Increase Mather.

THE ARTS 1601–1707

In the 1600s, a new style of art and sculpture called Baroque developed in Europe. Many new forms of music also began to appear during this period.

Molière (1622–1673) wrote plays to entertain the court of Louis XIV of France. Best known are his comedies, which laugh at human failings such as stinginess and snobbishness. Some said he couldn't take anything seriously. Both the Church and people who were powerful in society saw this as dangerous.

In Europe, in the Ottoman Empire, and in Japan and China, differences between the culture of ordinary people and that of the ruling classes were widening. Ordinary Asian people's culture went unrecorded, but a lot is known about Asia's high culture. However, in Europe, popular culture was increasing, due to the development of printing, theater, and town life. In Italy, there was a new kind of pantomime, called *commedia dell'arte*, in which a company of actors would make up their lines as they went along.

Meanwhile, there was a new style developing among rich Europeans called Baroque. Painters, sculptors, and architects used it to produce spectacular grand effects and also to represent reality. Artists such as Rubens, Rembrandt, and Van Dyck from the Netherlands and Velázquez from Spain were in demand to paint portraits in an almost photographic style. Ruisdael of the Netherlands, Salvator Rosa of Italy, and Claude Lorraine of France were the leading landscape painters of the day.

In Japan, even lunchboxes were works of art. This black lacquer lunchbox, with figures painted on it, and several compartments, was made in the 1600s.

Authors such as Cervantes, Milton, Pepys, and Bunyan wrote popular books about issues of common concern. Musical instruments such as lutes, harpsichords, organs, and violins became common. Upholstered, polished, and highly decorated furniture was made. European composers wrote the first orchestral concertos, sonatas, operas, and oratorios.

This picture shows an opera production in the 1600s.

Kabuki drama was developed in Japan in the 1600s. It was extremely formal, combining dialogue, songs, music, and dance. Men took all the parts in the plays, many of which are still performed in Japan today.

▲ Ballet and opera grew from court entertainments. Ballet was developed during the 1600s in France, by court composer Jean-Baptiste Lully and dancer Pierre Beauchamp. Women did not dance roles until 1681. Opera began in Italy, and the first public opera house opened in Venice in 1637. Italian composers brought opera to Germany and France.

Early ballet dancer

◀ This is "David Slaying Goliath" by Giovanni Bernini (1598–1680), who was the leading Italian sculptor and architect of his day. Bernini designed and decorated churches, chapels, and monuments, as well as the tombs of eight of the popes.

▲ "Belshazzar's Feast" was painted by the Dutch artist Rembrandt van Rijn (1606–1669). It shows the last king of Babylon seeing a vision at a banquet. In it, Belshazzar foresaw his own death and the fall of his empire. This exotic and magical theme illustrates the growing interest in unconventional ideas in the late 1600s.

The Ottomans were notable for their elaborate palaces, mosques, and state buildings. Qing royalty in China, detached from ordinary Chinese life, developed elaborate styles, fashions, and customs, which, by 1800, became more rigid and unconnected with reality. Tokugawa Japan was slightly different, because the country had undergone a modernization. Here, Kabuki drama, novels, and new forms of entertainment were developing.

▶ This elaborate *cloisonné* book cover was made in China in the late 1600s. Cloisonné is a method of decorating metal surfaces. The design is outlined with thin wires and the spaces in between are filled with different-colored enamels.

ARCHITECTURE 1601–1707

Like the art of the 1600s, the architecture that developed in western Europe is called Baroque. Cities worldwide were largely rebuilt in this grander style.

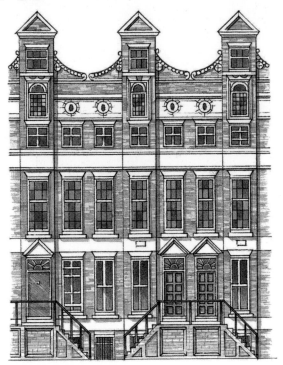

Townhouses in Amsterdam were made of brick and finely carved stonework. The Dutch built tall houses close together because land for building was scarce.

During the 1600s, great building projects were set in motion, both for practical reasons and for show. In India, the vast and elegant mosques, parks, and palaces of the Moguls took Islamic architecture to a new peak. In Qing China, a dramatic rise in the size of the population led to the building of new cities and public works. In the Ottoman Empire, the great architect Sinan had died in 1588, but during the 1600s his students built new mosques, bazaars, palaces, and public buildings in the style that he had initiated.

Europe was the scene of the greatest change. London was rebuilt after the Great Fire of 1666 by architects such as Sir Christopher Wren. At Versailles, southwest of Paris, a royal city was built for Louis XIV in the Baroque style. St. Petersburg, Russia's new capital, was designed and built by Europe's best Baroque architects; and in Berlin, capital of Brandenburg, new palaces, government buildings, and academies sprang up.

In England, Holland, and Germany, glass windows became more common in the late 1600s. Small panes of glass were held together by strips of lead. In the 1700s, improved production techniques meant that larger panes of glass could be used.

Functional buildings also took on a new look as European cities grew larger and more modern. Brick and stonework homes, warehouses, and streets, as well as public buildings and churches, displayed distinctive, modern styles that departed from the architecture of the past.

▼ The College of William and Mary in Williamsburg, Virginia, was founded in 1693. Originally named Middle Plantation, Williamsburg got its name in 1699, after Jamestown burned down and the capital was moved there. The name was changed in honor of King William III.

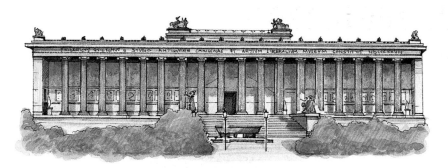

New town buildings featured large glass windows, straighter lines, bigger rooms, and well-designed fronts, reflecting a new sense of respectability among Europe's growing middle classes. The Puritan influence led to pleasingly simple, yet stylish buildings, as seen in colonial North America. In Amsterdam, Stockholm, Cologne, and Vienna, townhouses and streets took on a new shape. This set the patterns for the architecture that we know today. This period is considered the "early modern" period.

▲ A renewed interest in classical art resulted in many public buildings in Europe being modeled on Greek temples. The grand Baroque style of the Old Museum in Berlin uses Greek-style columns to give an appearance of power, age, and authority.

The Blue Mosque in Istanbul was designed by Mehmet Agha (pupil of the great Turkish architect Sinan) and built between 1606 and 1616. The complex, with its fine domes and courtyards, included a college, hospital, and libraries.

◀ After the Great Fire of London in 1666, Sir Christopher Wren was commissioned to rebuild St. Paul's Cathedral. Begun in 1675, the cathedral took 35 years to build, and was his masterpiece. Combining Renaissance and Baroque architecture at its finest, it towered proudly over the city.

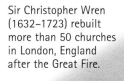

Sir Christopher Wren (1632–1723) rebuilt more than 50 churches in London, England after the Great Fire.

SCIENCE AND TECHNOLOGY 1601–1707

In the 1600s, scientists began to understand how nature worked and how they might control it. They made discoveries that led to great advances in technology.

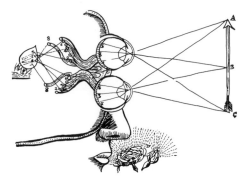

Early industrial machines, such as this screw press, made it much easier to handle large quantities of materials.

Jethro Tull (1674–1741), a prosperous English farmer and student of agricultural methods, invented the seed drill in 1701. The drill sowed seed evenly in straight lines that allowed weeding between each row. It was the first farm machine.

In the early 1600s, Francis Bacon, the great English philosopher, saw science as a study of God's creation by means of experimentation. In this way he forced a path between the religious beliefs of the past and the rise of reason and scientific inquiry. This century was an age of intellectual activity with science at its core. Until then, most thinkers rejected ideas if they broke with accepted religious beliefs. In the Age of Reason, unusual ideas and new information became acceptable. All the conclusions drawn from them were to be tested by experiment and observation.

Scientists now specialized in particular subjects. Notable breakthroughs were made by Robert Boyle in chemistry, William Harvey in medicine, and Sir Isaac Newton in physics and mathematics. Newton's idea that everything in heaven and on Earth could be understood by reason gave science a new, almost religious meaning. Meetings of scientists became popular in the 1640s. Academies, such as the Royal Society in London and the Royal Academy in Paris, were given royal patronage by the 1660s and led the way for the next 200 years.

The French René Descartes (1596–1650) argued that only ideas that could be proven by evidence or reasoning were true. This diagram illustrates his theory about the coordination of the senses.

All across Europe, new scientific ideas led to a flood of practical inventions. These were sought after by sailors, traders, generals, and kings, and there was a great deal of money to be made. Mechanical devices such as clocks, pumps, orreries, cannons, textile machines, and engineering tools were developed—sometimes by solitary geniuses, with little support.

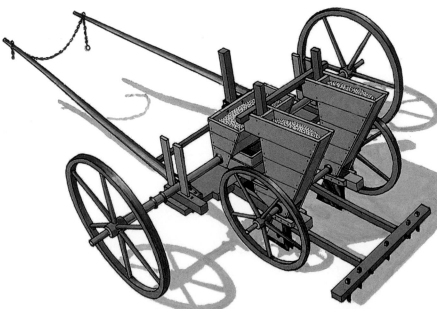

Galileo realized in 1582 that a swinging pendulum keeps accurate time, but it was not until 1657 that Christiaan Huygens designed the first successful pendulum clock.

Indian soldiers of the 1600s fought their battles dressed in coats of thick, quilted cloth. The cloth was tough enough to deflect the edge of a sword, but still allowed the wearer to move easily.

Thermometer   Barometer

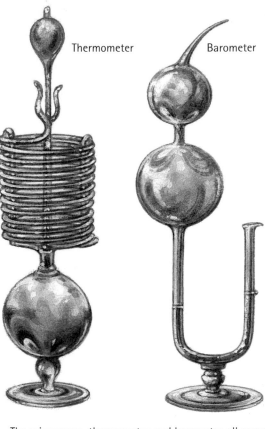

Microscope

The microscope, thermometer, and barometer all came into widespread use in the 1600s. They helped scientists carry out experiments more accurately.

WHEN IT HAPPENED

1608 Lippershey invents the telescope
1609 Drebbel makes the first thermostat
1644 Torricelli presents the barometer
1650 Von Guericke invents the air pump
1654 The first accurate thermometer used
1660 Royal Society is founded in London
1666 Royal Academy is founded in Paris
1668 Newton invents reflecting telescope
1687 Newton's Theory of Gravitation
1705 Edmund Halley predicts the return of Halley's comet in 1758

SCIENTIFIC ADVANCES

For the first time, heat could be accurately measured with the newly invented thermometer. Advances in mathematics kept pace with those in science. The invention of calculus, logarithms, and the slide rule enabled scientists to make detailed calculations to support their theories. Electricity was first identified by William Gilbert in 1600, but it was not until the 1800s that it was put to practical use. More great breakthroughs in steam engines, textile looms, and other machinery were to come in the 1700s. All this arose out of the ideas of the Renaissance and the research of the Age of Reason, which, as each century moved forward, laid the foundations of science and technology.

▼ Firearms such as these kept monarchs safely on their thrones. Only kings could afford to equip their armies with them. As a result, many kings grew too powerful to be overthrown by rebel subjects.

Double-barreled, wheel-lock pistol

Flemish matchlock

REVOLUTION AND INDEPENDENCE

1708–1835

The 1700s are often called "the century of revolutions." Between 1708 and 1835, there were revolutions against governments and growing colonial power in many parts of the world—some were successful, some were not. Political revolutions happened because people were dissatisfied with the way their countries were run. There were also revolutions in farming techniques, and industry, in science, technology, and medicine, in transportation, and in the arts—especially literature.

▲ The Jacobite Rebellion against Hanoverian rule in England ended at the Battle of Culloden in 1746, when the Jacobites were defeated by English troops led by the king's son, the Duke of Cumberland.

◄ Generals Rochambeau and Washington give orders for the attack at the siege of Yorktown during the American Revolution in 1781.

THE WORLD AT A GLANCE 1708–1835

In North America, the United States won its independence from British rule, but this brought problems for the Native Americans. Many people emigrated from Europe and took up more and more land. In Mexico and South America, the colonies fought for freedom from Spain and Portugal and won.

In Europe, Prussia and Russia rose to become major European powers, while the French Revolution of 1789 marked the end of the monarchy in France.

In Africa, the Fulani, Zulu, and Buganda peoples established new kingdoms. African states in the north threw off Ottoman control. The Mogul Empire in India collapsed and Britain and France fought for control of its land. China conquered Tibet, but faced problems at home. Japan banned contact with the West. In the Pacific, the arrival of Europeans threatened the traditional way of life.

NORTH AMERICA

The 1700s saw the birth of the United States of America and of Canada. The American Revolution had been caused by bad British colonial government. The United States became the world's first democratic, constitutionally ruled country, with a declaration of rights embracing everyone (except Native Americans and slaves). A declaration of independence was made, and after a while, the new republic began to spread its wings westward, reaching toward the Pacific Ocean. Migrants from war-torn Europe, seeking a new future, swelled the population. American towns, trade, and culture took shape and grew larger and richer. The British held on to Canada, which eventually gained greater control of its own affairs. Meanwhile, many Native Americans in the East were thrown off their lands, and made to migrate westward. In the South, slaves worked the cotton and tobacco plantations, catering for the appetites of Europe and fueling the wealth of their landowning masters.

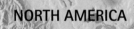

NORTH AMERICA

LATIN AMERICA

LATIN AMERICA

The Napoleonic Wars in Europe forced Latin Americans to think for themselves, and in the early 1800s, new independence movements fought against the Spanish and Portuguese for control of their colonies. The riches of the mines and slave-run plantations had declined in importance, and Latin Americans now had to fight for a place in a fast-changing world. But the independence movements were run by the landowners, so there was little gain for ordinary people. Native peoples suffered greatly under the rule of Europeans.

EUROPE

For much of the 1700s, a gap was developing in European society. Wealthy, autocratic rulers lived in great palaces, while the growing middle classes with "new money" developed a different, forward-thinking outlook. Society changed greatly. Cities grew, bankers and inventors were busy, foreign goods and ideas arrived. New inventions enabled factories to start making manufactured goods in large quantities. During the Napoleonic Wars, the old order was swept away across much of Europe, and the rule of law and business grew stronger. Russia expanded into the Far East, knocking on China's door. Europe now dominated the world, mainly as a result of trade, industry, bravado, and cannons, and its influence was still growing.

ASIA

During this time, India was slowly taken over by the British. China resisted such changes, growing conservative and refusing to entertain new ideas and foreign contact. Japan was still isolated, yet modernizing faster than China. Other Asian countries found themselves with both new friends and new enemies in the Europeans, who meddled in their affairs—always to their own advantage. Rivalry between Russia, China, and Britain for control of central Asia grew stronger. Asian traditions and stability were being undermined, and if Asian rulers resisted, the Europeans came in the back door.

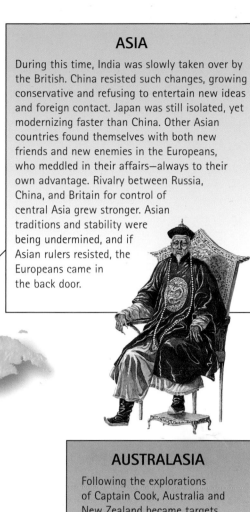

EUROPE

ASIA

MIDDLE EAST

AFRICA

AUSTRALASIA

AUSTRALASIA

Following the explorations of Captain Cook, Australia and New Zealand became targets for British colonization. Settlers started arriving in the early 1800. The Maoris, who were warriors, fought back, but the Aborigines of Australia, who lived simpler lives, were easily controlled.

AFRICA

Though Europeans and Arabs controlled a few coastal colonies, many African nations were now strong. However, their power came from trade with Europeans. Some tribes dominated others, and some, such as the Zulus and Ashanti, were aggressive toward their neighbors. African disunity made it easier for Europeans to turn one nation against another.

MIDDLE EAST

The Middle East was weak at this time because of the decline of the Ottomans. In North Africa and Egypt, Ottoman control was lost. Persia remained stable, largely unaffected by outside influences.

AUSTRIA AND PRUSSIA 1711–1786

The Austrian Empire was by now passing its peak, and Brandenburg–Prussia was growing stronger. They both sought to dominate the other states of Germany.

Maria Theresa (1717– 1780) was Hapsburg empress from 1740. She slowly improved conditions in the Austrian Empire with the help of well-chosen ministers, and reformed local government, education, and the army.

Charles VI, Archduke of Austria, became Holy Roman Emperor in 1711. This made him the most powerful man in Europe, and added the lands of the Holy Roman Empire to Austrian territory. After he died in 1740, three men claimed that they, not Charles's daughter Maria Theresa, should be crowned. The rivals were Charles of Bavaria, Philip V of Spain, and Augustus of Saxony.

The situation became more complicated as other European states got involved. The War of the Austrian Succession (1740–1748) began when the Prussians invaded the Austrian province of Silesia. Prussia was supported by France, Bavaria, Saxony, Sardinia, and Spain. But Britain, Hungary, and the Netherlands backed Maria Theresa. In the end, Maria Theresa kept her throne, but Austria was weakened, and Prussia kept Silesia. The balance of power in Germany shifted to Prussia, and the Holy Roman Empire declined. Over a century later, in 1870, it was Prussia which united Germany, and Austria was left out.

The enormous Schönbrunn Palace in Vienna, built between 1696 and 1730, is a grand example of decorative Rococo architecture.

BRANDENBURG–PRUSSIA

The Hohenzollern dynasty of Brandenburg inherited Prussia in 1618. By 1700, Brandenburg–Prussia had become a leading Protestant power, with Berlin as its capital. Its electors (kings) built an efficient government and helped its industries thrive. Prussia's rise to power began under Frederick William I. He reigned from 1713 to 1740 and built up the army. His successor, Frederick the Great, used the army to challenge Austria, France, and Russia. During his reign, he doubled the size of Prussia, improved its business and industry, and made it a cultural center of the Enlightenment. Over the next 100 years, Prussia gained more lands, and increasingly dominated Poland and northern Germany.

Frederick the Great (1712-1786) became King of Prussia in 1740. He was stern, brave, and ambitious. Under his leadership, Prussia became a strong nation. He established religious tolerance in Prussia and freed his serfs. But many men died as a result of the wars he entered.

In the Battle of Fontenoy in Belgium, in 1745, France had a major victory over Austria and its allies. In this painting, the French king Louis XV, points to the victor of the battle, Marshal de Saxe.

SCOTLAND: THE JACOBITES 1701–1746

During the early 1700s, the grievances of the Scottish people and Stuart claims to the English throne led to two fateful and bloody Scottish rebellions.

Charles Edward Stuart (1720–1788), or "Bonnie Prince Charlie" was half-Scottish, half-Polish, and raised in Rome. He led a rebellion in Scotland and was beaten at the Battle of Culloden in 1746.

Flora Macdonald (1722–1790) was the daughter of a laird who worked with the English, but she supported Bonnie Prince Charlie and helped him escape, disguised as her maid.

▲ The Jacobites were beaten at Culloden by English troops led by the Duke of Cumberland. He had all the wounded killed, and the others were chased and punished.

Scottish Highlanders, many of whom were Catholic, felt threatened by Mary, daughter of James II, and the Dutch and Protestant William III on the throne. They actively supported the return of a Scottish Stuart. To control such sentiment, the English tried to break down the Highland clan system. The lairds (clan chiefs) were forced to live in Edinburgh or London. As a result, they needed more money. They raised rents and cleared people from the highlands so that they could create large areas of farmland to increase production. Family feeling in the clans broke down, and relatives just became tenants, without any clan rights.

When Mary's sister Queen Anne died in 1714, her German cousin, George of Hanover, became king. He was the great-grandson of James I and a Protestant, but a foreigner. Some people felt that the Scottish James Stuart (1688–1766), son of James II, had a better claim. Many Scottish people were also unhappy about being joined with England in the "United Kingdom" in 1707.

The Jacobites supported James Stuart. They planned rebellions both in England and Scotland, but these failed. James returned from France in 1715, but it was too late; 26 soldiers were executed and 700 sent to the West Indies as punishment. In 1745, there was another uprising. James's son, popularly known as "Bonnie Prince Charlie," or the Young Pretender, landed secretly in Scotland. He overran Scotland, then invaded England. They got only as far south as Derby. In 1746, the Jacobites were cruelly defeated at the Battle of Culloden.

Bonnie Prince Charlie fled, and returned to France in disguise. The English gained control of the Highlands, and their revenge was severe. Highland lairds were executed and clansfolk disarmed. Until 1782, they were forbidden to wear kilts or play bagpipes. Over the years, clan lands were forcibly cleared of people to make way for grazing sheep, in order to earn money by supplying wool to the woolen mills of England. Clansfolk were sent to live in the cities, Northern Ireland, and the colonies.

▼ Bonnie Prince Charlie traveled from France and landed secretly in the Hebridean Islands off northwest Scotland on his way to lead the rebellion of 1745.

AGRICULTURAL REVOLUTION 1650–1800

During the 1700s, the landscape changed dramatically in parts of Europe as profitable new farming methods were introduced.

In many villages, the poor were forced to leave their homes to clear space for the new enclosed fields and modern farming methods.

This cartoon shows a farm worker carrying all the tools he needed to use on the new farms of the 1700s.

European farming methods had not changed for centuries. But by 1700, landowners, botanists, and breeders, particularly in England, were discussing better ways of running farms and growing crops. Scientists did research into animal breeding, land management, and raising crops. Cities and industries were rapidly growing larger, and there was more money to be made in farming. As profits rose, landowners studied and experimented even more. All this led to an agricultural revolution.

New plows were designed, and in 1701, the English farmer Jethro Tull (1674–1741) invented the horse-drawn seed drill, which allowed the mechanized planting of seeds in rows for ease of weeding. By rotating crops, soil fertility was increased, and by careful breeding, animals were improved. These methods all required financial investment and larger farms.

The rural landscape changed greatly during the 1700s. In many parts of England, land had been farmed in large, open medieval fields. Villagers rented strips of these fields, where they worked alongside their neighbors. This system provided enough food to keep people alive, but it did not produce a surplus to sell to town dwellers for profit.

▲ Thomas William Coke (1752–1842), Earl of Leicester, was a wealthy landowner and a member of Parliament. He was famous as a leader in the Agricultural Revolution. He changed the way soil was treated and the kinds of crops that were grown.

▶ Each year, Thomas Coke held a conference at his country house, Holkham Hall. Landowners and breeders from all over Europe met to discuss new farming and breeding methods. Here, he inspects some of his sheep with a visiting sheep breeder.

The British Royal Agricultural Society held outdoor meetings each year, to show pedigree animals and discuss farming. This meeting, near Bristol in southern England, took place in the early 1800s.

THE ACTS OF ENCLOSURE

Landlords decided that their fields could be farmed more efficiently if they were enclosed. Hedges and walls were built across fields, to create smaller units that were easier to work. The Acts of Enclosure, passed by Parliament between 1759 and 1801, also meant that common grazing land was enclosed. In total, 7,400,000 acres (3 million ha) of English land were enclosed during the Agricultural Revolution.

Many tenants lost their livelihoods, and had to move to towns. Rich landlords established enormous estates with grand houses. Their farms grew large, and some estates were redesigned as beautiful parkland by landscape gardeners like Lancelot ("Capability") Brown. This was all supported by the government, which itself was made up of landowners. But it brought hardship to ordinary farmers.

Experimental breeding of farm animals produced new, improved strains, such as this Old English breed of pig.

KEY DATES	
1701	Jethro Tull invents seed drill for faster planting
1730	Lord Townshend introduces the system of four-crop rotation
1737	Linnaeus develops a system of plant classification
1754	Charles Bonnet publishes a study of the food value of various crops
1804	French scientist Sussure explains how plants grow

Growing the same crop every year eventually weakens the soil. Using crop rotation increases soil fertility, especially if clover is sown every fourth year. This enriches the soil and lets it rest. Crops planted in the next three years grow better.

INDUSTRY: EARLY REVOLUTION 1708–1815

The Industrial Revolution began in Britain in the cotton industry. It brought a wealth of change—a rapid growth of cities, mines, canals, and factories.

The cotton gin was patented by Eli Whitney (1765–1825), in 1794. It was used to remove seeds and impurities from cotton fibers.

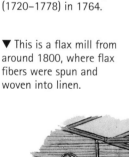

▲ The first multireel thread-spinning machine, the spinning jenny, was invented by James Hargreaves (1720–1778) in 1764.

▼ This is a flax mill from around 1800, where flax fibers were spun and woven into linen.

During the early 1700s, most people made goods in a traditional way, usually by hand, at home or in small workshops. The men were carpenters, blacksmiths, and weavers. Others were farm laborers, who worked on the land to grow crops to feed their families. Women worked at home, looking after the animals, cleaning sheep fleeces, and spinning wool into yarn for clothes. The Industrial Revolution changed all this. Many people began to move into towns to work for wages where employers were starting larger-scale production to increase profit.

The Industrial Revolution began in Britain in the textile industry. Machines, powered by waterwheels, speeded up the spinning, weaving, and finishing of cloth. Larger mills and factories were built. New towns sprang up in areas such as Yorkshire and Staffordshire in England, and the Ruhr Valley in Germany. Industrial cities such as Newcastle, Lille, Leipzig, and Rotterdam expanded rapidly. A network of canals was built to transport goods efficiently. Soon, steam engines were developed. Newcomen built a steam engine in 1712 for pumping water from mines, but it was not until 1774 that James Watt and Matthew Boulton built engines to power machines. In 1709, Abraham Darby began to smelt iron in a blast furnace using coke.

The fantail windmill was invented by Edmund Lee in 1745. The top rotated, steered by the fantail, so that the sails always turned toward the wind. It was used to pump water and grind grain.

Britain became known as the "workshop of the world." The Industrial Revolution began there because, unlike much of Europe, it was not ravaged by war. It had plentiful supplies of iron ore and coal; it was quick to develop a canal system; it had plenty of cheap labor (because of enclosures of farmland); and plenty of money was available from colonial profits.

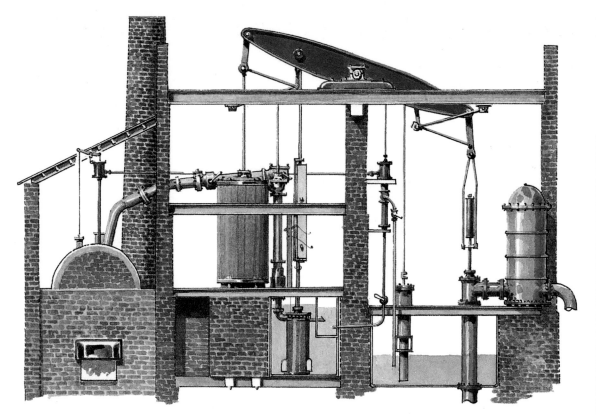

The first steam engine, built by Thomas Newcomen (1663–1729) in 1712, pumped water out of mines. Later designs were used to power factories.

KEY DATES

1709 Abraham Darby invents blast furnace
1712 Newcomen builds a steam engine for use in mines
1730 John Kay introduces mechanical textile machines
1759 Wedgwood's porcelain factory opens
1764 Hargreaves invents spinning jenny
1769 Thomas Arkwright invents a water-powered spinning machine
1769 Nicolas Cugnot builds a steam-powered vehicle for the French army
1773 Arkwright builds his first spinning mill (factory)
1794 Eli Whitney patents the cotton gin
1807 Robert Fulton's steamboat makes first trip

BRITAIN'S INDUSTRY BOOMS

By 1815, Britain's output of coal, textiles, and metals was equal to that of the rest of Europe. It had taken a century to reach that point. Tremendous social changes took place as people moved from the country to the towns—families and villages broke up, and workers were exploited by powerful factory owners. Many children died working in mines and mills. A new class of rich industrialists gradually evolved, as well as managers and professionals. London became the financial capital of Europe. Manufactured products were exported around the world, and raw materials such as silk, cotton, and timber were carried to new ports such as Liverpool and Glasgow, then taken inland by canal.

The Agricultural and early Industrial revolutions went hand in hand. The factories supplied new machines and tools to farmers, and farmers became more like businessmen who sold their products to growing populations in the towns. The personal relationships of local country life and local trade gave way to financial deals, middlemen, and contracts. The "dark, satanic mills" commented on by the poet William Blake were taking over.

The invention of the steam engine allowed railroads to be built to transport coal from mines to factories. In 1812, John Blenkinsop (1783–1831) designed steam rack locomotives that were used on the Middleton Railway in England.

INDIA IN TRANSITION 1707–1835

During the 1700s India suffered great devastation because of war and foreign interference. The Mogul Empire was replaced by the British Raj.

Robert Clive (1725–1774) was an administrator and soldier for the British East India Company in the 1750s and 1760s. By winning key battles against the French and Indians, and by diplomacy and bribery, he strengthened the British hold on India.

In 1707, the Mogul emperor Aurangzeb died. During his long reign he had spent many years trying to maintain power and hold the empire together. The religious tolerance that his predecessor Akbar had once encouraged had broken down. After Aurangzeb's death, India began a century of war as different groups tried to gain control. Local rulers, who were entrusted by Mogul emperors with responsibility for the protection of distant states, built up their own private kingdoms in Oudh, Hyderabad, and Bengal instead. In western India and the Punjab, rebellions were organized by the Hindu Maratha states and Sikh princes.

From 1740 to 1760, the Hindu Marathas conquered central India, taking over most of the Mogul lands. But their attempt to take over the Mogul Empire in 1761 was thwarted by invading Afghans.

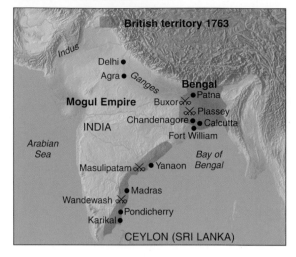

War in Europe between Britain and France spread overseas. Several major battles involving French, British, and Indian troops took place in India from 1756 to 1763.

In 1739, the Persians under Nadir Shah invaded the north and sacked Delhi, the Mogul capital, killing 30,000 people. The Sikhs of the Punjab had established virtual independence by 1762. The Nizam of Hyderabad took various lands in central and southern India. India was in chaos.

▲ As governor general of the French East India Company, Joseph-François, Marquis de Dupleix (1697–1763) built up a *sepoy* (native Indian) army and challenged British interests in southern India. The appointment of Robert Clive as commander of British troops finally defeated the French plans.

▶ The ruler of Persia (today's Iran), Nadir Shah (1688–1747), was a brilliant but ruthless general. In 1739, he led his troops in a successful attack on Delhi, the Mogul capital.

THE BRITISH TAKEOVER

The fragile Mogul Empire was also threatened by ambitious Europeans. The British and French East India Companies had acquired vast possessions in India, centered on their profitable trading posts. They made alliances with discontented Indian leaders, using a mixture of diplomacy, bribes, and bullying. The French were given Mogul land in southern India by the *Nawab* (local ruler) of Hyderabad, in return for military support. The British allied with the Marathas and Mysore. The British general, Robert Clive, fought and defeated the French in 1752. Then, in 1756, the ruler of Bengal seized the British base in Calcutta. The following year, the British victory at Plassey gained them Bengal. By 1761, the British had seized the French base at Pondicherry, and ended the French influence in India.

During the next hundred years, the British East India Company gained ever-larger territories, or forced independent states to obey them. It was only in 1858 that the Indian Raj, the company's rule in India, was taken over by the British government. Queen Victoria was made empress of India.

INDIA'S DOWNFALL

From 1707 to 1858, India went through a period of war and upheaval, followed by a gradual takeover by the British. In the early 1800s, the British overcame the Marathas and invaded central India, Sind, and the Punjab (now Pakistan). Christian missionaries were allowed in from 1813, roads were built, and a new class of English-educated Indians emerged to help run the vast country. There were many small independent states, but they survived only if they obeyed the British. India was not united, but it was under British control.

Robert Clive met Mir Jafar, a Mogul general, in 1757, and offered him money and other advantages if he changed sides. Mir Jafar's support helped the British win power in India.

▲ Ivory carving is an ancient Indian art form. This ivory comb, made in Mysore, in the 1700s, shows Lakshmi, the goddess of good fortune and prosperity.

◄ When the British took control, they tried to stop the feared practice of *thuggee*, in which members of a Hindu sect (thugs) attacked travelers and strangled them as a sacrifice to Kali, the goddess of death and destruction.

THE SEVEN YEARS' WAR 1756–1763

The Seven Years' War was a battle between the European powers for continental dominance, and for control at sea and of overseas colonies.

William Pitt, the 1st Earl of Chatham (1708–1778) was British secretary of state from 1756 to 1761. He directed the British involvement in the Seven Years' War with a sharp sense of strategy.

▼ The Seven Years' War was costly in lives and money for all the participants and fought on a large scale, as this skirmish involving Prussian and British soldiers demonstrates.

During much of the 1700s, Austria, Prussia, Russia, and France each wanted to take control of Europe. This was unfinished business left over from the War of the Austrian Succession, which ended in 1748. But none of the European powers was strong enough to win on its own, so they made alliances. As a result, there was an uneasy balance of power.

Austria, France, Sweden, Russia, and Spain were opposed to Prussia, Britain, and Hanover. Austria wanted to recapture Silesia from Prussia, and England and France were already fighting over their Indian and Canadian colonies. But wars were expensive in time, money, weapons, and lives, and they drained the warring states' resources. Fighting started in 1756 and lasted for seven years. At first, it seemed as if the Austrians and French would win.

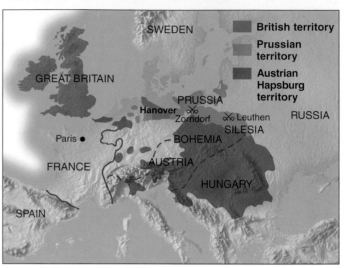

The Seven Years' War involved many nations, each with its own aims. Prussia and Britain gained the most. Prussia kept Silesia, and Britain gained greater control of Canada, India, and the seas.

Then the British, under secretary of state William Pitt ("Pitt the Elder"), joined the Prussians. Prussian victories in 1757 at the battles of Rossbach (against France), Leuthen (against Austria), and Zorndorf (against Russia), along with British success against the French at Plassey in India and in Quebec, restored the balance of power.

HOW THE WAR ENDED

In 1759, a British–Prussian army defeated the French at Minden in Germany, and the British navy defeated the French fleet at Quiberon Bay, northwest France. In 1760, the British took Montreal in Canada. Then, in 1761, William Pitt was forced to resign because his policies were unpopular with other politicians. Elizabeth, the czarina of Russia died in 1762, and the new czar, Peter III, withdrew Russia from the war. However, this did not bring an end to the hostilities. What actually ended it was the expense and destruction it brought to all sides as they ran out of money and military materials.

▼ The Battle of Zorndorf was fought between the Russians and the Prussians in 1758. The battle was fierce, and neither side really won, but Prussia benefited most, since it fended off a Russian invasion.

Ministers and diplomats now controlled governments and, after prolonged deprivation, many countries preferred to talk rather than make war. In the Treaty of Paris in 1763, it was agreed that Britain would get French lands in Canada and India, and the Prussians would keep the rich province of Silesia.

KEY DATES

1740–48	War of the Austrian Succession
1756	The Seven Years' War breaks out
1757	Battle of Plassey—British control of India grows
1757–58	Prussia battles for survival—victories at battles of Rossbach and Leuthen
1759	British gains in Canada and at sea; Battle of Minden—British–Prussian victory
1760	British take Montreal, Canada
1762	Russia withdraws from the war
1763	Treaty of Paris ends the war

In the Battle of Quiberon Bay, off Brittany in November 1759, the British navy defeated the French and, from then on, dominated the high seas.

This medal was made in honor of the alliance forged at Versailles in 1756 between Austria and France.

NORTH AMERICA 1675–1791

The mid-1700s saw a conflict for control of North America between settlers and the Native Americans, and between the English and the French.

Joseph Brant, also known as Thayendanegea, (1742–1807), was a Mohawk. He was befriended by an English official, who gave him an English name and education. Brant fought with the British when he was just 13, and became a captain in 1775. He later visited London and was received at the British court.

French and British colonists had been fighting for many years. First came King Philip's War (1675–1676), in which the New England Wampanoag tribes rose up against the settlers. The Wampanoag lost, but not before killing 10 percent of the adult males in Massachusetts. King William's War (1689–1697), between English and French settlers, did not achieve much. In Queen Anne's War (1702–1713), the English took Acadia (Nova Scotia) and destroyed Spanish St. Augustine in Florida. Finally, in King George's War (1744–1748), the British captured Louisbourg, a French fort, but it was returned in 1748 in exchange for Madras in India.

These wars were all related to European conflicts. Each side had one long-term aim: they wanted to control North America. Each side was helped by Native Americans, who fought in all the wars, hoping to receive support in their own disputes with colonists in return. But the Native Americans generally lost out to the settlers, who did not respect them. For example, between 1730 and 1755, the Shawnee and Delaware peoples were forced from their lands.

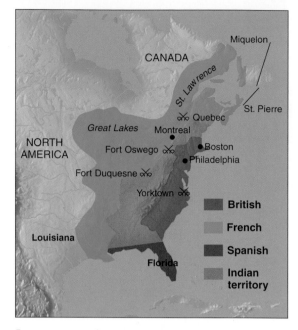

European possessions in North America at the beginning of the Seven Years' War in 1756. By the end of the war in 1763, Britain controlled most of France's lands.

PONTIAC'S REBELLION

In 1763, there was a Native American uprising. Pontiac (1720–1769) was chief of the Ottawa and of a confederacy of Algonquin tribes. To drive the British out, the tribes attacked places from the Great Lakes to Virginia. Some 200 settlers were killed. The British retaliated, and in 1766, Pontiac made peace. He was assassinated in Illinois in 1769 by a British-paid Native American.

CAPTURE OF ACADIA

Acadia, or Nova Scotia, was claimed by the French in 1603 and settled by them. Britain also claimed it, and attacked it several times during the 1600s. Finally, they captured it in 1710, though the French held on to nearby Cape Breton Island. In the late 1750s, the British threw out 10,000 of the Acadians. Many went to Louisiana, settling around the mouth of the Mississippi, where they became known as Cajuns. Nova Scotia was then populated by Scottish people, many of whom had lost their lands in the Highland Clearances.

The British taking of Quebec in 1759 meant the beginning of the end of New France. The battle took place in the fields outside the city. The British and French generals, James Wolfe (1727–1759) and the Marquis de Montcalm (1712–1759), both died during the fighting.

CANADA

The French and Indian War (part of the Seven Years' War) was fought from 1754. French colonists had settled in the Ohio Valley, and the British claimed it for themselves, so the French built a chain of forts and refused to leave. The French won some important battles in 1755 (Fort Duquesne) and 1756 (Fort Oswego). But the British captured Acadia in 1755, Quebec in 1759, and Montreal in 1760. The Treaty of Paris in 1763 gave Britain many former French colonies, and New France became British. Britain now controlled all of the lands east of the Mississippi River, and some French lands were given to Spain in exchange for Florida, which became British.

After the American Revolution, many colonists loyal to the crown, but with strong feelings about freedom, moved north to Canada. So, in 1791, the British Constitutional Act split Quebec into English-speaking Upper Canada (Ontario) and French-speaking Lower Canada (Quebec). The Act set up a government with an elected body in each of the two provinces. The British hoped that this would satisfy the growing demand for a government in which people felt they had a say. The French were also guaranteed continuing freedom of religion.

Through the death of General Montcalm near Quebec in 1759, the French lost their military leadership, and thus lost control of Canada.

KEY DATES

1675–76 King Philip's War
1686–97 King William's War
1710 Acadia taken by the English
1739–41 The British fight Spanish Florida
1744–48 King George's War
1754–63 French and Indian War
1760 British gain control of Canada
1763–66 Pontiac's Rebellion
1775 American Revolution begins

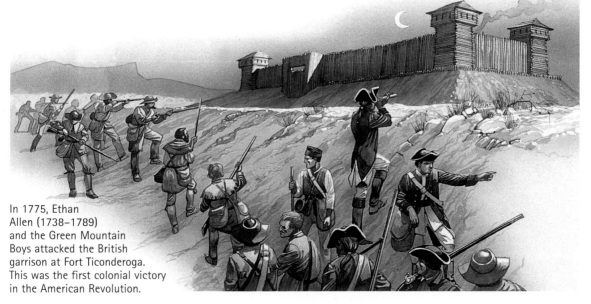

In 1775, Ethan Allen (1738–1789) and the Green Mountain Boys attacked the British garrison at Fort Ticonderoga. This was the first colonial victory in the American Revolution.

TRADE WITH CHINA 1700–1830

Trade with China was profitable, but the government there did not want "barbarian" influences introduced. European merchants looked for other ways to trade.

China reached its largest size during the reign of Qianlong, spreading its tentacles into central Asia and Tibet—but this expansion was expensive and brought few benefits except keeping out the British and the Russians.

Qianlong (1711–1795) ruled China for 60 years from 1735. He was a philosopher-emperor who supported the arts, wrote poetry, and created libraries.

Throughout the 1700s, Chinese silk, cotton, tea, lacquerware, and porcelain were highly prized in Europe. They were expensive and in short supply. Merchants from Portugal, Britain, Italy, and the Netherlands tried to expand trade with China. But the powerful Chinese emperors, who controlled all contact between their people and foreigners, were simply not interested. Qianlong (Ch'ien-lung), emperor for 60 years, was a scholar and traditionalist who had no time for "barbarians." The Europeans' problem was that they had to pay for everything in silver, because Chinese traders were not allowed to exchange foreign for Chinese goods. Also, Europeans were permitted to trade only in Guangzhou (Canton), where they were penned up in "factories" (fortified warehouses), and forced to trade through Chinese intermediaries. European traders were competitive, and fought to get the best Chinese goods and to ship them to Europe quickly to fetch the highest prices.

▲ These Chinese maps from around 1800 show China, the "Middle Kingdom," sitting at the center of the world. At the time, China was isolated—but the world was knocking at its door.

▶ In 1793, the British diplomat Lord Macartney visited the Chinese emperor to encourage trade relations. Such relations were rejected, so people resorted to illegal deals. China and Britain had little respect for each other.

THE OPIUM TRADE

Opium had long been used in China for medicinal purposes. Since European merchants were looking for other ways to trade, they established links with Chinese drug dealers, and sold them vast quantities of opium (5,000 barrels every year by the 1820s), from countries such as Burma. In return, they received precious Chinese goods for Europe. The trade grew steadily in the late 1700s, and the Qing government tried to stop it. By the 1830s, opium use was spreading through China, making people lazy, harming society and the economy, and costing China dearly.

THE QING DYNASTY

The Qing emperors were not keen to develop trade because they had urgent problems at home. Years of peace and prosperity had led to huge growth in the population (400 million by 1800), and there were now food shortages. Taxes were high, corruption was growing, and the population was moving from place to place.

The Qing were very conservative, remote, and stubborn. As as result, there were protests and uprisings, often organized by secret societies with political ambitions. The White Lotus sect caused a peasant rebellion which lasted from 1795 to 1804. The effect of this was to weaken people's respect for the Qing dynasty. Foreigners—Russians, Japanese, Tibetans, and other ethnic minorities, as well as the Europeans—were also nibbling at China's edges.

EUROPEAN INTERVENTION

The Qing emperors believed that China was the center of the world— "the Middle Kingdom, surrounded by barbarians." When a British ambassador traveled to Beijing in 1793, Qianlong refused to discuss trade. From then on, foreigners decided to get their way by other means, and the opium trade increased. By 1800, life was oppressive for many Chinese. They were heavily taxed, and He Shen, a corrupt official, had gained power. Smoking opium provided an escape. In 1839, when the Chinese tried to stop the trade, the British went to war. Even control of the world tea supply was almost at an end. During the 1840s, Robert Fortune stole several tea plants in China, took them to India, and set up rival plantations.

The foreign trading stations or "factories" at Guangzhou were the only places where trading with China was permitted. Europeans could not travel outside their compound, and they could trade only during certain months.

▲ The Temple of Heaven was rebuilt in 1751 during Qianlong's reign. The wooden prayer hall was enormous and highly decorated, and the roof was covered with blue ceramic tiles.

◄ Macao was a Portuguese colony on a peninsula not far from Guangzhou. It had been established in 1557, with imperial permission, and it was a center for Chinese and Japanese trade.

THE AGE OF LOGIC 1700–1789

The pursuit of logic and reason during the 1600s gave rise to further new social and political ideas in the 1700s. This is often called "The Enlightenment."

▲ Voltaire (1694–1778) was one of France's greatest thinkers and authors. He wrote poetry, plays, philosophical works, and the novel *Candide*. His openly critical attitude meant that he fell out of favor with the French court.

▼ An imaginary portrait by the British artist and poet William Blake (1757–1827). It shows Sir Isaac Newton calculating how the universe is held together by the law of gravitation.

The German philosopher Immanuel Kant wrote "Dare to know! Have the courage to use your own intelligence!" People were no longer interested in traditional beliefs. The scientific research of the 1600s had begun a widespread process of examination and exploration of the world and, as a result, in the 1700s great encyclopedias were published that recorded this knowledge.

Between 1751 and 1772, Denis Diderot compiled the 28-volume *Encyclopedia*, with 200 contributors. In 1755, Samuel Johnson published his *Dictionary of the English Language*, and the *Encyclopedia Britannica* was published between 1768 and 1771.

The Enlightenment also represented a search for happiness, justice, and knowledge, in music, romance, travel, philosophy, and politics. Many absolute rulers and powerful landowners enjoyed new ideas, but they feared the consequences of ordinary people reading and talking about them. Such ideas would soon lead to revolutions.

This cartoon of Thomas Paine (1737–1809) shows him as a champion of liberty. Paine supported and provided many of the ideas which lay behind both the American and French revolutions.

THE SPREAD OF IDEAS

The Enlightenment was led by philosophers such as Kant and Voltaire, the economist Adam Smith, the composers Haydn and Mozart, and political thinkers such as Rousseau, Locke, and Paine. Voltaire was a French writer who criticized intolerance, and rewrote the history of the world, as well as writing dramas and essays that commented on society and politics. Adam Smith, a Scottish economist, described the workings of modern economies and free markets. The French political thinker, Jean-Jacques Rousseau, wrote about social equality and democracy. Thomas Paine, a British-born revolutionary writer who visited America and France, wrote *The Rights of Man* which strongly influenced popular ideas.

It was also a time when people began to find things out by scientific experiment and observation. During this period, the basics of modern chemistry were established, and advances were also made in biology. These developments would help scientists in the future. Literature became more realistic as the first modern novels appeared. More people than ever could read, so new ideas spread more rapidly.

◄ The French philosophers and encyclopedists, Voltaire (with his hand up), Diderot, Abbe, Maury, Condorcet, and others, meet for dinner. In addition to compiling the *Encyclopedia*, they became the mouthpiece and focus for radical social ideas, and they criticized the *ancien régime* (the old order) for its conservative and authoritarian ways.

In a Europe battered by war, heavy taxes, inequalities, and oppressive governments, freethinking and freedom-seeking aspirations were becoming more prevalent. The first result of this bid for freedom occurred outside Europe, in the colonies of North America. Unexpectedly, a revolution was brewing there, which would encourage another revolution in France and further radical changes across the continent of Europe.

► Denis Diderot (1713–1784) was the editor of the *Encyclopedia*, published between 1751 and 1772. The 28 volumes included 17 books of text and 11 books of pictures. Each volume was censored by the publishers if they did not agree with his views.

Jean-Jacques Rousseau (1712–1778) was another of France's leading Enlightenment thinkers. In 1762, he wrote *The Social Contract* in which he emphasized the rights of people. In his novel *Émile*, he proposed a new theory of education.

KEY DATES

1721	J. S. Bach composes Brandenburg Concertos
1730	Peak of Rococo architecture
1743	American Philosophical Society founded
1749	Fielding's novel *Tom Jones* published
1750s	Capability Brown, landscape artist, at work
1751	Publication of the *Encyclopedia* starts
1752	Benjamin Franklin identifies electricity
1760s	Rousseau at work in France
1768	Royal Academy of Arts founded in England
1770s	Goethe, German poet and dramatist, at work
1776	American Declaration of Independence
1780s	Mozart and Haydn, composers, at work
1781	Kant's *Critique of Pure Reason* written
1790s	French Revolution takes place
1807	Abolition of slavery in England

AFRICA 1700–1830

Africa was now strongly affected by its increasing trade with Europeans and Arabs. Many African kingdoms grew strong and rich as a result.

Shaka Zulu (1787–1828) became Zulu leader in 1816. He taught them battle skills and expanded their lands in southeastern Africa.

During the 1700s, the continent of Africa was relatively peaceful. In the north, the Ottoman Empire, which controlled Egypt, continued to decline. The Ashanti people on the west coast grew increasingly rich by selling slaves. In the southeast, the Portuguese were slowly building up a colony in Mozambique. The lands of the east coast (now Kenya) were ruled from Oman, a kingdom to the north, on the Arabian Sea. At the southern tip, the Cape of Good Hope, Dutch settlers began to explore the inland territory.

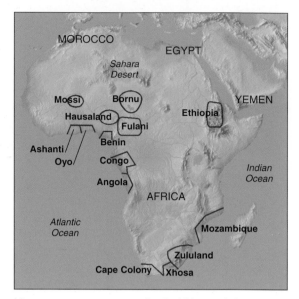

Many new states were growing in Africa, and there was much movement of peoples. Europeans and Arabs had small coastal colonies, but their influence inland was mainly felt through trade, rather than invasion.

NEW AFRICAN STATES

During the 1700s, an average of 35,000 slaves each year were being sent from western Africa to the Americas. But, by the end of the century, the British were having second thoughts, and in 1787, they established Sierra Leone as a refuge for freed slaves. In 1822, Liberia was founded for freed slaves from the United States. Most European countries stopped trading in slaves in the early 1800s, but Portugal continued until 1882.

The Yao and Nyamwezi empires in eastern Africa virtually emptied that area to provide slaves. Ashanti and Oyo dominated the West African slave trade into the 1800s, then they started selling timber, ivory, hides, gold, and beeswax to the Europeans instead. This changed the West African farming practice of growing cash crops for export. Meanwhile, in eastern Africa, slaves continued to be sent by the Omani Arabs to Arabia and India.

The Zulu nation in southern Africa, led by King Shaka, fought constantly with its neighbors. The bloodshed was so great that the years from 1818 to 1828 became known as *mfecane*, or the time of troubles. There were migrations from the Sudan, the Tutsi moved into Rwanda, and the Masai into Kenya from farther north.

Zulu warriors were armed with stabbing spears known as *assegai*. They wore battle headdresses and ornamental shields to frighten their enemies and also to recognize each other in battle.

AFRICAN MUSLIM STATES

On the southern edge of the Sahara, there was an Islamic revival. Many Muslims expected a *mahdi*, or savior, to appear, and various African caliphs, moved by this possibility, founded new, well-organized states such as Sokoto, Mossi, Tukulor, and Samori in inland West Africa. In Egypt, Mehmet Ali Pasha took control from the Mamluks in 1811, modernized the country, and invaded Sudan in the 1820s.

Africa was changing rapidly. Most of it still belonged to Africans, but they were not united against their common threat, the Arabs and Europeans. As a result, Africa was vulnerable.

▲ In 1809, the Hausa city of Kano in northern Nigeria was captured by the Muslim leader Usman dan Fodio, of the Hausa kingdom of Gobir. The Hausa cities converted to Islam, and became part of an Afro-Islamic state called the Sokoto Caliphate.

Mehmet Ali Pasha (1769–1849) was the Ottoman governor of Egypt, but he made Egypt virtually independent of the Ottomans and invaded the lands up the Nile River in Sudan, making Egypt the leading power in the eastern Mediterranean. He ruled Egypt from 1805 to 1848.

MASSACRE OF THE MAMLUKS

The Mamluks were originally slaves, captured in the 800s by Muslim armies in the Caucasus and Russia. They were mostly Cossacks and Chechens by origin, trained to serve as soldiers and administrators in Egypt. By 1200, they had become palace guards and ministers. They then overthrew the sultan and ruled Egypt from 1249 to 1517. When the Ottomans took Egypt, the Mamluks became the ruling class under the Ottomans. As Ottoman power declined in the 1700s, they regained power in Egypt. After Mehmet Ali Pasha conquered the Mamluks in 1811 and took control of Egypt, he invited all the surviving Mamluk commanders to a banquet in Cairo where he had them massacred.

MODERNIZING RUSSIA 1730–1796

The rulers who followed Peter the Great continued his strategy of westernization and expansion, making Russia into a great European power.

Peter III (1728–1762) was czar for half a year. A grandson of Peter the Great, he did not have the character to be czar, and he was not liked. Czarina Elizabeth forced him to marry Catherine.

▼ Winter was often a good time to travel in Russia, because the snow made progress faster. Catherine the Great traveled in an enclosed sled drawn by horses.

When Peter the Great died in 1725, his wife became Czarina Catherine I. However, she died after only a few years. Anna Ivanovna ruled for ten years from 1730, continuing Peter's pro-Western policies, and welcoming many foreigners at court. The Russian people themselves suffered. The czarina's court in St. Petersburg cared more about music, poetry, and wars against the Ottomans or the Europeans, than about the welfare of the peasants.

From 1741, Peter's daughter, Elizabeth (1709–1762), made Russia even more westward-looking and industrial, and she declared war on Prussia in the Seven Years' War. In 1745, she forced her son Peter, the heir to the Russian throne, to marry Catherine, who was from a poor but noble Prussian family. The marriage was not a happy one. When Elizabeth died in 1762, Peter III ruled briefly.

Catherine the Great (1729–1796) ruled Russia for 34 years. Other European leaders respected Catherine for her achievements in foreign policy, but feared her power.

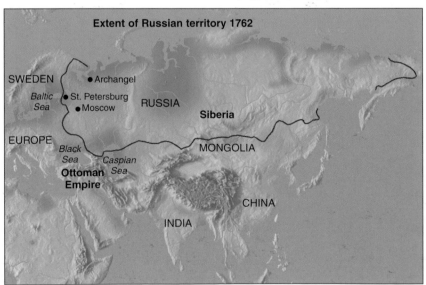

Extent of Russian territory 1762

SWEDEN — Archangel
Baltic Sea — St. Petersburg — Moscow — RUSSIA
EUROPE
Siberia
Black Sea — Caspian Sea
Ottoman Empire
MONGOLIA
CHINA
INDIA

CATHERINE THE GREAT

Peter III was a weak man, and Catherine despised him. Six months after his coronation, he was deposed and murdered. Catherine declared herself empress and ruled in his place. Although she was intelligent and cultured, she carried her private ruthlessness into public life.

To support Catherine's wars and her lavish court, Russia was drained of wealth in tax and young men. She planned to improve education and social conditions, but there were few educated officials to carry out these plans. So she asked the nobility for help, and gave them extra powers. This made the peasants' situation even worse, and led to Pugachev's Rebellion in 1773–1774. Rebels took the city of Kazan, and promised to abolish tax, serfdom, landlords, and military service. But Pugachev was brutally crushed.

◀ From the 1500s to the 1700s, the Russian Empire had more than doubled in size. During Catherine's reign, it gained ports on the coasts of the Baltic and Black seas.

FOREIGN POLICY

Catherine's appointment of a reform commission in the 1760s failed, so she chose autocratic rule, and divided the country into regions, each ruled by nobles. Then she left the nobles to take care of Russia's internal affairs.

Her claim to greatness comes from the way she expanded Russia's lands. This strategy of expansion was masterminded by two ministers, Count Alexander Suvarov and Grigori Potemkin. In the north and west, new lands were won from Sweden in 1790. Most of Poland was seized when it was partitioned (divided). These gains gave Russia important seaports on the Baltic coast.

In the south, Russia took Azov from the Ottomans, then the Crimea, and, by 1792, the whole northern shore of the Black Sea. The Ottomans no longer controlled the Black Sea and Russia built up a powerful navy. To the east, Russia's gradual development of Siberia was also stepped up.

But Catherine was very cruel. Courtiers were flogged, and peasants who dared to complain about their situation were punished. Many poor people faced starvation, yet Catherine continued to collect heavy taxes to pay for her wars and extravagant lifestyle.

KEY DATES

1741 Elizabeth becomes czarina
1756–63 Russia joins the Seven Years' War
1762 Catherine the Great becomes czarina
1772 First partition of Poland
1783 Russia annexes the Crimea
1792 Russia gains Black Sea coast
1793–95 Second and Third partitions of Poland
1796 Death of Catherine the Great

Life at the Russian court was rich and elegant, sheltered from reality, and out of touch. In contrast, the peasants lived in poverty. When Catherine the Great traveled through Russia in 1787 to see how her subjects lived, the streets of the towns were lined with healthy, well-dressed actors. The real peasants were kept hidden from view.

This painting of the inside of the Winter Palace in St. Petersburg shows how impressive life in St. Petersburg was. Tropical plants thrived indoors, while people sometimes froze to death just outside the palace.

EXPLORATION IN OCEANIA 1642–1820

The exploration of Oceania came about quite late compared with other parts of the world. It was pioneered by Tasman, Cook, and other explorers.

Between 1768 and 1779, the navigator Captain James Cook (1728–1779) made three voyages of discovery to the Pacific. In 1770, he landed at Botany Bay and claimed Australia for Britain.

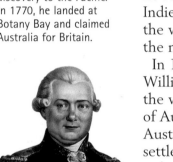

Jean-François La Pérouse (1741–1788) was sent by Louis XVI to sail around the world on a scientific expedition. He traveled the oceans with a crew of scientists, charting, observing, and collecting samples while visiting Canada, Siberia, and Australia. His ships disappeared in 1788.

During the 1600s, Dutch seamen explored the southern Pacific and Indian oceans. By the 1620s, they had found the northern and western coast of Australia, naming it "New Holland."

In 1642, the Dutchman Abel Tasman (1603–1659) discovered the island of Tasmania. He had sailed from Mauritius and traveled so far south that he did not sight Australia. Farther to the east, Tasman reached the south island of New Zealand. After a fight with its Maori inhabitants, he returned to Batavia in the Dutch East Indies, and discovered Tonga and Fiji on the way. The next year, he sailed along the northern coast of Australia.

In 1688 and 1699, the English navigator William Dampier (1652–1715) explored the western and northwestern coastline of Australia. These explorers proved that Australia was an island, but they did not settle there. The Pacific remained largely unknown since it was too distant and too poor to attract European trading interest.

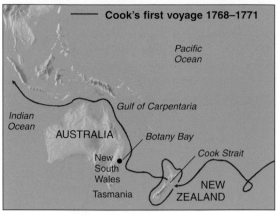

On Cook's first voyage, he sailed from the tip of South America to New Zealand and proved that there was no large continent in between as many people thought.

The first scientific exploration of these southern lands was undertaken by Captain James Cook, who made three voyages. The first voyage (1768–1771) took him around New Zealand. Then he landed at Botany Bay in Australia, claiming it for Britain. On his second voyage (1772–1775), he explored many Pacific islands and Antarctica. On his last voyage, started in 1776, he visited New Zealand, Tonga, Tahiti, and finally Hawaii, where he was killed in a quarrel with the islanders.

THE VOYAGES OF CAPTAIN COOK

Captain Cook was commissioned to sail to Tahiti to observe the passage of Venus in front of the sun. After this, he was secretly sent south to chart New Zealand and Australia for the British government. On his second voyage, he was the first explorer to visit the Antarctic, but he was driven back by pack ice. Cook discovered the value of carrying vegetables and fruit for his sailors, so preventing scurvy (caused by lack of Vitamin C). He also took well-trained artists with him because he was determined that the findings should be scientifically recorded. He died in Hawaii, in 1779, while on his third voyage.

NATIVE PEOPLES

The "new" lands explored by Cook had been inhabited for hundreds of years. The Maoris lived in New Zealand, and the Aborigines lived in Australia. Both peoples lived according to ancient traditions. Understandably, they were wary of Cook and his men—the first Europeans that they had ever seen.

Aborigines had lived in Australia for thousands of years, spread out over a vast continent. They lived by foraging and hunting, and using their advanced knowledge of nature. They were so different from Europeans, and there was such a culture clash, that Aboriginal culture was almost entirely destroyed.

The Maoris, it is thought, had sailed to Aotearoa (New Zealand) from Polynesia around A.D. 750, and were farmers, warriors, and village dwellers. They resisted the efforts of the Europeans to move into their land.

The first settlers in Australia arrived in 1788. They were convicts who had been transported there from Britain as punishment. Free settlers started to arrive in 1793. In New Zealand, whalers, hunters, and traders were soon followed by missionaries. Many of the early settlers came from Scotland, Ireland, and Wales. The settlers introduced diseases that often killed the local peoples.

KEY DATES

1642–44	Tasman's voyages to Tasmania and New Zealand
1688/1699	Dampier explores western and northwestern coastline of Australia
1766–68	Bougainville discovers Polynesia and Melanesia
1768–71	Cook's first voyage
1772–75	Cook's second voyage
1776–79	Cook's third voyage
1829	Britain annexes all of Australia
1840	Britain claims New Zealand

▲ The Maoris were skilled sailors and craftworkers who decorated their canoes with elaborate religious carvings. When Cook arrived, there were about 100,000 Maoris in New Zealand. Many were killed in later wars against British settlers and troops.

In 1779, while on his third voyage to the Pacific, Captain Cook was killed in a skirmish with Hawaiians over the theft of a boat. Initially, the British had been welcome, but after this event, his crews had to sail home without their captain.

JAPAN AND SOUTHEAST ASIA 1603–1826

Europeans were gradually making headway into Asia, as they sought to dominate trade. During the 1700s, these trade links turned into political battles.

The Japanese had very advanced ideas about cleanliness and hygiene. Public baths were very popular and socially acceptable in Japan.

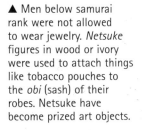

Sword guards protect the hand during fighting. This decorative Japanese sword guard dates from the 1700s.

Since 1603, Japan had been dominated by the Tokugawa shoguns, who ran the country very strictly, isolated from other lands. But they also brought peace and security. The country prospered under their rule. The population grew from 20 to 30 million in 150 years, and the output of farmers increased greatly. Towns flourished, and with them trade and the merchant classes. Skilled craftworkers made beautiful goods, especially clothes and fabrics in colored silks. Many Japanese people received a good education.

But Japan also had problems. Many Japanese had left the land, crowding into the cities, and the samurai class had fallen into debt. Heavy taxes led to riots, and many minor crimes were punished by death. In the 1740s, the enlightened shogun Yoshimune (1684–1751) lifted many harsh laws and allowed European books into the country. But the 1760s brought famine, earthquakes, and frequent uprisings, and an anti-shogun movement developed. A small number of Dutch traders were the only foreigners allowed into Japan. They were treated scornfully, but they made so much money that they put up with the insults.

▲ Men below samurai rank were not allowed to wear jewelry. *Netsuke* figures in wood or ivory were used to attach things like tobacco pouches to the *obi* (sash) of their robes. Netsuke have become prized art objects.

▶ This 1815 Japanese woodblock shows Minamoto Yoshitsune, a famous shogun of the 1100s. He continued to be popular long after his death, and many stories sprang up about his exploits. In one legend, supernatural spirits called *tengu*, who live in the mountains, taught Yoshitsune the skills he needed to be a warrior.

SOUTHEAST ASIA

In Southeast Asia, there was no such ban on traders. Arabic and European spice traders had visited the area since medieval times, and later, Europeans had established trading posts. The Dutch dominated the area, controlling Java and creating trading posts on many of the islands. Several Muslim-dominated states in the East Indies were either friendly with or under the control of the Dutch.

During the 1700s, trade links turned into political battles. The British were gaining more interest in the area. In 1762, they forced the Spanish to give up their monopoly over the sea route to Latin America. In 1786, they took control of Penang in Malaya, and in 1795, they took the port of Malacca from the Dutch.

During the Napoleonic Wars, the British occupied Batavia, the Dutch capital in Java. Later, they returned it, after the Dutch recognized their control of Malaya. The British established Singapore as a free port in 1819, giving special privileges to their own traders. This became a crucial stopover port for Chinese trade, and it quickly turned into the region's main commercial center. Goods from Britain and India traveled east, and goods from China and the East Indies went west.

LOCAL WARS

European nations became involved in wars between the Southeast Asian states. They used these local conflicts to settle European disputes among themselves. The British, French, and Dutch all fought in Siam (today's Thailand) at different times, though Siam remained independent. From 1824 to 1826, an Anglo-Burmese war flared up after Burma supported Britain's enemies, who lived close to the rich British-ruled lands of Bengal. The Europeans did not colonize mainland Southeast Asia, but they gradually made these countries dependent on them. By 1820, the Europeans had a very strong hold on Southeast Asia.

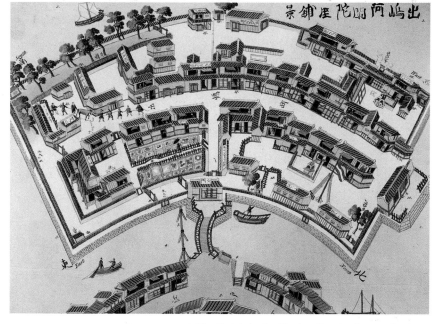

▲ The Dutch had a "factory," or trading post, at Desima Island near Nagasaki in southern Japan. This was the only foreign trading post allowed in the country. There, the Dutch exported silks and other fine Japanese products in exchange for silver.

◀ Sir Thomas Stamford Raffles (1781–1826) founded the British colonial port of Singapore in 1819. He worked hard to increase British power in Southeast Asia, and Singapore soon became the business center of the region.

THE CAPTURE OF RANGOON

In 1824, the British commander Sir Archibald Campbell led 11,000 soldiers on a river journey of 400 mi. (640km) to capture the Burmese capital, Rangoon. The raid was planned in revenge for the Burmese king's attack on British lands in India.

THE BIRTH OF THE U.S.A. 1763–1789

People in the Thirteen Colonies in America were dissatisfied with British rule. They fought for their independence, and a new nation was born.

George Washington (1732–1799) was an officer in the British army and a wealthy landowner. He was made commander in chief of the new American army, fighting the British. In 1789, he became the first president of the United States.

At the end of the Seven Years' War in 1763, both the British government in London and the English colonists in America felt satisfied. They had defeated France and gained territory from them in Canada, as well as land as far west as the Mississippi River. With the French threat gone, the colonists no longer needed the British to defend them.

But the British wanted to govern the old French territories and collect higher taxes to pay for soldiers to defend these newly won lands, so they raised taxes in the 13 colonies. Local colonial assemblies argued that it was unfair for Britain to tax the American colonies, since they had no say in running the British government. They said "taxation without representation is tyranny." The colonies decided to ban all British imports. On July 4, 1776, representatives from all 13 colonies adopted the Declaration of Independence, claiming the right to rule themselves.

The Boston Tea Party, in 1773, was a protest against British taxation. A band known as the Sons of Liberty, led by Samuel Adams (1722–1803), dressed up as Mohawks, boarded two ships in Boston Harbor, and threw tea chests into the sea. The British closed Boston Harbor until the lost tea was paid for.

▲ The British soldiers were well-drilled professionals, while the Americans were mostly volunteers. But the Americans were highly motivated because they felt strongly about their cause. On the left is a uniformed British grenadier, and on the right is an American revolutionary soldier.

At the Battle of Bunker Hill, near Boston, in 1775, the British lost twice as many men as the Americans. It took three uphill assaults for the British to win.

316

INDEPENDENCE

Guided by the ideas of Thomas Jefferson, and influenced by the Enlightenment, the American Declaration of Independence stated: "We hold these truths to be self-evident, that all men are created equal, that they are endowed by their Creator with certain inalienable Rights, that among these are Life, Liberty, and the Pursuit of Happiness."

The American Revolution had begun in 1775. At first the British were successful, despite the problems of fighting nearly 3,000 mi. (5,000km) from home. But the Americans had an advantage because they were fighting on home territory, and they believed in their cause. Six years after the conflict began, the British army surrendered at Yorktown, Virginia, having been defeated by Washington's troops. Britain eventually recognized American independence in the Treaty of Paris in 1783.

KEY DATES

1763	End of the Seven Years' War; British troops sent to North America
1764	Sugar Act taxes imported molasses
1765	Stamp Act adds tax on documents
1775	American Revolution begins; Battle of Bunker Hill takes place
1776	Declaration of Independence
1781	British army surrenders at Yorktown
1783	Britain recognizes American independence
1787	Draft American Constitution drawn up
1789	American Constitution becomes law; George Washington becomes first president
1791	Bill of Rights is adopted

THE U.S. CONSTITUTION

At first, the United States of America was run by the governing body that was set up during the Revolution, the Continental Congress, under the laws called the Articles of Confederation. But the Congress was weak. It was little more than an assembly of representatives from the states and could only make decisions that affected all of the states. It could borrow money, for example, but could not collect taxes from the states to raise money to repay the loan.

Some thought a whole new system of government that would unite the states into a nation was needed. In May 1787, at the Constitutional Convention in Philadelphia, they designed this system. They decided to have a president, elected every four years. He would rule with the help of a Congress (consisting of a House of Representatives and a Senate, made up of representatives from every state), and a Supreme Court.

In addition, each of the states would have an elected assembly, and run their state government as they liked. A system of checks and balances would make sure that neither the president, the Congress, nor the Supreme Court would be allowed to control the federal government.

Finally, many people worried that the Constitution did not protect all the rights they had fought so hard for. So, in 1791, ten amendments were added to the Constitution. They are the Bill of Rights.

The draft Constitution was worked out at the Constitutional Convention in Philadelphia in 1787. Fifty-five delegates attended, 39 signed the document. Copies were sent to each state to be agreed by its leaders.

A Liberty Medal was made to mark the victory of the Americans over the British in 1781.

The Liberty Bell in Philadelphia symbolizes American independence.

Thomas Jefferson (1743–1826) became the third president in 1801. He was a political leader whose ideas greatly affected American politics.

THE FRENCH REVOLUTION 1789–1799

In 1789, the discontented people of France overthrew their king, demanding freedom and equality. The revolution that followed changed France forever.

Marie Antoinette (1755–1793) was Louis XVI's Austrian wife. The people thought she was arrogant and extravagant.

▲ Maximilien Robespierre (1758–1794) became the leader of a revolutionary group called the Jacobins in 1793. He was the head of the Committee of Public Safety and backed the execution of the king and queen. Executions grew so frequent that this time was known as the Reigin of Terror. Robespierre may not have been responsible for this, but he did make enemies. In 1794, he was accused of treason and executed.

▶ On July 14, 1789, the people of Paris stormed the Bastille, a prison where many popular leaders had been imprisoned by the king. This was the real outbreak of the Revolution.

The French Revolution had been building up for years. It was caused by bad government and enormous differences between the rich and the poor, encouraged by new Enlightenment ideas about people's rights, and influenced by the American Revolution.

In the 1700s, France was in crisis. Food was scarce, prices were high, and the government was facing bankruptcy. To get more money, Louis XVI could either borrow it or raise state taxes. But first he needed approval and support from a traditional assembly, the Estates-General, which had not met for 175 years.

At the assembly, the representatives of the professional classes rebelled against the nobles and clergy. They took an oath to start a new National Assembly and demand reform. They wrote a new constitution that abolished the old order, nationalized Church lands, and reorganized local government. Louis sent troops to try and dismiss the Assembly.

Louis XVI (1754–1793) became king in 1774. He was shy and not a strong ruler. His wrong decisions led to the Revolution.

When the citizens of Paris heard this, they rebelled. On July 14, 1789, a mob stormed the Bastille, the king's prison in Paris. The riot marked the beginning of a bloody revolution in which the rebels demanded "Liberty, Equality, Fraternity."

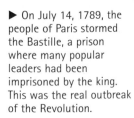

THE STRUGGLE FOR POWER

In 1791, Louis XVI fled, but was captured and imprisoned. In 1792, the monarchy was abolished, and the following year, Louis and his wife were tried and executed. By this time, the revolutionary government was at war with most other European states, who were afraid that revolution might spread to their countries.

Predictably, chaos broke out, and there was a struggle for power. The new revolutionary government began rounding up its rivals, royalist or popular, calling them "enemies of the revolution." There was a political battle between two groups, the Jacobins and Girondins, which the Jacobins won. They then dominated a new ruling body, called the Committee of Public Safety. The committee mobilized French armies against foreign invasion, and from September 1793 to July 1794, they executed all who opposed them in what is known as the Reign of Terror.

During the Terror, around 18,000 people were guillotined. Soon, one man, Robespierre, wielded dictatorial power. Even he was not safe, and in 1794, he was accused of treason and executed.

THE DIRECTORY

A new constitution was written in 1795 and a weak government, called The Directory, was formed. War had already broken out, and French revolutionary armies had conquered the Netherlands and south Germany. A young general, Napoleon Bonaparte, took over the army, and invaded Italy, Switzerland, and Egypt. The Directory came to rely on him. He grew popular and powerful. In 1799, he removed the Directory and took control.

The so-called *sans culottes* (named because they did not wear knee-length pants, like the middle class and aristrocracy), preserved public order in the streets during the Reign of Terror. Many people lost their lives as a result of the hatred of the *sans culottes*.

KEY DATES

1788	Estates-General called to a meeting
1789	National Assembly and storming of the Bastille; Declaration of the Rights of Man
1791	The New Constitution and Legislative Assembly
1792	The Revolutionary Wars and French Republic
1793–94	The Reign of Terror
1794	Robespierre's dictatorship; Holland invaded
1795–99	The Directory rules France
1796	Napoleon becomes chief army commander
1799	Napoleon takes power

THE REIGN OF TERROR

After Louis XVI had been executed in 1793, the Committee started to attack and execute anyone suspected of opposing the revolution. A Tribunal was set up to bring "enemies of the revolution" to trial, but these trials were often hurried and unfair. Aristocrats, royalists, priests, and any suspected people went to the guillotine. Once Robespierre had rid himself of rivals in the Committee of Public Safety, he ruled alone for a short time, until he too was sent to the guillotine in July 1794. The Reign of Terror then ended.

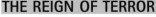

Here, people celebrate the end of the Reign of Terror by dancing around a tree decorated with rosettes in red, white, and blue, the national colors.

THE NAPOLEONIC WARS 1797–1815

Restoring order after the French Revolution, Napoleon attempted to change the whole of Europe. But Britain stood against him and Napoleon was finally exiled.

Napoleon was born in Corsica, the second son of an Italian lawyer. As a young man, he had joined the French army, and his courage and quick thinking led to rapid promotion. At the age of 24, he became a general. He led a number of successful campaigns, capturing northern Italy in 1797. The new government, the Directory, feared his popularity and power. They offered Napoleon the job of invading Britain, but he suggested invading Egypt to disrupt Britain's trade route to India. In 1789, he did invade Egypt, but his plan failed after the British, led by Lord Nelson, destroyed his fleet.

In 1799, Napoleon returned to France and seized control. He dismissed the government, and appointed three consuls (officials), to run the country. He made himself first consul, and ruled for 15 years. In 1804, he crowned himself emperor.

Napoleon introduced many lasting reforms that brought new laws, a better educational system, a reorganized government, and a new national bank.

In this 1803 cartoon, Napoleon is shown straddling the world while the comparatively tiny John Bull (representing Britain) tries to fight him off alone.

Napoleon wanted to create a society based on skill rather than on noble birth. To encourage achievement he founded the Legion of Honor in 1802 "for outstanding service to the state." Members of the Legion received a medal and a pension for the remainder of their lives.

In 1799, Napoleon (1769–1821), already a war hero, took over the government by force. Many disagreed, but France was in disorder and Napoleon became first consul.

He was a brilliant general, who moved his troops quickly and used new battle tactics. He also had a very large army, because Robespierre had introduced a draft system in which all adult men were forced to serve. The army numbered 750,000 soldiers in 1799, and another two million men joined up between 1803 and 1815. Napoleon used this massive force to try to conquer Europe.

THE BATTLE OF MARENGO

One of Napoleon's many military successes, the Battle of Marengo was fought against the Austrians in Italy in 1800. Napoleon was a brilliant leader, inspiring his troops with speeches, "leading from the front," and using very innovative tactics. He modernized warfare, used cannons and large armies, and outwitted his opponents. His control of Europe pushed many countries into the modern world.

THE NAPOLEONIC WARS

Napoleon defeated Austria and Russia at Austerlitz in 1805, Prussia at Jena in 1806, and Russia faced a second defeat at Friedland in 1807. Napoleon created new republics allied to France and ruled by placing his relatives in positions of power. He also created Europe-wide laws and governments—known as the Continental System.

In 1805, Britain won a major sea battle against France at Trafalgar in Spain. The British admiral, Horatio Nelson (1758–1805) died, but his victory saved Britain from invasion. In 1808, Napoleon invaded Spain. This began the Peninsular Wars in which Britain supported Spain and Portugal.

The British sent troops led by the Duke of Wellington to Spain. There, he won battles at Salamanca (1812) and Vittoria (1813), pushing the French out of Spain.

Napoleon's disastrous invasion of Russia in 1812 left over 500,000 French dead of cold or hunger, or killed. In 1813, he was also crushed at Leipzig by a combined European force, led by the Prussian general, von Blücher. Finally, in 1814, France was invaded, and Napoleon was exiled. He escaped and was defeated by Wellington and von Blücher at Waterloo in Belgium. He died in exile on the remote South Atlantic island of St. Helena in 1821.

KEY DATES	
1796–97	Napoleon invades Italy
1798	Campaign in Egypt
1799	Napoleon takes over French government
1804	Napoleon crowns himself emperor
1805	Battle of Austerlitz against Austria and Russia; Battle of Trafalgar—British sea victory
1807	Peace of Tilsit with Russia and Prussia
1812	Russian campaign
1813	Napoleon loses Battle of Leipzig; Spain freed at Battle of Vittoria
1814	France invaded; Napoleon exiled to Elba
1815	Napoleon's last battle, at Waterloo

Napoleon believed Russia had allied with Britain, so he invaded. When his army reached Moscow, the Russians had already burned it down. Eventually, the winter took its toll. Napoleon entered Russia with 510,000 men—but left with only 10,000.

Irish-born Arthur Wellesley, Duke of Wellington (1769–1852), fought Napoleon's armies in Spain where it took four years to push out the French. Wellington was involved in the Congress of Vienna after the Napoleonic Wars. A national hero, he became prime minister of Britain in 1828.

The Battle of Waterloo in Belgium, in 1815, was closely fought. It was Napoleon's last battle, fought against Wellington of Britain and von Blücher of Prussia.

THE END OF SLAVERY 1792–1888

The European colonies in the Americas depended heavily on slave labor. But by the mid-1700s, many people were questioning the morality of this.

William Wilberforce (1759–1833) was the member of Parliament for Hull, a busy slave trading port. The trade horrified him. He and other humanitarian Christians campaigned against the slave trade from 1788 onward.

Throughout the 1700s, Britain, France, and Spain grew rich on taxes and profits from their colonies. Much of this wealth was created by slave labor. Denmark, Sweden, Prussia, Holland, and Genoa (Piedmont) also traded in slaves. Africans were sold to Europeans by slave dealers and local rulers, who saw slave trading as a means of punishing criminals, getting rid of enemies, disposing of captives, and getting rich. Nobody knows how many slaves were sold in all, but historians have estimated that 45 million slaves were shipped between 1450 and 1870, although only 15 million survived—many died on the voyage across the Atlantic. Many Europeans disapproved of the slave trade, but they believed it was the only way to supply labor to colonial plantations.

However, some protested, saying it was against God's law and human decency. Rousseau, a French philosopher, wrote in *The Social Contract*, in 1762, "Man is born free, but everywhere he is in chains." His writings inspired the revolutions in America and France, and individual freedom became regarded as a social right, not a gift from a king. Rousseau's ideas also inspired people to fight on behalf of others who were unable to help themselves. Politicians, clergy, and ordinary people began to think how they might help the slaves. But moral arguments did not have as much force as the profits that slavery generated.

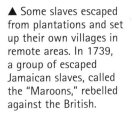

▲ Some slaves escaped from plantations and set up their own villages in remote areas. In 1739, a group of escaped Jamaican slaves, called the "Maroons," rebelled against the British.

▶ Conditions on slave ships were appalling and unhealthy, and many slaves died. Slaves were stacked on dark shelves and floors in the holds of ships, hardly able to move.

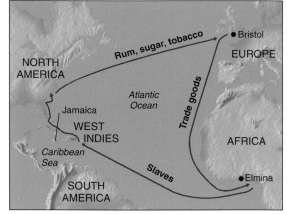

Before abolition, slave ships followed a triangular Atlantic sailing route, taking goods to Africa, slaves to the Americas, and products such as sugar back to Europe.

ENDING THE SLAVE TRADE

Between 1777 and 1804, slavery was made illegal in the northern United States. Denmark withdrew from the slave trade in 1792, and Britain in 1807. But slave smuggling continued. The British navy clamped down on slave trading from 1815, but slavery was still legal elsewhere. A slave revolt in the French colony of Santo Domingo in 1791–1793 led to abolition by France but, in 1803, they made slavery legal again. In 1831, a slave uprising in Virginia led by Nat Turner led to harsh laws and increased support for slavery among white southerners.

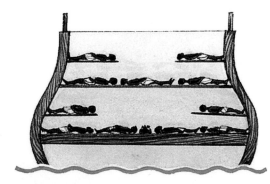

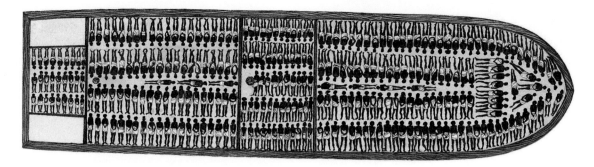

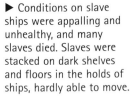

PHILANTHROPY

In Britain, Thomas Clarkson (1760–1846) and William Wilberforce had led an antislavery campaign, which resulted in the abolition of slave trading in 1807. However, slaves were not actually freed for some time. Wilberforce died just before all of the slaves in British hands were freed. Europeans had by now grown disgusted with slavery, and the British navy blocked slave-trading ships.

Slavery continued in Cuba, Costa Rica, Brazil, and the southern United States. The plantations had been built on slave labor. There was a thriving market in Europe for cheap, slave-grown cotton and tobacco, and plantation owners were reluctant to change.

In the U.S., the northern states supported freeing the slaves, but the situation in the South grew worse. Nat Turner's 1831 revolt in Virginia led to new laws designed to control the slaves. Slavery finally ended in the United States in 1863, in Cuba in 1886, and in Brazil in 1888. The Arabic slave trade in Africa ended in 1873.

◄ The leader of the Virginia slave revolt of 1831, Nat Turner (1800–1831), killed his master and 60 whites, and encouraged 75 slaves to revolt. Their revolt lasted for some weeks. He and his followers were eventually captured, tried and hanged.

The economy of the southern states relied on black slave labor. Cotton picking was one of the slaves' main jobs. The cotton was profitably exported to supply the cotton mills of industrial Europe.

KEY DATES

1517	Regular slave trading started by Spain
1592	British slave trading begins
1739	Jamaican "Maroon" slave revolt
1760s	Slave trading at its peak
1791–1804	Santo Domingo slave revolt
1792	Danish slave trade abolished
1807	British slave trade abolished
1834	Slavery abolished in British colonies
1865	13th Amendment abolishes slavery in U.S.
1888	Slavery abolished in Brazil

THE SLAVES' REVOLT IN SANTO DOMINGO

The French Revolution spread to French colonies overseas. In 1791, the National Assembly in Paris decided to give the vote to slaves in Santo Domingo (now Haiti) in the Caribbean. Plantation owners refused to obey. When they heard this, about 100,000 slaves rebelled. Many slave owners were killed, houses destroyed, and sugar and coffee plantations set on fire. Napoleon sent troops to the island and there was a long civil war led by Toussaint l'Ouverture (1746–1803), an ex-slave who declared himself ruler of the island in 1801.

THE BRITISH IN INDIA 1774–1858

The hold on India by the British East India Company gradually grew stronger. The British came to dominate Indian society, becoming its ruling caste.

This mechanical toy, called "Tipu's Tiger," shows a tiger devouring a European. It was made for Tipu Sahib of Mysore. Between 1767 and 1799, with French support, Mysore tried to resist British control of its lands.

By 1750, the British East India Company controlled the very profitable trade between Britain, India, and the Far East. Its officials were skillful businessmen who had built up a knowledge of Indian affairs, especially through the Indians they employed. They made friends with Indian princes, and struck bargains with both the friends and the enemies of the declining Mogul rulers. Many British people in India lived like princes themselves. By working for the East India Company many became very rich. Some of these "nabobs" (from the word *nawab*, for local ruler or rich man) built fine houses; they were designed by British architects, and furnished with luxuries from England, India, and the colonies. In Calcutta, they held horse races, tea parties, and dances. Gradually, wives and families arrived to share this way of life and a community developed.

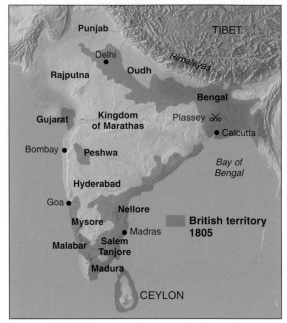

By 1805, the British controlled the rich clothmaking districts of Bengal in northeastern India, as well as the prosperous coastal lands in the south.

However, some British people were attracted to Indian art, culture, and architecture, even wearing Indian clothes, at least at home. They learned Indian languages and studied Indian religions and writings. They took Indian ideas back to Britain when they went home.

▲ Tipu Sahib (1749–1799) of Mysore owned an ivory chess set which was made up of pieces with Indian princes and men on one side, and East India Company administrators and soldiers on the other.

► At first, the British mixed easily with Indians. Here, the Scottish governor Sir David Ochterlony smokes a water pipe at an Indian musical performance.

BRITISH EXPANSION

By 1780, the East India Company controlled many of the more prosperous parts of India, but in 1784, the British government decided to stop it from expanding any further—a policy the company's managers were not happy about. Around 1800, the British were frightened by Napoleon's ambition to build an empire in India, and the government changed its policy. From 1803 to 1818, the company fought the Marathas, who ruled central India, and broke their power. In many cases, they took a soft approach, and used trade to favor certain Indian states, stationing troops there "for their protection."

The company fought in Burma, where the local rulers threatened Bengal, as well as on the Northwest Frontier and in Afghanistan, where they feared Russian influence. Between 1843 and 1849, they annexed Sind and the Punjab. Whenever a dynasty failed, or if a state was weakly governed, the company moved in. During the 1830s, the company's governor had arrogantly overruled local traditions, and brought in missionaries to convert Indians to Christianity. The company built roads, railroads, and buildings, and expanded British businesses. They insisted on using English as the language of education and business. As a result, Indian opposition gradually grew stronger.

THE INDIAN MUTINY

Trouble broke out among the *sepoys*, the Indian soldiers in the company's army. Sparked by a terrible famine, a mutiny started in 1857. Several towns, including the capital, Delhi, were captured by the sepoys, and British men, women, and children were massacred. The mutiny was suppressed violently by British troops. Each side now became suspicious of the other side. The British started to live a more separate life, and Indians were "kept in their place." The British government took control of the East India Company in 1858, and closed it down. While India was perhaps the richest and most developed European colony of all, the British had to work very hard to control it.

Some Indian rajahs and princes made friends with the British and gained many advantages as a result. To be protected by British soldiers guaranteed a prince's power, and the British gained from the deal by having easy influence and trade in a prince's state, without having to govern it.

HOMES FOR NABOBS

Nabobs were officers of the East India Company who had made fortunes in India. Many nabobs had themselves grown up in tough conditions, and had gone to India to escape hard times, seek a fortune, or build a new life. They worked hard, risking their lives through war or disease. They lived in conditions that reflected the opulence of Indian rulers and combined them with the trappings of the British aristocracy. They built great mansions in cities like Calcutta and Delhi, and often had many servants.

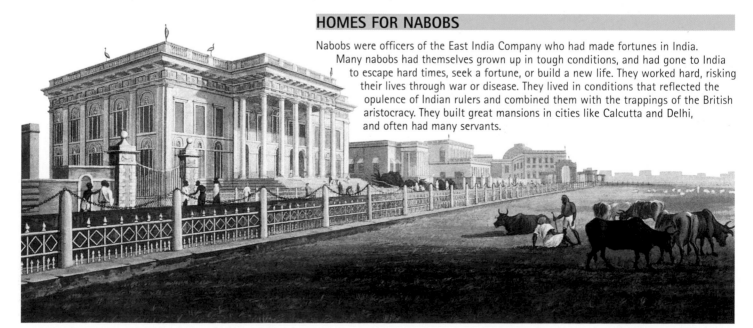

REVOLT IN LATIN AMERICA 1808–1825

While Europe was fighting the Napoleonic Wars, the settlers of Latin America grew restless, and an independence movement gathered strength.

Simón Bolívar drove the Spanish from Colombia and Venezuela, and joined with San Martín to free Peru. He became president of Gran Colombia, but he could not stop its breakup in 1830 and resigned.

José de San Martín was a revolutionary who joined the Argentinean independence movement. He marched his troops over the Andes to Chile, liberating it in 1818. In 1820, he took Lima, Peru.

Ever since Portugal and Spain had divided the New World between them in 1494, they had both ruled vast colonies in North, Central, and South America. For centuries, the colonies had suffered from distant European rule. In 1807–1808, Napoleon had marched into Portugal and Spain, and they became a battleground, as British, Spanish, and Portuguese troops fought against French soldiers. This period of confusion gave the colonies their chance. They began their fight for independence in 1808, refusing to accept Napoleon's brother Joseph as the new Spanish king, and their ruler.

INDEPENDENCE

Argentina declared itself free of Spanish rule in 1810, followed by Paraguay in 1811. Mexico became independent from Spain in 1821, as did Peru, and Brazil finally broke free from Portugal in 1822. Venezuela finally gained its independence in 1830. The independence movement in South America owed a great deal to two energetic leaders, Simón Bolívar (1783–1830) and José de San Martín (1778–1850), both of whom were inspired by the ideas of the French Revolution.

▼ Simón Bolívar's revolutionary troops won an important victory over the Spanish colonial government of Peru at Ayacucho in 1824. This was the final decisive battle of the Latin American wars of independence.

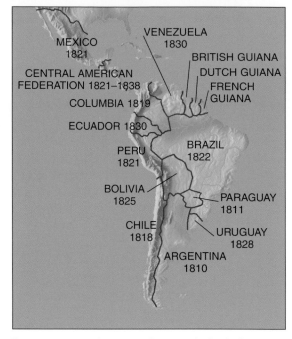

MEXICO 1821
VENEZUELA 1830
BRITISH GUIANA
DUTCH GUIANA
FRENCH GUIANA
CENTRAL AMERICAN FEDERATION 1821–1838
COLUMBIA 1819
ECUADOR 1830
PERU 1821
BRAZIL 1822
BOLIVIA 1825
PARAGUAY 1811
CHILE 1818
URUGUAY 1828
ARGENTINA 1810

Between 1808 and 1830, 13 former colonies in South America won their independence. However, wealthy colonial settlers still owned most of the land and governed it for their own profit.

In 1819, Bolívar and other Venezuelan aristocrats defeated the Spanish in New Granada (Colombia) and Peru. In 1824, Bolívar met up with San Martín, who had marched across the Andes to liberate Chile. In 1826, Bolívar proclaimed the Republic of Gran Colombia (Venezuela, Colombia, Ecuador, and Panama), but the republic later broke up. In 1825, Upper Peru took the name of Bolivia in his honor. Both Bolívar and San Martín had fought under very difficult conditions. But, in spite of independence, conditions did not really improve, because power was still held by the plantation owners.

UNREST IN BRITAIN 1811–1832

In the new industrial society of "dark, satanic mills," British workers were badly treated. They demanded better pay and improved working conditions.

Working conditions in factories were appalling. Women and children often worked for 12 hours every day, in dangerous jobs, for pitiful wages. Many workers died young.

The years of peace following the end of the Napoleonic Wars were a time of discontent. There was unemployment, and high food prices. The British government feared the growing trade union movement (workers who bargained for better working conditions), and in 1800, unions were made illegal. Life in industrial towns was grim, with poor housing, frequent accidents, and disease. But events abroad had shown British workers that they had a right to make their voices heard. They demanded improved working conditions and pay, as well as a say in government.

However, not all the protesters wanted change. From 1811 to 1813, craftsmen known as Luddites (after their leader, Ned Ludd) smashed new machinery in factories in northern England. They feared they would lose their jobs to machines. Six years later, a group of workers known as Blanketeers, wrapped in the woolen cloth they wove, marched from Manchester to London to ask the Prince Regent for his support.

Many people were destitute and not used to living in cities. Some turned to drinking gin to drown their sorrows. This engraving by William Hogarth, made in 1751, was called "Gin Lane."

Limited trade union activity was permitted from 1824. Many people campaigned for "one man, one vote." In 1832, the law was changed to reform election to Parliament, but it was still only men who owned property that were allowed to vote.

▲ This Luddite protester is dressed in women's clothes as a disguise. The Luddites were skilled craftworkers who opposed the introduction of new machinery that replaced their jobs. They were active from 1811 to 1813.

▶ The Peterloo Massacre took place in St. Peter's Fields, in Manchester, England, in 1819. Soldiers charged into a crowd of unarmed men and women who had gathered to listen to Henry Hunt, a famous campaigner for political change. Eleven people were killed and more than 400 injured.

327

WESTWARD MIGRATION 1776–1845

After independence, the fledgling United States started to develop rapidly. New immigrants spread westward, and took the lands of the Native Americans.

Meriwether Lewis was commissioned by President Jefferson to explore the West with William Clark.

William Clark, traveling with Lewis, reached the west coast in Oregon in 1805 and returned to report on their findings the next year.

In the early 1800s, the United States was still small and very much affected by European politics. During the Napoleonic Wars, Britain took control of the seas and blocked most sea traffic between Napoleonic Europe and the United States. This meant that Napoleon could not protect French Louisiana. Since the French controlled trade on the Mississippi River, the Americans held discussions with them. Napoleon decided to sell them Louisiana for $15 million. The Louisiana Purchase more than doubled United States territory.

THE WAR OF 1812

The British blockade of Europe was disastrous for American trade. In 1812, the United States declared war on Britain. The Americans tried to invade Canada, but without success. They won a few battles on the Great Lakes, and the British burned down Washington, D.C., the new capital. Little progress was made, and, weary of war, they signed a treaty in 1814 that returned all territories. The British blockade was lifted, because the Napoleonic Wars were ending, and the United States was able to restore its trade and economy.

Daniel Boone (1734–1820) was held captive by a group of Shawnee Indians. As a test of courage, he was forced to run the gauntlet between two rows of fierce warriors.

MIGRANTS AND SETTLERS

Settlers flocked to the United States after its independence in 1776. They came from all over Europe, seeking a new life in this land that seemed to promise freedom. The American population was around four million in 1803, but by 1861 it was 31 million. The first arrivals settled in the northeastern states, but as their numbers grew, they moved south and west.

The United States was like a new empire, rich in land and resources. Suddenly, the back country of the former eastern colonies became the new frontier. By 1820, this frontier crossed the Mississippi River. However, for Native Americans, American expansion meant hardship, and the settlers' prosperity and liberty became poverty and confinement for them.

The Lewis and Clark expedition left St. Louis in 1804 and spent the winter in the Dakotas before crossing the Rocky Mountains to Oregon in 1805. Sacajawea, a woman of the Shoshone tribe, traveled with the expedition and helped them communicate with other Native Americans they encountered.

THE TRAIL OF TEARS

The Native Americans had been promised that their traditional lands would become available for white settlement only with their permission. But the Northwest Ordinance Act, in 1787, paved the way for westward expansion—a direct threat to the tribal lands. Native Americans decided to confront the white settlers. A series of wars followed in the early 1800s.

In 1830, Congress passed the Indian Removal Act. This led to great suffering. The Five Civilized Tribes—the Cherokee, Chickasaw, Choctaw, Creek, and Seminole—refused to leave their lands and be placed in a so-called Indian Territory. The Cherokee won a Supreme Court decision to stay on their lands, but President Jackson ignored it. In 1838–1839, the army moved the five tribes 800 mi. (1280km) west to Oklahoma. Thousands of helpless, betrayed Native Americans died of hunger and exhaustion on what has become known as the Trail of Tears.

As the new country grew, more settlers arrived, looking for new land—always at the expense of the Native Americans. New migrant trails such as the Cumberland Road from Baltimore to St. Louis opened. Lewis and Clark headed farther west. The army protected settlers and the government passed laws protecting their land claims.

Settlers on the trail to the American West make overnight camp. They came from all over Europe, and hoped to make a new life in what they called "the land of the free."

The U.S. economy grew, and this benefited the growing towns in the east, where industries and businesses were located. The east was the backbone of the United States, and the west its empire. A new state could join the Union when it had a population of 60,000, and by 1821, there were 23 states in the Union.

Andrew Jackson (1767–1845), was president from 1829 to 1837. He fought in the War of 1812 and invaded Florida in 1818 in a war against the Seminoles. He believed in developing the frontier in the west, encouraging settlers, and supporting them against the Native Americans.

KEY DATES	
1783	British withdrawal from the Thirteen Colonies
1803	Louisiana Purchase from France
1805	Explorers Lewis and Clark reach the Pacific
1812-14	The War of 1812 against Britain
1819	Spain gives Florida to the United States
1820	Settler frontier reaches the Mississippi River
1830	Indian Removal Act allows their legal eviction; Chief Black Hawk leads a war against settlers
1838-39	The Cherokee "Trail of Tears" to Oklahoma
1845	The United States annexes Texas

BATTLE OF LAKE ERIE

The Battle of Lake Erie was fought between British troops and the small American navy in September, 1813. The Americans won the battle, led by Oliver Perry (1785–1819), here shown rowing through the battle to another American vessel after his own ship had been sunk. He then announced, "We have met the enemy, and they are ours."

THE ARTS 1708–1835

Increased trade and travel in the 1700s opened Europe up to new influences. This happened at a time when Europe was reaching new cultural peaks of its own.

Jane Austen (1775–1817) was the daughter of an English clergyman. She wrote six novels that commented on the society and manners of her time. Her novels, including *Emma, Sense and Sensibility*, and *Pride and Prejudice* are still read and enjoyed today.

In terms of power and innovation, Europeans now enjoyed worldwide dominance. European ideas and standards were entering other cultures, and the European style of moneymaking and trade affected far distant lands. Yet this trade also brought exotic, fresh influences into Europe.

Oriental china, African carvings, and Indian cotton goods arrived in Europe. Ideas, inspiration, and knowledge were drawn from the Far East, and from the new cultures of the Americas.

Painters, designers, and craftspeople found fresh inspiration in other countries and combined them with their own. European ceramics adopted Chinese styles, and textile designs featured Indian patterns. Many people welcomed these changes, but many others remained untouched by them or simply ignored the growing trend toward modernization.

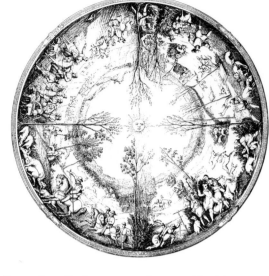

Scenes from the four seasons decorate this elaborate German ornamental shield from the 1700s. It shows a romantic interest in nature that was common at the time. Small, round shields like this were called bucklers.

The musical genius Wolfgang Amadeus Mozart (1756–1791) was already famous at the age of six, after playing for Maria Theresa, the empress of Austria.

◀ For many years, Europeans tried to copy the techniques used by Chinese porcelain makers. This figure was made in the Meissen factory near Dresden in 1765.

▲ This is a clavichord from the 1720s. It produces a clear, light, delicate sound. German composer Johann Sebastian Bach wrote many pieces of music especially for the clavichord.

This Japanese *netsuke* object demonstrates the fine, detailed skills of Japanese carvers of the 1700s.

The 1700s saw great achievements in art of all kinds. In China, jade carving showed great skill. In Japan, woodblock printing grew more advanced, and *haiku* poetry became popular.

EUROPEAN CULTURE

In Europe, three major influences were at work. The rich upper classes built extravagant mansions and opera houses, and paid artists large sums for portraits and records of scenes and events. In cities, pamphlets, coffeehouses, and street life bred a new popular culture. In the factories, new mass-produced products changed the designs and uses of everyday items, making them available to the growing populace. Society was changing, and so were its tastes.

In Europe, the composers Handel, Beethoven, Haydn, and Schubert wrote brilliant orchestral works. Constable, Ingres, Goya, and other painters were the famous artists of the day. Novelists, essayists, journalists, and publishers introduced new styles of writing. Neoclassical poets aimed for elegance, and the Romantics chose bold, emotional styles. In the theater, ballet developed and operas attracted enthusiastic audiences who demanded realistic plots and characters.

This Chinese carved jade pot from the 1700s was made during the Manchu period to hold brushes that were used in calligraphy (decorative writing).

▼ This painting by French artist Jacques Louis David (1748–1825) shows the Tennis Court Oath, one of the key events that sparked the French Revolution in 1789. Only 100 years later, important historical events would be recorded by photography.

ARCHITECTURE 1708–1835

The year 1800 marked a turning point in architecture. Traditional styles gave way to more modern buildings constructed using new technologies.

A cross the world, most cultures by now referred back to tradition to define their architecture—inventiveness and creativity were not at their height, except in Europe. Yet, even in Europe and North America, architectural innovations tended to imitate earlier styles such as those of Greece and Rome, or to adopt exotic styles copied from the colonies, especially India.

Two main influences were at work in European architecture. First, the growth of country estates and townhouses, where grand architecture with large windows was the fashion. Second, the influence of new industries, for which large factories and cities were built. European and American cities grew, and with this came new building styles, such as Georgian architecture in England and the Palladian style in the United States.

The outside of the Royal Pavilion, in Brighton, England, was completely redesigned in 1818 by the fashionable English architect John Nash (1752–1835) for the Prince Regent, the future George IV. He based his designs on Indian architecture, but added many extravagant ideas of his own. The interior design and furniture show clear Chinese and Japanese influences.

In 1784, the British government introduced a tax on windows. In order to save money, many people, especially the rich, blocked up some of their windows.

An urge to try out new industrial techniques led architects to design new types of buildings, using new materials. In 1779, cast iron was first used to construct a bridge over the Severn River in England. This trend toward the use of new materials was to flower during the Victorian period in the 1800s.

▼ In southern Africa, the Zulus lived in stockaded settlements gathered around a central cattle pen, or *kraal*. The huts were built with wooden poles covered with matting and straw. There was one for each wife of the man who built the kraal, plus some for storing grain.

▲ The building of the English city of Bath, near the port of Bristol, was financed with profits from the colonies and the slave trade. John Wood the Elder (1705–1754) was responsible for much of its design. The Royal Crescent is a group of 30 houses built in the late 1700s from plans by his son, John Wood the Younger. He was strongly influenced by classical Greek designs.

Russian settlers moved eastward into the vast lands of Siberia. Peasant houses were made of raw timber from the forests, built cheaply and easily in traditional, simple styles. They were decorated with local designs. Similar construction methods were used by early settlers in the American West for their log cabins.

In many parts of the world traditional designs using local materials remained popular. Settlers were building housing in the new territories of the United States and Russia, and in the growing European colonies in India, Africa, and South America. In most cases, this was practical, basic, and traditional. But the governors, bosses, and plantation owners also built grand houses to remind everyone of their wealth and status.

▶ In the southern states, plantation owners, many of them descended from rich Europeans, built impressive Greek-style mansions. This emphasized their superiority in a society where, in many places, the majority of people were black slaves.

The first cast-iron bridge in the world was built across the Severn River in England in 1779. The builders used the same methods of construction that they used for wooden buildings because they were not sure how cast iron would behave.

SCIENCE AND TECHNOLOGY 1708–1835

In Europe, major breakthroughs were being made in science and technology. New machines and processes brought revolutionary changes to people's lives.

There were many developments in science and technology, particularly in Europe, during this period. Discoveries were of two kinds: theoretical and practical. Throughout the 1700s, mathematicians, scientists, and philosophers researched, discussed, and published their investigations into how the world worked, while engineers and inventors developed new and successful machines and processes.

The latest theories inspired greater invention, and more technology encouraged theoretical scientists to make further discoveries in medicine, biology, mechanics, physics, and chemistry. By 1800, the new machines had brought revolutionary changes—to the workplace, transportation and communications, and eventually to the home.

Some of these inventions simply made it easier to produce things on a large scale—such as textile machines and foundries, which produced large quantities of cloth and metal objects quickly and cheaply. But some inventions brought completely new possibilities—such as the first batteries, steamboats, and locomotives. It would take decades for some of these inventions to make a big impact on the world. Yet their creation, and the sheer amount of imagination and risk-taking involved, marked the beginning of a modern, global, technologically-based economy of the kind that we live in today.

Lady Mary Wortley Montagu (1689–1762) pioneered vaccination against smallpox, which killed thousands every year. However, it was originally the Ottomans who discovered it.

In 1763, John Harrison (1693–1776) won a prize from the British government for inventing the marine chronometer. This accurate clock meant that for the first time sailors could measure their exact position at sea.

In 1800, Alessandro Volta (1745–1827) designed the first electric battery, the Voltaic pile. This was the beginning of a century during which electrical technology was developed.

► The metric system was introduced in France in 1795. It used liters to measure liquids, grams and kilograms for weight, and meters for length, with the number 10 as the standard scale. Napoleon introduced this system to the European countries that he conquered.

Claude Chappe (1763–1805) devised a system for sending messages, using semaphore signals and relay towers. The French used Chappe's system until 1850.

UNIFICATION AND COLONIZATION

1836–1913

The world map changed dramatically during this period—new nations were formed and some were unified. Africa was carved up by nations seeking new colonies, and China's power was fractured. There were more revolutions in Europe. The United States, Canada, and Russia expanded to the farthest frontiers of their countries. Railroads, telegraph wires, and steamships suddenly made the world seem smaller. New cities such as New York, Buenos Aires, Johannesburg, Bombay, and Shanghai became centers in a new global order.

▲ The coming of the railroad opened up North America, but also led to the first national strike. The strike spread along the railroad, from coast to coast, uniting the workers in their fight for decent wages.

◀ During the Second Boer War in South Africa, the Boers (Dutch settlers) were finally defeated by the British in 1902.

THE WORLD AT A GLANCE 1836–1913

In North America, settlers moved west to colonize the vast lands taken over by the United States and Canada. However, the opening up of these new territories caused much hardship for the native peoples, whose way of life was being threatened.

In Africa, religious wars strengthened the influence of Islam in the kingdoms of the north. European explorers and missionaries began to visit lands in the interior. Led by a desire to exploit the resources of Africa, European powers quickly established colonies throughout the continent. The power of the great trading nations of Europe grew.

In Asia, Europeans also took control of India, Burma, and Southeast Asia, and began to trade with China and Japan. Europe's expansion into other continents did not stop internal conflicts, and many wars were fought between countries or empires that wanted more power and territory.

NORTH AMERICA

The United States grew strong during this period. Its territories now extended west to Texas and California, and the Wild West was being opened up by railroads, settlers, and soldiers. This took place at great cost to the Native Americans, who were killed or squeezed into small, isolated reservations. Despite attempts to revive their fortunes, their culture was dying, and it gained little respect from the new Americans. In the 1860s, the Civil War broke out, a destructive, modern-style war over political principles. One result of it was the abolition of slavery. The cities of the East and the Midwest then grew larger and more industrial, and more settlers arrived from Europe. Canada was united, and it pushed west, too, becoming a prosperous independent dominion within the British Empire. By 1900, North America had become wealthy and strong. The United States became an imperial power itself. Its financiers, corporations, and armies were to help it dominate the world from the 1900s onward.

NORTH AMERICA

LATIN AMERICA

LATIN AMERICA

Latin America developed more slowly than North America, partly because of its dictatorial governments and controlling landowners. After the independence wars of the 1820s, a second wave of changes came about between the 1860s and 1880s, when South American countries fought each other. There followed a spate of development brought by railroads, population growth, and increasing wealth earned from exports. But the old Spanish ways lived on in the form of tough governments, rich landowners in their *haciendas* (ranches), and a large mass of poor people.

EUROPE

This was Europe's century. Europe's incessant wars almost stopped, and its armies went overseas, staking out claims to empires elsewhere. Industrial cities grew large, linked by railroads and telegraph wires. Politicians, industrialists, and the middle classes gained increasing power. The new working classes formed workers' movements, leading, by 1905, to the first—unsuccessful—workers' revolution, in Russia. Immense achievements were made in engineering, science, ideas, the arts, and in exploring the world. Europe now governed and financed the world, and grew rich as a result. Yet times were hard for some— there were famines, strikes, economic downturns, and mass emigrations. These hardships eventually led to another new invention—social welfare systems for the poor.

ASIA

Trouble hit China and Japan in the mid-1800s. Foreign traders forced their way in, and in China, major rebellions broke out. China's, isolationist Qing dynasty eventually fell in 1911. Japan, inspired by the West, began modernizing. In India, British rule became total—though not without being challenged by an Indian mutiny first. The West now dominated the East. For some Asians, employed by Westerners, this was advantageous. But many Asians simply became cheap labor on plantations and in Asian colonial cities. Railroads, missionaries, soldiers, and traders opened up the interior of Asian countries. But Asian traditions survived better than those of other cultures elsewhere.

EUROPE

ASIA

MIDDLE EAST

AFRICA

AUSTRALASIA

British settlers took over most of Australasia, and, in growing numbers, overwhelmed the indigenous peoples. Australia and New Zealand made a name for themselves as exporters of food, wool, and gold.

AUSTRALASIA

AFRICA

First came explorers, then traders, missionaries, governors, and administrators. In the 1880s, Europe carved up Africa and took over. Gold rushes made South Africa rich, though ruled by whites. The slave trade had now ended, but all of Africa fell to European exploitation and government instead,dominated by the British and the French.

MIDDLE EAST

The long, slow decline of the Ottomans continued, and the Persians had to fight the British to fend them off. The Middle East became something of a backwater, held in check by traditional rule, and untouched by change. By the same token though, it also avoided colonialization.

INDUSTRIAL REVOLUTION 1836–1913

The continuing revolution in industry was shaping a new world. The rapid growth of opportunities for employers and workers also brought exploitation and injustice.

Many children worked in mines and factories, but this was banned in most countries by 1900.

The British inventor Isambard Kingdom Brunel (1806–1859) built railroads, bridges, tunnels, train stations, ports, and the world's largest ship.

During the 1700s, many people in Britain worked at home, usually producing goods by hand. There were also many farmers and farm laborers who worked on the land to grow crops to feed their families. By the middle of the 1800s, all this had changed. Many British people now lived in towns and worked in enormous factories, or in stores, offices, railroads, and other businesses designed to serve the inhabitants of these industrial centers. Leading the world, British inventors continued to develop revolutionary new machines that performed traditional tasks such as spinning and weaving much faster than they could be done by hand. Machines were also used to make iron and steel. These metals were, in turn, used to make more machines, weapons, and tools.

▼ New factories were built near rivers or canals and railroads This meant that raw materials could be delivered, and finished goods taken away. Houses for workers were often built close to the factory.

Jobs in factories, such as textile mills, often required skill rather than strength. This gave women a chance to earn a living wage, both in the towns of the New England states and in the north of Britain.

Four factors brought about the change: coal mining, a canal system, capital (money), and cheap labor. Coal was used to smelt iron and steel and to make steam to power the new machines. Barges carried raw materials and finished goods along the canals. The profits from Britain's colonies gave businessmen the money to invest. And badly paid farmworkers flocked to the towns for better paid work.

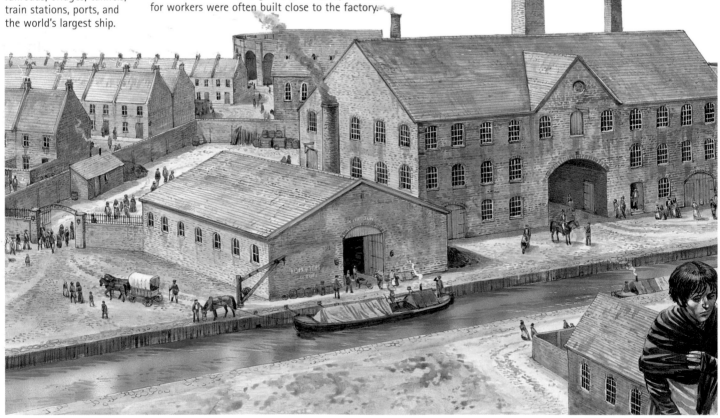

BUSINESS BOOM

New coal mines were dug to supply coal for steam engines and coke for ironworks. By the mid-1800s, Britain's canal and rail systems linked all the major industrial cities. The new machines made goods faster and more cheaply. Factory and mine owners made huge profits, some of which they spent on more machines, so creating new jobs. Investors saved small amounts of money in banks. The banks then lent large amounts to industrialists. This developing capitalist system raised money to build factories, offices, and houses.

For many workers, life in the factories and mines was hard and dangerous. Men, women, and children worked 12 or more hours a day, often for low wages. Many workers were killed or injured by unsafe machinery before new safety laws were enforced. Towns grew rapidly and without any real planning, leaving some areas without drains or clean water. Diseases such as cholera (from dirty water) became common and killed thousands of people.

In time, laws to shorten working hours and prohibit child labor were introduced. Trade unions, at first banned, campaigned for better pay and conditions for workers. Reformers won better working conditions, and schooling for all children. Slums were cleared and new laws were brought in to control factories and houses.

The arrival of the railroad opened up North America but also led to the first national strike—the Great Strike of 1877. When railroad workers had their wages cut, their protests stopped the trains.

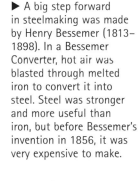

▶ A big step forward in steelmaking was made by Henry Bessemer (1813–1898). In a Bessemer Converter, hot air was blasted through melted iron to convert it into steel. Steel was stronger and more useful than iron, but before Bessemer's invention in 1856, it was very expensive to make.

In 1842, James Nasmyth (1808–1890) invented the steam hammer, used to make parts for the new steamships.

KEY DATES

1838	Brunel builds the steamship *Great Western*
1842	James Nasmyth invents first steam hammer
1865	George Pullman invents railroad sleeping car
1869	George Westinghouse invents air brake; Suez Canal completed, easing travel to India
1886	Samuel Gompers sets up American Federation of Labor
1893	Frank Sprague invents electric trolley
1900	United States and Germany both overtake Britain's steel production

TEXAS AND MEXICO 1835–1848

Gaining independence from Spain in 1821, Mexico soon found itself in conflict with Texas over land ownership. The conflict led to war.

Sam Houston (1793–1863) was twice elected president of the Republic of Texas. He became governor of the state in 1859.

▲ A contemporary cartoon shows the Aztec symbol for Mexico—a proud eagle perched on a cactus. Mexico's vast territories shrank after the United States gradually annexed the northern areas in the mid-1800s.

▶ Davy Crockett (1786–1836) was one of the defenders of the Alamo, a mission in San Antonio. In 1836, 186 men held out against the 5,000 strong Mexican army of General Santa Anna. Only two women and two children survived. Other heroes killed were Jim Bowie and William Travis. In the end, they ran out of ammunition and had to use their guns as clubs.

At the time Mexico gained its independence, its borders stretched much farther north and covered many areas now in the southern United States. Many U. S. citizens settled in Texas, which belonged to Mexico. In 1835, Texas declared its independence. The Texans appointed Sam Houston as their military commander. He captured the town of San Antonio. His opponent, the Mexican General Santa Anna, then led a large Mexican army into Texas to crush the rebellion. He laid siege to the Alamo, a mission in the center of San Antonio, and won the town back. Davy Crockett was one of the defenders of the Alamo, which was sometimes used as a fort. It became a symbol of Texan resistance during the war against Mexico.

Santa Anna was later defeated by Houston's forces at the battle of San Jacinto in 1836. Texas then became independent, and was known as the Lone Star Republic. After a few years of independence, the people of Texas voted to join the United States. In 1845, Texas became the 28th state. Clashes between Texans and Mexicans continued as Texas tried to increase its territory.

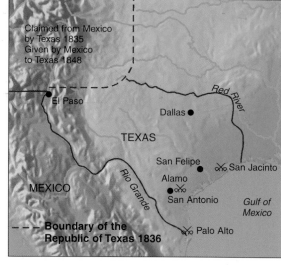

The land that the Texans and the Mexicans fought over lay between the Rio Grande and the Red River. In 1848, a treaty gave the United States large tracts of land.

WAR AND PEACE

President James Polk sent troops to the Rio Grande, invading land still claimed by Mexico. The Mexicans resisted, and the Mexican–American War broke out. U.S. troops captured the capital, Mexico City, in 1847, and the Mexicans surrendered. The treaty of Guadalupe–Hidalgo, in 1848, gave the United States huge new territories, including the modern states of California, Nevada, Utah, Arizona, and some of New Mexico, as well as Texas.

SOUTH AFRICA 1814–1910

South Africa saw enormous struggles for power and territory in the 1800s as the British, the Boers, and the Zulus all competed with each other.

Cecil Rhodes (1853–1902) was prime minister of the Cape Colony from 1890 to 1895 and sought to unite all of Africa under British rule.

Cetshwayo (1826–1884) was king of the Zulus from 1873 to 1879. He led his people in the Zulu battles against the British.

In 1836, the Cape Colony at the southern tip of Africa was ruled by the British. Dutch settlers, known as Boers (literally "farmers"), disliked British rule. The Boers left the Cape Colony and set out on the Great Trek. They traveled northward to the areas now known as KwaZulu-Natal and the Free State and defeated the African people who lived there. The British took over the Boer republic of KwaZulu-Natal in 1843, but they gave independence to the Transvaal and the Free State. A three-way struggle developed, with the British against the Zulus and both groups against the Boers.

In the Zulu war of 1879, the Zulus defeated the British at Isandlwana but lost to them at Rourke's Drift and Kambula. The Zulus were organized into *impis* (regiments) and fought bravely before their defeat. In 1880, the British tried to take over the Transvaal, and the First Boer War broke out. The Boers defeated the British, and the Transvaal remained independent.

Although only armed with simple weapons such as spears and knobkerries (round-headed clubs), the Zulus were often successful in inflicting heavy losses on their opponents.

CECIL RHODES

The prime minister of the Cape Colony at that time was Cecil Rhodes. He wanted to create a British Empire in Africa that would stretch from Cape Town to Cairo in Egypt. Rhodes planned the Jameson Raid, which was designed to overthrow the Boer government of the Transvaal. The raid failed, and in 1899, the Second Boer War broke out. Although the Boers won some of the early battles, such as Spion Kop, they were defeated by the British in 1902.

The Treaty of Vereeniging was signed in May 1902, and the Boer republics became part of the British Empire in exchange for a guarantee of self-government. In 1907, this promise was honored, and they joined KwaZulu-Natal and the Cape Colony as the founding provinces of the Union of South Africa in 1910.

The Great Trek is an important event in Boer history. A group of Boers left the Cape Colony with all their belongings loaded onto wagons and traveled northward into the areas where the African peoples lived.

THE OPIUM WARS 1830–1864

European merchants used the addictive power of opium to gain important trading links with China— a country that wished to remain closed to foreigners.

The wife of an opium smoker publicly destroys her husband's pipe. The sale and smoking of opium had been banned in China from the early 1700s, by order of the emperor.

The Chinese had almost no contact with the rest of the world for centuries. Many European merchants were eager to trade, especially in the rare Chinese silks and porcelain that were so popular in Europe. However, the Chinese government allowed trading to take place at only one port, Guangzhou (Canton). To get around this problem, foreign traders began to smuggle the drug opium into the country, so that the Chinese would trade their precious goods in exchange for the drug. The Chinese government tried to stop this. In 1839, Chinese officials, under the orders of Lim Tse-hsu, the Chinese high commissioner of Guangzhou, visited British warehouses where they seized and burned up to 20,000 chests of opium.

The British would not tolerate what they saw as the confiscation of private property. In response, they sent warships that threatened the Chinese and besieged the port. The Chinese refused to pay compensation, banned trade with Britain, and fired on the British forces. Thus started the First Opium War (1839–1842) fought by the Chinese and the British.

Ships, like this British merchant ship in Lintin Harbor, in 1834, would have carried quantities of opium. Foreign merchants traded the drug for the precious goods that were so greatly desired by customers in Europe.

Hong Kong Island became a British colony in 1842. It soon grew into a center of trade. In 1860, the Kowloon Peninsula was added, and in 1898, the British gained the New Territories on a 99-year lease.

TREATY OF NANJING

The war was one-sided. The British had superior forces, and they bombarded Guangzhou and captured Hong Kong from the Chinese. When this first war was over, the British forced the Chinese to sign the Treaty of Nanjing (Nanking), which opened up Chinese ports to Britain. China also had to pay compensation and give the island of Hong Kong to the British.

Britain's aggressive approach to the Chinese owed a great deal to the British foreign secretary Henry Temple, 3rd Viscount Palmerston. He was always ready to use force in what he saw as the defense of British interests overseas. In this, and later treaties, the Chinese were forced to give in to European demands. The Chinese, however, continued to fear that foreign trade meant that the country would come under foreign influence.

SOCIAL UNREST

Trouble, largely promoted by the British, erupted again in the mid-1850s and resulted in the Second Opium War (1856–1860). This war was also eventually won by the British and it ended with another treaty. The Treaty of Tianjin (Tientsin) was signed in 1858, and it forced the Chinese to open even more ports to trade with European merchants. Other countries, including France and the United States, also signed treaties, which gained their citizens special rights and increased Western influence in China. Eager traders and missionaries rushed in.

At the same time, the huge Chinese Empire was gradually breaking down. The ruling Qing dynasty was faced with rebellions started by starving peasants. The Taiping Rebellion (1851–1864) was begun by people who wanted the land to be divided equally among ordinary people. The foreign powers helped to crush the rebellion because they wanted the Qing dynasty to continue so that the treaties would be honored.

KEY DATES	
1839	Chinese officials destroy British opium stocks; Outbreak of First Opium War
1842	Chinese sign the Treaty of Nanjing
1844	Treaty of Wanghia with the United States; Treaty of Whampoa with France
1851	The Taiping Rebellion breaks out
1856	Outbreak of Second Opium War
1858	Chinese sign the Treaty of Tianjin
1898	Britain obtains 99-year lease on New Territories

Britain's vastly superior navy could easily destroy Chinese junks during the opium wars.

The Taiping Rebellion (1851–1864) was crushed by the Chinese with help from foreign powers who wanted Qing rule to continue.

EUROPE: YEAR OF REVOLUTION 1848

In 1848, protests broke out all over Europe. They demonstrated how unhappy people were with how they were governed.

Giuseppe Mazzini (1805–1872), seen here in prison, was a tireless campaigner for democracy and the unification of Italy.

The reasons for many of these rebellions were similar to those that sparked the French Revolution. One of the main factors was that people in many countries in Europe began to feel that they should have a say in their own government. In response to the rebellions and violent protests, many rulers just ignored the pleas of their people and tried to restore older systems of government, but the events of 1848 showed that change was inevitable.

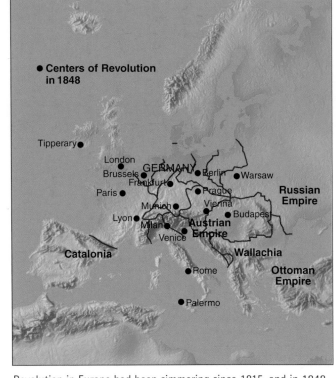

Revolution in Europe had been simmering since 1815, and in 1848, most European countries experienced rebellions. The map above shows where the most serious outbreaks were.

One powerful reason for the revolutions of 1848 was nationalism—the desire of people who spoke the same language to form their own independent nations. Nationalism was especially strong in Italy and Germany, which were divided into many small states, and in parts of the Austrian Empire. Other rebellions were led by people who wanted cheaper food, or changes in laws that would give land to working people.

▲ Paris revolutionaries demanding "Bread or Death" stormed government buildings in Paris. They overthrew the king, Louis-Philippe, and declared a republic with Louis Napoleon, nephew of Napoleon Bonaparte, as "prince president."

▶ The People's Charter, drafted by William Lovett (1800–1877) in 1838, demanded political reforms, including votes for all men. It gave its name to the Chartist movement. The last and biggest Chartist demonstration took place in London, in 1848.

CHARTISM

In some countries, people were demanding the right to vote. This was one of the reforms that the Chartist movement in Britain wanted. The People's Charter was first published there in May 1838. A petition said to have 1,200,000 signatures on it was handed in to Parliament in June 1839, but was rejected a month later. By February 1848, and following the revolution in France, a final petition was formed. When it was complete it was said to have over 3,000,000 names on it. On April 10, 1848 a mass march traveled across London to the Houses of Parliament to present the petition. Again, it was rejected, and Chartism lost its momentum.

Recent changes had made rebellion easier. More people were now able to read and newspapers told them what was happening in other countries. Few police forces existed, so troops had to be used against rioters. Most of the revolts of 1848 failed in their immediate demands, but over the next few years, nationalist feeling grew stronger, and many governments began to see that democratic reforms would soon be necessary.

The rebellions in Vienna and other cities resulted in the resignation of the Austrian chancellor, Prince Metternich, in March 1848. Emperor Ferdinand abdicated in favor of Franz Josef in December 1848.

Frankfurt, in Germany, also witnessed street fighting and rebellion. The people did succeed in forcing a change in their country's leadership. Peasants were given rights and protection.

REVOLUTION IN EUROPE

In France, the Second Republic was founded with Louis Napoleon, nephew of Napoleon Bonaparte, as "prince president." In the Italian states, revolts were widespread, but were crushed by the end of the year. The Austrian chancellor, Prince Metternich, was forced to flee, and the emperor abdicated in favor of Franz Josef.

There were uprisings in Berlin, Vienna, Prague, Budapest, Catalonia, Wallachia, Poland, and Britain. In Germany, the National Assembly met in Frankfurt, and in the Netherlands, a new constitution was introduced.

In Belgium, the *Communist Manifesto*, written by Karl Marx and Friedrich Engels, was published. Elsewhere, the armies and peasants remained loyal to their monarchs. Revolts were crushed in Prussia and Italy, but there were some reforms.

NEW ZEALAND 1792–1907

Having been the sole occupants of New Zealand for nearly a thousand years, the Maori people suddenly found themselves in competition for land.

Ko Tauwaki, chief of the Tukanu tribe of the Maori people. Maori folklore says that the North Island of New Zealand was created by the legendary hero Maui.

Whalers were among the first European settlers in New Zealand and the surrounding islands of the Pacific Ocean.

The first people to inhabit New Zealand were the Maoris, who had begun to settle in the early 800s, having arrived from other Pacific islands in their seagoing canoes. They settled mainly along the coast and rivers of North Island, but also established communities on South Island in smaller numbers. From the end of the 1700s, more and more settlements and trading posts were being established by missionaries and whalers, despite the objections of the Maoris. By the 1830s, the growing number of European settlers on New Zealand's North Island was beginning to cause problems. The settlers needed large areas of land to graze sheep. The Maoris, on the other hand, grew crops in addition to fishing and hunting, and they welcomed trade.

Maori folklore says that the North Island of New Zealand was created by the Maori hero Maui. They believed that all land should be held in trust for the next generation, so selling land went against their tradition. This is why they did not want to sell land to the Europeans settlers.

▼ Before the arrival of the Europeans, the Maoris had no outside enemies, but different tribal groups were often at war with each other. Tribes usually lived in fortified villages, such as this one above Lake Rotorua.

BRITISH SOVEREIGNTY

By the 1830s, the Maori numbers had been reduced by the diseases that the Europeans accidentally introduced. Both the settlers and the Maoris wanted the British to provide strong laws and they appealed to Britain for help.

In 1840, a representative of the British government, together with 50 Maori chiefs, signed the Treaty of Waitangi. The treaty set out that if the Maoris gave control of New Zealand to the British Empire and accepted Queen Victoria as their sovereign, the British would protect all Maori land ownership rights. Under this agreement, New Zealand also became a dependency of New South Wales in Australia. The Europeans continued to take Maori land. Many thought they had bought it legally. But because there were two versions of the treaty, the Maoris thought that they had only agreed to give the British "governorship." There were several violent Maori uprisings between 1845 and 1847.

The ceremony of *ongi*, or pressing of noses, is practiced by Maori women at Taranaki on the west coast of New Zealand's North Island. The 8,258-ft. (2517-m) peak of Mount Egmont can be seen in the distance.

KEY DATES

1790s	First European settlers arrived, often whalers
1839	New Zealand Company established in London
1840	Treaty of Waitangi signed by British and Maoris
1841	New Zealand becomes separate Crown colony
1845	First serious unrest breaks out among Maoris
1860	Full-scale war breaks out
1871	Peace permanently established
1882	First refrigerated ships allow export of meat
1907	New Zealand becomes a dominion within the British Empire

MAORI WARS

In 1860, war broke out between the Maoris and the colonists. Although they fought bravely, the Maoris were forced to retreat to the mountains. Peace was established in 1871. In 1907, New Zealand became a dominion of the British Empire. New Zealand prospered, and the numbers of Maoris began to grow again.

▲ Maori tribal groups often fought each other. Maori warriors decorated their faces with elaborate tattoos to identify each other in battle.

◄ Maori uprisings occurred between 1845 and 1847, and again between 1860 and 1870. After that date, the colonial settlers made concessions and a lasting peace was established.

THE CRIMEAN WAR 1853–1856

One of the few wars involving European nations in this period took place in the Crimea. It was sparked off by a struggle for the territory of the old Ottoman Empire.

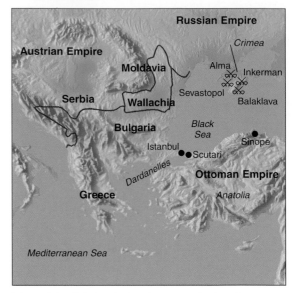

Most of the fighting during the war took place in the Crimean Peninsula, which projects southward from Russia into the Black Sea.

A defenseless Turkey is caught up in the merciless grip of Russia; Russia was seen as the main aggressor in the buildup to the Crimean War.

The Crimean War was originally a conflict between Russia and Turkey. The Russians felt that the Muslim Turks had failed to deal fairly with Christians in their Balkan territories or in the question of access to holy places in Palestine. In addition, the Russians also wanted access for their warships through the Black Sea via the Bosphorus and the Dardanelles. Negotiations between Turkey and Russia broke down, and the Turks, encouraged by the French, declared war on Russia. Russia then won the naval battle of Sinope, in the Black Sea, in 1853. Britain and France were concerned that Russia wanted to expand into the collapsing Ottoman Empire. They accordingly sent their fleets into the Black Sea to protect Turkish coasts, and quickly became Turkey's allies.

Russia also had quarrels with France, mainly to do with commercial and religious rivalry. The Turks were anxious to get rid of the strong Russian influence in their Balkan territories of Moldavia and Wallachia.

Florence Nightingale (1820–1910) founded the first training school for nurses in London in 1860. This was a direct response to the terrible sights she and other nurses had seen while serving in the Crimea. Some 4,600 British soldiers died in battle, and a further 17,500 died of disease.

CHARGE OF THE LIGHT BRIGADE

During the Battle of Balaklava on October 25, 1854, the British Light Brigade was ordered to charge an enemy position. The battle was won by the British, but because of the confusion of their officers, nearly 250 of the 673 men in the Light Brigade were killed or wounded during this misjudged engagement. The commanders thought that they were charging an isolated enemy outpost, but they were in fact charging a heavily fortified position.

KEY DATES

May	1853	Russians occupy Moldavia and Wallachia
Oct.	1853	Turkey declares war on Russia
Mar.	1854	France and Britain declare war on Russia
Sept.	1854	Allies win Battle of the Alma River
Oct.	1854	Siege of Sevastopol begins; Battle of Balaklava and Charge of the Light Brigade
Nov.	1854	Russians heavily defeated at Inkerman
Sept.	1855	Fall of Sevastopol
Feb.	1856	Fighting stops
Mar.	1856	Treaty of Paris signed

THE ALLIES

Anxious to put a check on Russia's plans for expansion, Britain joined France in declaring war on Russia toward the end of March 1854. They were also supported by actual forces from Piedmont–Sardinia, and were politically supported by Austria. The allied armies fought a bloody battle at the Alma River, and, in October, laid siege to the town of Sevastopol. Attempts by the Russians to relieve the siege led to the battle of Balaklava, with the disastrous charge of the Light Brigade, followed by the battle of Inkerman in early November. All three of these major engagements were won by the Allies. Although they were partially successful in recapturing Sevastopol, they were unable to take the dockside area, and it was not until September 1855 that Sevastopol finally fell. The Russians were held back because a lack of railroads prevented supplies and reinforcements from getting through. The war ended with the Treaty of Paris on March 30, 1856.

The British Rifle Brigade fought at the Battle of Inkerman in November 1854. This was another victory for the Allies. Cholera and frostbite took a far greater toll than the Russian forces.

The Crimean War marked the first time that the public was kept informed about the war by photographs and reports sent back by telegraph. Perhaps the most influential newspaperman was W. H. Russell of *The Times* in London—the first "war correspondent." Because of these reports in the British press, the war became notorious for the general level of incompetence shown by political leaders, and led, in January 1855, to the fall of the British government.

The Battle of the Alma River in September 1854 was one of the earliest encounters of the war. It was a clear victory for the Allied forces over Russia.

◀ The bombardment of Sevastopol by the Royal Navy in October 1854 was not enough to retake the whole town, and it was not until September 1855 that it finally fell.

JAPAN 1853–1913

Under the Tokugawas, Japan had been closed to foreigners for more than 200 years. In the early 1800s, it began to experience Western influence.

After 1868, the Meiji government improved educational standards. By 1914, the Japanese were among the best-educated people in the world.

During the first half of the 1600s, Japan's rulers decided that contact with the West must end. In particular, they feared that Christian missionaries might bring European armies to invade Japan. They therefore banned almost all foreigners from entering Japan and the Japanese from leaving their own country. As a result, people in the West were unable to appreciate the great beauty of the Japanese art of this period until the mid-to-late 1800s. In 1853, Millard Fillmore (1800–1874), the 13th President of the United States, sent four warships, under the command of Commodore Matthew Perry, on an important journey to Japan designed to bring about the opening of trade there.

The warships anchored in Tokyo Bay. The threat of American naval power helped Commodore Perry persuade the Japanese to resume trading with the West. The Japanese were impressed by Perry's steamships and by the other machinery he showed them. The two countries went on to sign the Treaty of Kanagawa a year later, in 1854, in which they agreed to open two ports to American trade.

The ships of Commodore Perry's fleet were the first steamships that the Japanese had ever seen. They realized that they would be unable to beat them.

▲ U.S. Commodore Matthew Perry (1794–1858) is known as the man who opened up Japan to trade with the rest of the world. In 1853, he sailed to Japan, and in 1854, signed the Treaty of Kanagawa with the Japanese.

Soon, similar treaties had been signed with Britain, the Netherlands, and Russia. The Tokugawa were criticized by their opponents for allowing these treaties to be signed, and for many other problems they could not solve.

▶ This Japanese woodblock print shows Yokohama Harbor in the late 1800s. Following the Treaty of Kanagawa, the Japanese agreed to open ports to trade with the United States and several European countries.

RESTORATION OF THE EMPEROR

People were tired of the near total isolation that the Tokugawa family had imposed for so long. In 1868, the Tokugawa were finally overthrown and the emperor, Mutsuhito, was restored as ruler (the Meiji Restoration). Now that their country had opened up to the West, the Japanese began to modernize.

Although the Japanese wanted to keep some of their own traditions, they were also eager to learn from the industrial nations of the West. They changed and adapted both their government and their schools. Improved education meant that by 1914 the Japanese were among the best-educated people in the world. They began to import machines and introduced new industries such as cotton manufacture. Many Japanese people adopted European fashions in music and clothes. At the same time, foreigners gradually learned to respect Japanese success and culture.

With industrialization, the Japanese soon began to expand their country. They tried to take over Korea, which led to a war with China in 1894. Japan also fought Russia over this issue in 1904–1905 and finally annexed Korea in 1910. This helped make Japan the most powerful nation in its region. By 1913, Japan had become an industrial power of great importance—the first country in Asia to make such advances.

▲ Russian soldiers flee after the Battle of Mukden, in northeast China, in which the Japanese won a decisive victory in March 1905.

▼ In May 1905, Japan's fleet, led by Admiral Togo, annihilated the Russian fleet. This led to the Treaty of Portsmouth and gave the Japanese control over Korea.

AMERICAN CIVIL WAR 1861–1865

By the mid-1800s, the United States was badly divided. The North and South strongly disagreed about questions of states' rights and ownership of slaves.

Union soldier

Confederate soldier

Ulysses S. Grant (1822–1885) was appointed commander of the Union forces in 1863. He was a tough and determined general.

Robert E. Lee (1807–1870) was in the U.S. army when civil war broke out. He resigned, and first advised, then took command of, the Confederate troops.

In 1850, the North had almost all of the manufacturing industries, thriving cities, and a growing railroad system. The South was a land of farms, and of large cotton and tobacco plantations that relied on slave labor. Slavery had long been banned in the northern states.

This division caused hostility between North and South. The Kansas–Nebraska Act (1854) gave new states the right to choose whether or not they allowed slavery. The Compromise of 1850 helped northern states protect the rights of runaway slaves—the South felt threatened.

The southern states were sure that the economy of the South would be ruined if the slaves were freed. Furthermore, the southern states believed that they had the right to make their own laws without interference from the federal government.

In 1860, Abraham Lincoln (1809–1865) was elected president. He belonged to the Republican Party, which opposed slavery, although he himself was not an abolitionist. Many southern states refused to live under such a government, and led

Union soldiers wore the blue uniform of the U.S. army. The Confederates usually wore gray.

by Jefferson Davis (1808–1889), they announced in December 1860 that they were seceding from (leaving) the Union and forming the Confederate States of America. The United States government declared they had no right to do this.

BATTLE OF GETTYSBURG

The Battle of Gettysburg (July 1–3, 1863) was a turning point in the Civil War. The battle was the bloodiest ever fought on American soil, but was an important Union victory by General George Meade. He stopped an invasion of the North by General Robert E. Lee's Confederate army. From this point onward, the South's chances of winning the war declined.

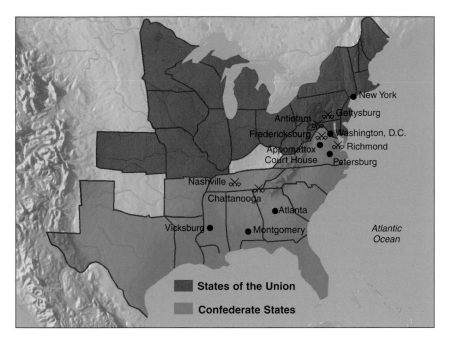

◀ This shows the division of the United States at the beginning of the Civil War. Eleven of the 34 states made up the Confederacy. Most of the battles were fought in the east and southeast.

▲ The Battle of Spotsylvania, Virginia, in May 1864, was one of the many Union victories of the Civil War. In all, more than 600,000 soldiers died on both sides in the conflict.

THE TWO SIDES

The North (Union), made up of 23 states, had more men, more money, and more industry than the South. The North also controlled the navy and started a naval blockade that prevented the South from receiving help or supplies from abroad. The 11 states of the South (the Confederacy) were much weaker, but they had the benefit of good generals and a great fighting spirit. Civil war broke out on April 12, 1861 when the forces of the South opened fire on Fort Sumter in South Carolina. The Confederates won a number of victories early in the war.

The South won the first battles in 1861, including Fredericksburg and Chancellorsville, but the turning point in the struggle came in July 1863, when the North won the biggest battle of the war, at Gettysburg. The Union forces, under the command of General George Meade, stopped an invasion of the North by General Robert E. Lee's Confederate army. Each side had over 20,000 soldiers killed or wounded.

Union flag

Confederate flag

During the Civil War, the Confederates rejected the Stars and Stripes and adopted their own flag.

For the first time in history, railroads played a vital part in warfare by moving troops, ammunition, and supplies swiftly over great distances.

Harriet Tubman (1820–1913) was an escaped slave who made trips through southern territory, helping slaves escape.

THE END OF THE CIVIL WAR 1865

Slavery was completely abolished in 1865, with the 13th Amendment to the Constitution. The country was reunited, but new problems emerged.

General Lee's presentation sword was not handed over during the surrender ceremony, as was customary. Instead, it remained by his side.

In 1864, despite Lee's skillful tactics, General Grant captured Richmond, the capital of the South. General Sherman marched through Georgia and the other southern states, capturing Atlanta. He followed this victory with a "march to the sea," during which he destroyed towns and farms. Short of men, money, weapons, and food, Lee surrendered on April 9, 1865, ending the Civil War. More than 600,000 soldiers had died, many from diseases such as typhoid and dysentery. Five days later, Abraham Lincoln was assassinated.

The Civil War settled two important questions. First, it confirmed that the United States of America was a single nation and that no state had the right to break away. Second, it brought slavery in the southern states to an end. After the Civil War, arguments raged over how the South should be "reconstructed." Ideas included the opening of schools and the building of railroads. Abraham Lincoln's successor, Andrew Johnson (1808–1875), a Democrat, wanted better conditions for black Americans. The Republicans wanted a harsher policy, and it was they who won the argument in the end.

General Lee surrendered to General Grant at Appomattox Court House, Virginia, on April 9, 1865. His men were outnumbered, exhausted, and starving.

The people of the South resisted most aspects of Reconstruction. Many former slaves who had fought on the Union side returned home expecting more freedom in the South. However, the Ku Klux Klan and other racist organizations began a campaign of murder and terrorism in 1866 that tried to stop black Americans from enjoying civil rights. Northern troops withdrew, Reconstruction ended, and the Democrats took over the South.

Abraham Lincoln (1809–1865) was the 16th President of the United States. Many people believe he was the greatest of all of the presidents. "Honest Abe" was known for his integrity and the force of his arguments.

THE GETTYSBURG ADDRESS

In November 1863, President Lincoln was invited to make a "few appropriate remarks" at the dedication of a national cemetery at Gettysburg. His speech lasted about two minutes and is today regarded as a masterpiece. Abraham Lincoln summed up the central issue of the war—the survival of a nation dedicated to freedom.

CANADA 1763–1913

The peace terms of 1763 effectively gave Canada over to British rule. In 1791, the British Constitutional Act split Canada into British- and French-speaking territories.

Louis Joseph Papineau (1786–1871) was a French–Canadian politician. He led the French-speaking Canadians' demand for reform and equality.

William Lyon Mackenzie (1795–1861) was a member of Canada's Reform Party. He wanted Canada to have more freedom from British rule. He led the 1837 rebellion in Upper Canada.

Opposition to British rule in Canada grew during the 1830s. Rebellions broke out in both Upper and Lower Canada in 1837, led by William Lyon Mackenzie and Louis Papineau respectively. The rebels wanted self-government and, although they had some support, the most influential people in the colonies did not agree with them. The rebels were soon defeated by British troops. The British government sent Lord Durham to Canada to investigate the causes of the rebellions. His report said that Upper and Lower Canada should be united and should have control over their own affairs.

The 1840 Act of Union united the two colonies, which became known as the Province of Canada. However, many Canadians still felt that these reforms did not go far enough. This was partly because the Canadians were concerned that the United States might invade if Canada looked weak. In 1867, the British North America Act was passed, and Canada became self-governing. The act united four Canadian provinces in a dominion. The French Canadians of Quebec were promised equality, and French and English became the official languages.

Winnipeg, a center of the fur trade, was still a small town in 1870. In that year, the settlement became the capital of the province of Manitoba.

WESTERN TERRITORIES

The vast lands to the west, which belonged to the Hudson's Bay Company, later also became part of Canada. The Northwest Territories joined the dominion in 1870, and the Yukon Territory in 1898. The Yukon had been the location of a gold rush in 1896, which led to tens of thousands of hopeful prospectors making their way over the Rocky Mountains to the goldfields and, they hoped, great wealth. Completion of the Canadian Pacific Railway in 1885 united the country. Unlike the American railroads, it formed one continuous system from the St. Lawrence River to the Pacific Ocean.

◄ The British North America Act of 1867 united the provinces of Nova Scotia, New Brunswick, Ontario (formerly Upper Canada), and Quebec (Lower Canada) in the Dominion of Canada.

▲ The Canadian Pacific Railway was completed in 1885. It linked the east and west coasts, reducing the journey time from five months to five days.

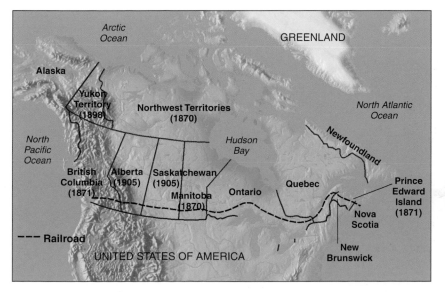

Map showing: Arctic Ocean, GREENLAND, Alaska, Yukon Territory (1898), Northwest Territories (1870), North Atlantic Ocean, North Pacific Ocean, Newfoundland, Hudson Bay, British Columbia (1871), Alberta (1905), Saskatchewan (1905), Manitoba (1870), Ontario, Quebec, Prince Edward Island (1871), Nova Scotia, New Brunswick, UNITED STATES OF AMERICA

--- Railroad

ITALY 1833–1878

The birth of the Italian nation was brought about with the help of an aristocrat, Count Camillo Cavour, and a man of the people, Giuseppe Garibaldi.

Victor Emmanuel II (1820–1878) was the popular king of Piedmont–Sardinia. He eventually became king of all Italy.

▼ Piedmont–Sardinia took the lead in uniting Italy in 1859–1860. Nice and Savoy were given to France in 1860.

I n the early 1800s, Italy was made up of a number of small states. Apart from the Kingdom of Piedmont–Sardinia and Rome, which was ruled by the pope, these states were governed by foreign countries. In the 1830s, an independence movement known as the *Risorgimento* ("resurrection") began to grow. In 1848, many revolutions against foreign rule broke out, but they were quickly suppressed. In 1849, Victor Emmanuel II became king of Piedmont–Sardinia (a northern state in the Piedmont region, which also ruled the island of Sardinia), and made Turin his capital. He was a very popular man, at least in part because he restricted the powers of the clergy, who were less well-regarded in the north than in the south. He was known as "the cavalier king."

The rebellion in Venice in 1848 was one of the last in Italy to hold out. Severely weakened by hunger and disease, the people of Venice gave up in August 1849.

SKILLFUL POLITICIAN

Count Camillo Cavour, an Italian aristocrat with very liberal views, became the chief minister of the Kingdom of Piedmont–Sardinia in 1852. He made an alliance with France in 1858. Together, they defeated the Austrians in 1859. Austria ceded Lombardy to France who then handed it to Piedmont in exchange for Savoy and Nice. Most of northern Italy then joined with Piedmont–Sardinia.

In 1860, rebellion broke out in southern Italy, which was part of the Kingdom of the Two Sicilies. Giuseppe Garibaldi led a revolt and conquered the kingdom. His men were known as "red shirts" because of their dress, and faithfully followed their romantic and patriotic leader. It took them a mere three months to conquer all of Sicily.

Cavour was now very concerned that Garibaldi, and his seemingly unstoppable men, would attack Rome, which might in turn lead Austria or France to come to the aid of the pope. Cavour invaded the Papal States (but not Rome) and then marched his army south. Garibaldi's forces had taken Naples, and Cavour, being careful to go around Rome itself, finally met up with him.

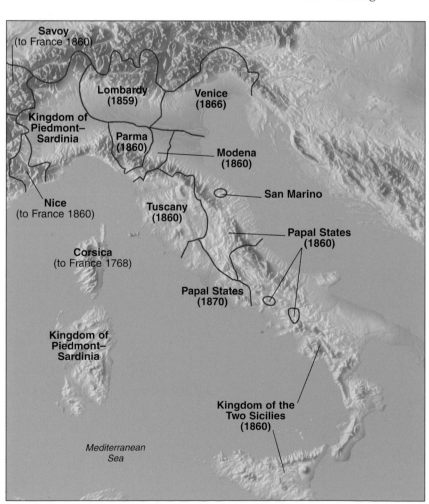

Savoy (to France 1860)

Lombardy (1859)

Venice (1866)

Kingdom of Piedmont–Sardinia

Parma (1860)

Modena (1860)

Nice (to France 1860)

Tuscany (1860)

San Marino

Corsica (to France 1768)

Papal States (1860)

Papal States (1870)

Kingdom of Piedmont–Sardinia

Kingdom of the Two Sicilies (1860)

Mediterranean Sea

Giuseppe Garibaldi (1807–1882) was a patriot who fought against foreign rule in Italy. With his "red shirts," he conquered the kingdom of the Two Sicilies in 1860, and it became part of the Kingdom of Italy.

Count Camillo Cavour (1810–1861) was the politician who made most of the plans for a unified Italy. He was also able to harness the talents of Giuseppe Garibaldi to help his own plans.

AGREEMENT AND UNITY

Count Cavour reached a detailed agreement with Garibaldi and his red-shirt soldiers that allowed the Kingdom of Piedmont–Sardinia to take over Sicily, Naples, and the Papal States. In February 1861, the first national parliament was held in Turin and, one month later, Victor Emmanuel II was proclaimed king of all Italy.

Two small areas were not included. Venice was still part of the Austrian Empire and Rome was ruled by the pope but occupied by France. Venice was given to Italy after Austria was defeated in the Austro–Prussian War (1866). In Rome, Pope Pius IX was totally unwilling to bend to what he still saw as a northern king. The Franco–Prussian War of 1870 forced the French to withdraw their garrison in Rome for other duties, and the Italian army immediately took over Rome. The city then became the capital of Italy. Pope Pius would not negotiate and thought of himself as a prisoner in the Vatican until he died in 1878. The people of Rome wanted unity and so it was that the ruling house of Piedmont–Sardinia reigned over a totally united country.

KEY DATES

1830s	Mazzini founds the "Young Italy" movement
1848	Revolutions break out in Europe
1849	Victor Emmanuel II–King of Piedmont–Sardinia
1852	Cavour–chief minister of Piedmont–Sardinia
1859	Piedmont–Sardinia and France defeat Austrians
1860	Garibaldi and his army conquer Sicily
1861	First national Italian parliament held
1870	Rome joins greater Italy

▼ A meeting between Victor Emmanuel II and Garibaldi at Teano, northeast of Naples, in 1860 eventually led to the unification of Italy.

GERMANY 1848–1871

In the second half of the 1800s, the military might of France was overtaken by a German state, Prussia. A new and powerful Germany emerged.

The diplomatic skills of Otto von Bismarck (1815–1898), prime minister of Prussia, kept his enemies isolated.

▲ Napoleon III (1808–1873) became emperor of France in 1852. He was captured at the Battle of Sedan during the Franco-Prussian War and sent into exile in 1871.

After the failure of the revolutions of 1848, the German Confederation, made up of over 40 states, stayed as disunited as it had been for centuries. The two strongest states, Austria and Prussia, jostled for power over all of Germany. Although weaker at first, Prussia's trade and industry grew in the 1850s. Its increasing strength was supported by the Prussian kaiser and his new prime minister, Otto von Bismarck.

Austria and Prussia went to war against Denmark over control of the duchies of Schleswig and Holstein. Although both duchies belonged to the royal family of Denmark, many Germans lived there. Denmark was defeated, and both duchies now came under German control. But Austria and Prussia soon clashed over how they should be administered.

WHO WOULD LEAD GERMANY?

In 1866, Bismarck dissolved the German Confederation, and Austria declared war on Prussia, confident of victory. They had, however, not taken sufficient account of the skill and strength of the Prussian army. The Prussian forces swept through the Austrian territory at an alarming speed. The power of the Austrian Hapsburg Empire was forever weakened when they were defeated on July 3, 1866 at the Battle of Sadowa. Bismarck then set up the North German Confederation, with Prussia as the most powerful member.

The Peace of Prague was an excellent example of the skillful diplomacy and statesmanship of Bismarck. He knew that it would be dangerous to humble Austria, and he wanted to make an ally and not an enemy. Accordingly, the Hapsburgs only lost the two duchies, which they did not really want anyway, and Venice. Prussia did, however, make huge gains within the rest of Germany.

▶ In September 1870, during the Franco–Prussian War, the Prussian army laid siege to Paris. Rather than make a full assault on the city, the Prussians simply surrounded it and waited. The poor were soon facing starvation, and the wealthy were reduced to eating the animals from the Tuileries Zoo. Peace came in May 1871.

THE BATTLE OF SEDAN

The Battle of Sedan, in northern France, on September 1–2, 1870, was the scene of an unequal conflict between Prussian forces and the French. The French forces were outnumbered two to one. Although Leboeuf, the French war minister, had claimed that the French preparation was total, once the battle began, it was found that not all of the French riflemen even had a rifle. Surrounded and unable to break out, Napoleon III, along with 85,000 French troops, was forced to surrender.

THE FRANCO–PRUSSIAN WAR

The French emperor, Napoleon III, a poorly supported, ill-advised leader, felt threatened by Prussia's increasing power. He demanded Germany hand over some of its territory to balance out the Prussian gains. Bismarck ignored this demand, and Napoleon's threats only served to bring the previously reluctant southern German states behind Prussia.

Bismarck provoked the French when he altered the report of a conversation between the Prussian king and the French ambassador so that it looked like an insult to France. When the document, the "Ems Telegram," was published in 1870, Napoleon III was furious and declared war. In the Franco–Prussian War, Prussia defeated France in 1871 and took over Alsace and Lorraine. The remaining German states also joined in 1871. Bismarck then formed the German Second Reich, with the king of Prussia (William I) as emperor.

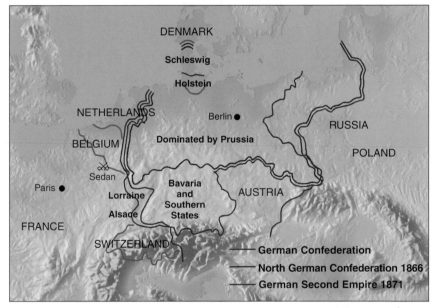

▲ The North German Confederation, dominated by Prussia, was formed in 1867. It was a union of states in which the members kept their own governments, but military and foreign policy was decided by a federal government.

KEY DATES

1852	Napoleon III becomes emperor of France
1862	Bismarck becomes Prussian prime minister
1864	Danish plans to take over Schleswig-Holstein
1866	Schleswig-Holstein taken over by Prussia
1867	North German Confederation formed
1870	Outbreak of the Franco–Prussian War
1870	French defeat at the Battle of Sedan, Napoleon III captured
1870	Prussian siege of Paris begins
1871	Franco-Prussian War ends at Peace of Frankfurt
1871	Second German Reich proclaimed at Versailles
1873	Napoleon III dies in exile

◀ This cartoon shows Bismarck and Kaiser Wilhelm riding on Napoleon III as a pig as they make their triumphal entry into Paris in 1871.

SCRAMBLE FOR AFRICA 1880–1912

With their greater wealth and technology, the major European powers were able to conquer large parts of the world. They claimed the territory as their own.

This cartoon shows the German eagle, poised to take as much of Africa as it can. Germany was just one of many European powers seeking new lands.

▼ During the latter part of the 1800s, rivalry between the different European powers played a large part in the scramble for Africa.

Toward the end of the 1800s, the European powers ceased to squabble among themselves for territories and trade within Europe itself. With the sudden emergence of the new force of Germany under the political control of Otto von Bismarck, all European nations looked farther afield for economic gain. Rival European nations now rushed to carve out their respective colonies in Africa. This process became known as the "scramble for Africa."

Britain and France undoubtedly led the scramble, but Germany, Belgium, and Italy were very close behind. Numerous conflicts flared up between Britain and France over colonies in West Africa. Where Britain had been happy to control a relatively small number of coastal towns and ports, by the end of the century they had taken over all of what is now Ghana and Nigeria, and effectively controlled Sierra Leone and The Gambia.

Dr. David Livingstone, lost while seeking the source of the Nile, had a historic meeting with Welsh-born American journalist H. M. Stanley by Lake Tanganyika in 1871.

THE SUEZ CANAL

Opened in 1869, the Suez Canal cut the sea journey between Britain and India from three months to three weeks. The Khedive of Egypt was in financial difficulties, and the British bought his half of the shares in the Suez Canal in 1875.

Relations between Britain and France worsened when the British occupied Egypt in 1882 to protect their interests during a local uprising against the Europeans. In 1885, General Gordon and many British soldiers were killed when the Mahdi, the leader in Sudan, took Khartoum on the White Nile. The Italians invaded Eritrea (now part of Ethiopia), and King Leopold of the Belgians took over the Congo.

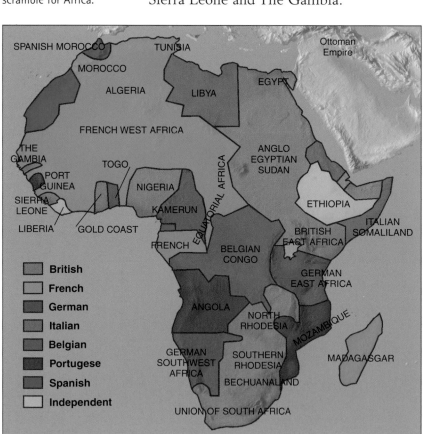

Europeans traded guns in exchange for gold and ivory. The guns had a devastating effect in Africa.

CONSTANT EXPANSION

The scramble for Africa became a formal process at a conference in Berlin in 1884. The rival European countries cut up Africa like a cake. Only Liberia and Ethiopia, which held off an Italian invasion, remained independent. The colonization of Africa had a number of effects on Africans. The Europeans took no notice of the different African nations and tribal boundaries when the new borders were drawn. They brought new forms of government to Africa, but few Africans could vote. Profits from the colonies went back to Europe, and European colonists often took the best farmland.

KEY DATES

1869	Suez Canal opens to shipping
1871	Stanley meets Livingstone at Lake Tanganyika
1876	Leopold II of Belgium takes over the Congo
1882	British occupy Egypt to protect the Suez Canal
1884	European nations meet in Berlin to divide Africa among themselves
1885	The Mahdi besieges Khartoum
1898	British defeat the Mahdi's troops at Omdurman
1893	The French take Timbuktu, Mali, West Africa
1899	British–Egyptian rule of Sudan
1912	The African National Congress (ANC) forms in South Africa

▲ The French conquest of Mali in West Africa was symbolized by the raising of the French flag in Timbuktu in 1893. Their advance along the Niger River was held up by the resistance of the local people, the Mande.

◀ Designed by French engineer Ferdinand de Lesseps (1805–1894), the Suez Canal considerably reduced the journey from Britain to India, and helped trade goods reach England more quickly. In 1875, the British, under the leadership of Disraeli, heard that the Khedive (viceroy) of Egypt faced bankruptcy, and they bought his share of the canal for £4 million.

IRELAND 1800–1913

Ireland went through a period of great suffering when disease struck the potato, the staple food of the poor. At least a million people died, and a million emigrated.

Daniel O'Connell (1775–1847) was a fighter for the rights of Catholic people in Britain. He was the first Irish Catholic to be elected to the British Parliament. He served from 1829 to 1847.

Most of the people of Ireland made a living by farming small plots of rented land or working on large estates for Anglo–Irish landlords. They were desperately poor and depended on potatoes, which were cheap, to feed large families. In 1845 and 1846, potato blight, a type of fungus, spread rapidly across the land, turning the potatoes black, diseased, and inedible. Famine relief, paid for by charities and public fund-raising, was too little and came too late. The government system for the relief of property was badly planned and run, and it broke down under the pressure.

The authorities believed that the food supply would adjust itself to meet the demand, and they opposed the distribution of free food until it was too late. Efforts to bring down the price of wheat by repealing the Corn Laws also came too late. Because landlords evicted tenants who could not pay their rent, entire families were left to starve to death by the side of the road.

▲ Irish tenant farmers were ruined when the potato blight struck in 1845. The harvest was poor and they could not pay their rent. Many of the farmers and their families starved to death.

On May 6, 1882, in Phoenix Park in Dublin, Lord Frederick Cavendish, the Irish chief secretary, and T.H. Burke, his undersecretary, were stabbed to death by Irish Nationalists. Five were later hanged for this offense.

IRISH EMIGRATION

To escape the famine, hundreds of thousands of Irish people emigrated, mostly to the British mainland, but great numbers also went to the United States and Canada. Blight also hit potato crops in Britain and other countries. But only in Ireland did it have such disastrous consequences, including the shadow it was to cast over Irish–British relations in future generations.

▶ Most Irish people lived a hard life with little food and comfort. Their homes were usually not very different from the barns in which their Anglo–Irish landlords kept their cattle.

During the potato famine, many Irish people had to choose between possible starvation or leaving their country. About one million people starved to death and another million emigrated over the next five years, mostly to England, Scotland, and Wales, as well as the United States. A typhoid epidemic in 1846–1847 is thought to have killed another 350,000 Irish people.

Charles Stewart Parnell was the leader of the Irish Nationalists in the British Parliament. He led the struggle for Irish home rule and supported the Land League, which wanted land to be given to Irish farmers.

The Irish Republican Brotherhood, or Fenians, was founded in 1858 by James Stephens (1825–1901). It was an organization that wanted to set up an Irish republic.

▼ The Fenians sometimes resorted to acts of violence in Britain. In 1867, they attacked a police van in Manchester to rescue some of their members.

IRISH LEADERS

The demands of Irish politicians, particularly Charles Parnell (1846–1891), became increasing vocal in the British Parliament. Parnell had entered Parliament in 1875, and became president of the Irish Land League in 1879. His party demanded rent reductions and resisted the evictions of tenant farmers. The Irish politicians, and the strength of public feeling among the Irish, led to some law reforms, especially relating to land ownership rights.

However, these reforms were not enough to keep the Irish happy with British rule. Almost all of the Irish wanted home rule, or self-government. After the failure of both the 1886 and 1893 Home Rule Bills, the British Parliament finally passed the third Home Rule Bill in 1912—but it was not put into operation because of the outbreak of World War I, in 1914.

KEY DATES

1801	Irish Parliament abolished by the British
1829	Daniel O'Connell enters the British Parliament
1845	First potato blight leads to widespread famine
1846	Second potato blight causes worse famine
1846	Typhoid epidemic kills 350,000 Irish people
1875	Charles Parnell enters the British Parliament
1879	Parnell becomes president of the Land League
1912	Third Home Rule Bill passed, but not enacted

SOUTHEAST ASIA 1800–1913

Southeast Asia was dominated by the Dutch, French, and British in the late 1800s. They grew rich on the profits from crops grown by local people.

In Malaya, the British ruled through the local sultans. This beautiful mural of the tree of life comes from a family home in Sarawak, now part of Malaysia.

Rubber packing in Ceylon (now Sri Lanka) in the late 1800s. Rubber plants were introduced to Southeast Asia by the British from seeds collected in Brazil.

Southeast Asia was colonized by Europeans who set up plantations that were worked by the native population. The French colony of Indochina included Cambodia, Laos, and Vietnam. The French gradually conquered the area during the 1800s, despite local resistance. In Annam, the emperor, Ham Nghi, waged a guerrilla war until 1888.

The Dutch had been established in Indonesia since the 1620s. They had already taken over Indonesian trade, and from 1830, they also took over agriculture. The peasant farmers were forced to grow the crops the Dutch wanted, especially coffee and indigo (a plant from which a blue dye was made).

By 1900, a nationalist= movement was growing in Indonesia itself. The Indonesians made efforts to improve education and to regain some control over their business and trade.

Faced with Burmese expansion at the end of the 1700s, the British colonized Burma and the Malay Peninsula during the 1800s because they wanted to protect India, which they regarded as the most valuable part of their empire.

The Burmese resisted British rule in a series of bloody wars between 1824 and 1885, but by 1886, Britain controlled the whole country and made it into a province of India. It was not until 1937 that Burma was separated from India and regained some independence.

In Malaya, the situation was calmer because of British rule through the local sultans. During the early part of the 1800s, the British East India Company had set up trading posts; in 1826, Singapore, Malacca, and Penang were united to form the Straits Settlements.

The merchant ships of the British East India Company were known as East Indiamen.

▲ Indonesian princes and Dutch colonists benefited from the profits made by growing cash crops on the islands. For ordinary Indonesians, this way of life meant great hardship.

▶ Tea was one of the important cash crops grown on large British-owned estates in India.

BRITISH INFLUENCE

In later years, the British went on to become responsible for other states in the Malay Peninsula and formed the Federated Malay States in 1896, with the capital at Kuala Lumpur. Demand for rubber grew rapidly in the 1800s, but the only source of supply was South America. Rubber seeds were collected in Brazil and shipped to Kew Gardens, in London, where they were raised. In 1877, 2,000 young plants were shipped and distributed to countries such as Ceylon, Malaysia, and Indonesia, where the plants flourished.

By the 1880s, British engineers, surveyors, and architects were helping to build railroads, roads, bridges, factories, and government buildings in Southeast Asia. They drew on the experience gained from the Industrial Revolution in Britain. Banking and investment were geared toward financing the empire by trading raw materials from the colonies for homemade manufactured goods.

The British also figured out how to improve the techniques used for mining the large deposits of tin and other precious metals that had been discovered in Malaya and other countries. Toward the end of the 1800s, many people went to live and work in Southeast Asia as traders, soldiers, engineers, diplomats, and government administrators.

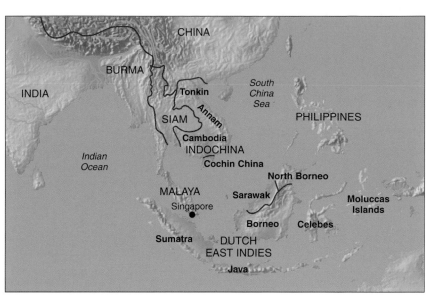

KEY DATES

1813	East India Company's trade monopoly ends
1819	Thomas Raffles of the East India Company founds Singapore as a free port
1824	British and Dutch interests settled by treaty
1859	French naval forces capture the citadel in Saigon
1867	Singapore and the Straits Settlements apply to be a Crown colony
1877	Brazilian rubber plants, grown in Kew Gardens, in London, exported to Southeast Asia
1884–1885	Chinese-French War
1885	At the Treaty of Tientsin China recognizes French rule over Annam and Tonkin
1886	British annexe Upper Burma
1887	Union of Indochina formed from Vietnam, Cambodia, and Laos
1898	U.S.A. takes Philippines from the Spanish

Southeast Asia was dominated by three European powers in the late 1800s—the French, British, and Dutch controlled every country except Siam.

▼ The French gradually conquered Indochina during the 1800s. Their forces captured the citadel in Saigon, Annam, on February 17, 1859. In 1862, the French signed a treaty with the local leader, Tu Doc.

THE BRITISH EMPIRE 1815–1913

During the 1800s, the British extended and consolidated their empire. Britain took over more land than any other nation in history.

When William IV died in 1837, the English crown passed to his niece, Victoria (1819–1901), who was just 18 years old. When Victoria died, her reign had lasted 63 years, the longest in British history.

▼ Between 1870 and 1913, the British Empire expanded further to take in land in Africa and Southeast Asia. This provided jobs for many British people. At its height, it included a quarter of the world's land and people.

At its height, during the reign of Queen Victoria, the British Empire included a quarter of the world's land and people. From the end of the Napoleonic Wars in 1815 to the start of World War I in 1914, Britain acquired so many new colonies that the empire stretched around the world. Britain was able to control this vast empire by its domination of the seas and world trade routes. Throughout the 1800s, British naval strength was unbeatable, and its boats constantly patrolled countries that belonged to the empire.

Because the empire covered both hemispheres it was known as "the empire on which the sun never sets." Colonies in the Caribbean, Africa, Asia, Australasia, and the Pacific were ruled from London, and were all united under the British monarch. Strategic harbors such as Gibraltar, Hong Kong, Singapore, and Aden came into British hands. Vital trade routes such as the Cape route to India, or the Suez Canal (via Egypt) to the spice and rubber plantations of Southeast Asia were also controlled by Britain.

Soldiers from the countries that were part of the British Empire were frequently used to make sure that British power and influence continued and expanded.

RAW MATERIALS

The empire provided the British with raw materials for manufacturing, and British demand for colonial products such as silk, spices, rubber, cotton, tea, coffee, and sugar led to the gradual takeover of many countries. Several countries became colonies when the British government acquired a bankrupt trading company. India was an example of a country where the British had come to trade and stayed to rule. It was the most prized colony in the empire. In 1850, India was still under the rule of the British East India Company. After the rebellion, of 1857, India was placed under the rule of the British government, and its policies were more cautious. British officials left control of local affairs to the Indian princes.

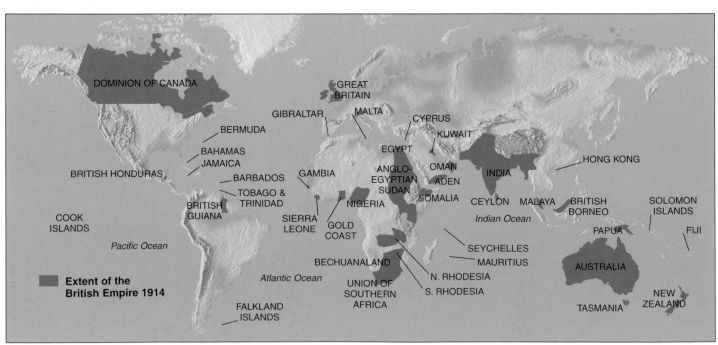

DOMINION OF CANADA · GREAT BRITAIN · GIBRALTAR · MALTA · CYPRUS · BERMUDA · KUWAIT · BAHAMAS · JAMAICA · EGYPT · HONG KONG · BRITISH HONDURAS · GAMBIA · ANGLO-EGYPTIAN SUDAN · OMAN · INDIA · BARBADOS · ADEN · TOBAGO & TRINIDAD · NIGERIA · SOMALIA · CEYLON · MALAYA · BRITISH BORNEO · SOLOMON ISLANDS · BRITISH GUIANA · SIERRA LEONE · GOLD COAST · Indian Ocean · COOK ISLANDS · PAPUA · FIJI · Pacific Ocean · SEYCHELLES · MAURITIUS · BECHUANALAND · AUSTRALIA · Atlantic Ocean · UNION OF SOUTHERN AFRICA · N. RHODESIA · S. RHODESIA · NEW ZEALAND · FALKLAND ISLANDS · TASMANIA

Extent of the British Empire 1914

CONSOLIDATION

The British took over Egypt in 1883 to guard the Suez Canal and the route to India. After a rebellion in the south of Egypt led by a religious leader, the Mahdi, Britain entered Sudan in 1898. The British set up trade links throughout the empire by appointing an agent in every port. They organized local produce for export and markets for British imports. The British navy protected their interests and kept the sea routes safe for shipping.

British influence extended into mainland settlements in Central and South America, and into China where it had trading outposts. Queen Victoria, herself empress of India since 1876, was a keen supporter of a foreign policy that pursued colonial expansion and upheld the empire. As more British people emigrated to countries within the empire, these lands were given more freedom to govern themselves. Many colonies, notably Canada, Australia, and South Africa, became dominions rather than colonies and were allowed self-government.

KEY DATES

1824	Penal colony established in Brisbane, Australia
1829	Britain claims West Australia
1837	Victoria becomes queen of England
1850	Australian Colonies Government Act gives limited independence to Australia
1852	New Zealand is granted a constitution
1857	Indian mutiny against British rule begins
1867	British North American Act grants home rule to Canada
1875	Britain buys controlling interest in Suez Canal
1876	Queen Victoria becomes empress of India
1884	Britain annexes southeastern New Guinea
1890	Zanzibar becomes a British protectorate
1901	New South Wales, Queensland, Victoria, South Australia, Western Australia, and Tasmania become the Commonwealth of Australia; Queen Victoria dies
1907	Dominion of New Zealand is founded

END OF EMPIRE

Toward the end of the 1800s, some colonies began to break away from British rule. Home rule was granted to Canada in 1867, and independence to Australia in 1901. Both countries became dominions although they remained part of the British Empire. The gradual loosening of ties with the British Empire reflected the fact that Britain had ceased to be the leading industrial nation in the world. Germany and the United States had overtaken it, with France and Russia close behind.

The British government passed the Australian Colonies Government Act in 1850. This gave limited independence to the country. In 1901, the colonies of New South Wales, Queensland, Victoria, South Australia, Western Australia, and Tasmania became the Commonwealth of Australia.

◄ This cartoon from the 1800s shows the colonies of the British Empire constantly worrying the imperial lion.

▼ In 1897, Victoria celebrated her Diamond Jubilee. The guests of honor included Indian princes, African chiefs, Pacific Islanders, and Chinese from Hong Kong.

THE PLAINS WARS 1849–1913

The plains of the American Midwest had once seemed vast and endless. In the 1800s, they became the scene of a struggle for land ownership.

The Pawnee were one of the Plains tribes. They lived by hunting buffalo.

General George Custer (1839–1876) died in the Battle of the Little Bighorn.

Sitting Bull (1831–1890) was a Dakota (Sioux) medicine man and war chief.

Many groups of Native Americans lived on the Great Plains of the American West and had done so for thousands of years. This vast area stretched from the Mississippi River in the east to the Rocky Mountains in the west, and from Canada in the north to Texas in the south. Until the 1600s, many Plains tribes were farmers. They grew corn, beans, and other food, but they also hunted buffalo, on foot, using bows and arrows. Their way of life on the plains began to change during the 1600s when the Spanish introduced the horse.

With horses, the Native Americans could easily follow the buffalo. The buffalo not only provided them with meat, but also with tools and weapons fashioned from the animals' bones, and tepees and clothing made with the skins. Some of the larger tribes of Native Americans became known as the Plains tribes. Early white settlers forced some tribes to move west from their original homelands east of the Mississippi River.

WESTWARD HO!

After the Civil War, the land between the Mississippi River and the Rocky Mountains was thought of as a wilderness of plains and mountains. The government encouraged pioneers to migrate westward. Settlers traveled west together in wagon trains for protection on the long journey across plains, rivers, and mountains, which could take up to eight months.

Native Americans depended on buffalo for their food, clothing, and shelter. Many buffalo were also killed to supply meat to workers laying track for the railroads.

SETTLERS MOVE WEST

The government encouraged people to migrate westward. Under the Homestead Act of 1862, a family could have 160 acres (65ha) for a small fee, as long as they did not sell the land for five years. More land was given to those who made improvements by drilling wells or planting trees. The Act encouraged farmers to move into and settle on the Great Plains.

The government also encouraged the building of railroads, which carried people into unsettled regions. It gave land to the railroads so generously that many lines were built simply to obtain land. By 1869, the Union Pacific Railroad was finished—connecting America from coast to coast.

STRUGGLE FOR SURVIVAL

The expansion of the railroads soon changed the face of the United States. They brought even more settlers to the Native American homelands. The two cultures came into conflict. Local Native American chiefs made land agreements with the settlers, without realizing that they were signing away their rights. The settlers' idea of private property meant nothing to the Native Americans. They thought they could continue to hunt on the land. Many bought guns and attacked the settlers' homesteads, their wagon trains, and the railroads.

Between 1860 and 1885, the number of buffalo was reduced—largely by white hunters—from 15 million to only 2,000. Starting in 1866, a series of wars took place. The goal was to claim land for white settlers. To do this, the Native Americans were driven onto reservations, or destroyed if they resisted. President Rutherford B. Hayes (1822–1893) said, in 1893, "Many, if not most, of our Indian wars had their origin in broken promises and acts of injustice." By then, it was too late—the few survivors of the Plains tribes had been forced onto the poor quality land of the reservations.

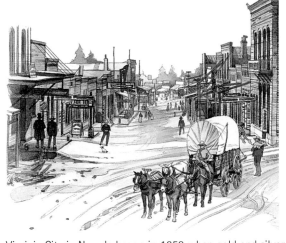

Virginia City in Nevada began in 1859 when gold and silver were found. By 1876, it was a large town, but when the gold and silver ran out, it became a ghost town.

The Native Americans were used to hunting and did not want to be farmers. They were not allowed to become American citizens and had few civil rights. Fierce battles with soldiers resulted in the deaths of thousands of Native Americans. The last battle was at Wounded Knee in South Dakota, in 1890, when soldiers slaughtered 200 Sioux. Soon, all the tribes were moved onto reservations, and the Native American way of life was changed forever.

In 1848, gold was discovered at Sutter's Mill, in California, and the gold rush started. By 1855, San Francisco's population had grown from 800 to 50,000.

▲ The possibility of making their fortune attracted people of many nationalities to the American goldfields. Thousands of Chinese people traveled to California in the 1850s and the 1870s to work as laborers.

◀ In the 1830s, the Chickasaw tribe was forced to move to a reservation in Oklahoma where they were told that the land was theirs "as long as the grass grows and the waters run." But the central and western parts were thinly populated, and very sought after by white settlers. In 1906, the Chickasaw rose up to stop their land from being taken, but were suppressed by the United States Cavalry.

THE BOXER REBELLION 1900

Under the weak Manchu government, the Chinese Empire appeared to be breaking up. Discontent at Western influence led to the Boxer Rebellion in 1900.

The last emperor of China was P'u-yi (1906–1967). He became emperor at the age of two and lost the throne when he was six.

KEY DATES

1898 The Hundred Days of Reform end when Empress Cixi comes to power. Britain gains Hong Kong on a 99-year lease from China.
1900 Foreign embassies in Beijing are besieged by Boxer rebels. American, Japanese, and European troops end the rebellion. The empress flees Beijing.
1905 Sun Yat-sen founds a group that becomes known as the Chinese Nationalist Party, or Kuomintang.
1911 The army backs a nationalist rebellion. Manchu rule ends, and a republic is declared. Sun Yat-sen becomes provisional president.

Much of the Chinese Empire under the weak and corrupt Manchu government was dominated by competing European powers. Many powerful groups struggled to preserve the country from Westerners, but the Chinese recognized that they would have to copy Western ways and set up new industries.

In 1898, the reformers gained power for a brief time. New laws were passed to turn China into a modern state. They sought to change the civil service and to deal with the day-to-day problems rather than rely on ancient and outdated texts. They founded a university in Beijing (Peking) and started to reform the army. But the "Hundred Days of Reform" ended when the dowager empress, Cixi (also known as Tz'u-hsi), regained power. Many reformers were executed.

In 1900, a revolt began in northern China against all foreigners, but especially Christians. It was led by a secret organization—the Society of Harmonious Fists, or "Boxers." They were secretly supported by the Manchu government.

THE END OF THE MANCHUS

In 1900, the Boxers attacked the European embassies in Beijing. They killed many Europeans, especially missionaries, as well as Chinese Christians. They held a number of embassies under siege for two months. An international force was set up, made up of American, British, French, German, Japanese, and Russian soldiers. An earlier, smaller, less well-equipped unit was unable to take Beijing, but in the summer, a second force successfully freed the embassies.

Having crushed the rebellion, the Chinese government was unable to prevent foreign interference. They were obliged to punish officials thought to be involved, to pay an indemnity payment, and to allow foreign troops into the embassies. Educated Chinese began to plot the overthrow of the Manchu regime.

In 1905, Sun Yat-sen founded what became the Chinese Nationalist Party, or Kuomintang. Plots and rebellions were organized by other groups. The Manchu government steadily lost control of the country. In 1911, a powerful general, Yuan Shikai, gave his support to a nationalist rebellion. Manchu authority collapsed, and a republic was declared.

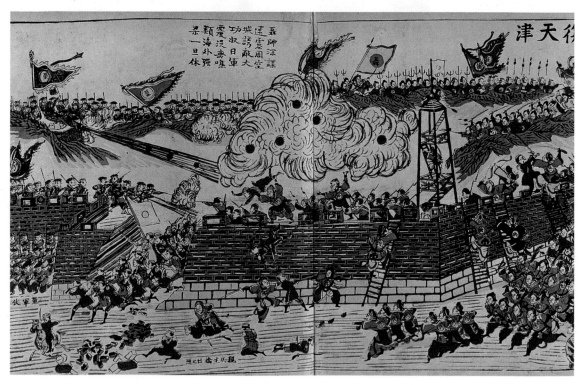

This Chinese woodcut of 1902 shows Boxer rebels storming and taking a mountain fortress in Tien Shin in northwest China.

WOMAN SUFFRAGE 1848–1928

During the 1800s and early 1900s, men and women in countries around the world were waging a campaign for woman suffrage—the basic right of women to vote.

With her daughter, Christabel, Emmeline Pankhurst (1858–1928) founded the National Women's Social and Political Union in 1903 and campaigned for women's rights in Britain.

With Lucretia Mott, Elizabeth Cady Stanton (1815–1902) organized the first women's rights convention in the United States in 1848. She went on to help found the National Woman Suffrage Association in 1869. The foundations of women's suffrage were laid in the face of fierce opposition.

▶ To draw attention to their cause, women in Britain (suffragettes) and the United States (suffragists) took to the streets in peaceful demonstrations to gain public support for their campaign to give women the vote.

During the early 1800s, only men who owned property could vote. The poor, women, and slaves were excluded. There were groups demanding reforms but only to extend the vote to all men. In the mid-1800s, some people began to say that everyone should be able to vote.

On July 20, 1848, a large group of men and women met in Seneca Falls, New York. The two organizers, Elizabeth Cady Stanton and Lucretia Mott, had met some years earlier while campaigning against slavery. But the fight for women's rights became their life's work. Improvements came in many small steps. In 1869, the Wyoming Territory gave women the right to hold public office. The same year, Susan B. Anthony and Elizabeth Cady Stanton founded the National Woman Suffrage Association. In 1872, another organization even nominated a woman to run for president. The campaign gained support in the 1900s. In 1920, the 19th Amendment granted voting rights to women.

Many suffragists were arrested and sent to prison for disturbing the peace, often going on hunger strikes to continue to draw attention to their cause.

New Zealand had been the first country to grant women voting rights in 1893. Finland was the first country in Europe to do so in 1906. In Britain, voting rights for women came in two stages: in 1918, for those over 30, and in 1928, for those over 21 (the same age as for men).

373

AUSTRALIA 1788–1913

The original inhabitants of Australia, the Aborigines, faced a growing threat to their way of life, as white settlers encroached ever farther into their territories.

Aborigines led a way of life based around tribal territories and customs. Although the spread of white settlements destroyed much of this, they still kept a strong cultural identity.

▲ Robert O'Hara Burke (1820–1861) and William Wills (1834–1861) were the first white men to cross Australia. Their expedition contained 18 men and set out in 1860 to travel north from Melbourne to the Gulf of Carpentaria. They suffered terribly from starvation and exhaustion on the way back and only one man survived.

▶ On arrival in Australia, immigrants were housed at first in large wooden buildings. This one was designed to accommodate more than 70 people.

During the 1800s, the new nation of Australia was created. More than 174,000 convicts had been shipped from Britain to Australia, mainly to Sydney, to serve their sentence in work gangs, for periods varying from a few years to life. Transportation to the colonies, which had begun in the reign of Elizabeth I, was an extension of the older punishment of banishment, and it did not end until 1868.

For many convicts, Britain held only bitter memories, so many of them chose to settle in Australia after their release. Early settlements were founded along the coast, but explorers gradually opened up the interior. They were followed by pioneers looking for grazing land for the ever-growing flocks of sheep.

As the wool industry grew, so did the demand for land. Many drove their sheep beyond the official settlement limits, earning themselves the name "squatters." Though they were later granted grazing rights, the name stuck. These early farmers gradually spread into the interior, acquiring land as they went. But eventually they came into conflict with the native Australians, the Aborigines.

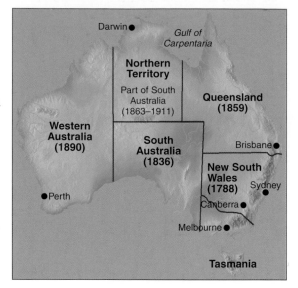

The colonies were granted self-government by 1890. New South Wales originally occupied all of eastern Australia, but was eventually divided.

ABORIGINAL PEOPLE

Australia's first inhabitants, the Aborigines, arrived from Southeast Asia 50,000 years earlier. They lived in nomadic groups, traveling around their territories, hunting with spears and boomerangs, fishing from canoes, and gathering fruit and vegetables. They had no written language, but passed on valuable knowledge by word of mouth and in song.

When the British settled in Australia, Aboriginal culture was threatened and their land was taken over by squatters. In the late 1700s, there were more than 300,000 Aborigines. Many were killed or driven off their land by settlers, and the population fell to under 45,000.

In Van Diemen's Land, later renamed Tasmania, the Aboriginal population was completely wiped out by the 1870s. Some had perished from European diseases, and white settlers had murdered the rest.

THE GOLD RUSH

In 1851, many people rushed to Australia at the news that gold had been found in New South Wales and Victoria. This event became known as the Gold Rush. Melbourne, the capital of Victoria, became a wealthy city, and Australia's population more than doubled. In 1854, gold miners at the Eureka Stockade rebelled against their colonial rulers, and put on pressure for reform and self-government.

GROWING UNREST

Squatter settlement also created problems when the immigrants and ex-convicts demanded that land be made available for farms. Many failed to gain land because of opposition from existing squatters. At the same time, a sense of nationalism was growing. Britain had granted self-government to all her colonies by the 1890s, and the leaders of the colonies had come to realize that some form of union was needed.

None of the Australian colonies were willing to give up their individual independence, so in 1890, after fierce arguments, the colonies agreed to unite in a federation. The Commonwealth of Australia was proclaimed on the first day of 1901, and the city of Canberra was chosen as the federal capital.

▲ In 1851, thousands of people from many countries moved to Australia after they heard that gold had been found in New South Wales and Victoria.

▶ Ned Kelly (1855–1880) and his gang of bushrangers roamed the country staging holdups and bank raids. Kelly, who often wore homemade armor, was hanged in 1880.

KEY DATES	
1797	Sheep ranching introduced to Australia
1836	City of Adelaide founded
1851	Gold Rush starts in New South Wales
1854	Rebellion of gold miners at Eureka stockade
1855	Van Diemen's Land renamed Tasmania
1860	Burke and Wills set out to cross Australia
1868	Britain stops sending convicts to Australia
1880	The outlaw Ned Kelly is captured and hanged
1901	Commonwealth of Australia declared

SHEEP RANCHES

Introduced to Australia in 1797, sheep ranching became the major agricultural activity in the country. Because the land was often far from fertile, enormous areas of pasture were needed to keep the sheep healthy and well fed. This meant that more and more land was taken from the Aborigines.

THE BALKAN WARS 1821–1913

The Balkan states in the southeastern corner of Europe had long been an area of turmoil. As the Ottoman Empire shrank, they wanted independence.

Peter I (1844–1921) was elected king of Serbia in 1903. He was exiled to Greece in 1916, but he returned in 1918 and was proclaimed king of the Serbs, Croats, and Slovenes.

The decline of the Ottoman Empire led to demands from the Balkan states for independence. There was also a rise in nationalism, which was encouraged by both Russia and Austria–Hungary, who did not want to see the other increase its influence in the region.

Britain and Germany supported Austria–Hungary, because they wanted to stop Russia from gaining access to any more ice-free ports in the Mediterranean or Black seas. Greece was the first to rebel, declaring independence as early as 1829. In 1878, Serbia, Montenegro, and Romania also became independent and Bulgaria gained self-government. Austria–Hungary occupied the Ottoman territory of Bosnia–Herzegovina in 1908, so that it would not fall under the growing power of the

The Balkan Peninsula 1912

The Balkans had long been a turbulent area. The power of the Ottoman Empire was fading, and Russian power was growing. Austria–Hungary was trying to hold its own.

Serbian nationalists in the region. Albania and Macedonia remained under Ottoman control. When Italy attacked the Turkish-held territory of Tripoli (Libya) in 1912, it showed how weak Turkey was militarily. The Treaty of Ouchy gave Tripoli to Italy.

▲ In 1906, Ferdinand I (1861–1948) proclaimed Bulgaria independent from the Ottoman Empire and became king. In 1912, his country joined the Balkan League against Turkey.

▶ The Ottoman Turks were defeated by the Balkan League in 1912, because they were also fighting the Italians in North Africa. The Young Turks movement was also battling against the ways of the old regime.

KEY DATES

1829   Greece declares its independence
1878   Montenegro, Serbia, and Romania declare
        their independence
1903   Peter I elected king of Serbia
1908   Austria–Hungary occupies Bosnia-Herzegovina;
        Bulgaria proclaims independence;
        Ferdinand I becomes king of Bulgaria
1912   Balkan League formed by Bulgaria, Serbia,
        Greece, and Montenegro
1912   First Balkan War
1912   Italian–Turkish War ended by Treaty of Ouchy
1913   Second Balkan War

FIRST BALKAN WAR

In March 1912, Serbia and Bulgaria made a secret treaty to join forces to attack Turkey and divide the Ottoman territory between themselves. The Balkan League of Serbia, Bulgaria, Greece, and Montenegro was formed in October. By the end of the month they were all at war with Turkey.

The First Balkan War ended in 1913 with the signing of the Treaty of London, after what appeared to the rest of the world as the easy defeat of the Turks. In many ways, the First Balkan War merely served to increase the rivalries of the Balkan states. Serbia and Greece gained territory in Macedonia, while Bulgaria extended its territory to the Aegean Sea.

During the Second Balkan War (June–August 1913), Bulgarian forces bombarded the Turkish town of Adrianopolis (now known as Edirne).

SECOND BALKAN WAR

Albania had declared itself an independent Muslim principality in December 1912. Austria–Hungary supported Albanian independencein order to stop Serbia expanding to the Adriatic. The peace settlement led to disagreements among the victors. Bulgaria had gained far more territory than Serbia, which wanted more in Macedonia. Its three former allies combined against Bulgaria.

The Second Balkan War broke out in June 1913, when Bulgaria declared war on Serbia and Greece. Romania and Turkey fought against Bulgaria. The Bulgarians were surrounded and overpowered. In August, the Treaty of Bucharest was signed. Macedonia was divided between Greece and Serbia, and Romania gained some of Bulgaria. This settlement greatly increased the size of Serbia. Count Otto von Bismarck had declared, before either of the Balkan Wars, that the next major European war would be caused "by some foolish thing in the Balkans." He words proved to be correct.

In November 1912, during the First Balkan War, the Bulgarian army captured Kirk-Kilisse from Turkish forces. The Bulgarians were allied with Greece, Serbia, and Montenegro.

In this cartoon of the time, the Balkan countries were seen by Europe as a boiling pot of troubles.

THE ARTS 1836–1913

For all the arts, the period between 1836 and 1913 was a time of change and experiment. Painting and music in particular developed and flourished.

This lamp by U.S. designer Louis Comfort Tiffany (1848–1933) is in the Art Nouveau style, popular from about 1890.

Mark Twain, the pen name of Samuel Langhorne Clemens (1835–1910), was a writer and humorist who wrote *The Adventures of Tom Sawyer*.

In the late 1800s, the French impressionists such as Claude Monet, Auguste Renoir, and Edgar Degas developed spontaneous styles, filling their canvases with bold strokes of color in an attempt to capture the fleeting effects of light. In England, a group of artists, poets, and writers called the Pre-Raphaelites rejected the position of Raphael as the ultimate master of painting.

In European literature, more and more novels were being written for a growing number of readers. Romantic adventure stories were written by novelists such as Sir Walter Scott—*Ivanhoe*—and Jules Verne—*20,000 Leagues Under the Sea*. The wretched life of the poor in the cities was described with great skill by Charles Dickens in novels such as *Oliver Twist*. William Thackeray evoked an image of country and town living among the middle and upper classes in *Vanity Fair*, and Elizabeth Gaskell depicted life in the new manufacturing cities of the north in books such as *North and South*.

▼ This is a scene from *David Copperfield* by Charles Dickens (1812–1870). Dickens's writing entertained and enlightened his readers about social problems.

This English daguerreotype (early photograph) is from about 1885. Three years later, George Eastman's Kodak box camera made photography available for everyone.

Wagner developed a new form of grand opera, and the Russian ballet changed ideas about dance. Beethoven's dramatic and expressive music had opened the way for the romantic period with composers such as Schubert, Mendelssohn, Schumann, Chopin, Berlioz, Verdi, Brahms, and Tchaikovsky producing works full of passion and drama.

Giuseppe Verdi (1813–1901) was one of the greatest Italian composers of opera. His works include *Rigoletto*, *La Traviata*, and *Aida*.

▲ "Dante's Dream" was painted by Dante Gabriel Rossetti (1828–1882), an English artist and poet who helped form the Pre-Raphaelite Brotherhood.

▶ Johann Strauss the Younger (1825–1899) toured Europe and the United States with his own orchestra. He was famous for his waltzes, such as *The Blue Danube*.

Drama became more realistic with plays by Ibsen, Chekhov, and George Bernard Shaw. In 1877, the British-born American photographer Eadweard Muybridge created the first motion picture sequences, and by the early 1900s, an entirely new form of performing art had appeared: the movies. Hollywood, in California, soon became the center of moviemaking.

▶ This bronze sculpture, *The Thinker*, by Auguste Rodin (1840–1917) went on show in France in 1904. His figures were expressive, conveying the power of emotion.

▼ Claude Monet (1840–1926) was the leader of the impressionists. He frequently worked outside and painted landscapes and scenes of simple middle-class life.

ARCHITECTURE 1836–1913

Architecture during the late 1800s reflected a new freedom of expression and a willingness to use modern technology.

The style of architecture used for a building can depend on several factors. One consideration is that of the materials available to the builders. Another is the purpose to which the building is to be put. Equally important is the imagination of the architects and their clients. The main feature of architecture in Europe and North America during the 1800s was a willingness to use all the great styles of the past, from ancient Greece to the 1700s. Sometimes, very different styles were used in the same building.

Later in the century, a new kind of architecture developed. It was based on the use of steel to form the framework, or "skeleton," of a building. Since the walls did not have to support their own weight, buildings could be higher. Steel-framed skyscrapers were first made practical in the United States by the elevator, invented in 1852 by Elisha Otis (1811–1861). In 1884, William Le Baron Jenney (1832–1907) built the world's first skyscraper in Chicago. At ten stories, it would not be a skyscraper today, but its metal-frame structure set a new trend.

The Eiffel Tower, named after its designer, Gustave Eiffel (1832–1923), was built for the Paris Exhibition of 1889. It is 989 ft. (300 m) high, made from iron, and held together by 2.5 million rivets.

Isambard Kingdom Brunel (1806–1859) designed the Clifton Bridge to cross the Avon River in England. It was completed in 1864. The road is suspended on cables high above the river.

The Statue of Liberty, in New York Harbor, was a gift from France in 1884. It is made from copper sheets on an iron framework, designed by Gustave Eiffel. The statue—the work of sculptor Frédéric Bartholdi—rises 307 ft. (93.5m) from the bottom of the pedestal to the tip of the torch, and weighs 254 tons. A famous poem by American writer Emma Lazarus is on a plaque at its base.

As towns and cities became more and more densely populated, it was vital that services such as fresh water and removal of sewage were adequate. New water pipes were built under cities, and when cast-iron pipes became available it became easier to build drains. As engineering knowledge improved, it was also possible to built bridges that spanned ever greater distances.

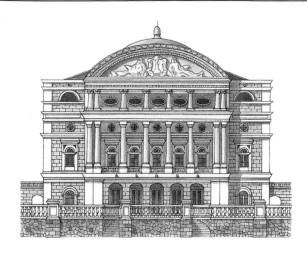

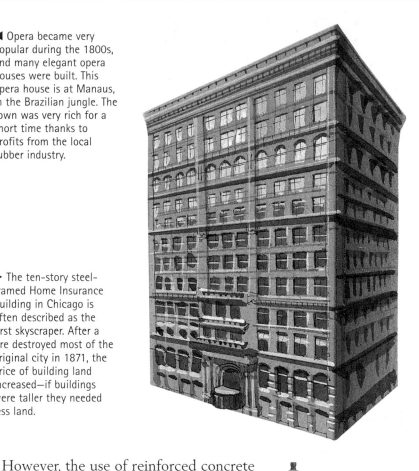

◀ Opera became very popular during the 1800s, and many elegant opera houses were built. This opera house is at Manaus, in the Brazilian jungle. The town was very rich for a short time thanks to profits from the local rubber industry.

NEW TECHNOLOGY

The architecture of the late 1800s was adapted to make use of the discoveries of engineers and the availability of iron and steel. In addition to skyscrapers, the use of steel frames also made possible structures such as the Eiffel Tower in Paris, built for the great exhibition of 1889, and the Statue of Liberty in New York Harbor, a gift and symbol of friendship from the people of France to the people of the United States to celebrate the centennial of the Declaration of Independence.

The railroad age brought with it many new opportunities for architects and builders. Railroad stations, symbolizing the wealth of the new industrial age, were built in cities around the world. These grand edifices combined the new technologies of iron and steel with styles from bygone periods.

▶ The ten-story steel-framed Home Insurance Building in Chicago is often described as the first skyscraper. After a fire destroyed most of the original city in 1871, the price of building land increased—if buildings were taller they needed less land.

However, the use of reinforced concrete in the early 1900s brought about a major change in architecture. Building design began to become simpler and less decorative. This "modern" style was to develop significantly after the end of World War I.

▲ During the 1800s in Europe and the United States, the prosperous middle classes lived in imposing townhouses set in quiet, tree-lined streets.

◀ The main railroad station in Bombay was opened in 1866. It was built in a mixture of the European Gothic and Renaissance styles, but the domes are Indian.

SCIENCE AND TECHNOLOGY 1836–1913

Technological progress continued at an ever-increasing pace. Major developments in communications and transportation were to change the world forever.

The telephone was invented by Alexander Graham Bell in 1875. The first public telephone exchange opened in Pittsburgh, in 1877.

An American, Whitcomb Judson, invented the zipper in 1891. The first one, called a clasp locker, looked like the hooks and eyes that it replaced.

The daguerreotype camera appeared in 1838. It was not until 1888 that George Eastman made photography available to all with the first roll film camera, the Kodak box.

Industry continued to develop, with new inventions, new products, and factories producing new types of goods. In 1850, coal and steam engines still provided the power for machinery, but by the early 1900s, electricity and oil were being used instead. In 1859, Edwin L. Drake found substantial reserves of oil at a depth of only 69 ft. (22m) in Oil Creek, Pennsylvania. Oil was to provide the fuel for the internal combustion engine. This, in turn, led to the invention of the first automobiles.

The German engineer Gottlieb Daimler invented the high-speed internal combustion engine in 1887. This was to prove convincingly better than the steam engines that had been used previously. In the United States, Frank and Charles Duryea produced their first vehicles in 1892, and Henry Ford made his first experimental car in 1893. Oil products also played a large role in the new chemical industry. They made possible the development of a huge range of materials such as plastics, detergents, fertilizers, paints, dyes, nylon, artificial rubber, and explosives.

The first bicycles were uncomfortable and dangerous. The "penny farthing" was invented by James Starley in the early 1870s, and had solid tires and no brakes.

The Scottish-born American inventor Alexander Graham Bell invented the telephone, and the first public exchange opened in Pittsburgh in 1877. That same year, prolific inventor Thomas Alva Edison produced the phonograph. This enabled sound to be recorded and played back on a foil-coated cylinder.

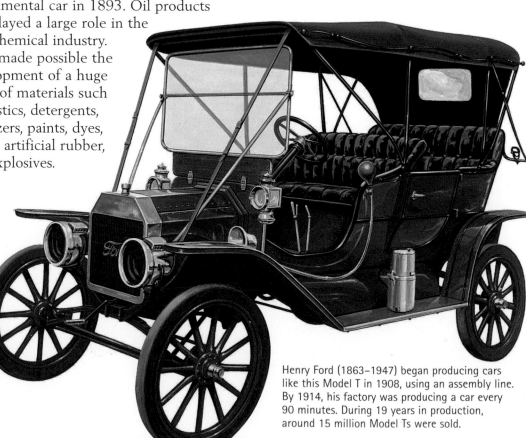

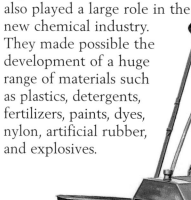

Henry Ford (1863–1947) began producing cars like this Model T in 1908, using an assembly line. By 1914, his factory was producing a car every 90 minutes. During 19 years in production, around 15 million Model Ts were sold.

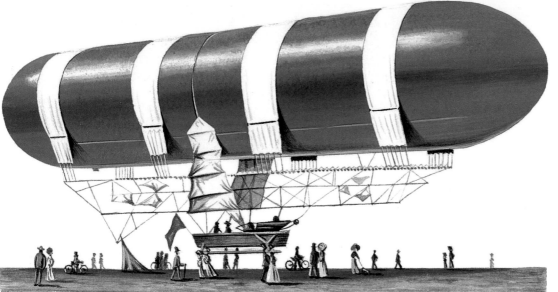

◀ Balloons were used for observation in the American Civil War. One of the observers was a retired German army officer named Zeppelin. He was an inventor of airships, which are sometimes called Zeppelins after him. Airships were more useful than balloons, because they could move under their own power.

In 1879, Edison demonstrated the electric lightbulb, and in 1882, the world's first large-scale electric power station, designed and installed by Edison, was completed in New York City. The kinetoscope, used to produce moving pictures, was invented in 1891, again by Edison, and he was able to synchronize this with his phonograph to produce the first talking motion pictures in 1913.

Thomas Edison was a pioneer of the electric lightbulb. In 1880, his system was first used to light a steamship.

▼ Wilbur and Orville Wright used gliders to test their experiments in controlled airplane flight. They made the first powered flight on December 17, 1903, at Kitty Hawk, North Carolina.

▼ An early radio, called a wireless, had glass tubes. No one knew that radio waves existed until German scientist Heinrich Hertz (1857–1894) proved it in 1888, by transmitting and receiving them in his laboratory.

WHEN IT HAPPENED

1837 Samuel Morse invents Morse Code
1856 Bessemer converter invented
1859 First oil well drilled in Pennsylvania
1867 Nobel invents dynamite
1868 Frenchman Georges Leclanché invents the dry-cell battery
1869 Mendeleyev devises periodic table
1875 First telephone call made by Bell
1877 Nikolaus Otto patents four-stroke internal combustion engine
1877 First public telephone exchange
1882 First hydroelectric power plant uses water to generate electricity
1885 First automobiles built in Germany
1887 Dunlop invents pneumatic tire
1896 Marconi invents first radio system
1903 First powered and controlled flight by the Wright brothers
1909 Leo Baekeland invents the first plastic, Bakelite

Scientists believed that all things were made up of atoms. Proof was provided by Ernest Rutherford's discovery of the atomic nucleus in 1911.

THE WORLD
AT WAR
1914–1949

In the years from 1914 to 1949, the world went through a period of rapid, intense, and painful change. The Great War, the "war to end all wars," was followed by a massive worldwide influenza epidemic. The 1917 Bolshevik Revolution made Russia the world's first socialist state. Then came the Great Depression, a collapse of capitalism that led to mass unemployment worldwide. This, followed by World War II, meant that European world dominance was replaced by that of the United States and the Soviet Union.

▲ World War I saw the first widespread use of aerial warfare. These early airplanes were used to spy on enemy positions and drop bombs.

◄ After the defeat of Nazi Germany in 1945, the victors, Marshal Zhukov (U.S.S.R.), General Eisenhower (U.S.A.), and Field Marshall Montgomery (Britain) meet in the ruins of Berlin.

THE WORLD AT A GLANCE 1914–1949

Almost the whole world was affected by World War I, the Great Depression, and World War II. In North America, the United States adopted a policy of isolation between the wars, but joined the Allies in World War II. In South America, right wing governments came to power in Argentina and Brazil.

In Europe, civil wars broke out in Ireland, Spain, and Greece, and revolution in Russia led to civil war there, too. In the Middle East, the Ottoman Empire collapsed after World War I, and Israel was founded in 1948 as a homeland for the Jewish people.

Italy's attempts to build an empire in Africa failed. Many countries began clamoring for independence. India gained independence from Britain, but it was partitioned to form Pakistan. Civil war divided China, while Japanese expansion was one of the causes of World War II, with the Pacific becoming a battle zone. Science, in the form of the atom bomb, ended the war.

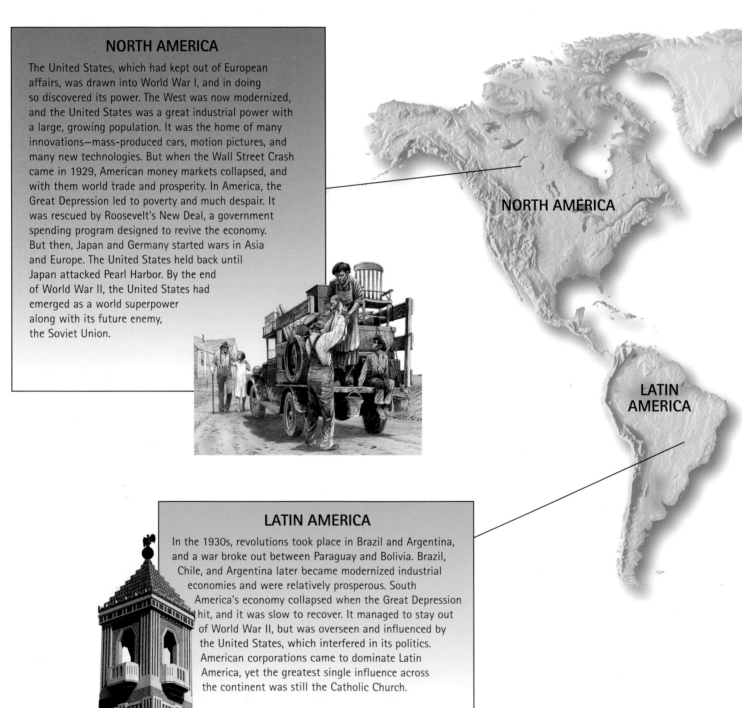

NORTH AMERICA

The United States, which had kept out of European affairs, was drawn into World War I, and in doing so discovered its power. The West was now modernized, and the United States was a great industrial power with a large, growing population. It was the home of many innovations—mass-produced cars, motion pictures, and many new technologies. But when the Wall Street Crash came in 1929, American money markets collapsed, and with them world trade and prosperity. In America, the Great Depression led to poverty and much despair. It was rescued by Roosevelt's New Deal, a government spending program designed to revive the economy. But then, Japan and Germany started wars in Asia and Europe. The United States held back until Japan attacked Pearl Harbor. By the end of World War II, the United States had emerged as a world superpower along with its future enemy, the Soviet Union.

LATIN AMERICA

In the 1930s, revolutions took place in Brazil and Argentina, and a war broke out between Paraguay and Bolivia. Brazil, Chile, and Argentina later became modernized industrial economies and were relatively prosperous. South America's economy collapsed when the Great Depression hit, and it was slow to recover. It managed to stay out of World War II, but was overseen and influenced by the United States, which interfered in its politics. American corporations came to dominate Latin America, yet the greatest single influence across the continent was still the Catholic Church.

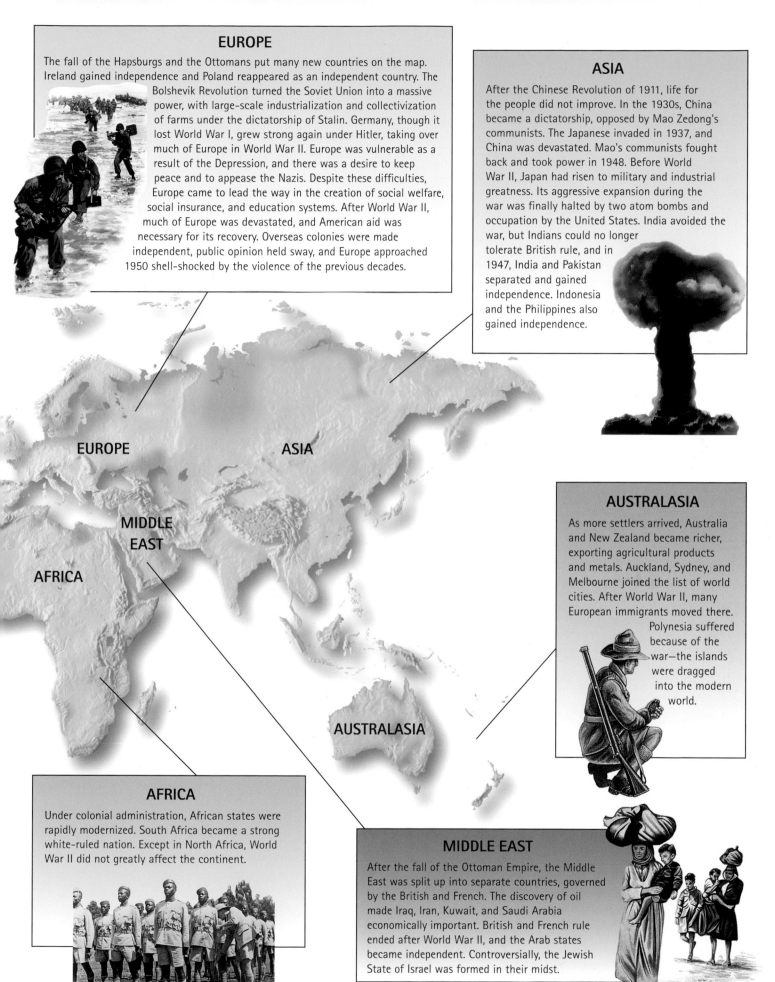

EUROPE

The fall of the Hapsburgs and the Ottomans put many new countries on the map. Ireland gained independence and Poland reappeared as an independent country. The Bolshevik Revolution turned the Soviet Union into a massive power, with large-scale industrialization and collectivization of farms under the dictatorship of Stalin. Germany, though it lost World War I, grew strong again under Hitler, taking over much of Europe in World War II. Europe was vulnerable as a result of the Depression, and there was a desire to keep peace and to appease the Nazis. Despite these difficulties, Europe came to lead the way in the creation of social welfare, social insurance, and education systems. After World War II, much of Europe was devastated, and American aid was necessary for its recovery. Overseas colonies were made independent, public opinion held sway, and Europe approached 1950 shell-shocked by the violence of the previous decades.

ASIA

After the Chinese Revolution of 1911, life for the people did not improve. In the 1930s, China became a dictatorship, opposed by Mao Zedong's communists. The Japanese invaded in 1937, and China was devastated. Mao's communists fought back and took power in 1948. Before World War II, Japan had risen to military and industrial greatness. Its aggressive expansion during the war was finally halted by two atom bombs and occupation by the United States. India avoided the war, but Indians could no longer tolerate British rule, and in 1947, India and Pakistan separated and gained independence. Indonesia and the Philippines also gained independence.

EUROPE

ASIA

MIDDLE EAST

AFRICA

AUSTRALASIA

As more settlers arrived, Australia and New Zealand became richer, exporting agricultural products and metals. Auckland, Sydney, and Melbourne joined the list of world cities. After World War II, many European immigrants moved there. Polynesia suffered because of the war—the islands were dragged into the modern world.

AUSTRALASIA

AFRICA

Under colonial administration, African states were rapidly modernized. South Africa became a strong white-ruled nation. Except in North Africa, World War II did not greatly affect the continent.

MIDDLE EAST

After the fall of the Ottoman Empire, the Middle East was split up into separate countries, governed by the British and French. The discovery of oil made Iraq, Iran, Kuwait, and Saudi Arabia economically important. British and French rule ended after World War II, and the Arab states became independent. Controversially, the Jewish State of Israel was formed in their midst.

THE START OF WORLD WAR I 1914

The assassination of Archduke Franz Ferdinand, heir to the Austro–Hungarian Empire, in Sarajevo in June 1914, triggered the bloodiest conflict in human history.

Jealous of Britain's trade and colonies, Germany—which already had the world's largest army—had begun to build up its navy. Kaiser Wilhelm II's ambition to acquire more colonies overseas, along with his aggressive foreign policy, worried other European countries. In the years leading up to 1914, Britain and Germany competed to build bigger and better ships for their navies. The rivalry of other European countries over trade, colonies, and military power had also been growing, and the European powers had grouped together in defensive alliances.

A British recruiting poster at the start of World War I featured the War Minister, Lord Kitchener.

Under Kaiser Wilhelm II (1859–1941), Germany built a battle fleet to rival Britain's navy.

DEFENSIVE ALLIANCES

The main alliance was the Triple Alliance: Germany, Italy, and Austria–Hungary. An attack on any one country would bring its allies to its defense. The purpose of the alliance was to block Russian aggression in the Balkans (mainly the European areas of the old Ottoman Empire).

The Triple Entente, between Britain, France, and Russia, was not a military alliance, but its members had agreed to cooperate against German aggression.

World War I began after Serbian terrorist Gavrilo Princip killed the heir to the Austro–Hungarian throne, Archduke Franz Ferdinand, in Sarajevo on June 28, 1914.

HOW THE WAR BEGAN

The war began when a Serbian terrorist, Gavrilo Princip, assassinated the heir to the Austro–Hungarian Empire, Archduke Franz Ferdinand, and his wife in Sarajevo on June 28, 1914. This led Austria to declare war on Serbia on July 28. Russia's Czar Nicholas II mobilized his country's troops to defend Serbia from Austria. In return, Germany declared war on Russia on August 1. Russian armies were defeated by the Germans at Tannenberg and in the Battle of the Masurian Lakes. To the south, the Austro–Hungarian armies were defeated by the Russians in September.

A WAR ON TWO FRONTS

Germany had always dreaded a war on two fronts, so it put the Schlieffen Plan into operation. Drawn up by General von Schlieffen, the plan aimed to defeat France in six weeks, so that Germany could concentrate its forces against Russia.

On August 3, Germany declared war on Russia's ally, France. When the German army marched into neutral Belgium to attack the French from the north, they were faced with determined Belgian resistance. This slowed down their advance and allowed the French, under General Joffré, time to reorganize their forces.

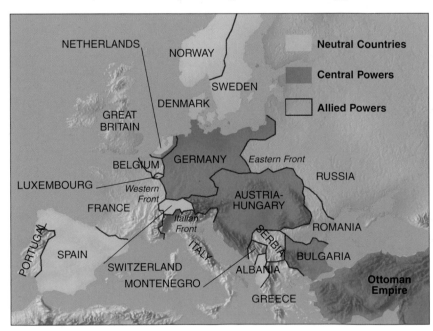

NETHERLANDS
NORWAY
SWEDEN
DENMARK
GREAT BRITAIN
BELGIUM   GERMANY   *Eastern Front*
LUXEMBOURG   *Western Front*   RUSSIA
FRANCE   AUSTRIA-HUNGARY
Italian Front   ROMANIA
PORTUGAL   SERBIA
SPAIN   ITALY   BULGARIA
SWITZERLAND   ALBANIA
MONTENEGRO   **Ottoman Empire**
GREECE

Neutral Countries
Central Powers
Allied Powers

◀ In 1914, Europe was divided in two. Britain, France, and Russia, known as the Allies, combined to fight the Central Powers, comprising Germany, Austria–Hungary, and its allies. Fighting took place simultaneously on an eastern front and a western front.

GERMANY INVADES FRANCE

The British then acted on the Treaty of London (1839), in which they had agreed to protect Belgian neutrality. It was on these grounds that Britain declared war on Germany on August 4. Britain went to Belgium's defense and sent the 100,000-strong British Expeditionary Force to France to help slow the German advance at Mons and Charleroi.

However, in the face of a determined German advance, Joffré retreated until he was behind the Marne River. Here, the French forces halted the Germans on September 8. Both sides then took up defensive positions and within three months, a line of trenches was dug from the English Channel to the Swiss frontier.

During the war, Britain, France, and Russia were known as the Allies, or Allied Powers. Germany, Italy, Austria–Hungary, and their allies were known as the Central Powers. Both sides raced to produce more and more deadly weapons, such as poison gas. They thought that by using these weapons they would shorten the war, but it lasted for four years and was the bloodiest conflict in human history. It has been estimated that the war cost the United States alone over $20 billion. The total number of men killed or wounded amounted to about 30 million.

KEY DATES

June 28	Archduke Franz Ferdinand assassinated in Sarajevo by a Serbian terrorist
July 28	Austria declares war on Serbia; Russia mobilizes its troops to defend Serbia
Aug. 1	Germany declares war on Russia
Aug. 3	Germany declares war on France
Aug. 4	Germany invades Belgium; Britain declares war on Germany
Sept. 8	German advance on Paris stopped at the Marne River

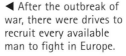

◄ After the outbreak of war, there were drives to recruit every available man to fight in Europe.

The French army had the difficult task of defending hundreds of miles of frontier against the enemy.

The German army was the largest and best trained in the world.

Britain had the smallest army, but it consisted of professional career soldiers.

◄ Motivated by patriotism and inspired by the call for volunteers to defend their countries in August 1914, millions of men of all ages across Europe joined up to fight the enemy.

BATTLES OF WORLD WAR I 1914–1917

In a series of horrific battles along the Western Front, millions of lives were lost to gain only a few miles. The land war soon reached a stalemate.

Gas masks were introduced in World War I to protect the troops against poison gas attacks by the enemy.

The Western Front stretched across Belgium and northeastern France. Millions of soldiers were killed in battles along it between 1914 and 1918.

During World War I, fighting took place in several areas. The Western Front was between Germany and northern France, and the Eastern Front between Germany and the Russian forces. There was also fighting at sea and in the Middle East, where the Allied Powers attacked the Ottoman Empire. In Africa, British and French troops attacked German colonies.

On the Western Front, French and British troops, together with thousands of men from the British Empire, occupied a network of deep trenches from September 1914. Facing them, across a few hundred yards of ground known as "no man's land," were trenches occupied by the Germans. Millions of men were killed on the Western Front in battles including Ypres, Verdun, and the Somme. One of the worst was the Third Battle of Ypres, or Passchendaele, in 1917. The troops had to wade through mud up to waist level. In 102 days, the Allies advanced just five miles at a cost of 400,000 lives.

For four years, the Western Front did not move more than 20 mi. (32km) in any direction. Barbed wire and machine-gun and artillery defenses made attack futile. Tanks, first used in 1916, could crush barbed wire or machine guns, but were unreliable. Aircraft were more successful, and were used to spot enemy troops, target shells, and drop bombs. The Eastern Front ran from the Baltic to the Black Sea and also had lines of trenches, to which the Russians retreated in September 1914.

▲ Only 12 years after the Wright brothers made their pioneering flight in North Carolina, aircraft were being used in warfare. Although control of the air was not a deciding factor in World War I, the war led to many advances in flight technology.

▶ In September 1914, the German advance toward Paris was stopped short of the capital when the Allies precariously held the line of the Marne River. The French government fled to Bordeaux. The Allied line held, and in their great counterattack, known as the First Battle of the Marne—regarded as one of the decisive battles of the war—the Allies drove the Germans back to the line of the Aisne River.

The war along the Western Front was fought from trenches guarded by barbed wire and machine guns. The conditions were appalling, with knee-deep mud, constant shelling, sniping, and raids. The battles of the Somme and Verdun in France in 1916 cost over two million casualties, but neither side was able to advance more than a few hundred yards.

Invented by two British scientists, Tritton and Wilson, the first tanks were used in the Battle of the Somme in 1916. These vehicles, fitted with machine guns, terrified the German soldiers, but suffered from too many mechanical failures to be fully effective.

THE WAR AT SEA

There were only two significant sea battles in World War I. The first, in 1914, was when a German fleet was destroyed by the Royal Navy off the Falkland Islands. In 1916, the Battle of Jutland took place and both Germany and Britain claimed victory. However, the German fleet did not leave the port of Kiel again until the end of the war, when it surrendered to the Allies.

German submarines, called U-boats, attacked ships bound for Britain and France. U-boats sank hundreds of Allied ships, nearly crippling Britain. When the U.S.S. *Housatonic* was sunk in 1917, the United States declared war on Germany.

Jutland was the major sea battle of World War I. Although the German fleet inflicted far more serious losses than they sustained, Britain and Germany both claimed victory. After the battle, on May 31, 1916, the German fleet escaped in darkness and returned to port, where they remained for the rest of the war.

DISASTER AT GALLIPOLI

Turkish officer

Australian private

During 1915, in an attempt to assist the Russians on the Eastern Front, Allied forces bombarded Turkish forts guarding the Dardanelles. Allied troops, including ANZAC forces from Australia and New Zealand, then landed at Gallipoli to try to capture the strategic positions overlooking the narrow straits. But the Allied powers grossly underestimated the strength of the Turkish forces. Almost 15 percent of Australian deaths in the war came from this battle.

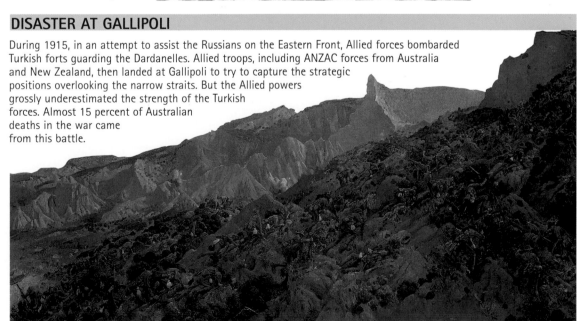

IRELAND: CIVIL UNREST 1916–1923

Irish frustration at home rule being first granted, and then delayed by World War I, led to rebellion and civil war. Southern Ireland became self-governing in 1921.

James Connolly (1868–1916) led the Irish Citizen Army. After the Easter Rising, he was shot in jail, even though he was already mortally wounded.

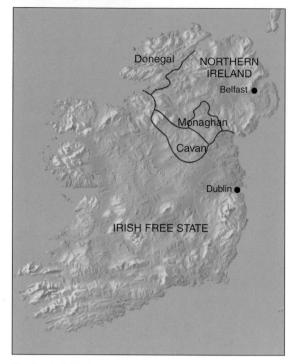

The Anglo-Irish Treaty of 1921 made southern Ireland into a self-governing country. In 1949, it became a republic, completely independent of Britain.

Many Irish people wanted home rule, and a Home Rule Bill was approved by the British Parliament in 1912. This would have become law, and given Ireland its own parliament to deal with domestic affairs, but it was suspended when war broke out in 1914.

In the north, Protestants opposed home rule because they would be a minority in a Catholic country. Some people (Republicans) wanted Ireland to be an independent republic. Many supported a political party called Sinn Féin ("We alone"). Some belonged to the Irish Volunteers, the Irish Republican Brotherhood, or the Irish Citizen Army.

On Easter Monday 1916, members of the Irish Volunteers and the Irish Citizen Army, led by Patrick Pearse and James Connolly, took control of public buildings in Dublin. This event became known as the Easter Rising. From their headquarters in the General Post Office, Pearse and Connolly declared a republic, but were soon defeated by the British army. In the 1918 election, Sinn Féin won 73 of the 105 Irish seats in the British Parliament.

Sinn Féin set up their own parliament, the Dáil Eireann, and declared Ireland to be an independent republic in 1919. This led to war between the Irish Republican Army (IRA) and the Royal Irish Constabulary (RIC). Armed police, the Black-and-Tans, were sent to support the RIC. The fighting continued until 1921.

▲ On Easter Monday, April 24, 1916, the Republicans made their headquarters inside Dublin General Post Office. Fighting went on for a week. The Republicans surrendered on April 29. The British army fired heavy guns at the building, and it caught fire.

▶ The remains of an automobile used as a barricade in the streets of Dublin during the 1916 Easter Rising. On one side of the barricades were the Republicans, and on the other were the British forces. Many civilians died in the shooting.

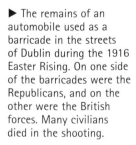

◀ Michael Collins (1890–1922), center, took part in the 1916 Easter Rising, and was arrested and imprisoned by the British. He became leader of Sinn Féin and head of intelligence in the Irish Volunteers. He was elected to the Irish parliament in 1918 and negotiated the peace treaty with Britain in 1921. He became head of the provisional government in 1922, but was killed in an ambush that same year.

▲ Éamon de Valera (1882–1975) was born in the United States. He was arrested and imprisoned by the British for his part in the 1916 Easter Rising. In 1926, he founded the Fianna Fáil ("Soldiers of Destiny") Party. Between 1937 and 1959, he served as prime minister of Ireland three times. He then became president until 1973.

THE ANGLO–IRISH TREATY

The British government wanted to divide Ireland into two countries, with six of the counties of Ulster, in the north, separate from the rest. Under the 1920 Government of Ireland Act, both countries would have some self-government. The six Ulster counties had a Protestant majority, who did not want to be ruled from Dublin. They agreed to the act and formed the new state of Northern Ireland. The Dáil Eireann, led by Éamon de Valera, opposed the act because they wanted complete independence for all Ireland.

In an attempt to bring peace to the country, the Anglo–Irish Treaty of 1921 made southern Ireland into a dominion of Great Britain. Called the Irish Free State, it was established in 1922. But this action led to civil war. On one side were the Free Staters who agreed to the treaty's terms. On the other side were the Republicans.

The civil war lasted until 1923, when de Valera ordered the Republicans to stop fighting. In 1926, he founded a new political party, called Fianna Fáil. In the general election of 1932, he defeated the Free Staters. The new constitution of 1937 changed southern Ireland's name to Eire, but it stayed within the British Commonwealth. It became independent and left the Commonwealth in 1949.

KEY DATES

1916	Easter Rising in Dublin is crushed by the British after a week
1918	In elections, Sinn Féin wins 73 of the 105 Irish seats in the British Parliament
1919	Sinn Féin declares Ireland independent—this leads to civil war
1922	Southern Ireland, known as the Irish Free State, becomes a self-governing dominion of Britain
1923	Civil war ends
1926	Fianna Fáil Party founded
1937	New constitution renames southern Ireland Eire

▼ Both the Free Staters and the Republicans were well supplied with weapons during the civil war. This gun belonged to the Free Staters and was used in County Limerick.

RUSSIA 1917–1924

After years of rule by a corrupt and inept government, the people of Russia rose against the czar and his advisers and seized power in November 1917.

Czar Nicholas II (1868–1918) was forced to abdicate in 1917. He and his family were then imprisoned and killed by the Bolsheviks in 1918.

Following the defeat of Russia by Japan in 1904, there were workers' strikes and revolts throughout Russia. The new czar, Nicholas II, issued a declaration promising civil rights and a national government, called the Duma. The Duma did not keep its promises. Elections were rigged so that reformers were kept out of government. Opponents of the government were arrested, and the leaders fled. But the Russian people thought that the czar was out of touch with the population and that his advisers were corrupt. The government, which had not been very efficient in peacetime, was even less effective during World War I. Soldiers who thought that they would be sent to fight in the war began to question their loyalty to their country.

During the March 1917 riots in Petrograd, many soldiers refused to obey orders and attached the Red Flag to their bayonets as a sign of support for the rioters.

Food and fuel were in short supply, and many people in the cities began to starve. The economy was on the way to collapse. In March 1917, riots broke out in the capital, St. Petersburg, which had been renamed Petrograd at the start of World War I. Rioting crowds were usually broken up by troops, but this time they refused to obey their orders. When the troops joined the rioters, the czar abdicated, and his advisers resigned. A temporary government was set up, led by Prince George Lvov.

Grigori Rasputin (1871–1916) was adviser to Czar Nicholas II and his wife Alexandra. They thought he was a holy man who could make their sick son better. But he was hated by the people of Russia.

Armed workers and Bolshevik-led soldiers and sailors attacked the Winter Palace in Petrograd on November 7, 1917. Although it was the headquarters of the czar's government, it was not well defended and was soon in Bolshevik hands.

394

◀ Vladimir Lenin (1870–1924) became a Marxist in 1887 after his brother was executed for trying to assassinate the czar.

Leon Trotsky (1879–1940) was the most influential person after Lenin in the revolution. During the Russian Civil War, he led the Red Army to victory. He hoped to become president after Lenin's death, but lost to Stalin.

THE BOLSHEVIKS SEIZE POWER

The government found it difficult to carry on with the war. Alexander Kerensky succeeded Prince Lvov as chief minister. After the March revolution, the Bolshevik Party was still determined to seize power. In April, their leader, Vladimir Lenin, returned from exile.

The Bolsheviks in Petrograd wanted Russia to become a communist state. After struggling with the government, the Bolsheviks, led by Lenin, seized power in November 1917. In March 1918, the new government signed the Treaty of Brest-Litovsk which made peace with Germany. It moved the capital from Petrograd to Moscow, broke up the large estates, and gave the farmland to the peasants. Control of factories was given to workers. Banks were taken into state control, and Church property was seized.

The White Russians (anticommunists) opposed these moves and, in 1918, the Russian Civil War broke out. The White Russians were finally defeated by the Bolshevik Red Army in 1922. By this time, around 100,000 people had been killed and two million had emigrated. That year, the country's name was changed to the Union of Soviet Socialist Republics (U.S.S.R.), or Soviet Union. Lenin led the U.S.S.R. until his death in 1924, when a new power struggle began between Leon Trotsky and Josef Stalin. Stalin won and dominated Soviet politics until 1953.

Josef Stalin (1879–1953) joined the Bolshevik Party in 1903. In 1922, Stalin became general secretary of the Communist Party and in 1924, leader of the U.S.S.R.

▶ When Josef Stalin became leader of the U.S.S.R. in 1924 he carried out the Great Purge—millions of people were arrested and murdered. He decided to strip farmers of their land in order to reorganize farming into larger state-owned units called collectives. His orders were brutally carried out by the army and secret police. Villages were burned and the villagers killed or evicted.

WORLD WAR I: THE AFTERMATH 1918-1923

Germany, freed from Russia, launched an assault on the Western Front in 1918. Newly arrived U.S. troops helped stop the attack and Germany asked for peace.

The arrival of American troops in Europe in 1917 meant that the Allies could launch fresh attacks on the Western Front. In 1918, Russia withdrew from the war, so German soldiers were no longer needed on the Eastern Front. By 1918, more than 3.5 million German soldiers were fighting on the Western Front. In March, they broke through the trenches and advanced toward Paris. The French counterattacked in July, and in August, British tanks broke the German line at Amiens. As the United States poured troops into France, the Germans retreated.

The fighting in World War I left many areas of Belgium and northeastern France devastated. Cities such as Ypres, in northwestern Belgium, were left in ruins.

By October, the fighting was nearing the German border and a naval blockade was causing starvation in Germany. Early on the morning of November 11, Germany signed an armistice. Kaiser Wilhelm II abdicated, and at 11 o'clock, fighting in World War I ended. Almost 10 million people had been killed and over 20 million wounded. Most were young men, and their loss changed the social structure of several countries. As a result, many women gained more equality and freedom than they had had before the war. In many places, they also gained the right to vote.

World War I involved whole populations. Women went to work to produce armaments and keep industries going while the men were at war.

▶ German submarines, or U-boats, attacked ships on the surface by firing torpedoes at them from under the water. They were so successful in attacking Allied ships that Britain came close to defeat in 1917.

▶ On January 31, 1917 the Germans announced to the world that they would begin unrestricted submarine warfare. This threatened U.S. ships. In February, U-boats sank a U.S. ship, the *Housatonic*. President Wilson cut off diplomatic relations with Germany, and on April 6, the United States declared war. The arrival of American troops in Europe tipped the balance in 1918 when the Germans launched a major, final attack on the Western Front.

THE TREATY OF VERSAILLES

World War I was formally ended by the Paris Peace Conference, which was held between 1919 and 1920. All the nations that had been involved in the war (except Germany) met to draw up a peace agreement, but the United States, Britain, France, and Italy led the process. Five separate treaties were proposed.

The most important was the Treaty of Versailles, which punished Germany for its part in World War I. Vast amounts of reparations (compensation) were to be given to the Allies. The size of Germany was reduced and seven million people were removed from German rule. Germany had to surrender all its overseas colonies and reduce its army to 100,000 men. The German economy collapsed and this led to hyperinflation. Other nations also suffered as they tried to pay back money they had borrowed during the war. This led to political and economic upheaval.

Further strife was caused by the redrawing of international boundaries in Europe following the collapse of the German, Austro–Hungarian, Russian, and Ottoman (Turkish) empires.

THE LEAGUE OF NATIONS

The League of Nations was also set up at the Paris Peace Conference. Its aim was to help keep world peace, settling disputes by discussion and agreement, but it failed. The reasons for this were that it had little power because the United States refused to join, and there were still rivalries among the 53 members. These weakened the League and reduced its power, so by the late 1930s, few countries took any notice of it.

The Treaty of Versailles was signed on June 28, 1919. It declared that Germany's rulers were solely responsible for the outbreak of war, and so Germany had to make reparations (pay money) to the Allies.

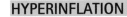
HYPERINFLATION

German industry was totally destroyed in the war and the country was unable to repay the reparations demanded by the Allies in the Treaty of Versailles. The Germans regarded the Treaty as unjust and indefensible. One of the outcomes was that the German economy was hit by hyperinflation in the 1920s. Hyperinflation is fast inflation that causes the value of money to drop very quickly. People needed enormous amounts of money to buy just a loaf of bread.

After the Paris Peace Conference (1919–1920), Germany gave back lands to France and Belgium. The Hapsburg monarchy was ended, and Poland, Czechoslovakia, Hungary, and Yugoslavia all became new states.

Because of hyperinflation, this million mark note issued in Germany during the 1920s was worth virtually nothing.

397

THE RISE OF FASCISM 1922–1939

The political philosophy known as fascism became popular in many European countries during the 1930s. To many, it offered a way out of economic decline.

Benito Mussolini (1883–1945) became the fascist dictator of Italy in 1922.

Young Italian fascists march past Mussolini during a March of Triumph in Rome in October 1935.

Fascist ideas gained support after World War I. The first fascist government appeared in Italy in the 1920s. The term "fascism" comes from the Latin *fasces*— a bundle of rods with an ax that was a symbol of power in ancient Rome. Fascism was based on the idea that a nation would only succeed through disciplined, ruthless action and a determined will. To many people, it offered a way out of economic decline.

Fascists believed that achieving a worthwhile aim made any action they took acceptable. Schools, religion, newspapers, and the arts and sciences were expected to serve the nation. Military power and a secret police organization supported the fascist governments. Fascists believed that their race was superior to others. They opposed communism and encouraged national pride and racism (prejudice against other races). In Germany, this hatred was directed especially at Jews and gypsies.

ITALY AND BENITO MUSSOLINI

In Italy, the Fascist Party was founded by Benito Mussolini in 1919, when economic depression and the threat posed by the communists helped its rise to power. In 1928–1929 he imposed one-party government.

To avenge a humiliating defeat in 1896, Mussolini's army invaded Abyssinia (Ethiopia) in 1935–1936. Britain, France, and other countries condemned the invasion. So, Italy, keen to become a major power, then formed an alliance with Germany. They became known as the Axis Powers. In May 1939, Mussolini and the German fascist dictator, Adolf Hitler, agreed a military treaty—the Pact of Steel. Mussolini's leadership led Italy to defeat in World War II, and he was dismissed and imprisoned by King Victor Emmanuel in 1943. He was later released by German soldiers and set up fascist rule in the north of the country. In April 1945, he was captured and executed by Italian partisans.

GERMANY AND ADOLF HITLER

The terms of the Versailles Treaty were harsh on Germany, and the economic recession of the early 1930s saw large-scale unemployment in the country. The fragile Weimar Republic was under threat from the communists and Adolf Hitler's National Socialist German Workers' Party (known as Nazis). Hitler promised to end unemployment and poverty, and to build the country into a great state after its humiliation in World War I. Amid political turmoil and violence, President Hindenburg appointed Hitler as chancellor in January 1933. As *Führer* (leader), Hitler crushed all opposition, and ordered the murder of millions of Jews, gypsies, and others. In 1939, he led Germany into World War II, but killed himself when faced with defeat.

THE SPREAD OF FASCISM

In other countries, economic difficulties and the threat of communism in the postwar period led to the establishment of many fascist governments. In Spain, the army leader, General Miguel Primo de Rivera, took power in 1923, and ruled until 1930. In 1933, his son José Antonio formed the fascist Falange Party.

To avenge Italy's humiliating defeat in 1896, Mussolini sent his army to invade Abyssinia. In 1936, Italian troops under General Badoglio victoriously entered the capital, Addis Ababa. The invasion led to a worldwide outcry and Italy's withdrawal from the League of Nations.

The Falangists supported General Francisco Franco's nationalist forces during the Spanish Civil War (1936–1939). With the support of Germany and Italy, they took power in 1939. Franco ruled as dictator until his death in 1975.

Fascism also won support in Portugal, Austria, the Balkan states, and South America in the years before World War II. Juan Perón ruled Argentina with his wife Eva in the 1940s and 1950s. Antonio Salazar was dictator of Portugal from 1932 to 1968. In England, former Cabinet minister Sir Oswald Mosley founded the Britsh Union of Fascists in 1931, during a period of economic depression and mass unemployment. His public meetings were known for the violence between his supporters and his opponents.

KEY DATES	
1919	Italian Fascist Party founded by Mussolini
1922	Mussolini becomes prime minister of Italy
1923	Primo de Rivera takes power in Spain
1928	Mussolini becomes dictator of Italy
1933	José Antonio Primo de Rivera forms Spanish Falange Party; Hitler appointed chancellor of Germany
1936	Italian troops invade Abyssinia
1939	General Franco becomes dictator of Spain; World War II begins

◀ Sir Oswald Mosley (1896–1980) resigned from Ramsay MacDonald's Labour government in 1931 to form the British Union of Fascists. The party stirred up anti-Semitism, especially in the East End of London, where many Jewish people lived.

This antifascist poster was issued by the Socialist Party of Catalonia in Spain.

José Antonio Primo de Rivera (1903–1936) founded the Spanish Falange nationalist movement in 1933.

Adolf Hitler rose from obscurity to found the National Socialist German Workers' Party. During political unrest in 1933, he was appointed chancellor.

U.S.A. BETWEEN THE WARS 1919–1941

After World War, I the United States went back to its isolationism. The booming economy of the 1920s was followed by the Depression of the 1930s.

Warren Harding (1865–1923) was elected 29th president in 1920. His health was affected when several cabinet members were involved in an oil scandal. He died suddenly while still in office.

B efore the outbreak of war in Europe, the United States had a policy of isolationism. This meant that the country only became involved in world affairs when it was necessary for self-defense. The United States was physically cut off from most of the world, preoccupied with its own affairs, and preferred to stay out of entangling alliances.

When World War I broke out, most Americans wanted to stay neutral. Between 1914–1917, President Wilson tried to mediate between the warring European countries. The United States did not enter the war until 1917, after its ships were attacked by German U-boats.

After World War I, the desire for isolationism grew stronger. The country had seen what happened in Europe because of alliances. Also, people were alarmed by what was happening in Russia. The Senate voted not to join the League of Nations—President Wilson's brainchild. By the early 1920s, the U.S. economy was coming out of the postwar slump, and industrial production began to grow.

In Chicago, gangs fought each other to gain control of illegal saloons called speakeasies. This scene depicts the murder of gangster John Dillinger in Chicago in 1934.

In 1920, newly-elected president Warren Harding promised "a return to normalcy." This meant not getting involved with other countries and strengthening law and order—including a ban on alcohol. This ban led to a lack of respect for the law and a growth of violence.

▲ Al Capone (1899–1947) was born in Brooklyn. From 1925, he led Chicago's South Side Gang, and dominated the city's criminal underworld. He was finally jailed for tax evasion in 1931.

▶ Charles Lindbergh (1902–1974) made the first solo nonstop flight across the Atlantic in 1927. He became a hero to people around the world.

PROHIBITION AND GANGSTERS

Before World War I, the Women's Christian Temperance Union and other pressure groups fought for Prohibition. They argued that alcohol is a dangerous drug that destroys family life and leads to crime. In 1920, their efforts led to the 18th Amendment to the Constitution. This banned the manufacture, sale, and transportation of alcoholic beverages in the United States. Many thought this would reduce crime, but the opposite happened. Gangsters set up illegal saloons called speakeasies, where they sold bootleg, or illegal liquor. Warfare between competing gangs became commonplace, and corruption in law enforcement agencies was rife. When it became clear that Prohibition was not working, the 21st Amendment was passed, and Prohibition ended in 1933.

BOOM AND BUST

Following World War I, the United States withdrew from the world stage and continued its policy of isolationism into the 1930s. The country even put restrictions on immigration. During the economic boom of the 1920s, the United States became the first country in which millions of people drove cars, listened to radio, and enjoyed movies. It was a time when the arts flourished. The motion picture industry was growing. The New York skyline kept changing as more new buildings were added. But in 1929, the Roaring Twenties—the Jazz Age—ended in total economic collapse. A new president, Franklin Delano Roosevelt, would have to use all his skills to rebuild his country and restore his people's faith.

THE END OF ISOLATIONISM

Roosevelt continued his country's isolationist policies after war broke out in Europe in 1939. But these policies ended abruptly when the Japanese attacked the U.S. Pacific Fleet at Pearl Harbor on December 7, 1941. President Roosevelt described December 7 as "a date which will live in infamy." The following day, Congress declared war on Japan, and the United States entered World War II. Isolationism had ended.

"Cootie" Williams and his jazz band play in the Savoy Ballroom in Harlem, in the 1930s. Jazz developed around 1900 in New Orleans. By the 1920s, the music was called Dixieland, and soon, Chicago, St. Louis, and New York were the centers of jazz.

▲ The Art Deco Chanin Building of 1929, in New York, is typical of the skyscrapers that were built in New York between the wars.

▲ Skyscrapers only became possible when Elisha Otis developed the elevator, and steel girders began to be used in construction in the late 1800s. In New York, the Woolworth Building, designed in 1913 by architect Cass Gilbert, was for a time the tallest building in the world.

◄ Prohibition agents examine some of the 3,000 bags of illegal liquor hidden in a coal steamer in New York Harbor.

KEY DATES

1917 The United States enters World War I
1918 World War I ends
1919 The Senate votes not to join League of Nations
1920 Warren Harding becomes 29th president; 18th Amendment introduced—Prohibition era begins
1925 Al Capone becomes leader of Chicago's South Side Gang
1929 Wall Street Crash and start of Great Depression
1931 The gangster Al Capone is jailed for tax evasion
1933 18th Amendment repealed—Prohibition ends
1941 Japanese attack Pearl Harbor; The United States enters World War II

CHINA 1911–1935

Following the fall of the Manchus in 1911, and the founding of the Republic of China, the country soon became embroiled in a long-running civil war.

When the Chinese nationalist leader, Sun Yat-sen (1866–1925) died, he was buried in this tomb on Zijin Mountain, just east of Nanjing.

Opposition to the rule of the Manchus eventually led to the 1911 Chinese Revolution and their downfall. The revolutionary leader Sun Yat-sen was named provisional president. The Republic of China was founded on February 12, 1912 with the official abdication of the imperial government. Sun Yat-sen's presidency did not last long—he resigned because of lack of support just three days later. China was then ruled by the military leader Yuang Shikai until his death in 1916, when the political situation in the country began to disintegrate.

The followers of Yuang Shikai set up a government in Beijing, and Sun Yat-sen's Kuomintang (nationalist) Party formed a rival government in Canton. For the next ten years, the country was embroiled in civil war. Student demonstrations against the terms of the Treaty of Versailles in 1919, when Japan took over German colonies in China, eventually led to the founding of the Chinese Communist Party in 1921. With help from the Russians, Sun Yat-sen reorganized the Kuomintang Party and allowed Communist Party members to join. When Sun Yat-sen died in 1925, leadership of China and the Kuomintang Party passed to Chiang Kai-shek.

CHINESE CIVIL WAR

In 1926, Chiang Kai-shek launched an expedition against the warlords in the north who wanted to overthrow the nationalist government. He was helped in this by the Chinese Communist Party. Together, they defeated the warlords. But in 1927, the Communist–Kuomintang alliance ended and the two sides started fighting each other. This fighting became known as the Chinese Civil War. Chiang Kai-shek set up his capital in Nanjing (Nanking). Later that year, the nationalists drove the communists out of Shanghai and into the Jiangxi hills. The nationalists claimed to have united China, but they still did not have control of the country.

▲ Chiang Kai-shek (1887–1975) took control of the Kuomintang Party in 1926. In 1927, he set up the nationalist government in Nanjing. After fighting against the Japanese invasion, he was ousted by the communists and fled to Taiwan (Formosa), where he established the Republic of China.

▶ This Shanghai poster, dated 1927, immortalizes Sun Yat-sen and shows his successor, Chiang Kai-shek, setting out with his nationalist forces to oust the communists from northern China.

THE LONG MARCH

In October 1933, the Chinese nationalist leader Chiang Kai-shek launched a massive attack against the communists in Jiangxi, southern China. In October 1934, 100,000 communists left Jiangxi and set out on what has become known as the Long March. Led by Mao Zedong, they traveled for nearly 6,300 mi. (10,000km) to northern China. They endured terrible conditions, cold, and hunger during the long journey. Only one fifth of them reached their destination.

THE RISE OF MAO ZEDONG

In 1931, taking advantage of the turmoil within China, the Japanese occupied Manchuria and set up the puppet state of Manchukuo in 1932. Meanwhile, the communists had set up a rival government (the Jiangxi Soviet) in southern China in 1931. In the same year, Mao Zedong became chairman of the Jiangxi Soviet. The communists built up their forces in Jiangxi and withstood four attempts by the Kuomintang to oust them. In October 1933, Chiang Kai-shek launched a massive attack against the communists with the intention of exterminating them. The communists resisted for a year, then in October 1934, 100,000 of them left Jiangxi and set out on the Long March.

THE LONG MARCH

Mao Zedong led the Long March for almost 6,300 mi. (10,000km) until they reached Yan'an in Shaanxi Province in northern China. It took them until October 1935, and only about 20,000 of the original 100,000 marchers survived to reach their destination. The Long March established Mao Zedong as leader of the Chinese communists.

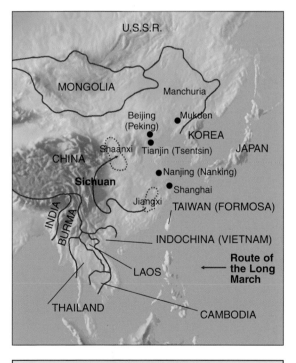

KEY DATES

1911	Chinese Revolution, end of the Manchus
1912	Republic of China is founded
1921	Chinese Communist Party founded
1925	Sun Yat-sen dies
1926	Chiang Kai-shek takes control of Kuomintang (nationalist) Party
1927	Chinese Civil War starts
1931	Japanese occupy Manchuria

During the Long March of 1934–1935, the communists fled from nationalist forces in Jiangxi, winding through southern and western China, and finally reaching Yan'an in Shaanxi Province. Here, Mao Zedong emerged as the leader of the communists.

Mao Zedong (1893–1976) became involved with the Chinese Communist Party in 1919, and in 1931 became chairman of the Jiangxi Soviet. During 1934–1935, he led the Long March. In 1949, he proclaimed the People's Republic of China.

THE GREAT DEPRESSION 1929–1939

After World War I the U.S. economy saw rapid growth. The Wall Street Crash of 1929 brought an abrupt end to this and led to worldwide depression.

During the Depression of the 1930s, thousands of poverty-stricken American families fled the East Coast and rural farming areas to search for work in the West, especially in California.

In October 1936, 200 men from Jarrow in northeast England marched to London with a petition. A major shipyard had closed down and caused unemployment to soar.

The Great Depression came at the end of a period of economic turbulence. In 1919, the Treaty of Versailles forced Germany to pay a lot of compensation to the Allies. Many Germans lost all their savings as the value of their money plummeted. In Britain, France, and the United States, industry struggled to adjust to peacetime trade. Millions of soldiers came home and looked for jobs, but there were none. Trade unions called on workers to strike against employers who imposed wage cuts. Food prices fell so low that many farmers were ruined and forced to give up their land.

During the 1920s, the U.S. economy grew at a tremendous rate. This was due to the continued development of industry and manufacturing. The growth was also encouraged by the economic policies of presidents Harding and Coolidge. Stock market share prices had been forced up beyond their real value by reckless speculators.

On October 29, 1929, the Wall Street Crash caused panic on the streets of New York. Share prices dropped so fast that many people lost all their money.

THE WALL STREET CRASH

In October 1929, people began to panic and sell their shares rapidly. On a single day, almost 13 million shares were sold on the New York Stock Exchange. This started the crisis known as the Wall Street Crash. It soon affected the whole world.

Many people lost all their money. Banks and businesses closed. Unemployment began to rise. By 1933, the worst year of the Depression, there were 12 million people unemployed in the United States alone. Those who still had jobs saw their salaries halved, and more than 85,000 businesses went under. President Hoover arranged for federal loans to banks and businesses, but refused to give anything directly to the unemployed. People lost all faith in him as a leader.

The situation was made worse by a drought on the Great Plains. The soil turned to dust in many places and blew away in the wind, leading to crop failure on a massive scale.

THE DUST BOWL

Because of a long drought in the 1930s, the soil in the southern Great Plains of the United States became very dry. A series of terrible dust storms swept across the area, which became known as the Dust Bowl. By 1933, hundreds of millions of tons of topsoil had been carried off by the winds, destroying the land. Faced with ruin, thousands of families fled the Dust Bowl looking for work in California and elsewhere.

Franklin D. Roosevelt (1882–1945) was elected governor of New York in 1928. In 1932, he was elected president, and in 1933, he introduced the New Deal to combat the problems caused by the Depression.

ROOSEVELT'S NEW DEAL

For the first two years of the Depression, President Hoover and the federal government took little direct action, believing that the economy would recover naturally. Franklin D. Roosevelt was elected president in 1932, and in 1933, he introduced the New Deal to combat the problems caused by the Depression. This was a set of laws designed to ease the worst of the poverty, provide support for the banks, and protect people's savings. Farm prices were subsidized, a minimum wage was introduced, and a huge construction program was started to create employment. The New Deal helped considerably, but it was not until 1939, when the outbreak of World War II gave an enormous boost to heavy industry, that the Depression came to an end.

▶ Although the U.S.S.R. escaped the worst effects of the Depression, Stalin's five-year plan caused other problems. Announced in 1928, the plan included a program to introduce collective farms. To put this into action, the richest peasant farmers were either executed or banished to Siberia. The rest of the peasants were forced to work on collective farms. This action severely disrupted agricultural production and led to a famine in 1933.

GLOBAL DEPRESSION

The Wall Street Crash led to the collapse of the system of international loans that handled war reparations. This affected Europe and North America directly. Other regions were also badly hit since much of their economies relied on selling food and raw materials to Europe and North America. As these markets collapsed, many people around the world lost their jobs. As a result, unrest increased, and nationalism grew in many countries.

Under Roosevelt's New Deal many unemployed people were given work on government projects. Here, young members of the Civilian Conservation Corps (CCC) lift seedlings from the ground in Oregon for the Forest Service.

WEIMAR AND HITLER 1919–1939

Adolf Hitler took advantage of the economic and social turmoil in Germany in the 1920s to promote fascism. He seized power in 1933.

Field Marshal von Hindenburg (1847–1934) was president of the German Republic. At his death, the chancellor Adolf Hitler became Führer of Germany.

Adolf Hitler (1889–1945) was born in Austria. In World War I, he served in the German army and won the Iron Cross. Hitler became leader of the Nazi Party in 1920.

Following Germany's defeat in 1918, Kaiser Wilhelm II abdicated and fled to the Netherlands. Germany became a republic, and its new government ruled from Weimar, instead of Berlin. From 1919 to 1933, Germany was known as the Weimar Republic. Following elections in January 1919, Friedrich Ebert, a socialist, became its first president. Under his leadership, the Weimar Republic accepted the harsh terms of the Treaty of Versailles. In 1922–1923, the Republic survived several attempts to bring it down, first by the Bolsheviks, then by financial pressure, and finally through an attempted political revolution led by an unknown Austrian fascist named Adolf Hitler.

Ebert died in 1925 and was succeeded by Field Marshal Paul von Hindenburg, who was by then 78 years old. Germany joined the League of Nations in 1926. However, the worldwide Depression of the early 1930s led to massive social and financial problems in Germany.

THE NUREMBERG RALLIES

German soldiers parade with the Standards of Victory at a Nazi Party rally in Nuremberg in 1933. The Nazi propaganda techniques of the 1930s were successfully used to create enormous public support for Hitler. His policies were popular because they promised to make Germany powerful.

THE RISE OF ADOLF HITLER

The next presidential election was in 1932, when Germany was in economic crisis, with sky-high inflation and unemployment. Hindenburg was elected as president again, with Adolf Hitler, by then the leader of the National Socialist German Workers' (Nazi) Party, in second place. By using intimidation and violence started by Hitler's followers, the Nazi Party won the most seats in the Reichstag (German parliament). Hindenburg reluctantly appointed Hitler as chancellor in January 1933.

When the Reichstag was burned down in February, Hitler brought in emergency powers and called for new elections. By April 1933, he had gained absolute power in Germany and established a single-party government. As a result, Germany withdrew from the League of Nations.

On the "Night of the Long Knives" in June 1934, Hitler had many of his rivals killed. When Hindenburg died in August, Hitler was appointed Führer (leader) of the Third Reich (German Empire). He set out to avenge the humiliation brought on Germany by the Treaty of Versailles and to make Germany a powerful empire.

THE RISE OF ANTI-SEMITISM

Blaming the Jews and the labor unions for Germany's problems, Hitler and his Nazi Party started persecuting them. The Nuremberg Laws of 1935 deprived Jews of their German citizenship and banned them from marrying non-Jews. Many Jews were forced to live in ghettos and to wear a yellow star to show that they were Jewish.

On *Kristallnacht* ("Night of Broken Glass") in November 1938, Nazi mobs attacked Jewish property and synagogues all across Germany. Around 30,000 Jews were arrested—the start of a full-scale massacre of Jews in Germany. During the next seven years, six million Jews from many areas of Europe were murdered as part of Hitler's plan to exterminate the Jewish population.

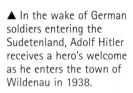

▲ In the wake of German soldiers entering the Sudetenland, Adolf Hitler receives a hero's welcome as he enters the town of Wildenau in 1938.

The deliberate burning of the Reichstag building in Berlin on February 27, 1933, was an excuse for Adolf Hitler to bring in emergency powers and call for new elections.

GERMAN MILITARY EXPANSION

In 1935, Germany abolished its agreement to the armament restrictions imposed by the 1919 Treaty of Versailles. In 1936, its forces entered the Rhineland, an area of Germany that had been demilitarized at the end of World War I. Germany entered into alliances with fascist Italy and the military rulers of Japan. German forces also became involved in the Spanish Civil War, where they supported the fascists, led by General Francisco Franco.

▲ In Hitler's Germany, most Jews were forced to wear a yellow star to show that they were Jewish.

KEY DATES

1919	Friedrich Ebert becomes first president of German Republic
1921	Adolf Hitler becomes leader of Nazi Party
1925	Ebert dies; Hindenberg becomes president
1933	Hitler is appointed chancellor
1934	Hindenberg dies, and Hitler becomes Führer. The "Night of the Long Knives" takes place
1935	Jews deprived of German citizenship
1936	German forces enter demilitarized Rhineland. Germany forms alliances with Italy and Japan
1938	Germany annexes Austria and the Sudetenland
1939	Germany annexes Czechoslovakia and invades Poland—World War II starts

▶ When Hitler came to power, he used every means to destroy opposition. This included the imposition of state censorship of newspapers, books, and radio. In support of this, students and members of the Nazi Party threw banned literature into a bonfire in Berlin in May 1933.

407

THE SPANISH CIVIL WAR 1936–1939

The Spanish Civil War was a battle between two opposing ideologies—fascism and socialism. Fascism won—to be followed by 36 years of dictatorial rule.

Francisco Franco (1892–1975) led the rebellion against the republican government in 1936. From 1939 until his death, he ruled Spain as dictator.

Before World War I, Spain sent military expeditions to strengthen its position in northern Morocco. In 1921, the Spanish forces were defeated by the Berber leader, Abd el-Krim, and it was not until 1927 that Spain was able to subdue the Berbers. In 1923, a military defeat in Morocco led to a fascist military dictatorship in Spain, headed by General Primo de Rivera.

Primo de Rivera ruled Spain until he fell from power in 1930. In the following year, King Alfonso XIII gave in to the demand for elections. The Republican Party won, and the monarchy was overthrown. During the following years, the government survived revolts in Asturias and Catalonia, and a new Popular Front government was elected in February 1936.

The new government under the presidency of Manuel Azana included members of the Socialist Workers' Party and the Communist Party. With their support, it opposed the power of the Roman Catholic Church in Spanish affairs. The Church was supported by the army and by the fascists.

Both men and women fought in the civil war. These republican women are defending a barricade on a Barcelona street in 1936. The U.S.S.R. and the International Brigade of volunteers helped the republicans.

FASCISM VERSUS SOCIALISM

On July 17, 1936, army generals in Spanish Morocco, in North Africa, began a rebellion. Led by General Francisco Franco, and supported by the nationalists, or Falange Party, they invaded Spain. They had the support of the fascist governments of Italy and Germany. The rebellion led to a bitter civil war. By the end of 1936, the nationalists controlled most of western and southern Spain.

FRIENDS OF THE SPANISH REPUBLIC
DONATIONS TO HAMPSTEAD FLAT I, 26 LYNDHURST GDNS

▲ During the Spanish Civil War, people from many countries volunteered to fight in support of their political ideals. This British poster was designed by the artist Roland Penrose to help raise funds for the republican side.

▶ The Nationalists were supported by the fascist governments of Italy and Germany. This photograph, by war photographer Robert Capa, shows nationalist militia in action against republicans on the Córdoba Front in September 1936.

BATTLEGROUND OF BELIEFS

The republicans, supported by the Soviet Union, held the urban areas in the north and east, including the cities of Barcelona, Bilbao, Madrid, and Valencia. The nationalists captured Bilbao in 1937. In support of the nationalists, German dive-bombers attacked the Basque town of Guernica on April 27 of that year and killed hundreds of civilians. This was the first time that unrestricted aerial bombing was used in wartime against civilians, and marked a turning point in modern warfare.

The Spanish Civil War was a battleground between the beliefs of fascism and socialism. People from many countries, supporting one side or the other, volunteered to travel to Spain to fight because of their political ideals.

Some 750,000 people were killed in the war before government forces surrendered Barcelona in January 1939, and Madrid in March, to the nationalists. General Franco was declared "Caudillo of the Realm and Head of State."

Franco banned any opposition to the Falange Party, restored power to the Roman Catholic Church and took Spain out of the League of Nations. Although sympathetic to Hitler, he kept Spain neutral during World War II. Franco ruled Spain until his death in 1975, when the monarchy and democracy were restored.

▲ General Franco's troops are shown in battle with the republicans in the streets of Madrid during 1936. The surrender of Madrid by the republicans in March 1939 marked the end of the civil war.

▼ A turning point in modern warfare was the unrestricted aerial bombing of civilians in the town of Guernica by German aircraft in 1937. The event is recorded in one of Pablo Picasso's most famous paintings.

CHINA AND JAPAN AT WAR 1931–1945

While the Chinese communists and nationalists were fighting a bitter civil war, Japan's expansionist policies and military strength were being felt in the region.

To keep control of the resource-rich region of Manchuria, in northeast China, the Japanese occupied the city of Mukden in 1931. In 1932, they set up a puppet state ruled for them by the last Chinese emperor, P'u-yi.

This German cartoon shows Japanese brutality toward any Chinese opposition during their 1931 invasion of Manchuria in northeast China.

By 1905, the Japanese had defeated both China and Russia and taken control of Korea and Taiwan (Formosa), becoming the strongest military nation in the region. With the help of foreign expertise, industry expanded rapidly in Japan from 1900 to 1925. Industrial investment depended on heavy taxes levied on peasants. However, the industries, especially silk production, depended largely on foreign markets. During the Depression, these markets collapsed and many Japanese factories came to a halt. Faced with a growing population and weak political leadership, the military began to expand Japan's influence over its neighbors.

At the same time, China was ready to try to reclaim Manchuria, which Japan had dominated since 1905. An explosion on the south Manchurian railroad in 1931 led the Japanese to occupy the city of Mukden in Manchuria. There they set up a puppet state called Manchukuo in 1932. Officially, it was ruled by P'u-yi, the last Chinese emperor, but in fact, the Japanese army was in control.

Chinese "big sword" troops were among the defenders of Chengteh (Jehol), northeast of Beijing, when the Japanese attacked the city in March 1933.

JAPAN INVADES CHINA

During 1935–1936, Inner Mongolia came largely under Japanese influence. In China, civil war between the nationalists and the communists continued. Chiang Kai-shek, leader of the nationalists, was captured by the communists in 1936. He was released when he agreed to stop fighting them and join the fight against the Japanese. The two sides became unwilling allies when Japan launched a full-scale invasion of China in 1937.

The better-equipped Japanese forces attacked Chinese cities, including Tianjin, Beijing, and Shanghai. Their massacre of over 100,000 Chinese in Nanjing (Nanking) came to be known as "the Rape of Nanking." Despite Chinese resistance, Japan controlled most of eastern China by 1938, and had installed puppet governments in Beijing and Nanjing. Chiang Kai-shek and his nationalist government moved to Szechwan, where they received military supplies from the United States and Britain.

Meanwhile, Mao Zedong's communists still controlled much of northwest China. When the Japanese tried to advance westward in 1939, they were stopped by the Soviet army. The Chinese–Japanese War lasted until 1945, when Japan surrendered in World War II.

▲ Following the takeover of Manchuria, Japan launched a full-scale attack on China. During 1937, the well-equipped Japanese forces made great advances, attacking many cities in the east of the country and massacring hundreds of thousands of civilians. After occupying Beijing, they launched a ferocious attack on Nanjing in December 1937.

▼ Thousands of civilians were killed when Japanese forces attacked the city of Shanghai in 1937. This photograph shows the terrible scenes of carnage at Shanghai station following the Japanese attack.

▲ During the reign of Emperor Hirohito (1901–1989), Japan had an aggressive policy toward its neighbors. After World War II, Japan became a strong industrial nation. Hirohito's death ended the longest reign in Japanese history.

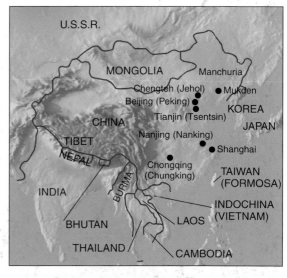

▲ Following its occupation of Manchuria, Japan invaded eastern China, attacking Tianjin, Beijing, Shanghai, and Nanjing. By 1938, they occupied most of eastern China.

GERMAN EXPANSION 1938–1939

Hoping to avoid another war, Britain and France tolerated Hitler's expansionist policies, and allowed Germany to annex Austria and Czechoslovakia.

After the signing of the Munich Agreement in September 1938, Britain's prime minister, Neville Chamberlain, declared, "I believe it is peace for our time."

▲ Artur von Seyss-Inquart (1892–1946), the leader of the Austrian Nazis, was a member of the Austrian government. He invited the Germans to occupy his country and make it a part of the Third Reich. The annnexation of Austria in March 1938 brought little criticism from Britain or France.

▶ German troops entered Prague in April 1939. To appease the Nazis, Czechoslovakia was forced to return the Sudetenland to Germany in 1938. However, this failed to appease Hitler, and German forces invaded Czechoslovakia on March 15, 1939.

One of Adolf Hitler's ambitions was to unite Germany and Austria. This union had been forbidden by the Treaty of Versailles in 1919, because France and other countries thought it would make Germany too powerful. By the early 1930s, however, many people in Germany and Austria wanted their countries to unite. In 1934, an attempted Nazi coup in Austria failed. In 1938, Hitler met with the Austrian chancellor, Kurt von Schuschnigg, and made new demands. With chaos and German troops threatening his country, Schuschnigg resigned in favor of Artur von Seyss-Inquart, leader of the Austrian Nazis. He invited German troops to occupy Austria, and the union, or *Anschluss*, of the two countries was formally announced on March 13, 1938.

Hitler also wanted to reclaim areas of Europe given to other states by the Treaty of Versailles. One of these was areas was Czechoslovakia's Sudetenland. The Munich Agreement of 1938 was signed as an attempt to keep peace in Europe.

German troops marched into Vienna in 1938. Hitler wanted to unite all German-speaking peoples into a Greater Germany, an important part of his vision of the third German Empire, or Third Reich.

This agreement gave the Sudetenland to Germany. This was seen as a reasonable concession to Hitler—a policy known as appeasement. But it was not enough for Hitler. He broke the agreement, and seized all of Czechoslovakia in March 1939.

THE START OF WORLD WAR II 1939

Hitler's confidence grew after years of appeasement by the rest of Europe. But his invasion of Poland led Britain and France to declare war on Germany.

Winston Churchill (1874–1965) became British prime minister in 1940 and led Britain during World War II.

Messerschmitt
Me 109

Supermarine
Spitfire

The three Axis Powers, German, Italy, and Japan, all wanted more territory. After his invasion of Czechoslovakia, Hitler did not expect any international military action against his plans to expand farther. To counter any military threat to the east of Germany, he signed a non-aggression pact, the Molotov–Ribbentrop Pact, with the Soviet Union in August 1939. The two countries secretly agreed to divide eastern Europe. Despite appeals from the United States, Britain and the Vatican, and feeling secure from any military threat, Hitler invaded Poland on September 1, 1939. Britain and France declared war on Germany two days later. Troops from the Soviet Union, which had signed the nonaggression pact with Germany, then invaded Poland from the east. Poland was divided between Germany and the U.S.S.R. In April 1940, German troops invaded Denmark and Norway, and in May, they invaded Belgium, the Netherlands, and France.

German forces attack the poorly equipped Polish army near the Vistula River in September 1939. Much of western Poland was taken into the Third Reich and many of its people were deported to Germany as forced labor.

In June, Italy declared war on the Allies. British troops sent to France were forced to retreat to Dunkirk, where hundreds of thousands of them were evacuated to Britain. With most of Europe under fascist control, Hitler planned to invade Britain. In July 1940, the *Luftwaffe* (German air force) started to attack targets in Britain. The United States remained in isolation.

▲ Between July and October 1940, the German air force (*Luftwaffe*) bombed British cities and attacked Britain's Royal Air Force (RAF). During these attacks, the RAF destroyed 1,733 Luftwaffe planes, while the RAF lost 915. By October 31, the British had won the Battle of Britain.

▶ On May 10, 1940, German forces invaded Holland and Belgium. British troops were sent to France in an unsuccessful attempt to halt the German advance. They were forced to retreat to the French port of Dunkirk. Between May 29 and June 4, 335,000 British and Allied troops were evacuated safely back to England from the beaches around Dunkirk.

WAR IN THE WEST 1939–1945

After German successes in Europe and North Africa, Allied victories at El Alamein and Stalingrad were a turning point in the war and led to Germany's defeat.

Erwin Rommel (1891–1944) was a leader of the German armored units. In North Africa, his tanks showed their superiority over the aging British machines.

Bernard Montgomery (1887–1976) led the British forces in North Africa and Europe. The victory of his Eighth Army at El Alamein was a major turning point in the war.

Georgy Zhukov (1896–1974) commanded the Soviet Red Army in their struggle against the German invaders.

Dwight D. Eisenhower (1890–1969) was Supreme Allied Commander during the war and was elected president in 1952.

The Battle of Britain lasted until October 31, 1940, and forced Hitler to abandon his plan to invade Britain. Instead, he turned his attention to bombing Britain's industry, cities, and shipyards. This lasted until May 1941, but failed to break the morale of Britain, which received substantial supplies and equipment from the United States.

GERMAN ADVANCES

Meanwhile, the Italians had invaded Greece and North Africa. British forces defeated the Italians in North Africa, but in April 1941, Hitler's troops occupied Greece and Yugoslavia to assist Mussolini's army. The Germans drove the British out of Greece and sent a large force, under General Rommel, to North Africa. His superior forces succeeded in driving the British back to Egypt.

In June 1941, encouraged by military successes in the West, and to capture oil supplies, Hitler's armies launched a massive attack on Russia. The Germans drove the Russian army back as far as Leningrad, Moscow, and Kiev. However, during the harsh Soviet winter they lost a large part of their recently gained territory.

British RAF pilots rest beside a Spitfire fighter plane during a lull in the Battle of Britain. Completely outnumbered, but with superior aircraft, British pilots halted the German air force's bombing of Britain.

THE TIDE TURNS AGAINST GERMANY

In August 1941, British prime minister Winston Churchill, and U.S. president Franklin D. Roosevelt, signed the Atlantic Charter—a declaration of freedom for all people. In December, the United States entered the war after a Japanese attack on Pearl Harbor. Meanwhile, Allied troops were sent to Africa to fend off Rommel's advance on Egypt. In November 1942, the Allies won the decisive battle of El Alamein against the Germans and the Italians. To the east, the Russians launched a counterattack against German forces at Stalingrad, forcing them to retreat. These two Allied victories marked the turning point of the war in the West.

A German mortar detachment moves off in support of the infantry during the Battle of Stalingrad. In November 1942, the Russians launched a surprise counterattack on the German forces attacking the city, and forced them to retreat.

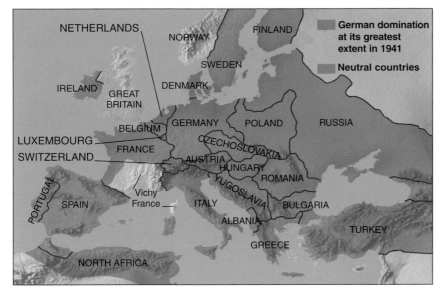

By 1941, Germany had conquered most of Europe apart from Britain, and was expanding into North Africa. From June 1940, Vichy France was ruled from the town of Vichy by Marshal Pétain as a puppet of the Germans.

Child prisoners stare through a barbed-wire fence at the Auschwitz death camp in southern Poland. Between 1940 and 1945, the Nazis killed at least 1.1 million people—mostly Jewish—at the camp, most of them in gas chambers. As well as Jews, the Nazis persecuted Slav and Roma peoples, homosexuals, and Germans of African descent.

Throughout 1942 and 1943, German U-boats attacked ships carrying supplies to Britain. In 1943, Britain and the United States started bombing German industry and cities. In July, British and U.S. forces landed in Sicily, and by September they had invaded Italy. This brought about the downfall of Mussolini and the surrender of Italy.

FINAL DEFEAT OF GERMANY

In the east, Russian troops were slowly driving back the Germans. A second front was opened on D-Day, June 6, 1944, with the Allied invasion of Normandy, France. The Germans launched a counteroffensive but had to retreat in January 1945. By March 1945, the Allies had crossed the Rhine and the Soviets had reached Berlin. Hitler killed himself on April 30. On May 7, Germany surrendered unconditionally.

THE HOLOCAUST

Germany's defeat revealed the true horror of the most extreme example of genocide in history—12 million people had been exterminated by the Nazis. Around half were Jewish. The killing had begun in 1939, when Poland's Jews were forced to move into ghettos. Around 500,000 people died of sickness or starvation. As the Nazis pushed into Russia, they rounded up and shot almost two million Jews. From 1942 to 1944, the Nazis murdered millions more in specially-built death camps.

When France fell in 1940, General Charles de Gaulle became the leader of the Free French. He served as president of France in 1945 and 1959-1969.

On D-Day (June 6, 1944), Allied forces landed on the coast of Normandy: 1,200 warships and 4,100 landing craft put 132,500 men ashore, and 10,000 aircraft attacked German positions. The D-Day landings allowed Allied troops to drive the Germans out of France.

WAR IN THE PACIFIC 1941–1945

The Japanese attack on Pearl Harbor catapulted the United States into World War II. After initial success, the Japanese were slowly driven back to their country.

Admiral Yamamoto Isoroku (1884–1943) planned Japan's attack on Pearl Harbor. In April 1943, while flying to inspect Japanese forces in the Solomon Islands, his route was located by Allied codebreakers who were listening to Japanese radio signals. He was killed when American fighters shot his plane down.

Since September 1940, Japan had allied itself with Germany and Italy, but had not been involved in the fighting. After Japan's invasion of China in 1937, it had come under increasing pressure from the United States to withdraw its forces from that country. The war in the Pacific began on December 7, 1941, when Japanese aircraft from six aircraft carriers launched an unprovoked attack on the U.S. naval base at Pearl Harbor, Hawaii. More than 2,400 U.S. soldiers and sailors were killed and 18 major naval vessels were destroyed or severely damaged. The Japanese lost fewer than 100 men. Japanese forces invaded Thailand on the same day. On the following day, Congress declared war on Japan. Germany and Italy then declared war on the United States.

The U.S. battleships *Tennessee* and *West Virginia* on fire after the Japanese attack on Pearl Harbor on December 7, 1941. In the attack, 18 major U.S. ships, including eight battleships, were destroyed or severely damaged.

JAPANESE KAMIKAZE PILOTS

Kamikaze means "divine wind," a reference to a heaven-sent gale that scattered the ships of a Mongol invasion fleet in 1281. Toward the end of the war in the Pacific, there was no shortage of Japanese pilots who volunteered to die for their emperor by diving their aircraft, laden with bombs, straight into an Allied ship. More than half of the 2,900 kamikaze attacks were launched during the defense of the island of Okinawa. The plane used most often in kamikaze attacks was the Zero fighter, because large numbers of them were available.

▼ Kamikaze attacks were first mounted by the Japanese Imperial Navy on October 25, 1944, during the Battle of Leyte Gulf. During the war, around 300 Allied ships were hit by kamikaze attacks.

▲ Kamikaze pilots often performed rituals before takeoff, and wore a special scarf.

On December 10, 1941, the British battleship *Prince of Wales* and the battle cruiser *Repulse* were sunk in the Gulf of Siam by Japanese aircraft. With American and British fleets severely damaged, the Japanese now thought that they had complete control of the Pacific. Within five months, their forces had overrun Burma, Hong Kong, Singapore, Malaya, the Dutch East Indies (Indonesia), Thailand, and the Philippines. They also invaded New Guinea and threatened the north coast of Australia. With most of its own troops and equipment helping the Allies in Europe, Australia had to turn to the United States for protection.

JAPANESE LOSSES AT SEA

Not all of the U.S. fleet had been sunk at Pearl Harbor. Three American aircraft carriers were at sea at the time of the attack and they were soon joined by two new carriers. Japanese hopes of further expansion were stopped in 1942 in two major sea battles.

The Battle of the Coral Sea (May 4–8) was the first in naval history in which opposing ships were out of each other's sight during the fighting. It was fought by aircraft launched from aircraft carriers. There was no clear winner, but the battle did halt Japanese plans to invade Australia. In June, the Japanese planned to invade the small but strategic island of Midway and the Aleutian Islands. But first they had to destroy American aircraft based on Midway. However, the United States had cracked the Japanese radio codes and were prepared for the attack.

In the Battle of Midway (June 4–6) the Japanese navy was so severely damaged by U.S. carrier-borne aircraft that it retreated. Midway was a decisive victory for the United States and a turning point in the war. With the Japanese advance halted, the task of recapturing territory began.

Over the following three years, U.S. forces regained the Gilbert, Marshall, Caroline, and Mariana islands. From there, they could bomb Japanese cities and industry. In September 1944, U.S. forces began to retake the Philippines, while the British Fourth Army began to reconquer Burma. After fierce fighting, U.S. forces took the Japanese islands of Okinawa and Iwo Jima in early 1945.

▲ After their victory at Midway, U.S. forces took the island of Guadalcanal in August 1942. Following in their footsteps, New Zealand troops come ashore at Guadalcanal Bay in November 1943.

▼ Dislodging the Japanese from the jungles of Burma was a difficult task. In the early stages of the war, a small British force under General Wingate, known as the Chindits, operated many miles behind Japanese lines.

KEY DATES	
1941	December 7—Japan attacks American Pacific Fleet in Pearl Harbor, Hawaii; United States declares war on Japan; Japanese sink British warships in Gulf of Siam
1942	Japanese overrun Hong Kong, Burma, Thailand, Singapore, Malaya, Dutch East Indies, and the Philippines; Battles of Coral Sea, Midway, and Guadalcanal
1944	Battle of Leyte Gulf; U.S. forces recapture the Philippines
1945	U.S. Air Force takes Okinawa and Iwo Jima; American air force drops atomic bombs on Hiroshima and Nagasaki; Japan surrenders on August 14

PEACE IN THE PACIFIC 1945–1948

With U.S. forces on their doorstep, the Japanese were prepared to fight to the bitter end. The dropping of atomic bombs forced them into surrender.

Japanese representatives wait to sign the formal statement of surrender with General Douglas MacArthur (1880–1964) on the deck of the U.S. battleship *Missouri* on September 2, 1945.

In the taking of the island of Okinawa, more than 100,000 Japanese and 12,000 American soldiers were killed. After these enormous losses, Allied commanders were fearful of the deaths that might result if they invaded the Japanese mainland. They knew that the Japanese would fight to their last drop of blood to defend their country, and estimated that up to a million Allied soldiers would die in the invasion.

In the United States, Roosevelt had been elected to his third term of office as president in 1944. Meanwhile, amid great secrecy, American scientists had been developing a new and terrible weapon—the atomic bomb. Roosevelt died in office on April 12, 1945, and his successor, Harry S. Truman, made the decision to drop the new atomic bomb on Japan.

JAPANESE SURRENDER

Truman argued that the use of atomic bombs would quickly end the war and possibly save millions of Allied soldiers' lives. At the end of July 1945, the Allies gave Japan an ultimatum, threatening complete destruction if Japan did not surrender. Japan gave no signs of surrendering, so an atomic bomb was dropped on Hiroshima on August 6, 1945. It killed about 130,000 people. Three days later a second atomic bomb was dropped on the city of Nagasaki and caused up to 750,000 deaths. Thousands more died later from injuries and radiation sickness. The use of the bombs finally forced the Japanese to surrender on August 14.

World War II ended when the Japanese formally surrendered on September 2, 1945. More than two million Japanese had been killed in World War II, 100 of their cities were destroyed by bombing, and industrial production had practically ceased. It took ten years for Japanese industry to regain its prewar levels.

THE BOMBING OF HIROSHIMA

The development of the atomic bomb by American scientists had been kept secret. Two atomic bombs were used in war. The five-ton "Little Boy" was dropped on Hiroshima (below) by an American B-29 Superfortress, the *Enola Gay* on August 6, 1945. Three days later a second atomic bomb, "Fat Man" was dropped from another Superfortress, the *Bockstar*, to destroy the city of Nagasaki.

The Boeing B-29 Superfortress was the largest bomber used in World War II.

THE UNITED NATIONS 1945–1948

At the end of World War II, the victorious Allied powers divided Germany into four zones. The United Nations was created to keep international peace.

Following the Yalta Conference, the division of Germany was confirmed by the "Big Three" Allied powers at the Potsdam Conference. By this time, Roosevelt had died and been replaced by Harry S. Truman as president. Britain was represented by Clement Attlee. Germany also lost some of its territory to Poland and the U.S.S.R. Countries conquered by Germany and Japan regained their former status. The influence of the Soviet Union increased when Bulgaria, Hungary, Poland, Romania, Czechoslovakia, Yugoslavia, and eastern Germany became communist states. The Truman Doctrine promised American aid to all free peoples that were threatened by communism, while the Marshall Plan provided help for economic recovery.

On April 25, 1945, the United Nations was formally set up at a conference in San Francisco. It was meant to keep world peace and solve problems by international cooperation.

At the Yalta Conference in February 1945, the "Big Three" Allied powers, represented by their leaders, Churchill (Britain), Roosevelt (U.S.), and Stalin (U.S.S.R.), decided to divide Germany into four zones after the war.

THE UNITED NATIONS

The term "United Nations" (UN) was first used in January 1942 when the Atlantic Charter was signed by the Allies.

In the Charter, they agreed to fight the Axis countries and not make any separate peace agreements. The UN was planned to be stronger than the League of Nations had been. It had a powerful Security Council to decide what should be done if disputes broke out. Members were to contribute arms and personnel to UN peacekeeping missions. In 1948, the UN issued a Universal Declaration of Human Rights.

▲ The Potsdam Declaration of 1945 made it possible to bring Nazi war criminals to justice in trials held in Berlin and then in Nuremberg. Here, former Nazi leaders Hermann Goering, Rudolf Hess, and Joachim von Ribbentrop await cross-examination at the trials. All three were found guilty and sentenced to life imprisonment (Hess) or execution. On December 10, 1948, the Nuremberg trials became the birthplace of the modern human rights movement when the UN adopted the Universal Declaration of Human Rights.

▶ On June 25, 1948, the Soviet Union set up a blockade around Berlin to try to force France, Britain, and the United States to give up their rights to the western part of Berlin. To feed the population, Britain and the United States flew supplies into the city for 15 months until the blockade was lifted.

ISRAEL 1948–1949

Growing demands for a separate Jewish state and the flood of refugees from Europe forced the British to withdraw from Palestine. Israel became a reality.

David Ben-Gurion (1886–1973) was born in Poland. As a young man he went to live in Palestine and in 1930 became leader of the Mapai Party. In 1948, he declared the State of Israel and became its first prime minister.

Until the end of World War I, Palestine was part of the Ottoman Empire. It was inhabited by Arabs and a growing number of Jews, some of whom wanted a Jewish homeland. When the Ottoman Empire collapsed, Palestine was ruled by Britain under a 1922 League of Nations' mandate. In 1917, the Balfour Declaration had promised British support for a Jewish homeland in Palestine, with specific protection for the rights of non-Jewish Palestinians. As problems grew in Europe, Jewish immigration increased.

Between 1922 and 1939, the Jewish population in Palestine had risen from 83,000 to 445,000. Tel Aviv had become a Jewish city with a population of 150,000. The Arabs resented this and fighting often broke out between the two groups. After 1945, Jewish immigration increased again. Under pressure from the Arabs, Britain restricted the number of new settlers allowed. Jewish terrorists then began to attack both the Arabs and the British.

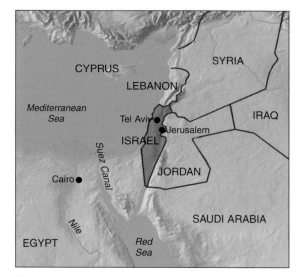

The new State of Israel was surrounded by Arab states. On May 14, 1948, the Arab League of Lebanon, Syria, Iraq, Jordan, and Egypt declared war on Israel and attacked it. They were defeated and Israel increased its territory.

A secret Jewish army called *Haganah* (self-defense) was formed in 1920. More extreme groups were later formed, notably Irgun and the Stern Gang. Both groups thought that Britain had betrayed the Zionist cause—to establish a Jewish state in Palestine—and took part in a violent terrorist campaign against the Arabs and the British. Jewish leaders such as Chaim Weizmann and David Ben-Gurion took a more peaceful approach.

▲ One result of the hostility between the Arabs and Jews in 1948 was the migration of nearly one million Arabs from Palestine. They left their homes and became refugees because they were afraid of the action Israel might take after the war with the Arab League.

▶ After World War II, the number of Jewish refugees from Europe trying to enter Palestine became a problem for the British. In October 1947, the ship *Jewish State* arrived at the port of Haifa with 2,000 illegal Jewish immigrants aboard.

By June 1945, an enormous number of Jewish refugees, displaced by the war in Europe, were clamoring to live in Palestine. Despite British efforts to stop them, the number of refugees entering the country continued to increase. The United States put pressure on Britain to allow the admission of 100,000 refugees, but Britain refused. It soon found itself involved in a full-scale war with Jewish terrorist organizations.

THE NEW STATE OF ISRAEL

Unwilling to be caught up in another bloody and costly war, Britain took the matter to the United Nations. In 1947, the UN voted to divide Palestine into two states. One would be Jewish and the other one Arab. Jerusalem, which was sacred to Jews, Muslims, and Christians, would be international. The Jews agreed to this, but the Arabs did not.

On May 14, 1948, Britain gave up its mandate to rule Palestine and withdrew its troops. On the same day, the Jews, led by Mapai Party leader David Ben-Gurion, proclaimed the State of Israel, and its legitimacy was immediately recognized by the governments of the United States and the Soviet Union.

Israel was immediately attacked by the surrounding Arab League states of Lebanon, Syria, Iraq, Jordan, and Egypt. Israel defeated them and increased its territory by a quarter. Nearly one million Palestinian refugees, afraid of Jewish rule, fled to neighboring Arab countries. The United Nations negotiated a cease-fire in 1949, but conflicts between Israel and its Arab neighbors continue to this day.

During the War of Independence, Jewish Haganah militiamen watch over the road to Jaffa. They captured this important position on April 17, 1948, after stiff Arab resistance.

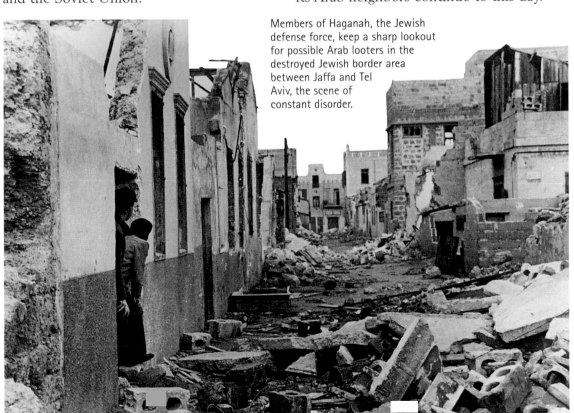

Members of Haganah, the Jewish defense force, keep a sharp lookout for possible Arab looters in the destroyed Jewish border area between Jaffa and Tel Aviv, the scene of constant disorder.

The Israeli flag was raised at Eilat on the Gulf of Aqaba in 1949. It is the southernmost point in Israel, and its only port on the Red Sea.

BRITISH COMMONWEALTH 1914–1949

In 1931, the countries that formed the British Empire joined together to form the Commonwealth. Over the next 60 years they were given their independence.

During both World Wars, soldiers from all corners of the British Empire and Commonwealth fought on the British side. Here, members of the Rhodesian Air Askari Corps practice square drill in 1943.

▼ Here, Commonwealth premiers pose with King George VI at Buckingham Palace while attending the Conference of Commonwealth Prime Ministers in London in April 1949.

The relationship between Britain and parts of its empire had begun to change by the beginning of the 1900s. Some of the larger countries were made independent as dominions. They were completely self-governing, but they maintained strong links with Britain—the "mother country." Dominions retained the British Crown (king or queen) as the symbolic head of state. Each dominion had a lieutenant governor, a native resident of that country, who represented the Crown.

In the 1920s, the dominions asked for a clear definition of their status. In the 1931 Statute of Westminster dominions were defined as "autonomous (self-ruling) communities within the British Empire, equal in status…united by a common allegiance to the Crown and freely associated as members of the British Commonwealth of Nations." After this, the name British Commonwealth of Nations was used instead of British Empire. Many colonies started to clamor for independence.

INDEPENDENT MEMBERS OF THE COMMONWEALTH

Antigua and Barbuda 1981	Namibia 1990
Australia 1901	Nauru 1968
Bahamas 1973	New Zealand 1907
Bangladesh 1972	Nigeria 1960
Barbados 1966	Pakistan 1947
Belize 1981	Papua New Guinea 1975
Botswana 1966	Rwanda 2009
Brunei 1984	St. Kitts-Nevis 1983
Cameroon 1995	St. Lucia 1979
Canada 1931	St. Vincent and the
Cyprus 1960	Grenadines 1979
Dominica 1978	Seychelles 1976
(Fiji suspended—2009)	Sierra Leone 1961
Gambia 1965	Singapore 1965
Ghana 1957	Solomon Islands 1978
Grenada 1974	South Africa 1994
Guyana 1966	Sri Lanka (Ceylon) 1948
India 1947	Swaziland 1968
Jamaica 1962	Tanzania 1961
Kenya 1963	Tonga 1970
Kiribati 1979	Trinidad and Tobago 1962
Lesotho 1966	Tuvalu 1978
Malawi 1964	Uganda 1962
Malaysia 1957	United Kingdom 1931
Maldives 1965	Vanuatu 1980
Malta 1964	Zambia 1964
Mauritius 1968	(Zimbabwe—suspended
Mozambique 1995	1980)

In 1932, the dominions received better terms for trading with Britain than countries outside the Commonwealth. Canada, Australia, New Zealand, and South Africa had all become dominions before World War I. The Irish Free State also became a dominion in 1921. The first three colonies to gain independence after World War II were India (1947), Ceylon (1948), and Burma (1948). India and Ceylon (now Sri Lanka) stayed in the Commonwealth, but Burma did not join, and the Republic of Ireland left in 1949.

COMMUNIST CHINA 1945–1949

After the defeat of Japan in 1945, the Chinese nationalists and communists resumed their civil war. In 1949, the People's Republic of China was declared.

The communists introduced collective farming to China. This meant that all the land, buildings, and machinery belonged to the community. Committees in each village decided what to grow. One improvement was that they replaced their oxen with tractors, which they called "Iron Oxen."

In 1936, the Chinese nationalist leader, Chiang Kai-shek, was forced to make an alliance with the Communist Party to fight against the Japanese in Manchuria. This alliance lasted until 1945 and brought China into World War II on the Allies' side. While the Chinese were fighting the Japanese, Britain and the United States gave them aid. After the defeat of Japan in 1945, the alliance collapsed and civil war broke out in 1946. The nationalists were weak and divided, but Mao Zedong's communists had the support of the people. The communists also had a large army, and by January 1949 they had taken Tianjin and Beijing (Peking). From there they moved southward, pushing the nationalists onto the island of Taiwan (Formosa), which became known as the Republic of China. It held a seat in the United Nations until 1971. The communist People's Republic of China was declared on October 1, 1949, but many countries refused to recognize it.

The People's Republic of China came into being on October 1, 1949. In the coming years, the Chinese communist leader Mao Zedong introduced reforms in the countryside in order to gain the support of the people. This 1949 poster for the Chinese Communist Party shows farmers and soldiers working together.

Large posters of Communist Party leaders formed the backdrop to speeches at a meeting of the Communist Party in Shanghai. When they took power in 1949, the communists soon moved to control the press and nationalized industries.

THE ARTS 1914–1949

The prewar drift away from traditional art forms in music, painting, and sculpture led to further experimentation and expression after World War I.

Charlie Chaplin (1889–1977) became the most successful Hollywood comedian of the silent movie era. At the height of his fame in the 1920s, he was known and loved throughout the world for his portrayal of the "Little Tramp" in films such as *The Gold Rush* (1925).

During and after World War I, new styles of art appeared. Dadaism, founded in Switzerland in 1915, soon influenced the American Man Ray and the French Marcel Duchamp. Their work was designed to shock, and to question established art forms. Surrealism was born out of the Dadaist movement. Surrealists, such as the Spanish Salvador Dali and the Belgian René Magritte, produced paintings that seemed to reflect dreams and the subconscious mind. The onset of World War II led many European Surrealists to work in New York.

Abstract art evolved before World War I in Germany, Holland, and Russia—artists grouped shapes and colors in patterns rather than painting objects in a realistic way. The American Georgia O'Keefe, the Dutch Piet Mondrian, and the Spanish Joan Miró were among the earliest abstract artists. Abstract expressionism started in the United States in the 1940s, and painters include Jackson Pollock, who developed a style using splashes of color, and Mark Rothko, who painted large areas of solid color. They were to influence European art in the 1950s.

Vaslav Nijinsky (1890–1950) studied ballet in St. Petersburg, then joined the Ballet Russe company. In 1912, he electrified Paris audiences with his interpretation of the title role in *The Afternoon of a Faun* by the French composer Claude Debussy (1862–1918).

MUSIC AND BALLET

Classical music was also going through a formative period of change and experimentation. There were many notable composers during this period. The Austrian Arnold Schoenberg explored music in an abstract way. In Russia, Igor Stravinsky was composing lively music for ballet, and in Hungary the composer Béla

The 1920's were prosperous, but still influenced by the horror of war. As a reaction, people tried to live life to the full, and they reveled in the ability to shock. The United States gave birth to the Roaring Twenties. In Europe, Berlin was the center of a wild nightclub culture—this chorus line of the Revue Girls was daring at the time.

▲ The Spanish artist Pablo Picasso (1881–1973), seen here at work in 1945, was one of the pioneers of cubism. Cubists tried to show the basic geometric shapes of the forms they painted. However, Picasso's personal style evolved greatly throughout his long and prolific career.

▲ The American composer George Gershwin (1898–1937) was born to Russian immigrant parents in New York. He incorporated elements of jazz and blues into his music. Among his works are *Rhapsody in Blue* and the opera *Porgy and Bess*.

Bartók was heavily influenced by his country's folk music. In the United States, Charles Ives composed a uniquely American style of classical music.

Western popular music was dominated by the United States. The folk music of black artists evolved into what became known as jazz—the Roaring Twenties are also called the Jazz Age. By the mid-1930s, big band music was popular, and U.S. bandleaders like Glenn Miller were well known throughout the world.

THE MOVIES

By 1920, Hollywood was the movie capital of the world. In 1927, *The Jazz Singer* was the first movie with sound. Moviemakers began to use color in the early 1930s, and had perfected it by the time *Gone With the Wind* was released in 1939. Movies reflect history. During the Depression, musicals cheered people up; in wartime, stories of courage and oppression stirred patriotism.

▼ The Spanish artist Salvador Dali (1904–1989), seen here in action in 1945, was a surrealist painter who also designed jewelry. In his paintings, he tried to show a different reality—that of dreams and the subconscious mind.

◀ Judy Garland (1922–1969) is known all over the world for her portrayal of Dorothy in *The Wizard of Oz* (1939). The movie, made by the Metro-Goldwyn-Mayer studios, was one of the first to be made in color.

▼ This jeweled watch was designed by Salvador Dali in the 1920s.

ARCHITECTURE 1914–1949

After World War I, developments in building design and construction in Europe and the United States became known as the "International Style."

In 1914, two styles of architecture were being developed in the West. The Art Nouveau style, based on natural forms, had flowing lines. Other architects' designs were based purely on function. This modern style, which became known as the International Style, used steel, glass, and reinforced concrete.

The Bauhaus school of art and design, created in 1919 by Walter Gropius, moved from Weimar to this building in Dessau in 1925. Its staff included world-famous painters such as Paul Klee and Wassily Kandinsky.

EUROPEAN DEVELOPMENTS

The trend toward more modern, functional design was led by architects such as Jacobus Oud and Gerrit Rietveld of Holland's de Stijl movement, Mies van der Rohe in Germany, and Le Corbusier in France, each with his own unique style. In Germany, Walter Gropius founded the Bauhaus school of design in 1919. The Nazis closed it in 1933, and in 1938, Gropius became professor of architecture at Harvard. In 1937, Mies van der Rohe had become professor of architecture in Chicago. This led to a new exchange of ideas.

The Moorish influence on Spanish architecture can be seen in the tower of the Bacardi Building in Havana, Cuba. The building, with a terracotta design, was built in 1931.

AMERICAN STYLE

Frank Lloyd Wright designed buildings that were in harmony with the landscape. His early "Prairie style" of two-storied buildings was admired in Japan and Europe. In the 1930s, he was joined by architects escaping persecution. In 1936, he built his most famous house, "Fallingwater," which was suspended over a waterfall. A shortage of space in cities led to the construction of skyscrapers. New York's 102-story Empire State Building, completed in 1931, was the tallest building in the world.

◀ Built in the Art Nouveau style, the Einstein Tower in Potsdam, Germany, was designed after World War I by Erich Mendelsohn. This was the workshop in which Albert Einstein tested his theory of relativity.

▲ The architect Le Corbusier was born in Switzerland, but worked in France. This apartment block in Berlin is an example of his use of reinforced concrete during the 1930s.

◄ During this period, the greatest American architect was Frank Lloyd Wright. He was a pupil of the eminent Louis Sullivan, the architect who developed steel-framed buildings in Chicago. This house, in Los Angeles, was designed by Wright to be in harmony with the landscape.

WORLD WAR II AND AFTER

The onset of World War II halted building development in Europe. But in South America, particularly in Brazil, the International Style and the work of Le Corbusier was influencing building design.

By 1945, in the capital cities of Europe, over 40 million new homes were needed to replace those destroyed in the war. The rapid building of new houses became a priority. In the United States, new prosperity saw many people buying homes, often for the first time. New suburbs and large housing tracts sprang up across the country.

▼ The Golden Gate suspension bridge in San Francisco, was completed in 1937. Its main span is 8,979 ft. (2,737m) long and its twin bridge towers are 745 ft. (227m) above sea level.

▲ The Chrysler Building in New York was designed by architect William van Alen and completed in 1930. It is a classic example of the Art Deco style that influenced building design between 1925 and 1939.

SCIENCE AND TECHNOLOGY 1914–1949

Between the two world wars, scientists developed many weapons of mass destruction. However, their work also led to new discoveries that had peaceful uses.

After World War I, new, innovative equipment made domestic chores easier. The first electrically driven washing machines appeared in 1914.

World War I saw the first use of chemical warfare and the first use of tanks on the battlefield. Aircraft were used for observation, aerial combat, and bombing. By World War II, scientists had developed weapons that were far more sophisticated. Aircraft could fly faster and carry more bombs. In 1940, the radar system was developed to locate distant objects such as enemy aircraft. In 1934, the physicist Enrico Fermi found that a chain reaction of nuclear fission could be achieved using uranium. This led to the Manhattan Project in 1941, in which scientists developed the atomic bomb at Los Alamos. Developments in atomic physics also led to the discovery of the most accurate method of measuring time.

Until the invention of transistors in 1948, radios used tubes and were built into large polished wooden cabinets, such as this 1928 Columbia set. Transistors allowed miniaturization in all forms of electronics.

SCIENCE FOR PEACE

John Logie Baird (1888–1946) invented an early television system. In 1926, he transmitted the first pictures of a moving object. His system was soon replaced by one developed by Russian-born U.S. scientist Vladimir Zworykin (1889–1982). The world's first high-definition public television service was started by the BBC, in England, in 1936.

The development of plastics and synthetic fibers in the 1930s meant that many consumer goods and clothes could be mass produced at prices that people could afford. Major advances were made in the development of computers. Early computers filled whole rooms and needed large amounts of electricity to handle a small amount of data. In 1948, the transistor was developed by the Bell Telephone Company. This brought about a revolution in electronics and led to the building of smaller and more powerful computers.

▲ Ferdinand Porsche (1875–1951) wanted to produce a car that people could afford. His Volkswagen was first planned in 1934 and first mass-produced in 1938.

▲ Developed from a military bomber, this British Handley Page HP42 Hannibal was used on Imperial Airways' flights from England to Egypt, South Africa, and India in the 1930s.

▲ Penicillin was discovered by Alexander Fleming in 1928. He saw that a mold in his laboratory killed the bacteria around it. It was not until the 1940s that penicillin was made stable enough for use in medicine.

Cures and prevention methods were found for diseases that had killed thousands. As a result of warfare, many advances were made in the treatment of injuries. Peacetime advances included the discovery of insulin in 1921, by the Canadians Dr. Frederick Banting and Dr. Charles Best, and the Scottish Dr. John Macleod. In 1937, the first blood bank opened in the United States; plasma was first used in 1940.

The introduction of mass-production meant that cars could be sold at affordable prices. Military aircraft were redesigned to carry civilians, and by the 1930s, commercial airlines flew passengers to most parts of the world.

▲ In 1943, the first completely electronic computer was developed in England. Known as Colossus, it successfully decoded top-secret messages sent by the Germans on their Enigma machines.

▶ The first nylon products appeared in 1939. This is an advertisement for American nylon stockings from the 1940s.

▶ A mushroom cloud rising after the explosion of an atomic bomb. In August 1945, the United States dropped atomic bombs on the Japanese cities of Hiroshima and Nagasaki. This forced the Japanese to surrender.

Albert Einstein (1879–1955) won the Nobel Prize for Physics in 1921. His work led to the development of the atomic bomb. After the war, he fought to control the use of nuclear weapons.

WHEN IT HAPPENED

1915 The sonar system is developed to detect submarines under water
1919 Ernest Rutherford splits the atom
1922 BCG tuberculosis vaccine used in France
1926 First liquid-fuel rocket launched in the U.S.A.
1928 Penicillin discovered by Alexander Fleming
1937 Frank Whittle designs first jet engine
1938 Lazlo Biro introduces first ballpoint pen
1939 First nylon stockings sold in the U.S.A.
1940 Radar system developed
1941 Scientists develop atomic bomb in the U.S.A.
1944 Jet-engined fighter planes first used in battle by Britain and Germany
1948 Atomic clock invented

THE MODERN WORLD

1950 – PRESENT DAY

The years between 1950 and the present day are recent history. Some of the events have occurred during our lifetime or we have seen reports of them on television. These years saw social, technological, and environmental changes on a scale never witnessed before. Politicians and policy-makers, as well as historians, have identified several important trends that will continue to transform our world: advances in science and technology, environmental pollution, ever-increasing population, changing family structures, and a growing gap between the rich and poor.

▲ Aircraft carriers from Britain and the United States played an important peacekeeping role in the 1990s in various world trouble spots, such as the Middle East and Yugoslavia.

◄ The space shuttle *Discovery* blasts off from the Kennedy Space Center at the beginning of its twenty-first spaceflight in July 1995.

WORLD AT A GLANCE 1950–PRESENT

This period was dominated by the Cold War between the communist East and the capitalist West. The United States and the U.S.S.R. played the leading roles. These two were also involved in the space race. The U.S.S.R. was the first to send a man into space, and the United States the first to put a man on the moon. The collapse and breakup of the U.S.S.R. led to the end of the Cold War, but the emergence of many independent states in the region led to new tensions and competition.

In western Europe, the European Union encouraged economic growth and expanded its membership. In Africa, many nations became independent, but faced droughts, famines, and severe economic problems. In Southeast Asia, technology and industry developed, and Japanese business became for a time the most successful in the world. China had a cultural revolution and launched a drive to modernize and expand its industries, while Indochina was devastated by a series of wars.

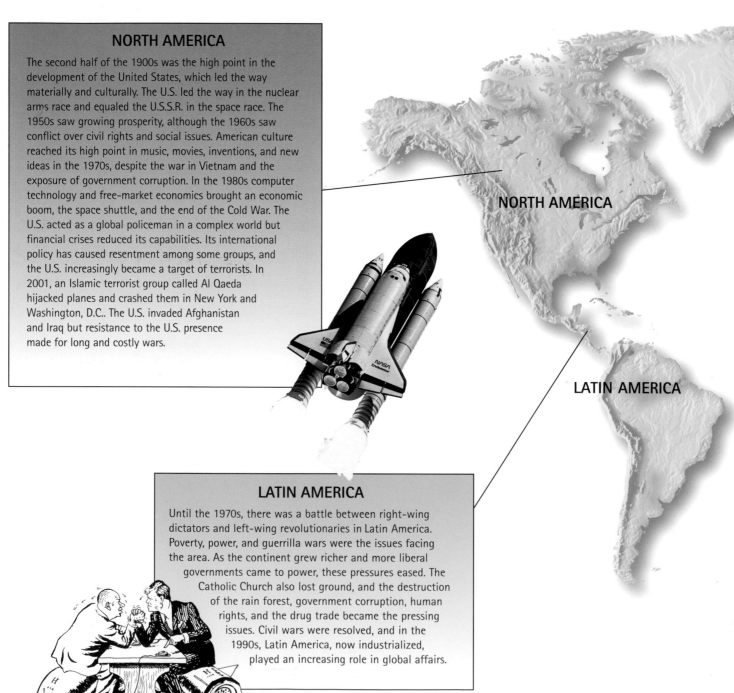

NORTH AMERICA

The second half of the 1900s was the high point in the development of the United States, which led the way materially and culturally. The U.S. led the way in the nuclear arms race and equaled the U.S.S.R. in the space race. The 1950s saw growing prosperity, although the 1960s saw conflict over civil rights and social issues. American culture reached its high point in music, movies, inventions, and new ideas in the 1970s, despite the war in Vietnam and the exposure of government corruption. In the 1980s computer technology and free-market economics brought an economic boom, the space shuttle, and the end of the Cold War. The U.S. acted as a global policeman in a complex world but financial crises reduced its capabilities. Its international policy has caused resentment among some groups, and the U.S. increasingly became a target of terrorists. In 2001, an Islamic terrorist group called Al Qaeda hijacked planes and crashed them in New York and Washington, D.C.. The U.S. invaded Afghanistan and Iraq but resistance to the U.S. presence made for long and costly wars.

NORTH AMERICA

LATIN AMERICA

LATIN AMERICA

Until the 1970s, there was a battle between right-wing dictators and left-wing revolutionaries in Latin America. Poverty, power, and guerrilla wars were the issues facing the area. As the continent grew richer and more liberal governments came to power, these pressures eased. The Catholic Church also lost ground, and the destruction of the rain forest, government corruption, human rights, and the drug trade became the pressing issues. Civil wars were resolved, and in the 1990s, Latin America, now industrialized, played an increasing role in global affairs.

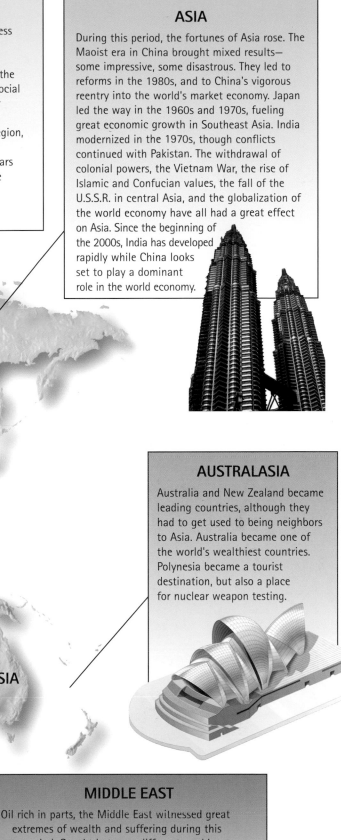

EUROPE

Ruined by World War II and overshadowed by the Cold War, Europe made a dramatic recovery between the 1950s and the 1970s, beginning a long process of cooperation through the founding of the European Union. The greatest breakthrough was the ending of the Cold War, which reunited Germany and brought reconciliation between East and West, though ugly scenes, such as the Yugoslavian civil wars of the 1990s, hindered progress. Environmental and social concerns were important, especially after the Russian nuclear disaster in Chernobyl in 1986. The European Union became the dominant economic and political organization in the region, extending its membership and launching a common currency—the euro. But the financal crises of recent years and difficulties integrating immigrant populations have troubled the European project.

ASIA

During this period, the fortunes of Asia rose. The Maoist era in China brought mixed results—some impressive, some disastrous. They led to reforms in the 1980s, and to China's vigorous reentry into the world's market economy. Japan led the way in the 1960s and 1970s, fueling great economic growth in Southeast Asia. India modernized in the 1970s, though conflicts continued with Pakistan. The withdrawal of colonial powers, the Vietnam War, the rise of Islamic and Confucian values, the fall of the U.S.S.R. in central Asia, and the globalization of the world economy have all had a great effect on Asia. Since the beginning of the 2000s, India has developed rapidly while China looks set to play a dominant role in the world economy.

EUROPE

ASIA

MIDDLE EAST

AFRICA

AUSTRALASIA

Australia and New Zealand became leading countries, although they had to get used to being neighbors to Asia. Australia became one of the world's wealthiest countries. Polynesia became a tourist destination, but also a place for nuclear weapon testing.

AUSTRALASIA

AFRICA

After a promising start in the 1960s, when most states gained independence, Africa was troubled by wars, corruption, famine, social crises, and the AIDS virus. Foreign interference and exploitation were common. In South Africa, torn by apartheid, reform came in 1990, and brought the dawn of a new, multiracial society. Zimbabwe, Somalia, and several other countries still suffer from political and economic turmoil.

MIDDLE EAST

Oil rich in parts, the Middle East witnessed great extremes of wealth and suffering during this period. Caught between different world powers, war and interference by foreign powers were common. The popular uprisings of the "Arab Spring" of 2011 toppled rulers in Egypt, Libya, and Yemen, and are likely to lead to further change.

THE COLD WAR 1945–1989

After the end of World War II, tensions between East and West and the buildup of nuclear weapons almost brought the world to the brink of war.

This 1962 cartoon, produced at the time of the Cuban missile crisis, shows the two superpower leaders arm-wrestling for power. The U.S.S.R.'s Nikita Khrushchev (1894–1971), on the left, is facing the U.S. president, John F. Kennedy (1917–1963). They are both sitting on nuclear weapons.

The U.S.S.R. and the United States fought as allies in World War II. But in 1945, these two superpowers became rivals and then enemies. This division became known as the Cold War, a conflict largely without any actual fighting. Both countries made threats and built up their armed forces and weapons. Each side also accumulated an enormous stockpile of nuclear weapons. The idea was to hold a kind of balance in which neither side would want to start a real war.

Friendly contacts ceased. The U.S.S.R. became shut off from the world. The great British statesman Sir Winston Churchill described the frontier between East and West as the "Iron Curtain" in a speech at Fulton, Missouri on March 5, 1946.

The Cold War dominated world politics for many years. On one side, the United States became the leader of NATO (North Atlantic Treaty Organization), a military alliance of Western nations providing collective defense against the communist powers. On the other side, the U.S.S.R. led the Warsaw Pact, a military alliance of East European states that backed communism.

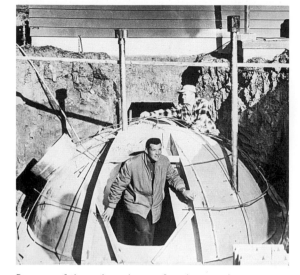

Because of the serious threat of nuclear war between East and West during the 1960s, many Americans built fallout shelters in their backyards.

BERLIN: A DIVIDED CITY

In 1945, the United States, France, and Britain took control of West Germany. The U.S.S.R. controlled East Germany. The capital, Berlin, inside East Germany, was also divided. In 1948, the Soviets closed all access to West Berlin. The Western powers brought in supplies by air, until the blockade was lifted in 1949. From 1949 to 1958, three million people escaped from East to West Berlin. In 1961, East Germany closed off this escape route by building the Berlin Wall across the city. It crossed tram lines and roads and created an area on either side known as No Man's Land.

▲ The Berlin Wall, built in 1961 to divide East and West Berlin, finally "fell" in November 1989.

▶ By 1949, most European states had joined rival alliances. Warsaw Pact countries supported the U.S.S.R. Members of NATO backed the U.S.A.

NATO countries in Europe

Warsaw Pact countries

FINLAND
NORWAY
SWEDEN
NETHERLANDS
IRELAND
DENMARK
U.S.S.R.
GREAT BRITAIN
EAST GERMANY
BELGIUM
WEST GERMANY
POLAND
LUXEMBOURG
CZECHOSLOVAKIA
SWITZERLAND
FRANCE
AUSTRIA
HUNGARY
ROMANIA
PORTUGAL
YUGOSLAVIA
SPAIN
ITALY
BULGARIA
ALBANIA
TURKEY
GREECE

CUBAN MISSILE CRISIS

Although the United States and the U.S.S.R. never fought, they came close. The world held its breath for a week in October 1962. President John F. Kennedy received Air Force photographs showing that the Soviet Union was building missile launch sites in Cuba. From there, the nuclear missiles could reach and destroy many U.S. cities. On October 22, the president ordered a naval blockade of Cuba. The United States made plans to invade Cuba, and the world braced itself for nuclear war. Finally, on October 28, Nikita Khrushchev, the Soviet leader, backed down and agreed to remove the missiles and destroy the Cuban launch sites. The crisis was over.

THE END OF THE COLD WAR

The friendly relationship between the American president Ronald Reagan and the Soviet leader Mikhail Gorbachev helped reduce Cold War tensions. By 1987, they had agreed to abolish medium-range nuclear missiles. In 1989, Gorbachev allowed the communist countries of Eastern Europe to elect democratic governments. And in 1991, the Soviet Union broke up into 15 republics. The Cold War was over. On March 12, 1999, Hungary, Poland, and the Czech Republic joined NATO. The joining ceremony was held at the Harry S. Truman Library in Independence, Missouri.

◄ Francis Gary Powers (1929–1977) was the pilot of an American U-2 spy plane that was shot down over Russian territory in 1960. He was released in exchange for the imprisoned Soviet spymaster Rudolf Abel (1903–1971).

▼ Czech students tried to stop Soviet tanks in Prague, in August 1968. The U.S.S.R. feared that independent actions by Warsaw Pact members might weaken its power, so it moved into Czechoslovakia.

► During the Cold War many groups of people, such as the Peace Pledge Union, were formed to try and influence governments and stop the spread of nuclear weapons.

◄ Here, supporters of the Campaign for Nuclear Disarmament (CND) march through London in 1983 to demonstrate against the deployment of Cruise and Trident nuclear missiles on British soil.

IN SPACE 1957–PRESENT

The space age began in 1957 when the U.S.S.R. launched *Sputnik I*. In 2000, the first crew of the International Space Station set up home in space.

The development of German rocket technology during World War II helped scientists realize that one day it might be possible for people to travel in space. At the end of the war, both the U.S. and the U.S.S.R. obtained German rocket equipment and expertise and started work—but the U.S. was surprised when, in 1957, the Soviets sent the first artificial satellite into orbit. This triggered a "space race" between the U.S. and the U.S.S.R., with a human moon landing as the ultimate goal. Both sides felt that winning the race would increase their prestige. They also hoped that space science would help them develop new, more powerful weapons.

Soon both sides were investing enormous amounts of time and money in space science. The U.S.S.R. achieved another first in 1961, when Yuri Gagarin became the first person in space. Other notable achievements by both countries included probes sent to the Moon, Venus, and Mars, further manned flights, space walks, and the launch of communication satellites.

The *Apollo* spaceflights enabled the United States to win the space race by landing men on the Moon. Between July 1969 and

Sputnik 1 was launched by Russia on October 4, 1957. The satellite was used to broadcast a radio signal and orbited Earth for three months.

This picture shows Russian cosmonaut Yuri Gagarin (1934–1968) in the cabin of *Vostok 1*, the spacecraft in which he became the first person to orbit Earth on April 12, 1961.

In the run-up to the *Apollo* flights, the American Gemini program was designed to teach astronauts how to cope with space travel. In November 1966, "Buzz" Aldrin carried out three space walks high up over Earth.

December 1972, the U.S. successfully carried out six of these missions.

After the Cold War, the two superpowers scaled down their space programs. In 1993, they agreed to work together to develop the International Space Station—the first parts of which were launched into orbit in 1998. The ISS received its first resident crew in 2000.

MAN ON THE MOON

In 1961, President John F. Kennedy said that his scientists would send a man to the Moon by 1970. In fact, the first manned Moon landing took place on July 20, 1969. The crew of the *Apollo 11* mission consisted of Neil Armstrong, the first man to set foot on the Moon, Edwin "Buzz" Aldrin, who was the second man to walk on the lunar surface, and Michael Collins, who remained in orbit in the command and service module. Armstrong described his first step on the Moon as "one small step for a man and one giant leap for mankind."

◀ *Apollo 11* was launched from Kennedy Space Center, Florida, on July 16, 1969. The first manned landing on the Moon was just three days later.

SPACE SHUTTLES

The National Aeronautics & Space Administration (NASA) developed a reusable space vehicle, the space shuttle, which could take off like a rocket and return to Earth like a plane. The launch of the first shuttle in 1981 marked a new phase in space exploration. For 30 years, space shuttles launched and repaired satellites and carried people and cargo to and from orbiting space craft and space stations. In 2003, the U.S. shuttle fleet was grounded after the shuttle *Columbia* exploded on its return to Earth, killing everyone on board. Flights began again in 2005 with the shuttle

▲ This picture of the Santa Maria crater, on Mars's dusty, rock-strewn surface, was created from images taken by the U.S. Mars rover *Opportunity* in 2010.

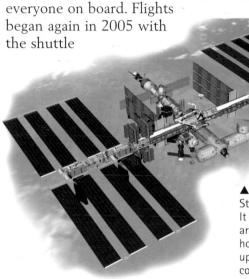

▲ The International Space Station is still being built. It is permanently in orbit around Earth, and is both a home and a workplace for up to seven astronauts and cosmonauts.

Discovery, which docked to the International Space Station. The shuttle program ended with the final flight of *Atlantis* in 2011.

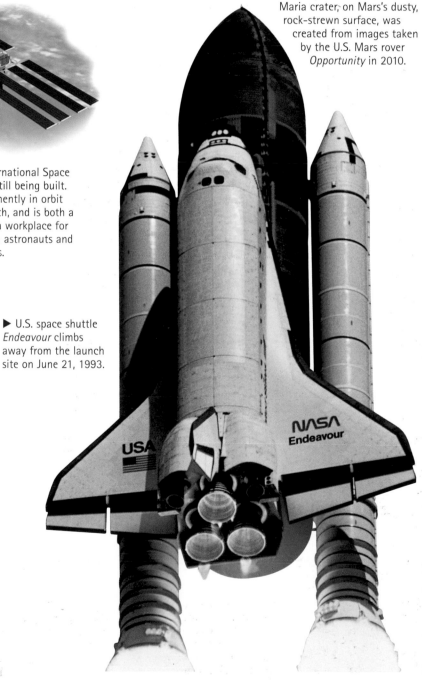

▶ U.S. space shuttle *Endeavour* climbs away from the launch site on June 21, 1993.

THE EXPLORATION OF DEEP SPACE

Unmanned space probes have flown by or landed on every planet in the solar system. Soviet probes landed on Venus in 1965 and sent back pictures in 1975. In 1977, the United States launched the two *Voyager* missions, which traveled around the solar system. Before they passed the last planet on their journey toward the stars, they transmitted valuable data and photographs.

The Hubble Space Telescope, launched in 1990, enabled scientists to produce images of objects billions of light years away, and provided information about the universe. In 2004, the U.S. rovers *Spirit* and *Opportunity* landed on Mars. Over the next eight years, they traveled over the red planet, responding to commands from Earth and sending back pictures.

CHINA 1949–PRESENT

In 1949, Mao Zedong and the Communist Party
came to power and reshaped battle-weary China.
Full political freedom has still not been achieved.

To reduce the growth rate of China's enormous population,
in 1980 the Chinese government introduced the one-child
policy, limiting families to one child each.

By the beginning of the
2000s, China had become
far removed from its
previous peasant economy.
All types of sophisticated
electronic equipment were
now being manufactured
and exported abroad.

▼ Mao Zedong sought
to solve the problem of
food shortages in China
by the creation of collective
farms. Nevertheless, China
continued to suffer periods
of extreme food shortages.

The Communist Party came to power
in China in 1949. Their leader, Mao
Zedong, became chairman of the new
People's Republic of China. Civil war and
the war with Japan had left the land poor
and many people were starving. Roads,
railroads, schools, and hospitals could not
meet the people's needs. Many in the new
government believed that they should
follow the example of the Communists in
Russia. Mao did not agree with the move
to industrialization, instead believing in a
peasant economy. He launched his Great
Leap Forward experiment in 1958, which
redistributed land to giant communes of
peasants to encourage development via
agriculture. This failed, and Mao lost much
of his influence, but in 1966, he started
the Cultural Revolution. With the help of
students and the People's Liberation Army,
he overthrew the party leaders.

Mao transformed China. Collective farms
grew basic foods, and industry produced
more iron and steel. "Barefoot doctors"
provided medical care to people in the
countryside, and children learned to read
and write. Mao wrote *The Thoughts of
Chairman Mao*. It was required reading,
and everyone carried a copy with them
wherever they went—even the simplest
peasants were able to quote from it.

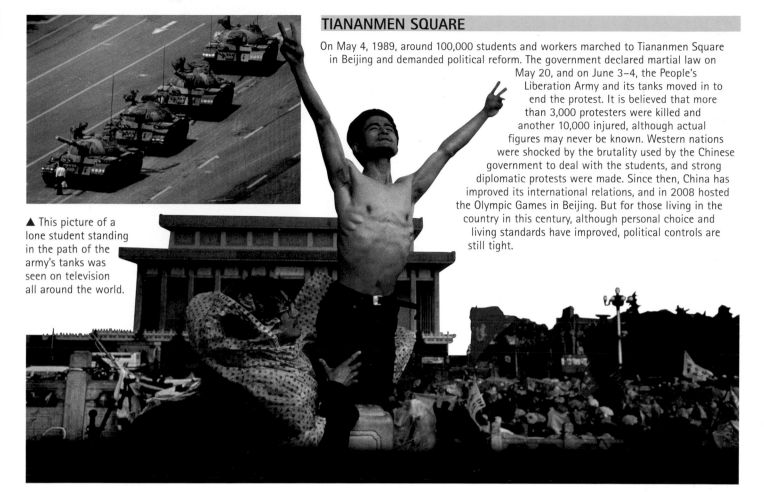

▲ This picture of a lone student standing in the path of the army's tanks was seen on television all around the world.

TIANANMEN SQUARE

On May 4, 1989, around 100,000 students and workers marched to Tiananmen Square in Beijing and demanded political reform. The government declared martial law on May 20, and on June 3–4, the People's Liberation Army and its tanks moved in to end the protest. It is believed that more than 3,000 protesters were killed and another 10,000 injured, although actual figures may never be known. Western nations were shocked by the brutality used by the Chinese government to deal with the students, and strong diplomatic protests were made. Since then, China has improved its international relations, and in 2008 hosted the Olympic Games in Beijing. But for those living in the country in this century, although personal choice and living standards have improved, political controls are still tight.

CIVIL RIGHTS

In the early 1960s, educated people were beginning to criticize communism. Mao feared opposition to his own extreme form of communism, and decided to take drastic action. During the Cultural Revolution, many of Mao's political opponents were executed, scholars were imprisoned and tortured, families were split up, and millions of people died from famine.

ECONOMIC GROWTH

After Mao's death in 1976, the Chinese government began to reform the economy by opening up to the rest of the world and encouraging foreign trade and investment. The economy grew so fast that by 2010, the gross domestic product (GDP) was ten times higher than in 1978, and the economy became the second largest in the world after the U.S. However, the country's rapid economic growth has resulted in environmental problems, especially concerning air pollution, soil erosion, energy usage, and water shortages.

POPULATION GROWTH

In 1980, the Chinese government introduced a one-child policy to try to reduce the country's population growth. The policy has been relatively successful and continues into this century, although it has resulted in problems such as a growing proportion of elderly people with fewer children to look after them.

▼ A magnificent fireworks display marked the return of Hong Kong to Chinese ownership on June 30, 1997—the official end of Britain's 99-year lease on the territory.

WORLD ECONOMY 1950 – PRESENT

The industrialized countries of the world improved their standard of living since 1950, but many poorer countries saw little or no improvement.

The OECD (Organization for Economic Cooperation and Development) was created to protect weak nations from powerful market forces and aid economic development.

This is the flag of the European Union (EU), the successor to the European Economic Community (EEC), first formed after the two Treaties of Rome in March 1957. The EU is made up of 27 member states from across Europe.

▼ Panic trading on the floor of the New York Stock Exchange in October 1987. In that year, world stock markets all suffered a dramatic fall in share prices. Roughly 20 years later the world economy suffered another major collapse.

After the end of World War II, countries such as the United States and those in Western Europe enjoyed rapid growth in their economies. After the war, there was an enormous amount of rebuilding to be done, particularly in Europe. There was full employment, and the amount people were paid, compared to what things cost to buy, steadily climbed. In other words, their standard of living rose. To a slightly lesser extent, this also applied to countries such as Australia and New Zealand, as well as Southeast Asian countries such as Hong Kong, Singapore, and Taiwan.

All this came to a sudden halt in 1973 when the price of crude oil started to increase. The Organization of Petroleum (oil) Exporting Countries (OPEC) was founded in 1960 to get the best price on world markets for its member states' oil. OPEC members include many Middle Eastern Arab states, as well as Venezuela, Algeria, Indonesia, Nigeria, and Gabon.

Between 1973 and 1974, OPEC quadrupled the price of oil, which led to a worldwide energy crisis. Poorer nations were badly hit by the rise in oil prices (by 1981, they had increased by almost 20 times), and their economies had to be supported by Western loans. In advanced nations, the energy crisis caused inflation because the rise in oil prices was passed on in the price of goods, and unemployment rose as fewer goods were exported.

COMMON MARKETS

Throughout the world neighboring countries or countries with shared economic interests have joined to form powerful associations. Some groups have also set up economic communities, known as common markets. Within them, members buy and sell at favorable rates. They also agree to protect one another from outside economic competition.

In Asia there are the Asia-Pacific Economic Cooperation Group (APEC) and the Association of Southeast Asian Nations (ASEAN). The North American Free Trade Agreement (NAFTA), originally between the United States and Canada, now also includes Mexico. The Group of Eight, or G-8, is a group of countries that meets to monitor the world economic situation. The European Union (EU) is the successor to the European Economic Community (EEC) of the 1950s. It is made up of 27 members from across Europe and forms a significant trading bloc. Many of the EU members share a single currency—the euro.

The collapse of the Soviet Union in the early 1990s meant that the former communist countries had to adapt to the new post-Soviet realities. Many of the former countries of the "Eastern Bloc" have recently accepted membership in the EU, a development that has raised tensions with Russia who tends to see these nations as part of its sphere of influence.

In 2009, the world's oil reserves amounted to more than 1.3 trillion tons, of which 746 million tons, or more than half, were to be found in the Middle East.

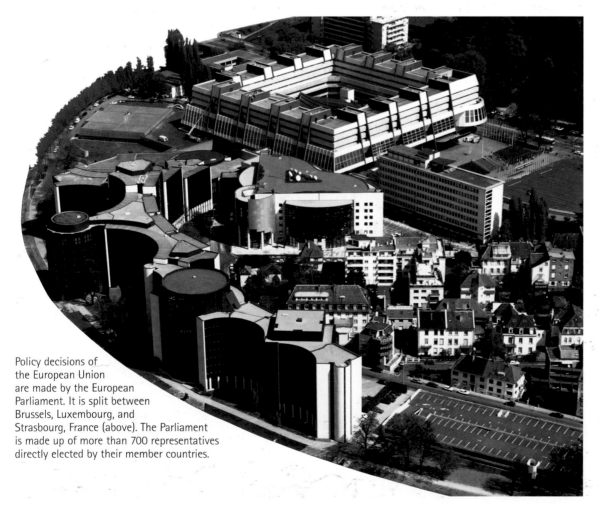

Policy decisions of the European Union are made by the European Parliament. It is split between Brussels, Luxembourg, and Strasbourg, France (above). The Parliament is made up of more than 700 representatives directly elected by their member countries.

▲ In January 2002 12 members of the European Union stopped using their own individual currencies and adopted a common currency called the euro. Now 17 countries use the common currency.

WARS IN ASIA 1950–PRESENT

Japan's defeat and the collapse of colonial rule led to fighting among political rivals. The superpowers took sides, based on economic interest or Cold War strategy.

Australian soldiers were part of the United Nations forces that, by the end of 1950, had pushed the North Koreans back as far as the border with China.

▼ Fighting between rival political groups flared up in many parts of Asia between 1946 and 1988. After Japan's defeat in World War II and the collapse of European colonial power, Asia became very unstable.

In 1950, many nations in the East had not yet recovered from Japanese invasions during World War II. People needed peace and stability, but many countries were soon at war. These wars caused further damage to people, cities, and land. Eastern countries wanted to be free of distant European powers. The old colonial masters (France, Britain, and the Netherlands) wanted to hold on to these potentially rich lands.

Fighting broke out in Vietnam and its neighbors Laos, Thailand, and Cambodia, and in Indonesia, Malaysia, Burma, and the Philippines. These wars were often complicated by political differences between rival groups seeking independence. The situation became even more dangerous when the Soviet Union, China, and the U.S. joined in, offering money, weapons, or technical advice to these rival groups.

In 1945, French colonial rule was restored to Vietnam. French Foreign Legion troops were sent to North Vietnam in 1953 to try to suppress a communist uprising.

THE KOREAN WAR

The Korean War began when communist North Korea attacked South Korea in June 1950. The United Nations quickly authorized its members to aid South Korea. The United States, along with 16 other countries, began sending troops. Within two months, North Korean troops had captured most of South Korea. In September, UN forces mounted a massive land, sea, and air assault at Inchon, near Seoul. The UN troops recaptured most of South Korea and advanced into the North. By November 1950, they had reached the North Korean border with China. Chinese troops then entered the fighting and forced the UN forces to retreat south. A cease-fire ended the war in July 1953.

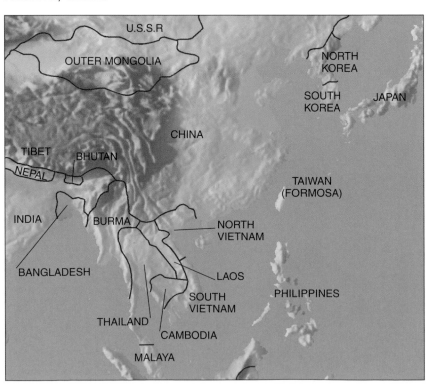

Between 1948 and 1960, British troops were sent to Malaya to fight a communist guerrilla offensive. Here, soldiers of a jungle patrol rest beneath a "basha" shelter.

444

During the war in Vietnam (1964–1975), large areas of the country were devastated. Many civilians were killed and injured. Others were made homeless, and fled as refugees to neighboring lands. Peace finally came in 1976 when Vietnam was united.

Ho-Chi Minh (1892–1969) was a founder member of the French Communist Party. As a revolutionary Vietnamese leader, he led the struggle against French colonial rule and American-supported South Vietnam.

WAR IN VIETNAM

After the French were defeated by Vietnamese communists in 1954, the country was temporarily divided into North and South. Planned elections for the country did not take place, and the communists in the North started giving aid to South Vietnamese communists, the Viet Cong, to help them overthrow the government of Ngo Dinh Diem.

In 1965, the United States sent the first troops to help the South—by 1969, there were over half a million U.S. troops in Vietnam. After Richard Nixon became president in 1969, he began to withdraw troops. A cease-fire was signed in 1973, and the remaining American soldiers returned home. During the war more than 57,000 Americans were killed or missing in action.

CIVIL WAR IN CAMBODIA

In Cambodia, a guerrilla army, the Khmer Rouge, was led by Pol Pot. They sought to overthrow the government of Lon Nol. The Khmer Rouge took over Cambodia in 1975 and Pol Pot became Prime Minister. His regime of terror was overthrown in 1979 by Vietnamese troops.

▲ After Richard Nixon (1913–1994) became president in 1969, he began to withdraw U.S. troops from Vietnam. In 1973, a cease-fire was signed and all U.S. troops were withdrawn.

◀ In Cambodia, Pol Pot (1926–1998) was the leader of the Khmer Rouge guerrillas. They fought a long civil war, beginning in 1963, and took over the country in 1975. Over the following three years, it is estimated that between two and four million people were executed or died of famine and disease.

KEY DATES	
1950	North Korean forces invade South Korea
1953	Cease-fire in Korea
1954	Vietnamese communists defeat the French
1962	Military coup in Burma ends democratic rule
1963	Civil war starts in Cambodia
1965	First U.S. troops land in Vietnam
1969	Richard Nixon becomes president
1973	All U.S. troops withdrawn from Vietnam
1975	Pol Pot takes over Cambodia
1979	Pol Pot deposed by Vietnamese forces
1993	First free elections in Cambodia for 20 years

CIVIL RIGHTS 1950–PRESENT

Civil rights are the basic freedoms and rights of people within a community. They are guaranteed by laws and customs that give everyone fair treatment.

The idea of civil rights in the West dates back to the writings of ancient Greek and Roman philosophers, and to the ideas of Judaism and Christianity. In some countries, civil rights are protected by a written constitution. In the United States and in other democratic countries, such as Britain, they consist of laws and customs built up over hundreds of years. Civil rights mean that people must be treated fairly and equally, no matter what their gender, religion, or ethnic origin. They are allowed freedom to express what they believe in speech or in the media. They also have the right to organize a political party, to have a fair trial, and to vote in elections. However, many oppressive regimes still abuse their power and ignore civil rights.

During 1989, Chinese students demonstrated in Beijing, demanding democracy in their country. The government sent in the army and thousands of students were killed.

Many rights have been won only after a long and painful struggle. During the 1950s and 1960s, Martin Luther King, Jr. led the civil rights campaign to win equality for black Americans.

Re-formed in the 1950s, the Ku Klux Klan harassed minority groups. They burned crosses to intimidate their victims.

In the early 1960s, many southern states practiced segregation. This taxi is clearly marked as being only for use by black people. Other forms of public transportation were similarly segregated.

MARTIN LUTHER KING

The Reverend Martin Luther King, Jr. (1929–1968) was a Baptist minister and the main leader of the U.S. civil rights movement of the 1950s and 1960s. On August 28, 1963, he led a march on Washington, D.C., where he gave a famous speech that began "I have a dream." His dream was of a future in which his country lived by the ideals of freedom and liberty on which it had been founded. On April 4, 1968, he was shot dead by James Earl Ray. Every year, the third Monday in January is designated a federal legal public holiday in his honor.

CIVIL RIGHTS ABUSES

In South Africa, Nelson Mandela was sent to prison in 1962 for opposing apartheid (the separation of whites and nonwhites). Many governments and people from all over the world campaigned to end apartheid by holding demonstrations. They boycotted goods from South Africa and stopped all sports links. F.W. de Klerk became president in 1989, and started to dismantle apartheid. Mandela was released in 1990, when apartheid was abolished. In 1994, he was elected as South Africa's first black president.

In 1976, Argentina was taken over by a military *junta* (ruling group). They suppressed opposition by arresting thousands of people and holding them in prison without trial. Between 20,000 and 30,000 people were never seen again by their families. They became known as *los desaparecidos*, or "the disappeared ones." Similar brutality was used by the military regime led by General Pinochet in Chile between 1973 and 1990.

PROTECTING CIVIL RIGHTS

International bodies, such as the United Nations and the European Court of Human Rights, protect civil rights. Other organizations, such as Amnesty International, campaign on behalf of people who are persecuted. However, some governments continue to ban civil rights. Dictators and single-party nations deny rights to their people because they do not want their own power threatened.

▲ In the 1970s and 1980s, Chile was ruled by a military *junta*. Many ordinary citizens were arrested, and many of those were never seen again. The Catholic Church denounced the violence against innocent people. They held religious services and vigils for people who were detained or missing.

◀ In the South African city of Johannesburg in the 1980s, many black and colored people were moved into slums and shantytowns to make more room for white people's homes.

When European settlers first arrived in Australia in the 1700s and 1800s, the Aborigines—the original inhabitants of the country—were driven off their traditional hunting grounds. Many also died from diseases brought in by the settlers. In February 2008, Australian Prime Minister Kevin Rudd finally issued an apology to the indigenous peoples for past wrongs.

447

TERRORISM 1952–PRESENT

From the 1950s, people increasingly began to use spectacular acts of violence to promote their particular political causes.

During 1981, some members of the Irish Republican Army (IRA) who were serving prison sentences in Northern Ireland for terrorist offences went on hunger strike. When one of them died, there was rioting.

▼ In 1988, an American jumbo jet was blown up by a bomb in midair over the Scottish town of Lockerbie, killing 270 people. In 2001, a Libyan spy was convicted of this terrorist act.

Some groups of people use violence (terrorism) to gain publicity and win support for a political cause. They are often called freedom fighters by their supporters. Terrorists murder and kidnap people, set off bombs, and hijack aircraft. The reasons behind terrorism are not always the same. Some terrorists want to spread their own political beliefs, while others (nationalists or liberationists) want to establish a separate state for peoples who do not have a country of their own. For example, in the Middle East, terrorists have kidnapped people and carried out bombing campaigns to draw attention to the cause of the Palestinian people, who do not have a homeland.

In Spain, the *Euzkada Ta Askatasuna* (ETA) began a terrorist campaign in the 1960s to pressurize the government into creating a separate state for the Basque people. Similarly, in Northern Ireland from the 1970s, nationalist groups such as the Irish Republican Army (IRA) escalated their terrorist campaign against British rule in the province.

In 2001, an Islamic terrorist group, called Al Qaeda, launched devastating terrorist attacks on the U.S. In 2002 and 2003, there

In April 1995, a bomb destroyed the Murrah Federal Building in Oklahoma City, and killed 168 people. The bomber, Timothy McVeigh, thought the federal government had too much control over people's lives.

were further attacks by the same group in Bali (Indonesia), Saudi Arabia, and Morocco. In 2004 there were triple the amount of serious international terrorist incidents, with 651 attacks reported. In Iraq attacks became almost routine. In July 2005, a series of coordinated suicide bomb attacks on the public transportation system hit London, England. Terrorists attacked public buildings in Delhi, India, in 2011.

▲ In March 2012, a car bomb set off by a suicide bomber in the center of Baghdad, Iraq, was one of a wave of terrorist attacks that killed at least 44 people. Since 2003, there have been many terrorist attacks on military targets and ordinary people in the country.

FAMINE IN AFRICA 1967–PRESENT

Africa has suffered periodic drought and famine since ancient times. More recently, civil war in newly independent states has only added to the misery.

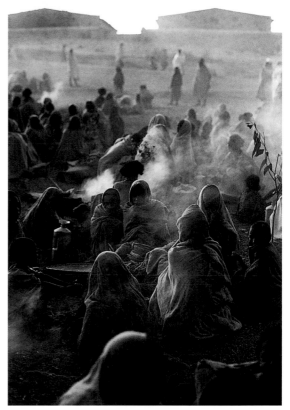

Ethiopia suffered from drought and famine for many years. Between 1977 and 2003, the combination of civil war and famine killed millions of Ethiopians.

Widespread famines have occurred periodically in most parts of sub-Saharan Africa since ancient times. Factors such as a failure of the annual rains, poor soil conditions, and low food reserves have all played a part in these tragedies. Following independence in the latter half of the 1900s, civil wars have added to the misery.

In 1985, musician Bob Geldof organized the Live Aid rock concert. They raised $70 million to help the victims of the famine in Ethiopia.

CIVIL UNREST AND FAMINE

Most of the worst famines during this period happened in countries that suffered civil unrest. In Nigeria, the people who lived in the east of the country were the Christian Ibo tribe. They were oppressed by the majority Islamic Hausa and Fulani peoples. When tens of thousands of Ibos were massacred, the Eastern Region declared its independence as the Republic of Biafra in May 1967. War continued between the two sides until January 1970. It is believed that over a million Biafrans died of starvation because the Nigerians stopped food getting through to them.

Civil strife in Mozambique in the 1980s led to the almost total collapse of health care, education, and food production. By the beginning of the 1990s, nearly a million people had been killed. Another one-and-a-half million had fled the country and were refugees.

In Somalia, civil war, violence, drought, flooding, and famine devastated the country from the early 1980s into this century.

▼ In 1994, the Democratic Republic of the Congo (formerly Zaire) was itself experiencing civil violence when the arrival of hundreds of thousands of refugees from the civil war and genocide in neighboring Rwanda prompted massive aid from international relief agencies. Often, war and civil strife have made it very dangerous for foreign aid workers to provide aid.

In Ethiopia, the combination of the withdrawal of aid from the U.S.S.R., drought, and a civil war in the 1970s and 1980s led to millions of people dying from famine. Through the Western media, people all around the world became aware of the catastrophe. International relief charities, such as the Red Cross, the Live Aid rock concert of 1985, and individual governments all provided vast amounts of aid for the victims.

▲ Foreign aid does more than supply food in emergencies or crises. Here, we see the results of a project to provide clean water for a community in Kenya. Projects like this help to improve the health of local people.

NEW NATIONS 1950–PRESENT

Following centuries of rule by colonial powers, many nations have gained independence—often achieved through war and terrorism as well as peaceful means.

Independence was granted to Ghana (formerly the Gold Coast) by Britain in 1957. The Duchess of Kent represented the British Queen at the ceremony in the capital, Accra. In the following years, the country suffered from government corruption and military coups.

After World War II, the leaders of many European-ruled colonial countries felt the growing pressure from their people for independence from foreign control. The days of colonial rule were rapidly coming to an end. During the 1950s and 1960s, many peoples in Africa and Southeast Asia fought for their independence. Their people believed that they had a right to own and control their own countries. Many of these independence movements were led by men and women of courage and vision. They were frequently imprisoned before they eventually gained power.

Often, these countries used military force to win independence from colonial rule. European nations would not give up their power, and so groups like the Mau Mau in Kenya launched terrorist campaigns. In some states, as in Egypt in 1952–1953, independence was achieved only after the army took control.

The British gained control of Malaya in 1786. In September 1963, Malaya, Singapore, Sarawak, and Sabah joined together to create the independent nation of Malaysia. To end tensions, Singapore withdrew in 1965.

RANDOM BORDERS

In Africa, numerous civil wars sprang up as the European powers gradually withdrew. One of the most common reasons for this was that when the land had been previously divided between the European settlers, little regard was shown for existing tribal boundaries. When the Europeans left, several tribes were often left to dispute the ownership and control of a country. When this happened in Nigeria, with the declaration of an independent Biafran state in 1967, millions of people died of starvation.

Britain granted full independence to Nigeria in 1960. Since then, the country, one of the largest in Africa and an important oil producer, has suffered from a major civil war, economic problems, and military rule.

After civil war in Sudan, the country split in two. In a referendum in 2011, the people of South Sudan voted for the split and South Sudan gained independence as a new country.

STRUGGLE FOR SURVIVAL

Today, nearly all former colonies are independent. Some maintain ties—as members of the Commonwealth, for example. Others have formed new alliances, such as the Organization for African Unity (OAU). However, many former colonies are still economically dependent. World trade is controlled by Europe, the United States, and Japan, and by multinational companies. It is hard for new nations not to fall into debt.

EASTERN EUROPE

The end of the Cold War, and the collapse of the U.S.S.R. at the end of the 1980s, led to the countries around Russia's borders gaining their freedom from Soviet rule. In Czechoslovakia free elections were held in 1990 for the first time since 1946. At the beginning of 1993, Czechoslovakia ceased to exist and was replaced by the separate states of the Czech Republic and Slovakia.

In 1991 and 1992, Yugoslavia broke up as the states of Slovenia, Bosnia & Herzegovina, Macedonia, and Croatia declared independence. Thousands of people were killed in the devastating civil wars that followed. In 2003, Serbia & Montenegro replaced Yugoslavia on the map. In 2006, this loose union broke apart to become independent nations, and in 2008, Kosovo also declared its independence from Serbia.

Turkmenistan, on the eastern coast of the Caspian Sea, became a republic of the U.S.S.R. in 1925. Following the breakup of the Soviet Union in 1991, this mainly Muslim country declared independence and joined the Commonwealth of Independent States (CIS), consisting of 12 of the 15 former Soviet republics.

▶ East Timor was the first new nation of the 2000s. It was recognized as independent in 2002.

▲ After the breakup of the Soviet Union in 1991, the Muslim state of Uzbekistan became independent and joined the Commonwealth of Independent States (CIS). Food shortages in 1992 led to civil unrest, and riots in the capital, Tashkent.

◀ Bosnia & Herzegovina became part of what was to be known as Yugoslavia at the end of World War I. Nationalist feeling grew after the death of President Tito in 1980. Independence was declared in 1992, against the wishes of the Serbian population, and a bitter civil war broke out. Thousands of people died, while others lost their homes and became refugees. In Bosnia & Herzegovina, the capital city of Sarajevo was under siege between 1992 and 1995, during which thousands of its citizens lost their lives.

451

MIDDLE EASTERN WARS 1956–PRESENT

Following the formation of the State of Israel in 1948, there have been many tensions in the Middle East that have led to bitter disputes and even war.

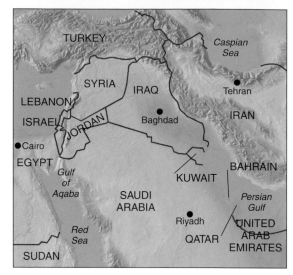

There have been many conflicts in the Middle East between Israeli, Palestinian, and Arab peoples, especially since 1948. Some areas of territory are still in dispute.

The Six-Day War took place between June 5–10, 1967. In a surprise attack, Israeli bombers destroyed Egyptian planes, and then sent in troops to capture the Egyptian soldiers left in Sinai.

▼ The Yom Kippur War started in 1973 when Egypt and Syria launched a surprise attack on Israel after it refused to give up land captured during the Six-Day War.

The lands around Jerusalem have long been believed by the Jewish people to be their traditional home. After World War II, many Jewish refugees settled in Palestine, although the area was occupied by Arab peoples. The State of Israel was formed in 1948, and fighting broke out with neighboring Arab countries and continued on and off for many years.

In 1956, Egypt took over control of the Suez Canal, which was owned by Britain and France. Because it felt threatened, Israel invaded Egyptian territory in the Sinai, and Britain and France attacked the canal area. There was international disapproval, and the United States and U.S.S.R. both called for a cease-fire. UN troops moved in to keep the peace after the withdrawal of Israeli, British, and French troops.

Tensions continued to grow in the 1960s between Israel and the Arab countries of Egypt, Jordan, and Syria. They were aided by several other Arab countries including Iraq, Kuwait, Saudi Arabia, Algeria, and Sudan. Both sides were hostile and unwilling to negotiate their differences. Both sides were also busy getting their troops ready for a possible armed conflict. In May 1967, Egypt closed the Gulf of Aqaba to Israeli shipping.

In 1980, Iraq invaded Iran. The two countries fought a long and bitter war. It did not end until August 1988, and cost the lives of over a million soldiers, and almost two million wounded.

SIX-DAY WAR

In June 1967, the Israeli air force launched a surprise air attack on the Arab forces' air bases, which took them completely out of action. They then swiftly moved their army to occupy the Gaza Strip and parts of the Sinai. They also pushed their border with Jordan back and captured the Golan Heights from Syria.

IRAQI AGRESSION

In 1979, the Shah of Iran was deposed and replaced by Islamic fundamentalist Shiite Muslims led by the Ayatollah Khomeini. Tension between Iran and Iraq finally resulted in Iraq's invasion of the oil-rich Iranian territory of Khuzistan in 1980. Iraq feared the power of the new Iranian government set up by the Ayatollah Khomeini. When the war ended in 1988, neither country had made any gains but the cost was enormous—over a million dead, and nearly two million injured.

Rivalries within the Arab world have often been caused by the region's oil deposits. In 1990, Iraq invaded Kuwait to improve its sea access. The UN Security Council demanded that Iraq immediately withdraw its troops. When Saddam Hussein refused, a multinational force led by the United States forced him to withdraw. Retreating Iraqis caused huge ecological damage because they set fire to most of Kuwait's oil wells.

In 2003, concerned that Iraq was developing weapons of mass destruction, a U.S.-led coalition invaded Iraq and destroyed Saddam Hussein's regime. The invasion was followed by the eight-year Iraq War, in which occupation forces faced violent resistance. The coalition forces started to withdraw from Iraq in 2007 and completed their withdrawal in 2011.

Saddam Hussein (1937–2006) was the leader of Iraq from 1979–2003. He fought a costly war against Iran (1980–1988) and invaded Kuwait in August 1990. In 2003 a U.S.-led military campaign overthrew him. He was executed in 2006.

▼ A U.S.-led coalition invaded Iraq in 2003. In December of that year, U.S. forces mounted an operation that captured Saddam Hussein, who had been hiding at a farm near his home town.

KEY DATES	
1948	Independent State of Israel declared; fighting with Arab neighbors erupts
1956	Suez Crisis
1964	Palestinian Liberation Organization (PLO) founded in Lebanon
1967	Six-Day War between Israel and Egypt
1973	Yom Kippur War in Israel
1979	Shah of Iran deposed
1980	Iraq invades Iran
1988	Iran-Iraq War ends
1990	Iraq invades Kuwait
1991	Iraq forced out of Kuwait
2003–2011	Saddam Hussein overthrown; Iraq War

SCIENTIFIC REVOLUTION 1950–PRESENT

The second half of the 1900s was a period of rapid development in science and technology. The arrival of the computer age revolutionized people's lives.

Scientists and business people were able to develop the discoveries made earlier in the century and put them to practical use. Industry and business realized that there were enormous financial benefits to be made by working with universities and other academic centers and a great deal of important research was done in partnership between the two.

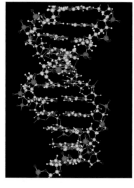

Since lasers were invented in the early 1960s, they have been used for a wide range of tasks, including eye surgery, construction work, mapping, and weapon guidance systems.

The silicon chip microprocessor, developed in the United States in 1971, caused a technological revolution. The chips were printed with tiny electronic circuits so that computers could process and store information.

ELECTRONICS

The most important breakthrough was the silicon chip, a tiny electronic component that could be cheaply mass-produced. It replaced old, bulky, and fragile pieces of equipment, and allowed much smaller, but more powerful, electronic machines to be built. Microprocessors—complex circuits fitted on a single chip—became widely used in all electrical devices ranging from computers and space rockets to robots and telephones. The silicon chip changed life radically in the late 1900s.

▲ The double helix of DNA was discovered by Crick and Watson in 1953. It carries the blueprint for all of an organism's cells, along with all the instructions that control their activities. This discovery helped scientists understand the cause of many diseases.

▶ By 1990, repetitive tasks, such as the assembly line manufacture of cars, was being done by computer-controlled robots. This meant greater efficiency for industry, but reduced the human workforce.

THE COMPUTER AGE

The developments in electronics also led to a revolution in communications. Copy and fax machines meant that office workers could handle vast amounts of information more quickly than ever before. They could also communicate rapidly with other people around the world. As the means of communications improved, information became more freely available. By the end of the 1900s, anyone with a personal computer and a telephone line could contact millions of other people around the world in an instant using the Internet.

In industry, electronics also brought about a new industrial revolution. By the 1990s, most aspects of the manufacturing process in a wide range of industries were computer controlled. Repetitive tasks on assembly lines were carried out by electronic machines or robots. Stock control, distribution, and administrative systems also came under the control of computer technology.

MEDICAL BREAKTHROUGHS

First developed in the 1960s, lasers were used in surgery to burn away diseased tissue and perform delicate eye operations. In the 1950s, American and British scientists discovered the structure of DNA, the basic building blocks from which living cells are made. This knowledge led eventually to the production of new drugs by genetic engineering, which helped cure serious diseases. The discovery of DNA means that many genetic illnesses, passed down through families, will be curable.

Genetic engineering also raised the possibility of creating new or improved strains of plants and animals, resistant to disease. This technology has helped to feed people in poorer countries by increasing the amount that the land can support.

◄ The Hubble Space Telescope was launched into orbit by the U.S. space shuttle *Discovery* in April 1990. It allowed scientists to capture images of objects billions of light years away in space.

▲ The first communication satellite was launced in 1960. The introduction, in 1964, of geosynchronous satellites, which remain over the same place on Earth, meant that any two places on Earth could be linked almost instantly.

THE WORLD WIDE WEB

The World Wide Web (WWW) was invented in 1990, so that users could "surf" the Internet quickly and easily. By clicking on the screen with a mouse, users can move between pages of information located on a vast network of computers around the world. Each page has links that lead to further pages.

▼ Search engines greatly speed up the process of finding Web pages and specific pieces of information on the Internet.

▼ The Web allows people to watch live video clips of a current U.S. space mission.

▲ Many goods and services can be ordered and paid for over the Internet.

► Using e-mail, people can send messages and pictures to each other across the world within minutes.

◄ Information on sports, movies, museums, and many other types of entertainment can be found on the Internet.

THE ENVIRONMENT 1950–PRESENT

Unlike any other species on Earth, humankind has the power to destroy the world. People only recently grasped that their environment was being threatened.

In the latter half of the 1900s, people began to realize that Earth was in danger, threatened with pollution and overexploitation from ignorance and greed. At first, only a few naturalists, like Rachel Carson, dared to speak up. Her book *Silent Spring* caused a sensation when it was published in 1962. It showed how widespread the damage was when pesticides were overused, and led to the banning of DDT (an insecticide) in the United States and many other countries.

Then, pressure groups such as Greenpeace and Friends of the Earth also began to campaign. It slowly became clear that the environment had been seriously damaged.

The oceans in many parts of the world have been overfished, and in many cases scientists believe that for stocks to return to their previous levels, fishing would have to stop completely for between five and ten years. Car exhausts and factories pump fumes into the air. Some of these gases mix with clouds to form acid rain, which kills plants. In many cities, like Los Angeles, the air quality is so poor that smog forms over them. Continual exposure to smog causes serious breathing problems and premature death.

On the night of March 24, 1989, the *Exxon Valdez*, a 985-ft. (300-m) oil tanker, ran aground in Prince William Sound, Alaska. The ship leaked over 35,000 tons of toxic petroleum over the next two days and was the biggest oil spill in American history. It destroyed much wildlife and required a major cleanup operation.

▼ Cities such as São Paulo in Brazil suffer from dangerous levels of air pollution from motor vehicles and industry.

Hundreds of oil-well fires were lit by Iraqi troops retreating from Kuwait in 1991, causing widespread pollution in the desert. It took a year to extinguish them.

PROTECTING THE ENVIRONMENT

In the 1970s, British scientists working in Antarctica discovered that the ozone layer above them was becoming thinner. The ozone layer is vital to all life on Earth because it blocks much of the sun's harmful ultraviolet radiation. It was discovered that the protective barrier was being seriously damaged by the release of chemicals called CFCs. They were used in refrigeration and as a propellant for aerosols. These chemicals have now been banned in many countries.

By the 1980s, some governments had passed laws to protect the environment, but in the 2000s, scientists concerned with global warming believed that these goals to protect our planet were becoming more urgent. At first, change was slow to take effect, because people did not believe that our planet really is in danger. New studies are being conducted and information is being collected by scientists that prove that the threat is real.

It took environmental disasters like accidents at nuclear reactors in the United States and the U.S.S.R., explosions at chemical plants in Italy and India, and oil spills at sea to show people that new technology could be deadly.

Public opinion gradually forced many governments to take action and to reduce pollution. Laws were passed to protect the environment and encourage conservation and recycling.

▲ Huge tracts of the tropical rain forests in South America were being destroyed so that local farmers could graze cattle.

In the poorer countries of the world, however, people's only income still comes from farming or forestry, which often damage the land. Their governments do not like being told by the developed world to slow their growth to reduce pollution.

▲ In 1900 the world's population was around one billion. By 2011, it had risen to seven billion. In the year 2025, more than eight billion people will be living on Earth.

RENEWABLE ENERGY

Most of the world's energy is produced by burning coal, oil, or gas. These fuels are known as fossil fuels, and there is a limited supply of them to be taken from Earth. Many countries are developing renewable energy technologies, which use the energy from moving water, sunlight, and wind. These are nonpolluting sources that will not run out.

▼ Nonpolluting wind turbines are built on exposed sites where wind power is used to generate electricity. They are not perfect and can cause significant noise pollution.

► Solar power uses energy from sunlight to provide a clean, nonpolluting source of energy.

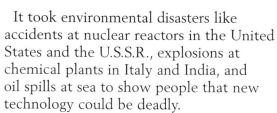

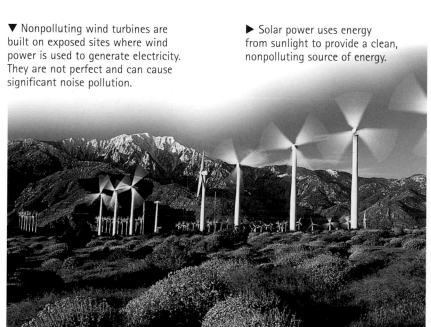

ASIAN "TIGER" ECONOMIES 1970–PRESENT

With the help of Western aid, economic growth in the countries of Southeast Asia was very rapid. It soon outstripped that of Europe and the United States.

Japan is one of the world's largest producers of electronic and other high-tech goods, motor vehicles, and steel. Japanese factories use advanced equipment to produce goods for export to the rest of the world.

In Japan, government and business had to rebuild their economy after World War II. They took a different approach than China and planned a complete industrial redevelopment of their country and rapid capitalist growth. The United States had occupied Japan and encouraged it to move toward a democracy. They also helped Japan financially, and after the war, the United States was providing money at the rate of more than ten million dollars a week. The Japanese brought in industrial and land reforms and greatly improved the education system for their children. Free elections were held, and women were not only allowed to vote for the first time, but some were also elected to the Japanese parliament. In the 1970s and 1980s, Japan's economic growth was one of the most rapid in the world.

Along with other stock markets around the world, the Tokyo Stock Market saw panic selling in October 1987. In one day it traded over one billion shares.

OTHER ECONOMIES

Although it took longer to get started, by the late 1970s and 1980s, South Korea's industrialization was growing by nearly ten percent every year, far more than Western countries. Again the United States supplied aid and so did Japan. Hong Kong also became a major Southeast Asian financial trading center, attracting much outside investment.

Malaysia became a major exporter of both raw materials—oil and natural gas, rubber, palm oil, timber, and metals such as tin—and manufactured goods such as electrical machinery and semiconductors.

Singapore started to build up its industry in the 1960s. Shipping played a growing part in the economy along with the establishment of oil refineries. Singapore became a major exporter of petroleum products, rubber, and electrical goods.

By the beginning of the 1990s, economies gradually suffered from the downturn in world markets. Japan's export-led economy, worth more than half of the region's total, had been in poor shape since 1989 and over the next ten years its stock-market value fell by two thirds. This had a knock-on effect on the other countries in the region, which slowed their growth dramatically. Since 2000 Japan's economy has recovered, and in 2011 it was the third largest in the world. Its neighbors are big world economic players, too.

Built as a symbol of Malaysia's once-booming economy, the twin Petronas Towers in Kuala Lumpur are among the world's tallest office buildings at a height of 1,483 ft. (452m).

PEACEKEEPING 1950–PRESENT

In 1945, the United Nations was formed by the international community to guarantee civil liberties and to work for peace and stability on a global scale.

Fifty countries formed the United Nations after World War II. By 2011, the membership had increased to 193.

The United Nations was formed after World War II with the intention of trying to make sure that such a war could not happen again. It was established to maintain international peace and security; to develop friendly relations among nations; to achieve international cooperation in solving economic, social, and cultural problems; and to encourage respect for basic human rights and fundamental freedoms.

Delegates from 50 nations attended what was known as the United Nations Conference on International Organization in San Francisco, in April 1945. The United Nations Charter was approved in June and permanent headquarters for the organization were built in New York City.

During the 1990s, Britain used its significant naval presence to support UN peacekeeping and humanitarian missions in many parts of the world.

THE SECURITY COUNCIL

Keeping international peace is the job of the UN Security Council. The permanent members are China, France, Great Britain, the United States, and Russia, plus ten other members elected for two-year terms.

The civil war in Lebanon between Christians and a Muslim–PLO alliance during 1975–1976 caused much destruction and bloodshed. United Nations forces were sent in as a peacekeeping force.

▶ During conflicts in the former Yugoslavia in the 1990s, UN peacekeeping troops were fired on by more than one side. Here, French UN troops keep a watchful eye out for snipers in Sarajevo's notorious sniper alley. The region of Kosovo was supervised by UN peacekeeping forces from 1999–2008 as it worked toward independence.

WORLD PEACEKEEPING

The first use of a United Nations peacekeeping force was during the Korean War in 1950. They remained there until 1953, when an armistice was signed. Further deployment happened in Egypt during the Suez Crisis in 1956—UN forces supervised the withdrawal of invading British, French, and Israeli forces.

The first large-scale UN operation in Africa went into action in 1960. Belgium had granted independence to the Democratic Republic of the Congo (Zaire), but civil unrest threatened the new country. UN troops were able to provide aid as well as security. In the following years, UN peacekeeping forces were involved in many troubled areas of the world, including Cyprus, Lebanon, Somalia, and Rwanda.

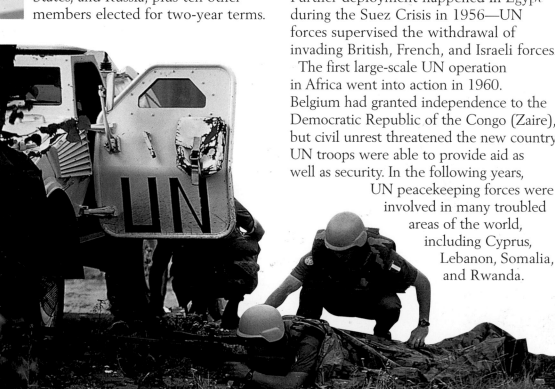

WORLD TROUBLE SPOTS 1950–PRESENT

After World War II, border disputes and wars between countries continued. Sometimes the wars involved other nations with strategic and commercial interests.

The end of World War II did not result in peace for all of the peoples of the world. Border disputes and wars between countries continued. In Korea and Vietnam, wars involved other nations, such as the United States, the U.S.S.R., and China. In other places, the superpowers supplied weapons and finance to third parties without getting directly involved. In 1979, the U.S.S.R. moved its army into Afghanistan to fight Islamic rebels, while the United States secretly provided training, arms, and financial support to the rebel groups.

Many parts of the world have been troubled by civil wars. Families have been divided, and economies have been weakened and torn apart by famine, disease, and death. These conflicts have often happened because political boundaries between nations sometimes did not coincide with traditional geographic, cultural, linguistic, or religious frontiers.

▲ The Tamil Tigers fought for independence from Sri Lanka from the 1970s. In 2009, government forces captured the last fighters and killed their leaders.

▼ Indian soldiers inspect a captured Pakistani tank after border clashes over disputed territory in Kashmir during the Indo-Pakistani conflict of 1965.

In 1995, the UN sent a peacekeeping force to Rwanda after the death of President Habyarimana led the Hutu people to murder around half a million Tutsi people.

CONFLICT OVER KASHMIR

When the Indian subcontinent gained its independence from the British Empire in 1947, the division between Pakistan and India involved the movement of millions of people. Around three and a half million Hindus and Sikhs moved from their homes in what was about to become Pakistan. Around five million Muslims moved from India to Pakistan. Such a vast disruption caused great problems, and the ownership of the territory of Kashmir, between the two countries, soon came to be a matter of dispute. There were many border skirmishes after this partition, and India managed to take over about two thirds of the state. The dispute became of great importance to the world when it was revealed in 1998 that both countries had nuclear weapons. After more violent clashes in 2010, the Indian government said that it would be willing to give some

degree of local autonomy to the people of Kashmir, but Pakistan replied that the people of Kashmir should decide how they are governed so the dispute continues.

THE BREAKUP OF YUGOSLAVIA
Following the death of President Tito in 1980, Yugoslavia was soon split apart by its many ethnic and religious peoples demanding independence. Macedonia, Croatia, Slovenia, and Bosnia & Herzegovina all declared their independence from Yugoslavia in 1991 and 1992. The Serbs declared war, and fighting in Croatia lasted for seven months. In Bosnia, Muslims, Croats, and Serbs all fought each other. Thousands of Muslims were killed by the Serbs in what was called "ethnic cleansing." In 1999 NATO, the Western military alliance, resorted to military force in an attempt to protect Albanians living in Kosovo.

ISRAEL AND PALESTINE
The conflict over Palestine continues to be a major trouble spot. Israel occupied the West Bank and Gaza after conquering them in the Six Day War in 1967. After a series of Palestinian uprisings against Israeli occupation, called the "Intifadah," Israel pulled out of Gaza, and forced some Jewish settlers to be uprooted. It has annexed much of the territory of the West Bank into the Jersualem city limits and more recently has built a huge wall, which it calls a "Security Barrier," to prevent Palestinians from entering Israel and committing acts of terrorism. The wall has cut many Palestinians off from their land and makes their lives even more difficult.

THE FIGHT FOR FREEDOM
Groups such as the Basques in Spain, the Shan peoples in Burma (Myanmar), and the Eritreans in Ethiopia felt trapped within a larger state. In Northern Ireland, the Protestant majority wanted to remain part of the U.K. but a Catholic community wanted to unify the whole island. The "troubles," as this situation became known, resulted in many deaths. The collapse of the U.S.S.R. also meant that many peoples had to re-establish their national identity. At the start of the 2000s, many of the world's people still sought justice and freedom.

▲ Bosnia declared its independence from Yugoslavia in 1992, against the wishes of the local Serb population. A bloody civil war broke out between the many different ethnic and religious groups in the country.

◀ Soviet forces entered Afghanistan in 1979 in support of the left-wing government. During the 1980s, Islamic Mujiahideen rebels, armed by the West, fought a guerilla campaign—forcing Soviet forces to withdraw in 1989—and the rebels overthrew the government.

▲ Although the war between North and South Korea ended in 1953, the border between the two countries is still heavily guarded. Both countries still view each other with suspicion.

◀ The "Security Barrier" is a long barrier of fences and high concrete walls that separates Israel from the West Bank. Controversially, some West Bank land is on the Israel side of the barrier, and it makes it difficult for Palestinians living nearby to work and travel freely.

461

SOUTH AFRICA 1990–PRESENT

South Africa was the last bastion of imperialist, white minority rule in Africa. The release of Nelson Mandela from prison in 1990 signaled the end of apartheid.

Frederick W. de Klerk (1936–) became president of South Africa in 1989, after P. W. Botha resigned because of his health. He worked toward ending apartheid.

▲ Nelson Rolihlahla Mandela (1918–) shared the Nobel Peace Prize with F. W. de Klerk in 1993 for their work in ending apartheid. Following free elections in 1994, he became the first black president of South Africa in 1994.

▶ Under apartheid, many black South Africans were moved out of cities and forced to live in shabby and crowded conditions in shantytowns on the outskirts. Their movement was severely restricted.

Apartheid, the separation of people according to their color or race, was started by the Boers in South Africa at the beginning of the 1900s. It separated the people of South Africa into whites, black Africans, and "coloreds"—people of mixed race. People of Indian origin later became the fourth group. The African National Congress (ANC) was formed in 1912 to fight these repressive laws.

The South African, white-dominated government passed a series of harsh laws to try to suppress opposition. In 1960, it made all black political parties illegal after the violent antiapartheid riots at Sharpeville. In the mid-1970s, the government relaxed its controls a little and started to allow some unions. In the mid-1980s, the government allowed coloreds into Parliament, but not black people.

The ANC and other political parties wanted a true democracy in which everyone had a vote, regardless of their color or race. P. W. Botha, president of South Africa from 1978, was the first white leader to want reform.

As Archbishop of Cape Town and head of the Anglican Church in South Africa, Desmond Tutu won the Nobel Peace Prize for his fight against apartheid in 1984.

THE REFORMER: F. W. DE KLERK

Although Botha had made some changes to make life fairer for blacks, these did not made any radical difference. His health failed him, and he resigned in 1989. A reformer, F. W. de Klerk, then became president, and in 1990, ended the ban on black people's political parties, including the ANC. In order to show he really wanted change, he also had many black political prisoners released from prison. One of these was Nelson Mandela, who had been in prison since 1964. De Klerk had regular meetings with him, both while he was in prison, and after his release.

THE END OF APARTHEID

Nelson Mandela became the leader of the ANC. He campaigned for the civil rights of his people, but he also argued strongly for a peaceful settlement. By working closely with de Klerk, it was possible for both white and black people to work for change. In 1992, de Klerk organized a whites-only referendum, asking them whether they would like to end apartheid. Two thirds of the voters were in favor of ending apartheid.

After a great deal of negotiation, the first free election, in which black people could also vote, was held in South Africa, in April 1994. The ANC won a decisive victory, and Nelson Mandela became the first black president of South Africa when de Klerk handed over power to him in May. Although the ANC now formed a government, de Klerk stayed on as one of two vice presidents.

A great victory for equality had been won, and since the 1990s, South Africa has made real progress in both political equality and economic stability. However, the new democracy still faced enormous problems, which would take many years to improve. The first part of the 2000s saw rising crime rates, ethnic tensions, and a huge gap between the rich and the poor in terms of housing and education. The rise of the AIDS pandemic continued to have a major impact on the nation's health.

The modern city of Johannesburg is the financial center of South Africa and lies in the area known as Witwatersrand, at the heart of the gold-mining area.

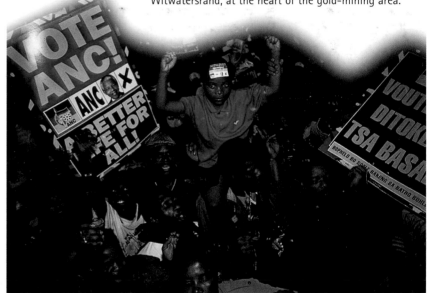

▲ Supporters of Nelson Mandela celebrate the triumph of the African National Congress after the first free elections in South Africa, in 1994. The ANC was the clear winner, and Nelson Mandela became president. He led the country until he retired in 1999.

◄ Following the end of apartheid, some white South African farmers were concerned about their property. They thought that the huge farms that they lived on would be taken away from them by the government and given to black farmers in land redistribution.

WAR ON TERROR

The early years of the 21st century saw an increase in global terrorism, with attacks on Western countries and citizens by Islamic fundamentalists.

Firefighters struggle to recover survivors after two hijacked airplanes were crashed into the twin towers of the World Trade Center in New York City on September 11, 2001.

A statue of Saddam Hussein is pulled down after U.S.-led forces overthrew the Iraqi leader's military regime in April 2003.

On September 11, 2001, members of an Islamic militant group called Al Qaeda hijacked four airplanes. Two of the planes were crashed into the World Trade Center, another into the Pentagon, and the fourth in a field in Pennsylvania. In total, around 3,000 people died.

The world responded with shock and outrage to these terrorist attacks, and the U.S. government pledged to find those responsible. The president at the time, George W. Bush, with the support of other countries, launched a "war on terror." Hundreds of suspected terrorists were arrested in more than 50 countries and several countries changed their laws to enable the arrest of alleged terrorists.

TERRORIST NETWORK
Al Qaeda was set up by the Islamic militant Osama Bin Laden. His terrorist network opposed the U.S.'s Middle Eastern policies and support for Israel. Bin Laden had already been linked to other terrorist attacks—a bomb in the World Trade Center in 1993, attacks on U.S. embassies in East Africa in 1998, and on a U.S. warship in 2000.

Bin Laden was believed to be hiding in Afghanistan. This Asian country was run by a fundamentalist Islamic regime called the Taliban. In October 2001, a U.S.-led coalition invaded Afghanistan in order to find Bin Laden and close down Al Qaeda training camps. The Taliban regime was overthrown, but it took until May 2011 to find Bin Laden. He was killed by a small U.S. force transported by helicopters to the compound in Pakistan, in which he was hiding.

WAR IN IRAQ
In January 2002, President Bush described Iran, Iraq, and North Korea as an "axis of evil." He argued that these countries were dangerous because they were developing nuclear, biological, and chemical weapons.

UN weapon inspectors had been monitoring the development of weapons of mass destruction in Iraq since the Gulf War in 1991. By 2003, the U.S. and Great Britain were calling on the UN to consent to military action against Iraq, opposed by France, Russia, and Germany. They wanted to destroy the chemical weapons that Iraq's leader, Saddam Hussein, was believed to be holding. The UN Security Council was divided over what action to take and eventually, the U.S., Great Britain, and other nations invaded Iraq without UN backing. Iraq's military regime was overthrown in April 2003, and Hussein was captured on December 13, 2003. He was executed in December 2006.

A WORLD UNDER THREAT
Since September 11, 2001, Al Qaeda has been blamed for more attacks in Jordan, Kenya, Saudi Arabia, Indonesia, Turkey, Great Britain, Israel, and Algeria. Depsite Bin Laden's death, Al Qaeda is believed to be plotting more terrorist attacks, and security in cities and airports around the world continues to be on high alert as people live with the threat of terrorism.

READY
REFERENCE

40,000 B.C.–PRESENT DAY

READY REFERENCE

ANCIENT EGYPTIAN DYNASTIES

PERIOD	DYNASTY	DATES (B.C.)	PRINCIPAL PHARAOHS
Early Dynastic	1–3	c.2925–2575	Menes (Aha)
			Zoser (Djoser)
Old Kingdom	4–7/8	c.2575–2130	Khufu (Cheops)
First Intermediate Period	9–11	c.2130–2040	
Middle Kingdom	11–14	c.2040–1600	Mentuhotep II
Second Intermediate Period	15–17	1630–1540	Hyksos kings rule Lower Egypt
			Ahmose reunites Upper and
			Lower Egypt
New Kingdom	18–20	1550–1070	Amenhotep I–III
			Thutmose I–IV
			Queen Hatshepsut
			Akhenaten (Amenhotep IV)
			Tutankhamen
			Ramses I–XI
Third Intermediate Period	21–25	1070–656	Sheshonq I
			Rule of Nubians
Late Period	25–31	664–332	Psammatichus I
			Rule of Persians (D. 27 and 31)
			Nectanebo II
			Conquest of Alexander the Great

CHINESE DYNASTIES

DYNASTY	DATE	DETAILS
Xia	c.2200–1766 B.C.	
Shang	1766–1122 B.C.	
Zhou	1122–221 B.C.	
Qin	221–206 B.C.	Shi Huangdi, first emperor of unified China
Early Han	202 B.C.–A.D. 9	Emperor Wu Di also rules Korea and southern China
Hsin	A.D. 9–25	Wang Mang takes power
Later Han	25–220	Han rule restored
The Three Kingdoms	220–280	China breaks into three kingdoms—the Wei, Shu, and Wu
Western Jin	265–317	
Eastern Jin	317–420	
Southern dynasties	420–589	
Sui	589–618	China reunified
Tang	618–907	Golden age of culture; includes reign of Emperor Taizong
The five dynasties and ten kingdoms	907–960	Period of civil wars
Liao	907–1125	Northeastern China ruled by Mongol Khitans
Song	960–1279	Dynasty rules parts of China only
Northern Song	960–1127	
Western Xia	990–1227	
Chin	1115–1234	
Southern Song	1127–1279	
Yuan (Mongol)	1279–1368	All of China ruled by the Mongols, led by Kublai Khan
Ming	1368–1644	Reestablishment of a native Chinese dynasty
Qing (Manchu)	1644–1911	
Republic of China	1911–1949	Government set up under Sun Yat-sen, followed by disunity and the warlord era
People's Republic of China	1949–	Mao Zedong is first chairman of the Communist Party

ROMAN RULERS

KINGS OF ROME

Romulus	753–716 B.C.	Tarquinios Priscus	616–579
Numa Pompilius	716–673 B.C.	Servius Tullius	579–534
Tullus Hostilius	673–640 B.C.	Tarquinius Superbus	534–509
Ancus Martius	640–616 B.C.		

THE REPUBLIC OF ROME   509–27 B.C.

Dictatorship of Sulla	82–78 B.C.	Dictatorship of Julius Caesar	45–44
First Triumvirate	60–53 B.C.	Second Triumvirate	43–27
(Julius Caesar, Pompey, and Crassus)		(Octavian, Mark Anthony, and Marcus	
Dictatorship of Pompey	52–47 B.C.	Lepidus)	

EMPERORS OF THE ROMAN EMPIRE

Augustus (previously Octavian)	27 B.C.–A.D. 14	Gallus and Hostilianus (Volusianus)	251–253
Tiberius I	A.D. 14–37	Aemilianus	253
Caligula (Gaius Caesar)	37–41	Valerian and Gallienus	253–260
Claudius I	41–54	Gallienus	253–268
Nero	54–68	Claudius II (Gothicus)	268–270
Galba	68–69	Quintillus	269–270
Otho	69	Aurelianus	270–275
Vitellius	69	Tacitus	275–276
Vespasian	69–79	Florianus	276
Titus	79–81	Probus	276–282
Domitian	81–96	Carus	282–283
Nerva	96–98	Carinus and Numerianus	283–284
Trajan	98–117	Diocletian (divides empire)	284–305
Hadrian	117–138	Maximilian (jointly)	286–305
Antoninus Pius	138–161	Constantius I	305–306
Marcus Aurelius	161–180	Severus	306–307
Lucius Verus (jointly)	161–169	Licinius (jointly)	308–324
Commodus	177–192	Constantine I (reunites empire)	312–337
Pertinax	193	Constantine II (jointly)	337–340
Didius Julianus	193	Constans (jointly)	337–350
Septimus Severus	193–211	Constantius II (jointly)	337–361
Caracalla	198–217	Magnentius (jointly)	350–353
Geta (jointly)	209–212	Julian (the Apostate)	361–363
Macrinus	217–218	Jovianus	363–364
Elagabulus (Heliogabalus)	218–222	Valentinian I (rules West)	364–375
Alexander Severus	222–235	Valens (rules East)	364–378
Maximinius I (the Thracian)	235–238	Gratian (rules West)	375–383
Gordian I	238	Magnus Maximus (usurper in West)	383–388
Gordian II	238	Valentinian II (rules West)	375–392
Balbinus and Pupienus Maximus	238	Eugenius (usurper in West)	392–394
Gordian III	238–244	Theodosius I (the Great)	379–395
Philip (the Arab)	244–249	(rules East, then unites East and West)	
Decius	249–251		

EMPERORS OF THE EASTERN ROMAN EMPIRE

Arcadius	395–408	Leo II	474
Theodosius II	408–450	Zeno	474–491
Marcian	450–457	Anastasius	491–518
Leo I	457–474	Justinian	527–565

EMPERORS OF THE WESTERN ROMAN EMPIRE

Honorius	395–423	Majorian	457–461
Maximus	410–411	Severus III	461–467
Constantius III	421	Anthemius	467–472
John	423–425	Olybrius	472
Valentinian III	425–455	Glycerius	473–474
Petronius Maximus	455	Julius Nepos	474–475
Avitus	455–456	Romulus Augustus	475–476

POPES

The head of the Roman Catholic Church is chosen by the cardinals of the Church. Occasionally, rival popes have been elected in opposition to the chosen pope; the rivals are known as antipopes (A.P.). There were many other popes before these; the first pope was St. Peter in A.D. 42.

Sylvester II	999	Gregory VIII	1187	Adrian VI	1522
John XVII	1003	Celestine III	1191	Clement VII	1523
John XVIII	1004	Innocent III	1198	Paul III	1534
Sergius IV	1009	Honorius III	1216	Julius III	1550
Benedict VIII	1012	Gregory IX	1227	Marcellus II	1555
Gregory (A.P.)	1012	Celestine IV	1241	Paul IV	1555
John XIX	1024	Innocent IV	1243	Pius IV	1559
Benedict IX	1032	Alexander IV	1254	St. Pius V	1566
Sylvester III	1045	Urban IV	1261	Gregory XIII	1572
Benedict IX	1045	Clement IV	1265	Sixtus V	1585
Gregory VI	1045	Blessed Gregory X	1271	Urban VII	1590
Clement II	1046	Blessed Innocent V	1276	Gregory XIV	1590
Benedict IX	1047	Adrian V	1276	Innocent IX	1591
Damasus II	1048	John XXI	1276	Clement VIII	1592
St. Leo IX	1049	Nicholas III	1277	Leo XI	1605
Victor II	1055	Martin IV	1281	Paul V	1605
Stephen IX (X)	1057	Honorius IV	1285	Gregory XV	1621
Benedict X (A.P.)	1058	Nicholas IV	1288	Urban VIII	1623
Nicholas II	1059	St. Celestine V	1294	Innocent X	1644
Alexander II	1061	Boniface VIII	1294	Alexander VII	1655
Honorius II (A.P.)	1061	Blessed Benedict XI	1303	Clement IX	1667
St. Gregory VII	1073	Clement V	1305	Clement X	1670
Clement III (A.P.)	1080	John XXII	1316	Blessed Innocent XI	1676
Blessed Victor III	1087	Nicholas V (A.P.)	1328	Alexander VIII	1689
Blessed Urban II	1088	Benedict XII	1334	Innocent XII	1691
Paschal II	1099	Clement VI	1342	Clement XI	1700
Theodoric (A.P.)	1100	Innocent VI	1352	Innocent XIII	1721
Albert (A.P.)	1102	Blessed Urban V	1362	Benedict XIII	1724
Sylvester IV (A.P.)	1105	Gregory XI	1370	Clement XII	1730
Gelasius II	1118	Urban VI	1378	Benedict XIV	1740
Gregory VIII (A.P.)	1118	Clement VII (A.P.)	1378	Clement XIII	1758
Callistus II	1119	Boniface IX	1389	Clement XIV	1769
Honorius II	1124	Benedict XIII (A.P.)	1394	Pius VI	1775
Celestine II (A.P.)	1124	Innocent VII	1404	Pius VII	1800
Innocent II	1130	Gregory XII	1406	Leo XII	1823
Anacletus II (A.P.)	1130	Alexander V (A.P.)	1409	Pius VIII	1829
Victor IV (A.P.)	1138	John XXIII	1410	Gregory XVI	1831
Celestine II	1143	Martin V	1417	Pius IX	1846
Lucius II	1144	Eugene IV	1431	Leo XIII	1878
Blessed Eugene III	1145	Felix V (A.P.)	1439	St. Pius X	1903
Anastasius IV	1153	Nicholas V	1447	Benedict XV	1914
Adrian IV	1154	Callistus III	1455	Pius XI	1922
Alexander III	1159	Pius II	1458	Pius XII	1939
Victor IV (A.P.)	1159	Paul II	1464	John XXIII	1958
Paschal III (A.P.)	1164	Sixtus IV	1471	Paul VI	1963
Callistus III (A.P.)	1168	Innocent VIII	1484	John Paul I	1978
Innocent III (A.P.)	1179	Alexander VI	1492	John Paul II	1978
Lucius III	1181	Pius III	1503	Benedict XVI	2005
Urban III	1185	Julius II	1503		
Clement III	1187	Leo X	1513		

RULERS OF ENGLAND

SAXONS

Egbert	829–839	Edred	946–955
Ethelwulf	839–858	Edwy	955–959
Ethelbald	858–860	Edgar	959–975
Ethelbert	860–865	Edward the Martyr	975–978
Ethelred I	865–871	Ethelred II, the Unready	978–1016
Alfred the Great	871–899	Sweyn Forkbeard	1013–1014
Edward the Elder	899–924	Ethelred II, the Unready (restored)	1014–1016
Athelstan	924–939	Edmund Ironside	1016
Edmund	939–946		

DANES

Canute	1016–1035	Harthacanute	1040–1042
Harold I Harefoot	1035–1040		

SAXONS

Edward the Confessor	1042–1066	Harold II	1066

HOUSE OF NORMANDY

William I, the Conqueror	1066–1087	Henry I	1100–1135
William II	1087–1100	Stephen	1135–1154

HOUSE OF PLANTAGENET

Henry II	1154–1189	Edward I	1272–1307
Richard I, the Lionheart	1189–1199	Edward II	1307–1327
John	1199–1216	Edward III	1327–1377
Henry III	1216–1272	Richard II	1377–1399

HOUSE OF LANCASTER

Henry IV	1399–1413	Henry VI	1422–1461
Henry V	1413–1422		

HOUSE OF YORK

Edward IV	1461–1483	Richard III	1483–1485
Edward V	1483		

HOUSE OF TUDOR

Henry VII	1485–1509	Mary I	1553–1558
Henry VIII	1509–1547	Elizabeth I	1558–1603
Edward VI	1547–1553		

RULERS OF SCOTLAND

Malcolm II	1005–1034	Malcolm IV	1153–1165
Duncan I	1034–1040	William the Lion	1165–1214
Macbeth (usurper)	1040–1057	Alexander II	1214–1249
Malcolm III (Cranmore)	1057–1093	Alexander III	1249–1286
Donald Bane	1093–1094	Margaret of Norway	1286–1290
Duncan II	1094	(Interregnum	1290–1291)
Donald Bane (restored)	1094–1097	John Balliol	1292–1296
Edgar	1097–1107	(Interregnum	1296–1306)
Alexander I	1107–1124	Robert I, the Bruce	1306–1329
David I	1124–1153	David II	1329–1371

HOUSE OF STUART

		James III	1460–1488
Robert II	1371–1390	James IV	1488–1513
Robert III	1390–1406	James V	1513–1542
James I	1406–1437	Mary, Queen of Scots	1542–1567
James II	1437–1460	James VI (I of Great Britain)	1567–1625

RULERS OF ENGLAND AND SCOTLAND

HOUSE OF STUART

James I	1603–1625	Charles I	1625–1649

COMMONWEALTH **1649–1653**
PROTECTORATE **1653–1660**

Oliver Cromwell	1653–1658	Richard Cromwell	1658–1659

HOUSE OF STUART

Charles II	1660–1685	William III (jointly)	1689–1702
James II	1685–1688	Anne	1702–1714
Mary II (jointly)	1689–1694		

RULERS OF GREAT BRITAIN

HOUSE OF HANOVER

George I	1714–1727	George IV	1820–1830
George II	1727–1760	William IV	1830–1837
George III	1760–1820	Victoria	1837–1901

HOUSE OF SAXE–COBURG

Edward VII	1901–1910

HOUSE OF WINDSOR

George V	1910–1936	George VI	1936–1952
Edward VIII	1936	Elizabeth II	1952–

PRIME MINISTERS OF GREAT BRITAIN

	IN OFFICE	PARTY
Sir Robert Walpole	1721–1742	Whig
Earl of Wilmington	1742–1743	Whig
Henry Pelham	1743–1754	Whig
Duke of Newcastle	1754–1756	Whig
Duke of Devonshire	1756–1757	Whig
Duke of Newcastle	1757–1762	Whig
Earl of Bute	1762–1763	Tory
George Grenville	1763–1765	Whig
Marquess of Rockingham	1765–1766	Whig
William Pitt the Elder (Earl of Chatham)	1766–1768	Whig
Duke of Grafton	1768–1770	Whig
Lord North	1770–1782	Tory
Marquess of Rockingham	1782	Whig
Earl of Shelburne	1782–1783	Whig
Duke of Portland	1783	Coalition
William Pitt the Younger	1783–1801	Tory
Henry Addington	1801–1804	Tory
William Pitt the Younger	1804–1806	Tory
Lord Grenville	1806–1807	Whig
Duke of Portland	1807–1809	Tory
Spencer Perceval	1809–1812	Tory
Earl of Liverpool	1812–1827	Tory
George Canning	1827	Tory
Viscount Goderich	1827–1828	Tory
Duke of Wellington	1828–1830	Tory
Earl Grey	1830–1834	Whig
Viscount Melbourne	1834	Whig
Sir Robert Peel	1834–1835	Tory
Viscount Melbourne	1835–1841	Whig

Sir Robert Peel	1841–1846	Tory
Lord John Russell	1846–1852	Whig
Earl of Derby	1852	Tory
Earl of Aberdeen	1852–1855	Peelite
Viscount Palmerston	1855–1858	Liberal
Earl of Derby	1858–1859	Conservative
Viscount Palmerston	1859–1865	Liberal
Earl Russell	1865–1866	Liberal
Earl of Derby	1866–1868	Conservative
Benjamin Disraeli	1868	Conservative
William Gladstone	1868–1874	Liberal
Benjamin Disraeli	1874–1880	Conservative
William Gladstone	1880–1885	Liberal
Marquess of Salisbury	1885–1886	Conservative
William Gladstone	1886	Liberal
Marquess of Salisbury	1886–1892	Conservative
William Gladstone	1892–1894	Liberal
Earl of Rosebery	1894–1895	Liberal
Marquess of Salisbury	1895–1902	Conservative
Arthur Balfour	1902–1905	Conservative
Sir Henry Campbell-Bannerman	1905–1908	Liberal
Herbert Asquith	1908–1915	Liberal
Herbert Asquith	1915–1916	Coalition
David Lloyd George	1916–1922	Coalition
Andrew Bonar Law	1922–1923	Conservative
Stanley Baldwin	1923–1924	Conservative
James Ramsay MacDonald	1924	Labour
Stanley Baldwin	1924–1929	Conservative
James Ramsay MacDonald	1929–1931	Labour
James Ramsay MacDonald	1931–1935	National Coalition
Stanley Baldwin	1935–1937	National Coalition
Neville Chamberlain	1937–1940	National Coalition
Winston Churchill	1940–1945	Coalition
Winston Churchill	1945	Conservative
Clement Atlee	1945–1951	Labour
Sir Winston Churchill	1951–1955	Conservative
Sir Anthony Eden	1955–1957	Conservative
Harold Macmillan	1957–1963	Conservative
Sir Alec Douglas-Home	1963–1964	Conservative
Harold Wilson	1964–1970	Labour
Edward Heath	1970–1974	Conservative
Sir Harold Wilson	1974–1976	Labour
James Callaghan	1976–1979	Labour
Margaret Thatcher	1979–1990	Conservative
John Major	1990–1997	Conservative
Tony Blair	1997–2007	Labour
Gordon Brown	2007–2010	Labour
David Cameron	2010–	Conservative–Liberal Democrat Coalition

HOLY ROMAN EMPERORS

Dates given are period of reign

Charlemagne	800–814	Louis II	855–875
Louis I (the Pious)	814–840	Charles II	875–877
Lothair I	843–855	Charles III	881–891

HOUSE OF SPOLETO

Guy	891–894	Lambert	894–898

CAROLINGIAN DYNASTY

Arnulf	896–899	Louis III	901–905

HOUSE OF FRANCONIA

Conrad I	911–918

CAROLINGIAN DYNASTY

Berengar	915–924		

SAXON DYNASTY

Henry I	919-936	Otto III	983–1002
Otto I, the Great	936–973	Henry II	1002–1024
Otto II	973–983		

FRANCONIAN DYNASTY

Conrad II	1024–1039	Henry V	1106–1125
Henry III	1039–1056	Lothair III, Duke of Saxony	1125–1137
Henry IV	1056–1106		

HOHENSTAUFEN DYNASTY

Conrad III	1138–1152	Otto IV of Brunswick	1198–1214
Frederick I, Barbarossa	1152–1190	Frederick II	1212–1250
Henry VI	1190–1197	Conrad IV	1250–1254
Philip of Swabia	1197–1208		

INTERREGNUM

Electors gain power	1254–1273		

TRANSITION PERIOD

Rudolf I of Hapsburg	1273–1292	Frederick of Austria (co-regent)	1314–1326
Adolf of Nassau	1292–1298	Charles IV, of Luxembourg	1347–1378
Albert I, King of Germany	1298–1308	Wenceslas of Luxembourg	1378–1400
Henry VII of Luxembourg	1308–1314	Rupert, Duke of Palatine	1400–1410
Louis IV of Bavaria (co-regent)	1314–1347	Sigismund of Luxembourg	1410–1437

HAPSBURG DYNASTY

Albert II	1437–1439	Leopold I	1658–1705
Frederick III	1452–1493	Joseph I	1705–1711
Maximilian I	1493–1519	Charles VI	1711–1740
Charles V, King of Spain	1519–1556	War of the Austrian Succession	1740–1748
Ferdinand I	1558–1564	Charles VII of Bavaria	1742–1745
Maximilian II	1564–1576	Francis I of Lorraine	1745–1765
Rudolf II	1576–1612	Joseph II	1765–1790
Matthias	1612–1619	Leopold II	1790–1792
Ferdinand II	1619–1637	Francis II	1792–1806
Ferdinand III	1637–1657		

HAPSBURG EMPERORS OF AUSTRIA

Francis II	1804–1835	Francis Joseph	1848–1916
Ferdinand	1835–1848	Charles	1916–1918

HOHENZOLLERN EMPERORS OF GERMANY

William I (of Prussia)	1871–1888	William II	1888–1918
Frederick III	1888		

RULERS OF GERMANY

WEIMAR REPUBLIC

Friedrich Ebert	1919–1925	Paul von Hindenburg	1925–1934

THIRD REICH

Adolf Hitler	1934–1945		

POST WORLD WAR II

Germany under Allied control	1945–1949		

CHANCELLORS OF THE FEDERAL REPUBLIC OF GERMANY (WEST GERMANY)

Konrad Adenauer	1949–1963	Willy Brandt	1969–1974
Dr. Ludwig Erhard	1963–1966	Helmut Schmidt	1974–1982
Kurt George Kiesinger	1966–1969	Helmut Kohl	1982–1990

CHAIRMEN OF THE DEMOCRATIC REPUBLIC OF GERMANY (EAST GERMANY)

Walter Ulbricht	1949–1971	Egon Krenz	1989–1990
Erich Honecker	1971–1989		

CHANCELLORS OF UNITED GERMANY

Helmut Kohl	1990–1998	Gerhard Schröder	1998–2005
Angela Merkel	2005–		

RULERS OF FRANCE

THE CAROLINGIANS

Charles II, the Bald	843–877	Robert	922–923
Louis II	877–879	Rudolph	923–936
Louis III	879–882	Louis IV	936–954
Charles III	884–887	Lothair	954–986
Eudes	888–898	Louis V	986–987
Charles III	898–922		

THE CAPETS

Hugh Capet	987–996	Louis VIII	1223–1226
Robert II, the Pious	996–1031	Louis IX	1226–1270
Henry I	1031–1060	Philip III	1270–1285
Philip I	1060–1108	Philip IV	1285–1314
Louis VI	1108–1137	Louis X	1314–1316
Louis VII	1137–1180	Philip V	1316–1322
Philip II	1180–1223	Charles IV	1322–1328

HOUSE OF VALOIS

Philip VI	1328–1350	Louis XII	1498–1515
John II	1350–1364	Francis I	1515–1547
Charles V	1364–1380	Henry II	1547–1559
Charles VI	1380–1422	Francis II	1559–1560
Charles VII	1422–1461	Charles IX	1560–1574
Louis XI	1461–1483	Henry III	1574–1589
Charles VIII	1483–1498		

HOUSE OF BOURBON

Henry IV, of Navarre	1589–1610	Louis XV	1715–1774
Louis XIII	1610–1643	Louis XVI	1774–1793
Louis XIV	1643–1715	Louis XVII	1793–1795

THE FIRST REPUBLIC AND FIRST EMPIRE

Napoleon Bonaparte (first consul)	1799–1804	Napoleon I (emperor)	1804–1814

RESTORATION OF MONARCHY

Louis XVIII	1814–1824	Louis-Philippe	1830–1848
Charles X	1824–1830		

SECOND REPUBLIC

Louis Napoleon Bonaparte (president)	1848–1852	Napoleon III (emperor)	1852–1870

THIRD REPUBLIC

Louis Adolphe Thiers	1871–1873	Paul Deschanel	1920
Marshal Patrice de MacMahon	1873–1879	Alexander Millerand	1920–1924
Paul Grévy	1879–1887	Gaston Doumergue	1924–1931
Marie Carnot	1887–1894	Paul Doumer	1931–1932
Jean Casimir-Périer	1894–1895	Albert Lebrun	1932–1940
François Faure	1895–1899	Vichy government (under Germans)	1940–1944
Émile Loubet	1899–1906		
Armand C. Fallières	1906–1913	Provisional government	1944–1946
Raymond Poincaré	1913–1920		

FOURTH REPUBLIC

Vincent Auriol	1947–1954	René Coty	1954–1959

FIFTH REPUBLIC

Charles de Gaulle	1959–1969	François Mitterrand	1981–1995
Georges Pompidou	1969–1974	Jacques Chirac	1995–2007
Valéry Giscard d'Estaing	1974–1981	Nicolas Sarkozy	2007–

RULERS OF SPAIN

HAPSBURG DYNASTY

Charles I (V of Germany)	1516–1556	Philip IV	1621–1665
Philip II	1556–1598	Charles II	1665–1700
Philip III	1598–1621		

BOURBON DYNASTY

Philip V	1700–1724	Charles IV	1788–1808
Louis I	1724	Ferdinand VII	1808
Philip V (restored)	1724–1746	Joseph Bonaparte	1808–1814
Ferdinand VI	1746–1759	Ferdinand VII	1814–1833
Charles III	1759–1788	Isabella II	1833–1868

OTHER MONARCHS

Amadeus of Savoy	1870–1873

FIRST REPUBLIC

1873–1874

RESTORATION OF MONARCHY

Alfonso XII	1874–1885	Alfonso XIII	1886–1931
General Miguel Primo de Rivera (dictator)	1923–1930		

SECOND REPUBLIC

Niceto Alcalá Zamora	1931–1936	General Francisco Franco	1939–1975
Manuel Azaña	1936–1939		

RESTORATION OF MONARCHY

Juan Carlos	1975–

PRIME MINISTERS

Admiral Luis Blanco	1973	Felipe González Márquez	1982–1996
Carlos Navarro	1973–1976	José María Aznar López	1996–2004
Adolfo Suárez	1976–1981	José Luis Rodríguez Zapatero	2004–2011
Leopoldo Calvo Sotelo y Bustelo	1981–1982	Mariano Rajoy	2011–

PERIODS OF JAPAN

Yamato	c.300–592	
Asaka	592–710	Empress Suiko (592–628)
		Emperor Temmu (673–686)
Nara	710–794	Emperor Kammu (781–806)
Heian	794–1185	Japan ruled from Heian (now called Kyoto)
Fujiwara	858–1160	Fujiwara clan rules
Taira	1159–1185	Taira clan takes control

Kamakura	1185–1333	Minamoto Yoritomo defeats Taira clan; in 1192 he became a shogun	
Namboku	1334–1392	End of shogun rule in 1333; Emperor Godaigo rules alone 1333–1339; imperial line splits into northern and southern courts	
Ashikaga	1338–1573	Ashikaga Takauji becomes shogun in 1338	
Muromachi	1392–1573	Two rival courts are unified	
Sengoku	1467–1600	Emperor Gonara (1527–1557)	
Momoyama	1573–1603	Oda Nobunaga, a *daimyo* (baron), deposes the shogun and becomes dictator to 1582	
Edo	1603–1867	Tokugawa Ieyasu becomes shogun in 1603; Tokugawa shoguns rule until 1867	
Meiji	1868–1912	Emperor Mutsuhito, Meiji restoration; he ends the shogunate and modernizes Japan	
Taisho	1912–1926	Emperor Yoshihito	
Showa	1926–1989	Emperor Hirohito	
Heisei	1989–	Emperor Akihito	

CZARS OF RUSSIA

Ivan III, the Great, ruler of Russia	1462–1505	Catherine I	1725–1727
Vasili, ruler of Russia	1505–1533	Peter II	1727–1730
Ivan IV, the Terrible, first czar	1533–1584	Anna	1730–1740
Fyodor I	1584–1598	Ivan VI	1740–1741
Boris Godunov	1598–1605	Elizabeth	1741–1762
Fyodor II	1605	Peter III	1762
Demetrius	1605–1606	Catherine II, the Great	1762–1796
Basil (IV) Shuiski	1606–1610	Paul I	1796–1801
(Interregnum	1610–1613)	Alexander I	1801–1825
Michael Romanov	1613–1645	Nicholas I	1825–1855
Alexis	1645–1676	Alexander II	1855–1881
Fyodor III	1676–1682	Alexander III	1881–1894
Ivan V and Peter I, the Great, joint rulers	1682–1689	Nicholas II	1894–1917
Peter I	1689–1725		

EFFECTIVE RULERS OF THE UNION OF SOVIET SOCIALIST REPUBLICS

Vladimir Lenin	1917–1924	Leonid Brezhnev	1964–1982
Joseph Stalin	1924–1953	Yuri Andropov	1982–1984
Georgy Malenkov	1953	Konstantin Chernenko	1984–1985
Nikita Khrushchev	1953–1964	Mikhail Gorbachev	1985–1991

PRESIDENTS OF RUSSIA

Boris Yeltsin	1991–2000	Vladimir Putin	2000–2008
Dmitry Medvedev	2008–2012	Vladmir Putin	2012–

PRESIDENTS OF THE UNITED STATES OF AMERICA

George Washington	1789–1797	Federalist
John Adams	1797–1801	Federalist
Thomas Jefferson	1801–1809	Democratic Republican
James Madison	1809–1817	Democratic Republican
James Monroe	1817–1825	Democratic Republican
John Quincy Adams	1825–1829	Democratic Republican
Andrew Jackson	1829–1837	Democrat
Martin Van Buren	1837–1841	Democrat
William H. Harrison	1841	Whig
John Tyler	1841–1845	Whig
James K. Polk	1845–1849	Democrat
Zachary Taylor	1849–1850	Whig
Millard Fillmore	1850–1853	Whig
Franklin Pierce	1853–1857	Democrat
James Buchanan	1857–1861	Democrat
Abraham Lincoln	1861–1865	Republican

Andrew Johnson	1865–1869	National Union
Ulysses S. Grant	1869–1877	Republican
Rutherford B. Hayes	1877–1881	Republican
James Garfield	1881	Republican
Chester Arthur	1881–1885	Republican
Grover Cleveland	1885–1889	Democrat
Benjamin Harrison	1889–1893	Republican
Grover Cleveland	1893–1897	Democrat
William McKinley	1897–1901	Republican
Theodore Roosevelt	1901–1909	Republican
William Taft	1909–1913	Republican
Woodrow Wilson	1913–1921	Democrat
Warren Harding	1921–1923	Republican
Calvin Coolidge	1923–1929	Republican
Herbert Hoover	1929–1933	Republican
Franklin D. Roosevelt	1933–1945	Democrat
Harry S. Truman	1945–1953	Democrat
Dwight Eisenhower	1953–1961	Republican
John F. Kennedy	1961–1963	Democrat
Lyndon Johnson	1963–1969	Democrat
Richard Nixon	1969–1974	Republican
Gerald Ford	1974–1977	Republican
Jimmy Carter	1977–1981	Democrat
Ronald Reagan	1981–1989	Republican
George Bush	1989–1993	Republican
Bill Clinton	1993–2001	Democrat
George W. Bush	2001–2009	Republican
Barack Obama	2009–	Democrat

PRIME MINISTERS OF CANADA

Sir John Macdonald	1867–1873	Richard Bennett	1930–1935
Alexander Mackenzie	1873–1878	William King	1935–1948
Sir John Macdonald	1878–1891	Louis St. Laurent	1948–1957
Sir John Abbott	1891–1892	John Diefenbaker	1957–1963
Sir John Thompson	1892–1894	Lester Pearson	1963–1968
Sir Mackenzie Bowell	1894–1896	Pierre Trudeau	1968–1979
Sir Charles Tupper	1896	Charles (Joe) Clark	1979–1980
Sir Wilfrid Laurier	1896–1911	Pierre Trudeau	1980–1984
Sir Robert Borden	1911–1920	John Turner	1984
Arthur Meighen	1920–1921	Brian Mulroney	1984–1993
William King	1921–1926	Kim Campbell	1993
Arthur Meighen	1926	Jean Chrétien	1993–2003
William King	1926–1930	Paul Martin	2003–2006
		Stephen Harper	2006–

PRIME MINISTERS OF AUSTRALIA

Sir Edmund Barton	1901–1903	Sir Arthur Fadden	1941
Alfred Deakin	1903–1904	John Curtin	1941–1945
John Watson	1904	Francis Forde	1945
Sir George Reid	1904–1905	Joseph Chifley	1945–1949
Alfred Deakin	1905–1908	Sir Robert Menzies	1949–1966
Andrew Fisher	1908–1909	Harold Holt	1966–1967
Alfred Deakin	1909–1910	Sir John McEwen	1967–1968
Andrew Fisher	1910–1913	John Gorton	1968–1971
Sir Joseph Cook	1913–1914	William McMahon	1971–1972
Andrew Fisher	1914–1915	Edward Gough Whitlam	1972–1975
William Hughes	1915–1923	John Fraser	1975–1983
Stanley Bruce	1923–1929	Robert Hawke	1983–1991
James Scullin	1929–1932	Paul Keating	1991–1996
Joseph Lyons	1932–1939	John Howard	1996–2007
Sir Earle Page	1939	Kevin Rudd	2007–2010
Sir Robert Menzies	1939–1941	Julia Gillard	2010–

PRIME MINISTERS OF NEW ZEALAND

Sir Joseph Ward	1906–1912	Keith Holyoake	1960–1972
Thomas MacKenzie	1912–1915	Sir John Marshall	1972
William Massey	1915–1925	Norman Kirk	1972–1974
Sir Francis Bell	1925	Hugh Watt	1974
Joseph Coates	1925–1928	Wallace (Bill) Rowling	1974–1975
Sir Joseph Ward	1928–1930	Robert Muldoon	1975–1984
George Forbes	1930–1935	David Lange	1984–1989
Michael Savage	1935–1940	Geoffrey Palmer	1989–1990
Peter Fraser	1940–1949	Michael Moore	1990
Sir Sidney Holland	1949–1957	James Bolger	1990–1997
Keith Holyoake	1957	Jenny Shipley	1997–1999
Sir Walter Nash	1957–1960	Helen Clark	1999–2008
		John Key	2008–

PRESIDENTS OF THE REPUBLIC OF ITALY

Alcide de Gasperi (acting head of state)	1946	Giovanni Leone	1971–1978
Enrico de Nicola (provisional president)	1946–1948	Amintore Fanfani	1978
Luigi Einaudi	1948–1955	Alessandro Pemini	1978–1985
Giovanni Gronchi	1955–1962	Francesco Cossiga	1985–1992
Antonio Segni	1962–1964	Oscar Luigi Scalfaro	1992–1999
Giuseppe Saragat	1964–1971	Carlo Ciampi	1999–2006
		Giorgio Napolitano	2006–

PRIME MINISTERS

Alcide de Gasperi	1946–1953	Francesco Cossiga	1979–1980
Guiseppe Pella	1953–1954	Arnaldo Forlani	1980–1981
Amintore Fanfani	1954	Giovanni Spadolini	1981–1982
Mario Scelba	1954–1955	Armintore Fanfani	1982–1983
Antonio Segni	1955–1957	Bettino Craxi	1983–1987
Adone Zoli	1957–1958	Giovanni Goria	1987–1988
Amintore Fanfani	1958–1959	Luigi Ciriaco de Mita	1988–1989
Antonio Segni	1959–1960	Giulio Andreotti	1989–1992
Fernando Tambroni	1960	Giuliano Amato	1992–1993
Amintore Fanfani	1960–1963	Carlo Azeglio Ciampi	1993–1994
Giovanni Leone	1963	Silvio Berlusconi	1994
Aldo Moro	1963–1968	Lamberto Dini	1995–1996
Giovanni Leone	1968	Romano Prodi	1996–1998
Mariano Rumor	1968–1970	Massimo D'Alema	1998–2000
Emilio Colombo	1970–1972	Giuliano Amato	2000–2001
Giulio Andreotti	1972–1973	Silvio Berlusconi	2001–2006
Mariano Rumor	1973–1974	Romano Prodi	2006–2008
Aldo Moro	1974–1976	Silvio Berlusconi	2008–2011
Giulio Andreotti	1976–1979	Mario Monti	2011–

PRESIDENTS OF THE REPUBLIC OF INDIA

Dr. Rajendra Prasad	1949–1962	Neelam Reddy	1977–1982
Dr. Sarvepalli Radhakrishnan	1962–1967	Giani Zail Singh	1982–1987
Dr. Zakir Hussain	1967–1969	Ramaswamy Venkataraman	1987–1992
Varahagiri Giri	1969–1974	Shankar Dayal Sharma	1992–1997
Fakhruddin Ahmed	1974–1977	K. R. Narayanan	1997–2002
Basappa Jatti	1977	Abdul Kalam	2002–2007
		Pratibha Patil	2007–

PRIME MINISTERS

Jawaharlal Nehru	1947–1964	Rajiv Gandhi	1984–1989
Gulzarilal Nanda	1964	V. P. Singh	1989–1990
Lal Shastri	1964–1966	Chandra Shekhar	1990–1991
Gulzarilal Nanda	1966	P. V. Narasimha Rao	1991–1996
Indira Gandhi	1966–1977	Atal Bihari Vajpayee	1996
Shri Morarji Desai	1977–1979	H. D. Deve Gowda	1996–1997
Charan Singh	1979–1980	I. K. Gujral	1997–1998
Indira Gandhi	1980–1984	Atal Bihari Vajpayee	1998–2004
		Dr. Manmohan Singh	2004–

MAJOR WARS

DATE	NAME OF WAR	WARRING PARTIES
c.1250 B.C.	Trojan Wars	Myceneans vs .Trojans
431–404 B.C.	Peloponnesian War	Athens vs. Sparta
264–241 B.C.	First Punic War	
218–201 B.C.	Second Punic War	Rome vs. Carthage
149–146 B.C.	Third Punic War	
1096–1099	First Crusade	
1147–1149	Second Crusade	Saracens vs. Christians over Palestine
1189–1192	Third Crusade	
1202–1204	Fourth Crusade	
1337–1453	Hundred Years' War	England vs. France
1455–1485	Wars of the Roses	House of York vs. House of Lancaster
1562–1598	French Wars of Religion	Huguenots vs. Catholics
1642–1648	English Civil War	Cavaliers vs. Roundheads
1618–1648	Thirty Years' War	Catholic League (Germany, Austria, Spain) vs. Denmark, Sweden, France
1689–1697	War of League of Augsburg	France vs. the League, England, and the Netherlands
1700	Great Northern War	Sweden vs. Russia, Denmark, Poland, and the Netherlands
1701–1713	War of Spanish Succession	Spain, France, and Bavaria vs. England, the Netherlands, Austrian Empire, and Portugal
1730–1738	War of Polish Succession	Russia and Poland vs. France
1740–1748	War of Austrian Succession	Austria and Great Britain vs. Prussia, Bavaria, France, and Spain
1756–1763	Seven Years' War	Great Britain and Prussia vs. France, Austria, and Russia
1775–1783	American Revolution	American colonies vs. Great Britain
1793–1815	Napoleonic Wars	France vs. Great Britain, Austria, Sweden, Russia, and Prussia
1821–1829	Greek War of Independence	Greece vs. Ottoman Turkey
1846–1848	Mexican–American War	Mexico vs. U.S.
1854–1856	Crimean War	Russia vs. Great Britain, France, and Turkey
1859	War for Italian Independence	France and Piedmont–Sardinia vs. Austria
1861–1865	American Civil War	Confederates vs. Unionists
1866	Austro–Prussian War	Prussia vs. Austria
1870	Franco–Prussian War	France vs. Prussia
1894–1895	Chinese–Japanese War	China vs. Japan
1899–1902	Boer War	Great Britain vs. Boers (Dutch) in South Africa
1904–1905	Russo–Japanese War	Russia vs. Japan
1914–1918	World War I	Germany and Austria–Hungary vs. France, Russia, Great Britain, and other nations
1918–1921	Russian Civil War	Bolsheviks vs. White Russians
1931–1933	Chinese–Japanese War	Japan vs. China
1936–1939	Spanish Civil War	Nationalists (Franco) vs. Republicans
1939–1945	World War II	Great Britain, France, U.S.S.R., U.S., and other nations vs. Germany, Italy, and Japan
1950–1953	Korean War	North Korea vs. South Korea
1967	Six-Day War	Israel vs. Arab states
1964–1973	Vietnam War	North Vietnam vs. South Vietnam and U.S.
1980–1988	Iran–Iraq War	Iran vs. Iraq
1982	Falklands War	United Kingdom vs. Argentina
1991	Persian Gulf War	Iraq vs. combined international forces
2001–present	Afghanistan War	Combined international forces vs. Taliban-controlled Afghanistan and Al Qaeda terrorist network
2003–2011	Iraq War	U.S. and international coalition forces vs. Iraq

INTERNET LINKS

The British Museum: http://www.britishmuseum.org
Cluny Museum: http://www.musee-moyenage.fr/ang/index.htm
German Historical Museum: http://www.dhm.de/ENGLISH
The History Channel: http://www.history.com
History for Kids: http://www.historyforkids.org
Hyperhistory Online: http://www.hyperhistory.com/online_n2/History_n2/a.html
Museum of Art and Archaeology: http://maa.missouri.edu/
Smithsonian Institution: http://smithsonianeducation.org/students/index.html
Virginia War Museum: http://www.warmuseum.org/index.php

INDEX

484

mystery plays 187

N

Nabopolassar 36
Nadir Shah 298
Nagasaki 244, 417, 418, 431
Nagashino, Battle of (1575) 232
Nalanda University 79
Nan Chao 136
Nanjing (Nanking) 180, 344
Nanjing, Treaty of (1842) 344
Napata 30
Napoleon Bonaparte 319, 320, 321, 325, 326, 334
Napoleon III, Emperor (Louis Napoleon) 346, 347, 360, 361
Napoleonic Wars 368
Nara 85
Narses, General 100
Narva, Battle of (1700) 278
Naseby, Battle of (1645) 260
Nash, John 332
Nasmyth, James 341
Natal 343
National Aeronautics and Space Administration (NASA) 439, 455
nationalism:
  rise of in Europe 145
native Americans:
  European settlers 248, 302
  Pontiac's rebellion 303
NATO see North Atlantic Treaty Organization
Navajo tribe 111
navigation:
  astrolabes 238
  compasses 94, 95, 142, 143, 238
  instruments 238
  in the Renaissance 201
Nazareth 72, 73
Nazca people 50, 129
Nazis 399, 406, 428
Neanderthals 6, 7
Nebuchadnezzar I, king of Babylon 25, 36
Nefertiti 26
Nehru, Jawaharlal 421
Nelson, Admiral Horatio 321
Nero, Emperor 67
Nestorian church 73
Netherlands:
  Calvinism 214, 215, 228
  East India Company 259
  revolt against Spain 228, 229
  slaves 259, 270, 271
  spice trade 258
  Thirty Years' War 215, 243, 246, 250, 252, 253, 254, 255, 257, 266
  trade with China 304
  War of the Spanish Succession 257, 279
  West India Company 259
  see also Austrian Netherlands; Spanish Netherlands
netsuke ix, 314, 331
Neva River 276
Nevarre 200
New Deal 405
New England 230, 248, 249
New France 303
New Guinea 5, 88
New Mexico 281
New Model Army 260
New Netherland 259
New South Wales 374
New Territories 344
New York:
  skyscrapers 380, 381, 401

Statue of Liberty 380
  terrorist attack 448, 464
New York Stock Exchange 404, 442
New Zealand:
  Captain Cook visits 89, 291
  Dutch visit 243
  in British Empire 348
  Maoris 88, 89, 140, 141, 147, 291, 348
  Polynesians settle in 5, 51, 88, 89, 99
  whaling 348
  women's rights 373
Newcomen, Thomas 296, 297
Newfoundland 248, 249
Newton, Sir Isaac 268, 269, 286, 287
Niani 60
Nicene Creed 73
Nicephorus, Emperor 112
Nicholas II, Czar 388, 394
Niger River 31, 208, 363
Nigeria: 309
  1100–1480 166, 167
  see also Benin; Dahomey; Nok culture
"Night of the Long Knives" (1934) 406
Nightingale, Florence 350
Nijinsky, Vaslav 426
Nijo Castle, Kyoto 244
Nile River 10, 309, 362
Nineveh 22, 23, 37
Nixon, Richard M. 445
Nobel, Alfred 383
Nobunaga, Oda 232
Nok culture 31, 51, 60, 95
nomads 8, 50
Nördlingen, Battle of (1634) 251, 253
Normandy 131, 415
Normans:
  architecture 140, 141
  in England 123, 131, 132, 133
  in Sicily 133
North Africa:
  and the Ottoman Empire 290,
  see also individual countries
North America: 290
  European settlers 302, 338
  exploration of 338
  farming 230
  railroads 337
  Temple Mound culture 98, 110
  Vikings in 131
  wars between British and French 302
  see also Canada; Mexico; Native Americans; United States of America
North Atlantic Treaty Organization (NATO) 436, 437
North American Free Trade Agreement (NAFTA) 443
North Carolina 280
North German Confederation 360
Northern Ireland (Ulster):
  fighting between Catholics and Protestants 274, 275
  see also Britain
Norway:
  Vikings 130
Nostradamus 239
Nova Scotia 302
Novgorod 113, 131, 226
Nubia 11, 30, 31
nuclear weapons
  see also atomic bombs
Numitor, King 34

Nur Jahan, Empress 265
Nuremberg Laws 407
Nuremberg rallies 406
Nuremberg war trials 419
Nyamwezi 308
nylon 431

O

Oba 166, 212
Oba Ewuare 166
Ochterlony, Sir David 324,
O'Connell, Daniel 364
Octavian see Augustus, Emperor 64, 65, 66
Odyssey, The 38
Offa, king of England 122
Ogodai Khan 170
Ohio Valley 303
oil:
  Iraq invades Kuwait 453, 456
  pollution 456
Old Pretender see Stuart, James
Old Testament 25
Olmecs 32
Oman 308, 506
O'Neill, Sir Phelim 274
opera 282
opium wars 344
Orange Free State 343
Organization for African Unity (OAU) 451
Organization of Petroleum Exporting Countries (OPEC) 442
Orkney Islands 13, 45
Orleans, Siege of (1428-1429) 177
Ormonde, James Butler, Duke of 274
Ormuz 213
Orissa, India 189
orrery 269, 286
Orthodox Church 101, 112, 113
Osiris 2, 11
Osman I, Sultan 216
Osman II, Sultan 266
Ostrogoths 90
Oswald, king of Northumbria 122
Oswy, king of Northumbria 122
Ottakar II, king of Bohemia 121
Otto I, emperor of Germany 120, 124
Ottoman Empire: 290
  arts and crafts 234, 235
  besieges Vienna 216, 267, 279
  captures Constantinople 100, 101, 182, 183
  Crimean War 350
  decline of 243, 266
  fall of Constantinople 101, 182, 183
  golden age 195
  Janissaries 182, 183, 266
  makes peace with Safavid Empire 266
  Süleyman the Magnificent 216, 266
  war with Egypt 291
  war with Russia 310
  see also Turkey
Ouchy, Treaty of (1912) 376
Oudenarde, Battle of (1708) 279
Oudh 298
Oxenstierna, Count Axel 250
Oxfam 449
Oyo Empire 273, 308
ozone layer 456

P

Pachacuti 173, 199
Pacific Ocean:

Polynesians 88, 89, 99
paganism 122
Paine, Thomas 306
Pakistan:
  ancient history 5, 14
Palenque 77
Palestine:
  Crusades 99, 109, 144, 145, 148, 149
  see also Israel
Palestine Liberation Organization (PLO) 453
Panama 271
Pankhurst, Emmeline 373
pantomime 282
papacy see popes
Papal States:
  annexed by Cavour 358, 359
  Piedmont–Sardinia invades 358, 359
  see also popes
papermaking 94, 143, 190
Papineau, Louis Joseph 357
papyrus viii, 10
Paracelsus 239
Pardoner's Tale 187
Paris:
  Black Death 109, 146, 147, 178, 179
  Eiffel Tower 380
  Franco–Prussian War 359
  French Revolution 290, 307, 346
  Hundred Years' War 176, 177
  Second Republic 347
Paris, Treaty of (1856) 351
Parliament (Britain):
  execution of Charles I 261
  Gunpowder Plot 246
Parnell, Charles 365
Parni 74
Parthenon 92
Parthians 74, 75, 80
Passchendaele, Battle of (1917) 390
Pataliputra 74
Patrick, St. 154, 155
Paul, St. 72, 73
Paul III, Pope 215
Pavia 236
Pawnee tribe 230, 231, 370
Pearl Harbor 401, 414, 416, 417
Pearse, Pádraig 392
peasants, farming 440
Pechenegi 113
Peel, Sir Robert 364
Peking see Beijing
Palestinian Liberation Organization (PLO) 453
Peloponnesian War 53, 56
Pembroke, Richard de Clare, Earl of ("Strongbow") 154, 155
penicillin 431
Penn, William 280
Pennsylvania 280
Pepin the Short, king of the Franks 114, 115
Pepys, Samuel 269, 282
Pericles 54
periods of Japan 474
Perry, Commodore Matthew 352
Perry, Oliver 9
Persepolis 40, 41
Persia:
  Alexander the Great conquers 41, 56
  the arts 234, 235
  attack on Delhi, 298
  windmills 238
  Safavid dynasty 195, 209, 217, 243
  Sassanian Empire 74, 75, 106

ACKNOWLEDGMENTS

The publishers wish to thank the following for their contributions to this book:

Photographs

(*t* = top; *b* = bottom; *m* = middle; *l* = left; *r* = right)

Cover front: *t* Shutterstock/Galyna Andrusko; *r* Corbis/Sandro Vannini; *bl* Shutterstock/meunlerd; *bm* Corbis/Gianni Dagli Orti; flap Shutterstock/sculpies; cover back NASA Images; Shutterstock/alysta; Shutterstock/Kellis; Shutterstock/Elina Pasok; Shutterstock/Lukas Hlavac; Shutterstock/Kamira; page i *bl* ET Archive, *ml* Bridgeman Art Library; iii *mtl* Werner Forman Archive, *m* ET Archive; vi-vii Gavin Hellier/Robert Harding Picture Library; viii *bl* ET Archive; 1 *m* ET Archive; 2 Robert Harding Picture Library; 14 ET Archive; 15 Ancient Art & Architecture Collection Ltd; 16 AKG; 17 *t* ET Archive, *ml* AKG; 18 ET Archive; 19 ET Archive; 20 *tl* ET Archive, *bl* ET Archive, *br* ET Archive; 21 ET Archive; 25 Ancient Art & Architecture Collection Ltd; 28 Ancient Art & Architecture Collection Ltd; 29 Ancient Art & Architecture Collection Ltd; 30 ET Archive; 32 ET Archive; 34 AKG; 35 ET Archive; 36 ET Archive; 39 ET Archive; 40 *t* ET Archive, *b* ET Archive; 42 AKG; 43 *m* ET Archive, *b* ET Archive; 45 Mick Sharp; 48 Roy Rainford/Robert Harding Picture Library; 56 ET Archive; 57 Robert Harding Picture Library Ltd; 61 *t* Ronald Sheridan/Ancient Art & Architecture Collection Ltd, *b* Ronald Sheridan/Ancient Art & Architecture Collection Ltd; 73 Robert Harding Picture Library; 76 Robert Harding Picture Library; 78 Richard Ashworth/Robert Harding Picture Library; 79 Richard Ashworth/Robert Harding Picture Library; 81 ET Archive; 83 *t* ET Archive, *b* ET Archive; 85 Ancient Art & Architecture Collection Ltd; 93 *tl* ET Archive, *tr* G&P Corrigan/Robert Harding Picture Library; 96 Robert Frerck/Robert Harding Picture Library; 97 Bridgeman Art Library; 100 Bridgeman Art Library; 101 *t* ET Archive, *b* ET Archive; 103 ET Archive; 107 ET Archive; 108 ET Archive; 109 *t* ET Archive, *bl* Bridgeman Art Library, *br* AKG; 111 Robert Harding Picture Library/James Gritz; 113 *tl* Ancient Art & Architecture Collection, *tr* Bridgeman Art Library, *b* Bridgeman Art Library; 114 ET Archive; 115 The Bridgeman Art Library; 118 Ancient Art & Architecture Collection/C.Blankenship; 119 R. Sheridan/Ancient Art & Architecture Collection; 120 *mr* R. Sheridan/Ancient Art & Architecture Collection, *b* ET Archive; 121 *t* ET Archive, *b* ET Archive; 125 AKG; 126 *l* Bridgeman Art Library, *r* AKG; 127 *t* AKG, *m* Bridgeman Art Library; 129 *t* Robert Harding Picture Library, *b* Robert Harding Picture Library; 132 Bridgeman Art Library; 135 *t* R. Sheridan/Ancient Art & Architecture Collection, *m* Ancient Art & Architecture Collection; 136 *t* ET Archive, *b* ET Archive; 137 *tl* ET Archive, *tr* ET Archive; 139 *tl* ET Archive, *tr* ET Archive; 141 ET Archive; 143 ET Archive; 144 ET Archive; 152 ET Archive; 154 ET Archive; 155 ET Archive; 160 ET Archive; 161 *t* ET Archive, *b* ET Archive; 162 ET Archive; 163 ET Archive; 164 *m* ET Archive, *b* ET Archive; 165 Robert Harding Picture Library/S. Sassoon; 167 Robert Harding Picture Library/Geoff Renner; 169 Robert Harding Picture Library; 176 ET Archive; 180 ET Archive; 181 *m* ET Archive, *b* ET Archive; 183 *t* ET Archive, *b* Robert Harding Associates; 184 Robert Harding Picture Library; 185 A. Barrington/Ancient Art & Architecture Collection; 186 *t* ET Archive, *b* ET Archive; 187 Robert Harding Picture Library; 189 Robert Harding Picture Library; 192 ET Archive; 201 *tl* ET Archive, *tr* ET Archive, *b* ET Archive; 202 ET Archive; 204 Bridgeman Art Library; 205 ET Archive; 208 *tl* Ancient Art & Architecture Collection Ltd, *b* Werner Forman Archive; 209 Ancient Art & Architecture Collection Ltd; 212 *tl* Werner Forman Archive, *tr* Werner Forman Archive, *bl* Werner Forman Archive; 213 Bridgeman Art Library; 215 ET Archive; 218 Bridgeman Art Library; 227 *t* Ancient Art & Architecture Collection Ltd, *b* Bridgeman Art Library; 228 Bridgeman Art Library; 229 *t* AKG, *b* AKG; 234 *bl* Bridgeman Art Library, *br* Ancient Art & Architecture Collection Ltd; 235 ET Archive; 238 ET Archive; 239 ET Archive; 240 Margaret Collier/Robert Harding Picture Library; 243 *mr* ET Archive, *br* ET Archive; 244 Werner Forman Archive; 245 Werner Forman Archive; 247 Bridgeman Art Library; 250 *l* ET Archive, *b* AKG; 251 ET Archive; 252 *tl* ET Archive, *ml* AKG; 253 *t* AKG, *m* AKG, *b* AKG; 255 *t* ET Archive, *b* Ancient Art & Architecture Collection Ltd; 256 *tl* ET Archive, *b* Bridgeman Art Library; 257 *t* ET Archive, *b* ET Archive; 259 Bridgeman Art Library; 261 ET Archive; 262 Bridgeman Art Library; 263 *t* Bridgeman Art Library, *m* Werner Forman Archive; 264 AKG; 266 *t* ET Archive, *b* ET Archive; 267 *t* ET Archive, *b* ET Archive; 269 Bridgeman Art Library; 272 Bridgeman Art Library; 273 *t* AKG, *m* ET Archive; 274 *t* Bridgeman Art Library, *b* Bridgeman Art Library; 275 Bridgeman Art Library; 276 ET Archive; 277 ET Archive; 278 *tl* ET Archive, *ml* Bridgeman Art Library; 282 ET Archive; 283 *t* ET Archive, *b* Bridgeman Art Library; 285 Robert Harding Picture Library; 286 Bridgeman Art Library; 288 ET Archive; 292 ET Archive; 293 ET Archive; 294 *l* Bridgeman Art Library, *b* Bridgeman Art Library; 295 *t* ET Archive, *m* ET Archive; 297 ET Archive; 298 *tl* Bridgeman Art Library, *b* Ancient Art & Architecture Collection Ltd; 300 ET Archive; 301 ET Archive; 303 ET Archive; 305 *t* Bridgeman Art Library, *b* Bridgeman Art Library; 306 ET Archive; 307 *t* ET Archive, *b* ET Archive; 309 *t* ET Archive, *b* ET Archive; 310 *tl* ET Archive, *tr* ET Archive; 311 ET Archive; 312 *tl* ET Archive, *ml* ET Archive; 313 ET Archive; 314 *ml* ET Archive, *b* ET Archive; 315 ET Archive; 323 Peter Newark's American Pictures; 324 ET Archive; 325 ET Archive; 327 *t* ET Archive, *b* ET Archive; 329 Peter Newark's American Pictures; 330 ET Archive; 331 *t* Bridgeman Art Library, *r* ET Archive, *b* ET Archive; 332 Edifile/Lewis; 336 ET Archive; 339 ET Archive; 342 Peter Newark's American Pictures; 344 *tl* ET Archive, *b* ET Archive; 345 *t* ET Archive, *b* ET Archive; 346 ET Archive; 347 *t* ET Archive, *b* ET Archive; 348 *tr* ET Archive, *b* ET Archive; 349 *t* ET Archive, *mr* ET Archive, *b* ET Archive; 351 *t* ET Archive, *m* ET Archive, *b* ET Archive; 352 ET Archive; 353 *t* ET Archive, *b* ET Archive; 355 Hulton Getty Picture Library; 356 Hulton Getty Picture Library; 357 AKG; 358 ET Archive; 359 ET Archive; 360 ET Archive; 361 ET Archive; 363 ET Archive; 364 *tr* Hulton Getty Picture Library, *ml* Hulton Getty Picture Library, *b* ET Archive; 365 ET Archive; 366 *t* Hulton Getty Picture Library, *b* ET Archive; 367 ET Archive; 368 ET Archive; 369 ET Archive; 370 *ml* Peter Newark's American Pictures, *bl* Peter Newark's American Pictures; 371 Mary Evans Picture Library; 372 ET Archive; 373 *t* Hulton Getty Picture Library, *b* ET Archive; 374 ET Archive; 375 ET Archive; 377 *t* ET Archive, *b* ET Archive; 378 *tr* ET Archive, *mr* Mary Evans Picture Library, *br* ET Archive; 379 *tl* ET Archive, *tr* ET Archive, *bl* ET Archive; 384 ET Archive; 386 ET Archive; 387 Imperial War Museum; 388 ILN; 389 *t* Hulton Deutsch Collection, *b* Hulton Getty Picture Library; 390 ET Archive; 391 *b* ET Archive; 392 Hulton Getty Picture Library; 393 Hulton Getty Picture Library; 394 *tl* ILN, *ml* ILN, *tr* ILN; 395 *tl* ET Archive, *tr* ILN, *mr* ILN; 396 *tl* Imperial War Musem, *tr* ET Archive, *b* ET Archive; 397 *tr* ET Archive, *mr* ILN; 398 *tl* ILN, *b* Hulton Deutsch Collection; 399 *t* Hulton Getty Picture Library, *mr* ET Archive, *br* ILN, *bl* ET Archive; 400 *tr* ET Archive, *ml* Corbis-Bettmann/UPI, *bl* Corbis; 401 *tr* Corbis-Bettmann, *m* Corbis, *mr* ET Archive, *bl* Corbis-Bettmann; 402 ET Archive; 403 *tr* Hulton Getty Picture Library, *br* ILN; 404 *tl* Hulton Getty Picture Library, *tr* Hulton Getty Picture Library, *bl* Hulton Getty Picture Library; 405 *mr* Corbis, *b Novosti*; 406 *tl* AKG, *ml* ILN, *b* ET Archive; 407 *t* ILN, *tr* AKG, *br* AKG; 408 *tl* ILN, *ml* ET Archive, *tr* Magnum Photos, *b* Magnum Photos; 409 *tr* ET Archive, *b* ET Archive; 410 *tr* Hulton Getty Picture Library, *b* Hulton Getty Picture Library; 411 *tr* ET Archive, *bl* Hulton Deutsch, *mb* ILN; 412 *tl* AKG, *ml* AKG, *tr* ET Archive, *b* AKG; 413 *tl* ILN, *tr* ET Archive, *b* ET Archive; 414 *tr* ILN, *b* ET Archive; 415 *tr* Hulton Getty Picture Library, *m* ILN; 416 ET Archive; 417 *tr* Imperial War Museum, *b* ET Archive; 418 *tl* ET Archive, *b* ET Archive; 419 *tl* ET Archive, *tr* ET Archive, *ml* ILN, *br* Hulton Getty Picture Library; 420 Imperial War Museum; 421 *mr* ILN, *b* Magnum Photos; 422 Hulton Deutsch Collection; 423 *tr* Hulton Getty Picture Library, *bl* Hulton Getty Picture Library; 424 *tl* Imperial War Museum, *b* Hulton Getty Picture Library; 425 ET Archive; 426 *tr* Kobal Collection, *b* AKG; 427 *tl* ILN, *tr* Corbis-Bettmann, *bl* Kobal Collection, *br* ILN; 428 *tl* ET Archive, *bl* James Neal/Arcaid, *tr* AKG, *br* Michael Jenner/Robert Harding Picture Library; 429 *tl* Richard Bryant/Arcaid, *tr* Simon Harris/Robert Harding Picture Library, *b* Steve Myerson/Robert Harding Picture Library; 430, *tr* Science Museum/Science & Society Picture Library, *bl* Science Museum/Science & Society Picture Library, *b* Quadrant Picture Library, *br* ET Archive; 431 *tl* ET Archive, *tr* ET Archive, *mr* Advertising Archives, *bl* ILN; 432 Science & Society Picture Library; 434 NASA/Science Photo Library; 435 *tl* Rex Features, *tr* Rob Francis/Robert Harding Picture Library, *br* Stuart Franklin/Magnum Photos, *bl* G.Mendel/Magnum Photos; 436 *tr* Popperfoto, *bl* Rex Features; 437 *t* Hulton Getty Picture Library, *m* Magnum Photos, *br* ET Archive, *bl* Hulton Getty Picture Library; 438 *ml* Novosti/Science Photo Library, *bl* NASA/Science Photo Library, *tr* NASA/Science Photo Library; 439 *t* NASA/JPL, *b* NASA/Science Photo Library; 440 *tl* Robert Harding, *b* Marc Riboud/Magnum Photos, *tr* Eve Arnold/Magnum Photos; 441 *tl* Stuart Franklin/Magnum Photos, *t* Stuart Franklin/Magnum Photos, *b* Paul Lowe/Magnum Photos; 442 *tr* OECD, *b* Elliot Erwitt/Magnum Photos; 443 *t* Abbas/Magnum Photos, *mr* Popperfoto/Reuters, *b* European Parliament/Airdiasol; 444 *tl* Hulton Getty Picture Library, *tr* Roger-Viollet, *bl* Corbis; 445 *t* Magnum Photos, *b* Griffiths/Magnum Photos; 446 *tl* P. Jones Griffiths/Magnum Photos, *tr* S. Franklin/Magnum Photos, *ml* Danny Lyon/Magnum, *b* Bob Adelman/Magnum Photos; 447 *t* Chris Steele-Perkins/Magnum Photos, *m* Magnum Photos, *b* Thomas Hoepker/Magnum Photos; 448 *tl* James Natchwey/Magnum Photos, *tr* Rex Features, *l* Rex Features, *br* Getty/Khalil Al-Murshidi/AFP; 449 *tr* F. Scianna/Magnum Photos, *bl* Liba Taylor/Robert Harding Picture Library, *br* Robert Harding Picture Library; 450 *tl* Hulton Getty Picture Library, *tr* Popperfoto, *bl* Marilyn Silverstone/MagnumPhotos, *br* Getty/Ashraf Shazly/AFP; 451 *t* Pinkhassov/Magnum Photos, *m* Pinkhassov/Magnum Photos, *bl* Shutterstock/Orhan Cam, *br* Getty/Jewel Samad/AFP Burt Glinn/Magnum Photos, *b* Jones-Griffiths/Magnum Photos; 453 *t* Jean Gaumy/Magnum Photos, *mr* Stuart Franklin/Magnum, *br* Getty/Cis Bouroncle/AFP; 454 *tl* Hank Morgan/University of Massachusetts at Amherst/Science Photo Library, *ml* Alfred Pasieka/Science Photo Library, *b* Brian Brake/Science Photo Library, *t* Tim Davis/Science Photo Library, *tr* Dr. Jeremy Burgess/Science Photo Library; 455 *t* NASA/Science Photo Library, *mr* NASA/Science Photo Library; 456 *tr* Steve McCurry/Magnum Photos, *b* Bruno Barbey/Magnum Photos; 457 *tl* G.Peress/Magnum Photos, *tr* Thomas Hopker/Magnum Photos, *bl* Russell D. Curtis/Science Photo Library, *br* Martin Bond/Science Photo Library; 458 *tl* Robert Harding Picture Library, *bl* Rob Francis/Robert Harding Picture Library, *tr* Rene Burri/Magnum Photos; 459 *ml* Micha Bar-Am/Magnum Photos, *br* Paul Lowe/Magnum Photos; 460 *tl* Steve McCurry/Magnum Photos, *tr* Paul Lowe/Magnum Photos, *b* Marilyn Silverstone/Magnum Photos; 461 *tr* Luc Delahaye/Magnum Photos, *m* Steve McCurry/Magnum Photos, *mr* Martin Parr/Magnum Photos, *b* Bruno Barbey/Magnum Photos; 462 *tl* G.Mendel/Magnum Photos, *ml* G.Mendel/Magnum Photos, *b* Frank Spooner Pictures/Gamma, *tr* Gideon Mendel/Magnum Photos; 463 *t* Frank Spooner Pictures/Gamma, *m* Frank Spooner Pictures/Gamma, *b* Frank Spooner Pictures/Gamma; 464 *tl* Eli Reed/Magnum Photos, *b* Detlev Van Ravenwaay/Science Photo Library

Artwork archivists Wendy Allison, Steve Robinson

Artists Jonathan Adams, Hemesh Alles, Marion Appleton, Sue Barclay, R. Barnett, Noel Bateman, Simon Bishop, Richard Bonson, Nick Cannan, Vanessa Card, Tony Chance, Harry Clow, Stephen Conlin, Peter Dennis, Dave Etchell, Jeff Farrow, James Field, Ian Fish, Michael Fisher, Eugene Fleury, Chris Forsey, Dewey Franklin, Terry Gabbey, Fred Gambino, John Gillatt, Matthew Gore, Jeremy Gower, Neil Gower, Ray Grinaway, Allan Hardcastle, Nick Harris, Nicholas Hewetson, Bruce Hogarth, Christian Hook, Richard Hook, Simon Huson, John James, Peter Jarvis, John Kelly, Deborah Kindred, Adrian Lascombe, Chris Lenthall, Jason Lewis, Chris Lyon, Kevin Maddison, Shirley Mallinson, Shane Marsh, David MacAllister, Angus McBride, Stefan Morris, Jackie Moore, Teresa Morris, Frank Nichols, Chris D. Orr, Sharon Pallent, R. Payne, R. Philips, Jayne Pickering, Melvyn Pickering, Malcolm Porter, Mike Posen, Mike Roffe, Chris Rothero, David Salarya, Mike Saunders, Rodney Shackell, Rob Shone, Mark Stacey, Paul Stangroom, Branca Surla, Smiljka Surla, Stephen Sweet, Mike Taylor, George Thompson, Martin Wilson, David Wright, Paul Wright